SCRIBNER ECONOMICS

ROGER LEROY MILLER

SCRIBNER EDUCATIONAL PUBLISHERS
NEW YORK

MACMILLAN PUBLISHING COMPANY
NEW YORK

COLLIER MACMILLAN PUBLISHERS
LONDON

Author
Roger LeRoy Miller
Center for Policy Studies
Clemson University
Clemson, South Carolina

Roger LeRoy Miller graduated Phi Beta Kappa from the University of California at Berkeley, where he also won the Departmental Prize in Economics. He was a Woodrow Wilson Honor Fellow, National Science Foundation Fellow, and Lilly Honor Fellow at the University of Chicago, where he received his Ph.D. in economics in 1968. Now at Clemson University, Dr. Miller has taught at the University of Washington and the University of Miami. He has also taught methodology to teachers of high school economics for the Joint Council on Economic Education. Among the more than 70 books he has written or co-authored are works on economics, statistics, law, consumer finance, and government. Dr. Miller also has operated several businesses and served as a consultant to government agencies, private corporations, and law firms.

Reviewers

Mildred J. Almond
Social Studies Teacher
Middleton High School
Charleston, South Carolina

Dorothy A. Barnett
Social Studies Teacher
Mankota West High School
Mankota, Minnesota

Dr. G. Leland Burningham
State Superintendent of
Public Instruction
Utah State Office of Education
Salt Lake City, Utah

Dr. Gloria Contreras
College of Education
University of Texas
Austin, Texas

William D. Siedlecki
Arsenal Technical High School
Indianapolis, Indiana

Academic Consultants

Dr. Jack Adams
Professor of Education
Department of Economics
and Finance
University of Arkansas
Little Rock, Arkansas

Dr. Calvin A. Kent
Professor of Private Enterprise
Hankamer School of Business
Baylor University
Waco, Texas

Contributors

Mary Bolenbaugh
Economics Consultant
Radnor Township School District
Wayne, Pennsylvania

Ronald E. Eckstein
Chairperson, Social Studies Department
Hudson High School
Hudson, Florida

Karen Hallows
Assistant Director
Center for Economic Education
University of Nebraska
Lincoln, Nebraska

Abbejean Kehler
Assistant Director, Central Ohio
Center for Economic Education
The Ohio State University
Columbus, Ohio

Linda McPheron
Economics Teacher
St. Petersburg High School
St. Petersburg, Florida

Bonnie Meszaros
Assistant Director, Center for
Economic Education
University of Delaware
Newark, Delaware

Alfred Salesky
Former Economics Teacher
James Monroe High School
New York, New York

Nort Seever
Economics Teacher
Westwood High School
Austin, Texas

JoDean Wara
Economics Teacher
Vacaville High School
Vacaville, California

Scribner Educational Publishers
Macmillan Publishing Company
866 Third Avenue
New York, New York 10022
Collier Macmillan Canada, Inc.
Printed in the United States of America
ISBN 0-02-255500-5
9 8 7 6 5 4 3 2 1

CONTENTS

V

GRAPHS AND CHARTS

SOURCE MATERIAL: READINGS

HOW TO USE THIS BOOK

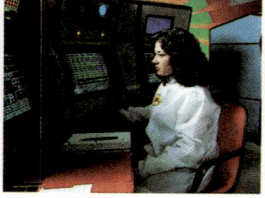

CHAPTER **13**

CHAPTER OUTLINE
1 Who Is the Labor Force?
2 Supply and Demand in the Labor Market
3 Organized Labor
4 Collective Bargaining
5 The Future of Unions

THE AMERICAN LABOR FORCE

You may already be working, but if not, you probably will be joining the American labor force sometime in the future. What kinds of jobs exist for you? What kind of training will you need for them? Which jobs are growing the fastest? How are wages determined? This chapter will help you answer these important questions. The chapter also presents a time line of the labor movement in the United States and describes how unions and management arrive at contract agreements. You will also read about the possible future of unions as technology changes the workplace. Learning Economic Skills discusses job possibilities for your future.

CHAPTER OBJECTIVES After you have studied this chapter, you will be able to:

1 • identify jobs by the type of work performed and by the education and/or training needed.

2 • describe the workings of supply and demand in the labor market.

3 • summarize the history of organized labor in the United States.
 • describe union organization in the United States.
 ★ use information from the *Occupational Outlook Handbook* to determine the future of some jobs.

4 • list the major issues involved in collective bargaining.

5 • describe the possible future of unionism in the United States.

ECONOMICS VOCABULARY
civilian labor force
blue-collar
white-collar
service worker
unskilled worker
semiskilled worker
skilled worker
professional
minimum wage law
labor union
craft union
industrial union
local union
closed shop
union shop
agency shop
right-to-work law
collective bargaining
mediation
arbitration
strike
picketing
cost-of-living adjustment
boycott
lockout
injunction

The American labor force is comprised of over 100 million men and women who work at an amazing variety of occupations in businesses and industries. Unions have made important contributions to many workers, but union membership has declined in recent years.

316   317

In Developing *Scribner Economics,* the author and editors designed a number of features to explain what each unit and chapter is about to help you recognize important ideas, and to make locating special material easier.

The first page of each unit lists the chapters and illustrates the main themes of the unit.

> **REVIEWING ECONOMIC PRINCIPLES**
>
> 1. What is the minimum wage law?
> 2. In the labor market, who creates: **a.** supply? **b.** demand?
> 3. **a.** What three factors underlying supply and demand affect wages in the labor market? **b.** Which factor seems to benefit workers most?
> 4. **Critical Thinking: Interpreting Information.** What are the disadvantages of imperfect competition in the labor market?
>
> **SUMMARY OF IMPORTANT PRINCIPLES**
>
> 1 • Every business involves five elements: advertising, expenses, receipts, record keeping, and risk.
> • A potential entrepreneur must also gather the factors of production and decide what type of business organization he or she wishes to form. Entrepreneurs must also learn about the laws, regulations, and tax codes that apply to the business.
>
> 2 • The advantages of sole proprietorships involve taxes. Disadvantages are unlimited liability and uncertainty about the life of the business. The following categories involve both advantages and disadvantages: profit and losses, management, personal satisfaction, and financing growth.

The first page of each chapter begins with a summary of the most important ideas in the chapter; a list of objectives, or goals; and a list of economics vocabulary in the chapter. The number before the objectives indicates the sections in which they are found. The star indicates the economic skill you will be learning. The section names are listed at the top of this page. By reading this page before you begin a chapter, you will discover the important items to look for and remember as you read.

At the end of each section is a series of questions called *Reviewing Economic Principles.* By answering the questions correctly, you will be mastering chapter objectives to which these questions relate. A Critical Thinking question will help you apply thinking skills to what you have learned.

The end of each chapter has a *Summary of Important Principles.* These principles follow the order of the section objectives listed at the beginning of the chapter and summarize the important information relating to each objective.

7 | CHAPTER REVIEW

PRACTICING YOUR COMMUNICATION SKILLS: DISCUSSION

During this course you have undoubtedly been participating in class discussions, as you probably have been since you first began school. You may not think about it, but any time you have a conversation with someone about a specific topic, you are taking part in a discussion, too. However, you may not be getting as much out of discussions or contributing as much as you might. Below are some tips to help you become an effective discussant (dis-KUHS-nt).

- If you are going to participate in a class discussion, be sure you are prepared. Read your assignment so that you have something to contribute.
- Be open-minded. Although you have probably formed some opinions ahead of time, you should not have made up your mind about the issue.
- Be willing to share your ideas and opinions. Everyone has something to contribute because everyone's viewpoint is unique.
- Respect the opinions of others. Everyone has a right to his or her ideas.
- Do not make disagreements personal. It is all right to disagree with another's ideas, but not with the person.
- Be clear in expressing your ideas when you speak.
- When listening, try to distinguish between the main argument and side issues. Concentrate on the main argument.
- If you agree with the person speaking, listen for additional information that will support your opinion.
- If you disagree with the person speaking, listen carefully to his or her point of view and the reasons used to support it. In that way, you will be able to argue against that view more effectively when it is your turn.

Activity: Practice these tips the next time you are part of a discussion, and see if you find that you contribute more ideas more effectively. If you have difficulty with one particular item on the list, concentrate on working on that in the next discussion.

VOCABULARY REVIEW

For each of the following terms, write a sentence using the term: maturity of a bond, preferred stock, over-the-counter market, compound interest, simple interest, common stock.

PRACTICING YOUR ECONOMIC SKILLS

1. **Analyzing Graphs.** The line graph below shows how $100 will grow at five different

How $100 Grows at Various Rates of Interest

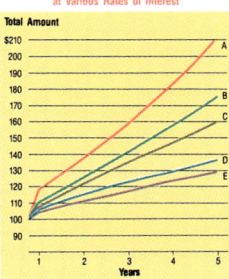

rates of annually compounded interest. Use the compound interest table on p. 163 to answer the following questions. **a.** Which curve represents an interest rate of 5 percent? **b.** Which curve represents an interest rate of 12 percent? **c.** Between which two curves would a curve based on 9 percent interest be drawn?

2. **Drawing Line Graphs.** Using the compound interest table on p. 163, create a line graph similar to the one on p. 178. Draw one line on the graph to show how $100 will grow over 15 years at 8 percent annually compounded interest. Draw another line to show how the same amount of money will grow during that period at 8 percent simple interest. **a.** What is the difference in the shape of the two curves? **b.** What causes this difference?

3. **Creating a Table.** Use the material in this chapter to create a table comparing these investments: passbook savings accounts, NOW accounts, Super NOW accounts, money market accounts, CDs, common stocks, bonds, tax-exempt bonds, U.S. savings bonds, mutual funds. Include the following information for each type of investment: possible return on investment (how much investors can expect to make); access to money (how easily investors can get their money); and amount of risk (how much chance is there of losing the original investment).

DISCUSSING ECONOMIC QUESTIONS

1. There are many different reasons why people save and many different savings plans they can use. What reasons would be best suited to short-term investments like savings accounts? What purposes would be best suited to longer-term methods such as CDs?

2. Most teenagers have a limited source of income. Should they nonetheless put a small amount of what they earn or are given in a savings account? Why or why not?

APPLYING CRITICAL THINKING SKILLS

1. **Researching Financial Services.** With your class, decide on several different types of financial institutions in your area and then divide into groups. Visit one of the institutions and find out about the services offered and rates of interest on the different savings plans. Use this information to make a table comparing services.

2. **Doing Research.** Using newspaper or magazine articles from 1980, research the provisions of the Depository Institutions Deregulation and Monetary Control Act. Then write a one-paragraph description of one way in which the act affects banks.

3. **Gathering and Analyzing Information.** Choose two stocks on the New York or American stock exchange, and follow their prices for two weeks in the financial pages of a newspaper. You will need to read only the last columns of figures. Note the daily closing prices, and then make a line graph showing the stocks' performance over the two weeks.

READINGS

Brown, Betty J., and Clow, John E. *General Business: Our Business and Economic World.* Boston: Houghton Mifflin, 1982. Savings accounts, insurance, and investing in stocks and bonds, real estate, and other investments.

Gupta, U. "How to Read the Financial Pages." *Black Enterprise,* April 1982. p. 27

Heilbroner, Robert, and Thurow, Lester. *Economics Explained.* Englewood Cliffs, N.J.: Prentice-Hall, 1985. Chapter 6, "Savings and Investing."

Ruby, Linda. "How to Pick a Mutual Fund to Match Your Money Needs." *Woman's Day,* 1 September 1982, p. 14.

Thoryn, Michael. "Good News for the Economy: IRAs Are Off to a Running Start." *Nation's Business,* June 1982, pp. 49–52.

The *Chapter Review* will help you develop your reading, writing, study, or communication skills with economic materials. It also has a vocabulary review and questions called *Practicing Your Economic Skills* to help you review and apply the economic skills you have learned in the text. *Discussing Economic Questions* presents thought questions, and *Applying Critical Thinking Skills* provides project and research ideas to extend the material in the text. *Readings* list books and articles to help you with research or for further reading about topics in the chapter.

Economics Vocabulary, the terms of economics, are listed on each chapter-opening page. In the text, they appear in bold type and are defined the first time they are used. *Vocabulary Builders,* words that you might not know, are defined in the margins. They also are listed on the unit-opening page of the teacher's manual or are listed on the Chapter Preview blackline worksheets. The economics vocabulary also are given in the Glossary at the end of the textbook. Vocabulary words are reviewed at the end of sections, chapters, and in the tests.

By issuing stock, a company obtains funds for use in expanding its business, and it hopes, in making a large profit. Table 7-2 describes the two types of stock that a corporation can sell. You will read more about ways to finance business operations in Chapter 11.

Stockholders—owners of stock—make money from stock in two ways. One is through **dividends,** the money return a stockholder receives on the money he or she invested in the company.

The corporation may declare a dividend at one or more times during a year. However, dividends are paid only when the company makes a profit. The other way people make money on stock is by selling it for more than they paid for it. Some people buy stock just to speculate (SPEK-yuh-layt). That is, they buy stock hoping that the price will increase greatly so they can sell at a profit. They do not buy it for the dividends.

issue: to offer new stock for sale

---

right-to-work law: state law forbidding contracts that require employees to join a union or pay union dues (p. 325).

robotics: the sophisticated computer-controlled machinery that forms part or all of an assembly line (p. 479).

satellites: structures that orbit the earth to relay signals to and from earth stations (p. 485).

saving: nonuse of income for a period of time so that it can be used later (p. 156).

short-term financing: borrowing by a business for a period of time less than a year (p. 277).

simple interest: interest figured only on the original amount deposited (p. 162).

skilled worker: person who has a trade or craft (p. 319).

smokestack industries: industries that manufacture heavy goods such as steel or automobiles (p. 478).

social cost: total cost that society must pay for any economic activity (p. 51).

stock: share of ownership in the company that issued the stock; entitles owner to a certain part of company profits and sometimes to a vote in certain matters, such as electing a board of directors (p. 160).

stockholder: person who owns stock in a company and thus holds a claim against a certain part of its profits (p. 161).

store of value: use of money to store purchasing power for later use (p. 377).

straight life insurance: insurance that combines insurance coverage

Putting Economics to Work

SURPLUS: SALE MERCHANDISE

It is the end of January, and Teresa Cintron is taking inventory—counting what she has—in her clothing store. Each summer and winter, Teresa holds a sale of the previous season's remaining items. In her latest end-of-season inventory, Teresa has found that she is left with 90 blouses and tops. The 90 items are divided almost equally among three price ranges. There are 40 blouses selling for $30 each, 30 tops for $20 each, and 20 tops for $15 each.

To sell these remaining winter items, Teresa lowers the prices on the 90 blouses and tops by 20 to 50 percent. To bring customers into her store, Teresa advertises the $15 tops at $7.50 each. This price is about

Putting Economics to Work, the summary case study at the end of the chapter, uses a real-world situation to explain an economic principle that you learned in the chapter. For instance, the example to the left is about the use of a sale to clear a store of unsold merchandise at the end of a selling season. The case study is at the end of the chapter; it explains supply and demand and illustrates a real-world application of the concept of surplus.

Learning Economic Skills

USING INDEXES OF CONSUMER PRICES

The consumer price index (CPI) is the measure of inflation with which you are probably most familiar. It is the one most often quoted in news reports and articles. This index, however, is just one of many measures of consumer prices published by the Bureau of Labor Statistics. Although the CPI indicates the average rise in prices, it is not necessarily the best guide to how much your own cost-of-living has gone up.

As you read earlier in this chapter, the CPI is based on the price of all items in a market basket of goods and services. The Bureau also publishes separate price indexes for each of the ten major groups making up the market basket. These are: food, residential rent, home ownership, home purchase, fuel oil and coal, gas and electricity, clothing, private transportation, public transportation, and medical care.

1967. But prices for fuel oil and coal have gone up about 410 percent over the same period. Although clothing is more expensive now than it was in 1967, the cost of clothing compared to most products on the market has actually decreased.

The rise in your own cost of living will depend on which consumer goods and services you use most. For example, if you live in a rented apartment and walk to work or school, your daily costs have probably gone up less than they have for a homeowner who drives to work. Rent increased an average of 172 percent between 1967 and 1986. However, during the same period, the cost of homeownership went up 236 percent. The cost of owning a car has also gone up considerably. The prices of automobiles, gasoline, garages, automobile insurance, as well as of highway and bridge tolls, have all increased.

Your own cost of living also depends on the mix of products you buy. To remain consistent, the market basket that the Bureau uses to compute the CPI is always the same. In reality, however, individuals vary the products and services they buy based on price. For example, if the price of beef increased steeply, you might buy less beef and more chicken. Because of careful shopping and substitution of goods, your own cost might go up less than the consumer price index would show.

Price Indexes for Selected Consumer Groups*

	Food	Rent	Home-owning	Fuel	Clothes	All Items
1965	94.4	96.9	92.7	94.6	93.7	94.5
1970	114.9	110.1	128.5	110.1	116.1	116.3
1975	175.4	137.3	181.7	235.3	142.3	161.2
1980	254.6	191.6	314.0	556.0	178.4	246.8
1981	274.6	208.2	352.7	675.9	186.9	272.4

Learning Economic Skills is a feature of one, two, or three pages in every chapter that explains some skill related to economics, such as understanding the use of statistics, recognizing trends, choosing a career, knowing which records to keep for income tax purposes, and how to fill out a tax form. Besides explaining a particular skill, each *Learning Economics Skills* feature provides exercises for you to practice your mastery of that skill.

Case Study

THE STORY OF THE APPLE

The story of the Apple computer is one of the great success stories in modern American business. In creating the Apple Company, two young men, Steven Wozniak and Steven Jobs, combined their technical genius with marketing flair to start what became the multi-billion dollar personal computer industry. Apple's co-founders were self-taught electronic wizards, who introduced their first computer, the Apple I, in 1976. The account of their success is a present-day version of the classic rags-to-riches stories that were so familiar in the earlier days of America's industrial history. Andrew Carnegie, Henry Ford, Thomas Edison, and countless other business pioneers made fortunes for themselves and in the process changed the daily lives of all Americans.

Wozniak and Jobs first teamed up when Jobs was a high school student in Palo Alto, California. Their most successful early product was a device that enabled a caller to make free long-distance telephone calls! From this questionable start, the

years, the Apple II earned $140 million. The success of the Apple Company was ensured when in 1980 it became a publicly owned company. With the sale of shares in the company to the public, Steven Wozniak and Steven Jobs became multi-millionaires.

Apple Computer, Inc. continued to be a pace-setter in the computer field, marketing new, more powerful and versatile machines like the Macintosh computers. But in 1986 the company experienced internal problems that led to the departure of both Wozniak and Jobs from Apple. The departure was painful for both of Apple's founders. However, Jobs organized a new company to develop education-oriented computer software. Some of Apple's key employees joined Jobs' company, leaving Apple with a potential "brain-drain."

An additional feature, the *Case Study,* appears in many chapters. The case studies provide a variety of material. They present the accomplishments of well-known members of business and industry. They show the American economy in action and provide real examples of the benefits of the market system.

Accompanying many chapters is a feature called a *Biography*. This feature appears in the text near the material it best illustrates. The biographies highlight the contributions of important economists of the past and present and will help you to understand how competing schools of thought have developed.

The *Readings*, which are part of the end-of-chapter materials, are primary and secondary source materials. They enable you to learn what economists and others actually said or thought about the economic concepts and topics you have just learned. There is one reading per section, and each focuses on a key critical thinking skill. Content and critical thinking questions on the reading will help you analyze and relate the sources to the text.

At the end of each unit, there is a special featured titled *Issue*, which presents various viewpoints on some topic of national interest mentioned in the unit, such as the conflict among national goals or the controversy over the national debt. Each *Issue* is followed by thought questions to help you weigh the evidence on both sides and decide what you think about the issue.

HOW TO STUDY YOUR TEXTBOOK

In writing and editing *Scribner Economics,* the author and editors had one goal in mind: to help you learn economics and the skills needed to use that knowledge in your everyday life. Economics, as you will discover, is not just a textbook subject. It relates to all aspects of your life—every day.

Before you begin your study of economics, we want to describe a five-step method for studying that will help you develop these skills and make learning economics—and other subjects—easier. It is called the SQ3R method. The letters stand for Survey, Question, Read, Recite, and Review. As you use the SQ3R method in studying *Scribner Economics,* you will find that you are better able to remember what you read.

SURVEY Before you begin reading an assignment, survey it. This means to look quickly through it to get an idea of what the material is about. *Scribner Economics* is organized to help you with this step. Each chapter contains the following highlights for skimming:

- **Chapter opening page.** The page at the beginning of each chapter summarizes the main ideas of the chapter and lists the objectives, or goals, to be achieved by reading it. It also lists the title of each of the chapter sections. Skim the lists to help you decide what is most important in the chapter.
- **Economics Vocabulary.** Skim this list of words for a preview of what is to come. Identify any words that are unfamiliar to you.
- **Headings.** Each chapter is organized like an outline. The chapter title is like the title of the outline. Major headings for each section, those that are numbered and in capital letters, are similar to the topics of an outline. Within the sections are headings in both capital and small letters, which are similar to the subtopics. Skim the headings of each chapter before you begin reading. This will give you the structure, or framework, for reading and understanding the chapter.
- **Reviewing Economic Principles.** These review questions at the end of the text following

each major heading relate back to the list of objectives at the beginning of the chapter. Use the questions to check yourself. Skim them to see how well you did in deciding what was most important.

- **Graphics.** There are pictures, charts, graphs, diagrams, and tables throughout the book. As you skim the text, look at them briefly to get a mental picture of the type of statistics, people, and events that relate to the concepts in the chapter.

QUESTIONS After you have skimmed the chapter, ask yourself questions based on each heading. In other words, turn each heading into a question. This will help you decide what facts to look for as you read. When you first practice the SQ3R method, we suggest that you actually write out your questions. Also, ask yourself if you understand all the Economics Vocabulary in the list. However, if there are any vocabulary words you do not know, look them up in the Glossary before you begin to read.

READ Read one heading at a time and the text that follows. Look for the answer to the question that you write for that heading.

RECITE Recite the answers to your questions aloud. Also, make notes on the answers. Your spoken answers and notes should come from memory and should be brief. They should be the main points for each topic and subtopic only.

REVIEW Review the chapter. Read over the main points once again. You can use the chapter opening page as your guide. If there are any of your own questions or any of the Reviewing Economic Principles questions that you could not answer or could not answer correctly, reread the sections that explain those points. Then answer these questions again.

You can use the SQ3R method with any textbook you have. Just look for special features like the chapter opening page, and adjust the skimming step to the features in that textbook.

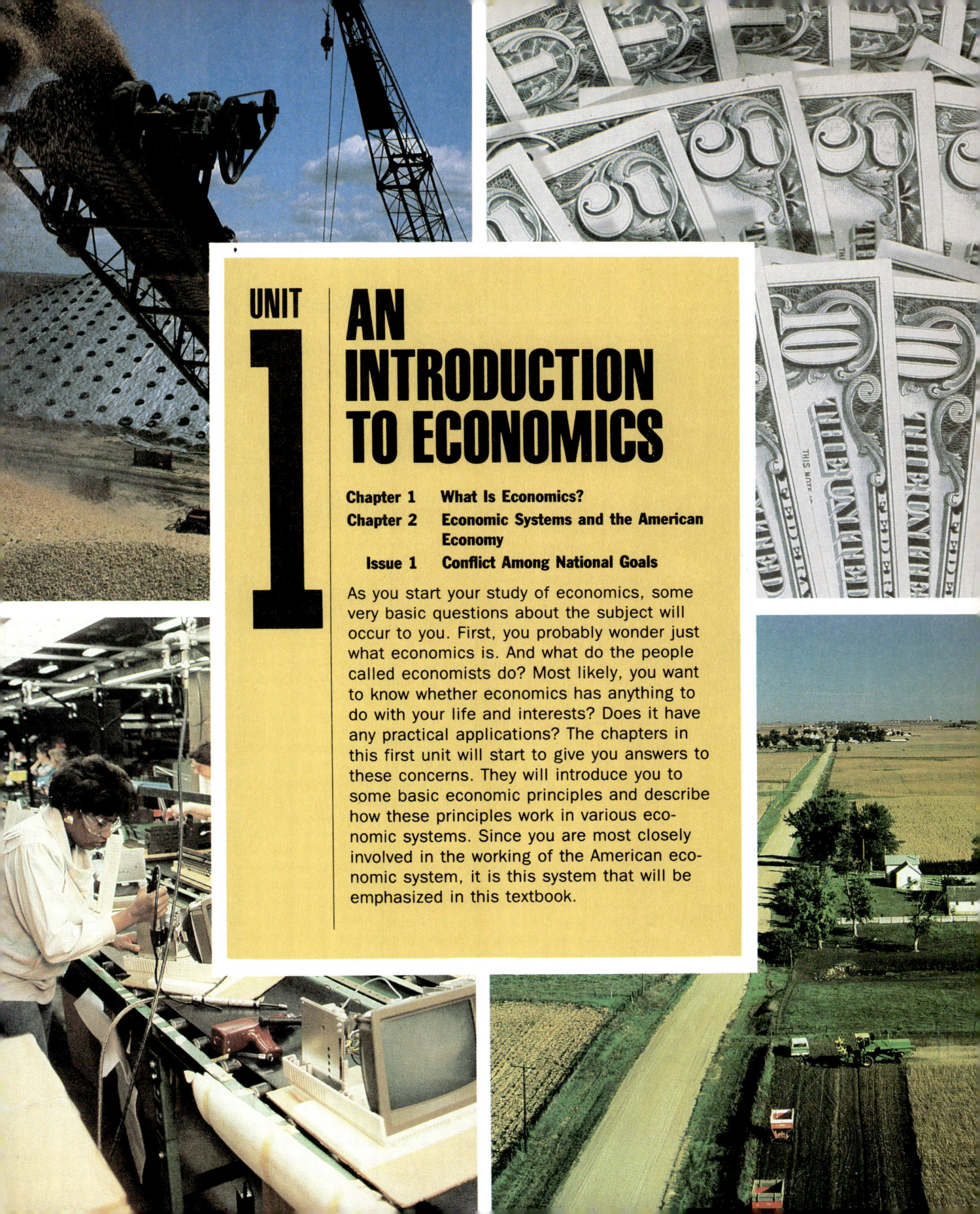

UNIT 1

AN INTRODUCTION TO ECONOMICS

As you start your study of economics, some very basic questions about the subject will occur to you. First, you probably wonder just what economics is. And what do the people called economists do? Most likely, you want to know whether economics has anything to do with your life and interests? Does it have any practical applications? The chapters in this first unit will start to give you answers to these concerns. They will introduce you to some basic economic principles and describe how these principles work in various economic systems. Since you are most closely involved in the working of the American economic system, it is this system that will be emphasized in this textbook.

CHAPTER 1

Land, labor, and capital—machines, tools, and money—are resources that every economy needs. The choices people make in using these limited resources help shape their nation's economy.

WHAT IS ECONOMICS?

This chapter explains what economics is and how economists work. It also explains why studying economics is important to you as a present or future employee, employer, entrepreneur, consumer, saver, investor, and citizen. By describing the use of economic models and the principles of scarcity of resources, trade-offs, opportunity costs, and production possibilities, the chapter introduces you to some basic economic principles that you will be studying throughout the text. Learning Economic Skills deals with reading tables and graphs.

CHAPTER OBJECTIVES After you study the sections of this chapter, you will be able to:

1 • state the basic problem in economics.
   • explain the importance for you of studying economics.
   • identify the types of resources available to satisfy needs and wants.
   ★ determine that tables and graphs can be used to present economic information in visual form.

2 • explain the trade-offs involved with production possibilities.

3 • describe the use of economic models by economists.
   • explain why economists do not work with values.

ECONOMICS VOCABULARY

economics
resource
hypothesis
generalization
scarcity
wants
land
labor
capital
productivity
entrepreneurship
factors of production
goods and services
technology
trade-off
statistics
bar graph
line graph
pie graph
opportunity cost
production possibilities
economy
economic model
values

The United States has chosen to use some of its resources for space telecommunications. How does this communication satellite benefit Americans?

Economics is the study of how individuals and nations make choices about how to use scarce resources to fill their needs and wants. A **resource** is anything that people can use to make or obtain what they need or want. You may be asking yourself at this point how economics will help you, a student. Also, you may be wondering how scarce resources is a problem for a nation like the United States that has such abundant resources.

It may surprise you to know that many of the decisions you will face as a citizen deal with how the United States should use its resources. Learning economic principles can help you make decisions about candidates for political office, political and social issues, and the goals the United States should set for itself, such as how to spend government revenues. Many people are familiar with the benefits of government programs such as job training and Medicare, but how many people are aware of the costs of these programs? Economics can help you to understand both costs and benefits and, therefore, help you to make better decisions.

Because economics examines facts in order to make choices, it can teach you some basic skills for making decisions. Being able to make reasoned, well-informed decisions will be important to you as an employee, employer, entrepreneur, saver, and investor, as well as a citizen. The economic principles that underlie your different roles in life are the same. This chapter introduces you to some of these basic concepts.

1 | WHY STUDY ECONOMICS?

Ask yourself as you read:
- What is scarcity?
- What are the factors of production?

As a student, you probably have a small amount of money—from an allowance or a part-time job—to spend. As a result, you have to make choices about its use. Whenever you make such a spending decision, each available choice competes with every other available choice. Suppose you have $10 to spend. You could use it to buy lunch for five days or one record album or a sweatshirt or two movie tickets, and so on.

THE PROBLEM OF SCARCITY

The need to make choices arises from the fact that everything that exists is limited, even though some items may appear to be in overabundant supply. At any one moment in the United States, or anywhere, there is a fixed, or set, amount of resources available. At the same time, people may have different, competing uses for these resources. This is the problem of scarcity. It is the basic problem of economics. **Scarcity** means that people do not and cannot have enough income, time, or resources to satisfy their every desire. What you can buy with your

fixed: limited, set at a certain amount

income as a student is limited by the amount of income you have. In this case, your income is the scarce resource.

The problem of scarcity faces businesses as well as individuals. Businesspeople must choose constantly among the possible uses for their resources. Decisions are made daily about what to produce now, what to produce later, and what to stop producing. These decisions in turn affect people's income and their ability to buy. Nations, too, face the problem of choosing how to spend their scarce resources. The United States, for example, must decide each year how much to spend on defense, how much on Social Security benefits, and on aid to higher education. How people make these choices is the subject of economics.

WANTS AND NEEDS

How many times have you said that you "need" something? How often do you think about what you "want"? The distinction, or difference, between wants and needs is not a clear one. Everyone needs certain basic things—enough food, clothing, and shelter to survive. People think there are certain basic needs for a nation, too, such as a strong military defense. Americans also consider a certain number of years of public education and adequate health care as needs.

Everything other than these basic needs are called **wants** by economists. People want better and more clothing, bigger places to live, new cars, personal computers, and the like. Although more and more people have these items, this does not mean that anyone actually needs them. For example, people entertained themselves and informed themselves of news long before the invention of the radio. But as the wonders of radio were advertised and more people bought radios, more people began to believe they needed one. What began as a luxury, or want, became to many people a necessity. This cycle of wants and perceived needs is repeated over and over. In economics, however, there are only a few true needs, such as food and shelter. You may believe you need a videocassette recorder (VCR). But is it really a need or just a want?

TYPES OF RESOURCES

Besides the question of whether you need or want a VCR there is the issue of whether there will be enough VCRs to allow every person to own one. Also, not everyone would have enough money to buy one. As you have just read, only a certain amount of resources exist, regardless of wants and needs. Traditionally, economists have classified resources into three types, depending on their economic use: 1. land, 2. labor, and 3. capital.

The term **land** refers to natural resources, not just to surface land. Natural resources are all the things found in nature—on or in water and the earth—such as fish, animals, forests, and minerals as well as land and water. Among the most important natural resources in economic terms are land and mineral deposits such as iron ore. In economics, the location of land is also important. In the United States today, location is

The problem of scarcity affects each consumer's purchases of food and all items. Why must this shopper make choices when she purchases food?

perceived (puhr-SEEVD): believed to be

probably more important than natural resources in establishing the value of land.

Labor refers to the work that people do. It includes all kinds of jobs—bus driver, doctor, teacher, business executive, plumber, assembly-line worker, and so on. Anyone who works is a part of the labor resource.

Capital is all the property—machines, buildings, and tools—that people use to make other goods and services. For example, the machines used to make automobiles are capital. The cars themselves are not considered capital unless they are used, for example, as taxicabs, to produce services. Combining capital with land and labor resources increases the value of all three resources by increasing their productivity. **Productivity** is the ability to produce greater quantities of goods and services in better and faster ways. A person using a tractor, for example, can plow many more acres a day than a person using a wooden plow and a team of horses.

A related resource is **entrepreneurship** (ahn-truh-pruh-NER-ship), which refers to individuals' ability to start new businesses, to introduce new products and techniques, and to improve management techniques in existing businesses. All changes in business organization are part of entrepreneurship. It involves initiative, and individual willingness to take risks and to experiment with new ideas that could lead to profits. Entrepreneurs, or those who use these entrepreneurial skills, succeed when they produce new products, improve an existing product or produce it more efficiently, or reorganize a business to run more smoothly.

Together these resources are called the **factors of production.** They are the things used to produce **goods and services.** Goods are the things that people buy. Services are the activities done for others for a fee. For example, butchers and bakers sell goods, while doctors, teachers, and auto mechanics sell services. Sometimes the term *goods* is used to mean both goods and services because individuals may provide a good and a service.

Today some economists add another item to the list of resources: technology. The first use of fire by early people is an example of technology. Any use of land, labor, and capital that produces goods and services more efficiently is technology. For example, the tractor is a technological advance over the horse-drawn plow.

Today, however, **technology** usually describes the use of science to develop new products and new methods for producing and distributing goods and services. In modern economics, land, labor, capital, and advanced technology are interrelated. Advanced machinery and new production and distribution methods increase the productivity of the other resources. For example, without modern drilling machinery, the amount of oil pumped from the ground would be far less than it is. It would also be impossible to tap the oil resources of the ocean without modern equipment. Modern technology has many benefits. It creates leisure time, highly skilled workers, efficient use of resources, lower prices, and a high quality of goods and services.

1. Define these terms: **a.** economics, **b.** resource, **c.** scarcity, **d.** land, **e.** labor, **f.** capital, **g.** productivity, **h.** entrepreneurship, **i.** factors of production, **j.** goods, **k.** services, **l.** technology.
2. Why is scarcity the basic problem in economics?
3. **a.** What is the difference between needs and wants? **b.** Give two examples of each.
4. **Critical Thinking: Identifying Main Ideas. a.** List three types of resources available to satisfy wants. **b.** Describe each and include one example. **c.** Why are entrepreneurship and technology sometimes included as resources?

2 | TRADE-OFFS

Ask yourself as you read:
- What factors must be considered in making economic choices?
- What kind of graphic aid will show trade-offs and opportunity costs?

Scarcity forces people to make choices about how they will use their resources. Those choices affect not only how people live today, but how people will live in the future. It is important to realize that the economic choices people make involve exchanging one good or service for another. If you choose to buy a cassette for your videocassette recorder, you are exchanging your money for the right to own the cassette. Exchanging one thing for the use of another is called a **trade-off.**

Individuals, businesses, and nations are forced to make trade-offs every time they use their resources in one way and not another. For example, as a student you may be faced with a decision about going to college or vocational school to increase future earnings, or going to work right after high school. Consider some other possible trade-offs that individuals, businesses, and nations face:
- saving to satisfy future wants or spending income now.
- continued automobile pollution or higher car manufacturing costs.
- more defense spending or more aid to education.

People make trade-offs every day. They are a part of making choices, which are unavoidable because of the problem of scarcity.

OPPORTUNITY COSTS

Another way to describe a trade-off is in terms of the cost of what a person gives up in order to get something else. When you decide to study economics for one hour, you are making a choice. You are giving up many other things you could do. You could watch television, read a book, talk on the telephone, listen to music, and so on. Because time is a scarce resource—there are only so many hours in a day—you must decide how to use it.

Nutritious food is a necessity for everyone. How do school cafeterias satisfy this need?

In other words, there is a cost involved in spending time studying this book. Economists call it an **opportunity cost.** This is the next best alternative that had to be given up for the alternative that was chosen. Whatever you consider as the value of the next best alternative to studying—watching television, for example—is the opportunity cost of your studying for one hour.

Consider an example at the national level. Suppose Congress votes $2 billion for projects to clean up polluted rivers. The opportunity cost of their vote is the next best alternative use of those same tax dollars. For example, instead of voting for clean water projects, Congress could have voted for increased spending on space research. Then the opportunity cost of clean rivers would be fewer space flights.

Being aware of opportunity costs and trade-offs is important in making economic decisions of all kinds. For example, you will be able to make wiser use of your own resources if you know the opportunity costs and trade-offs involved. You will be able to vote more intelligently if you are aware of the choices your elected officials face. Businesspeople, too, must consider opportunity costs and trade-offs. They must constantly decide on the most efficient way to produce goods and services.

PRODUCTION POSSIBILITIES

The term *mix* brings up another fact about resources. How do people determine how much of each thing to produce? What are the trade-offs and opportunity costs involved in each decision? The concept of production possibilities is useful in examining this problem. **Production possibilities** are all the combinations of goods and services that can be produced from a fixed amount of resources in a given period of time. For each situation, only a limited number of factors are considered. There are a fixed amount of resources and a given period of time.

The classic example for explaining production possibilities in economics is the trade-off between guns and butter. *Guns* refers to all military defense, and *butter,* to all civilian goods. The extremes for a nation would be using all its resources to produce only guns or only butter. Figure 1-1 shows the two extremes. Point A represents all resources being used to produce only guns. Point E represents the other extreme— all resources being used to produce only butter.

Of course, no nation produces all of one or the other. Countries produce combinations, or mixes, of goods. That is shown by the curve between points A and E. The curve represents the production possibilities between guns and butter in a nation during one year. Any point on the curve AE is a possibility. If a nation were at point D, it would be producing mostly civilian goods and some military goods. If a nation were at point B, it would be producing mostly military items and some civilian goods. The decision about where on the production-possibilities curve the nation will be is determined by the federal government. The government takes income from citizens through taxes. It uses this revenue, which could have been used for butter, to produce guns. "The nation"

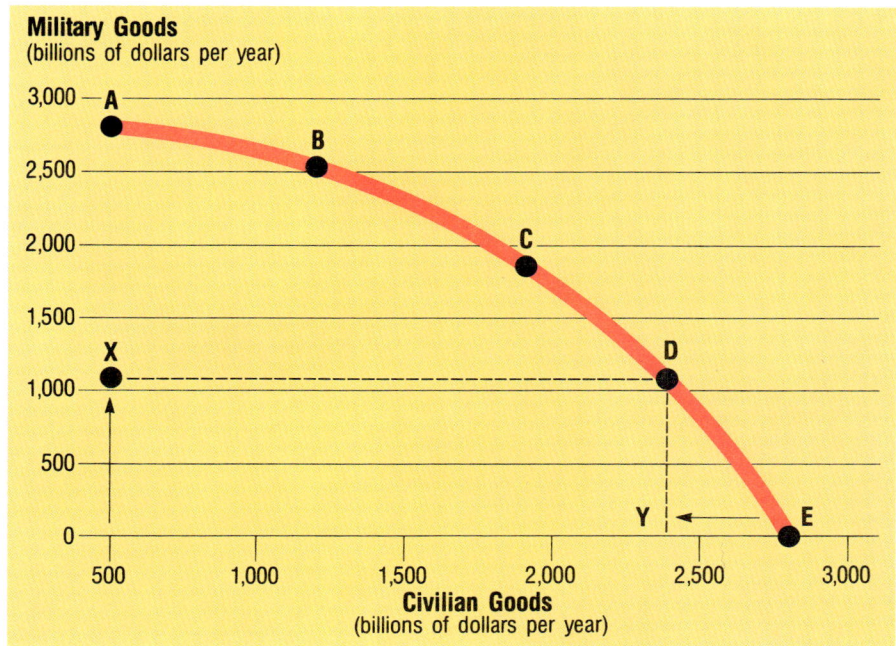

Figure 1–1: PRODUCTION POSSIBILITIES

Military Goods
(billions of dollars per year)

Civilian Goods
(billions of dollars per year)

The quantity of guns made per year is shown by the vertical distance from point 0 to point A. What is shown by the horizontal distance from point 0 to point E?

on the curve is Congress and the President, who make decisions for the public.

Production-possibilities curves are a good way to show trade-offs and opportunity costs visually. As you can see from the graph, a nation or a business cannot produce more of one thing without giving up something. For example, if a nation starts with all butter production and no military production—point E—it can only get to point D—some weapons production—by giving up some butter production. In other words, the price of having some weapons production (represented by the vertical distance from O to point X) is giving up some butter production (represented by the horizontal distance from point E to point Y). The amount of butter production given up is the opportunity cost for increasing weapons production.

By using a production-possibilities curve, a nation or a business can decide how best to use its resources. By "best" is meant using resources most efficiently for economic growth. Such a curve is useful in locating the opportunity costs if a particular course of action is followed.

REVIEWING ECONOMIC PRINCIPLES

1. **a.** Define trade-off. **b.** Define opportunity cost. **c.** How are trade-offs and opportunity costs related?
2. **Critical Thinking: Analyzing Data. a.** What is the balance between military and civilian production represented by point C in Figure 1-1? **b.** What type of production must be reduced to move from point C to point B?

Learning Economic Skills | READING TABLES AND GRAPHS

Statistics are data presented in numerical form. They are important in understanding the nation's economy and in making good economic decisions. Statistics are sometimes quoted in text material, but most are organized into tables and graphs. These are some of an economist's most important tools. Knowing how to read them is essential to understanding economic information in newspapers, magazines, financial reports, reference books, and this book.

TABLES

You were undoubtedly familiar with tables before you began this course. You may have used a logarithmic table in math, or a train or bus schedule on a trip. Tables present data in rows and columns according to topics. Each column contains only one topic and where columns cross, the data is related. Tables make information, especially statistical data, easier to read than if it were presented in text form.

How Americans Traveled In A Recent Year

Form of Transportation	Passenger Miles in Billions	Percent Distribution
Private Automobile	1,287	83.4
Airlines	213	13.8
Bus	27	1.7
Train	12	.8
Inland waterways	4	.3

Practicing Your Skills

1. What was the most frequently used form of passenger transportation in this year?
2. How many billions of passenger miles were traveled on: **a.** buses? **b.** trains?

GRAPHS

Graphs are a visual presentation of statistical data and are often easier to read than tables. There are three types: bar graph, line graph, and pie, or circle, graph. On bar and line graphs, the bottom line is called the horizontal axis and the line on the side, the vertical axis. When you read a graph, be sure to read its title and all labels carefully to find out the kind of data shown.

BAR GRAPHS

Bar graphs usually compare differences between things at one point in time. They can also show the change in amounts of things at different times. Read the bar graph below. It shows the number of people employed in seven industries in a recent year.

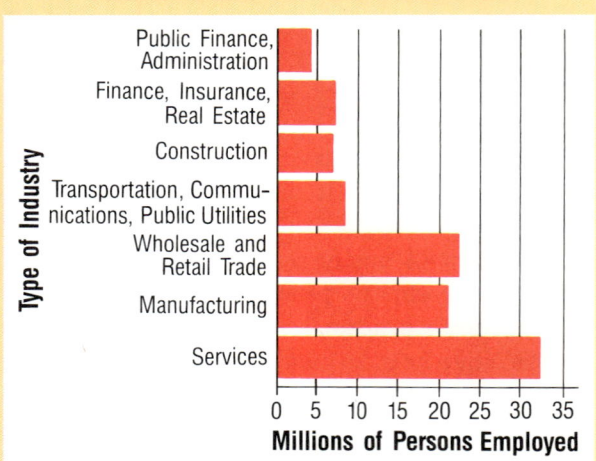

Numbers of Persons Employed in Selected Industries in a Recent Year

Source: *Statistical Abstract of the U.S.*, Bureau of the Census

Now look at the next bar graph. It shows the number of men and women in the labor force in the United States from 1960 to 1990. The labor force is the total number of people employed or able and willing to work and looking for a job.

Men and Women in the U.S. Labor Force, 1960-1990

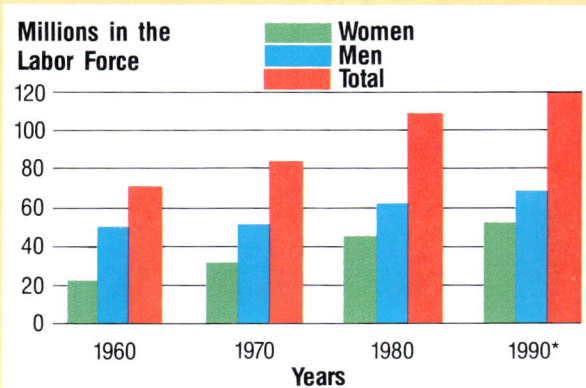

Source: *Statistical Abstract of the U.S.*, Bureau of the Census

Practicing Your Skills

1. Which industry employed the largest number of workers in the year shown?
2. How many were employed in: **a.** construction? **b.** manufacturing?
3. How large was the labor force in 1960?
4. How many workers were women: **a.** in 1960? **b.** in 1990?

LINE GRAPHS

A **line graph** shows the change in the same item over a period of time. The line of the graph is called the curve. Often one graph will compare changes between two or more items by using several curves. The horizontal axis of a line graph shows units of time. The line graph here shows the change in the percentage of the country's population that has graduated from high school.

Practicing Your Skills

1. What is shown on the vertical axis?
2. What period of time does the graph cover?
3. What percentage of the population had graduated: **a.** in 1940? **b.** in 1980?

High School Graduates as Percentage of U.S. Population Over 25 Years Old, 1940-1990

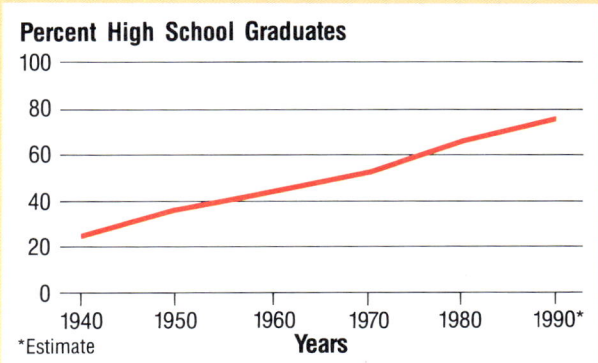

Source: U.S. Department of Labor, Bureau of Labor Statistics

PIE GRAPHS

As you will read in Chapter 2, percent means parts per hundred. A pie graph is a good way to show percentages. Each section of the pie represents a percentage of the total. The percentages in all sections must always add up to 100. Read the pie graph shown here carefully to answer the questions. Gross national product (GNP) is the total value of all final goods and services produced by a nation during a given period.

Gross National Product in a Recent Year

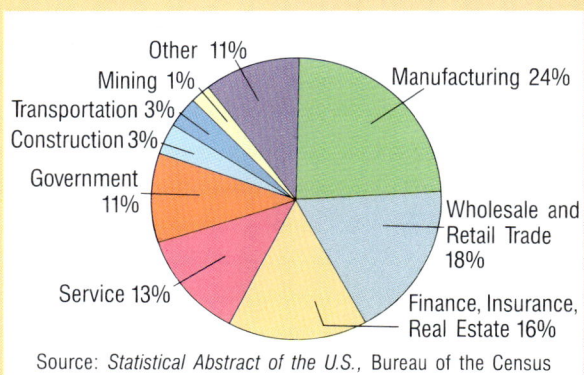

Source: *Statistical Abstract of the U.S.*, Bureau of the Census

Practicing Your Skills

1. What percentage of the gross national product in a recent year came from: **a.** wholesale and retail trade? **b.** mining and manufacturing?
2. What is the percentage of all other areas combined?

MISLEADING GRAPHS

Although graphs are helpful in visualizing statistical data, they can be used to mislead. The most common way to distort a graph is to stretch the scale on either the vertical or the horizontal axis. Try to imagine the bar graph shown on page 11 as if the vertical axis were twice as long as it is now. The line would be much taller, which might give you the idea that the numbers were much greater than they actually are.

Now look at the line graph shown on page 11 and imagine that the horizontal axis has been doubled. What would this do to the curve on the graph? What impression might you get of the changes in the number of Americans over 25 years of age who have graduated from high school during the last 40 years or so?

The two graphs shown on this page present the same information—a recent increase in the consumer price index. By studying the changes in this index, economists can measure changes in the average cost of a certain number of goods and services that people buy year after year. Study these graphs carefully to answer the following questions.

Practicing Your Skills

1. **a.** What are the differences in the way the scales on the two graphs are drawn? **b.** What effect do these differences have on the shape of each graph's curve?
2. What are the different impressions the two graphs give of how steep the rise in prices has been?

Consumer Price Index, 1979-1988

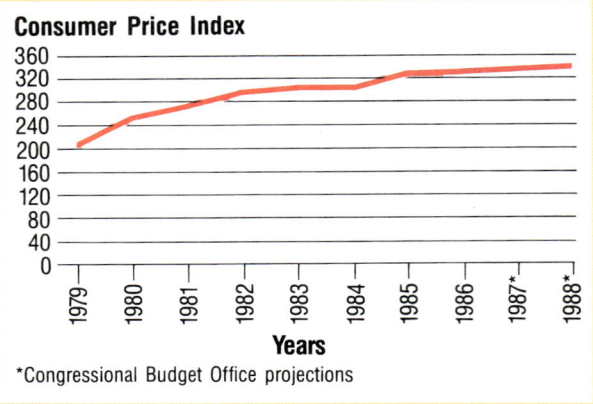

*Congressional Budget Office projections

Source: *Statistical Abstract of the U.S.,* Bureau of the Census

Consumer Price Index, 1979-1988

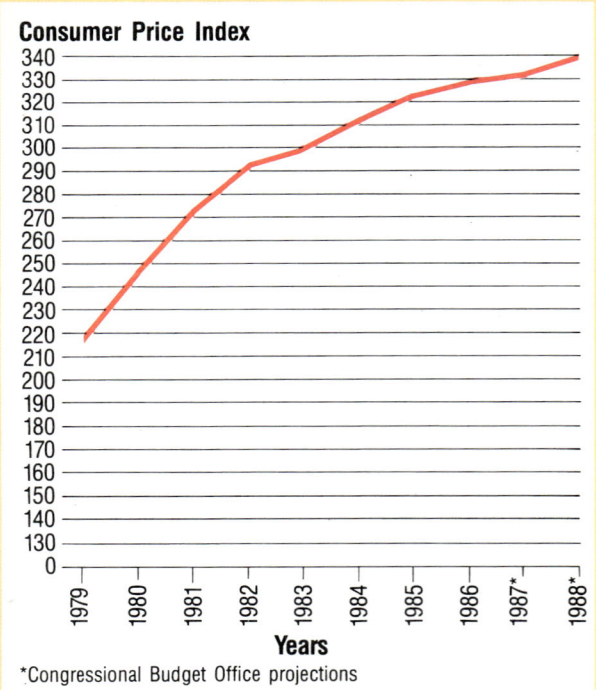

*Congressional Budget Office projections

Source: *Statistical Abstract of the U.S.,* Bureau of the Census

3 | WHAT DO ECONOMISTS DO?

Ask yourself as you read:
- What topics do economists study?
- Why do economists use economic models?

Economics, as you read, is concerned with the ways individuals and nations choose to use their scarce resources. Much of the work of economists deals with describing and analyzing causes and their effects and with comparing and contrasting information. For example, economists might investigate the causes of unemployment among teenagers or compare unemployment among different groups within the economy.

The American Economic Association lists 14 major topics that economists study. Among them are labor economics; business administration, marketing, and accounting; money, credit, and banking; international economics; urban economics; and regional economics. This textbook will introduce you to many of these topics and to the basic concepts of economics. You will learn how your personal economic decisions work with those of labor, business, and government to form the nation's economy. You will then see how the nation's economy fits into international economic activity. By the term **economy** is meant all the activity in a nation that together affects the production, distribution, and use of goods and services.

To carry out their investigations, economists often gather information from the real world. These data then become the basis for testing theories that explain an event, such as unemployment, or offer a solution to a problem—more federal aid for job training. The theories or solutions then become the basis for actual decisions about how to use resources. Those decisions may be made by private business or by government agencies. Because of the importance of economics, economists are employed by government agencies and large corporations as well as many smaller companies.

data (DAT-uh): facts, information

ECONOMIC MODELS

In their work, economists use economic models, or theories. An **economic model** is a simplified representation of the real world. Physicists, chemists, biologists, and other scientists also use models to explain in simple terms the complex workings of the world.

Economic models show the way people react to changes in the economy. The most frequently used model explains how people react to changes in the prices of things they want to purchase. An economist has three ways of presenting such a model: through an explanation in words, in a graph, or with a mathematical equation. Whichever method is chosen, the information in the model is the same. In the case of prices, the model—a graph—shows that consumers respond to higher prices by purchasing less of more expensive items. People respond to lower prices by purchasing more of less expensive items. For example, your local record store lowers the price of albums of a particular popular singer or group if it wants to sell more albums by those performers. The record store also hopes to attract more customers to the store by cutting prices.

No economic model records every detail and relationship that exists about a problem to be studied. A model will show only the basic factors needed to analyze the problem. Suppose, for example, an economist for General Motors is studying the reaction of buyers to an increase in the price of its subcompacts. The economist will find that hundreds of factors influence buyers. However, most of these factors will not appear in the economist's model. It is not that these factors are unimportant. But economists have found that they need to analyze only three basic factors to determine buyer reaction to price changes. These factors are: 1. the price of the item, 2. the income of the average buyer, and 3. the price of alternatives.

factor: fact or situation that influences another

alternative (awl-TER-nuh-tiv): possible choice

THE PURPOSE OF MODELS

As you study economics, it is important to keep in mind the purpose of economic models. They are not supposed to account for all the possible factors that might influence a problem. They take into account only the most important ones. Remembering this should help you from being confused as you read this or any economics textbook. Much of what is discussed in economics is described in terms of economic models.

An economist considers a model *good* if it provides useful material for analyzing the way the real world works. As in forming a hypothesis, an economist begins with some idea about the way things work, then collects facts and discards those that are not relevant. Once a conclusion is reached, the only way an economist can find out whether a model is good is to test it. Suppose an economist has developed a model stating that when the federal government requires employers to pay higher wages to teenagers, unemployment among that group increases. The economist goes about testing the model, or theory, by collecting data on the amount of teenage unemployment every year for the last 30 years. He or she also gathers information on the frequency of federal legislation increasing the minimum, or legal, wage paid to teenagers. Suppose the economist finds that every time the legal wage rate increased, teenage employment decreased. The economist can be fairly satisfied with the model. Suppose that the data do not seem to show a relationship between teenage unemployment and increases in the minimum wage. The economist then will have to develop another model to show the relationship between minimum wages and teenage unemployment.

You should understand that much of the work of economists is involved with predicting how people will react in a particular situation. Individual human behavior is not always predictable, however. As a result, an economist's answer to a problem may turn out not to work for everyone. For example, to stimulate the economy, some economists be-

Writing about Economics: Robert L. Heilbroner (1919–   )

The well-known economist Robert L. Heilbroner combines scholarship with literary style when he communicates his ideas about our economic world. Heilbroner has been fascinated by the economic theories of Smith, Marx, and Mills ever since he first studied about them at Harvard University in 1936. After a brief career in government and business, Heilbroner received his doctoral degree at the New School for Social Research in New York City, and he has taught there since 1972.

A prolific writer, Heilbroner has written a dozen books on economics. His first book, *The Worldly Philosophers,* was published in 1953 and helped to popularize the famous economists he wrote about. Heilbroner not only examined the ideas of these great economic thinkers but he brought them to life as people whose ideas helped shape our world. His presentation in *The Worldly Philosophers* of Adam Smith's theories and those of Thomas Malthus and David Ricardo clearly set forth the ideas and insights of these pioneers of economics.

He took special interest in the English business owner and early Utopian socialist, Robert Owen. Heilbroner describes how Owen's thinking developed in the early 1800s. England, emerging from the Napoleonic Wars, was beginning to industrialize its economy. Owen was greatly disturbed by the terrible conditions faced by laborers in the early textile mills and factories. And he became convinced that the solution was a system of capitalism based on social responsibility. This theory of utopian socialism would end the abuse of children working in the factories and the long hours, low wages, and unsafe working conditions that adult laborers also were forced to endure. Owen argued that factory conditions would be greatly improved without loss of profits for the owners. Heilbroner also described the economic doctrines of Karl Marx and John Maynard Keynes in his book. *The Worldly Philosophers* today remains one of the best accounts of some of the great economists and their place in history.

Heilbroner's later books include *The Future as History* (1960), *The Great Ascent* (1963), *Between Capitalism and Socialism* (1970), *The Nature and Logic of Capitalism* (1985), and two works in which he is coauthor with Yale economics professor Lester Thurow, *The Making of Economic Society* (1979) and *Marxism: For and Against* (1980).

Heilbroner's writings reflect his firm belief that economics is a dynamic science filled with exciting ideas and endless possibilities. He understands that great economists of the past had the power to shape history, and he regards their ideas as a valuable legacy to our modern world. This is seen in his statement in the introduction to *The Worldly Philosophers:* "They took the whole world as their subject and portrayed that world in a dozen bold attitudes—angry, desperate, hopeful. The evolution of their heretical opinions into common sense, and their exposure of common sense as superstition, constitute nothing less than the gradual construction of the architecture of contemporary life."

1. Why was Heilbroner's book *The Worldly Philosophers* so important?
2. What did Heilbroner mean when he wrote "the great economists of the past had the power to shape history"?

15

lieve that taxes should be cut and government spending increased. These economists believe that cutting taxes will increase personal spending, which, in turn, will increase production. However, people's fears about the future may cause them to save the extra money rather than spend it. As this illustrates, economists cannot predict all the factors that may influence people's behavior.

SCHOOLS OF ECONOMIC THOUGHT

school of thought: group that agrees on certain principles or ideas

Economists deal with facts. Their personal opinions and beliefs may nonetheless influence how they view those facts and fit them to theories. The government under which an economist lives also shapes how he or she views the world. As a result, all economists will not agree that a particular theory offers the best solution to a problem. Often, economists from competing schools of thought claim that their theory alone will produce a certain result. Throughout this text, you will be reading about men and women who have contributed to economic thought at various times and in various countries. Their views often represent differing sides of the same economic issue.

At any one time, a nation's political leaders will agree with one school of economic thought and develop policies based on it. Later, leaders may agree with another group of economists. For example, from the 1930s to the 1970s, one group of economists believed that increased government intervention in the economy was needed to control unemployment and inflation. Since the beginning of the 1980s, however, a different economic philosophy has been widely accepted. This philosophy stresses the role of businesses and consumers rather than of the government in preventing increased unemployment and inflation. You will read about all of these schools of thought later in the text.

VALUES AND ECONOMICS

Economics will help you to predict what may happen if certain events occur or certain policies are followed. However, economics will not tell you whether the result will be good or bad. That judgment will depend on your values. **Values** are the beliefs or characteristics that a person or group considers important, such as religious freedom, equal opportunity, individual intitiative, freedom from want, and so on. Suppose, for example, that you believe the nation should do something to lower unemployment among teenagers. This belief is a value judgment on your part. If you were a legislator, you might show your commitment to this value by introducing a bill to decrease teenage unemployment. The economists who help you research the causes of teenage unemployment will not tell you whether your bill is good or bad. They will tell you whether the proposed solution may be workable or not.

People's values differ. Therefore, they will have varying opinions about whether or not something should be done to lower teenage unemployment. Having the same values does not mean that people will agree about solutions, strategies, or interpretation of data. For example,

Table 1-1: USING A HYPOTHESIS

From physical science and history classes, you are probably familiar with the term **hypothesis**—an educated guess, or prediction, used as the starting point for investigation. The list below reviews the steps involved in making and testing hypotheses. In working with models, economists use these same steps.

1. Define the problem.

2. From the possible alternatives, state a hypothesis that appears to offer the best solution to a problem or explanation of an event.
   An economist may also talk about reaching a goal.

3. Gather data to test the hypothesis.
   Besides using facts from the real world, an economist must identify economic principles involved.

4. Evaluate the data and discard any that are not relevant, or related to the immediate situation, or that are not objective. Objective data are those that are based on fact, not influenced by personal feelings.

5. Make sure there are enough data to test the hypothesis thoroughly.

6. Develop a conclusion based on the data.
   To do this, an economist evaluates whether the alternative is the best in view of its consequences and trade-offs.*

7. If the hypothesis appears to be proved, retest it with new data to see if the same results can be obtained again.
   An economist may test another alternative to see if it offers a better solution.

8. If the hypothesis appears to be proved, form a generalization that can be applied to other cases. A **generalization** (jen-uhr-uh-luh-ZAY-shuhn) pulls together common ideas among facts and is true in most cases.
   For an economist, this step may involve developing an economic policy based on the best alternative.

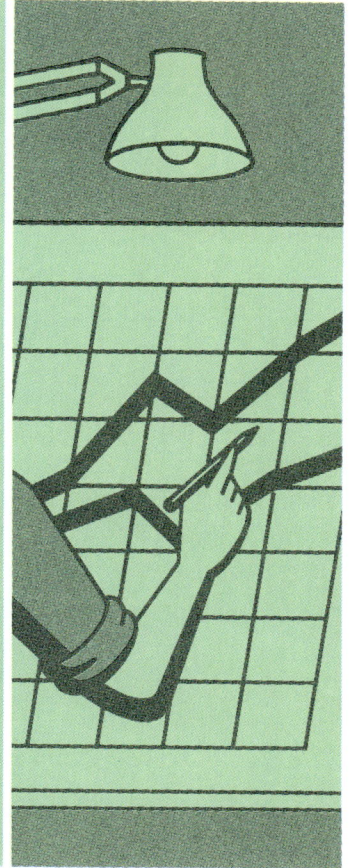

those in favor of decreasing teenage unemployment may disagree about the best way to solve this problem. Some may want the federal government to pay for training programs, while others may favor business-sponsored trainee programs, and still others may want the government to require young people to stay in school until they are 19 years of age. Therefore, people who disagree strongly about something may share the same values.

REVIEWING ECONOMIC PRINCIPLES

1. Write a sentence defining each of the following economic terms: **a.** economy, **b.** values.
2. **a.** An economic model is a simplified representation of the real world. What does this mean? **b.** What factors do economic models take into account?
3. **Critical Thinking: Analyzing Ideas.** What is the reason that economists cannot tell you whether a possible solution to a problem will be good or bad?

17

SUMMARY OF
IMPORTANT PRINCIPLES

1
- Economics is the study of how individuals and nations choose to use their scarce resources to fulfill their needs and wants.
- Because economics involves examining facts to make choices, it can teach some basic skills for decision making.
- Scarcity is the basic problem in economics. Everything that exists is limited. Although resources are scarce and there are few true economic needs, people's wants are unlimited.
- Land, labor, and capital are the traditional categories of resources available to satisfy needs and wants. Some economists today also include entrepreneurship and technology as types of resources.
- Together land, labor, capital, and entrepreneurship are called the factors of production. They are used to produce goods and services. Goods are the items that people purchase. Services are activities that provide something useful or necessary such as a haircut.

2
- Exchanging one thing for the use of another is called a trade-off. An opportunity cost is the cost of what a person gives up in order to get a chosen alternative. It is the next best alternative that had to be given up for the alternative that was chosen.
- A production-possibilities curve can help a nation or business decide how best to use resources to produce the most efficient combination of goods and services.
- Tables and graphs can show economic information in visual form. Depending on how graphs are drawn, they can be helpful or misleading.

3
- Economic models take into account only the most important factors that might influence a problem.
- Economics will help to predict what may happen if certain events occur or certain policies are followed. It will not tell whether the result will be good or bad. That judgment depends on a person's values.
- Economists examine economic data from the real world and offer solutions to economic problems. Economists specialize in many fields of economic study and are hired by businesses and all levels of government.

Putting Economics to Work

MAKING DECISIONS

In this chapter, you read about forming and testing hypotheses. Whenever people make a decision, they go through these same steps. For example, Al and Liz Smith decided to buy a new car. Then they talked about it, "We need to buy a new car, but we don't know what kind to buy." A statement like this is stating the problem (step 1).

The Smiths then read some ads and visited some car dealers. Using the criteria of appearance and roominess, they narrowed down their choice to models A, B, and C (step 2).

To decide which one to buy, Al and Liz gathered facts about different cars. They also checked car magazines and consumer magazines and talked to friends and relatives who own these cars (step 3).

Relevant facts would be purchase price, gas mileage, maintenance and repair costs, and safety records. The magazines checked had good reputations. They ignored opinions of friends and relatives that did not seem factual. As a result, their information was as reliable as they could obtain. To make sure they had enough information, they made a table. The columns across the top read: Criteria, Car A, Car B, Car C. The columns down the left read: Purchase price, gas mileage, maintenance and repair record, safety record. Blanks showed where more facts were needed (steps 4 and 5).

Now that they had gathered their information and checked it for relevancy, accuracy, and adequacy, they reached their conclusion (step 6). Because the purchase prices and maintenance and repair costs were all very high, they decided to look at other cars. The Smiths even considered a used car. They were prepared to go through the same steps again in making their new decision. You can see from this example that making and testing hypotheses are what everyday decisions are all about.

1. Using Table 1-1, state the Smiths' hypothesis?
2. What was their conclusion? What alternatives did they consider?

criteria (kry-TIR-ee-uh): rules by which something is judged

Readings in Economics

ECONOMICS—A MAJOR PREOCCUPATION
Skill: Making Inferences

John Kenneth Galbraith is an outspoken and controversial economist. In this reading, however, he discusses something on which most economists will agree—the importance of economics.

[British Prime Minister Winston Churchill] said he couldn't get his mind around economics, but he did know that shooting Montagu Norman would be a good thing. Montagu Norman was then the head of the Bank of England.

Alfred Marshall, the great Cambridge economist who dominated the accepted British—and American—economic teaching from the 1880s to the 1920s, said that economics is merely the study of mankind in the ordinary business of life. I would now add reference to organization—to the study of the way people are organized for economic tasks by corporations, by trade unions and by government. Also, of how and when and to what extent organizations serve their own purposes as opposed to those of the people at large. And of how the public purposes can be made to prevail. . . .

To have a working understanding of economics is to understand the largest part of life. We pass our years, most of us, contemplating the relationship between the money we earn and the money we need, our thoughts suspended, as it were, between the two. Economics is about what we earn and what we can get for it. So an understanding of economics is an understanding of life's principal preoccupation.

There is another thing it can do for you. The newspaper headlines . . . are largely concerned with the economic decisions of governments. If people make no effort to understand these decisions, do not have an intelligent position and do not make that position known, they obviously surrender all power to those who do understand, pretend to understand or believe they understand. And you can be sure that the decisions so made will rarely be damaging to those who make them or to the people they represent.

1. In your own words, tell what Galbraith suggests is "life's principal preoccupation."
2. What can you infer about how economics can help us make these decisions?

John Kenneth Galbraith and Nicole Salinger, *Almost Everyone's Guide to Economics*. Boston: Houghton Mifflin Company, 1978. pp. 1, 2.

WHAT DETERMINES VALUE?
Skill: Drawing Conclusions

Sometimes scarcity alone determines a good's value, while often the amount of labor that has been used to produce the good is also a determinant of value. David Ricardo, the leading 18th-century British economist, discusses the value of commodities in this reading.

It has been observed by Adam Smith [the famed 18th-century Scottish economist] that "the word Value has two different meanings, and sometimes expresses the utility [usefulness] of some particular object, and sometimes the power of purchasing other goods which the possession of that conveys. The one may be called *value in use*; the other *value in exchange*. The things," he continues, "which have the greatest value in use have frequently little or no value in exchange; and, on the contrary, those which have the greatest value in exchange, have little or no value in use." Water and air are abundantly useful; they are indeed indispensable to existence; yet, under ordinary circumstances, nothing can be obtained in exchange for them. Gold, on the contrary, though of little use compared with air or water, will exchange for a great quantity of other goods. . . .

Possessing utility, commodities derive their exchangeable value from two sources: from their scarcity and from the quantity of labor required to obtain them.

There are some commodities, the value of which is determined by their scarcity alone. No labor can increase the quantity of such goods, and therefore their value cannot be lowered by an increased supply. Some rare statues and pictures, scarce books and coins . . . are all of this description. Their value is wholly independent of the quantity of labor originally necessary to produce them, and varies with the varying wealth and inclinations of those who are desirous to possess them.

These commodities, however, form a very small part of the mass of commodities daily exchanged in the market. By far the greatest part of those goods which are the objects of desire are procured by labor; and they may be multiplied, not in one country alone, but in many, almost without any assignable limit, if we are disposed to bestow the labor necessary to obtain them.

1. Ricardo writes that sometimes the scarcity of a good can determine its value. The same can also be said of services. Using this reasoning, explain why salaries of professional athletes are so high.
2. What does Ricardo give as an example of goods that have value in use but not value in exchange?

David Ricardo, *Masterworks of Economics*, edited by Leonard Dalton Abbot; *Principles of Political Economy and Taxation*. Garden City, N.J.: Doubleday, 1953. pp. 277, 278.

THE DISMAL SCIENTISTS LOOK AT THE COST OF UNCONFINED JOY

Skill: Making Inferences

Economists have always noted the trade-offs and opportunity costs due to scarcity. In this reading American economist Kenneth E. Boulding explains that some people think that scarcity has ended and that production possibilities are limitless.

Economics is first and foremost the science of scarcity. This is why it is a dismal science. Its problems arise only if there is not enough to go around. One of its greatest principles, though not necessarily the truest, I have sometimes called the "Duchess's Law," enunciated by the Duchess in *Alice in Wonderland:* "The more there is of yours, the less there is of mine." . . .

Economics is the good, gray, rational science.

How is the concept of scarcity illustrated by this picture of a busy electronics equipment plant?

. . . Even when St. Francis urges to give and not to count the cost, the economist says that somebody has to count the cost; and when somebody wants a Great Society, the economist says: "Who is going to pay for it?" It is no wonder that the economist is not very popular.

At this point someone is sure to come up and say, "But we have changed all that. Science and technology have produced the age of affluence. Scarcity has been abolished. Let us eat, drink, and be merry; there is plenty for all." Among biology, automation, and systems engineering, we can produce all we need with a fraction of the labor force, and today not even the sky is the limit. There are a good many voices today urging that we can have both guns and butter, "more for everybody and more for me too," and that economists can be put in the ash can.

This view seems to me to involve delusions of grandeur and a totally unwarranted euphoria [sense of well-being] derived from the careless and poorly sampled observations of a few special cases. . . .

1. What can you infer from Boulding's article regarding the idea that "scarcity has been abolished"?
2. What is the trade-off described in the "Duchess's Law"? What does it mean?

1 CHAPTER REVIEW

PRACTICING YOUR READING SKILLS: MAIN IDEAS AND SUPPORTING DETAILS

The main idea is the key point or topic of a paragraph, chapter, or article. It is the person, place, or thing that the material is about. In economic writings, the main idea might be a concept such as scarcity or an issue such as the federal budget deficit. It might also be a period of time like the Great Depression. Supporting details are the information that explain the main idea. In reading a paragraph, you will often find that the main idea is stated directly in the first sentence. Sometimes, however, a writer will place it in the middle or at the end of the paragraph.

For longer pieces such as a magazine article or book chapter, a writer may state the main idea of the entire piece in the first paragraph or place it somewhere in the middle or at the end. The main idea of each paragraph within the article or chapter develops the main idea of the entire article. The main ideas of the separate paragraphs act as supporting details for the topic of the entire article or chapter.

Sometimes, you will find that the main idea is suggested rather than stated. Then you will have to infer it. That is, you will have to analyze and evaluate the material to decide what it is about. To check yourself to see if you have found the main idea, always look for supporting details. Do they explain what you think the main idea is?

Activity: Read the following passages from Chapter 1. Write a sentence for each stating the main idea. Then list as many supporting details as you can.

1. The paragraph under the heading "Values and Economics," page 16.
2. The second paragraph under the heading "Economic Models," page 13.
3. a. What is the main idea of the chapter?
   b. List four supporting details.

VOCABULARY REVIEW

1. Write the letter of the definition in Column B that correctly defines each term in Column A.

Column A	Column B
1. entrepreneur	a. insufficient resources to satisfy wants and needs
2. scarcity	b. exchanging one thing for use of another
3. hypothesis	c. risk taker in forming and managing businesses
4. productivity	d. ability to produce greater quantities of goods in better and faster ways
5. trade-off	e. prediction at the start of an investigation

2. Explain the difference between a trade-off and an opportunity cost.

PRACTICING YOUR ECONOMIC SKILLS

1. **Drawing a Pie Graph.** Use the table How Americans Traveled in a Recent Year, p. 10, to draw a pie graph showing the percentage of people that used each form of transportation.

2. **Drawing a Line Graph.** Use the figures below to create a line graph showing the increase in GNP between 1982 and 1986.

1982	$3,170 billion
1983	3,440
1984	3,750
1985	3,998
1986	4,110

3. a. **Making an Economic Model.** Use the quantities listed in the two columns on the top of page 23 to graph the production possibilities for a toy manufacturer that makes two truck models: dump trucks and cement mixers.

Dump Trucks	Cement Mixers
400	0
350	25
300	50
250	75
200	100
150	125
100	150
50	175
0	200

b. How many more cement mixers can be produced when the production of dump trucks is reduced from 350 to 300?

4. **Studying Tables.** The table below shows the production possibilities for food and manufactured goods in a fully employed economy. An increase in the production of food causes a decrease in manufactured goods. Use the table to determine the opportunity cost in manufactured goods as food production increases from 0–10, 10–20, 20–30, 30–40.

Production Possibilities

	A	B	C	D	E
Food	0	10	20	30	40
Manufactured Items	100	90	70	40	0

DISCUSSING ECONOMIC QUESTIONS

1. The concept of scarcity may be new to you. If it is, how might learning about it change the way you use your own time and money? How might the idea of scarcity affect the way you evaluate such government policies as health care, aid to education, social security, military spending, and so on?

2. The following are the main ways of allocating scarce goods: first-come, first-serve; force; lottery; plan; sharing; and market mechanisms. Choose a scarcity problem that affects you as a student. Then describe the best way to solve the problem by evaluating the pros and cons of each of the strategies mentioned.

APPLYING CRITICAL THINKING SKILLS

1. **Gathering and Analyzing Information.** From newspapers or magazines, clip one article showing an example of an opportunity cost on a national or international level. Write a statement explaining how the concept of opportunity cost is involved.

2. **Writing a Research Report.** Entrepreneurship is an important factor of production. Research and write a report on one of America's major entrepreneurs. Explain which entrepreneurial skills were partly responsible for his or her success.

3. **Researching a Topic.** Choose a branch of economics that interests you. Then from college catalogues in the library, find out what courses are available for that branch of economics. Summarize your findings and share them with the class.

READINGS

Heilbroner, Robert L., and Thurow, Lester C. *Economics Explained.* Englewood Cliffs, N.J.: Prentice-Hall, 1986.

Silk, Leonard. *Economics in Plain English: Everything You Need to Know About Economics in Language You Can Understand.* New York: Simon and Schuster, 1986.

Swartz, Thomas R., and Bonello, Frank J., eds. *Taking Sides: Clashing Views on Controversial Economic Issues.* Guildford, Conn.: Dushkin, 1984.

CHAPTER 2

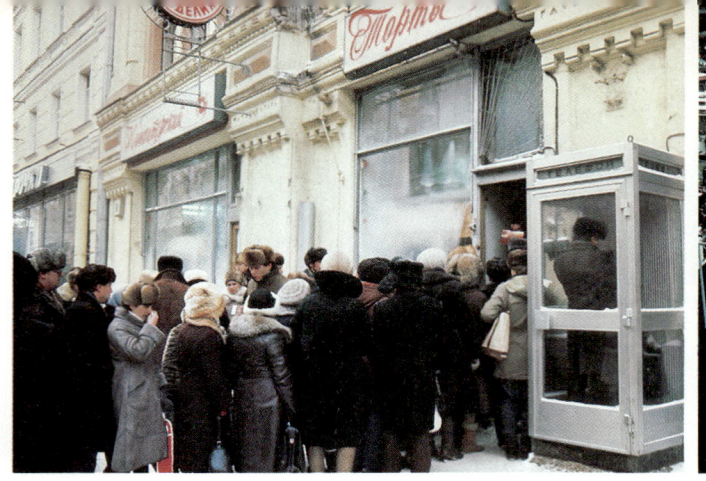

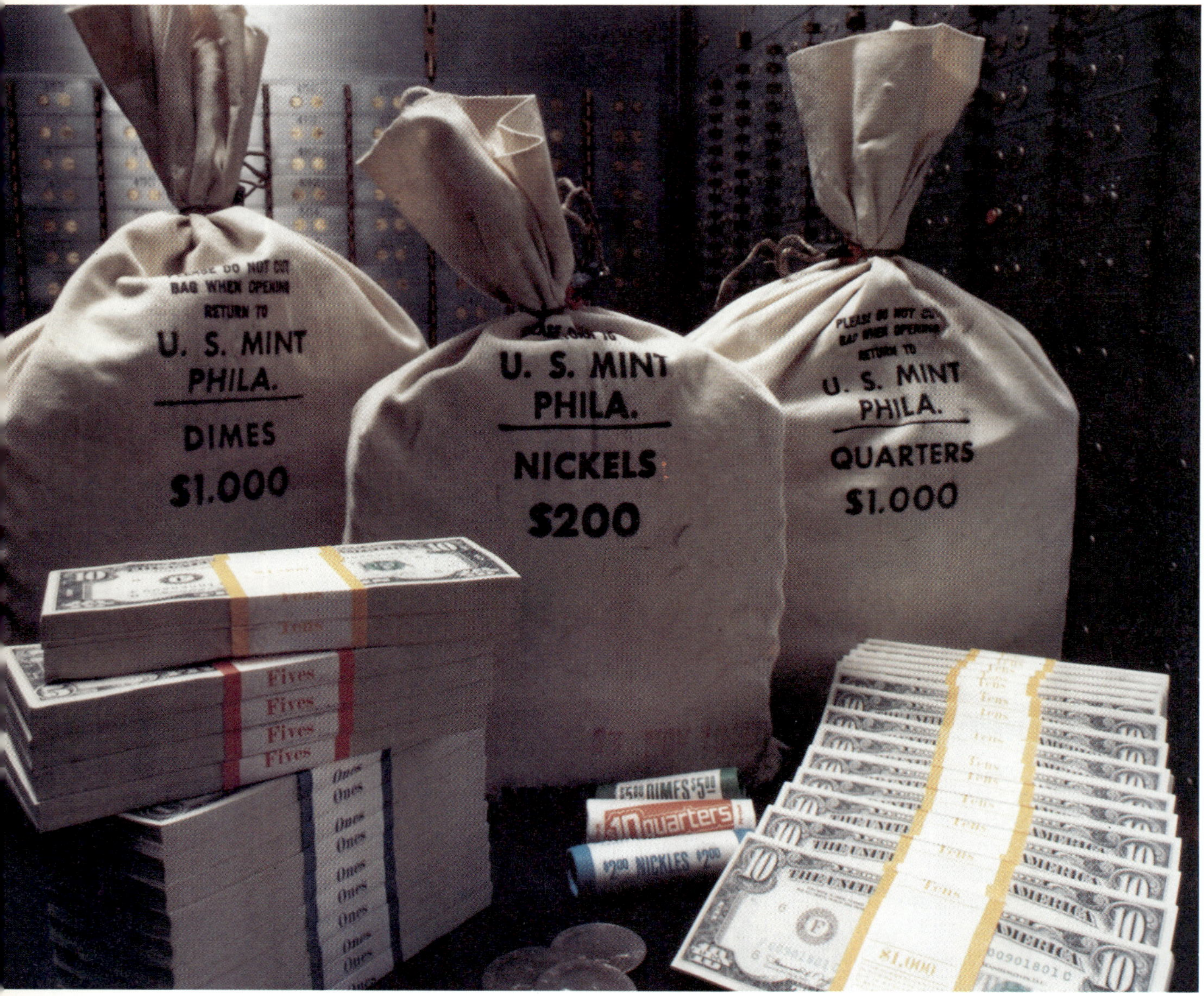

There are several different economic systems in today's world. They include the market economy of the United States, the command economy of the Soviet Union, and the traditional economy of some developing nations.

ECONOMIC SYSTEMS AND THE AMERICAN ECONOMY

Chapter 1 explained some basic economic principles. This chapter describes how these principles affect the way individuals, businesses, and nations make economic decisions. You will read about various types of economic systems and the four basic economic questions that every society must answer. Because you live in the United States, the characteristics of the American market economy are given in detail. You will also read about how a nation's goals determine its answers to the four basic questions. In Learning Economic Skills you will be working with statistics as percentages, means, and medians.

CHAPTER OBJECTIVES After you study the sections of this chapter, you will be able to:

1 • explain each of the four basic questions that all economic systems must answer.

2 • compare and contrast traditional, command, and market economic systems.
 • describe what is meant by the term *mixed economy*.
 • explain Adam Smith's theory of the invisible hand.

3 • describe the role of government in the American economy.
 ★ use statistics to figure percentages, means, and medians.
 • describe how freedom of enterprise, freedom of choice, and the right to private property encourage entrepreneurship.
 • explain the relationship between profit incentive and competition.

4 • explain the effect a nation's goals has on the type of economic system that nation develops.
 • discuss the benefits of the free enterprise system.

ECONOMICS VOCABULARY

economic system
traditional economic system
command economic system
market economic system
market
mixed economy
capitalism
percent
mean
median
free enterprise system
private property
profit
profit incentive
competition
economic efficiency
economic growth
equity
standard of living
invisible hand
laissez faire

As a young adult, you probably have set some goals for your life, even if they are short-term. They might be no more distant than finishing this year in school or getting a part-time job. Or you may have long-term goals such as going to vocational school or to college, learning a trade or profession, getting married, opening a business, and so on. Personal goals are influenced by parents, friends, teachers, religion, and the media. But more than you may think or even realize, your personal goals are influenced by the economic system in which you live. An **economic system** is the way in which a nation uses its resources to satisfy its people's needs and wants. If you were to make a list of your personal goals and compare it with a list made by a person of your age in parts of Africa, the People's Republic of China, the Soviet Union, or Sweden, the lists would be very different. One of the reasons the lists would be different is that each of these nations has a different economic system.

the media (MEE-deeuh): television, radio, newspapers, and so on

1 | FOUR BASIC QUESTIONS FOR EVERY ECONOMIC SYSTEM

Ask yourself as you read:
- What questions must all economic systems answer to determine the use of resources?

Although nations approach the use of their resources differently, every nation is faced with answering the same four basic questions. These are: What goods and services and how much of each should be produced? Who should produce them? How should they be produced? Who should share in their use? The way each economic system answers these questions affects how every person within that system produces and uses goods and services.

WHAT AND HOW MUCH SHOULD BE PRODUCED?

In Chapter 1, you learned that this is a world of scarcity and trade-offs. If more of one item is produced, then less of something else will be produced. For example, an automobile manufacturer must decide how to use its supply of labor, steel, rubber, and so on. Should it produce subcompacts or full-sized automobiles? Maybe it should produce both as well as compacts and intermediate, or medium-sized, models. But how much of each? Regardless of the type of good or service being produced, these questions must be answered. Within every economic system, there are signals, such as prices, that tell the controllers of limited resources what they should do with those resources.

intermediate (in-tuhr-MEE-dee-it): medium-sized

WHO SHOULD PRODUCE WHAT?

Within each economic system, different people do different jobs. But who decides which people will produce which goods and services? This question relates directly to choice of career. Should a person become an

Americans are free to choose a career they like and are qualified for. This woman is a medical lab technician.

auto mechanic, a paralegal aide, an elementary school teacher, an electrician, a lawyer, a college professor, or what? The type of economic system in a nation determines who makes these decisions and how they are made.

HOW SHOULD GOODS AND SERVICES BE PRODUCED?

The question of how goods and services should be produced concerns methods. Its answer lies in the right mix of the factors of production—land, labor, and capital, discussed in Chapter 1. For each good and service produced, there is always a trade-off possible among the available factors of production. For example, a farmer could use ten laborers with horse-drawn plows to plow a field or one tractor and driver. Depending on available resources and their prices, what mix will be the most efficient? In other words, what combination of available resources will get the best results for the least cost? Owners and/or managers of businesses must ask themselves this question constantly. Today, technology plays an important part in the answer.

WHO SHOULD SHARE IN WHAT IS PRODUCED?

This last question relates to how goods and services are distributed among the members of an economic system. This does not mean just money payment for work. It also means such things as the amount of health care, education, food, and so on, that each person receives. Do some people have more than others? How is this decided? Are goods and services distributed according to the amount of work people do? Or does everyone receive the same amount regardless of what she or he contributes to the economic system? What about the unemployed, the old, the disabled, and children? How are they provided for? What part, if any, does government play in deciding how goods and services are divided?

REVIEWING ECONOMIC PRINCIPLES

1. Write a definition for the term *economic system.*
2. List the four basic questions that each economic system must answer.
3. Using your own examples, explain each of these four questions.
4. **Critical Thinking: Forming an Opinion.** Discuss which of the four questions affects students most directly.

2 | TYPES OF ECONOMIC SYSTEMS

Ask yourself as you read:
- What are the major differences among the various types of economic systems?
- What is meant by the term *mixed economy?*
- What is Adam Smith's theory of the invisible hand?

society (suh-SY-uh-tee): people living together as a group

Each society answers the four basic questions according to its view of how best to satisfy the needs and wants of its people. In other words, the values and goals that a society sets for itself determine the kind of economic system it will have. Economists have identified four types of economic systems: traditional; command, or controlled; market, or capitalist; and mixed. Remember as you read this section that the economic systems described are pure, or ideal, types. They are economic models, not examples of the real world. Most economic systems today are mixed. Generally, they are identified by the way in which most economic activity in the nation is organized. The United States, for example, has a mixed economy but is considered to have a market economic system because it mainly responds to the market. Yugoslavia also has a mixed economy. However, it is said to have a command economy because most economic activity there is planned by the government.

TRADITIONAL SYSTEM

A pure **traditional economic system** answers the four basic questions according to tradition. Things are done "the way they have always been done." Economic decisions are based on customs, beliefs—often religious—and ways of doing things that have been handed down from generation to generation. Traditional economic systems exist today in parts of Asia, the Middle East, Africa, and Latin America.

For example, the Bushmen of the Kalahari (kah-lah-HAHR-ee) Desert of South Africa continue to live in a traditional economy. They are nomadic, or roving, hunters and plant gatherers. They live and travel in groups of 40 to 60 relatives and friends. The men hunt and trap antelope and other desert animals, which are used for food and clothing. Their method of hunting is the bow and poisonous arrows. The women gather plants, roots, and berries to add to the food supply. The group shares whatever food there is. When the food in an area is used up, the group moves on in search of new food supplies.

An individual does not choose his or her role. It is dictated, or must be followed, by what people have done in the past. Each generation answers the basic economic questions in the same way that each previous generation has answered it—by tradition.

COMMAND, OR CONTROLLED, SYSTEM

The traditional economic system is in some ways similar to a pure command economic system. In a pure **command economic system,** the individual has little, if any, influence over how the basic economic questions are answered. Government controls the factors of production and, therefore, makes all decisions about their use. This is why this form of economic system is also called a controlled economy.

The government may be one person, a small group of leaders, or a group of central planners in a government agency. These people choose how resources are to be used at each stage in the production and decide the distribution of goods and services. They even decide who will do what. The government, through a series of regulations about the kinds and amount of education available to different groups, guides people into certain jobs.

During the Middle Ages in Europe, the command economy was the major economic system. The landholder of each manor decided what and how much to produce, who should produce each good or service, how, and for whom.

MARKET, OR CAPITALIST, SYSTEM

The opposite of a pure command economic system is a pure **market economic system**—or capitalism. In a pure market economic system, government does not intervene. Individuals own the factors of production and decide for themselves the answers to the four basic economic questions. These decisions are made through the free interaction of individuals looking out for their own best interests in the market. **Market** in this sense is not a place. Rather, it is the freely chosen activity between buyers and sellers of goods and services. That is, buyers and sellers freely choose to do business with those who best satisfy their needs and wants. The exchange of goods and services may take place in a worldwide market for a good such as crude oil. Or it may take place in a neighborhood market for the services of someone to mow lawns, deliver papers, or shovel snow.

In a traditional economic system, many jobs are still performed in much the same way as in the past. What are these workers in India doing?

intervene (in-tuhr-VEEN): to come between, to interfere

Figure 2-1: CIRCULAR FLOW OF ECONOMIC ACTIVITY IN THE MARKET

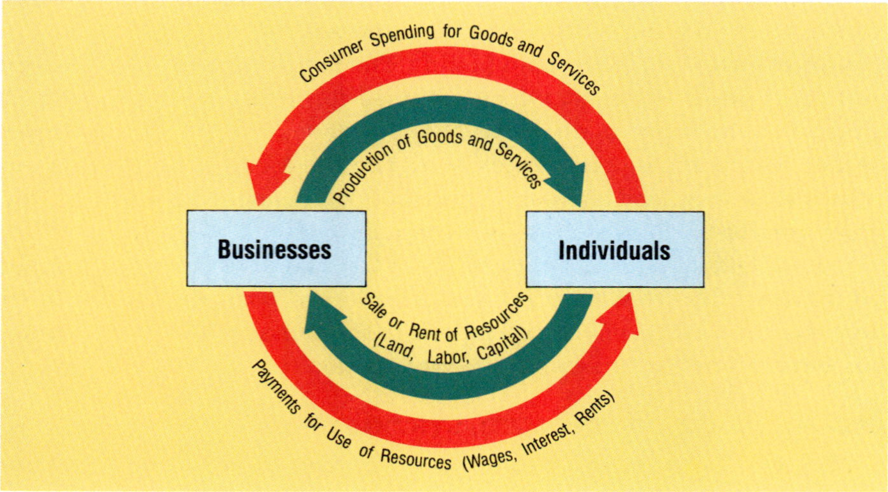

Consumer Spending for Goods and Services

Production of Goods and Services

Businesses

Individuals

Sale or Rent of Resources (Land, Labor, Capital)

Payments for Use of Resources (Wages, Interest, Rents)

This flow chart shows how income and products flow between individuals and businesses in the economy. Beginning with the role of individuals, explain the flow of economic activity through the market.

In a pure market economic system, producers of goods and services decide how to use their resources based solely on signals from the market. Government planning has no part in the decisions. Whether people buy a certain good or service or not indicates to producers the various ways to use or not use their resources. Suppose, for example, more people begin buying the compact discs (CDs) of a particular singing group. This increase in demand signals the record company to invest more resources—time, money, effort—into producing CDs by that group. If, however, few people are buying CDs by a particular group, the CD company will not sign that group again. Buyers have signalled that they do not want more CDs by that group.

People are also free in a pure market economic system to sell their labor as they wish. They may take, refuse, or change jobs whenever they choose. This assumes, of course, that there is a demand for their labor.

Figure 2-1 illustrates the flow of economic activity through the market in the capitalist system. The inside arrows show individuals selling the factors of production to businesses, who use them to produce goods and services. The flow of money from businesses to individuals in the form of rent, wages, and interest, and its return to business as consumer spending, is illustrated on the outside of the figure.

MIXED ECONOMIC SYSTEM

With the exception of the traditional economic system, it is doubtful whether these pure or ideal systems ever existed. They are useful models for analyzing existing systems, however. Today, almost all economic systems are what economists call mixed economies. A **mixed economy** contains characteristics of a command economy and a pure market economy. The mix will vary so that any one economic system leans more toward one pure type than another.

The United States, for example, tends much more toward the market system than toward the command system. However, all decisions are not made by individuals reacting to the market. Federal, state, and local governments make laws regulating some areas of business. Among these, for example, are the rates that electric companies may charge.

The Soviet Union, on the other hand, tends much more toward the command type than toward the pure market system. For example, the Soviet system of agriculture is based largely on collective farms. These are large farms in which the land, buildings, and equipment are owned by the government. Central government planners make decisions about how to use these resources, such as how many acres or hectares of wheat or sugar beets to plant and harvest. Hundreds of individuals may work together on one collective farm to meet these targets. However, the Soviet economy also has some characteristics of the market system. Many Soviet farmers are allowed small plots of land to grow crops or livestock to use themselves or to sell for whatever price the market will bring. No central planner decides what and how much the farmers should grow on their personal plots or how or to whom they should sell, or at what prices.

Economists classify economies according to the pure system that their activities are closest to. As a result, the United States is said to have a market economy, and the Soviet Union, a command economy. No two economies, even if they share many of the same characteristics, are exactly the same.

REVIEWING ECONOMIC PRINCIPLES

1. Write a definition for each of the following economic systems:
   a. traditional, **b.** command, **c.** market.
2. What type of economic systems do most nations have today?
3. **Critical Thinking: Making Inferences.** How does each system differ from the other in its answers to the four basic questions of economics? You will have to infer some of the answers from the information given.

3 | CHARACTERISTICS OF THE AMERICAN ECONOMY

Ask yourself as you read:
- What role does government play in the American economy?
- What freedoms are needed for entrepreneurship to flourish?
- What is one of the main causes of economic competition?

A pure market economic system has six major characteristics: 1) little or no government control, 2) freedom of enterprise, 3) freedom of choice, 4) private property, 5) profit incentive, and 6) competition. These characteristics are interrelated, and to varying degrees all are present in the American economy. The role of government, however, is much greater than it would be if the United States were a pure market system. Since the nation's founding, government involvement in individual economic choices has grown greatly. As the role of government grows, it can influence the degree to which individuals can freely exercise their economic freedoms and rights.

CAPITALISM

In his book *The Wealth of Nations,* Adam Smith in 1776 described a system in which government has little to do with economic activity. He said that individuals left on their own would work for their own self-interests. In doing this, they would be guided as if by an "invisible hand" of competition to achieve the maximum good for society.

Smith's idea of the ideal economic system is called capitalism, another name for the market system. Economists argue whether capitalism in its pure form, as Smith describes it, has ever existed. Today certainly, capitalism as practiced in the United States differs from Smith's idea. **Capitalism** today would be best defined as an economic system in which private individuals own the factors of production. As a result, individuals have the right to use those resources in any way they choose within the limits of the law. In other words, individuals have a voice in how they use their labor and the things they own, such as machines, to produce income. The law sets certain restrictions on these rights, however.

THE ROLE OF GOVERNMENT

Smith did see the need for government to intervene in some areas, however. He believed that government should provide for the national defense and eliminate any business practices that limited trade. Government was also needed to issue money, tax people for public works, and settle legal disputes. The founders of the new United States were influenced by Smith and others who believed in as little government control as possible. This philosophy was written into the Constitution. The new government would deal mainly with national defense and keeping peace. It limited its powers over individual economic choices.

Since the 1880s, the role of government—federal, state, and local— has increased significantly in the United States. This is especially true in the areas of regulating business and providing public services. The first federal regulatory agency, the Interstate Commerce Commission, was established in 1887 to ensure competition in the railroad industry. Today, it regulates many other areas of commerce, such as interstate trucking and inland waterways. Other federal agencies regulate the quality of various foods and drugs, watch over the nation's money and banking system, inspect workplaces for hazardous conditions, and guard against damage to the environment, to name only a few. In the last 20 to 30 years, through such programs as Medicare, Medicaid, and food stamps, the federal government has used tax money to provide

Founder of Modern Economics: Adam Smith (1732–1790)

In 1776, the Declaration of Independence was drafted by the Second Continental Congress in Philadelphia. In that same year, *An Inquiry into the Nature and Causes of the Wealth of Nations* was published in Great Britain. Its author was Adam Smith. Like the Declaration of Independence, Smith's work emphasized freedom, but it was economic freedom.

Smith was the first major supporter of free, or unrestricted, activity in the marketplace. He believed that people's self-interest would lead them to do what was best not only for themselves, but for the economy and society as a whole. This idea underlies Smith's theory of the **invisible hand,** which symbolizes economic competition.

According to Smith, when all individuals are allowed to do as they wish to improve their standard of living, the economy is guided as if by an invisible hand to maximize the welfare of all of society. There is no need for government to intervene to make things work smoothly. Smith, however, recognized that government should do certain things for its citizens, such as provide for national defense. But it should not control economic activity in any way. Another term used to describe Smith's theory of economics is *laissez faire* (les-ay FAIR). This is a French term meaning "do not interfere."

Smith also wrote about industrialization and the production process, especially the division of labor. He was one of the first to understand the advantages of having individuals do only certain tasks in a job rather than the complete job. If individuals concentrate only on specific productive activities, they can pool their talents to produce more and thereby consume more.

Most economists consider Adam Smith the founder of modern economics for these theories and for his writings on free trade. He believed that even in trade between nations, governments should not intervene. This was in direct conflict with the mercantilist policies of the British government at the time. Mercantilism is an economic theory that colonies exist only to make the governing country richer. Colonies supply raw materials to the governing country and buy manufactured goods only from that country. This policy was one of the causes of the American Revolution.

Smith's ideas have taken on increasing importance in today's world. An interest in returning to a more free-market economy was evident in the United States by the late 1970s. With the election in 1980 of Ronald Reagan, who supported less government, Smith's theories gained greater visibility and popularity. A growing number of American economists, citizens, and politicians took up his call for laissez-faire capitalism. Smith's ideas also stand out in sharp contrast to what has happened in a number of countries in this century. Most countries have moved toward greater—in some cases almost total—government control of economic activity.

1. Describe Adam Smith's theory of "the invisible hand."
2. Why is Smith considered the founder of modern economics?

benefits to certain groups. State and local governments have also expanded their roles in recent years in such areas as education, job training, recreation, support for the arts, and care for the old.

In the past, citizens through their elected representatives have chosen to enlarge the role of government. Citizens can also limit it if they choose. In recent years, the role of government within the United States, especially that of the federal government, has been the subject of much public debate. Some people feel that government rather than private individuals and groups should provide certain services in the areas of health care, mass transportation, and energy. Others maintain that the government should decrease its role in the economy. It should remove many regulations affecting business and cut the amount of money it spends on social programs. As in the past, you and other citizens will decide at the polls whether either view or one somewhere in the middle will dominate.

FREEDOM OF ENTERPRISE

The American economy is also called the **free enterprise system.** This term emphasizes the fact that individuals are free to own and control the factors of production. For example, if you decide to go into business for yourself, your abilities and resources will help you decide the good or service to produce, the quantity, and the methods of production. Of course, you may lose your money. There is no guarantee that you or any entrepreneur will succeed. The freedom to make money includes the risk of losing it.

There are certain legal limits to freedom of enterprise, however. You cannot make, sell, or buy anything illegal. Certain industries such as prescription drug manufacturers are regulated by law. State governments require professionals such as lawyers and teachers to pass examinations before they can be licensed to practice. In most states, teenagers must be 16 before they can work, and then laws set limits on how many hours they can work. Federal, state, and local governments require individuals and businesses to pay taxes.

FREEDOM OF CHOICE

Freedom of choice is the other side of freedom of enterprise. By freedom of choice is meant that buyers make the decisions about what should be produced. The success or failure of a good or service in the marketplace depends on individuals freely choosing what they want. The earlier example of people buying or not buying a particular group's CDs and the effects on the CD company illustrates this idea. The company, in reality, may choose to continue making CDs with the group anyway, even though it knows it will not make a lot of profit.

Although buyers are free to exercise their choice, the marketplace has become increasingly complex in this century. As a result, the government has intervened in various areas of the economy in an attempt to protect buyers. Laws set safety standards for such things as toys,

Many young people work at part-time jobs in their neighborhood. What business skills might they learn in these jobs?

appliances, and automobiles. In industries where only a few companies provide services, government regulates the price they may charge. This has happened with public utilities, those companies providing essential services such as gas, water, or electricity.

PRIVATE PROPERTY

Private property is simply things owned by individuals or groups rather than by government—federal, state, or local. An owner's rights to private property and its use are guaranteed by the Constitution. You as an individual are free to buy whatever you can afford whether it is land, a business, a home, an automobile, and so on. You can also control how your property is used, when, and by whom. If you own a business, you can keep any profit you make. **Profit** is the money left after all the costs of production—wages, rent, and so on—distribution, and taxes have been paid.

Within the United States, government at all levels controls some property. Parks, firefighting and police equipment, military bases, and post offices are some examples of government-owned property.

PROFIT INCENTIVE

Whenever a person invests time, know-how, money, and other capital resources in a business, that investment is made with the idea of making a profit. The desire to make a profit is called the **profit incentive** (in-SEN-tiv), and it is mainly this hope that moves people to produce things that others want to buy. After all, if no one buys what a seller produces, there will be no profit, only losses. For example, if you went into business mowing lawns, you would expect to make enough money to cover your expenses and make some profit.

The risk of failing is part of the free enterprise system. However, some industries are so large that their failure would seriously damage the economy and throw thousands of people out of work. In the past several decades, the federal government has passed laws providing special private loan guarantees to big corporations such as Lockheed and Chrysler, and even to the city of New York. The federal government has also aided farmers by providing them with loans.

COMPETITION

Competition is the rivalry among producers or sellers of similar goods to win more business by offering the lowest prices or better quality. In many industries, it requires a large number of independent buyers and sellers. This large number of competitors means that no one company can noticeably affect the price of a particular product. If one company attempts to raise its prices, potential customers can simply go to one of the many other sellers. In the ideal world, this is how competition would work. In practice, however, the federal government over the past 100 years has regulated some business practices in an attempt to make sure that competition exists. You will read in Chapter 10 about

public utility (yoo-TIL-uh-tee): company providing essential services, such as gas, water, or electricity

This teenager delivers newspapers after school to earn money. What benefits of our free enterprise system does this illustrate?

Learning Economic Skills

UNDERSTANDING STATISTICS

Average, percent, actual number, mean, median—these are all terms used with statistics. Throughout this textbook, you will be reading and using statistics. Some are mentioned within the text, and some are used in graphs and tables. Economists use statistics to describe different population characteristics—occupations, income, amounts spent on various budget items, and so on. Population, as statisticians (stat-uh-STISH-uhnz) use the term, can be a group of people, businesses, or branches of government.

You may not realize it, but the data that statisticians gather can be helpful to you in making your own decisions. For example, when you are trying to choose a career, it would be useful to know the average income in the occupations that interest you. If you are thinking of becoming a construction worker or actor, it would also be useful to find out the number of weeks in a year that the typical construction worker or actor is employed. You can also turn your own information into statistics. For example, in planning a budget, you might want to decide on the percentages of your income that you are willing to pay for items, such as food.

PERCENTAGES

Percent means parts per hundred. If you have ever had to figure the sales tax on a purchase, you have worked with percents. If you buy a book that costs $12.00 and the sales tax is 6 percent, you have to add $.06 for every $1.00 of the price:

$$.06 \times \$12.00 = \$0.72$$

The total cost of the book is $12.72.

All percents may be expressed as decimals. In the above example, 6 percent became .06. You find the decimal equivalent of a percent by moving the decimal point two places to the left and removing the percent sign. To find the percent equivalent of a decimal, reverse the steps.

FIGURING PERCENTAGES

There are various kinds of percentages that you should be able to calculate. One is figuring what percent one number is of another. If a stockbroker tells you that he or she has predicted market trends correctly 18 out of the last 60 times, you can determine the percent of the time that the broker has been correct. Divide the number of correct predictions by the total number of predictions:

$$18 \div 60 = .30 \text{ or } 30\%$$

On the other hand, if a stockbroker tells you that he or she is right 30 percent of the time and the total number of predictions is 60, you can find the number of times the stockbroker has been correct. Multiply the total number of predictions by the percent of success:

$$60 \times .30 = 18$$

This is using a percent of a total number to find a part of that number.

PERCENT AND ACTUAL NUMBER

What if the broker's success record improves to 60 percent for 120 predictions? Does that mean that the actual number of successful predictions has also doubled? No. Although the percentage has doubled, the total number of successful predictions has increased, but not doubled. The actual number of successful predictions is:

$$120 \times .60 = 72$$

When you are reading statistics, do not become confused if the material says the percentage has doubled or tripled or declined by half, and so on. This does not mean that the same change has occurred in the actual number.

Practicing Your Skills

1. In 1970, 58.5 million American homes had television sets. There were 4.5 million subscribers to cable television. What percent of homes with television also had cable?
2. By 1980, there were 76.3 million homes with television sets and 15.5 million cable subscribers. What percent of homes had cable in 1980?

AVERAGES: MEAN AND MEDIAN

Economic information is often summarized in averages. However, people sometimes use the word *average* when they should really use the terms *mean* or *median*. Economists use means and medians to give an overall view of a population or to summarize various statistics.

MEAN

The **mean** is the average of a series of items. It is found by adding the items and then dividing by the number of items in the series. The list below gives the weekly salaries of seven students in one class who all have part-time jobs after school. You can find the mean salary by adding the weekly wages and then dividing by the number of students, seven.

$$
\begin{array}{r}
\$ \ 20 \\
32 \\
34 \\
41 \\
53 \\
65 \\
\underline{\$175} \\
\$420 \div 7 = \$60
\end{array}
$$

The mean weekly salary for these students is $60.

MEDIAN

Sometimes using the mean to interpret a set of statistics can be misleading. This is especially true if one or two numbers in the series are much larger than the others. A median can be more accurate.

The **median** (MEE-dee-uhn) is the midpoint in any series of numbers arranged in order. For example, in the list of salaries above, $41 is the median weekly wage. The number of students that earn more than $41 a week is equal to the number that earn less than $41 a week.

In this case, the mean of the series, $60, is much larger than the median, $41. This is because one of the students earns $175 a week, more than twice as much as any other student.

This one large salary pushes the mean much higher than it would be if only the other six salaries were averaged. The median, or $41, is a more accurate description of how much the typical student in this class earns.

If there are an even number of figures in a series, the median is the mean of the two middle numbers. For example, suppose the four students with the highest salaries in the list above all worked for the same construction company. If you wanted to find their median weekly income, you would arrange the incomes in order, add the second and third numbers, and then divide by two:

$$
\begin{array}{rl}
\$41 & \\
53 & \$53 \\
65 & \underline{+ 65} \\
175 & \$118 \div 2 = \$59
\end{array}
$$

Practicing Your Skills

1. Below is a listing of the number of farm employees for a five-year period. During that period, what was the mean number of workers employed on farms?

   3,774,000
   3,383,000
   3,321,000
   3,179,000
   3,241,000

2. Below are the typical hourly wages for workers in different areas of the timber industry. What is the mean wage of workers?

Lumber	$7.14
Logging	8.90
Sawmills	6.80
Plywood	6.40
Paper	8.10

3. Using the same list, determine the median wage in the timber industry.

4. What is the difference between the mean wage and the median wage in the list in question 2?

Businesses must plan their operations carefully to be profitable and to compete with other companies. What are some decisions these business leaders must make?

regulations against business combinations and other practices that limit competition.

It is the opportunity to make a profit that encourages competition. Suppose that only one business makes a particular product such as a personal computer. It could charge as much as people who really want a personal computer are willing to pay. They have no alternative seller to turn to. Suppose a second company enters the market with a similar computer at a lower price. Then competition for buyers between the two businesses would force the price down.

Businesses have to keep prices low enough to attract buyers yet high enough to make a profit. This forces businesses to keep the costs of production as low as possible. Competitors who succeed do so because they are able to produce those goods that people want most. They are also able to produce them at a price that makes people want to buy.

Competition also requires that companies can enter or exit any industry they choose. Those who feel that they could make more profit in another industry are free to get out of the industry they are in. Some companies expand into new industries while staying in their old one. A company might conclude that manufacturing mimeograph machines is less profitable now because most people's needs for quick reproductions can be met more easily with photocopying machines. The company may decide to move out of its old business and to begin building photocopiers. Or it may divide its production between 80 percent photocopiers and 20 percent mimeograph machines.

Economists say that such an economy has weak barriers to entry and exit from industries. For the most part, this is true in the United States. However, some industries have tougher barriers to entry. For example, a person cannot become a doctor until he or she has passed through an approved medical school and received a license from a state government to practice medicine. Government approval is needed to start a public utility or set up a television or radio station.

REVIEWING ECONOMIC PRINCIPLES

1. Write a sentence using each of the following concepts: **a.** capitalism, **b.** free enterprise system, **c.** private property, **d.** profit incentive, **e.** competition.
2. What are the six major characteristics of a pure market system?
3. Based on what you read in Chapter 1 about entrepreneurship, how do you think entrepreneurship is encouraged by: **a.** freedom of enterprise? **b.** freedom of choice?
4. **a.** How does profit incentive encourage competition? **b.** State the two factors that are necessary for an economy to be competitive.
5. **Critical Thinking: Analyzing Information.** Choose any two characteristics of the American economy and show how government has a role in each of them.

4 | THE GOALS OF THE NATION

Ask yourself as you read:

- What are the major goals of a market economy?
- What are the benefits of the free enterprise system?

Nations—and the United States is no exception—have national values and set goals for themselves based on these values. These goals are evident in government policies and in the actions of people like yourself and those around you. As you read earlier in the chapter, the values and goals of a nation determine which of the several kinds of economic systems it will have.

AIMS OF A MARKET ECONOMY

As you have just read, the United States tends toward a market, or capitalist, system. Therefore, the major characteristics of a market economy should be evident in its goals. Among the national goals of Americans are efficiency, growth, stability, security, equity, and individual freedom. These goals are described below in economic terms because this is an economics text. However, these goals have moral, social, and religious elements as well. Most people agree on the goals, but not everyone agrees on how these goals should be accomplished. Such differences are one of the major reasons for the existence in the United States of several political parties rather than one.

By **economic efficiency** is meant the wise use of resources so that people will be better off in an economic sense. This value is related to **economic growth**—an expansion of the economy to produce more goods, jobs, wealth. No one likes the idea of never becoming better off, but there is some disagreement today about whether or not economic growth too often causes problems such as environmental pollution.

Again, most people agree that everyone should be secure. People should be protected against poverty and supplied with the means to provide for a medical emergency. This goal relates to the question of who should share in the distribution of the nation's goods and services. In the last 20 to 30 years, this goal of providing security has resulted in an increasing number of social programs. Here again is government intervention. These programs have been directed to the old, the disabled, the very young, and the sick who are unable in some degree to care for themselves.

Security relates to another goal—**equity.** The dictionary defines equity (EK-wuh-tee) as that which is fair and just. People usually have some idea of what they think is fair treatment for themselves and others. Such a principle can be used to evaluate economic policies of both private business and government. Do price rises based on a rise in costs, for example, hurt people more than they help companies stay in business? Business failures, after all, put people out of work.

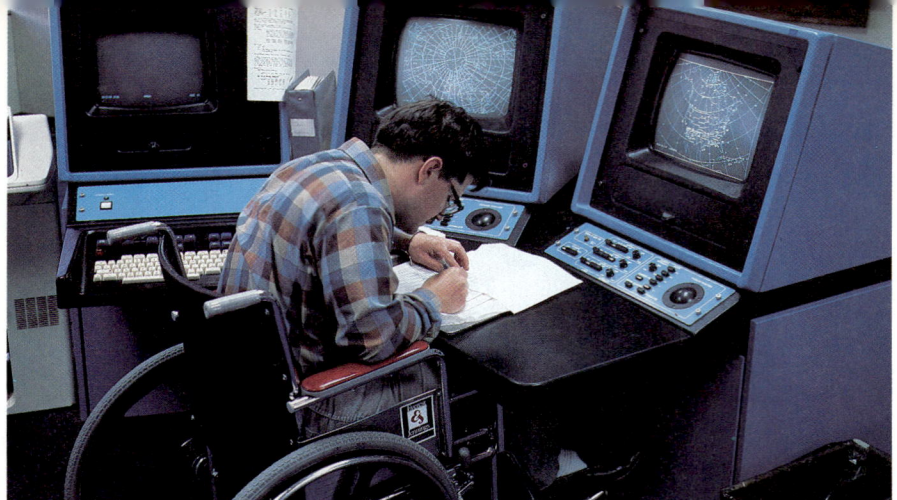

Many workers in a market economic system must have special training in order to secure skilled jobs. What skills might this weather forecaster need?

During the depression of the 1930s, about one-fourth of the workers in the United States were out of work. But there have been periods when year after year the economy is growing and everyone is doing better and better. The goal of stability seeks to reduce to a minimum these extreme ups and downs in the standard of living. **Standard of living** is the material well-being of an individual, group, or nation measured by the average value of goods and services used by the average citizen during a given period of time.

Earlier in the chapter you read that the freedoms of enterprise, choice, and private property are characteristics of a market system. The goal of individual freedom allows each member of society to enjoy these freedoms and to make his or her own decisions in the marketplace. It is not a contradiction, however, to say that the presence of law within the market economy protects these freedoms.

presence (PREZ-ns): act of being present

TURNING NATIONAL GOALS INTO REALITY

It is not enough that people consider certain goals important and would like to see them achieved. A plan of action must be developed in order to accomplish these goals. Such a plan often involves economic policy making by elected or appointed officials. They are the ones who must also deal with the reality of scarcity. Since all resources are scarce, when one person gets something, that something will not be available for anyone else.

Consider the goal of economic security. Many individuals can afford to buy private insurance policies and retirement plans. The government, however, has public policies such as Social Security, Medicare, and Medicaid that offer income security and health care. What does it mean when the government provides for such plans? It means that some people in society must agree to give up some of their income in order to transfer it to people in need. These people may be in need because they are too poor to care for themselves, or because they have not saved enough for emergencies or retirement.

In a world of scarcity, achieving national goals requires sacrifices by certain members of society. Any program to provide more security, more justice, or more equitable treatment of people involves a trade-off. Once you understand this, you will be well on your way to understanding not only the nation's economic system but also its political system. It is this system that makes many of the decisions about how resources are used in the nation. Such an understanding will help you realize that not all political desires can be turned into economic reality.

equitable (EK-wuh-tuh-buhl): fair, just

BENEFITS OF THE FREE ENTERPRISE SYSTEM

Those who support the American free enterprise system emphasize the many benefits that it provides for its citizens. These benefits include:

- **A high level of economic and personal freedom.** Proponents of the free enterprise system point out that of all nationalities, Americans enjoy perhaps the highest degree of freedom to start their own businesses and to pursue their own economic choices. This freedom extends to all aspects of life.

- **A high standard of living.** Supporters of the American economy explain that the nation has more individuals enjoying a high standard of living than almost anywhere else in the world. They believe that the ability of Americans to enjoy such high standards of living is directly tied to the ability of individuals to work where they want, how they want, and with whom, and to invest in whichever businesses they think will make profits. This is true for all industrialized capitalist economies.

- **Diverse lifestyles.** The great variety of economic opportunities in the United States allows for a wide range of lifestyles. People may choose to work nights, part time, at two jobs in different parts of the country for parts of the year, and so on. In contrast, command economies result in much less diversity in styles of living.

Critics of the system point out that in spite of its benefits, the free enterprise system has drawbacks. They say, for example, that free enterprise does not take care of the nation's poor people, nor do private businesses necessarily produce what is good for the nation as a whole. As you read the following chapters, ask yourself whether the free enterprise system provides the benefits just listed.

REVIEWING ECONOMIC PRINCIPLES

1. Define the following economic terms: **a.** economic efficiency, **b.** economic growth, **c.** equity, **d.** standard of living.
2. How do the goals of a nation affect the type of economic system that develops within that nation?
3. **a.** List six national goals evident in the United States. **b.** Choose one and explain it.
4. **Critical Thinking: Making Analogies.** Using an example of your own as an illustration, explain the difficulty in turning a national goal into reality.

SUMMARY OF
IMPORTANT PRINCIPLES

1
- Every economic system must answer four basic questions: What goods and services and how much of each should the nation produce? Who should produce them? How should they be produced? Who should share in their use?
- Each economic system answers the four basic economic questions based on its particular beliefs of how best to satisfy its people's needs and wants.

2
- There are four types of economic systems: traditional; command, or controlled; market, or capitalist; mixed.
- Adam Smith believed that people's self-interest would lead them to do what was best not only for themselves but also for the economy as a whole. This underlies Smith's theory of the invisible hand.
- A traditional economic system answers the four basic questions according to tradition.
- In a pure command economy, the individual has little, if any, influence over how the basic economic questions are answered. The government controls the factors of production.
- In a pure market economic system, individuals and companies own the factors of production and decide for themselves the answers to the four basic economic questions. This is done through the interaction of individuals looking out for their own best interests in the market.
- A mixed economy contains characteristics of command and market economic systems. Most, if not all, economies today are mixed. However, each leans more toward one type than another and is referred to by the name of the predominant system.

3
- The market economy of the United States has to some degree each of the six major characteristics of a pure market economic system: government, freedom of enterprise, freedom of choice, private property, profit incentive, and competition. All are interrelated. However, the role of government is much greater than it would be if the United States were a pure market system. As the role of government increases, it influences the degree to which the individuals can freely exercise their economic freedoms and rights.
- Statistics are useful tools for writing about and understanding economics. Percentage, mean, and median are some ways statistics are used.

4
- The values and goals of a nation determine which of the several kinds of economic systems will develop within that nation. The goals are evident in government policies and actions of individuals.
- Among the goals of the United States are economic efficiency, growth, stability, security, equity, and individual freedom.
- In a world of scarcity, achieving national goals requires sacrifices by certain members of society. Everything has an opportunity cost.
- Among the benefits of the free enterprise system are a high level of economic and individual freedom, a high standard of living, and a diversity of economic lifestyles.

Putting Economics to Work

TRADE-OFFS: MAKING POLITICAL DECISIONS

Donna Wong has just turned 18 and has registered to vote. In November, she will be voting for several local candidates, a state Senator, and the Representative from her Congressional district. Donna takes her job as a citizen-voter seriously. She listens to the speeches of the candidates, reads their literature, and follows their campaigns in the media.

Some of the candidates are asking for more government aid to education, the poor, space research, and defense. Donna realizes that increased government spending for any one of these programs means less spending for some other program. She understands that the concept of scarcity applies to government as well as to business and individuals. Keeping this in mind, Donna has decided that she must choose among candidates on the basis of those programs in which she believes most strongly. As far as Donna is concerned, those programs will have to come before any others. Donna believes that this approach will help her to cut through much of the campaign talk and televised appearances by the candidates and get down to the basics—how much each of these programs will cost, who will pay for them, and who will benefit most from each of these programs.

1. If government decides to increase spending in one area, must it always reduce spending in other areas?
2. **a.** What other alternatives does government have in trying to pay for programs? **b.** Consider the consequences of these alternatives.

Readings in Economics

THREE FUNDAMENTAL THINGS TO ANSWER THE FOUR BASIC QUESTIONS

Skill: Applying Information

The four basic questions—What goods and services and how much of each should be produced? Who should produce them? How should they be produced? and Who should share in their use?—must be answered by every economy, though different systems will answer them differently. Sumner H. Slichter, professor of Economics at Harvard University, restates them as three goals in this reading.

Every economic system must provide some way of doing three fundamental things: (1) getting goods produced; (2) determining what share each person shall have in the total product; and (3) regulating the consumption of goods, that is, determining who shall consume this good and who that. The manner in which these three basic economic processes are performed stamps the economic system with its most essential characteristics. How does the existing economic order organize and regulate the production, distribution, and consumption of goods?

There are several ways in which these activities might be organized and regulated:

1. On the basis of family autonomy. Each family might produce everything which it uses, relying upon others for nothing. In such a society there would be no trade.

2. On a communistic basis. What is produced and what each person does might be determined by the group as a whole and the product might be the property of the group, to be divided in accordance with socially determined rules.

3. On a despotic basis. The things produced and the tasks of each person might be decided by a despot or a despotic class, the product in all or in part being the property of the despot to be shared with the others as he saw fit.

4. On the basis of custom and heredity. Instead of choosing his own work or having it se-

lected for him by the group or a despot, each person might be born into his occupation. He might be expected to do the thing which his father did, and other occupations might be closed to him. Likewise the share of each person in the product and the things which he is permitted or forbidden to consume might also be determined by custom.

All of these methods of organizing and controlling economic activities have been more or less prevalent in the past and, indeed, instances of them still exist. They are not, however, the meth-

Under the economic system of Europe in the Middle Ages, lords and ladies like those shown here, lived lives of ease. The serfs did the farming and other hard work on the nobles' estates.

ods which prevail today in the United States. It may seem a strange way of doing [things], but we organize industry by, in effect, saying to each individual, "Choose your own occupation. Produce what you like. What you do, to whom you sell, what or from whom you buy, the prices you get or give, are all your own concern. You are free, subject to a few restrictions, to produce whatever you wish regardless of whether or not it is needed, regardless of whether or not too much of it already exists. You are likewise free to refrain from engaging in any occupation no matter how acute may be the shortage of goods or how pressing the need for your help. You are free to buy from whoever is willing to sell and to sell to whoever is willing to buy. You are equally free to refuse to buy or sell whenever you please and for any reason or no reason."

1. Economists often refer to types of economic systems as 1) market, 2) command, 3) tradition, or 4) mixed, which includes elements from any or all of the other three. Using these categories, classify Slichter's ways of organizing and regulating an economy.
2. List the basic economic questions which are included in Slichter's first goal of "getting things produced."

Sumner H. Slichter, "Free Private Enterprise" in *Readings in Economics*. Edited by Paul Samuelson, Robert Bishop, and John Coleman. New York: McGraw-Hill, 1955. Reprinted from *Modern Economic Society*. New York: Henry Holt & Co., Inc., 1928.

THREE FUNDAMENTAL THINGS TO ANSWER THE FOUR BASIC QUESTIONS

Skill: Classifying Information

Economic systems developed to hold human societies together and ensure their survival. In this reading, economist Robert Heilbroner describes two different economic systems and the emergence of a third, which led to the development of a profession that until then had been unnecessary.

A modern community is at the mercy of a thousand dangers. . . . Every day the community faces the possibility of breakdown—not from the forces of nature, but from sheer human unpredictability.

Over the centuries man has found only three ways of guarding against this calamity.

He has ensured his continuity by organizing his society around tradition, by handing down the varied and necessary tasks from generation to generation according to custom and usage: son follows father and a pattern is preserved. . . .

Or society can solve the problem differently. It can use the whip of central authoritarian rule to see that its tasks get done . . . [thus ensuring its] economic survival by the edict of one authority and by the penalties that supreme authority sees fit to issue.

For countless centuries man dealt with the problems of survival according to one or the other of these solutions. And as long as the problem was handled by tradition or command, it never gave rise to that special field of study called economics. Although the societies of history have shown the most astonishing economic diversity, although they have exalted kings and commissars, used dried codfish and immovable stones for money, distributed their goods in the simplest communistic patterns or in the most highly ritualistic fashion, so long as they ran by custom or command, they needed no economists to make them comprehensible. . . .

For the economists waited upon the invention of a third solution to the problem of survival. They waited upon the development of an astonishing game in which society assured its own continuance by allowing each individual to do exactly as he saw fit—provided he followed a central guiding rule. The game was called the "market system," and the rule was deceptively simple: each should do what was to his best monetary advantage. In the market system the lure of gain, not the pull of tradition or the whip of authority, steered each man to his task. And yet, although each was free to go wherever his acquisitive nose directed him, the interplay of one man against another resulted in the necessary tasks of society getting done. . . .

It was this paradoxical, subtle, and difficult solution to the problem of survival that called forth the economists. For unlike the simplicity of custom and command, it was not at all obvious that with each man out only for his own gain, society could in fact endure. . . .

1. Why did the "game" of the market system seem a threat to society?
2. Compare the similarities of the traditional economy and the command economy that made the work of the economist unnecessary.

Robert Heilbroner, *The Worldly Philosophers.* Fourth ed. New York: Simon & Schuster. Copyright © 1953, 1961, 1972, by Robert Heilbroner. Reprinted by permission of Simon & Schuster, Inc.

WHEN IS GOVERNMENT AN OBSTACLE TO FREEDOM?

Skill: Applying Information

SECTION 3

Many people disagree about the role that government should play in the American economy. In this reading, economist Milton Friedman describes one view of how freedom should be balanced with government power in the American economy.

In a much quoted passage in his inaugural address, President Kennedy said, "Ask not what your country can do for you—ask what you can do for your country." It is a striking sign of the temper of our times that the controversy about this passage centered on its origin and not on its content. Neither half of the statement expresses a relation between the citizen and his government that is worthy of the ideals of free men in a free society. . . . To the free man, the country is the collection of individuals who compose it, not something over and above them. He is proud of a common heritage and loyal to common traditions. But he regards a government as a means, an instrumentality, neither grantor of favors and gifts, nor a master or god to be blindly worshipped and served. He recognizes no national goal except as it is the consensus of the goals that the citizens severally [individually] strive.

The free man will ask neither what his country can do for him nor what he can do for his country. He will ask rather "What can I and my compatriots do through government" to help us discharge our individual responsibilities, to achieve our several goals and purposes, and above all, to protect our freedom? And he will accompany this question with another: How can we keep the government we create from becoming a Frankenstein that will destroy the very freedom we establish it to protect? Freedom is a rare and delicate plant. Our minds tell us, and history confirms, that the great threat to freedom is the concentration of power. Government is necessary to preserve our freedom; it is an instrument through which we can exercise our freedom; yet by concentrating power in political hands, it is also a threat to freedom. . . .

How can we benefit from the promise of government while avoiding the threat to freedom? Two broad principles embodied in our Constitution

The Amish people, who reject the conveniences of modern life, thrive in the free atmosphere of the American economy.

give an answer that has preserved our freedom so far. . . .

First, the scope of government must be limited. . . .

The second broad principle is that government must be dispersed.

1. According to Friedman, what two constitutional principles help us balance government's benefits with its threats to our freedom?

2. Friedman states that a free person would support neither of the ideas expressed in the famous Kennedy quote. How would a free person reword Kennedy's quote to better reflect his or her views on the role of government in a market economy?

Milton Friedman, *Capitalism and Freedom.* Chicago: University of Chicago Press, 1962. pp. 1—3.

AN ECONOMIC PROGRESS REPORT: THE STATE OF THE UNION

Skill: Making Inferences

Each year the President of the United States reports to the American people on the progress of the nation in a State of the Union address. In this reading from President Reagan's 1986 State of the Union speech, the President describes the progress made and his hopes for the nation's future.

I have come to review with you the progress of our nation, to speak of unfinished work and to set our sights on the future. I am pleased to report the state of our union is stronger than a year ago, and growing stronger each day. Tonight, we look out on a rising America—firm of heart, united in spirit, powerful in pride and patriotism. America is on the move!

But, it wasn't long ago that we looked out on a different land—locked factory gates, long gasoline lines, intolerable prices and interest rates turning the greatest country on earth into a land of broken dreams. Government growing beyond our control had become a lumbering giant, slamming shut the gates of opportunity, threatening to crush the very roots of our freedom.

What brought America back? The American people brought us back—with quiet courage and common sense; with undying faith that in this nation under God the future will be ours, for the future belongs to the free.

Tonight the American people deserve our thanks—for 37 straight months of economic growth; for sunrise firms and modernized industries creating 9 million new jobs in three years; interest rates cut in half, inflation falling from over 12 percent in 1980 to under 4 percent today; and a mighty river of good works, a record $74 billion in voluntary giving just last year alone.

And despite the pressures of our modern world, family and community remain the moral core of our society, guardians of our values and hopes for the future. Family and community are the co-stars of this great American comeback. They are why we say tonight: private values must be at the heart of public policies.

What is true for families in America is true for America in the family of free nations. History is no captive of some inevitable force. History is made by men and women of vision and courage. Tonight, freedom is on the march. The United States is the economic miracle, the model to which the world once again turns. We stand for an idea whose time is now: Only by lifting the weights from the shoulders of all can people truly prosper and can peace among all nations be secure. . . .

1. President Reagan's speech explains how private values and goals can bring about public good. Explain how this supports or reflects the philosophy of a market economy.

2. Politicians and leaders often use rousing rhetoric to appeal to our emotions. President Reagan's statement "What is true for families in America is true for America in the family of free nations" is an example of a powerful, although vague, message. What message is the President attempting to communicate?

Ronald Reagan, "State of the Union" speech delivered February 4, 1986, Washington, D.C. *Vital Speeches of the Day*, Vol. LII, No. 10. March 1, 1986.

2 | CHAPTER REVIEW

PRACTICING YOUR READING SKILLS: COMPARING AND CONTRASTING

When you compare things, you look for similarities; when you contrast them, you look for differences. Throughout your study of economics you will be comparing and contrasting data. It may be to analyze the standard of living in two nations, or to decide on the kind of insurance to buy. Sometimes information will be presented as statistical data, in graphs or tables. More often, however, you will need to draw information from your reading. When you need to make comparisons, look for such key words and phrases as *similarly, likewise,* and *as well as.* When you are making contrasts, look for such words and phrases as *however, but,* and *on the other hand.* You will also find that sometimes you will need to infer part of a comparison or contrast because they will not be pointed out specifically in the passage or passages that you are reading.

Activity: Organizing the data to be compared and/or contrasted into a table can help you discover similarities and differences. Reread the sections on pure command and pure market economies in the chapter to answer the following questions.

1. Compare and contrast the two types of economies by putting the information in table form. Label one column *similarities* and the other *differences.* As you fill in your table, keep in mind the four basic questions that all economic systems must answer. You may have to infer some of the data to complete your table.
2. Write one sentence stating how the pure market and pure command systems are the same.
3. Write another sentence stating how the pure market and pure command economic systems differ.

VOCABULARY REVIEW

Write the letter of the definition in Column B that correctly defines each term in Column A.

Column A	Column B
1. market	a. attempt by sellers to win business from sellers of similar goods
2. competition	
3. standard of living	b. money left after costs of production are subtracted
4. free enterprise	
5. profit	c. activity between buyers and sellers of goods and services
	d. system in which individuals own the factors of production and are free to choose what should be produced
	e. what is measured by the average value of goods and services used during a given period of time

PRACTICING YOUR ECONOMIC SKILLS

1. **Figuring Percentages. a.** A local insurance company has 671 employees. Five years ago, it had 550 employees. What was the percentage increase in employees over five years? **b.** If during the same period employment had increased 16 percent, how many employees would the company now have?
2. **Finding the Mean. a.** The list below gives the income of five workers at one factory during a certain year. Using this list, determine the group's mean annual income. **b.** What would the workers' mean annual income be for the following year if it increased by 8 percent?

$10,675	12,250	19,365
11,510	17,450	

3. **Determining Median Income. a.** Using the list from question two, determine the difference between the median income of the four highest-paid workers and the median income of the four lowest-paid workers. **b.** What percentage of the larger figure is the smaller figure?

4. **Using a Line Graph.** The line graph that follows shows passenger car sales. Use it to answer these questions: **a.** Did sales of domestic cars increase or decrease between 1981 and 1985? **b.** What happened to the sales of imported cars during the same time period? **c.** Approximately what percentage of total sales did domestic cars account for in 1985?

Sales of New Passenger Cars, 1981-1986

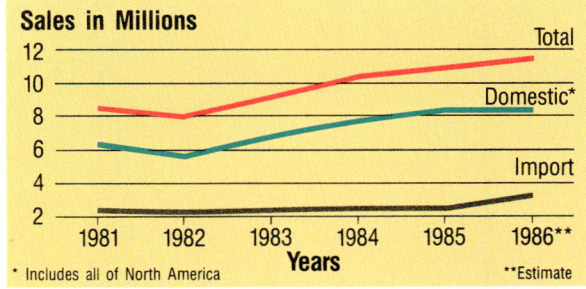

Sales in Millions

Total
Domestic*
Import

12
10
8
6
4
2

1981 1982 1983 1984 1985 1986**

* Includes all of North America   **Estimate

Years

Source: *Statistical Abstract of the United States,* Motor Vehicle Manufacturers Association of the United States, *Ward's Automotive Reports.*

DISCUSSING ECONOMIC QUESTIONS

1. Based on your reading of the chapter, discuss how the market economy operates in the United States. For example, who decides on career choice? How do controllers of resources decide what to produce or stop producing?

2. Discuss which, if any, national goals of the United States you would change and why. Which do you consider the most important goals? Are there any you would add to the six discussed in the text? What?

APPLYING CRITICAL THINKING SKILLS

1. **Analyzing Graphs.** Look through the business sections of newspapers or newsmagazines for bar and line graphs to bring in for a bulletin board display. Label each graph *helpful* or *misleading*, based on whether you found it a helpful or misleading aid in understanding the article it illustrated. Was it drawn in such a way as to distract your attention from the true meaning of the statistics?

2. **Analyzing News Stories.** Read the newspaper or listen to radio or television news for a week. List the stories that discuss some aspect of the government's role in the economy. Then, for each story, write a sentence or two explaining the government's involvement in the situation. Possible stories might be environmental or safety regulations or municipal funding for a service such as the public library.

3. **Gathering Statistics.** Go to a library and find the *Statistical Abstract of the United States,* published each year by the Bureau of the Census. Choose a topic such as education, population, or agricultural production, that gives statistics for each state. List three statistics about that topic for your state.

READINGS

Friedman, Milton. *Capitalism and Freedom.* Chicago: University of Chicago Press, 1981.

Greaves, Bettina B., ed. *Free Market Economics: A Basic Reader.* New York: Foundation for Economic Education, 1975.

Mishan, E.J. *The Economic Growth Debate.* Reading, Mass.: Allen & Unwin, 1977.

Okun, Arthur M. *Equality and Efficiency: The Big Tradeoff.* Washington, D.C.: The Brookings Institution, 1975.

Schumacher, E.F. *Small is Beautiful: Economics as if People Mattered.* New York: Harper & Row, 1975.

ISSUE 1

CONFLICT AMONG NATIONAL GOALS

After you study this Issue, you will be able to understand why a nation's goals may conflict.

social costs

As you read in Chapter 2, the United States as a nation has a number of goals: efficiency, economic growth, security, stability, individual freedom, and equity. Some of these goals may be familiar to you because they form part of your own value system. For example, you may believe strongly in an individual's right to make his or her own economic choices without intervention from the government. People who lived through the Great Depression, a time during the 1930s when millions of people were out of work, may put economic security far ahead of other goals, including economic freedom.

GOALS IN CONFLICT

Certainly, not everyone agrees on the order of importance of the nation's goals. This is in part because the goals are themselves in conflict. For example, the right of an individual to act as he or she chooses in the marketplace can conflict with another's economic security. An inventor may discover a new method for making television sets that uses only one-tenth the number of workers other companies use. The inventor's company may become richer, but many workers in the television industry may be put out of work.

Using resources in the most efficient way possible does not guarantee that everyone will be treated fairly or justly. The use of more technology may increase productivity in a particular industry.

However, it may also cause some people in that industry to lose their jobs.

Economic growth and stability can be in opposition. A city, for example, might enjoy a period of rapid economic growth, during which large numbers of new residents and new industries move to the city. Many people in the city might view such growth as positive. However, if growth only occurs in certain parts of the city's economy, some people may enjoy a period of prosperity while others are out of work. If after a period of rapid growth, business activity drops off again, some businesses may close and many people may lose their jobs.

There are no right or wrong ways to solve these conflicts. The answers come about through the decisions of citizens, businesspeople, and politicians about which goals are the most important at certain times and how they should be achieved.

ECONOMIC GROWTH *VERSUS* ENVIRONMENTAL CONCERNS

To understand how goals can be in opposition with one another, it may be helpful to examine in some detail the conflict between economic growth and environmental protection.

Land, air, and water not only provide industry with the raw materials of production, but they are also affected by the way industry uses them. For the sake of economic growth, air, land, and water are often polluted with chemical wastes, and land is made undesirable by harmful mining and lumbering practices. There was a time when many people believed that air and water could carry

Above left is a construction project in Houston, Texas. Above are containers of hazardous waste in an Eastern state that must be disposed of. At left is a city trash dump. These scenes represent the conflict between economic growth and environmental concerns. Why does economic activity have an impact on the environment? What can be done to try to deal with this problem?

away industrial wastes without being harmed themselves. However, with the increase in population and the increase in the amount of goods produced and used, this is no longer true.

In recent years, protecting natural resources has become an important goal of the national, as well as state and local, government. When Americans began to realize the social costs involved in polluting, they began to demand change. **Social costs** are the total costs that society has to pay for any economic activity. For example, the social cost of producing a ton of steel includes the cost of labor, raw materials, energy, and any pollution of the air and water around the steel mill. Govern-

ment at all levels has passed regulations to protect the environment from the effects of industrial pollution. For example, cars must be built with emission control devices to cut down on air pollution. Manufacturing plants must scrub—clean— the smoke that pours from their smokestacks. There are regulations to prohibit the dumping of chemical wastes, of stripping forests of trees, and of clearing land and building on it without guarding against soil erosion.

Businesspeople, however, find that such regulations raise the cost of manufacturing. As a result, prices are raised. Business also believes that these regulations reduce productivity and, therefore, cut back on the money available for new investments. These results of regulation hold down national growth. By the early 1980s, business was lobbying the federal government to lift or ease some of these environmental regulations as a way of helping the national economy grow.

On the other hand, the Environmental Protection Agency (EPA) and other regulatory agencies as well as private groups believe that the regulations produce long-term social benefits that cannot be measured in dollars. They believe the regulations are good for the economy because a better environment results in healthier workers, lower medical costs, conservation of resources for the future, more and better recreation and wildlife areas.

Discussing Economic Questions

1. Using examples from the news, choose two national goals and explain how they are in conflict with one another. Is there any solution that would satisfy both sides? Consider possible compromises that might be reached by opponents.

2. Some people believe industry should be responsible for the costs of cleaning up or of preventing pollution. Others believe that the public as buyers of goods and services should share the costs of preventing pollution through higher prices. With which of these two arguments do you agree? Explain your opinion.

UNIT 2

PRACTICAL ECONOMICS: HOW THEORY WORKS FOR YOU

Unit 1 explained why it is important to understand economic principles. But you may still wonder how useful economics will really be to you. Unit 2 explains the way these principles affect you in your various roles in the American economy. You should then find it easier to understand the ideas presented in the rest of this text.

CHAPTER 3

The goods and services that American consumers enjoy make it possible for them to have the highest standard of living in the world.

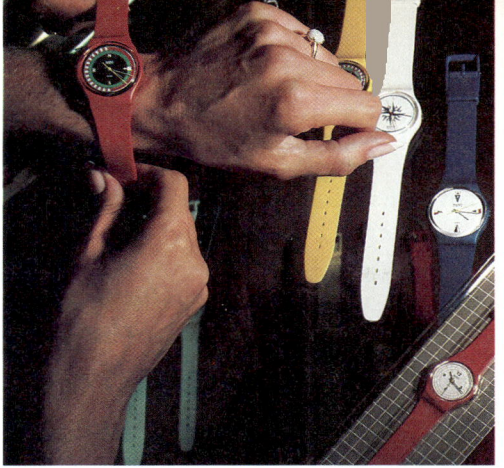

YOUR ROLE AS A CONSUMER

What determines the amount of money you have to spend? How do you decide what to buy? Do you always feel that you get the most for your money? If you find yourself with a faulty product or an item that breaks soon after purchase, do you know what to do to have it repaired or replaced by the store or manufacturer? This chapter will answer these questions for you. After describing the relationship between income and consumption, the chapter provides a checklist for making consumer decisions. You will also find a list of buying principles to follow and the names of agencies and groups that help consumers with problems. Learning Economic Skills explains ways to handle consumer problems.

CHAPTER OBJECTIVES After you study the sections of this chapter, you will be able to:

1 • describe the relationship between consumption and income. List two scarce resources involved in consumer decision making.

2 • explain the three steps to every consumer decision.
   • explain how a consumer would use each of the three buying principles to reach a decision about a purchase.
   • compare and contrast the advantages and disadvantages of buying brand-name products.

3 • identify the purpose of the consumer movement.
   • based on the information in the case study, describe the development of the consumer movement in the United States.
   ★ list the information a consumer needs to include in a letter of complaint.
   • read a table to see the kinds of help available from the federal government for consumers.
   • list the rights and responsibilities of consumers.

ECONOMICS VOCABULARY

consumer
disposable income
discretionary income
competitive advertising
informative advertising
bait and switch
comparison shopping
brand name
consumerism
warranty

Many students work a few evenings a week, on weekends, or throughout the summer and holidays. A number of these students work for a specific purpose, such as saving to buy a car, to go on vacation, or to pay for special lessons. However, other young people work because they have to help their families or provide for themselves. For these young people, as for most adults, spending money wisely is of primary concern.

1 | CONSUMPTION AND INCOME

Ask yourself as you read:
- What role do you as a consumer play in the economic system?
- Why does spending require consumers to make decisions constantly?

You and everyone around you are consumers and, as such, play important roles in the economic system. A **consumer** is any person or group that buys or uses goods and services to satisfy personal needs and wants. As consumers, people buy a wide variety of things—food, clothing, dental and medical care, automobiles, stereos, and so on.

To see how typical consumers spend their money, study the pie graph in Figure 3-1. It shows that the major share of money spent by American consumers is for food and housing. Together these expenses add up to 37 percent. The next largest category is taxes and Social Security, accounting for 18 percent of every dollar Americans spend. Transportation, medical and personal care, and clothing are the next most important categories. The least money is spent on recreation, only

Figure 3-1: CONSUMER SPENDING IN A RECENT YEAR

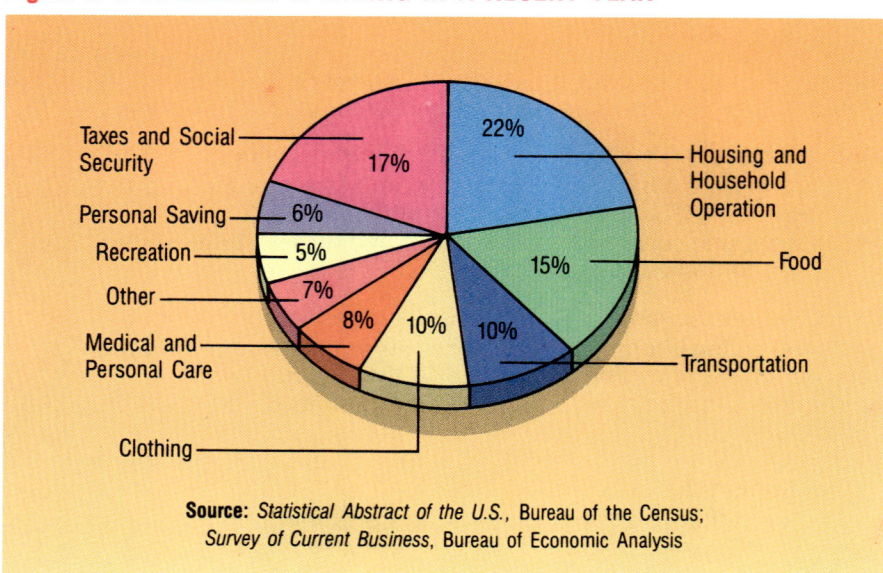

Source: *Statistical Abstract of the U.S.*, Bureau of the Census; *Survey of Current Business*, Bureau of Economic Analysis

The pie graph shows how Americans spend their income. Do any of the statistics surprise you? Which ones? Why?

5 percent of each dollar consumed. That may not seem like much in terms of percentages, but for the entire United States economy spending for recreation amounts to about $200 billion a year!

DISPOSABLE AND DISCRETIONARY INCOME

A person's role as a consumer depends on his or her ability to consume. This, in turn, depends on the income available and how much of it a person chooses to spend now or save for the future. Income can be both disposable and discretionary (dis-KRESH-uh-nair-ee). **Disposable income** is the money income a person has left after all taxes have been paid. People spend their disposable income on many kinds of goods and services. First, they buy the necessities: food, clothing, and housing. Once these needs have been taken care of, there may be some money left. This money, which can be spent on extras such as entertainment, is called **discretionary income.** The consumer's choice, or wants, is his or her guide in spending this money. Obviously, some people have more disposable and discretionary income and can afford to spend more than others.

Education, occupation, age, sex, and health can all make differences in a person's earning power and, therefore, in his or her ability to consume. Where a person lives can also influence how much he or she earns. City dwellers tend to earn more than those who live in rural areas. Wages in some regions of the country tend to be higher than those paid in others. How much a person has to spend can also be influenced by inheriting money or property.

Regardless of the size of a person's income, spending that income requires constant decision making. As a consumer, each person has a series of choices to make.

DECISION MAKING AS A CONSUMER

The first decision a consumer must make is whether to buy an item or not. This may sound so basic as to be unnecessary to mention. But how many times do you actually think about the purchase you are about to make? Do you think about whether you really need the item? Do you consider the trade-offs? Part I of the Checklist for Consumer Decision Making on p. 58 will help you analyze this first consumer decision.

Once you have decided to make a purchase, at least two scarce resources are involved—income, as you have just read, and time. The time you spend making a decision to buy something cannot be used for anything else. Once you have decided to spend your money, you need to invest time in obtaining information about the product you wish to buy. Suppose you decide to buy a bicycle. The time spent visiting stores checking models and prices is time you cannot spend doing anything else. It is a cost to you. But as you will see in reading this chapter, it may be a cost well worth paying.

Making consumer decisions involves three steps. The Checklist for Consumer Decision Making can help to guide you through them.

model: type; name given by manufacturer to a particular design

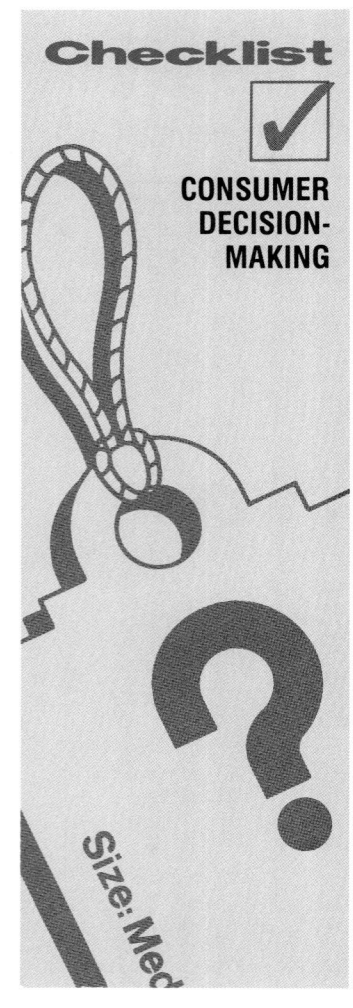

Checklist

CONSUMER DECISION-MAKING

Size: Med

Part I. Deciding to Spend Your Money

Before you buy anything, you should ask yourself:

1. Do I really need this item? Why? Remember the discussion about wants and needs in Chapter 1. Real needs are few, but wants are unlimited. Unless you answer this question honestly, you may find your wants are always greater than your ability to satisfy them.

2. Is this good or service worth the time I spent earning the money to pay for it?

3. Is there any better use for my money now? Should I save instead for future needs?

Part II. Deciding on the Right Purchase

Once you have made up your mind to buy a certain good or service, you are faced with more questions:

1. Do I want high, medium, or low quality? Quality refers to appearance, materials used, and the length of time a product will last. Most goods are of medium or average quality. For a higher price, you can usually get higher quality. For a lower price, you can usually expect a product that may not be as attractive or as long-lasting. At times such a purchase may suit your needs very well, however.

2. If I am buying an appliance or car, do I want one that will be the most efficient—least costly—to operate each year? The answer will probably involve a trade-off. A small automobile, for example, may use less gasoline than a larger one, but it provides less protection in an accident.

3. Does this particular item—a Brand Y stereo, for example—require more service than Brands A, B, and C? If so, do I want this additional problem and expense?

4. Should I wait until there is a sale on the item I want? Sales of certain items are seasonal. For example, winter clothes are on sale after Christmas and children's clothes, in August.

REVIEWING ECONOMIC PRINCIPLES

1. **a.** What is the difference between disposable and discretionary income? **b.** How does a person's disposable income affect his or her ability to consume?

2. What two scarce resources are involved in every consumer decision?

3. **Critical Thinking: Applying Principles. a.** According to the Checklist for Consumer Decision Making, what three steps does every consumer go through in making a decision? **b.** Suppose you have a part-time job and need transportation. You do not have a driver's license so you consider buying a bicycle. Use this example to go through the Checklist in the chapter and answer the questions.

5. If I am looking for an expensive item, such as a stereo, should I buy it new or used? What things are better to buy new than used? How can I protect myself if I buy a used item?

6. Should I choose a product with a well-known brand name* even though it costs more than a similar product without a brand name? Are there any benefits to buying a brand-name product for what I am buying now? What are they?

7. Does anyone I know own this product so that I can get a first-hand opinion?

8. Is the warranty on this particular product comparable to warranties of similar items? A **warranty** is a promise made by a manufacturer or a seller to repair or replace a product if it is found to be faulty within a certain period of time.

9. Is the return or exchange policy where I am thinking of buying a product comparable to the policies of other stores selling similar items?

10. What do consumer magazines say about it?

Part III. Deciding How to Use Your Purchase

Decision-making for you, the consumer, does not stop after you have bought an item. It continues for as long as you have a choice about using it. Once you own something—whether it is clothing, a videocassette recorder (VCR), or an automobile—you must decide:

1. How much time and effort should I spend on repairs and maintenance?

2. How much money should I spend on repairs and maintenance?

3. At what point should I replace this item? Why? (This brings you back to number 1 under Deciding to Spend Your Money.)

*You will read about brand names later in this chapter.

2 | BUYING PRINCIPLES, OR STRATEGIES

Ask yourself as you read:

- How will the basic buying principles help consumers to make wise purchases?
- In what ways will the study of advertisements help purchasers get the best buys?

Because of the problems of scarcity of income and time, every consumer's goal should be to obtain the most satisfaction from his or her limited income and time. There are three basic buying principles that can help consumers achieve this goal. They are: **1.** gathering as much information as is worthwhile; **2.** using advertising wisely; **3.** getting the best deal by comparison shopping. Part II of the Checklist for Consumer Decision Making can be especially useful to you in applying these three principles. All this information, of course, is based on the belief that your first decision—to make a purchase—was a wise one.

GATHERING ENOUGH INFORMATION

Again suppose that you are going to buy a bicycle. Once you have decided that, you have to decide on a brand and a model. How?

You first have to obtain information about bicycles. You can search it out by reading advertisements, or spending time testing out friends' bicycles. You could also go to different stores and discuss the good and bad points of various makes and models with salespeople. Actually, as a wise consumer, you would do some of each of these. But remember that information is costly because obtaining it involves your time. So you are faced with the problem of deciding how much information to obtain.

In this case the buying principle to follow is: Obtain as much information as is worthwhile. What is meant by *worthwhile?* The value of your time and effort spent in gathering information should not be greater than the value you receive from making the best choice of product for yourself. You would not, for example, want to go to every bicycle store in your town or city and spend two hours with every salesperson discussing every model. On the other hand, you would probably want to spend more than two minutes reading one advertisement about one model. In other words, the less valuable a person considers his or her time, the more comparison shopping he or she should do. A nonworking college student generally has more time for comparison shopping than a business executive.

make: name of the manufacturer

Supermarket customers benefit when they use buying principles to decide on the right purchase. What information might this shopper need?

Checking advertisements is a good, inexpensive way to find out about new products and services or changes in existing ones. But there are some things you should be aware of as you read or listen to advertisements. There are also certain types of information that you should be able to find in an ad. As you read ads, you should ask yourself:

1. Does the advertisement appeal to my emotions? Look beyond the appeal to your vanity to find out what the ad is really saying about the product or service.

2. What are the special features of the product? Do these special features make any sense in terms of my needs? Suppose you are looking for a clock radio to wake you up in the morning. Then you should not spend much time on an ad about a radio featuring push-button station selection, separate stereo speakers, and automatic shut-off.

3. If I am interested in an automobile or appliance, does the ad tell me anything about operating costs?

4. Does the ad tell me anything about a product's durability or ability to last?

5. Does the advertised price compare favorably with the price of similar products?

6. Is the advertised price the entire price? Sometimes an ad will show a low price in large print, and in small print you will discover that you have to pay separately for installation or buy separate parts, such as batteries.

USING ADVERTISING WISELY

Advertising is all around you. Whenever you turn on the radio or television, you will more than likely hear a commercial. Wherever you go, you see advertising on billboards, on posters on buses, and so on. There are two kinds of advertising: competitive and informative.

Competitive advertising attempts to persuade consumers that the product being advertised is different from and superior to any other. Its purpose may be to take customers away from competitors. Or its purpose may be defensive—to keep competitors from taking away customers. Ads for well-established brand names and products, such as General Motors and Green Giant, are often of this type. They are meant to keep the public aware of a company's name and products.

Informative advertising gives information about a product. In most cases, informative ads benefit consumers. From such ads, you, as a consumer, can learn about the existence, price, quality, and special features of products without spending much time or effort. Informative advertising may also be competitive.

The checklist for analyzing advertisements gives you some tips for reading ads. Unfortunately, advertising can be misleading. Although most advertisers try to present their products accurately, some do use deceptive, or false, advertising. Sellers may misrepresent the quality, features, or, most often, the price of goods. One of the most widely used methods of deceptive advertising is **bait and switch.** The bait is an unrealistically low-priced item advertised in the newspaper, on television, or on the radio. When the consumer gets to the store, he or she will find that item is no longer available. Or the salesperson will point out all the bad features of the advertised item and how dissatisfied the customer will be with it. The salesperson then shows higher-priced models and points out all their good features. This is the switch. Instead of being able to buy a $199 washer, for example, the customer finds all the available ones are $300 or more. This is not only deceptive but illegal.

GETTING THE BEST DEAL BY COMPARISON SHOPPING

Once you have gathered the information and made a decision about the type of bicycle—or any product you want—you must decide where to buy it. That decision is affected by the price you will have to pay for the make and model you want. Because you have limited income, the more cheaply you can buy it, the more income you will have to spend on other things. In other words, you will be best off as a consumer when you are able to pay the lowest price for what you want.

How do you find out which store has the lowest price? You can read newspaper advertisements, make telephone calls, and visit different stores. Remember, however, that finding out price information requires the use of your time. You probably would not want to visit every store in your area before deciding where to buy your bicycle. Nevertheless, you will want to shop around.

This suggests a third buying principle. Whenever you decide to make a purchase, it is generally worthwhile to get information on the types and prices of products available from different stores or companies. This is known as **comparison shopping.** It is a consumer principle that will be emphasized throughout this unit.

BRAND-NAME PRODUCTS—ANOTHER FACTOR TO CONSIDER

Even when you apply these three buying principles to actual consumer decision making, you may still find that being a wise consumer is not always easy. This is a complex world with many sellers of many products. Some sellers do not always include complete or reliable information about their products. Others may not repair or replace the products they sell if those products turn out to be faulty. Some consumers find that national brand-name products are worth the often higher prices that have to be paid for them, whether they be food or stereos.

logo (LOH-goh): trademark

A **brand name** is a word, picture, or logo on a product that helps consumers tell it from similar products of competitors. Brand names are usually sold nationwide and are backed by major national or even international companies. Food products, which are sometimes regional brands, may be an exception. Because a major company such as Sony or Nabisco manufactures a product, consumers can be reasonably sure that it will be of the same quality each time they buy it. Occasionally there may be differences, however, the wise shopper can often find non-brand name items of equally high quality and reliability if he or she follows the shopping steps outlined on pages 58 and 59. There are numerous small companies throughout the United States that produce high-quality products at a fair price.

Case Study

LET THE SELLER BEWARE—THE CONSUMER MOVEMENT

For hundreds of years, the relationship between the buyer of a product and the seller was governed by the principle of *caveat emptor*—a Latin phrase meaning "let the buyer beware." Under this principle, if you had bought a faulty product, you had to complain directly to the person you bought it from and hope that the seller would fix what was wrong or replace it, although he or she had no legal obligation to do so.

In the United States, the principle of *caveat emptor* no longer applies, for the seller of a product is required by law to provide products that are safe and in good working order. For example, many states have so-called "lemon laws." These laws state that if an automobile company sells a defective car—a "lemon"—it must repair it so that it runs properly, or replace it with one in good running order. In the United States the principle of let the buyer beware has mainly been replaced by the principle of let the seller beware.

Such consumer protection is part of a general movement that began at the end of the 19th century known as **consumerism.** Consumerism works to protect consumers from low-quality products, unsafe products, and fraudulent advertising. One of the most successful periods for consumerism in the United States was 1965 to 1975. In 1965, a young lawyer named Ralph Nader published a book called *Unsafe at Any Speed.* In it, he accused General Motors (GM) of selling automobiles that were faulty and even dangerous to the public. GM fought back by trying to discredit Nader. The company hired private detectives to uncover anything in Nader's private life that could damage his reputation. Nader then sued GM and was awarded $280,000, which he used to continue his fight for consumer protection.

In the years following his battle with GM, Nader helped persuade Congress to pass a series of major laws aimed at protecting the health and safety of consumers and workers. Nader organized a group of investigators, called "Nader's Raiders," to look into abuses against consumers, and he established an organization called Public Citizen to look into health care, tax reform, and other consumer issues. In the 1970s, private groups were organized in many cities to deal with such problems as poor housing, discrimination against minorities and women in granting credit, and business inaction on consumer complaints.

In more recent years, political leaders, economists, and concerned citizens have become aware of the costs of government regulation in the marketplace. In a world of scarcity, additional production costs that are required to make automobiles safer, for example, by installing airbags, are ultimately paid for by purchasers of automobiles. Legislation to benefit consumers always carries with it a price tag. It is perhaps because members of Congress realize this price tag that Congress has not established a federal consumer protection agency. Or perhaps the reason it has not done so is that the consumer movement has already achieved many of its goals.

1. What are some of the achievements of the consumer movement?
2. Why has Congress not established a federal consumer protection agency?

1. Write a definition for each of the following advertising terms: **a.** comparative advertising, **b.** informative advertising, **c.** bait and switch, **d.** comparison shopping, **e.** brand name.
2. What three buying principles does the author list as important?
3. Choose one and describe a situation in which you use the buying principle to make a purchase such as a stereo, personal computer, or car. For example, how would you go about gathering enough worthwhile information? (Be sure to explain how much information would be worthwhile in this situation.) How could you use the Checklist for Analyzing Advertising? How would you do comparison shopping?
4. **Critical Thinking: Analyzing Information. a.** What are the advantage(s) of buying brand-name products? **b.** What are the disadvantage(s)? **c.** Why do some people buy brand-name products regardless of the disadvantage(s)?

3 | CONSUMERISM

Ask yourself as you read:
- What is the consumer movement?
- Which federal agencies aid consumers?

Today the decisions Americans face as consumers are increasingly complex. Many Americans are greatly concerned with the safety and reliability of the products and services they use. Since the early 1960s, **consumerism,** or the consumer movement, has grown steadily. Its advocates, or supporters, wish to educate consumers about the purchases they make and to demand better and safer products from manufacturers. Many government agencies at the local, state, and federal levels and private groups work to ensure the well-being of consumers. Business can no longer assume it is only the buyer's responsibility to know whether a product is safe, food is healthful, or advertising is accurate.

advocate (AD-vuh-kit): supporter

This woman is shopping for clothing. What rights does she have as a consumer?

CONSUMER RIGHTS

In 1962, President John F. Kennedy sent the first consumer protection message to Congress. In that message, Kennedy stated four consumer rights:

- the right to safety—protection against goods that are dangerous to life or health;
- the right to be informed—information for use not only as protection against fraud but also as the basis for reasoned choices;
- the right to choose—the need for markets to be competitive (have many firms) and for protection by government in those markets, such as electric service, where competition does not exist;
- the right to be heard—the guarantee that consumer interests will be listened to when laws are being written.

To the four rights listed by Kennedy, most consumer advocates would add a fifth:

- the right to redress—the ability to obtain from manufacturers adequate payment in money or goods for financial or physical damages caused by their products.

redress: relief from distress or wrong

Depending on the item, a dissatisfied consumer can complain to the store manager or write to the manufacturer. He or she can also hire a lawyer or take the case to small claims court where a lawyer is not necessary. There are also many private and public agencies that can help consumers. Since the 1960s consumer education has become widespread and consumer legislation has increased considerably. The right of consumers to receive compensation for physical damages received when using a product is generally recognized.

Because the consumer movement had attained many of its goals by the early 1980s, it began to lose its force. However, problems still remain and the private and public consumer groups and agencies that were formed as a result of its actions continue to watch business practices and to educate consumers about products and the marketplace.

PRIVATE HELP FOR CONSUMERS

Among the private groups that aid consumers are local citizens' action groups and local chapters of the Better Business Bureau. Many major cities and some smaller ones have better business bureaus. They provide information on selling practices and products to consumers and help settle disagreements between consumers and sellers. Citizens' action groups and the Better Business Bureau can be found through local telephone directories. Some newspapers and television and radio stations have Action Line or Hot Line services to handle complaints.

Trade associations in some industries also provide consumer information. A trade association is a group of companies in the same business that work together to promote the industry. Some trade associations handle consumer problems. Through Consumer Action Panels the automobile, furniture, and major appliance industries deal with complaints that consumers have with a store or manufacturer.

Table 3-1: FEDERAL AGENCIES AND CONSUMERISM

Agency	How It Helps the Consumer	For More Information
Consumer Information Center Program	Provides free catalog of government publications on such consumer topics as health, food, nutrition, energy, automobiles, and money management.	*Consumer's Resource Handbook,* Consumer Information Center Pueblo, Colorado 81009
Federal Trade Commission	Promotes free and fair competition by enforcing laws against monopolies, price fixing, false advertising, and other illegal business practices. Also regulates packaging and labeling of products and protects the public against violations of consumer credit laws.	Federal Trade Commission 6th Pennsylvania Avenue, N.W. Office of Public Information Washington, D.C. 20580
Consumer Product Safety Commission	Protects the public against unreasonable risk of injury from consumer products. Sets product safety requirements, forbids the production and sale of dangerous consumer products, and conducts research and education programs on safety concerns for industry and the public.	Office of the Secretary, Consumer Product Safety Commission Washington, D.C. 20207
Government Printing Office	Sells over 15,000 different government publications on a wide variety of topics. Lists those of interest to consumers in free booklet: *Consumer Information Subject Bibliography.*	Superintendent of Documents Government Printing Office Washington, D.C. 20402
U.S. Postal Service	Through Inspection Service protects public from mail fraud and other violations of postal laws. Through Consumer Advocate's office acts on complaints and suggestions from individual customers and provides information on past and present schemes used to cheat the public.	Consumer Advocate U.S. Postal Service Washington, D.C. 20260

In addition, two national organizations provide consumer information. The Consumers Union of the United States, Inc., publishes a monthly magazine called *Consumer Reports.* This is an informational magazine that accepts no advertising. A competing publication is *Consumers' Research Magazine,* published by Consumers' Research, Inc. Both are good sources of information about many kinds of products, especially major ones such as appliances and automobiles.

Table 3-1: FEDERAL AGENCIES AND CONSUMERISM *(continued)*

Agency	How It Helps the Consumer	For More Information
U.S. Department of Agriculture	Inspects and grades meat, fish, poultry, dairy products, and fruits and vegetables through the department's Food Safety and Quality Service. Also ensures that food production is sanitary and that products are labeled truthfully. Is good source of information for consumers on best way to spend food dollars.	Office of the Consumer Adviser Administration Building U.S. Department of Agriculture Washington, D.C. 20250
U.S. Office of Consumer Affairs (Department of Health and Human Services)	Coordinates all federal activities on behalf of consumers, advises President on consumer affairs, and works for and testifies on behalf of consumer legislation. Through Complaint Coordination Center helps government agencies and industry solve consumer problems and educates public on how to get complaints answered.	U.S. Office of Consumer Affairs Humphrey Building 200 Independence Avenue Washington, D.C. 20201
Food and Drug Administration (Department of Health and Human Services)	Protects the public against impure and unsafe foods, drugs, and cosmetics. Researches and tests new products in these areas and ensures accurate labeling. Publishes *FDA Consumer* magazine and maintains regional consumer affairs offices.	Food and Drug Administration 5600 Fishers Lane Rockville, Maryland 20857
National Highway Traffic Safety Administration (Department of Transportation)	Sets requirements for automobile safety, maintenance, and fuel economy and tests products for compliance, or the fulfillment of requirements. Researches ways to save fuel and make highways safer and investigates complaints from consumers about vehicle safety. Publishes regular consumer protection bulletins.	National Highway Traffic Safety Administration Department of Transportation Washington, D.C. 20590

FEDERAL AGENCIES THAT HELP CONSUMERS

Numerous federal agencies have programs to aid consumers. Table 3-1 lists these agencies and what they do. Much of the information that now appears on product labels and in warranties is a result of federal regulations to protect consumers.

Each state has a consumer affairs council or agency, often within the state attorney general's office, whose job it is to respond to the needs

HANDLING A CONSUMER PROBLEM

Dealing with a faulty product or with a repair that was done incorrectly are two common consumer problems. The Office of Consumer Affairs in its *Consumer's Resource Handbook* suggests several steps to take to get satisfaction for a complaint.

1. Report a problem as soon as possible. Do not try to fix the product yourself because this may cancel the warranty.
2. Clearly state your problem and the solution you believe would be fair and just—replacement, money back, and so on.
3. Include all important details, along with copies of documents, such as receipts, guarantees, contracts, and so on, to support your case.
4. Describe what action you have taken.
5. Keep a record of efforts to have your problem solved, including names of people you speak to, times, dates, and similar information.
6. Allow each person you contact a reasonable period of time, such as three weeks, to solve the problem before contacting another source.
7. Never become angry or insulting. The person you are dealing with is not responsible for your problem, but may be able to solve it.

As a responsible consumer, you should follow these steps whether you deal with the problem in person or by writing a letter to the manufacturer. You will find that most businesses and manufacturers will solve your problem easily and quickly. They would rather have a happy repeat customer than an angry ex-customer.

Although you can sometimes handle a complaint in person with a store, you may need to write to the manufacturer. The following letter is a sample suggested by the *Consumer's Resource Handbook*. It could also be used for writing about a faulty repair job. If possible, type your letter. If you write it, be sure your writing is neat and easy

---

Your Address
Your City, State, Zip Code
Date

Customer Service Department
Company Name
Street Address
City, State, Zip Code

Dear Mr., Ms., Mrs.:

I bought a (product name and serial and model numbers) at (location and date of purchase). Unfortunately, (state problem; give history of the problem and efforts to solve it).

Therefore, to solve the problem, I would appreciate your (state specific action you want taken). Enclosed are copies of the following records: (list and enclose copies of all documents connected with the problem).

I am looking forward to your reply and resolution of my problem and will wait (state a reasonable time period) before seeking third-party assistance. Contact me at the above address or by phone at (work and home phone numbers).

Sincerely,
Your Name

---

to read. Keep a copy of it and all related information for your records.

Practicing Your Skills

Suppose that you bought a stereo and found after a week that one speaker did not work. Answer the following questions about how you would handle your complaint.

1. Sometimes an item must be returned to a manufacturer's service center or to the manufacturer for service rather than to the store. Using the sample, write a letter to the manufacturer.
2. What documents would you copy to send with the letter and the speaker?
3. If you do not receive satisfaction in a reasonable time, what agencies could you call?

This young shopper is comparing prices on clothing. What decisions does he need to make to purchase the item that is right for him?

and questions of consumers. Usually, counties also have their own consumer affairs departments.

CONSUMER RESPONSIBILITIES

So far you have been reading about consumer rights, but consumers have responsibilities, too. Their first responsibility is to themselves. Each consumer should learn as much as possible about the product or service he or she wishes to buy. This will enable the consumer to purchase the best product at the best price. Before agreeing to buy, a good consumer reads all contracts and warranties and asks about return and refund policies. After the purchase, he or she reads any instruction booklet and follows the directions for proper use of the product.

A second responsibility consumers have is to respect the rights of producers and sellers of goods and services. A responsible consumer will not try to return an item because he or she has seen it elsewhere for a lower price. Nor will a consumer misuse an item and then attempt to return it, saying it was defective—that is, faulty or broken—when bought. If it becomes necessary to file a complaint, the responsible consumer goes through the steps suggested on p. 68.

defective (di-FEK-tiv): faulty, broken

REVIEWING ECONOMIC PRINCIPLES

1. What is consumerism?
2. What are the major purposes of the consumer movement?
3. Using the biography of the consumer movement as the basis for your answer, list in correct time order the development of the consumer movement in the United States. (You might find it helpful to make a time line.)
4. According to the table Federal Agencies and Consumerism, what three types of help do these agencies give to consumers?
5. **Critical Thinking: Making Distinctions. a.** What consumer rights are important to you as a consumer? **b.** What two major consumer responsibilities do you have?

SUMMARY OF
IMPORTANT PRINCIPLES

1
- To consume, people must have income. It can be both disposable and discretionary. The amount available to spend depends on a person's earning power. This, in turn, is influenced by education, occupation, age, sex, ethnic group, geographical location, and inheritance.
- All buying decisions are affected by two scarce resources: time and income.

2
- Consumers go through a three-step decision making process each time they make a purchase. These three steps are: deciding whether to buy, choosing the right product, owning and using the product.
- There are three basic buying principles: gathering as much information as is worthwhile to find the right product; using advertising wisely; getting the best deal by comparison shopping.
- Obtaining as much information as is worthwhile means that the value of the person's time and effort in gathering the information should not be greater than the value he or she will receive from making the best choice of product.
- Checking advertisements is a good, inexpensive way to find out about new products and services or changes in existing ones. But consumers should be aware that some ads appeal to emotions rather than a consumer's need to know. A consumer should be able to learn from an ad such information as a product's special features, operating costs, durability, and price.
- Brand-name products are generally slightly higher in price than other goods, but people tend to consider them more reliable and of better quality than non-brand-name items.

3
- The purposes of the consumer movement are to educate consumers about the purchases they make and to demand better and safer products from manufacturers.
- One of the earliest consumer laws was passed in 1872 when mail fraud was made a federal crime. In the early part of the 20th century, muckrakers alerted the public to abuses against consumers. As a result, government regulations were passed, especially in the food and drug industries. Afterwords, the movement made little headway until efforts of Ralph Nader and others in the 1960s and 1970s. By the 1980s, consumer groups had won many of their goals.
- Many government agencies and departments provide information to consumers, regulate business practices, and do research in a   s of interest to consumers. Many private groups also assist co   rs.
- The first responsibility of consumers is to themselves to l   as much as possible about the product or service they want to buy. The second responsibility is to respect the rights of producers and sellers.
- In handling a complaint, a consumer should report a problem as soon as possible, state the problem and desired solution, include all important details and documents, describe past steps to solve the problem, never become angry or insulting, allow reasonable time for a solution, and keep a record of all efforts to solve the problem.

Putting Economics to Work

CONSUMER DECISION MAKING: DECIDING TO BUY A CAR

Tina Said has to travel 6 miles (about 10 kilometers) each day to and from her part-time job. The bus costs her an hour of time plus bus fare each day she goes to work. Tina decided to buy a used car with the help of her parents. She made this decision by comparing the value of the time she would save by having a car with the amount of money she must spend to buy it. In other words, she evaluated the trade-off involved.

Once the decision was made to buy a car, Tina made a list of the features she wanted. They included economy in gas use, safety, and reliability. To find out about economy, Tina read reports from the Environmental Protection Agency (EPA) published by the Department of Energy (DOE). These reports told her about the gas mileage that various makes and models could be expected to get.

While she was in the library, she also read issues of *Consumer Reports* to find out the reported repair records of cars owned by readers of that magazine. Finally, she wrote the National Highway Traffic Safety Administration in Washington, D.C., to obtain the latest information on the safety of various makes and models of cars.

In the end, Tina found that she could get economy and reliability—a good repair record—but would have to sacrifice some safety. The trade-off existed because many smaller economical cars do not protect their occupants in an accident as well as larger cars.

1. List the step(s) on the Checklist for Consumer Decision Making that Tina has completed.
2. Which questions does she still have to answer?
3. What trade-offs did she make in deciding to buy a car?
4. What kind of information did Tina have to gather to decide on her last trade-off?
5. Do you think this research was worthwhile to Tina in making her decision? Why or why not?

Readings in Economics

1851 FAMILY BUDGET: $10.37 A WEEK
Skill: Making Inferences

When we, as consumers, plan our expenditures, we must keep in mind today's prices for the items we wish to purchase. In this reading, we see how the prices as well as some of the items themselves have changed since 1851.

As one of America's most influential newspaper editors, Horace Greeley of the New York *Tribune* was full of advice, and he imparted it to the nation at every opportunity. "Go to the West," was perhaps his most famous injunction. But he also had plenty to say about business and economics. . . .

He . . . urged persistence, frugality, and the recognition of the value in money of one's time. . . . Implicit in his advice was the belief that business had a philosophical justification: it helped mankind. He ended with a criticism that underscored his message. "We are energetic," he said about the American people. ". . . We are confident in our capacities and in our national destiny; but we are not a systematic, a frugal, economical people."

. . . In 1851 he estimated the needs of the average skilled workman and four dependents and proposed this weekly budget for them:

Barrel of flour, $5, which will last eight weeks	$ .62
Sugar, 4 lbs. @ 8¢	.32
Butter, 2 lbs. @ 31½¢	.63
Milk	.14
Butcher's meat, 2 lbs. beef a day	1.40
Potatoes, ½ bushel	.50
Coffee and tea	.25
Candle light	.14
Fuel, 3 tons of coal per year, $15; matches, etc.	.40
Salt, pepper, vinegar, starch, soap, soda, yeast, cheese, eggs	.40
Household articles, wear and tear	.25
Rent	3.00
Bedclothes	.20
Clothing	2.00

Greeley, quite naturally, added twelve cents a week for newspapers and came up with a total of $10.37 for a family of five. It was high for most workers. . . . But Greeley felt that by following his budget, every workingman could eventually make his way upward on the economic ladder.

1. What expenses on Greeley's budget would probably not be incurred by a family today?
2. What are some of the expenses today's families have that an 1851 family did not have?

© 1972 American Heritage Inc. Reprinted with permission from *The History of American Business* by Alex Groner and the editors of *American Heritage* and *Business Week*.

WITH PRICES DOWN, CONSUMERS ARE UP
Skill: Making Inferences

Changing economic conditions in the 1980's have greatly increased consumer power. This reading discusses how new consumer power due to falling prices affects consumers' buying decisions.

For American consumers these would be heady days—if they weren't so confusing. Who, after all, needs all these questions? Do you buy a car while GM offers cut-rate financing, or do you wait for Chrysler to . . . chop sticker prices in May? What about a house? Buy now? Or are mortgage rates coming down even farther? Flying to Florida for a spring vacation? What "discount" airline is giving the best price? . . .

. . . Not since the 1950s has more buying power been concentrated in the hands of buyers. . . . "There used to be a general consensus that the consumer would buy whatever we put out," says Ross Roberts, a marketing executive at Ford Motor Co. "Those days are gone. . . ."

American companies, however belatedly, understand that—and are changing the way they do business. The automakers are now prodding dealers to take care of customers not only when they walk in to buy a car, but when they return for maintenance or repairs. . . . And home-computer makers know that they won't sell their product until people are really convinced they need a home computer. Price is not the issue. . . . Consumers, says William Campbell, Apple Computer sales and marketing executive, "aren't buying technology. They're buying utility."

The shift in the balance of power from corporations to consumers happened swiftly. In the late 1970s with prices rising at double-digit rates, the buying attitude of consumers was clear: buy now, because prices are going up later. Today, argues Prudential-Bache economist Edward Yardeni, the opposite is true: "I think increasingly people are sitting back and saying, 'Why buy now when prices are going lower tomorrow?'"

1. With less of an emphasis on price, what tactic did home-computer manufacturers take to try to sell computers to parents?
2. Create an advertisement that focuses on trying to convince people that they really need a home computer.

"The Consumer Is King—Again." *Newsweek.* March 31, 1986, pp. 34, 35.

THE ROLE OF THE FDA
Skill: Interpreting Information

 **Federal agencies that protect consumers often cause difficulty for manufacturers bringing new products onto the market because of all the regulations, testing, and paperwork involved. In this reading, James E. Wavle, Jr., president of a major American drug manufacturing company, addresses the issues of delays due to the Food and Drug Administration regulations.**

The industry's dependence on the FDA is a fact of life. So is the 32 months it takes for the average new drug application to wend its way through the approval process. . . .

Now we realize that new drug review is only one of the many FDA responsibilities. And we know that some consumer activists are constantly demanding that more attention should be paid to regulation enforcement and less to approving new medicines. And that regulators often have to drop everything else to deal with emergencies. . . . And there's no getting away from the reality that the FDA is overburdened, understaffed, underequipped and underfinanced. . . .

So perhaps the pharmaceutical industry should accept with better grace the lengthy, costly, frustrating drug approval procedure it has been forced to live with for the last quarter century—and take satisfaction from knowing that the process solidifies the underpinnings of safety and efficacy we build into the drugs we bring into the world.

There's just one trouble with that scenario: if we accept it, our nation will be forced to move to the sidelines while one of the most exciting and satisfying developments in human history is being played out in the world arena. I refer to the revolution in medical science. If we accept it, we must leave that revolution to others. For the revolution will go on. New medicines will continue to be discovered. It's just that people in other countries will have the benefit of their use long before we do.

This is not a matter of national pride we're discussing. We're talking about a much more important matter, in fact a matter of life and death.

A few years ago the FDA approved a beta-blocker to treat victims of heart attacks. In announcing the approval, the FDA commissioner predicted the drug would save 7,000 to 10,000 lives in this country every year.

That was the good news. Here's the bad news.

That same drug had been approved six years earlier in Sweden to prevent second heart attacks. Six years! If we just take the lower estimate of 7,000 lives the drug could have saved in this country a year and multiply it by six, we get 42,000 heart attack fatalities that might never have occurred. That's about the same number as U.S. traffic deaths last year.

1. What are some of the reasons for the FDA's delay in reviewing and approving new drugs?
2. How might the actions of the FDA in withholding new medicines be interpreted as a paradox, that is, of having the opposite effect from that intended?

James E. Wavle, Jr., "Do Regulators Have a Future?" From a speech delivered May 21, 1986, in Atlantic City. *Vital Speeches of the Day.* Vol. LII, No. 18, July 1, 1986. p. 570.

3 | CHAPTER REVIEW

PRACTICING YOUR READING SKILLS: CAUSE AND EFFECT

Cause and effect describes the relationship between events. One event results in, or causes, the other. Distinguishing between cause and effect is one of the major methods that economists use to analyze and describe the economy. In the process, economists have to be careful not to conclude that because two events occur around the same time, one caused the other. For example, because the price of gasoline increased in the mid-1970s and the sale of large-sized American cars dropped, an economist could decide that the first caused the second. That may be true. However, to be certain, an economist would need a model showing the effects of price increases on the sale of automobiles before he or she could form a valid conclusion about cause and effect. Without the model, an economist might also conclude that the decrease in the size of American families caused the decrease in the sale of large-sized cars.

In your reading, you will not be called upon to use models the way economists do. But you will have to analyze the conclusions that economists reach to decide on causes and effects. Certain words and phrases can help you identify these relationships. Among them are *according to, because, as a result of, since, therefore, if . . . then.* Sometimes the relationship will be directly stated. For example, on page 57, there is the following statement: " . . . ability to consume . . . in turn, depends on the income available and how much of it a person chooses to spend. . . . " The phrase *in turn* helps you to see that the effect of having disposable income results in the ability to consume.

Sometimes the relationship will not be directly stated. You will have to infer it. Turning statements into questions or substituting the words *cause* and *effect* may help you decide if one event is the cause or effect of another.

1. According to the text under the heading "Buying Principles, or Strategies," what is the effect of the problems of scarcity of income and time?
2. According to the text under the heading "Using Advertising Wisely," what are two effects of competitive advertising?
3. What is the cause-and-effect relationship expressed in number 2 in the Checklist for Analyzing Advertisements?
4. What has been the effect of consumerism on business?

VOCABULARY REVIEW

Write the letter of the definition in Column B that correctly defines each term in Column A.

Column A	Column B
1. disposable income	a. deceptive advertising intended to defraud the consumer
2. warranty	b. getting information about similar types of products and prices
3. bait and switch	c. money income left after taxes have been paid
4. comparison shopping	d. attempts to persuade consumers that its products are different and superior to others
5. competitive advertising	e. written guarantee of a product for a certain period of time

PRACTICING YOUR ECONOMIC SKILLS

1. **Reading a Pie Graph.** The pie graph on p. 56 is based on a year in which total consumer spending equalled $2,250 billion. **a.** How many dollars were spent on food that year? **b.** How many dollars were spent on food and housing combined?

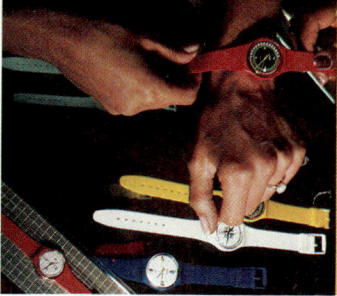

United States Production of Selected Metals in a Recent Year

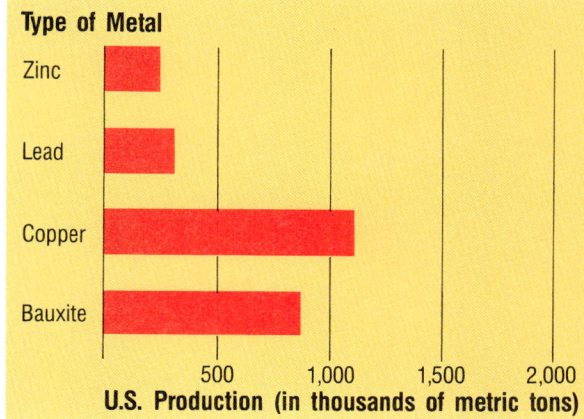

Type of Metal

Zinc

Lead

Copper

Bauxite

| 500 | 1,000 | 1,500 | 2,000 |

U.S. Production (in thousands of metric tons)

Source: Department of the Interior, Bureau of Mines

2. **Reading a Bar Graph.** The bar graph above gives United States production statistics for four selected metals in a recent year. **a.** How many metric tons of bauxite were produced in this year? **b.** Which two metals were produced in relatively small quantities? **c.** In 1970, the United States production of zinc was about 200 percent greater than for the year shown in the graph. About how many metric tons of zinc were produced in 1970?

DISCUSSING ECONOMIC QUESTIONS

1. According to the text, the three basic buying principles are gathering as much information as is worthwhile, using advertising wisely, and comparison shopping. Do you agree with these? Why or why not? Would you add any other buying strategies to this list? What?
2. Do you agree with the text that it is difficult to be a wise consumer? Why or why not?
3. Who do you think has the main responsibility for ensuring product quality and reliability, the seller or the consumer? Why? What should the role of government be?

APPLYING CRITICAL THINKING SKILLS

1. **Analyzing Ads.** Choose an advertisement from a newspaper or a magazine, and use the checklist on page 61 to analyze it. Write a sentence to answer each of the questions on the checklist. Do you think it is a competitive or informative ad or both?
2. **Consumer Decision Making.** Imagine that, like Tina Said on p. 71, you have decided to buy a car but you still have to decide on the type (not the make and model but the size). Go through the same steps she did to research your decision. Keep a record of the information you find to bring in for the class.
3. **Shopping Wisely.** Using the Checklist for Consumer Decision Making and the three buying principles listed in the text, shop for one of the following: 10-speed bicycle, tape recorder, video game, or personal computer. Keep a record of the steps you take and the information you gather to compare with others in the class.
4. **Gathering Information.** Choose one of the agencies listed on pages 66–67 and write to it, asking for information about the services it provides.

READINGS

Friedman, Milton, and Friedman, Rose. *Free to Choose: A Personal Statement.* New York: Harcourt Brace Jovanovich, 1981, Chapter 7, "Who Protects the Consumer?" pp. 189–227.

Leftwich, Richard H., and Sharp, Ansel M. *Economics of Social Issues.* Plano, Texas: Business Publications, Inc., 1984. Chapter 8, "Consumerism: The Regulators Versus the Regulatees," pp. 187–202.

Mauser, Ferdinand F., and Schwartz, David J. *American Business: An Introduction.* New York: Harcourt Brace Jovanovich, 1982. Marketing, advertising, and selling.

Porter, Sylvia. *Sylvia Porter's New Money Book for the 80's.* New York: Avon, 1980.

MORE FOR *you*

Many Americans use credit to buy the goods and services they want. Learning to manage your income and use credit effectively will help make you be a wise consumer.

GOING INTO DEBT

Being a wise consumer goes hand in hand with being a wise spender. One way to become a wise spender, whatever your income, is to learn how to manage that income. This chapter describes the use of credit and the many types of credit available. You will be reading about reasons for borrowing, and some guidelines for when to pay cash and when to use credit. Applying for credit and its costs are described as well as sources of loans, types of charge accounts, and credit cards. Learning Economic Skills describes budgeting and how to decide on a safe debt load.

CHAPTER OBJECTIVES After you study the sections of this chapter, you will be able to:

1 • compare making a credit purchase and taking out a loan.
  • contrast the advantages and disadvantages of repaying a loan over a long period of time.
  • identify two reasons people use credit.
  • explain how borrowing or using credit is basically a question of comparing costs and benefits.

2 • contrast the six major sources of loans.

3 • compare and contrast the three different kinds of charge accounts.

4 • describe three costs of using credit cards.
  • explain the importance of knowing annual percentage rates for credit.
  • explain the various methods of computing finance charges on charge accounts and credit cards.
  ★ state the methods for making a budget and deciding on a safe debt load.

5 • describe the process for obtaining credit.

6 • determine the purposes of regulations governing the credit industry.

ECONOMICS VOCABULARY

credit
principal
interest
installment debt
consumer durables
mortgage
commercial bank
savings and loan association
savings bank
credit union
finance company
consumer finance company
charge account
credit card
regular charge account
credit limit
revolving charge account
installment charge account
finance charge
annual percentage rate
budget
fixed expense
flexible expense
credit bureau
credit check
credit rating
collateral
secured loan
unsecured loan
cosigner
usury laws

Suppose you are eating in a restaurant with a group of friends. When the bill comes, you find that you do not have enough money to pay for your share. What do you do? Usually you borrow from a friend, promising to repay the money later. In most cases, the friend is willing to lend you the money because he or she is certain you will repay it. Many people borrow and lend in this friendly way without giving it a second thought.

1 | AMERICANS AND CREDIT

Ask yourself as you read:
- Why is credit important to the nation's economy?
- What are the advantages and disadvantages of going into debt?

For the nation as a whole, though, the total amount of money borrowed and lent each year is enormous. The federal, state, and local governments all borrow each year. The nation's economy depends on individuals and groups being able to buy and borrow on credit. **Credit** is the receiving of money either directly or indirectly to buy goods and services in the present with the promise to pay for them in the future. The amount owed—the debt—is equal to the principal plus interest. The **principal** is the amount originally borrowed. The **interest** is the amount the borrower must pay for the use of someone else's money. That someone else may be a bank, credit card company, store, or the like. Figure 4-1 shows the total amount of private debt owed each year in the United States since 1973.

As you read this chapter, remember that any time you receive credit, you are borrowing money and going into debt. The act of taking out a loan for $100 is the same as buying an item for $100 on credit. In both cases, you have gone into debt for $100. In both cases, someone has extended you credit—lent you $100. In both cases, you pay for the privilege of using the $100 by paying interest for the use of that someone else's $100 of purchasing power.

INSTALLMENT DEBT

One of the most common types of debt is the **installment debt.** The repayment of this type of loan is divided into equal amounts, or installments, over a period of time, for example, 36 months. Many people buy such consumer durables as automobiles, refrigerators, washers, and other appliances on an installment plan. **Consumer durables** are manufactured items that people use for long periods of time before replacing. People can also borrow cash and pay it back in installments.

The length of the installment period is important in determining the size of the borrower's monthly payments and the total amount of interest he or she must pay. The longer the repayment period is, the smaller the monthly payment. For example, if the repayment of a loan is spread over three years, the monthly payments will be smaller than if the loan were repaid in two years. However, there is a trade off. The longer it takes to repay an installment loan, the greater is the total interest you pay.

The largest form of installment debt in this country is the money people owe on home mortgages. A **mortgage** is an installment debt owed on real property—houses, buildings, or land. Most people who owe only home mortgages do not consider themselves deeply in debt. They do not think of a home mortgage as similar to other kinds of debt, but it is. Somebody has provided the homeowner with money to purchase property. In return, the homeowner must repay the loan with interest in installments over a number of years.

WHY PEOPLE USE CREDIT

Most Americans are accustomed to borrowing and to buying on credit. In fact, at times, especially when buying such expensive consumer durables as automobiles and fine furniture, they consider borrowing necessary. In a sense, people feel forced to buy items on credit because they believe they need them immediately. They do not want to wait. Of course, consumers are not really "forced" to buy anything. They could decide instead to save the money needed for their purchases.

To illustrate this point, a savings bank once ran a clever advertisement on buying a car. The ad noted that if a person saved for 36 months to buy a $12,000 car, the car would cost only $11,000. The remaining $1,000 would be made up by the interest paid on the savings over the

Figure 4-1: OUTSTANDING DEBTS, 1978-1988

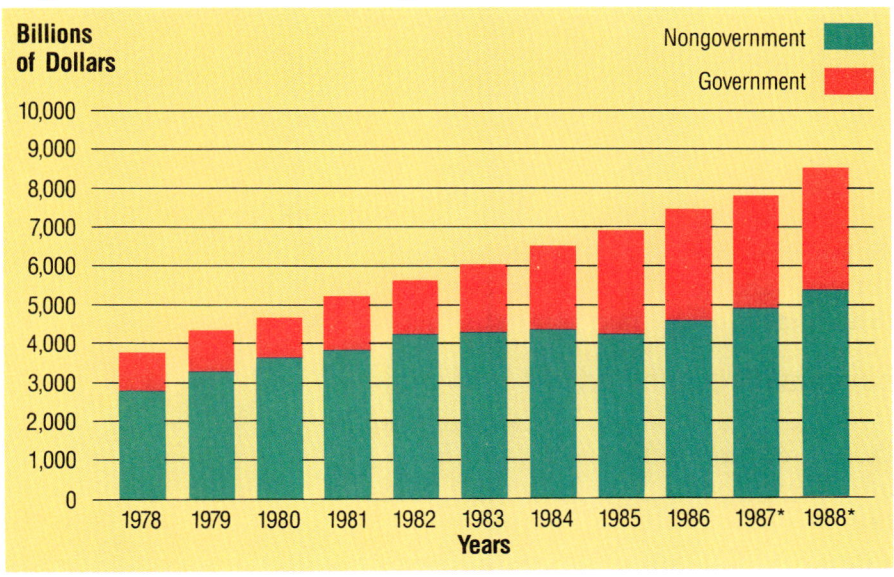

Source: Statistical Abstract of the U.S., Bureau of the Census
*Estimate

How much was private debt in 1978? By how many billion dollars did it grow in ten years? How much was government debt in 1978? By what percent did it grow in ten years?

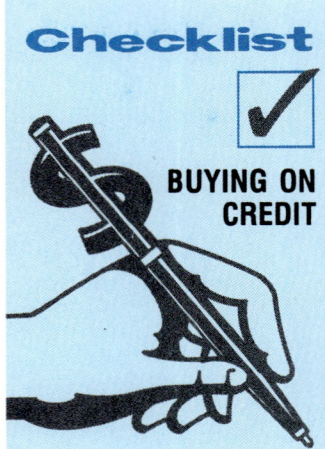

three years. On the other hand, according to the ad, if the person bought the $12,000 car immediately on a 36-month installment plan, the actual cost would be $15,000. The $3,000 difference would be the interest the person would have to pay on the borrowed money. In addition, the person would not receive any interest on savings.

Obviously, there is a big difference between $11,000 and $15,000. According to the ad, it is better to save now and buy later than to buy now and go into debt. But the ad omitted a couple of important points. First, during the three-year saving period, the person would not be able to enjoy the use of the car. Many people would not wait that long for something they want. They would rather buy on credit and enjoy the use of the item now rather than later. Second, the price of the car would probably have risen during this three-year period.

Another reason for going into debt is to have payments correspond to the use per time period of the item being purchased. For example, people do not buy a car to have it sit in their garages. What they buy is the availability of the automobile for use each day, week, month, and year that they own it. Suppose you decide to buy a car that costs $11,000 and you plan to keep it for five years. At the end of that time, it will be worth only $1,000. That means that over that five-year period you will get approximately $2,000 worth of use per year, or $166 per month, from the car. By buying an automobile on the installment plan, a person is able to make monthly payments that more or less correspond to the value of the use he or she receives from the car each month.

DECIDING TO USE CREDIT

Borrowing or using credit is a question of whether the satisfaction the borrower gets from whatever he or she buys is greater than the interest payments. It is basically a question of comparing costs and benefits. The benefit of borrowing is being able to buy and enjoy the good or service now rather than later. The cost is whatever the borrower must pay in interest or lost opportunities to buy other items. The

correspond (kor-uh-SPAHND)**:** to match

benefit of borrowing is something only you can decide for yourself. However, you and every other borrower should be aware of the costs involved in borrowing.

The Checklist For Buying on Credit, p. 80, and the chapter's Learning Economic Skills on budgeting and determining a safe debt load can help you decide when to use credit. It can also help you avoid the improper use of credit by overspending. Every day in the United States, thousands of families overextend their use of credit and get into financial trouble. Why? Because they have generally ignored the total costs of all their borrowing. They have too many credit cards and too many charge accounts and own too expensive a home with too large a mortgage. Just because someone offers you credit or allows you to borrow does not mean that you must accept. Buying on credit is a serious consumer activity. You should keep this Checklist in mind before you take the credit plunge.

REVIEWING ECONOMIC PRINCIPLES

1. Write sentences defining each of the following economic terms: **a.** credit, **b.** principal, **c.** interest, **d.** installment debt, **e.** consumer durables, **f.** mortgage.
2. In what three ways is making a purchase on credit the same as taking out a loan?
3. **a.** What are the advantages to repaying a loan over a long period? **b.** What are the disadvantages?
4. **a.** What are two reasons people give for using credit? **b.** What kinds of things do people buy on credit? Give three examples.
5. The Checklist for Buying on Credit is based on what three economic principles that you read about in Chapter 1?
6. **Critical Thinking: Making Decisions.** In deciding whether to pay cash or use credit for a personal purchase, what is: **a.** the cost involved? **b.** the benefit?

2 | SOURCES OF LOANS

Ask yourself as you read:
- How do the six types of loan institutions differ from one another?
- Which loan institutions charge the highest rates of interest?

As you read earlier in the chapter, borrowing money directly by taking out a loan is one of the two major types of credit. There are many sources for loans: commercial banks, savings and loan associations, savings banks, credit unions, and finance and consumer finance companies. Each of these sources, however, works in the same way, by charging interest on the money it lends.

Borrowing money by taking out a loan requires planning and comparison shopping. What information might this man request from the loan officer?

As with other items you buy, you should comparison shop for your loan. Based on the information in this chapter, you should check various lending agencies. Visit or phone several to find out how their interest rates and repayment terms differ.

COMMERCIAL BANKS

The first place you might think to go for a loan is a **commercial bank.** There are about 15,000 such banks in the country. Their main functions are: to accept deposits; to lend money; and to transfer funds among banks, individuals, and businesses. Commercial banks today control the largest amount of money and offer the widest range of services, many of which you will be reading about in Chapter 15.

Originally, commercial banks were the banks of business and commerce, or trade. But beginning in this century, commercial banks began to offer checking, savings, and loan services to individual consumers. Today, about a third of all loans that commercial banks make are for homes, cars, and other consumer goods. The loan departments of commercial banks make about 32 percent of all mortgages in the United States and about 45 percent of all other types of consumer installment loans. A commercial bank will often charge lower rates to customers with a checking or savings account at that bank.

SAVINGS AND LOAN ASSOCIATIONS

A **savings and loan association** (S&L), like a commercial bank, accepts deposits and lends money. When S&Ls were first established in the United States in the mid-19th century, they were called "building societies." Members of a society would combine their money over a period of time and take turns borrowing until each member was able to build a home. Today, there are over 4,500 S&Ls in the United States, and most savings deposits still come from individuals and families.

Recent changes in federal laws and regulations have greatly enlarged the activities of S&Ls. They may now offer many of the same services including checking-type accounts and business and consumer loans, as commercial banks. However, most loans at S&Ls are still used to buy homes. These loans account for slightly less than half of all home mortgages. S&Ls make only about 7 percent of all other consumer loans. Rates can vary widely from association to association.

SAVINGS BANKS

Savings banks are similar to S&Ls in that most of their business comes from savings accounts and home loans. Since 1980, savings banks, like commercial banks have been able to offer services similar to checking accounts. Savings banks were first set up in the United States in the early 19th century. They were meant to serve the small savers who were overlooked by the large commercial banks. Savings banks often include such words as *farmers', seamen's,* and *dime* in their names to indicate the group for whom the bank was originally intended.

Today there are about 440 savings banks. The majority of them are located in New England and the Mid-Atlantic states. Most of their loans are for home mortgages, although they do make personal and auto loans. Because of their small number, savings banks account for only about 8 percent of the country's home mortgages and about 3 percent of other consumer installment debt. Their interest rates for loans, like those of S&Ls, are often slightly less than those for commercial banks.

CREDIT UNIONS

Union members and employees of many companies often have credit unions. A **credit union** is owned and operated by its members to provide savings accounts and low-interest loans to its members only. In general, credit unions offer higher interest rates on savings and lower interest rates on loans than the institutions listed here. The approximately 20,000 credit unions account for about 14 percent of all consumer installment loans other than mortgages in the country. They make mostly personal, auto, and home improvement loans, though some larger credit unions offer home mortgages as well. They also offer share drafts, which are similar to checking accounts at commercial banks.

FINANCE COMPANIES AND CONSUMER FINANCE COMPANIES

You should not be confused by the terms *finance company* and *consumer finance company*. A **finance company** takes over contracts for installment debts from stores and adds a fee for collecting the debt. The consumer pays the fee in the form of slightly higher interest than he or she would pay to the retailer. Retailers use this method to avoid the risks involved in lending money to consumers. Finance companies also make loans directly to consumers.

retailer: person or store that sells directly to consumers

Consumer finance companies make loans directly to consumers at high rates of interest. These rates are often more than 20 percent a year. Some states, however, allow consumer finance companies to charge as much as 36 percent a year on small amounts of money. Consumers who use these companies are usually unable to borrow from commercial banks or other sources with lower rates. This inability to obtain lower-price credit may be because of nonpayment of loans in the past or an uneven employment record. Consumer finance companies are the largest supplier of installment cash loans for purposes other than buying consumer durables. People will often borrow money from consumer finance companies to pay off a series of bills. They trade making several payments a month for making just one, but this may increase interest costs.

There are more than 2,700 finance and consumer finance companies in the United States. Together, they account for about 23 percent of all consumer installment credit other than mortgages.

1. Define the differences among the following loan institutions: **a.** commercial bank, **b.** savings and loan association, **c.** savings bank, **d.** credit union, **e.** finance company, **f.** consumer finance company.
2. What are the six major sources of loans?
3. Using the information on pp. 82–83, make a table showing the following for each type of financial institution: **a.** name, **b.** number, **c.** percentage of the country's consumer installment loans accounted for by each type of institution, **d.** other characteristics.
4. **Critical Thinking: Assessing Information. a.** Which of these sources would you go to first for a loan for a word processor? **b.** Why?

3 | CHARGE ACCOUNTS AND CREDIT CARDS

Ask yourself as you read:

• What are the different types of charge accounts?
• How does a credit card differ from a charge account?

The other major type of credit is extended directly to an individual, without that person's having to borrow money first. This credit may be in the form of a charge account or a credit card. A **charge account** allows a customer to buy goods or services from a particular company and pay for them later. Department stores, for example, offer their customers three types of charge accounts: regular, revolving, or installment.

A **credit card,** like a charge account, allows a person to make purchases without paying cash. The difference is that most credit cards can be used at many kinds of stores, restaurants, hotels, and so on, throughout the United States and even in other countries. Many large stores issue their own credit cards, as you will read. Some companies, such as American Express, issue credit cards directly to individuals. Others, like Visa and MasterCard, issue cards through banks that can be used to purchase items in stores and restaurants where such cards are accepted. Bank credit cards also allow you to borrow money up to a certain limit. This means you have access to a money loan at all times without having to make application for it. In addition, many oil companies such as Gulf issue their own credit cards for use at their service stations. Using credit at places you shop regularly is one way to slip into debt very easily.

REGULAR CHARGE ACCOUNT

A **regular charge account,** also known as a 30-day charge, has a credit limit such as $500 or $1,000. A **credit limit** is the maximum amount of goods or services a person or business can buy on the promise to pay in the future. You and usually any member of your family can charge items up to this limit. At the end of every 30-day period, the store sends a bill for the entire amount. No interest is charged, but the entire bill must be paid at that time. If it is not, interest is charged on that part of the account. Some private credit card companies such as American Express also expect payment in full at the end of each billing period.

REVOLVING CHARGE ACCOUNT

A **revolving charge account** allows you to make additional purchases from the same store even if you have not paid the previous month's bill in full. Usually you must pay a certain portion of your balance each month, for instance one-fifth of the amount due. Interest is charged on the amount you do not pay. In many states, the rate is 1.5 percent per month, or 18.0 percent per year. Of course, if you pay everything you owe each month, no interest is charged. This type of account also has a credit limit.

balance: amount not paid

For both regular and revolving charge accounts, stores often issue their own charge cards. These cards are plastic, wallet-size, and imprinted with the customer's name and charge account number at that particular store. A store charge card is used the same way a credit card from an oil company, bank, or credit card company is used. However, it can be used only at the store for which it is issued.

INSTALLMENT CHARGE ACCOUNT

Major items such as stereos, televisions, and refrigerators are often purchased through an **installment charge account.** The items are purchased and paid for through equal payments spread over a period of time. Part of the amount paid each month is applied to the interest, and part is applied to the principal. At the end of the payment period, the borrower owns whatever he or she has made payments on.

This woman is using a credit card to make a purchase. What costs are involved in the use of a credit card?

CREDIT CARDS

Today, more than three-fourths of all American families have at least one credit card not issued by an oil company. In fact, more than one-fourth of all American families have three or more credit cards. The most popular are Visa, MasterCard, American Express, Diner's Club, Carte Blanche, and Chargex.

As with all scarce resources, credit issued on a credit card has a cost. Stores that allow people to use Visa, for example, must pay a certain percentage of credit purchases, usually 4 percent, to the credit card company or bank that issued the card. This is a fee for the services of the company. Stores include this cost in the price they charge their customers—credit card and cash customers alike. In other words, prices are higher than they would be if credit card purchases were not accepted.

In addition, credit card users are charged a monthly interest rate of around 1 or 1½ percent, or a yearly interest rate that is anywhere from 12 to 20 percent. This charge is added to the amount owed each month. It is similar to a revolving charge account at a store. Some credit card companies also charge a yearly fee for owning a card. This fee, which is often around $20, must be paid even if the card is never used.

REVIEWING ECONOMIC PRINCIPLES

1. Define the following credit terms: **a.** charge account, **b.** credit card, **c.** regular charge account, **d.** credit limit, **e.** revolving charge account, **f.** installment charge account.
2. **a.** What characteristics do regular, revolving, and installment charge accounts have in common? **b.** How are they different?
3. What three costs are involved in using credit cards?
4. **Critical Thinking: Comparing and Contrasting.** How do the various types of credit cards differ? What features do they have in common?

4 | THE COST OF CREDIT

Ask yourself as you read:
- What is a finance charge?
- What are the four methods of computing finance charges?

As you read earlier in this chapter, interest is the cost that people pay for credit. It is also the compensation the creditor gets for giving up part of his or her purchasing power to lend money. There is no single interest rate for credit. Rates for charge accounts and credit cards vary, depending on the repayment conditions and state laws regulating rates. For loans, the length of the loan and the risk also affect interest rates.

UNDERSTANDING INTEREST RATES

The terms *finance charge and annual percentage rate* tell the consumer the same thing—the cost of credit—but each is expressed in a different way.

The **finance charge** is the cost of credit expressed in dollars and cents. It must take into account interest costs plus any other charges connected with credit. For example, yearly membership fees for the use of a credit card are included in the finance charge. The **annual percentage rate** (APR) is the cost of credit expressed as a yearly percentage. Like the finance charge, the APR must take into account any noninterest costs of credit such as a membership fee. Say you charge on your credit card $200 worth of clothes to go back to school. The interest rate charged to you, let's say, is 10 percent, but the annual fee for the credit

REFERENCE NUMBER	PAYMENTS	PAYMENT DATE	CREDITS	PURCHASES	
17720284	25.00	10/26/82	4.42	9.24	14.44
				4.42	13.52
				23.67	23.00

SEND INQUIRIES CONCERNING YOUR ACCOUNT TO

THE BELK CENTER INC
P O BOX 30363
CHARLOTTE, NC 28230

COLOR YOUR WARDROBE WITH OUR
NEW FALL FASHION PALETTE. FIND
ALL THE EXCITING FASHION COLOR
OPTIONS THROUGHOUT OUR STORE.

ACCOUNT NUMBER ▶ 123 456 789 0
BILLING DATE ▶ 10/28/82
PAYMENT DUE DATE ▶ 11/28/82

PREVIOUS BALANCE	PURCHASES	PAYMENTS AND CREDITS	AVERAGE DAILY BALANCE	FINANCE CHARGE	NEW BALANCE	MINIMUM PAYMENT NOW DUE
242.92	88.29	29.42	272.70	4.09	305.88	35.00

FORM NO. 93398 R 2/82

FINANCE CHARGE RATES	APPLIED TO AVERAGE DAILY BALANCE OF	MONTHLY PERIODIC RATE	ANNUAL PERCENTAGE RATE
	272.70	01.50%	18.00%

PAYMENTS MADE AT YOUR LOCAL BELK STORE WILL BE CREDITED WITHIN FIVE DAYS, TO AVOID **FINANCE CHARGE** THE 'NEW BALANCE' MUST BE RECEIVED BY THE PAYMENT DUE DATE.

card is $5.00. Your APR will be $20 of interest, plus the $5.00 fee, or 12½ percent. The APR is always larger than the interest because it includes the noninterest cost of extending your credit.

Understanding and using APRs makes it easier to shop around for the best deal on credit. For example, if you are looking for a car, creditor A might ask for a large downpayment and offer in return small monthly payments. Creditor B might not require a downpayment at all, but charge large monthly payments instead. Creditor C might ask for small payments over a much longer period of time.

Knowing which creditor is charging the most for credit would be difficult without some guide to compare them. The APR provides that guide by allowing consumers to compare costs regardless of the dollar amount of those costs or the length of the credit agreement. Suppose creditor A is charging an APR of 16 percent, while creditor B is charging 17 percent, and creditor C is charging 18½ percent. On a yearly basis, creditor C is charging the most for credit and creditor A the least. Choosing which deal is best for you will still depend on such personal factors as your monthly income and the amount you have for a downpayment.

COMPUTING FINANCE CHARGES

The way finance charges are computed is another important factor in determining the cost of credit. The method can vary from creditor to creditor. Store charge accounts and credit cards use one of four methods to determine how much people pay for credit: previous balance, average daily balance, adjusted balance, past due balance. Each

It is important to know how finance charges are calculated. You should know the APR and how interest is computed. What other information do you need to decide which charge account or credit card offers the best deal?

compute (kuhm-PYOOT): to calculate, to figure out

Learning Economic Skills

BUDGETING AND DECIDING ON A SAFE DEBT LOAD

As you have already learned, everyone has a limited income. Thus, every time someone spends part of his or her income, that person must go without something else or take on large debts. To stay within a safe debt load, individuals and families must have ways to control expenditures. Making a **budget**—a plan for spending and saving income—is one such way.

BUDGETING

When individuals make a budget, they keep a record of how much income they expect to receive and to spend during a given period of time. A budget forces you to be aware of the decisions you make about spending and saving.

Suppose you are the head of a household and need to make a budget for the coming year. How would you begin? One way is to list the family's major goals. Does a leaky roof need to be repaired? Does the car need to be replaced? After the goals have been decided on, follow the steps listed below to create a spending plan. As a guide, refer to the previous year's expenses. Old bills, receipts, canceled checks, and income tax information will help you plan the kinds of expenses to expect.

1. Determine disposable income.
2. List **fixed expenses.** These expenses include rent or mortgage payments, car payments, insurance, and so on. Usually the amounts of payments that occur only once or twice a year, such as a yearly insurance premium, are known. Divide the total cost by 12 and add one month's payment for each expense into your monthly budget. The money should be set aside each month so it is available when you need it. This money should not be considered part of your monthly savings.
3. Determine **flexible expenses.** These are payments for food, clothing, heat, phone, and so on that vary greatly from month to month. To help you estimate these expenses accu-

CASH AVAILABLE		
	Estimated	**Actual**
Cash balance at end of previous month	_____	_____
net pay*	_____	_____
borrowed	_____	_____
other income	_____	_____
Total Cash Available	_____	_____

EXPENSES		
Fixed Expenses		
mortgage or rent	_____	_____
life insurance	_____	_____
homeowners insurance	_____	_____
car insurance	_____	_____
savings	_____	_____
taxes	_____	_____
loans or other depts	_____	_____
other expenses	_____	_____
Total Fixed Expenses	_____	_____
Flexible Expenses		
food	_____	_____
clothing	_____	_____
water	_____	_____
electricity	_____	_____
heat	_____	_____
telephone	_____	_____
car (gas, oil and filter changes, and so on)	_____	_____
medical/dental	_____	_____
contributions	_____	_____
entertainment	_____	_____
recreation	_____	_____
Total Flexible Expenses	_____	_____
Total Expenses	_____	_____

SUMMARY		
Total Cash Available	_____	_____
Total Expenses	_____	_____
Cash balance, end of period (Cash minus Expenses)	_____	_____

*Pay minus income tax and payments for social security

Item	ANNUAL AMOUNT
Payment for car loan	$ _____
Payment on installment debts (charge accounts, and so on)	$ _____
1.	$ _____
2.	$ _____
3.	$ _____
Payments on loans:	
1.	$ _____
2.	$ _____
3.	$ _____
YOUR DEBTS	
income after taxes	$ _____
expenditures on housing, etc.	$ _____
Subtract expenditures from income	$ _____
Divide difference by three	$ _____
YOUR SAFE DEBT LOAD	¢ _____

rately, keep a record for several months to see how much you actually spend. For some flexible expenses such as medical bills, you should use the previous year's bills to determine how much you spent and then divide the total by 12. Figure this amount into your monthly budget. Plan for savings.

4. Balance fixed and flexible expenses with available income. If there is not enough money, reexamine flexible expenses and cut back on one or more. If there is money left, then it can be applied to the family's goals.

A budget is not just for a family. It can be helpful to you as a student, too, in managing your money. Many of a student's expenses are similar to those a family faces. For example, having a car involves insurance and operating costs. In general, however, a student will be deciding how to divide income among flexible expenses.

DETERMINING A SAFE DEBT LOAD

If you do not use credit wisely, you may find yourself with more debts than you can pay. To avoid this, you should figure out the limit of debt that it is safe for you to carry. List all your debts and then total them. This tells you how much of your income is needed to pay for your present debts. To determine whether this is too much debt:

1. List your annual income after taxes.
2. Add up annual expenses for housing, food, clothing, and transportation.
3. Subtract these expenses.
4. Divide the difference by three. This is to include expenses not specifically listed.

By comparing this last number with the income needed to pay actual debts, you can determine the amount of income you have left after paying debts. You should then ask yourself: would it be financially wise to take on another debt?

Practicing Your Skills

Use the table to answer the following questions.

1. a. What is the family's safe debt load? b. Is this family's safe debt load less or more than the yearly income needed to pay its debts?
2. a. What is the debt load? b. How much less is the safe debt load than the payments?
3. Do you think this family should add to its existing debt load? Why or why not?

MONTHLY EXPENSES	
Payments on car	$ 225
Monthly payment on store revolving charge account	$ 46
Monthly payment on credit cards	$ 52
Monthly payment on loan for last year's vacation	$ 41
Monthly total	$ 364
Total for Year $364 x 12 ½	$4,368

ANNUAL EXPENSES	
Housing	$ 5,000
Food	$ 3,750
Clothing	$ 1,250
Transportation	$ 500
Total	$10,500
FAMILY'S TOTAL AFTER TAX INCOME:	$21,000

Table 4-1: DIFFERENT METHODS FOR COMPUTING FINANCE CHARGES

Type of Method	How Finance Charge Is Computed	Example: Account has opening balance of $300. A payment of $150 is made halfway through the month. Annual percentge rate is 18%; monthly interest rate is 1.5%.
Previous balance	Computed on the month's opening balance, even if the bill has been paid in full by the time the finance charge is figured. There is no benefit in paying off a debt early with this method.	Amount on which interest is due: $300, despite payment Calculation: $300 x .015 = $4.50 Finance Charge: $4.50 Balance Due: $154.50
Adjusted balance	Payments made during the month are deducted from the opening balance. Charge is then computed on the balance due the last day of the month. With this method you are best off paying your bill as soon as possible.	Amount on which interest is due: $150, balance on last day of billing period Calculation: $150 x .015 = $2.25 Finance Charge: $2.25 Balance Due: $152.25
Average daily balance	Charge is applied to the sum of the actual amounts owed each day during the billing period, divided by the number of days in that period. Payments and credits—return of goods—are subtracted on the exact date of payment. With this method you are best off paying your bill as soon as possible.	Amount on which interest is due: $225 Calculation: 15 days x $300 = $4,500 15 days x $150 = $2,250 30 days total = $6,750 $6,750 ÷ 30 = $225 $225 x .015 = $3.38 Finance Charge: $3.38 Balance Due: $153.38
Past due balance	No finance charge is applied so long as full payment is received within a certain period, usually within 25 days after the date of the last billing statement. If full payment is not received, then a finance charge for the unpaid amount is added on to the next month's bill.	Amount on which interest is due: $0 Calculation: $150 x .00 = 0 Finance Charge: $0 Balance Due: $150 Finance Charge of $2.25 (.015 x $150) will be added to next month's bill.

method applies the interest rate to an account's balance at a different point during each month. The different methods can result in widely varying finance charges. Table 4-1 describes these four methods and shows the difference in finance charges that can result. Creditors must inform their customers in writing of which method they use for computing finance charges. This method, along with the finance charge and APR, must appear on each monthly statement.

REVIEWING ECONOMIC PRINCIPLES

1. Define the following financial terms: **a.** finance charge, **b.** budget, **c.** fixed expenses, **d.** flexible expenses.
2. How will knowing annual percentage rates help you in deciding to take out a loan?
3. **a.** Using an opening balance of $450 and a payment of $225 after 10 days, compute the interest due under each of the four methods shown on the table Different Methods for Computing Finance Charges. **b.** Which is the best method for consumers?
4. According to the billing statement on p. 87, what is the: **a.** finance charge, if any? **b.** APR? **c.** method used by the store to compute finance charges?
5. **Critical Thinking: Expressing Opinions.** "Our way of life would change drastically without the use of credit cards." Do you agree or disagree with the statement? Why or why not?

5 | APPLYING FOR CREDIT

Ask yourself as you read:
- What should consumers know before they apply for credit?
- How are secured loans different from unsecured loans?

When you apply for credit, you will usually be asked to fill out a credit application. Once you have filled out the application, the store, bank, or other lending agency will hire a **credit bureau,** a private business, to do a **credit check.** This investigation will reveal your income, any current debts, details about your personal life, and how well you have repaid debts in the past.

THE CREDIT RATING

The information supplied by the credit bureau provides the creditor with a **credit rating** for you. This is a rating of the risk—good, average, or poor—involved in lending money to a specific person or business. If a person has a history of poor credit use—always late in paying debts— he or she will receive a poor credit rating. As a result, the creditor reviewing the credit check will be less willing to lend that person money.

Though past history of credit use is important in deciding credit-worthiness, the creditor also looks at three other factors that a credit check reveals. These are: **1.** capacity to pay, **2.** character, and **3.** collateral (kuh-LAT-uhr-uhl).

Capacity to pay is related to income and any current debts. If you have been working for several years at the same job, your capacity to repay a loan or credit will be rated more highly. If your employment has been spotty, your capacity to pay will be considered questionable. The amount of debt that you are already carrying is also a factor. The more debts a person has the greater the chance that he or she may have difficulty keeping up payments on them all.

Character refers to a person's reputation as a reliable and trust-worthy person—whether or not he or she has had any problems with the law, educational background, and any other factors that might indi-

The reasons a loan application may be turned down are: insufficient income, credit history, inability to prove employment, existing large debt, and insufficient time of residence in the community.

LIBERTY
THE BANK OF MID-AMERICA

LOAN APPLICATION

APPLICANT

| APPLICANT'S NAME (FIRST, MIDDLE, LAST) | | | | | SOCIAL SECURITY NUMBER |

ADDRESS (NUMBER & STREET) — CITY — STATE — ZIP — HOW LONG?

PREVIOUS ADDRESS (NUMBER & STREET) — CITY — STATE — ZIP — HOW LONG? — NO. YRS. IN CITY

HOME PHONE — BUSINESS PHONE — DATE OF BIRTH — NO. OF DEPENDENTS — DO NOT CHECK MARITAL STATUS BELOW UNLESS YOU ARE APPLYING FOR SECURED CREDIT ☐ MARRIED ☐ UNMARRIED ☐ SEPARATED

NAMES OF TWO NEAREST RELATIVES NOT LIVING WITH YOU — ADDRESS — WHAT RELATION?
(1.)
(2.) — ADDRESS — WHAT RELATION?

EMPLOYER (NAME AND ADDRESS) — HOW LONG? — POSITION — MONTHLY SALARY

PREVIOUS EMPLOYER (NAME AND ADDRESS) — HOW LONG? — POSITION — MONTHLY SALARY

ALIMONY, CHILD SUPPORT OR SEPARATE MAINTENANCE INCOME NEED NOT BE REVEALED IF YOU DO NOT WISH TO HAVE IT CONSIDERED AS THE BASIS FOR REPAYING THIS OBLIGATION.

OTHER INCOME $ — SOURCE — TOTAL MONTHLY INCOME $

JOINT APPLICANT OR OTHER PARTY

IF YOU ARE APPLYING FOR JOINT CREDIT WITH ANOTHER PERSON OR IF YOU ARE APPLYING FOR INDIVIDUAL CREDIT BUT ARE RELYING ON INCOME FROM ALIMONY, CHILD SUPPORT, OR SEPARATE MAINTENANCE, OR ON THE INCOME OR ASSETS OF ANOTHER PERSON AS THE BASIS FOR REPAYMENT OF THE CREDIT REQUESTED, COMPLETE THIS SECTION.

NAME OF JOINT APPLICANT OR OTHER PARTY — DATE OF BIRTH — ADDRESS

EMPLOYER (NAME AND ADDRESS) — HOW LONG? — POSITION — MONTHLY SALARY $

ASSETS AND CREDIT INFORMATION

IF THE JOINT APPLICANT OR OTHER PARTY SECTION ABOVE HAS BEEN COMPLETED, THIS SECTION SHOULD BE COMPLETED GIVING INFORMATION ABOUT BOTH THE APPLICANT AND THE JOINT APPLICANT OR OTHER PERSON. PLEASE MARK INFORMATION ABOUT THE APPLICANT ONLY WITH AN "A". IF THE JOINT APPLICANT OR OTHER PARTY SECTION WAS NOT COMPLETED, LIST ONLY INFORMATION DEALING WITH THE APPLICANT IN THIS SECTION.

CAR (MAKE & MODEL) — ESTIMATED VALUE — LIFE INSURANCE COMPANY — FACE VALUE OF POLICY — CASH VALUE

CAR (MAKE & MODEL) — ESTIMATED VALUE — STOCKS & BONDS (DESCRIBE) — VALUE

AUTO INSURANCE — AGENT — POLICY NUMBER — REAL ESTATE MARKET VALUE

NAME OF LANDLORD OR MORTGAGE COMPANY — ☐ OWN ☐ RENT — MONTHLY PAYMENT — MORTGAGE BALANCE (IF APPLICABLE)

NAME OF YOUR BANK — BANK SERVICES PRESENTLY USED — ☐ CHECKING ACCOUNT ☐ SAVINGS ACCOUNT ☐ LOAN ☐ SAFE DEPOSIT BOX — ☐ BANK CREDIT CARD ☐ CERTIFICATE OF DEPOSIT

DEBTS

TO WHOM OWED	BALANCE OWED	MONTHLY PAYMENT	TO WHOM OWED	BALANCE OWED	MONTHLY PAYMENT
VISA ACCT. NO.					
MASTERCHARGE ACCT. NO.					

ARE THERE ANY UNSATISFIED JUDGMENTS AGAINST YOU? ☐ YES ☐ NO — HAVE YOU BEEN DECLARED BANKRUPT WITHIN THE LAST 14 YEARS? ☐ YES ☐ NO — TOTAL MONTHLY PAYMENTS $

I/WE WISH TO BORROW $ _____ FOR _____ MONTHS, FOR THE PURPOSE OF

I/WE OFFER THE FOLLOWING AS SECURITY

EVERYTHING THAT I/WE HAVE STATED IN THIS APPLICATION IS CORRECT TO THE BEST OF MY/OUR KNOWLEDGE. I/WE UNDERSTAND THAT YOU WILL RETAIN THIS APPLICATION WHETHER OR NOT IT IS APPROVED. YOU ARE AUTHORIZED TO CHECK MY/OUR CREDIT AND EMPLOYMENT HISTORY AND TO ANSWER QUESTIONS ABOUT YOUR CREDIT EXPERIENCE WITH ME/US.

SIGNATURE — DATE — SIGNATURE (IF APPLICABLE) — DATE

11890

Case Study

CREDIT CARDS—THE GREAT PLASTIC WAR

"How much do you know about your BankAmericard? Do you know you get $150,000 automatic travel accident insurance? Do you know your BankAmericard is accepted at *5 million places* worldwide? Do you know you earn Bonus points for free travel and gifts when you use your BankAmericard?" So reads one bank's advertisement in the "Great Plastic War," the battle to broaden consumer credit-card use.

The typical American's wallet already holds seven credit cards. But companies such as American Express, Citicorp, Bank of America, and Sears are going "head-to-head" in an attempt to get even more customers to use their cards. Citicorp alone spends from $150 million to $200 million a year to promote its cards. The reason for this plastic war is that the credit-card business is extremely profitable.

Credit cards are a bright spot in the banking industry. Banks charge annual interest rates of 13 percent to 22 percent for unpaid balances on their cards. In addition, they charge an annual fee that averages $18 dollars per card. They also charge merchants a percentage of every credit-card transaction. American Express charges businesses 3 percent to 5 percent of every bill their customers charge to American Express. In addition, there is an annual fee that cardholders must pay. American Express cardholders pay $35 a year for its basic membership. It is estimated that the company nets $250–$300 million a year on its credit-card business, a sizable share of its total profits. No wonder there is such intense competition to win over consumers.

A major tactic used by competing companies is the promotion of "prestige" cards. American Express initiated the trend in the 1960s when it in-troduced its gold card, for which it charges $65 a year. In addition, in an attempt to lure the buying elite it now offers a platinum card. This super-prestige card costs $250 a year and features extras such as travel insurance, travel services, and the use of private clubs.

Credit card companies are interested not only in the "big spenders." A prime target is the "baby-boom" generation. Americans in their thirties and forties are the target of much of the advertising for new credit-card customers. Some banks are after an even younger market and are issuing cards to college students.

There is growing concern over the high interest rates charged credit-card users. With interest rates generally declining to less than 10 percent by the late 1980s from the inflationary rates of the early 1980s, the double-digit rates still charged on consumer credit have been criticized. Congress has expressed interest in dealing with this issue, but mounting competition between banks may be the force that prompts them to cut rates on their own. The "Great Plastic War" may well continue as long as Americans feel the need for easy access to credit.

1. What are the advantages and disadvantages of using credit cards?
2. Why do so many Americans use so many credit cards?
3. Despite intense competition, many credit-card companies do not lower interest charges. Why is this true?

cate something questionable. Character is the most difficult to determine in reviewing a person's creditworthiness. The judgment is based on how the creditor interprets what certain facts may mean.

Finally, **collateral** is something of value that a borrower can use as a promise to repay the loan. Do you have investments? Do you own a home? a car? The size of your capital, or personal wealth, is important because it indicates your past ability to save and accumulate. It also indicates your present ability to pay off a loan, even if you lose your job. Why? Because, if necessary, you could sell some of your belongings in order to make the payments.

SECURING A LOAN

Usually when a bank, S&L, or other financial institution makes a loan, it will ask for collateral from the borrower. The borrower then signs a legal agreement allowing the lender to claim the collateral if the loan is not repaid. A loan that is backed up with collateral in this way is called a **secured loan.** The collateral may be the item purchased with the loan money, such as a house or car. Or it may be something of value the borrower already owns. For example, a borrower might offer his or her car as collateral to obtain cash for home improvements.

Usually a young person will have little to offer as collateral. When dealing with a trusted customer, financial institutions will sometimes lend money on the person's reputation alone. This is called an **unsecured loan.** It is not guaranteed by anything other than a promise to repay it. Most young people have not had enough experience with borrowing and repaying money to have established this type of trust either. A bank will sometimes lend money to such a person if he or she has a cosigner. A **cosigner** is a person who signs a loan contract along with the borrower and promises to repay the loan if the borrower does not.

REVIEWING ECONOMIC PRINCIPLES

1. Write a definition for each of the following loan terms: **a.** credit bureau, **b.** credit check, **c.** credit rating, **d.** collateral, **e.** secured loan, **f.** unsecured loan.
2. **a.** How does a creditor obtain a credit rating on a possible borrower? **b.** Besides past history of credit use, what other factors are important in determining creditworthiness? **c.** Why might you as a student need a cosigner for a loan?
3. Look at the loan application on p. 92. **a.** Why might you need to list someone else's income or assets? **b.** Why would a creditor want to know what your rent is if you are a renter?
4. **Critical Thinking: Inferring Information.** What credit factors do you think creditors look for in loan cosigners?

Most financial institutions require collateral from anyone who borrows money. What are some forms of collateral?

6 | GOVERNMENT REGULATION OF CREDIT

Ask yourself as you read:

- What is usury?
- What are the major consumer credit laws?

Both the federal and state governments regulate the credit industry. Most states, for example, have set a maximum on the interest rates that can be charged for certain types of credit. The federal government has also passed laws designed to increase the flow of credit information to consumers and to protect consumers from unfair credit practices.

The Truth in Lending Act of 1968 was the first series of major federal laws that greatly expanded the government's role in protecting users of consumer credit. Table 4-2 summarizes five of these laws.

STATE USURY LAWS

A law restricting the amount of interest that can be charged for credit is called a **usury** (YOO-zhurh-ee) **law.** Often states set up different maximum rates for different types of consumer credit. Rates on charge accounts and credit cards, for example, are often around 18 percent a year, or 1½ percent per month. Consumer finance agencies, on the other hand, are often allowed to charge considerably more because their loans involve higher risks.

The ceilings for usury laws have become a controversial question in recent years. In the past, interest ceilings in many states were as low as 6 or 10 percent. When interest rates in general began to rise in the early 1970s, many lenders complained that they could not keep within such ceilings and still make a profit. In states that were slow to raise interest ceilings, some lenders cut back on the amount of credit they offered. Others stopped lending money completely. Many consumers, particularly those who were poor credit risks, found it hard to obtain credit. People opposed to raising interest ceilings claimed people with lower incomes would not be able to afford credit. Supporters of higher ceilings claimed that low rates made credit less available because it was less profitable for lenders. Low rates actually hurt those they were supposed to help. Today most usury laws make credit more available.

Table 4-2: MAJOR FEDERAL LAWS REGULATING CONSUMER CREDIT

Name of Law	Main Purpose	Major Provisions
Truth in Lending Act (1968)	Ensures that consumers are fully informed about the costs and conditions of borrowing.	• Creditors must keep borrowers informed in writing of a credit agreement's annual percentage rate, the way in which finance charges and any other fees are calculated, and the schedule under which the credit must be repaid. • Borrowers must be told 15 days in advance of any changes in the items listed above. • Consumers have a 3-day cooling-off period in which to cancel certain contracts. This applies to most contracts other than first mortgages that use a home as collateral. • Consumers are liable for only the first $50 in unauthorized purchases made on a credit card before it is reported lost or stolen. They are not liable for any purchases made after the loss is reported.
Fair Credit Reporting Act (1970)	Protects the privacy and accuracy of information in a credit check.	• If refused credit because of an unfavorable credit report, a consumer can request from the lender the name and address of the credit bureau issuing the report. • The credit bureau, if requested, must provide at least a summary of a consumer's credit file and help in interpreting the information. • If the consumer claims an important part of the file is in error, the bureau must investigate and either correct the record or explain why it thinks the information is correct. • A consumer can have a statement of disagreement placed in his or her file about the item. • Old and outdated information must be removed from a consumer's file after a certain period of time. • Credit records can be shown only to those with a true business need.
Equal Credit Opportunity Act (1974)	Prohibits discrimination in giving credit on the basis of sex, race, color, religion, national origin, marital status, age, or receipt of public assistance.	• The same guidelines for creditworthiness must be applied to all borrowers. • Lenders cannot extend credit to an individual on terms different from those given another individual in a similar economic situation. • Questions about age, sex, and marital status can be asked only if those questions relate directly to a person's ability to repay a loan. • Loan applicants must receive notice of a decision within 30 days. If the loan is denied, the lender must give the reasons or inform the applicant of the right to request the information.

Table 4-2: MAJOR FEDERAL LAWS REGULATING CONSUMER CREDIT *(continued)*

Name of Law	Main Purpose	Major Provisions
Fair Credit Billing Act (1974)	Sets up a procedure for the quick correction of mistakes that appear on consumer credit accounts.	• Consumers may challenge a billing statement for such errors as charges for unauthorized purchases or for items that were never delivered, failure to credit a payment, and so on. • Consumers have 60 days to notify a creditor of a disputed item. The creditor must investigate and within two billing periods (but not more than 90 days) either correct the mistake or explain why the charge is not an error. • While the mistake is checked, the consumer can withhold payment of the disputed sum but must pay for other items on the account. • Under certain circumstances, a consumer can withhold payment for merchandise that has been purchased and found defective. • Creditors must supply consumers with a statement of their rights under the act when an account is first opened and at least twice every year.
Fair Debt Collection Practices Act (1977)	Prevents abuse by professional debt collectors. Act applies to anyone employed to collect debts owed to others. It does not apply to banks or other businesses that collect their own accounts.	• Collectors can contact a person other than the debtor only to discover the debtor's location. • The debtor cannot be contacted at an inconvenient time or place—in the middle of the night or at a place of employment if the employer objects. If the debtor has an attorney, all contact must be made through that person. • All harassing behavior is prohibited. This includes the use or threat of violence, the use of annoying or repetitive phone calls, making the debt publicly known, and so on.

REVIEWING ECONOMIC PRINCIPLES

1. What is a usury law?
2. Choose the federal law regulating credit that applies to each of these situations: **a.** Susan Hayashida has been denied a credit card in her name and believes that it is because she is married. **b.** John Levy received a department store charge bill that shows a purchase he did not make. **c.** Tony Ryan had his credit card stolen. **d.** Ken Moore was denied a car loan and wants to find out why. **e.** Ann Neri has been hired by a debt collection agency.
3. **Critical Thinking: Explaining both sides of an issue.** Give the arguments for and against high ceilings in usury laws.

SUMMARY OF
IMPORTANT PRINCIPLES

1
- Taking out a loan is the same as buying an item on credit. In both cases, there is a debt, extension of credit, and payment of interest.
- The longer the repayment period for a loan is, the smaller the monthly payments. The longer it takes to repay an installment loan, the greater is the total interest that must be paid.
- People use credit because they do not want to wait to enjoy the use of an item. People also use credit to match payments to the use per time period of the item being purchased.
- The benefit of credit is being able to buy and enjoy the good or service now rather than later. The cost is whatever the borrower must pay in interest or lost opportunities to buy other items.

2
- Commercial banks often charge less on loans for customers with a checking or savings account. Savings and loan associations and savings banks make most of their loans for home mortgages. Credit unions offer members loans at low interest rates. Finance companies make some loans directly to consumers, but mostly they buy contracts for installment debts from stores. Consumer finance companies offer loans at high rates to consumers who have difficulty getting loans.

3
- A regular charge account has a credit limit, and the entire bill must be paid each month. A revolving charge has a credit limit and a certain portion of the bill must be paid each month. An installment charge account divides repayment into equal parts over a period of time.

4
- Credit card companies charge a service fee to stores that allow purchases with credit cards. This cost is included in the prices stores charge customers for their products. Credit card users are also charged interest on the amount of their purchases, and some credit card users must pay a yearly membership fee.
- Knowing the annual percentage rate allows a consumer to compare costs regardless of downpayment or length of the credit agreement.
- Budgeting is a way of managing income. By comparing amount of income needed to pay current debts with his or her expenses, a consumer can decide whether it is safe to take on more debt.

5
- After an applicant has filled out a credit form, the creditor hires a credit bureau to do a credit check, which provides a credit rating. The creditor then decides whether to extend credit to the applicant.

6
- Most states have usury laws that place a maximum on interest rates. The Truth in Lending Act ensures that consumers are informed about the costs and conditions of borrowing. Fair Credit Reporting Act protects the privacy and accuracy of information in a credit check. The Equal Credit Opportunity Act prohibits discrimination in giving credit. Fair Credit Billing Act sets up a procedure for the correction of mistakes on credit accounts. Fair Debt Collection Practices Act prevents abuse by debt collectors.

Putting Economics to Work

CONSUMER DECISION MAKING: CHECKING ANNUAL PERCENTAGE RATES

Helene Morgan has been working for several years and has had a bank credit card from the same bank for much of that time. As costs rose generally in the 1980s, many banks began charging higher annual percentage rates in return for the use of their credit cards. One day, Helene received a notice that her bank was raising its APR. There would also be an additional fee of $18 a year to use the card. Before this, the bank had never charged a fee for using its credit card. Needless to say, Helene was not happy about this increase in the cost of using her card.

Helene decided to shop around for a new credit card. She picked up an advertisement and application form from another bank. As she read through it, she found that nowhere did the application state the interest rate. It did not state whether there was a membership fee or what the method of computing interest on past due amounts was.

Helene then decided to check the applications for several other bank cards and found that the situation was the same in all the other applications there as well. There was no information on rates, fees, or methods of figuring interest.

1. What can Helene do to find out about interest rates, fees, and method of computing interest?
2. The maximum rate of interest that can be charged is set by state law. Since most businesses would charge the maximum, would Helene gather enough worthwhile information by finding out the maximum rate? Why or why not?

Readings in Economics

OFFERING CREDIT THROUGH THE MAIL

Skill: Drawing Conclusions

 Many Americans are using more and more credit because banks and credit-card companies are eagerly persuading them to do so. In this reading, Louis Rukeyser, writer and television-show host, describes how some banks tried to "give" him some money.

Even throughout a period in which we were told continually how "tight" [unavailable] money was supposed to be, the pressures . . . to go further into debt have been all about us. I have before me as I write two recent examples from my own unsolicited mail:

(1) A major New York City bank has sent me what looks like (but is not) a check for $15,000; this sum can truly be mine, the bank's computer informs me, if I will merely complete a short form and return it in a postage-paid envelope. These swell guys want to give me this money, it seems (no mention of anything so vulgar as interest rates appearing in the friendly letter—though the figure, it transpires, would be 19.75 percent), simply because I'm exactly their sort of fellow. "We believe," the word-processed billet-doux [love letter] continues, "an appropriate 'get acquainted' step is to provide you with an opportunity to borrow funds you may need right now." Can you imagine anything so thoughtful? . . . I can be their buddy even if I don't take everything they're offering: "Should you require less money, simply cross out the $15,000 and write in the amount you wish—minimum $3,500." (Anything less, I presume, is regarded as such petty cash as to be unworthy of us both.)

(2) Two more unsolicited checks arrive almost simultaneously, this time from some pals I didn't know I had at a big bank in Chicago. One of these checks has already been filled out for $500 and requires only my greedy signature to be negotiable [valid]; the other is for me to write myself, for what could be a much greater amount. And why am I so fortunate, so beloved by the financiers along the shores of Lake Michigan? Why, because

my First Card credit is being raised substantially, in tribute to the bank's "determination," after a "careful review" of my credit history, that I have managed my account "in a superior manner." Gosh, isn't that terrific? And these fellows don't mention interest rates even in the finest of print—though, to be sure, there is something . . . informing me that "the checks are for use in obtaining credit under the terms previously disclosed." . . . Could it be that these grand new friends were simply trying to get me in over my head—so that I would have to . . . start foundering in debt like I was supposed to be? Perish the ungenerous thought.

1. What strategies are the banks using to persuade customers to borrow money?
2. What can you infer about a bank's willingness to lend money and attract customers when interest rates are high?

Louis Rukeyser, *What's Ahead for the Economy?* New York: Simon and Schuster. Copyright © 1983 by Louis Rukeyser. Reprinted by permission of Simon and Schuster, Inc.

IT USED TO BE SIMPLE

Skill: Making Comparisons

 In 1980 Congress passed the Depository Institutions Deregulation and Monetary Control Act. This act allowed banking institutions much more freedom in determining the interest rates they could charge and the kinds of loans they could give. This article indicates some of the consequences of deregulation for consumers.

The rules of the banking game have been rewritten. Until a few years ago, financial institutions were heavily regulated. Laws prescribed how much interest they could pay on deposits, how much interest they could charge on loans, what kind of services they could offer and where they could offer them.

This regimented system made life simple for consumers. . . .

But the old order that had governed banking since the 1930s has now crumbled. . . .

Banking institutions of various types are competing both with each other and with companies not formerly in banking. Some of the services you could once buy only at commercial banks are now available through savings-and-loan associations, savings banks, and credit unions. . . .

Banks have shifted some of their financial risk to consumers by issuing adjustable-rate loans, which rise or fall with prevailing interest rates. Before deregulation, fixed-rate mortgages and installment loans were the norm. Today, roughly half of all newly issued home-mortgage loans carry adjustable rates.

Fixed-rate loans, when they're available, carry a stiffer price tag than they used to. Though many factors influence interest rates, deregulation has surely played its part in raising rate levels. Fixed-rate mortgage loans with 8 or 9 percent rates have become dinosaurs—pet dinosaurs, to be sure.

Borrowers may also experience higher loan costs as some financial institutions gradually switch them from installment loans to revolving charge accounts that offer credit limits as high as $25,000.

Historically, revolving charge accounts (at 15, 18, or 21 percent interest) were high-cost loans primarily used for small purchases. Credit lines on them were low, usually not exceeding $500. These loans typically carried higher rates than installment loans because of the greater expense of processing small balances. For big purchases, most consumers used installment loans, which generally carried lower rates. By encouraging consumers to use revolving charge accounts for large purchases, financial institutions are in effect switching consumers to higher-priced loans.

1. Compare installment loans and revolving charge accounts. Include categories such as interest rates, loan limits, purpose of loan, etc.
2. Using your answer from question 1, what can you conclude regarding the benefits the banks received by shifting borrowers from installment loans to revolving charge accounts?

"You and the Banks," *Consumer Reports*, September 1985, pp. 508–516.

THE SUPER CARD
Skill: Predicting Outcomes

 **SECTION 3**

One of the most recent developments in the burgeoning credit-card industry is the "super card." The following article describes this new kind of credit card and indicates some of the remarkable possibilities it offers to users and the far-reaching changes it will bring to consumer banking.

The historic evolution of plastic money began in the 1970s, when the magnetic stripe appeared on the back of credit cards. In 1985, we were introduced to the "smart card," a credit card with a built-in computer chip that allowed the card to make choices, follow alternative decision paths and be read on a television screen or personal computer.

Now we are told that the next generation credit card is about to revolutionize the way we use plastic money. It's called the "super card." Visa . . . will offer a credit card that combines a calculator-like keyboard and display unit with a microcomputer chip.

Super card holders could literally carry their banks around in their wallets or purses, initiating off-line transactions, authorizing transactions in their checking, savings, credit-card accounts, and updating their balances—all within the card and without the need for terminal equipment at merchant locations.

Besides replacing automatic teller machines, the super card will allow the card holder to automatically keep track of purchases, keep tax records, serve as a clock and keep notes and reminders.

Charles Russell, president of Visa, said, "We believe the super card represents the most significant development in consumer banking since the advent of the automated teller machine."

1. What are some advantages of the "super card"?
2. Predict what problems might arise with widespread use of this new card.

From "A 'Super' Credit Card that Tries to Do It All" by Jim Jorgensen, in *San Francisco Chronicle* May 20, 1986. Reprinted by permission of the author.

Readings in Economics

READ THE FINE PRINT

Skill: Interpreting Information

Many consumers have had to learn the hard way that failure to understand the terms of a contract can lead to pain and hardship. In the following reading, written by **Upton Sinclair** in 1906, this message is clear, and it is as relevant for today's consumer as it was for consumers 80 years ago.

. . . They had begun to question the old lady as to why one family had been unable to pay, trying to show by her figures that it ought to have been possible; and [she] had disputed their figures. "You say twelve dollars a month; but that does not include the interest."

Then they stared at her, "Interest!" they cried.

"Interest on the money you still owe," she answered.

"But we don't have to pay any interest!" they exclaimed, three or four at once. "We only have to pay twelve dollars each month."

And for this she laughed at them. " . . . They never sell the houses without interest. Get your deed, and see."

Then, with a horrible sinking of the heart, Teta Elzbieta unlocked her bureau and brought out the paper. . . . Now they sat round, scarcely breathing, while the old lady, who could read English, ran over it. "Yes," she said, finally, "here it is, of course: 'With interest thereon monthly, at the rate of seven per cent per annum*'."

And there followed a dead silence. "What do you mean?" asked Jurgis finally, almost in a whisper.

"That means," replied the other, "that you have to pay them eight dollars and forty cents next month, as well as the twelve dollars." . . .

In the morning . . . Ona and her stepmother were standing at the door of the office of the agent. Yes, he told them, when he came, it was quite true that they would have to pay interest. . . . The agent was as bland as ever. He was deeply pained, he said. He had not told them, simply because he had supposed they would understand that they had to pay interest upon their debt as a matter of course.

1. Consumers in the marketplace should heed this advice: "Buyer beware." What do you think this phrase means? How does it apply to this reading?
2. Can "ignorance of the law" be used as an excuse for not fulfilling a contract? What are the responsibilities of each party in signing a contract?

From *The Jungle* by Upton Sinclair, 1906.

THE RUSH FOR REFINANCING

Skill: Predicting Outcomes

When low interest rates for loans are available, many people refinance old higher-interest loans at the new low rates. This reading describes how low mortgage rates in 1986 made applying for credit a difficult process.

Mortgage loan officers are getting as difficult to see in some cities as doctors. In many places, borrowers just can't walk in off the street and talk to a loan officer. Some lenders are requiring appointments three to five weeks in advance. And if you're not already a customer, some lenders are advising people refinancing mortgages to go elsewhere. A few are even requiring "reservation fees" that can be applied against closing costs in order to weed out halfhearted borrowers.

Even those lenders that aren't having difficulty coping with the volume of mortgage applications say it's taking two to three weeks longer to close mortgage applications because appraisers, attorneys, title companies and credit bureaus are swamped.

The lowest mortgage rates in more than seven years have sent mortgage volume soaring just about everywhere. . . .

"It's refi-mania," says Felix Beck, chairman of Margaretten & Co., a New Jersey-based mortgage banker. Says James Wooten, president and chief operating officer of Lomas & Nettleton: "This is way beyond the experience that any of us have ever had. It's fun at first, but the practicality of service gets tough."

*per year

102

The Federal National Mortgage Association's latest forecast anticipates $290 billion in new mortgages being written in 1986, a 23% increase over last year. But the activity levels of the past few weeks are leading many to believe that the total will easily top $300 billion.

Lenders are having a hard time coping. Margaretten is limiting refinancing so that it can concentrate on mortgages to home buyers. Mr. Beck says, "What we're telling our branches is: Refinance those who currently have mortgages with us—if you can."

Says Mr. Wooten, "In some of our branches, borrowers have to make appointments three to five weeks in advance. At others we're at the stage that we have to say we're sorry but we can't help you."

1. What caused the increase in demand for mortgage loans?
2. Which consumers received preferred treatment in applying for loans?

Robert Guenther, "Mortgage Hunting? Be Ready for Delays and Waiting Lists." *The Wall Street Journal*, April 2, 1986. Reprinted by permission of *The Wall Street Journal*, © Dow Jones & Company, Inc., 1986. All Rights Reserved.

IS THERE A CURE FOR BAD CREDIT?

Skill: Making Inferences

In a credit society, those who are refused credit sometimes become an easy target for the numerous "credit clinics" that have sprung up around the nation. Their aim is to assist consumers who have a bad credit rating obtain credit or credit cards, but some of their methods worry law-enforcement agencies. The following reading describes how such clinics operate.

"Is bad credit ruining your life? We erase black marks. . . ."

"Now get major credit cards easy!"

"Bankruptcy no problem!"

Such are the claims of hundreds of "credit clinics" that have sprung up around the country. The companies say they can clean up an individual's credit history and help the desperate obtain credit cards.

But while some are legitimate, others have drawn fire from law-enforcement agencies for allegedly false or misleading advertising. . . .

Law-enforcement officials say their biggest concern is that many of the companies' advertisements either imply or guarantee that all negative information can be wiped off a credit report. "That just isn't true as an unqualified promise," says . . . a deputy attorney general in San Diego.

The credit-repair companies do have ways to remove some negative information, however. A tactic used by some of them is inundating credit agencies with requests that they verify information in consumers' files. A customer's creditors often don't respond in time, and the information is erased. . . .

So some clinics now appeal directly to a customer's creditors to remove negative entries in exchange for payment of outstanding debts. . . .

This irks credit agencies. "It's unethical for creditors to remove accurate information on the reports," says . . . [a] spokesman for Associated Credit Bureaus in Houston. . . . "The credit clinics are a threat to the entire credit-reporting system," he adds.

Many credit clinics also claim to help people get credit cards. According to a report by the Better Business Bureau in Los Angeles, however, most of their advertisements don't indicate that an individual often must deposit money in an out-of-state savings and loan to get a "secured" card. The deposit . . . becomes the . . . credit line.

Most financial institutions don't offer secured credit cards, because the rate of delinquent payments is usually higher than for unsecured cards. Even those issuing secured cards often require customers to meet minimum credit standards.

1. According to the article, what methods are used by "credit-repair" companies to clean up an individual's credit history?
2. Imagine that you are the manager of a "credit clinic." What advice would you offer your clients to help them obtain credit and avoid future debt problems?

Kathleen A. Hughes, "Credit Clinics May Make It Sound Too Easy to Clean Up a Bad Record." *Wall Street Journal*, June 16, 1986. Reprinted by permission of *The Wall Street Journal*, © Dow Jones & Company, Inc., 1986. All Rights Reserved.

4 | CHAPTER REVIEW

PRACTICING YOUR READING SKILLS: CLASSIFYING

Classifying means organizing data into a system by topic or category. The table "Different Methods for Computing Finance Charges" in this chapter is one way to organize data. It is often easier to make comparisons and contrasts or to find information when the data are in table form. If, for example, you did all of the exercises in the Reviewing Economic Principles for Section 2, you made a table of the different sources of loans. In so doing, you classified information.

Authors also use classifying when they write in text form. They may enumerate (ih-NOO-muh-rayt), or list items, and use such clue words as *first*, *second*, and *finally* to signal that the ideas that follow are connected. Other signal phrases are *the reasons for*, *the factors that*, *the following characteristics*, and *for example*. Such words and phrases can signal that details are about to be given that explain or expand on the main idea. If you are having trouble locating the main idea, look for details and see if there are any connections among them.

Activity: The headings in a textbook can also help you to see connections between or among ideas. In this text, the major ideas are all in capital letters. Supporting ideas are in capital and small letters, or they are in bold type. In many books supporting ideas are shown in different kinds of type or in another color. Reread the chapter to answer the following questions.

1. **a.** On what page is a list given? **b.** What is the connection among the different items?

2. What are the categories used to organize the heading "Charge Accounts and Credit Cards" called?

3. **a.** What is the main idea of the heading Americans and Credit? **b.** What are the supporting details?

VOCABULARY REVIEW

Write the letter of the definition in Column B that correctly defines each term in Column A.

Column A	Column B
1. principal	a. restricts the amount of interest that can be charged for credit
2. usury law	b. requires only a promise to repay
3. collateral	c. amount of money borrowed in a loan
4. annual percentage charged	d. something of value that a borrower uses as a promise of loan repayment
5. unsecured loan	e. cost of credit expressed as a yearly percentage

PRACTICING YOUR ECONOMIC SKILLS

1. **Computing Finance Charges.** Suppose you borrow $150 for a year. The monthly interest rate is 2 ½ percent, but there are no other charges. a. What is the monthly finance charge? b. What is the APR?

2. **Using Tables.** The table below shows how a typical family of four spends its disposable income. Using this table, determine the family's safe debt load if its annual, after-tax income is $18,000.

Food	20%
Housing	30
Transportation	13
Clothing	8
Medical care	13
Recreation	7
Other	9
Total	100%

3. **Computing Finance Charges.** Suppose some-one borrows $2,400 for a period of six months at an 18 percent annual interest rate. Repayment is by month. What will the amount of each monthly payment be? What will be the total amount of interest?

4. **Computing Finance Charges.** Suppose a person borrows $2,000 for three months and repays the loan at an annual interest rate of 8 percent. What is the total amount that the borrower will have to pay?

DISCUSSING ECONOMIC QUESTIONS

1. Some people think Americans buy too many items on credit. Is borrowing necessary for most Americans today? Can people in an industrialized nation such as the United States live without ever borrowing money? Why or why not?

2. Some people do buy such consumer durables as cars with cash. What is the benefit of paying cash for such goods? What are the disadvantages?

3. Why do families of the same size and income level often save different percentages of their incomes? Do you think that people with smaller incomes sometimes save more of their incomes than people with larger incomes? Why or why not?

4. Why do many people prefer to use charge accounts and credit cards instead of paying cash for purchases and services? How does the use of credit increase the costs for merchants, borrowers, and consumers?

5. Every year, and especially in recent years, the per capita consumer debt increases in the United States. Why do you think this happens? What are some possible effects of this trend?

APPLYING CRITICAL THINKING SKILLS

1. **Gathering Information.** Sometimes, credit cards are lost or stolen. The owner must take steps to keep his or her card from being used by an unauthorized person. Research the Truth in Lending Act to find out what a credit cardholder must do.

2. **Compiling a Table.** Working with several other members of the class, call or visit several sources of loans, and check interest rates for car loans and personal loans. Make a table of the data.

3. **Holding a Class Discussion.** Create a loan application that is appropriate for high-school students and circulate it in class. Based on the application, discuss why it is or is not difficult to decide who should receive loans. Is it difficult to decide who should not receive loans?

4. **Researching a Topic.** Savings banks have had many difficulties within the past 15 years or so. From business magazines and newspapers, find out why many savings banks have had a difficult time surviving. Write a short report on the topic.

5. **Finding Out About Local Laws.** With a few other members of your class, visit a local tax office or bank. Interview the officers to find out what the state usury laws are. Summarize your findings.

READINGS

Brown, Betty J., and Clow, John E. *General Business*. Boston: Houghton Mifflin, 1982.

Clawson, Elmer. *Our Economy: How It Works*. Menlo Park, Calif.: Addison-Wesley, 1980.

"Credit Cards." *Changing Times*, July 1982, pp. 54–56.

Friedrich, Otto. "The American Way of Debt." *Time*, 31 May 1982, pp. 46–49.

CHAPTER 5

Food and clothing are necessities on which Americans spend a large part of their incomes. Learning good consumer principles for buying these items will help you get the most value from your spending.

BUYING THE NECESSITIES: FOOD AND CLOTHING

Because food and clothing take so much of Americans' incomes, it is important to know good consumer principles for buying these items. After showing how buying strategies can be applied to food shopping, the chapter describes various trade offs connected with buying food. You will then read about factors that should be compared in deciding clothing value. Learning Economic Skills explains the importance of labels and warranties and the use of grades and standards for product labeling.

CHAPTER OBJECTIVES After you study the sections of this chapter, you will be able to:

1
- state three buying principles for food shopping.
- compare the trade-offs involved in shopping in supermarkets, food stores, convenience stores, and food cooperatives.
- compare the costs and benefits of buying different kinds of brands.
- explain the trade-offs involved in using trading stamps, cents-off coupons, and convenience foods.

2
- list three factors involved in comparing clothing value.
- ★ describe how warranties and grades and standards in product labeling can protect consumers.

ECONOMICS VOCABULARY

warehouse food store
convenience store
generic brand
net weight
unit price
guarantee
full warranty
limited warranty
implied warranty
standard
grade

mobile (MOH-buhl): move-able, on the move

Most people would place food, shelter, and clothing at the top of a list of life's necessities. Together, these three items add up to more than half of every American's annual budget. Not surprisingly, the food, housing, and clothing industries are big business. They account for over $1,086 billion of the nation's consumer spending each year. In this mobile nation, many people would also consider transportation—public or private—a necessity. American consumers spend over $350 billion a year on transportation. This chapter will discuss good consumer practices for buying food and clothing. The next chapter will describe buying principles for housing and transportation.

Although these goods may be considered necessities, their purchase is still subject to the basic principles of scarcity and trade offs. Because every family and individual has a limited income, the purchase of any one item, including necessities, means that less of something else can be bought. To get maximum satisfaction from their limited budgets, consumers need to apply the buying principles from Chapter 3 to these purchases.

1 | SHOPPING FOR FOOD

Ask yourself as you read:
- What are the three buying principles for food shopping?
- What types of food stores are available for shoppers?
- What are convenience foods?

Americans consume more than 30 percent of the agricultural output of the world. They can choose from thousands of different food products and buy them at over 300,000 stores. Hundreds of brands offer numerous choices: sliced carrots, whole carrots, carrots with peas—canned or frozen. In all, American consumers spend over $500 billion a year on food. This represents 16 cents of every dollar consumers spend.

COMPARISON SHOPPING

Because the average American family spends so much for food, comparison shopping is important. But it is important only to a point. It does not pay a shopper to go far out of his or her way to shop at a store that has only a few needed items at low prices. Any savings would be outweighed by the additional costs of time and transportation. As you learned in Chapter 3, a consumer should do only as much comparison shopping as is worthwhile to that person.

As you also learned in Chapter 3, reading advertisements is a good, inexpensive way to comparison shop. Food store ads describe sales and often contain cents-off coupons. Generally, stores set aside particular days of the week for sales on certain items. One store might have a sale on meat every second Thursday of the month. Another store might set aside every first Wednesday for a sale on fruits and vegetables. By read-

Checklist

FOOD SHOPPING

ing store ads, you can quickly become familiar with each store's schedule of sales.

Comparison shopping involves making comparisons among brands and sizes as well as stores. You need to decide not only where to shop but what to shop for. Learning Economic Skills in this chapter describes what to look for in labels, grades, and standards. The Checklist for Food Shopping will also be a useful guide.

FOOD STORES

There are three major types of stores and each has its own characteristics. Just about anything in the way of meats, fresh vegetables, paper products, canned goods, and so on, can be bought in a supermarket. Prices are high, however, so it is important to be aware of supermarket sales.

The **warehouse food store** has only a limited number of brands and items. However, they are less expensive than if bought in supermarkets. In many of these discount stores, goods are sold by the case only. Some stores offer only regional-brand items, but some carry slightly damaged cases of national-brand products. Warehouse food stores are best for consumers who can buy in large quantities to take advantage of lower prices.

Convenience stores seem to be everywhere. They are usually open 16 to 24 hours a day and carry a limited selection of items. The price per unit of almost anything is higher than in a supermarket or discount store. This is because you are paying the cost of convenience. Wise shopping dictates that only limited, emergency shopping be done in such stores.

BRAND-NAME PRODUCTS

As you may recall from Chapter 3, brand names help consumers determine the quality goods they wish to purchase. Most of what you will find in food stores are national-brand items. They are usually the most expensive. Food stores may also carry regional brands. These are brands found only in certain areas of the country.

Supermarkets often carry their own private, or store, brands for soft drinks and certain canned and packaged goods. These are usually cheaper than national brand names. But often the makers of the brand-name products also produce the private brands, and the quality is similar. Some products are labeled only with a **generic** (juh-NER-ik) **brand.** This is a general name of a product, such as *Dishwasher Soap* or *Applesauce,* rather than a specific manufacturer's trade name. Generic-brand items are usually the least expensive. It can be worth your time to try private-brand and generic-brand items to see if their quality meets your needs.

TRADING STAMPS AND COUPONS

Some supermarkets give trading stamps, such as S&H Green Stamps, Gold Stamps, Blue Stamps, and Plaid Stamps. These stamps have a cash value of one-tenth of a cent a piece (10 stamps equal one cent). The consumer must paste the stamps in a special book and take or mail the books to a trading stamp center. There, the books are exchanged for goods or money. Trading stamps are not free. Someone has to pay for them, and that someone ultimately is the consumer who buys at stores that give stamps. The store has to purchase the stamps and in order to keep their profits as high as possible, stores raise the prices of goods. Suppose you refuse trading stamps or throw them away. Then you are paying extra food costs without receiving the value of the goods or money you could get by redeeming the stamps.

redeem (ri-DEEM)**:** to convert into something of value

Many manufacturers give cents-off coupons. To take advantage of them, a consumer has to buy the brand, size, and quantity on the coupon. The store then reduces the price paid by the amount printed on the coupon. The manufacturer, in turn, pays the store. If you make a habit of using coupons, you can reduce your food bill by as much as 5 percent over a one-year period. But the use of such coupons requires time—the time to collect and match them to items when shopping. Since time is a scarce resource, you have to decide if the money you save using coupons is worth the time you spend.

CONVENIENCE FOODS

In most food stores, you can buy either foods that require preparation, such as fresh meat and vegetables, or foods that require little or no preparation, such as complete frozen dinners. The latter are called convenience foods and usually require no work other than heating. Some nutritionists (noo-TRISH-uh-nists)—experts on food and health—believe that convenience foods are unhealthy. They believe they con-

Women who work at jobs outside the home often prepare quick convenience food for their meals. What trade-offs does this involve?

tain too many added chemicals, too much sugar, and too many preservatives. But there is also an economic issue involved.

The purchase of a convenience food involves a trade-off. Convenience foods are more expensive to buy than foods that must be prepared. Because of the higher price you are paying when you buy convenience foods, you are sacrificing the purchase of other things. However, you are gaining more time for leisure or making extra money, because convenience foods require less work. This is one of the situations in which the consumer must choose between having more free time or having more money.

preservative (pri-SER-vuh-tiv): chemical that prevents decay

REVIEWING ECONOMIC PRINCIPLES

1. **a.** How much time should a consumer spend comparison shopping among food stores? **b.** Why is it important to read food store ads? **c.** Besides comparison shopping among food stores themselves what else should consumers compare?
2. List the advantages and disadvantages of shopping in each of the following type of food store: **a.** supermarket, **b.** warehouse food store, **c.** convenience store.
3. Which of the above type of store would you shop in if you wanted: **a.** a large quantity of canned goods? **b.** a quart of milk in a hurry? **c.** groceries of various kinds for a week's meals?
4. **a.** What is the benefit of buying name-brand items? **b.** Why might it be worth trying private- or generic-brand items?
5. What is the cost involved in refusing trading stamps?
6. **Critical Thinking: Applying Principles.** What is the trade-off for you in using: **a.** cents-off coupons? **b.** convenience foods?

111

Being a wise consumer involves being able to understand the labels on food, clothing, and so on. It means knowing how products are graded and what standards are used to grade them. Understanding warranties is also important.

READING A LABEL

You will find labels on nearly every item you buy, from canned and frozen food to furniture. In general, you should examine a label for the following information: quantity or size, contents or ingredients, quality, use and care, any specific warnings, and guarantee or warranty.

QUANTITY

Whether you are buying detergent or coffee, you will want to know the quantity of the product you purchase. On any label or package, you will find stated the number of grams or ounces the package contains. This is called the net weight. **Net weight** is the actual weight of the food or other product without the weight of the packaging. Once you know the actual quantity, you can use this information to compare prices of different brands.

Unit pricing is also useful for comparing prices. The **unit price** is the price of a product in terms of a common unit of measure—the cost per ounce or gram, for example. This price is usually found directly below the item in stores. Otherwise, to find the unit price, divide the cost of the item by the net weight. In this way, you can compare the prices of different brands as well as different sizes of the same brand. Is the 12-ounce (340-gram) package of cereal a better buy than the 10 ounce (283-gram) size? Is the unit price the same?

QUALITY

A wise consumer considers the quality of an item before buying. For food, you can do this by checking the ingredients on the package or label. Ingredients must be listed in the descending order of the amounts of each in the product.

Whole Kernel Corn

INGREDIENTS: CORN, WATER, SUGAR, SALT
NUTRITION INFORMATION—PER ONE CUP SERVING
SERVINGS PER CONTAINER—APPROX. 2

CALORIES	150	CARBOHYDRATE	36g
PROTEIN	4g	FAT	1g

PERCENTAGE OF U.S. RECOMMENDED DAILY
ALLOWANCES (U.S. RDA) PER ONE CUP SERVING

PROTEIN	6	NIACIN	10
VITAMIN A	8	CALCIUM	0
VITAMIN C	25	IRON	4
THIAMINE (VIT. B_1)	6	PHOSPHORUS	10
RIBOFLAVIN (VIT. B_2)	8	MAGNESIUM	10

WT. OF CORN (283g/10 OZ.) BEFORE ADDITION OF
LIQUID NECESSARY FOR PROCESSING
Net Wt. 17 oz.   (1 lb. 1 oz.)   482g

Many food labels, for example, those for canned goods, show nutritional information as well as ingredients. This information lists the calories, protein, vitamins, and minerals in each serving. You can compare and contrast the nutritional value of different brands of the same product to be sure you are getting your money's worth. Checking cosmetic and drug labels is also a good practice.

Clothing labels describe the fabric—whether it is cotton, wool, or polyester or a blend of fibers. This information is a clue to the item's durability as well as to any need for special care.

SPECIAL INFORMATION AND WARNINGS

Often labels will give special instructions or warnings. For example, if you wish to buy a skirt labeled "Dry Clean Only," you will have to figure the

100% WOOL
DRY CLEAN OR HAND WASH
IN COOL WATER
LAY FLAT TO DRY
MADE IN
U.S.A.

cost of cleaning it into the cost of your purchase. Appliances often give safety instructions to prevent accidents, such as not using a hair dryer near water. Cosmetics and drugs also enclose in their packaging warnings or special advice about use.

GUARANTEES AND WARRANTIES

Many products carry a **guarantee** of satisfaction. A guarantee is the manufacturer's promise that the product is what it is represented to be. If it is found defective, the manufacturer will replace it.

Most appliances come with a written warranty. It is similar to a guarantee, but the manufacturer may repair rather than replace the item. There are full warranties and limited warranties. A **full warranty** provides for repairs or replacement of faulty merchandise within a reasonable period of time.

Most warranties are **limited.** For example, a warranty might require you to notify the manufacturer within 30 days of discovering a defect.

When you purchase an appliance, look for the warranty to see any limitations the manufacturer has set. Some manufacturers will provide a card for you to fill out and return. This becomes your proof of purchase. Should you fail to return the card, the manufacturer still must honor the warranty as long as you have other proof of purchase.

According to law, almost everything that is sold is protected by an **implied warranty** whether there is a written one or not. This means the product must do what it claims to do. Otherwise, the manufacturer must replace or repair the item or refund the purchase price. Exceptions are goods sold "as is" or second hand.

WARRANTY

Finetune, Inc., warrants this product against defects in manufacturing for a period of two (2) years from the date of purchase when installed and operated according to the enclosed instructions.

Finetune will repair or replace the product, at our option, without charge for labor or parts. This warranty covers the product whether in the possession of the original owner or a subsequent owner.

The product must be delivered to a Finetune Service Center with evidence of the date and place of retail purchase. You are responsible for the cost of insuring and mailing the product to the Finetune Service Center. Finetune will pay for the cost of returning the product to you, within the continental U.S.

This warranty does not cover accessories, damage to recordings, or damage to the product from misuse, accident, or alterations.

Implied warranties are limited to the warranty period of two (2) years. Some states do not allow limitations on the period of implied warranties. This warranty gives you specific legal rights, and you may have other rights which vary from state to state.

FINETUNE, INC.
Manufacturers of quality sound systems

ENERGY GUIDE

(Name of Corporation)

Refrigerator-Freezer   Model(s) AH503, AH504, AH507
Capacity: 23 Cubic Feet   Type of Defrost: Full Automatic

Estimates on the scale are based on a national average electric rate of 4.97¢ per kilowatt hour. Only models with 22.5 to 24.4 cubic feet are compared in the scale.

Estimated yearly energy cost

Model with lowest energy cost $68 ▼	$91 THIS ▼ MODEL	Model with highest energy cost $132 ▼

Your cost will vary depending on your local energy rate and how you use the product. This energy cost is based on U.S. Government standard tests.

How much will this model cost you to run yearly?

Ask your salesperson or local utility for the energy rate (cost per kilowatt hour) in your area.

IMPORTANT Removal of this label before consumer purchase is a violation of federal law (42 U.S.C. 6302).

		Yearly cost Estimated yearly $ cost shown below
Cost per kilowatt hour	2¢	$36
	4¢	$73
	6¢	$109
	8¢	$146
	10¢	$182

ENERGY EFFICIENT LABELS

The cost of energy skyrocketed in the late 1970s. Since that time, manufacturers of large appliances have usually been required to include an energy guide to help consumers meet energy prices. The guide shows a scale comparing the cost of running one appliance with the cost of running different models of the same appliance. In comparison shopping, compare and contrast this average cost with the average costs on energy guides of similar appliances.

Practicing Your Skills

1. According to the label on the can of corn: **a.** what is the net weight? **b.** what is the actual weight of the corn before processing? **c.** what is the recommended serving size?
2. The label is from a wool jacket. Wool is very durable. How might your decision to buy the jacket be affected by: **a.** the fabric type? **b.** the care instructions?
3. According to the manufacturer's warranty for the stereo, what are **a.** your responsibilities? **b.** the manufacturer's?
4. According to the energy guide how does the cost of running this model compare to the cost of running similar models?

STANDARDS AND GRADES

Many products, from eggs to meat, are graded according to standards set by the Department of Agriculture. A **standard** is a basis of comparison for determining the quality or value of an item. That level of quality is called the **grade**. For example, there are four grades of most fresh produce— fruits and vegetables. Produce standards are based on size, shape, color, and any bruises.

Grades are listed on packaging and on the signs and tags in the market. Read these carefully, and then decide which grade best suits your needs. For example, you might prefer to pack a U.S. Extra Fancy grade apple for your lunch, but you will buy only U.S. No. 1 apples for a pie. The table on this page explains the grades used for meat, poultry, eggs, dairy products and produce.

Practicing Your Skills

1. U.S. Grade AA eggs cost more than U.S. Grade A eggs. The difference for grading purposes is appearance. Which is a better buy for baking?
2. What grade(s) would you find on butter?

Department of Agriculture Food Grades

Product	Grades
Meat (beef, veal calf, lamb, mutton)	USDA Prime USDA Choice (cut most often sold in stores) USDA Good (lean)
Poultry (Chicken, turkey, duck, geese)	U.S. Grade A U.S. Grades B and C (rarely used on poultry labels)
Dairy products (butter, dry milk, cheese)	U.S. Grade AA (butter) U.S. Grade A (butter) U.S. Extra Grade (nonfat dry milk) Quality Approved (cottage cheese, process cheese, sour cream)
Eggs	U.S. Grade AA U.S. Grade A (grade most often found in stores) U.S. Grade B (not usually found in retail stores)
Canned and frozen fruits and vegetables	Grade A Grade B Grade C
Fresh fruits and vegetables	U.S. Fancy or Extra Fancy U.S. No.1 (most often found in stores) U.S. Nos. 2 and 3

2 | CLOTHING CHOICES

Ask yourself as you read:

- How do values influence one's clothing purchases?
- What questions should consumers ask themselves in order to shop for clothing wisely?

Figure 5-1 shows how Americans spent their money on clothing and other personal products in a recent year. Most people could buy a few very durable, sturdy, and even good-looking pieces of clothing that would last much longer than their owners might want to keep them. By purchasing such clothing, consumers could reduce their clothing budget considerably. These clothes would protect them from the cold, sun, wind, and so on. However, the clothes would not serve another purpose—variety. Variety is just one factor involved in clothing choice. Custom, attitude about one's self, and values are other factors that cannot be judged statistically.

It was only by custom that for centuries men in European and American countries wore pants while women wore skirts. Clothing that appeals to and makes people feel attractive is one of the strongest influences on what people buy. People's behavior is also determined by the values they hold important. In this sense, the clothing that a person buys makes a statement about his or her values. For example, it may not be important to you to have special clothes to wear for a date, while it may be important to someone else. An individual's values are linked to the larger value system—family, friends, and culture.

culture: a people's language, beliefs, values, and manner of living

Figure 5-1: SALES OF CLOTHING AND PERSONAL PRODUCTS IN A RECENT YEAR

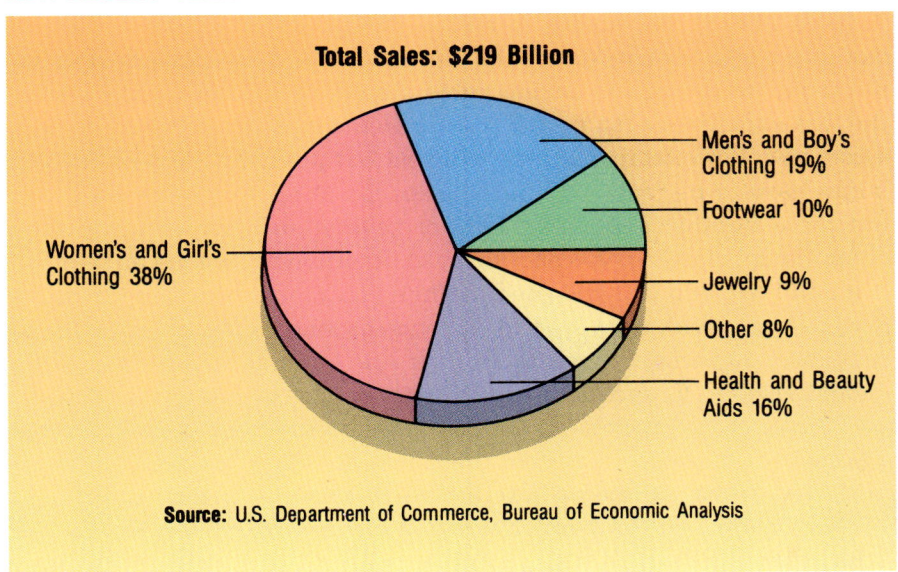

Total Sales: $219 Billion

Men's and Boy's Clothing 19%
Footwear 10%
Jewelry 9%
Other 8%
Health and Beauty Aids 16%
Women's and Girl's Clothing 38%

Source: U.S. Department of Commerce, Bureau of Economic Analysis

Personal care and clothing are huge industries in the United States. How many dollars does each category on this graph represent?

Consumers often comparison-shop when buying clothing. What information should you look for on clothing labels? What other factors should you consider in deciding to buy an item of clothing?

COMPARING CLOTHING VALUE

Comparison shopping is an important part of buying wisely. But comparing value in clothing does not mean simply purchasing an item from the store that offers the best price. Clothing value depends on at least three other factors: **1.** style, **2.** durability, and **3.** cost of care.

You may be able to buy the minimum amount of clothing that you need at very low cost. However, you will generally give up style to do it. Wearing clothes that are stylish—up to date—is usually expensive because you need to buy new clothes each year. In other words, wearing current styles costs more than wearing what are called classic styles. These are the more basic clothing designs and colors that do not change much through the years. Again, you are faced with a trade-off. Should you buy stylish clothes each year to keep up with fashion and have less money to spend on other things? Or should you buy less stylish clothes that you can wear from year to year and have more money?

Durability is the ability of an item to last. The longer a piece of clothing—or any item—lasts, the more durable it is. A consumer would not really be comparing similar value if he or she automatically bought the less expensive coat, dress, or shirt. In the long run, it might be more expensive. For example, an inexpensive but poorly made pair of pants might have to be replaced after one season. A slightly more expensive but more durable pair might last for several seasons. In comparison shopping for clothing, you should try to determine how long an item will last and how long you will need it. Then you should compare it to price. Suppose you think Coat A will last twice as long as Coat B, and Coat A costs only 20 percent more. Then Coat A is a better buy. However, you should also try to decide if the coat will still be in style in a year.

Finally, the cost of care is another important factor in deciding value. Two shirts or blouses may cost the same, but one may need dry cleaning. That is an expensive alternative to hand or machine washing. When deciding on the best choice in a clothing purchase, or any purchase that is meant to last, you must consider maintenance costs.

A Trailblazer in the Profession: Juanita Kreps (1921–   )

Juanita Kreps was a student at Berea College in Kentucky during the Great Depression of the 1930s, where she majored in economics courses. Her love of economics continued, and she soon achieved great success as an economist. Later in her career, she became the first woman to serve as Secretary of Commerce, when she held that job in President Carter's cabinet from 1977 to 1981.

After she graduated from Berea College in 1942, Kreps pursued her graduate studies in economics at Duke University, where she received her master's and her doctoral degrees. She then taught economics at Denison University and returned to Duke in 1955. From 1969 to 1972, Dr. Kreps served as Dean of the Women's College and Assistant Provost at Duke before being named James B. Duke Professor of Economics, the university's most prestigious endowed teaching position. In 1973, she was appointed Vice-President of the university.

As a highly respected economist, Kreps attracted the attention of several of America's largest corporations who were looking for qualified women to serve on their boards of directors. Kreps accepted offers on the boards of AT&T, United Airlines, the Chrysler Corporation, Citicorp, Western Electric, the J.C. Penney Company, R.J. Reynolds, and Eastman Kodak. She also served on the board of the New York Stock Exchange from 1972 to 1977.

A gracious and gifted person, Kreps was outspoken on many issues. As Secretary of Commerce, Kreps explained that she considered the department's role was not only to aid businesses but also to provide support for everyone who participates in the competitive marketplace, including consumers and employees. She hoped to use her position to increase corporations' social responsibility. She pledged to work to create employment opportunities and to improve the nation's productivity through a public works program.

One of her best-known books, *Sex in the Marketplace: American Women at Work,* examined women's role in the labor market. She sought answers to basic questions of why women in the 1960s entered the same occupations year after year, why so few women studied for advanced degrees, and why so many women exchanged their jobs as housewives for low-paying jobs outside the home.

Dr. Kreps offered this explanation to the problem women faced in the 1960s: "The woman who is considering the occupational options may be discouraged from trying to enter a male's field because she accurately perceives employers' reluctance to hire women for these jobs, or because the investment required of her may exceed her estimate of the return, given her expectation of withdrawal from work for a time, and the uncertainty surrounding her subsequent worklife." As the mother of three children, she also reflected on her experience: "The big problem with being a professional woman with a family is that [unlike a man] you simply have less time to give to the profession." By the 1980s, women's roles in the workforce had changed, and many had achieved job equality.

1. Describe some of Juanita Kreps's accomplishments as an economist.
2. Explain why Kreps was a trailblazer in the field of economics.

Checklist

☑

DETERMINING CLOTHING NEEDS

In deciding on clothing purchases, ask yourself the following questions:

1. **What do I already have?** Check the condition of the clothes you have, and see what you need to replace.

2. **What clothes do I need for:**
   - school?
   - job?
   - social life?
   - recreational activities?

3. **How many changes of clothes do I need to meet my minimum requirements for:**
   - cleanliness?
   - variety?
   - social status, or standing in society?

4. **How do my answers to questions 1 through 3 compare with the amount of money I have to spend?**

5. **Should I pay cash or charge my purchases?** Consider the trade-offs involved in paying cash or using credit.

CLOTHING SALES

Clothing sales are numerous throughout the year and it is easy to become a bargain fanatic. This is someone who buys sale items just because they are on sale. He or she may not really need or even want the items. Before going shopping, you should make a list of the clothing that you have and decide what you are lacking or need to replace. The Checklist for Determining Clothing Needs can help you evaluate your needs. Take your list with you when you go shopping. It will help you to keep your spending within limits. Remember, too, that finding the best deal involves using your time. Only you can decide how valuable that is.

There are several things to remember about clothing sales. Generally, a clothing sale is one in which a store owner is trying to get rid of goods that he or she could not sell during the regular selling season. That means in many cases you are buying clothes that you will not be able to wear until the following year. For example, you might be buying winter clothes at the end of the winter or summer clothes in late August. You might also be buying items that may not be in style in a year.

REVIEWING ECONOMIC PRINCIPLES

1. What four factors influence the kind of clothing choices people make?

2. In comparing clothing value, what three factors should a consumer consider?

3. State two things consumers should remember about clothing sales.

4. **Critical Thinking: Applying the Main Idea.** What main idea of Section 2 is important for you to apply to your personal shopping needs?

SUMMARY OF
IMPORTANT PRINCIPLES

1
- Three buying principles for food shopping are: a consumer should do only as much comparison shopping as is worthwhile to that person; reading advertisements for sales and cents-off coupons is a good, inexpensive way to comparison shop; comparison shopping involves comparisons among brands and sizes of products, as well as among stores.
- There are three major types of stores, each one with its own characteristics. Supermarkets contain just about everything in the way of meats, fresh vegetables, paper products, and so on, but prices are high. Warehouse food stores have a limited number of brands and items, are less expensive than supermarkets, may offer only regional-brand items or slightly damaged cases of national-brand products, are best for those who want to buy in quantity. Convenience stores are widespread, usually open from 16 to 24 hours a day, carry a limited selection, have high prices, and should be used for limited emergency shopping only.
- It is sometimes worth the time to try private-brand and generic-brand items to compare them and see if their quality meets a shopper's needs.
- In refusing or throwing away trading stamps, a consumer is paying extra food costs without receiving the value of the products that could be received by redeeming the stamps. The use of cents-off coupons involves a trade off between the time to collect and match the coupons to items and the money saved. Because of the higher cost of convenience foods, less money is available to spend on other things. Time is gained, however, because convenience foods require less time to prepare.
- Food is often graded based on standards set by the Department of Agriculture. The information on labels and in warranties is useful to consumers in making buying decisions and in understanding their rights and responsibilities.

2
- Style, durability, and cost of care are important to consider in comparing clothing value.
- Before going to clothing sales, wise shoppers will determine exactly what and how many clothes they need, and how much money they can afford to spend or put on their credit card or charge accounts.

Putting Economics to Work

USING SCARCE RESOURCES: BUDGETING

Tim Taylor has just moved into an apartment to live on his own for the first time. Although he is going to a vocational school full-time, he works 20 hours a week as a cashier in a drugstore. Each month his parents also send him a certain amount of money. As a result, Tim knows exactly what his income will be for the month.

To help him use that income in the most efficient way possible, Tim makes a budget at the beginning of each month. He writes down the amount of money he will spend on food, rent, clothing, and such flexible expenses as recreation. He then tries to follow this budget during the month. Tim also practices some good consumer buying principles. For example, when he shops for food, Tim first reads the food ads in the local newspaper to find which supermarket in his immediate area has the items he wants at the lowest prices. He also clips out cents-off coupons to use as he shops. Tim stocks up on bread, noodles, rice, and canned goods if they are on sale. He has learned enough about nutrition not to spend his food dollars on snacks and convenience foods. But when studying for a test, Tim does buy convenience foods. He feels the time cost of preparing a regular meal is too high then.

His clothing decisions are easier. Tim buys washable jeans only. He had decided not to buy more stylish clothes until he is out of school and making a better income. Tim's recreation expenses are small. He uses comparison shopping there, too. For example, he finds out which theaters offer reduced rates for early evening movies.

1. Suppose Tim began working more hours per week and his income increased. How might his budget change?
2. What principles of budgeting can you find in Tim's actions?
3. What principles of comparison shopping does Tim follow?
4. How has he answered questions on the Clothing Needs Checklist?

THE FOOD AND HEALTH INDUSTRIES
Skill: Drawing Conclusions

 **SECTION 1** Unlike many populations around the world, Americans are striving hard to eat less, not more. The following reading describes the "battle against their bulges" being waged by many Americans in this land of plenty.

In the battle against their bulges, Americans spent about $5 billion last year. They snatched up newly published diet and fitness guides in such quantities that at least one of the primers made best-seller lists each week. They bought some $200 million worth of over-the-counter diet drugs containing caffeine and amphetamine-related compounds and paid millions more for off-the-wall remedies like kelp and grapefruit extract. They loaded grocery baskets with low-calorie frozen foods, sales of which rose 15% annually for the past several years, according to Pathmark, one of the nation's largest food chains. They carted home low-cal cheeses, low-fat . . . milk, and stocked refrigerators with diet sodas. . . .

Determined to sweat off unsightly fat, many overweight citizens are enrolling in health clubs. Those who can afford to pamper their plumpness away register at pricy health spas. At least a million join self-help groups like Weight Watchers; . . . others visit diet doctors and nutrition gurus. The very fat . . . check into clinics and go on supervised fasts or have surgery. . . .

For all too many, however, the only certain result is a thinner wallet. Almost as quickly as the pounds drop off, they begin creeping back on. . . . Indeed, at least two-thirds of those who lose weight gain it all back, and then some, within a few years. After seven years, only 2% can still flaunt svelter [thinner] selves. . . .

1. How have producers responded to consumers' desire to lose weight?
2. What other industries have emerged in response to consumer demand for help in losing weight?

Anastasia Toufexis, "Dieting: The Losing Game." *Time*, January 20, 1986. Copyright 1986 Time Inc. All rights reserved. Reprinted by permission from *Time*.

WHICH COMES FIRST, FASHION OR COMFORT?
Skill: Contrasting Ideas

 **SECTION 2** People choose clothing not only because of its comfort or durability but also because of the way it looks on them and appears to others. Thorstein Veblen, economist and critic of those who consume only to impress others, distinguishes between "clothing" and "dress" in this reading from an essay written in 1894.

In human apparel the element of dress is readily distinguishable from that of clothing. The two functions—of dress and of clothing the person—are to a great extent subserved by the same material goods. . . .

But, however the two purposes may be served by the same material goods, . . . the elements of clothing and of dress are distinct. . . .

Of these two elements of apparel, dress came first in order of development, and it continues to hold the primacy to this day. The element of clothing, the quality of affording comfort, was from the beginning . . . some sort an afterthought. . . .

The first principle of dress . . . is conspicuous expensiveness. . . . A corollary under this principle inculcates [teaches] the desirability . . . of wearing nothing that is out of date. In the most advanced communities of our time . . . this principle expresses itself in the maxim that no outer garment may be worn more than once.

This requirement of novelty is the underlying principle of the whole of the difficult and interesting domain of fashion. Fashion does not demand continual flux and change simply because that way of doing is foolish; flux and change and novelty are demanded by the central principle of all dress—conspicuous waste.

1. What are the two functions of clothing? In what way is dress "conspicuous waste"?
2. Contrast attitudes toward clothing and dress today with attitudes in the 1890s.

Thorstein Veblen, "The Economic Theory of Woman's Dress." Reprinted from *Popular Science Monthly*, Vol. XLVI, November, 1894. *Essays in Our Changing Order*, edit. by Leon Ardzrooni. New York: August M. Kelley, 1964. pp. 65, 66, 71, 72.

5 | CHAPTER REVIEW

PRACTICING YOUR STUDY SKILLS: SCANNING AND RECALL

Sometimes in studying you may find it difficult to locate specific pieces of information or to remember them. Scanning can help you with the first problem. In the SQ3R method that you learned about at the beginning of the book, you read about skimming, which is reading to get a general idea of a text. Scanning is reading for specific information. It is useful for finding answers to assignments, taking open-book texts, researching, and so on.

1. To scan, do not read the text. Let your eyes run down the page.
2. Keep in mind the specific data that you are seeking. Do not let yourself become distracted and begin reading.
3. A text often contains visual clues that will help you. These include headings, tables, lists, and words in special type. Also look for numbers such as percentages and dates.

Activity: Practice your skill at scanning by answering the following questions about this chapter.

1. How much of their total income do Americans spend on food?
2. What are three types of food stores?
3. On what three things besides price does clothing value depend?
4. Besides price, what else should a person consider in buying a refrigerator from a particular dealer?

Often when faced with learning a great deal of information, you may find it difficult to remember what you have read or heard. However, there are methods you can use to improve your ability to recall information. Choose from the following five tips listed the ones that will be most helpful to you.

1. Really concentrate when you read or listen.

2. Study only small amounts of information at a time, and study for only short periods of time. It is more difficult to learn a lot of information during a long study period.
3. Use the SQ3R method outlined in the introduction to this book.
4. Make up acronyms. An acronym is a word put together from the first letters of the phrase you wish to remember. For example, SAM is an acronym for shared-appreciation mortgage, a type of mortgage described in Chapter 6.
5. Make up a nonsense rhyme or sentence. Especially useful are sentences or rhymes in which the first letter of each word is also the first letter of the words you are trying to recall. For example, in the phrase *Samantha Dozed in a Carload of Clothes*, the capital letters stand for the three factors of clothing value you read about earlier in the chapter: Style, Durability, and Cost of Care.

Activity: Practice your skills with recall by doing the following activities:

1. Use the SQ3R method to study the material on Clothing Choices.
2. Make up a nonsense rhyme or sentence for the six kinds of information you should look for on a label.

VOCABULARY REVIEW

For each of the following vocabulary terms, write a sentence using the term: grade, unit price, warehouse food store, guarantee, net weight.

Practicing Your Economic Skills

1. **Determining Unit Price.** One orange juice container holds 6 fluid ounces (177 milliliters) and sells for $.69. Another holds 12 fluid ounces (345 milliliters) and sells for $1.08. **a.** What is the unit price of each container? **b.** Which is the better buy?

2. Converting Graphs to Tables. The following graph shows how one person with an after-tax monthly income of $600 might spend his or her money. Use this graph to make a table showing the dollar amount spent on each of the seven categories shown on the graph.

How a Typical Person Spends After-Tax Income

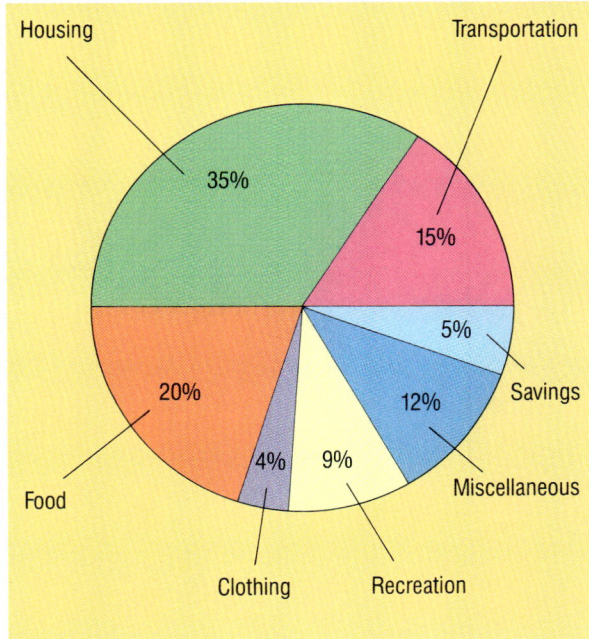

3. Compiling Information. Read the labels on five pieces of your clothing to determine how many items require dry cleaning rather than machine or hand washing. List the types of fabrics that require dry cleaning.

DISCUSSING ECONOMIC QUESTIONS

1. Single people tend to buy more convenience foods than families. Why?
2. According to the text, one reason people buy clothes is for variety. Do you agree with this? Why or why not?

APPLYING CRITICAL THINKING SKILLS

1. **Reading Labels.** Check the labels for one of the following: canned peaches, frozen peas and carrots, canned beef stew, frozen beef stew, chicken soup, tomato juice, cereal, cookies. Write down the information to use as the basis of a class discussion comparing the types of information that are given on food labels.
2. **Checking Warranties.** Visit a department store and check the labels and/or warranties for one of the following: shirt, raincoat, hair dryer, electric razor, sofa, videocassette recorder. Write down the information to use as the basis of a class discussion comparing the type of information on labels and warranties.
3. **Making Graphs.** Using the *Statistical Abstract of the United States* as a reference, draw one graph each to show: a. the number of bushels of wheat harvested per acre during a recent year in four states in your area; b. the amount of personal consumption expenditures for clothing, accessories, and jewelry for the last five years there. Remember bar graphs are best for showing differences between things at one point in time; and line graphs are the best kinds of graphs to use for showing the change in the same thing over a period of time.

READINGS

Brown, Betty J., and Clow, John E. *General Business: Our Business and Economic World.* Boston: Houghton Mifflin, 1982

Brown, Paul B. "Branded Foods." *Forbes,* 4 January 1982, pp. 207–209. *Competition from generic foods.*

Eliot, E., and Susco, W. "Defective Products." *Working Woman,* February 1982, pp. 58–59.

Flax, S. "Wholesalers." *Forbes,* 4 January 1982, pp. 222–223.

CHAPTER 6

Housing and transportation are the necessities for which most Americans spend the largest part of their income. Learning the steps in making sound decisions here will contribute to your economic well-being.

BUYING THE NECESSITIES: HOUSING AND TRANSPORTATION

This chapter describes the advantages and disadvantages of different types of housing and of *owning* versus *renting*. You will also learn two ways to estimate how much housing you can afford to buy. If you choose to rent, the chapter describes the rights and responsibilities of both renters and landlords. The steps involved in choosing and buying a car are also described, as well as the costs of operating a car. Learning Economic Skills describes various types of insurance.

CHAPTER OBJECTIVES After you study the sections of this chapter, you will be able to:

1 • compare the economic advantages and disadvantages of different types of housing.
  • determine the trade-offs involved in owning and renting housing.

2 • state two ways a household can determine how much it can afford to pay to buy a home.

3 • identify rights and responsibilities of renters and landlords.
  ★ explain the purposes of various kinds of insurance.

4 • list the steps involved in choosing and buying a car.
  • describe the trade-offs involved in choosing a particular car.
  • state the costs of buying a car.
  • state the costs of operating a car.

ECONOMICS VOCABULARY

condominium
lease
real estate tax
equity
security deposit
depreciate
closing costs
points
insurance
premiums
liability insurance
deductible
no-fault insurance
homeowners policy
term life insurance
death benefits
decreasing term insurance
straight life insurance
excise tax

Chapter 5 describes good consumer practices for buying food and clothing. This chapter deals with two of the largest purchases you may make: buying housing and buying a car.

Housing may be the rental of an apartment or a house or the actual purchase of a place to live. Today, there are more than 60 million houses, about 26 million apartments, and over 10 million mobile homes in the United States. As Figure 6-1 shows, an average of more than 2 million housing units are started each year. Americans also spend more than $21 billion a year remodeling existing housing.

Although many people, especially city dwellers, do not own cars, by the 1980s, 85 percent of all American households did. Some households owned two, three, or more cars. Owning a car involves more than making monthly payments on a car loan. It also means insuring and maintaining that car. According to the Department of Transportation, the cost of maintaining a standard-sized auto is about $.30 a mile. Over a ten-year period and 100,000 miles, this amounts to $30,000.

household: anyone living in a single housing unit; may be an individual or a group such as a family

1 | HOUSING NEEDS AND WANTS

Ask yourself as you read:
- What kind of housing is available for Americans?
- What are the most expensive types of housing to buy and maintain? the least expensive?

The average American family spends nearly one-third of its annual income on housing. In the United States, there are more than 100 million housing units, of which about two-thirds are owned by the people living in them. The rest are rented. A family or an individual is not just buying or renting a place to live. They are also paying for the pleasure or satisfaction gained by living in a place called "home." The amount of satisfaction depends on many things. Among them are the size of the dwelling, the neighborhood, the quality of construction and furnishings, and how well it suits the family's or individual's needs.

There are several types of housing available in the United States for single people, for families, and for different age groups. These include single-family homes, town houses, condominiums, cooperatives, and mobile homes.

SINGLE-FAMILY HOUSE

The single-family house is one that is separate from neighboring homes and has some land around it. This type of housing usually is the most expensive type to buy and maintain. The single-family house perhaps is also the type of housing that most Americans hope to own. It is part of the American dream, and more than in any other country it is a symbol of success and happiness.

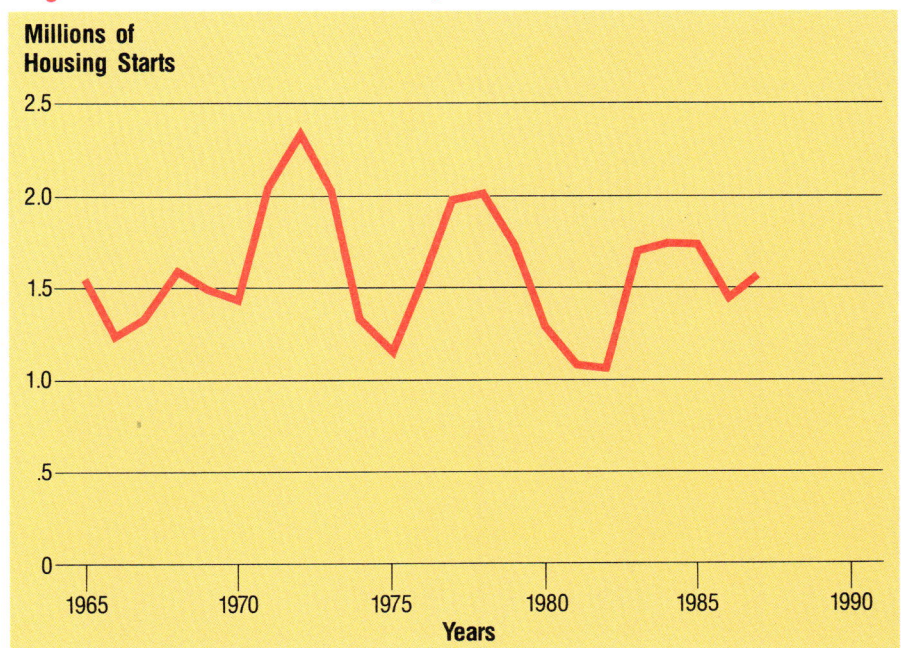

Figure 6–1: NEW HOUSING STARTS, 1965–1987

Millions of Housing Starts vs. Years

Source: *Statistical Abstract of the U.S.,* Bureau of the Census
*1987 data is estimated.

As you will read in Chapter 14, the number of new housing units started each year is an indicator of the health of the economy. According to this graph, which were not good years for the economy?

TOWN HOUSES

A town house is a house of two or more floors with a front and backyard but with common sidewalls. The advantage of a town house is its economy of construction. Its style saves on the amount of land, insulation, windows, foundation, roof, and walls needed, which makes it less expensive to buy and maintain. Unfortunately, noise often carries through the common walls.

CONDOMINIUMS

Some town houses are condominiums. A **condominium** (kahn-duh-MIN-ee-uhm) is a single unit in an apartment building or in a series of town houses that is owned separately. Common areas such as hallways, lobbies, recreational facilities, and the land on which the building is built are owned in common by the owners of the single units. Owners pay a monthly maintenance fee for upkeep of these common areas. Ownership rights in a condominium are similar to those in a single-family house, with some exceptions. Owners are free to make any changes they wish within their own units. However, the need for repairs to common areas is usually determined by a majority vote of the owners of all the units. The owners form an association to deal with such issues. Condominiums first became popular in resort areas as second homes. Now they are also popular among younger, single people, small families, and senior citizens who want to invest in real estate rather than pay rent.

facilities (fuh-SIL-uh-teez): equipment used in an activity

127

Table 6-1: ADVANTAGES AND DISADVANTAGES OF OWNING AND RENTING

Advantages	Disadvantages
Ownership provides a family or individual with: • freedom of use. Owners can remodel whenever or however they choose. • the pride of ownership. People tend to take better care of things they own. • greater privacy. • a good investment that in the past has risen in value as much as, or more than, the general rise in prices. • significant income tax benefits. • creation of **equity** (EK-wuh-tee), the amount of money invested in the property minus the debt—mortgage payments—still owed. • a good credit rating if mortgage payments are made on time. • property to use as collateral for other loans.	**Ownership has the following drawbacks:** • less mobility, especially in years when interest rates on mortgages are high and it is difficult to sell housing. • less feeling of being able to sell one property to move to another because the present one is too small, too big, and so on. • necessity of a large outlay of money for a down payment. • maintenance costs, real estate taxes, and possible depreciation. • less money for other purchases because of high monthly mortgage payments. • possibility of overextending a family's debt load to make home improvements.
Renting provides an individual or family with: • greater mobility. A renter does not have to worry about trying to sell property quickly if he or she must move. • a feeling of freedom to choose another place to live if dissatisfied with current rental unit. • having to only pay a small security deposit rather than a large outlay of money for a down payment. A **security deposit** is money the renter gives to the owner to hold in case the rent is not paid or the apartment is damaged. • no maintenance costs, real estate taxes, or depreciation. • a good credit rating if rent is paid on time. • more money for other purchases because monthly rental payments are often less than monthly mortgage payments. • no temptation to overspend on home improvements.	**Renting has the following drawbacks:** • no freedom of use. Renters may not remodel or even paint without permission of the owner. • no return on rental money. A renter will never own the property regardless of how much rent he or she pays or over how long a period of time. • little in the way of tax benefits. • lack of privacy. • little feeling of responsibility for seeing that the property is well taken care of. • no property for use as collateral. • need to wait for maintenance work at the convenience of the owner.

COOPERATIVES

Owners of cooperative apartments, on the other hand, own equal shares in the company that owns the apartment building and the land on which the building stands. They do not own their apartments but hold leases on their apartments. A **lease** is a long-term agreement describing the terms under which the property is being rented. All operating costs such as real estate taxes and maintenance are divided equally among the owners. **Real estate taxes** are those paid on land and buildings. A major problem with cooperative apartments is that individual members must obtain approval from the co-op before remodeling, renting, or selling their units.

MOBILE HOMES

Mobile homes are a popular form of low-cost housing in the United States. One reason for this is the favorable tax treatment they receive. In some states, mobile homes are taxed as motor vehicles rather than as real estate. Another reason for their popularity is that they often are the least expensive to buy and maintain. However, owners of mobile homes face problems that owners of other kinds of housing do not. The purchase of a mobile home does not always guarantee a space in a mobile home park in the area where the owner may want to live. Mobile homes are also more likely to suffer damage during storms than are other types of housing. Third, mobile homes, like automobiles and boats, **depreciate** (di-PREE-shee-ayt)—decline in value over time—as the mobile homes or the fixtures that are part of them wear out or become outdated in style.

THE DECISION TO BUY *VERSUS* RENT

No matter the type of housing a family or individual decides to live in, there is a decision that must be made—to buy or rent. Today many people rent apartments, town houses, or houses even though they can afford to buy. Table 6-1 compares the advantages and disadvantages—both economic and psychological—of owning and renting.

REVIEWING ECONOMIC PRINCIPLES

1. Write a sentence defining each of the following economic terms: **a.** lease, **b.** real estate tax, **c.** equity, **d.** security deposit, **e.** depreciate.
2. What are the advantages and disadvantages of buying and maintaining each of the following types of housing: **a.** single-family home? **b.** town house? **c.** condominium? **d.** cooperative? **e.** mobile home?
3. Based on the table Advantages and Disadvantages of Owning and Renting, choose: **a.** two advantages to owning that might appeal to younger people, **b.** two disadvantages to owning for older people, **c.** two disadvantages to renting for younger people, **d.** two disadvantages to renting for older people. Explain the reasons for your choices.
4. **Critical Thinking: Making Judgments.** Why do you think that condominiums and cooperatives have become increasingly popular among Americans?

2 | BUYING HOUSING: HOW MUCH CAN YOU AFFORD?

Ask yourself as you read:
- What costs are involved in buying housing?
- What kinds of mortgages are available for home buyers?

Should you decide to buy housing, it is important that you do not take on financial obligations that are beyond your budget. There are several things you can do to guard against this. First, you should figure the amount of your monthly income for the first one-third of all mortgage payments that will be due. Depending on the term, or repayment period, of the mortgage, this could be ten years. Next, you should estimate your monthly housing expenses. These include mortgage payments, insurance, taxes, and the costs for heating, electricity, water, sewage, and similar services. Table 6-2 on page 131 shows monthly costs for a typical housing purchase. You should also estimate first-year occupancy costs such as new or additional curtains, rugs, furniture, and landscaping. First-year occupancy costs are those costs that you will pay to make the housing attractive and livable when you move in. They probably will not occur again for some years.

Savings and loan associations use certain rules to help buyers determine how much housing they can afford.

term: repayment period

Rule 1. Purchase Price—Annual Income = 2.5 or less
Rule 2. Mortgage Payment—Monthly Take-Home Income = less than 33⅓ percent
Rule 3. Loan Amount—Value of the Housing = 95 percent or less (usually 80 percent)

According to Rule 1, the purchase price divided by an individual's or family's income should be 2.5 or less. Rule 2 shows that monthly mortgage payments should be no more than one-third of monthly take-home

Besides the down payment, what other costs will this couple have to pay when they sign the mortgage papers for their new home?

Table 6-2: ESTIMATING MONTHLY EXPENSES IN BUYING HOUSING

Monthly costs: Payments for items such as taxes and insurance are often made every three months. To determine monthly cost, divide amount paid annually by 12. The expenses are based on actual costs in a midwestern city.

Item	Description	Example Cost
Mortgage payment	Monthly payment for principal and interest	$607
Taxes	Amount paid for real estate taxes	50
Homeowners insurance	Amount paid for protection against loss from fire, storm, wind, theft, and so on	20
Mortgage life insurance	Amount paid for insurance that will pay off mortgage in case of death of insured (Optional)	13
Private mortgage insurance	Amount paid to protect lender against loss in case borrower defaults on the mortgage. Lender often requires this insurance if the down payment is less than 20 percent	0
Utilities and services	Payments for electricity, gas, water, sewer, and garbage services	170
TOTAL	Total for the above items	$860

pay. Rule 3 indicates that most savings and loan associations will not lend more than 95 percent of the purchase price. Generally, the maximum that a lender will give is closer to 80 percent and may even be as low as 65 percent.

Today it is almost impossible to finance 100 percent of the purchase price of housing. In addition to the cash down payment, you will need money for **closing costs.** These are costs involved in arranging for a mortgage or in transferring ownership of the property. Closing costs can include fees for such items as the title search, legal costs, loan application, credit report, house inspections, and taxes. Although the person buying the house usually pays these fees, the seller may agree to pay part or all of them if this will make it easier to sell the house.

In arranging for a mortgage, it is important to know about **points,** which are included in closing costs. Points are the fee paid to the lender and computed as percentage points of the loan. Each point equals 1 percent of the amount borrowed. Points are charged when the bank, savings and loan, or other lender believe that the current interest rate is not high enough to pay the expenses involved in handling the mortgage and still make a profit. The usual charge is from two to four points. For example, on a $48,000 mortgage for a $60,000 house, the lender might charge three points, which equals $1,440.

Table 6-3: TYPES OF MORTGAGES

Type of Mortgage	Interest Rate Changes	Monthly Payment Changes	Term Changes	Description
Standard Fixed Rate Mortgage	No	No	No	Interest rate and monthly payments remain the same over the term of the mortgage. Term is fixed, usually at 25 or 30 years. Until recently, standard fixed rate mortgages were the only type lenders could offer. Changes in state and federal law have allowed the increasing use of alternative mortgages.
Flexible Rate Mortgage	Yes	Yes	Yes	Any of several mortgage plans in which the interest rate and monthly payments float up or down along with interest rates in general. How much and how often rates change are limited by state or federal regulations. Usually, rates can increase by no more than a few percentage points over the life of a mortgage, while there is often no limit on the amount of decrease. The term on some mortgages can be extended, thereby reducing monthly payments by stretching them over a longer period of time. Three such plans are variable rate mortgage (VRM), adjustable rate mortgage (ARM), and renegotiable rate mortgage (RRM). Each plan operates under different state or federal regulations.
Federal Housing Administration (FHA) Mortgage	No	No	No	The FHA will insure the entire amount of its mortgages. This added security makes it possible for borrowers to obtain a larger loan than they could with an uninsured mortgage. Large loans mean that small down payments are possible.

FINANCING A HOUSING PURCHASE

One of the major problems facing today's home buyer is that of financing. Almost every home buyer has a mortgage. Mortgages are available from savings and loan associations, savings and commercial banks, and often from the seller of the house, co-op, or condominium.

Table 6-3: TYPES OF MORTGAGES *(continued)*

Type of Mortgage	Interest Rate Changes	Monthly Payment Changes	Term Changes	Description
Graduated Payment Mortgage (GPM)	No	Yes	No	Interest rate and term are usually fixed for the life of the mortgage. Monthly payments are small at the beginning and increase gradually over the years. In effect, the homeowner is borrowing the difference between the full payments he or she would make with a fixed rate mortgage and the reduced amount being paid. The amount of outstanding principal increases during the first years of the loan. Over the long run, this borrowed money is repaid with interest. GPMs are used by people who expect their incomes to increase steadily from year to year.
Shared Appreciation Mortgage (SAM)	Varies	Varies	Varies	Interest rate is usually low, but the borrower agrees to share with the lender a large amount (usually between 30 to 50 percent) of the increase in the home's value after a certain number of years or when the property is sold. The various types of SAMs are often called shared-equity plans. The lender can be an institution or a private group.
Veteran's Administration (VA) Mortgage	No	No	No	These loans can be obtained only by qualified veterans or their widows. The interest rate is generally lower than for other mortgages. The VA guarantees a large percentage of the loan, which is usually administered through a bank or other mortgage-lenders. Loans with no down payment are possible under the VA program.

Every mortgage usually involves a down payment and interest. If you buy a house for $100,000 and make a $20,000 down payment, you will need to obtain a mortgage for the remaining $80,000. The mortgage will then be repaid in monthly installments that include interest on the loan. Table 6-3 shows several kinds of mortgages that are available.

1. Define the following mortgage terms: **a.** closing costs, **b.** points.
2. **a.** What kinds of income and costs should an individual or family figure out before deciding to purchase housing? **b.** What rules can people use to decide how much they can afford to pay to purchase housing?
3. **Critical Thinking: Analyzing Information.** From the table Types of Mortgages, which two types of mortgages appear best suited to the needs of young people buying their first home?

3 | RENTING: A MATTER OF LEASES

Ask yourself as you read:
- What should be included in an apartment lease?
- What happens when a lease is broken?

When most young people first start living on their own, they usually rent housing rather than buy. Renting may seem like a simple matter, and, in many cases, it is. However, you should be aware of some important aspects of the legal rights and responsibilities of renters.

RIGHTS AND RESPONSIBILITIES

Most renters sign a lease, which describes the rights and responsibilities of both tenant and landlord. Most leases are for one to three years. Each item in the lease is usually written as an individual clause—or section—in the lease. Among the rights of tenants is the use of the property for the purpose stated in the lease. For example, if an apartment is rented for use as a living area, it may not be turned into a business office. Tenants have the right to a certain amount of privacy. A landlord usually cannot enter an apartment any time he or she chooses.

Finding the housing you can afford and best meets your needs is an important decision. What advantages and disadvantages of renting have this couple had to consider?

Case Study

AN AMERICAN BUSINESS HERO: LEE IACOCCA

On November 2, 1978, Lee Iacocca became the head of Chrysler Corporation, an automobile company that was on the verge of collapse. Quarterly losses had reached the highest in company history, and nothing seemed to indicate that things would get any better.

It was clear that only drastic measures could save the corporation from bankruptcy. Sales were down and cost-saving measures alone could not return the company to profitable operations. Worsening economic conditions in the nation made it all but impossible for the company to survive without large infusions of money. Attempts to attract investors—everyone from the Volkswagen Corporation to wealthy Arab oil sheiks—were futile. The only alternative seemed to be a government "bailout." For Iacocca, a strong believer in the free market system, this was a difficult decision to make. His answer to his critics was, "What choice do I have? It's the only game in town."

Once the decision to seek the federal government's aid was made, Iacocca zealously prepared his case. He discovered that Congress had appropriated money for aid to other troubled corporations in the past. Airplane manufacturer Lockheed, steel companies, and even American Motors, a rival automobile company, had received government-guaranteed loans. Iacocca found himself in the awkward position of defending government intervention in the economy. Yet it was his firm belief in the free market and competition that caused him to pursue these loan guarantees. Why? Because Iacocca was convinced that a government loan would insure Chrysler's ability to survive and to compete effectively with General Motors and Ford.

Iacocca's arguments at congressional committee hearings were eloquent and persuasive. It was difficult for Congress to argue against his evidence that showed, among other things, that if Chrysler failed it would cost the country $2.7 billion during the first year alone in unemployment insurance and welfare payments because of the layoffs of workers that would result. Iacocca persisted against stiff congressional and public opposition until he had convinced Congress that loan guarantees were the only way Chrysler could survive and repay its loans.

The result of Iacocca's efforts has been that Chrysler has survived and prospered. The government-guaranteed loans provided Chrysler with the funds to continue to operate. Thousands of workers were kept on the payroll. Moreover, the company's success enabled it to repay all of the loans seven years ahead of schedule.

Although Iacocca obviously did not single-handedly save Chrysler, to the public it seems as though he did. He was the "salesman," the "star" in the nationwide media campaign launched by Chrysler to sell its cars. He was visible, and he was likeable. His autobiography proved to be one of the best-selling books of recent times. (An excerpt from this book is found in the primary and secondary sources in Chapter 8.)

1. Why did Iacocca find it difficult to ask for a government-backed loan?
2. What economic justification did Iacocca use to support his request to Congress for aid?
3. Should the federal government make a policy of guaranteeing loans to companies in great financial difficulties? Give reasons for your answer.

Checklist

CLAUSES IN HOUSING LEASES

You should be aware of several types of clauses to avoid in leases.

1. According to a confession-of-judgment clause, the lawyer for the owner of the rental unit has the right to plead guilty for you in court in the event the owner thinks his or her rights have been violated. If you sign a lease with a confession-of-judgment clause, you are admitting guilt before committing any act. Such a clause is, in fact, illegal in some states.

2. According to the inability-to-sue clause, you give up your right to sue the owner if you suffer injury or damage through some fault of the owner, such as neglected repair work.

3. Leases may include arbitrary clauses, or those based on one's wishes rather than a rule or law. These give the owner the right to cancel the lease because he or she is dissatisfied with your behavior. Some leases include clauses that:
   - forbid hanging pictures.
   - forbid overnight guests. This is usually done to make sure the apartment is occupied only by the renter and members of the renter's immediate family.
   - forbid subleasing, or the leasing of the apartment by the tenant to someone else.
   - allow the owner to cancel the lease if you are only one day late in paying the rent but hold you legally responsible to pay the rent for the rest of the lease.
   - allow the owner or a representative, such as a plumber, to enter your apartment when you are not home.
   - make you legally responsible for all repairs.
   - make you obey rules that have not yet been written.

If you have the opportunity, these are some clauses that you should have added to your lease.

1. If the person renting the unit to you says that it comes with dishwasher, garbage disposal, and air conditioner, make sure the lease lists them.

2. If you have been promised the use of a recreation room, a parking lot, or a swimming pool, make sure that the lease states this. Also have it indicate whether or not you must pay extra for their use.

3. If the owner has promised to have the apartment painted, have this stated in the lease. If you wish to be able to choose the color, also have this stated in the lease.

4. In certain cases, you may be able to cancel your lease if you are transferred to a job in another city or state. Usually, however, you must agree to pay a certain amount to do this. The amount should be stated in the lease.

5. If you plan to put in lighting fixtures, shelves, and so on, and wish them to remain your property when you move, have this stated in the lease. Otherwise they become part of the apartment and you may not take them.

A landlord may enter only to make necessary repairs or to show the apartment to a potential renter when the current tenant is moving.

In turn, the tenant must pay the rent on time and take reasonable care of the property. If major repairs such as replacing a leaky roof are needed, the tenant is responsible for notifying the landlord. Often a lease will limit how an apartment can be used. The lease may forbid pets, for example, or forbid anyone other than the person named on the lease from living there. In signing a lease, the tenant is usually required to give a security deposit. This is usually equal to one month's rent and

Landlords' and tenants' rights are described in the rental lease. This landlord is installing a smoke detector as a safety measure. What should you look for as a tenant when you sign a lease?

is returned after the tenant has moved. The purpose of the security deposit is to pay for repairing any damages that the tenant caused, such as cracked plaster from hanging pictures. The amount returned depends on the condition of the apartment, as determined by the landlord. The tenant is also required to give notice, or a formal warning, if he or she plans to move before the term of the lease is up. In this event, the landlord may ask for several month's rent to pay for any time the apartment is empty before a new tenant moves in.

notice: formal warning

LANDLORD RESPONSIBILITIES

Landlords also have responsibilities. In many states, they must make sure apartments have certain minimum services, such as heat, and that their apartments are fit to live in. Landlords may also have to obey building safety laws. For example, fire escapes and smoke detectors may be required. Leases usually call for the landlord to make repairs within a reasonable amount of time. In many states, a tenant has the right to pay for the repairs and withhold that amount of rent if the landlord does not make the repairs.

A number of states and cities have laws that define the rights and responsibilities of both landlords and tenants. These laws often require a landlord to go to court before he or she can evict a tenant. Some cities have set up agencies to help settle disputes between landlords and tenants without the time and expense of going to court.

evict (ih-VIKT): to remove a tenant through a legal process

REVIEWING ECONOMIC PRINCIPLES

1. State one right and one responsibility of each of the following:
   a. tenants, **b.** landlords.
2. State two clauses that renters should: **a.** avoid in leases, **b.** try to have added to leases.
3. **Critical Thinking: Summarizing the Main Idea.** Why is it to the advantage of renters to sign a lease?

Learning Economic Skills | BUYING INSURANCE

Suppose one thousand people drive cars in a given area. Past experience for this group shows that a certain number will be involved in automobile accidents each year. However, no driver can know whether he or she will be one of those in an accident. Rather than risk paying large costs for damages, repairs, and injuries resulting from an accident, the drivers could share, or pool, the possible costs.

Each driver could contribute a small fee to a general fund, and this money could then be used to pay for repairs and injuries. In this way, no one driver would have to bear the full costs of an accident. Suppose that the total cost of automobile accidents for the group of 100 drivers is $10,000 a year. If they shared the risk, each driver would pay 1/100 of the cost, or $100 a year.

This is basically how all **insurance** works. It spreads the losses of a few over a large group. In doing so, it protects an individual against risk. Insurance enables an individual to deal with the financial problems resulting from accidental loss that might otherwise be disastrous.

Insurance companies sell individual insurance agreements—called policies—to cover almost any type of risk. The risks that consumers most often protect themselves against are those connected with their cars, their homes, and their lives. The fees paid for this protection are called **premiums.** The amount of a premium depends on statistics put together by insurance companies indicating risks for different individuals in different situations. In general, the higher the risk, the higher the insurance premium will be.

The principles of comparison shopping also apply to buying insurance. It is important to talk to insurance agents representing different companies and to compare their policies and services.

AUTO INSURANCE

The first kind of insurance you buy will probably be automobile insurance. Most states require car owners to have at least some **liability insurance** for automobiles and their drivers. This type of insurance pays for bodily injury and property damage. It covers you, or anyone you allow to drive your car, against financial obligations for injury or death to others and for property damage caused by your car. Liability insurance is usually described by the amount of coverage, for example, 100/300/50. This means the insurance company would pay up to $100,000 for any one person injured in the accident, up to a total of $300,000 for all personal injuries suffered in the accident, and up to $50,000 for damage to private or public property.

The table lists various types of auto insurance, including liability. Most people buy auto insurance that covers several of the risks listed. Each

Types of Auto Insurance

Bodily injury liability	Protects you against financial obligations for injury or death to others in an accident. Policies usually have a limit, such as $100,000, for each person injured in an accident, as well as a limit for the total amount paid out for each accident.
Property damage liability	Covers you against property damage in an accident. Property can include other cars, lamp posts, telephone poles, buildings, and so on.
Medical	Covers the cost of health care and hospitalization resulting from an accident for you, your family, and any passengers.
Collision	Covers the cost of repairs to your car resulting from an accident.
Comprehensive physical damage	Protects you against damage or loss of your car due to fire, flood, theft, vandalism, and so on.

additional type of coverage adds to the amount of the premium. Insurance rates for teenagers and young adults usually are higher because many younger people drive more recklessly than older ones and are in more car accidents.

One way of reducing the cost of car insurance is to request a high deductible on collision coverage. The **deductible** is the portion of the cost of repairs that you must pay before the insurance company pays anything. The amount is stated in the policy. For example, if your policy has a $200 deductible and repairs from an accident cost $700, you would pay $200 and the insurance company would pay the remaining $500. Repairs costing less than $200 you would pay. The greater the deductible that you pay, the lower the premium.

In recent years, several states have passed **no-fault insurance** laws. This means that in the case of an accident, each driver's insurance company pays for damages and medical bills for that driver without trying to determine who was at fault. No-fault insurance is intended to do away with the costly procedure of using lawyers and the courts to determine who should be made to pay.

Practicing Your Skills

1. Why might the owner of an old used car choose not to buy collision insurance?
2. What does a 25/50/15 policy mean?
3. Suppose you have an accident while driving your brother's car, with his permission. You and your passenger are hurt slightly; you also run over somebody's fence, damage a traffic light, and smash the front end of the car. **a.** Whose insurance policy will pay for the damages—yours or your brother's? **b.** Which types of auto insurance will cover each part of the accident?

HOME INSURANCE

If and when you buy a home, you will no doubt want to protect your investment with some type of

Types of Homeowners Insurance

Basic coverage	Insures against: • fire or lightning • loss of property removed from a home endangered by fire or other disaster • windstorm or hail • explosions • riot • aircraft • vehicles • smoke • vandalism • theft • broken glass
Broad coverage	Insures against all of the above plus: • falling objects • weight of snow and ice • building collapse • broken steam or hot water heating system • damage caused by water or steam leaking from a plumbing, heating, or air conditioning system • frozen plumbing • injury from faulty electrical wiring
Comprehensive coverage	Insures against all disasters *except:* • flood • earthquake* • war • nuclear accident • others as stated in your policy *Special policies for flood and earthquake insurance are available in some areas.

insurance. Most people realize that fire is a danger that must be insured against, but homeowners can also buy protection against windstorms, ice damage, vandalism, and so on. Insurance companies offer several plans—called **homeowners policies**—that insure a dwelling and its owners against a wide range of dangers. The table on p. 140 summarizes the three most common homeowners policies. As you might expect, the broader coverage means higher premiums.

Most policies also insure your home and any other buildings on your property, as well as your personal possessions. The latter are insured even if they are stolen or damaged away from home. If your home is damaged so badly that you must move out while it is being rebuilt, your homeowners policy will pay your living expenses. Homeowners policies also provide liability coverage if others are injured on your property. Apartment renters and owners of condominiums and mobile homes can purchase special policies with similar coverage. Like auto insurance, homeowners policies usually have a deductible of $100 or more.

Practicing Your Skills

1. a. Which homeowners policies protect a home from damage due to riot? b. Which policies cover damage caused by frozen plumbing?
2. Which of the disasters listed in the table are more likely to happen in the area in which you live than in other areas of the country?

LIFE INSURANCE

Life insurance is a way of protecting your family against the loss of your income if you die. There are many ways a life insurance policy can be set up, but there are two basic types: term insurance and straight or whole life insurance.

Term life insurance provides life insurance protection for a certain period of time—usually one or five years. If you die during that time, the insurance company will pay your survivors a certain amount in **death benefits.** This is the amount—for example, $50,000—that the company pays if you die while the insurance policy is in effect. Term insurance can be renewed at the end of the period. The premium is slightly higher because, as you grow older, risk of death increases.

Over a period of years, some term insurance policies, called **decreasing term insurance,** reduce the death benefits the company will pay. This is because as children grow older and move away from home, parents need less insurance to provide for them. Because it decreases in value over time, decreasing term insurance costs less than renewable term insurance. Some decreasing term insurance policies also pay off home mortgages or other debts if the insured dies.

Straight life insurance, also called whole life or ordinary life, combines insurance coverage with a savings plan. The premiums you pay over the life of the policy are more than enough to provide insurance coverage. The extra money builds over time and earns interest. If you, as the insured, cash in the policy, you receive the savings and accumulated interest. However, the amount of interest paid on this type of policy is usually less than can be earned on other forms of savings.

Practicing Your Skills

1. Life insurance is usually bought to protect a family against the loss of income of the person insured. Based on this information, which of the following individuals or families need life insurance the most: Carolyn Greene, a single working woman; Natalie and Peter Monahan, a couple with both persons working; Jan and Betsy Wolansky, a couple with two teenage children, with Jan working outside the home; Stu Kim, a single working father with one small child?
2. Mr. and Mrs. Hathaway are both around 55 years old. Their three children are grown and working. Mr. and Mrs. Jensen are about the same age. However, two of their grandchildren live with them and depend on them for support. Which couple would be better off with renewable term insurance rather than decreasing term insurance?

Most Americans own their own automobiles. What are the major trade-offs you will face in deciding which car to buy?

4 | BUYING AND OPERATING AN AUTOMOBILE

Ask yourself as you read:
- What are the costs of buying an automobile?
- What are the ongoing costs of owning and operating an automobile?

In most places in the United States an automobile is a necessity. Some Americans rent or lease cars because they do not have the down-payment or because they wish to gain a tax advantage by leasing or renting for business purposes. Nevertheless, the majority of people prefer to own their own automobiles. Therefore, it is probable that at some point in your life you will buy a car. The buying principles that were listed in Chapter 3 apply to this purchase, too. But there are some specific things you should be aware of as you shop for a car. The Checklist for Buying an Automobile on page 142 will help you.

Your choice of an automobile, like all other decisions, involves trade-offs. Here are the major trade-offs:

- Usually, the less gas an automobile burns, the smaller the engine. This makes it less costly to operate, but the car will accelerate more slowly.
- The newer the automobile, the more improvements it might already have compared to older ones. As a result, it will require fewer repairs in the immediate future. But it will cost you to obtain this benefit.
- The smaller the automobile, the more energy-efficient it is and the easier to park and turn. But, in general, in an accident, larger automobiles protect passengers better than smaller ones.

THE COSTS OF BUYING AN AUTOMOBILE

Buying a car involves opportunity costs. One is the amount of money (and time) spent shopping for the car. Another is the amount of money (and time) spent in actually purchasing the car. Because people are

These tips will help you in making a good choice of a new car or used car:

1. Ask friends and relatives about their satisfaction or dissatisfaction with their cars.

2. Read articles about different makes and models in car magazines such as *Car and Driver* and *Road and Track*.

3. Read *Consumer Reports* and *Consumers' Research Magazine* for their reviews of new automobiles. Read their reports on repair records of different models carefully.

4. Visit various dealers and read the material they hand out about their automobiles. Remember that these pamphlets are really advertising and promote the best features.

5. Personally inspect various makes and models.

6. Check what is covered by the service warranty for each make and model as you compare automobiles. Warranties may vary from manufacturer to manufacturer. If you are buying a used car that is only a year or two old, check to see if it is still covered under the original manufacturer's warranty. Also, some dealers offer their own limited warranties for used cars.

7. Once you decide on the particular make and model that you want, compare the prices offered by several dealers.

8. If you are buying an automobile off the lot rather than ordering one, check the options on the car and their prices. Options are the extra features and equipment on a car—such as air conditioning, stereo

faced with limited resources, most people have to take out a loan to buy a car. The costs of the loan are the interest, the down payment, and then the monthly payments on the principal. Interest is an important cost of buying an automobile on credit, but buying a car with cash has a cost, too. By paying cash, a person loses the ability to purchase other goods and services.

THE COSTS OF OPERATING AN AUTOMOBILE

As with other purchases, a consumer's responsibilities do not end with the purchase of the automobile, nor do the costs. Ongoing costs include: registration fee, normal maintenance, major repairs, depreciation, and insurance.

REGISTRATION FEE

The owner of an automobile must pay a state licensing fee, or a **registration fee,** to use the car. Usually, the fee must be paid annually. In most states, the amount of the fee varies depending on the car's age, weight, type, and value.

NORMAL MAINTENANCE AND MAJOR REPAIRS

The amount of normal maintenance—oil and filter changes and minor tune-ups—that an owner gives a car depends on the amount the

speakers, special paint, and so on—that you must pay for in addition to the basic price. If you do not want any of the options, such as white sidewall tires, you may be able to get the dealer to take some additional money off the price.

9. If you are buying a used car, have an automobile diagnostic (dy-uhg-NAHS-tik) center or a mechanic not connected with the dealer check it. Add to the dealer's price the cost of any repairs the mechanic thinks the car will need. This then becomes the real cost of the automobile to you.

10. Make sure the price given you includes federal excise tax and dealer preparation charges. **Excise** (EK-syz) **tax** is a tax on the manufacture, sale, or use within the country of specific products, such as liquor, gasoline, and automobiles. Dealer preparation charges cover the costs of taking a car as it arrives from the factory and preparing it to be driven away. This can include the costs of cleaning, installing certain options, and checking the car's engine. The price given by the dealer will not include state and local sales taxes. These will be added later.

11. Check various dealers for the reputation of their service departments. Your warranty usually allows you to take your car to any dealer selling that make of car. However, it may be most convenient to return for maintenance and repair work to the service department of the dealer who sold you the car.

12. Do not put a deposit on a car unless you are sure you are going to buy it. People sometimes have problems getting a deposit back if they change their minds.

car is driven and how carefully the owner chooses to maintain the car. Maintenance involves a trade-off. The more maintenance an owner gives a car, the better service it will give and the longer it will last. But the owner will have less money available for other things.

Major repairs are those that are unexpected and expensive. They include rebuilding the transmission and replacing the exhaust system. There is no way to guarantee that an automobile will not require major repairs while you own it. But there are ways to reduce the probability. As you read in the Checklist for Buying an Automobile, you should check the repair records of different cars before deciding on a particular make and model. If you are considering a used car, you should also take it to a diagnostic center, or have a mechanic check it.

One way to guard against having to pay for major repairs is to buy extended warranty coverage. New-car warranties protect owners for all major repairs except tune-ups and damage resulting from improper use of the automobile. But new-car warranties usually last only one or two years, or up to a certain limit of miles or kilometers. These warranties can often be extended for another one, two, or three years by paying additional money when the car is purchased. Sometimes dealers offer warranties for used cars as well, but usually for a limited period of time, such as 30 days, or you can purchase a warranty covering a longer period of time for a used car.

DEPRECIATION

Depreciation—a decline in value over time—takes place as an item wears out or becomes outdated. Age, obsolescence, and wear and tear cause a car to depreciate. Age is the major factor. A car loses value every year even if it is not driven. This is because an automobile is a consumer durable, and all consumer durables deteriorate, or become worse. Second, as new makes and models are produced, older models may not have as many features. Compared to newer models, they are not worth as much. This is related to obsolescence (ahb-suh-LES-ns), being out of date or out of style. Each year auto makers produce new models, making the previous year's models obsolete.

Physical wear and tear depends on how hard a car is driven, how many miles or kilometers it is driven, and how well it is maintained. The Department of Transportation publishes statistics on the average costs of operating an automobile for ten years. The largest cost is always for depreciation. For a standard car, it is $9,935 out of total costs of $29,000. For a subcompact it is $6,465 out of total costs of $23,200.

INSURANCE

A major cost of owning an automobile, especially for someone under 25, is insurance. Many states require that liability insurance be purchased before an automobile can be licensed. Insurance companies classify drivers in various ways, usually according to age, sex, and marital status. Depending on the category into which a person fits, he or she will be charged a certain amount that is different from that of someone in another category. These amounts are based on statistics that show that different types of drivers have different accident rates.

Young people almost always have to pay higher insurance rates. For example, single males in the 16—25 age group have the highest accident

deteriorate (di-TIR-ee-uh-rayt): become worse

Maintenance and repairs are part of the ongoing costs of owning a car. What are some other costs of driving your car?

Table 6-4: FACTORS AFFECTING AUTOMOBILE INSURANCE RATES

When you buy automobile insurance, the rate you are charged is determined, in addition to your age and sex, by the following:

1. The type of car you drive. Insurance companies consider the safety record of a car and the costs to repair it if it is involved in an accident.

2. Where you drive. If the rate of thefts and accidents is high in an area, the risk to the insurance company is greater. A city, for example, would have more thefts and accidents than would a rural area. Therefore, the rate the insurance company charges in a city will be higher.

3. What you use the car for. If you drive your car for business on a daily basis, the rate will be higher than if you use it only for errands and occasional trips.

4. Marital status. In general, married men and women have lower accident rates than single men and women and, therefore, pay lower insurance rates,

5. Safety record. If you have a history of accidents and traffic tickets, then you will be charged a high rate. Whether a new driver has had driver education is often considered in determining a rate.

6. Number of drivers. The number of drivers using a car increases the insurance rate. The age and sex of the drivers may further increase the insurance rate.

rate of all drivers. Not surprisingly, insurance companies charge these drivers the highest insurance rates. Married women 25–45 have the fewest accidents and are, therefore, charged the lowest rates. Table 6-4 on p. 145 shows factors in addition to age and sex that affect the insurance rates people pay. Insurance rates vary slightly, as insurance companies try to attract customers. Rates cannot vary much because states regulate the rates companies can charge within their borders.

REVIEWING ECONOMIC PRINCIPLES

1. According to the Checklist for Buying an Automobile, what steps would you take: **a.** to decide on the make and model you want? **b.** to choose the actual car you want? **c.** What special step would you take if you were buying a used car?

2. What are two costs of buying a car with a loan?

3. **a.** List costs involved in operating a car. **b.** Over which costs does a car owner have control? **c.** Over which costs has a car owner no control?

4. **Critical Thinking: Applying Information.** Based on the text and the table Factors Affecting Automobile Insurance Rates, which of the following drivers do you think would have the lowest insurance rate: Driver A: 21, female, single, drives a subcompact to school daily, no traffic offenses. Driver B: 30, male, married, drives a subcompact on weekends only, one traffic ticket. Driver C: female, 40, married, drives a full-sized car to work daily, no traffic offenses. What reasons do you have to support your choice?

SUMMARY OF
IMPORTANT PRINCIPLES

1
- The single-family home is the most expensive type of housing to buy and maintain. The economy of construction makes a town house less expensive to buy and maintain. A condominium is a single unit in an apartment building or in a series of town houses that is owned separately; common areas are owned by owners of the single units; ownership rights are similar to those in a single-family house except that repairs to common areas are decided by a majority of owners. Owners of cooperatives own equal shares in the company that owns the apartment building and the land on which it stands; they do not own their apartments but hold long-term leases; operating costs and real estate taxes are shared; individuals must get approval to remodel, sell, or rent. Mobile homes are the least expensive to buy.

2
- A household can determine how much it can afford to pay to buy housing by figuring monthly income for the first one-third of all mortgage payments, then estimate monthly housing expenses and first-year occupancy costs. Another way is to use the rules given on p. 131.

3
- Among a renter's rights are to: use the rental unit for the purpose stated in the lease, have privacy, withhold part of the rent to pay for repairs if the landlord does not make them within a reasonable amount of time. A renter's responsibilities include paying the rent on time, taking reasonable care of the property, telling the landlord if major repairs are needed, giving notice if leaving before the lease is up.
- A landlord's rights include limiting how an apartment may be used and being paid additional rent if a tenant is moving early. A landlord's responsibilities include: making sure apartments have minimum services, obeying building safety rules, making repairs.

4
- In deciding on a car, a consumer should: ask friends and relatives about their cars; read articles in car and consumer magazines; read advertising material; personally inspect various makes and models; check what is covered by the service warranty for each make and model; having decided on a particular make and model, compare prices from several dealers; if buying an automobile off the lot, check options to see if a better deal can be made; if buying a used car, take it to a diagnostic center or have a mechanic check it; make sure the price given includes federal excise tax and dealer preparation charges; check the reputation of various dealers' service departments; do not put a deposit down until sure about the choice.
- The costs of buying a car with a loan are the interest charge, down payment, and monthly payments on principal.
- The costs of operating an automobile include: registration fee; normal maintenance; major repairs; depreciation caused by age, obsolescence, and wear and tear; insurance.
- Five major types of auto insurance are bodily injury liability, property damage liability, medical, collision, and comprehensive physical damage. Homeowners insurance can protect a home against a wide range of possible disasters. Life insurance protects a family against the loss of an individual's income if that person dies.

Putting Economics to Work

DECIDING ON TRADE-OFFS: CHOOSING A PLACE TO LIVE

Maria Alvarez has been offered a new job in another city. She is preparing to move and has a decision to make. Maria has found an apartment not far from where she will work. The rent is high—almost half of her take-home pay—but she can walk to work and will not need a car. The apartment is also very small—one room with a kitchen and a bathroom attached. However, it is in a safe neighborhood near stores, restaurants, and theaters. Most other areas in the city that she would want to go to can be reached by bus.

Maria also has an offer from a friend for another place to live. The friend has suggested that she and Maria share a rented house that is a 40-minute drive from the city. The house is a two-story farmhouse with a large yard and garden. It is located in a rural area, near several other farms and a lake. The nearest store is four miles (about seven kilometers) away, and the nearest movie theater is in the city. Maria's share of the rent would be only half as much as the rent for the apartment in the city. However, moving to the farmhouse would mean that she would have to buy a car and take turns with her roommate driving into and out of the city each day.

1. What are two trade-offs in this situation that involve money? What are two trade-offs that involve personal values more than they do money?
2. What information can Maria gather to help her decide which of the trade-offs involving money is a better deal for her?
3. Which living situation seems the best to you? Why?

Readings in Economics

THE GOOD LIFE

Skill: Making Inferences

For a majority of American families, the good life involves owning one's own home. The idea of home ownership—the American dream—is explored in this excerpt by Dolores Hayden.

When Americans discuss the good life, they still speak about their hopes or their fears in terms of buying houses. Home ownership has not only symbolized a family's social status, but also guaranteed its economic security. The homeowner has been an owner-speculator, an identity acknowledged by one Florida developer who advertises his homes with the slogan, "To her, it's a nest; to him, a nest egg." The "nest egg" explains why Americans struggle to "climb the ladder of life from renter to owner." After years of mortgage payments to the bank (and substantial income tax deductions), some older homeowners have needed a speculative profit from the sale of the house to provide adequate retirement income. . . .

Because home ownership has been closely associated with an individual's tax position and retirement income, it has created a sense of progress through life for the two-thirds of American families who have managed to attain it. The process of entering the market has been a rite of passage for thirty-year-olds equipped with the savings, marriage, and children that make this choice seem logical. Ownership and intense participation in the culture of home have characterized the middle years of life. For the retirees who sell their houses, detachment from gender roles has come with age and the speculative bonus of leaving suburbia.

Of course, one-third of American families have never had a chance to participate in these rituals. The roots of this problem lie in the five groups of Americans that were excluded from home ownership in the late 1940s. First, white women of all classes were expected to gain access to housing through their husbands. Second, the white elderly working class and lower middle class, who were no longer wage earners in the prime of life. . . .

Third, minority men of all classes [who] were excluded from suburban home ownership. . . . Fourth, minority women of all classes. . . . Fifth, the minority elderly of all classes [who] were left in the central cities.

1. What economic and social benefits of home ownership appeal to Americans?
2. Why do you think that the five groups of Americans mentioned in this article never had a chance to own a home in the suburbs?

John Maynard Keynes, *General Theory of Employment, Interest, and Money.* Copyrighted by and reprinted by permission of Cambridge University Press.

DON'T BUY IF YOU'RE ON THE MOVE

Skill: Analyzing Information

Many costs must be considered when deciding whether or not to buy a house. In this reading, author and real estate appraiser John H. Denton recommends that you do not buy if you are not planning to stay in your home awhile.

The most obvious characteristic of real estate is that it can't be moved, and the dominant feature of the American family is that it is often on the move. This contradiction must be considered by every home purchaser. It is the first and perhaps the most important problem that the prospective home owner must face. Hurried sales of real estate usually result in a loss to the owner, and the costs of home ownership for a year or a year and a half are frequently greater than rent. Thus, it is best not to buy until you can look forward to a stay of two or more years, and it is probably best not to buy at all if you will have to sell in a hurry. With good luck a short-term owner or a hurried buyer will be able to keep his costs of home ownership at about what rent would be, but who can count on good luck? . . .

Costs of home ownership may be divided into two categories: those which are incurred only once and those which are incurred each year. The recurrent costs are as follows:

Town houses, like these in Columbia, Maryland, have become popular in many parts of the nation. Owners of town house condos have combined the advantages of home ownership with those of renting an apartment.

(a) Real estate taxes
(b) Repairs and maintenance
(c) Insurance
(d) Depreciation
(e) Interest . . .

The one-time costs of home ownership are largely those that are involved in the sale of the property. These will include:

(a) Broker's commission for selling
(b) Cost of title search or title insurance
(c) Lawyer's fee or escrow charges
(d) Transfer taxes, Internal Revenue Stamps, recording fees, service charges, etc. . . . .

Will you be moving in a year or two? If so, purchasing a home will probably result in a loss. The reason for this is that the costs of selling will raise the average monthly expenses of home ownership to a figure in excess of what rent would be for a similar house.

1. What are the two categories of the costs of home ownership? Give examples of each.
2. Why is it financially unwise to buy a home if you plan to move within two years?

John H. Denton, *Buying or Selling Your Home.* New York: M. Barrows and Company, 1961. pp. 6–12.

THE ECONOMICS OF RENTING
Skill: Defending Opinions

Traditionally, many Americans have accorded home renters an inferior status to home buyers. It is often assumed that those who rent do so because they can't afford to buy. The following reading points out that in some cases it makes more economic sense to rent rather than buy.

Homeownership has long been America's Holy Grail. From an investment viewpoint, it was close to a sure bet: Uncle Sam would subsidize mortgage payments, the home would appreciate nicely and the owner would get favorable tax treatment upon selling.

But times change—and so has the economics of homeownership. So much, in fact, that renting is becoming an attractive alternative for many people.

The slowdown in the meteoric rise of home prices during the 1970s is the key to this change. In most areas, the days of leveraging a small down payment into a quick profit are gone. Moreover, buying is discouraged by real interest rates

Readings in Economics

that remain high by historical standards. . . .

If you're willing to spend a few hours with a calculator, you can gauge whether it's better to buy or rent.

To start, figure all the costs of owning a home for a given period, say five years. That includes mortgage payments, taxes, insurance, utilities and repairs. From that, subtract anticipated tax benefits. Then, estimate how much you could get for the house if you sold it in five years, subtracting broker and closing costs. Assuming you've made a profit and you're not buying another home right away, capital-gains taxes must also be figured in.

Then, calculate the cost of renting a similar house. Include rent and utilities, making allowances for annual hikes and the foregone interest on any security deposit. As a renter, you won't have to make a down payment, so you should estimate what kind of after-tax return you could get by investing that money. Compare that income with your costs to determine the . . . tab for leasing.

If this sounds too daunting, Cornell University will do a computerized buy-rent analysis for $25. . . .

USN&WR [*U.S. News and World Report*] asked Cornell to look at one possible scenario: A family of four earning $45,000 buys a $100,000 home. It gets an $80,000, 30-year, fixed mortgage at 10.75 percent and puts $24,000 down. Property taxes and utilities come to $3,080 a year. The alternative is to rent the house for $600 a month and pay the monthly utilities of $140. Inflation is assumed to be 4 percent.

The computer's conclusion: Under these conditions, buying the home and then selling it after five years would be the financial equivalent of paying $903 a month to rent. That's considerably higher than the $740 it would cost . . . to lease.

1. List some of the reasons the author gives for renting instead of buying a home.
2. Even if it can be shown mathematically that renting costs less than owning a home, why do you think many Americans still view owning a home as more desirable?

Manuel Schiffres, "Renting a Piece of the American Dream." Excerpted from *U.S. News & World Report*, March 10, 1986. Copyright 1986, U.S. News and World Report.

CAR COSTS INCLUDE OWNING AND OPERATING
Skill: Classifying Information

SECTION 4 There are many costs involved in owning a car that are not immediately apparent to the prospective buyer. This reading lists these costs, broken down into two categories.

Soon these hundreds of shiny new cars will be sold to consumers. Many of these new car owners may not realize owning a car includes many costs, such as depreciation, repair, and maintenance, they had not counted on.

Most owners think of costs only in terms of outlays for gasoline, oil, tires, and tolls. A more careful examination shows that some costs occur whether or not the vehicle is driven, while others are directly related to the amount of travel. The travel-related group is generally referred to as operating costs and the other group as ownership costs.

Ownership Costs. Ownership costs include depreciation, insurance, registration and titling fees, scheduled mainenance, and any taxes applied to these items. No matter how little a vehicle is driven, some portion of each of these items is incurred.

Depreciation is the loss in value of the vehicle during its lifetime due to the passage of time, its mechanical and physical condition, and the number of miles it is driven. . . .

Insurance Costs are determined by the amount and type of coverage selected, the purpose for which the vehicle is used, and the location in which it is operated. . . .

Registration and Titling or Sales Taxes are payments to the State in which the vehicle is registered. The registration fee customarily is due each year, and the titling or sales tax is due only once—when the vehicle is purchased. . . .

Scheduled Maintenance includes the services shown in the owner's manual. Generally, the suggested maintenance intervals are expressed in miles driven or period of time owned. The services include maintenance of the emissions control and cooling systems, oil changes, safety checks, tune-ups, and lubrication. . . .

Accessory Costs cover the value of any add-on feature for a car or van which has no effect on its mechanical operations. These items customarily include extra wheels for snow tires, protective floor mats, seat covers, and miscellaneous items such as litter containers. . . .

Finance Charges may be approximated with relative ease. Most vehicle buyers either pay interest on money they borrow to buy their vehicles, or they forego interest they would have earned if they elect to use savings or other investments to pay for their vehicles outright. . . .

Operating Costs. Operating costs include repairs and maintenance, gasoline, oil, tires, parking, tolls, and the taxes applied to these items. These costs are each a function of vehicle usage.

Unscheduled Repairs and Maintenance services include such items as brake shoes, carburetor overhaul, shock absorbers, and ball joints. Also included are smaller, but no less important items such as fan belts, light bulbs, wiper blades, and washing and waxing. Some of these repairs and replacements must be made more than once in the life of the vehicle.

Gasoline is a major cost item for vehicles of all sizes. The difference in gasoline costs alone between the 1981 large-size car and the subcompact over the lives of the vehicles is $3,380. . . . The difference between the large and compact car is striking, when considering the large car provides only 15 percent more interior space for the 40 percent larger fuel cost.

Oil costs for a new or relatively new vehicle are mainly dependent on the car manufacturer's instructions for oil changes, because little, if any, oil is burned in these vehicles. . . .

Parking and Tolls include metered curb parking, fees charged in parking lots, and toll charges for using private or public highways, tunnels, and bridges.

Taxes on gasoline and oil are the primary component of operating cost taxes. These taxes are paid to the government on a per-gallon basis. . . .

1. Fixed costs are those that are constant and do not vary. Variable costs change and may increase or decrease. What analogy can be made between fixed costs and variable costs and ownership costs and operating costs of an automobile?
2. The article states that the difference in fuel cost between a large car and a compact car is striking when you consider that the larger car provides only 15% more space for a 40% larger fuel cost. Do you think the additional space is worth the cost? Why or why not?

"What Does It Cost to Own a Car?" *Consumer's Research Magazine*, July 1983, pp. 16–18.

PRACTICING YOUR WRITING SKILLS: WRITING A PARAGRAPH

As you read in Chapter 1, being able to locate main ideas and supporting details is important to understanding what you read. When you write, you can use main ideas and supporting details to make your material clear and interesting. In writing, however, the main idea is called the topic sentence. The topic sentence states what your paragraph is about and the supporting details explain it. Often, the topic sentence is the first sentence of a paragraph, but it may be placed anywhere in the paragraph. All details should be presented clearly and simply. Often, words such as *first, then, next, most important, the following* are used to list details. A good paragraph also has a concluding sentence to summarize ideas.

Later in this book, you will be asked to write essays and research reports and to organize material for speeches. Being able to write a good paragraph will be very helpful because paragraphs are the foundation of all longer writing.

Activity: Choose one of the following topics and write a paragraph about it. Try to build your paragraph to use at least three supporting details. You may make the first sentence the topic sentence or write it into the middle or end of the paragraph.

1. The Advantages to Renting Housing

2. The Advantages to Owning Housing

3. Why a Car Depreciates

VOCABULARY REVIEW

Write the letter of the definition in Column B that correctly defines each term in Column A.

Column A	Column B
1. equity	a. pays for bodily injury or property damage
2. depreciate	b. provides insurance protection during a certain period of time
3. term life insurance	c. to decline in value over time
4. liability	d. amount of money invested in property minus debts such as mortgage
5. closing costs	e. fee charged by lender for paperwork, taxes, and other necessary activities

PRACTICING YOUR ECONOMIC SKILLS

1. **Writing a Letter of Complaint.** The sample letter in Chapter 3 for handling a consumer problem can be used for a tenant's complaint, too. Suppose you have a window that has been leaking for two months and the superintendent has not fixed it, although you have called five times. Adapt the letter to show this.

2. **Determining a Safe Debt Load.** Suppose you have an annual salary of $21,000 and pay 15 percent in taxes. Your annual expenses for food are $4,620 and those for clothing, $1,260. You are carrying a debt load of $985. Using the form for determining a safe

Monthly Payment Required to Amortize (pay off) a loan at 9.75%

TERM		1 Year	5 Years	10 years	15 Years	20 Years	25 Years	30 Years
Amount	$100,000	8779.97	2112.43	1307.71	1059.37	948.52	891.14	859.00

Monthly Payment Required to Amortize (pay off) a loan at 10.25%

TERM Amount		1 Year	5 Years	10 years	15 Years	20 Years	25 Years	30 Years
	$100,000	8803.23	2137.03	1335.40	1089.96	981.65	926.39	896.11

debt load on p. 89 to determine how much more debt you can safely take on?

3. Use the amortization tables on these two pages to do the following exercises.
   a. How much will the monthly payments be on a $100,000 loan for 30 years at 9.75% interest? What is the total cost of the loan?
   b. How much will the monthly payments be for a $100,000 loan for 30 years at 10.25% interest? What is the total cost of the loan?
   c. What would be the effect on consumers of an increase in home mortgage interest rates to 14% and 15%?
4. **a.** Compute the total cost of a $12,500-car for which you pay $1,500 down and finance for four years at 5% interest. In addition to these costs, your yearly registration fee will be $250.00 and your automobile insurance will be $500.00. **b.** What other costs can you expect to pay while you own the car?

DISCUSSING ECONOMIC QUESTIONS

1. The American Dream for many people is to own a home. From an economic point of view, do you think it is wiser to buy rather than rent a home? Remember that mortgage payments are usually larger than rent payments. How will Americans feel about this?
2. Most Americans depend on cars for local transportation. Do you think this will still be true in 50 years? What things would have to happen for mass transit to replace private autos for local use for most Americans?
3. Why do some states require drivers to carry personal injury insurance and property damage liability insurance?

APPLYING CRITICAL THINKING SKILLS

1. **Researching Housing Statistics.** In the library, look up the section of the most recent Census of Housing entitled *Selected Housing Characteristics by States and Counties.* Make a table listing the following statistics for your state, the county you live in, and two nearby counties: number of total housing units; number of year-round housing units (those used throughout the year); number of units occupied by owners; number occupied by renters.
2. **Understanding Warranties.** Borrow a copy of a car warranty from a friend or relative, and check what is covered under the 12-month or 12,000-mile section if the car is new. If the warranty is for a used car, see what, if anything, is covered. Make notes to use as the basis for a class discussion on car warranties.
3. **Doing Research.** Select one type of insurance plan discussed in the chapter. Find out about this plan by collecting pamphlets and insurance forms from local insurance brokers. Write a summary of the plan and present your findings to the class.

READINGS

Hartman, Chester. *Housing & Social Policy.* Englewood Cliffs, N.J.: Prentice-Hall, 1975.
"How to Rent a Car." *Consumers' Research Magazine,* April 1982, pp. 19–20.
Sherman, D. "Some Numbers You Can Trust, Others You Can't." *Car and Driver,* April 1982, p. 21. Misleading data in ads.

CHAPTER 7

Most Americans save and invest some of their income. The decisions they make about ways to save their money and to invest it in stocks and bonds can help increase their income, now and in the future.

SAVING AND INVESTING

The first four chapters of this unit have dealt with ways to spend money wisely. This chapter describes ways to save and invest it. You will learn about different plans for saving and the trade offs for each. The differences between stocks and bonds are explained as well as the way they are bought and sold. Special retirement plans, life insurance, and real estate as forms of savings and investment are also described. The chapter ends with a discussion of the facts to consider in deciding how to save and invest. Learning Economic Skills will help you understand how interest is figured so you will receive the most return on your money.

CHAPTER OBJECTIVES After you study the section of this chapter, you will be able to:

1 • explain the purpose of saving income.
  • explain the trade-offs involved in different types of savings plans.

2 • describe the difference between saving and investing.
  ★ explain the difference between simple and compound interest.
  • contrast the differences between stocks and bonds.
  • describe how stocks and bonds are bought and sold.
  • list the advantages of mutual funds for investors.
  • describe the purpose of securities laws.

3 • state the tax benefits of a Keogh or an IRA plan.
  • describe how straight life insurance can be used as a form of savings.
  • state the trade-off involved in investing in real estate.

4 • list the decisions that must be made in saving and investing one's money.

ECONOMICS VOCABULARY

saving
interest
passbook savings account
statement savings account
NOW account
money market account
maturity
certificate of deposit (CD)
simple interest
compound interest
stock
stockholder
dividend
bond
tax-exempt bond
savings bond
Treasury bill
Treasury note
Treasury bond
common stock
corporation
preferred stock
over-the-counter market
capital gain
capital loss
mutual fund
money market fund
Keogh Plan
Individual Retirement
  Account (IRA)

Suppose you have a part-time job that pays you $60 a week and you want to buy a stereo that costs $240. As your monthly income equals the price of the stereo, how will you be able to get enough money to buy the stereo and pay your other monthly expenses? An adult could charge the stereo, but as a dependent you probably have no credit rating. You will have to save the money. Economists define **saving** as the nonuse of income for a period of time so that it can be used later. You may already be setting aside some of your income for some future use.

dependent (di-PEN-duhnt): someone supported by another person

1 | WHY SAVE?

Ask yourself as you read:
- What are the major ways of saving money?
- What types of savings institutions are available?

Any saving that you do now may be only for purchases that require more money than you usually have at one time. When you are self-supporting and have more responsibilities, you will probably save for other reasons. For example, you may save to have a source of money in case of emergencies, such as losing your job, and for your retirement. Most Americans who save do so for these reasons. Saving evens out a person's ability to spend throughout his or her lifetime. Figure 7-1 shows the rate of personal saving in recent years.

The saving of any individual benefits the economy as a whole. This saving provides money for others to invest or spend. Additional savings also allow businesses to expand, which provides income for consumers. Extra income makes a higher standard of living possible.

Generally, when people think of saving, they think of putting their money in a savings bank or a similar institution where that money will earn interest. In Chapter 4, you read that interest is the payment a person must make to obtain credit. The payment people receive when they lend money—allow someone else to use their money—is also called **interest.** A person receives interest on his or her savings account or similar savings plan for as long as there is money in the account.

WHERE TO PUT YOUR SAVINGS

There are many places and ways to invest your savings. The most common places are commercial banks, savings and loan associations, savings banks, and credit unions. Before depositing your money, you should investigate the different types of financial institutions in your area and the services they offer. Each institution usually has several types of savings plans, each paying a different interest rate. In comparison shopping for the best savings plan for you, you need to consider the trade-offs. Some savings plans allow you immediate access to your money, but pay a low rate of interest. Others pay higher interest and allow immediate use of your money, but require a large minimum balance.

access (AK-ses): right to use

Figure 7-1: PERSONAL SAVING EXPRESSED AS A PERCENTAGE OF DISPOSABLE INCOME, 1978–1987

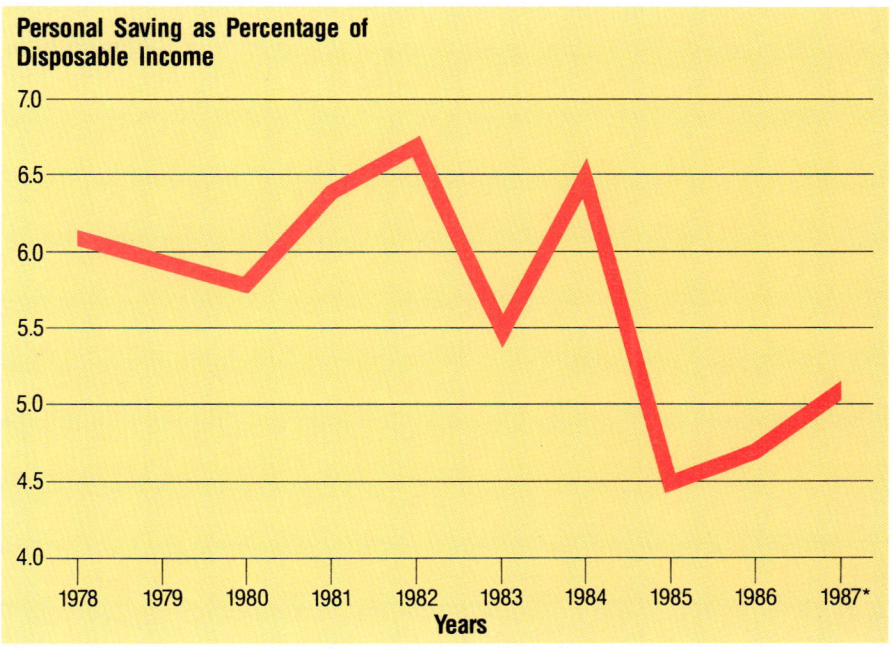

Personal Saving as Percentage of Disposable Income

Years

Source: *Survey of Current Business,* Bureau of Economic Analysis
*Estimate

In 1978 Americans saved about 6.1 percent of their disposable income. In 1985 the figure was only 4.5 percent. Why?

SAVINGS ACCOUNTS

Passbook savings accounts are also called regular savings accounts. With a **passbook savings account,** the depositor receives a booklet in which deposits, withdrawals, and interest are recorded. A customer must present the passbook each time one of these transactions, or business operations, takes place. A **statement savings account** is basically the same type of account. However, instead of a passbook that must be presented for each transaction, the depositor receives a monthly statement showing all transactions. The chief appeal of these accounts is that they offer easy availability of funds. You can usually withdraw money at any time without paying a penalty, that is, forfeiting any money. But there is a trade-off. The interest paid on these accounts is low compared to the interest on other savings plans. Savings accounts are called share accounts at credit unions.

A **NOW account** combines the benefits of both checking and savings accounts. NOW stands for Negotiable Order of Withdrawal. By using a NOW account, you earn interest on any unused money in your account. Although a NOW account allows you the convenience of writing checks, it is not the best way to save. Until 1986, the interest rate for NOW accounts was set by law at 5¼ percent. After that time, the federal government no longer regulated the interest that could be paid on accounts. Banks and other institutions now are free to pay whatever rates

transaction (tran-ZAK-shuhn): single act in a business process

negotiable (ni-GOH-shuh-buhl): something that can be transferred to another

157

they think will attract the most customers and still allow them to make a profit. NOW accounts, however, still pay low interest compared to that for other savings plans. This will be the trade-off between a depositor's being able to have his or her funds quickly without paying a penalty and still earn interest. Because of the low interest rate, it may be wise to keep as little money as possible in a NOW account. Since January 1983, banks and savings institutions have offered Super NOW accounts paying high rates of interest. However, at most banks the account must be at least $2,500, although the minimum balance can vary from institution to institution.

Money market deposit accounts (MMDAs) are another type of account paying high rates of interest and allowing immediate access to money. The trade-off is that these accounts also have a $1,000 to $2,500 minimum balance requirement. Customers can usually make withdrawals from a money market account in person at any time, but are allowed to write only three checks a month against the account.

TIME DEPOSITS

The term **time deposits** refers to a wide variety of savings plans that require a saver to leave his or her money on deposit for a certain period of time. The period of time is called the **maturity,** and may vary from 7 days to 8 years or more. Time deposits are often called **certificates of deposit** (CDs) or savings certificates. They state the amount of the deposit, the maturity, and the rate of interest being paid. The amount of deposit and interest rates vary widely. Some CDs, particularly those paying higher interest, require a minimum deposit. The minimum may be as small as $250 or as large as $100,000. CDs at credit unions are called share certificates.

Time deposits offer higher interest rates than passbook or statement savings accounts. The longer the maturity is, the higher the interest rate that is paid. For example, a CD with a short-term maturity of 90 days pays less interest than a CD with a two-year maturity. But there is a trade—off for this higher interest rate and that trade—off is the longer maturity period. Savers who decide to cash a time deposit before maturity pay a penalty.

Financial institutions also offer a number of special CDs. One example is the Small Savers Certificates. Their rates are tied to the current interest rates the federal government pays on certain types of borrowing that it does.

Most savings institutions in the United States are insured by one of several federal agencies. This means that each depositor's money is insured up to $100,000. If an insured bank or other institution fails, each depositor will be paid the full amount of his or her savings up to $100,000. Table 7-1, Different Types of Savings Institutions, lists the federal agencies that insure each type of institution. The table will also help you compare the various places where you can save your money. Keep in mind that different institutions may offer different rates on the

Table 7-1: DIFFERENT TYPES OF SAVINGS INSTITUTIONS

Institution	Savings Services Offered	Insured by	Number of Institutions	Amount of Savings and Time Deposits (in billions)	
Commercial banks	NOW accounts, Super NOW accounts, Passbook and statement savings accounts, Certificates of deposit, Money market accounts	Federal Deposit Insurance Corporation (FDIC)	15,000	$801.4	
Savings and loan associations	NOW accounts, Super NOW accounts, Passbook and statement savings accounts, Certificates of deposit, Money market accounts	Federal Savings and Loan Insurance Corporation (FSLIC)	4,500	566.8	
Savings banks	NOW accounts, Super NOW accounts, Passbook and statement savings accounts, Certificates of deposit, Money market accounts	Federal Deposit Insurance Corporation* (FDIC)	442	195.3	
Credit unions	Share drafts** Share accounts Share certificates	National Credit Union Share Insurance Fund	20,000	105.4	

*Some insured by FSLIC.
**Interest-earning account similar to checking account; pays higher interest than NOW accounts.

same type of savings. Or they may use different methods for figuring interest. Some savings institutions are not insured, or they carry private insurance. Those who put their money in these institutions run a higher risk of losing their funds if the institution fails.

REVIEWING ECONOMIC PRINCIPLES

1. Write a sentence defining the following economics terms: **a.** interest, **b.** passbook savings account, **c.** statement savings account, **d.** NOW account, **e.** money market deposit account, **f.** maturity, **g.** certificate of deposit.
2. What is the purpose of saving money?
3. **Critical Thinking: Applying Principles.** What is the trade-off involved in each of the following types of accounts: **a.** passbook and statement savings accounts? **b.** NOW accounts? **c.** CDs? **d.** money market accounts?

Table 7-2: COMMON STOCK AND PREFERRED STOCK

Common Stock	Preferred Stock
1. **Common stock** is issued by all corporation; it is the stock most often bought and sold. A **corporation** is an organization owned by many people but treated by the law as though it were a person: it can own property, pay taxes, make contracts, sue and be sued, and so on.	1. Many corporations do not issue **preferred stock.**
2. Holders of common stock have voting rights in a corporation. As a group, they elect the board of directors.	2. Holders of preferred stock have no voting rights.
3. Common stock pays dividends based on a corporation's performance. If the company does well, dividends may be high; if it does poorly, the dividends may be low.	3. Preferred stock pays a fixed dividend. This amount must be paid before holders of common stock receive any dividends. If a company is unable to pay a dividend on time, it must usually make up the missed payment at a later date.
4. Value of common stock rises and falls in relation to the corporation's performance and what investors expect it to do in the future.	4. Value of preferred stock changes in relation to how well the company is doing.
5. If a corporation fails, holders of common stock are the last to be paid with whatever money is left after paying all creditors.	5. If a corporation fails, holders of preferred stock must be paid before any holders of common stock.

2 | INVESTING: TAKING RISKS WITH YOUR SAVINGS

Ask yourself as you read:
- What are stocks and bonds?
- What are the major ways of investing?

People usually distinguish between saving and investing. People have savings plans because they want a sure, fixed rate of interest. However, if people are willing to take a chance on earning a higher rate of return, there are various ways they can invest their money, such as stocks and bonds. It is usually impossible, however, to get a higher rate of return without taking some risk. Of course, the very nature of risk implies that such investment may yield a lower rate of interest, too.

STOCKS

Stock, or shares of stock, entitles the buyer to a certain part of the future profits and assets of the corporation selling the stock. The person buying the stock, therefore, becomes a part owner of that corporation.

By issuing stock, a company obtains funds for use in expanding its business and, it hopes, in making a large profit. Table 7-2 describes the two types of stock that a corporation can sell. You will read more about ways to finance business operations in Chapter 11.

issue: to offer new stock for sale

Stockholders—owners of stock—make money from stock in two ways. One is through **dividends,** the money return a stockholder receives on the money he or she invested in the company.

The corporation may declare a dividend at one or more times during a year. However, dividends are paid only when the company makes a profit. The other way people make money on stock is by selling it for more than they paid for it. Some people buy stock just to speculate (SPEK-yuh-layt). That is, they buy stock hoping that the price will increase greatly so they can sell at a profit. They do not buy it for the dividends.

BONDS

Instead of buying stock, people with money to invest can buy bonds. A **bond** is a certificate issued by a company or government in exchange for borrowed money. It promises to pay a stated rate of interest over a stated period of time, and then to repay the borrowed amount in full at the end of that time. In other words, a bondholder lends money for a period of time to a company or government and is paid interest on that money. At the end of the period, the full amount of borrowed money is repaid. The period of time is called the bond's maturity.

Unlike buying stock, buying a bond does not make a bondholder part owner of the company or government that issued the bond. The bond

Stockholders in a corporation receive stock certificates like these. Why is owning a share of stock a form of saving?

Learning Economic Skills

UNDERSTANDING INTEREST

As you have read in this chapter, people save for different purposes. But one reason for putting savings into a financial institution is to increase that money by earning interest. There are two types of interest: simple and compound. Figuring interest is similar to figuring percents.

SIMPLE INTEREST

Simple interest is figured only on the original amount deposited, not on any interest earned. For example, $100 in a savings account paying 6 percent simple interest will earn $6 interest (.06 × $100) the first year. The account's balance at the end of the year will be $106—the original amount plus the first year's interest. The second year the interest will also be $6 even though the account has grown. The total amount in the savings account at the end of the second year will be $112 ($100 + $6 + $6). The account will continue paying $6 in interest year after year, despite the accumulated interest.

Practicing Your Skills

1. What is the simple interest paid in the second year on $50 at 5½ percent?
2. What is the total savings at the end of the second year for $50 saved at 5½ percent simple interest?
3. How much interest will $250 earn over three years at 7 percent simple interest?

COMPOUND INTEREST

With **compound interest,** interest is paid on the original amount deposited plus any interest that has been earned. If you deposit $100 in an account earning 6 percent interest compounded annually, it will earn $6 the first year and $6.36 (.06 × $106) the second year. With compound interest, your savings the second year will amount to $112.36 ($100 + $6 + $6.36).

The difference between simple and compound interest may seem small, but over a long period of time, or with large sums of money, the difference can be quite large. For example, if you keep $100 in an account that pays 6 percent simple interest for 15 years, the account will grow to $190 at the end of that time. On the other hand, if you keep the $100 in an account paying 6 percent interest compounded annually, it will grow to $239.70 in the same amount of time.

The rate at which interest is compounded is also important in deciding on a savings plan. The sooner interest is added to your account, the sooner it begins earning more interest. In the example above, the interest was compounded annually. That is, at the end of each year the interest earned was added to the account. In reality, many financial institutions compound interest on savings accounts more often. They may compound interest semiannually (twice a year), quarterly (every three months) or daily.

For example, suppose a bank is paying 6 percent interest on an account compounded semiannually. Another way of stating this is to say the bank is paying 3 percent interest on the original amount and the accumulated interest every six months. If $100 is in the account, it will earn $3 during the first six months (.03 × $100) and $3.09 during the second six months (.03 × $103). The account at the end of the year will total $106.09. In the same way, if the account was compounded quarterly, it would pay 1½ percent every 3 months.

Instead of paying $6.09, your account would pay $6.13. The additional $.04 may not seem like much. However, multiplied by several thousand dollars and over a long period of time, the additional interest could be considerable. Interest can also be compounded daily. Then it would pay ⅟₃₆₅ of 6 percent each day.

As you might imagine, it would be very slow and difficult to figure compound interest far into the future without the help of a compound interest table. The table below is based on $1 compounded at different interest rates and for different periods of time. To figure interest compounded annually, find the column with the correct percentage figure for your account at the top, and then read down the row at the left to find the correct number of years. Once you have found these two factors, read down the column and across the row to locate how much $1 will grow at that rate during that time period. Multiply this number by the amount in your account to find how much your savings have grown. For example, $1 at 8 percent interest compounded annually for 3 years will grow to $1.26. If you have $200 in this account, your total will be $252 ($200 × 1.26).

You can also use the table to figure interest compounded more often than annually. Each compounding counts as one time period. Suppose in the example above you save $200 for 3 years at 8 percent interest compounded quarterly instead of annually. Remember, this is the same as paying 2 percent on the account every three months.

To figure your interest, read down the column marked 2 percent, and across the row marked 12 (the number of 3 month periods in 3 years). That $1 will grow to $1.278 in this time, so $200 will grow to $254.

Practicing Your Skills

1. What is the interest paid in the second year on $50 compounded annually at 8 percent?
2. What is the interest paid in the second year on $50 compounded quarterly at 8 percent?
3. If you had $350 deposited in a savings bank that paid 6 percent interest compounded semiannually, how much would you have in your account after seven years?
4. If you had $2,500 in a 91-day certificate of deposit paying 12 percent simple interest, how much interest will your money have earned when the certificate of deposit matures?

Compound Interest Table for $1

Period	1%	2%	3%	4%	5%	6%	7%	8%	9%	10%	11%	12%	13%	14%	15%	16%	17%	18%
1	1.01	1.02	1.03	1.04	1.05	1.06	1.07	1.08	1.09	1.10	1.11	1.12	1.13	1.14	1.15	1.16	1.17	1.18
2	1.02	1.04	1.06	1.08	1.10	1.12	1.15	1.17	1.19	1.21	1.23	1.25	1.28	1.30	1.32	1.35	1.37	1.39
3	1.03	1.06	1.09	1.13	1.16	1.19	1.23	1.26	1.30	1.33	1.37	1.41	1.44	1.48	1.52	1.56	1.60	1.64
4	1.04	1.08	1.13	1.17	1.22	1.26	1.31	1.36	1.41	1.46	1.52	1.57	1.63	1.69	1.75	1.81	1.87	1.94
5	1.05	1.10	1.16	1.22	1.28	1.34	1.40	1.47	1.54	1.61	1.69	1.76	1.84	1.93	2.01	2.10	2.19	2.29
6	1.06	1.13	1.19	1.27	1.34	1.42	1.50	1.59	1.68	1.77	1.87	1.97	2.08	2.20	2.31	2.44	2.57	2.70
7	1.07	1.15	1.23	1.32	1.41	1.50	1.61	1.71	1.83	1.95	2.08	2.21	2.35	2.50	2.66	2.83	3.00	3.19
8	1.08	1.17	1.27	1.37	1.48	1.59	1.72	1.85	1.99	2.14	2.31	2.48	2.66	2.85	3.00	3.25	3.52	3.80	4.11	4.44
9	1.09	1.20	1.31	1.42	1.55	1.69	1.84	2.00	2.17	2.36	2.56	2.77	3.00	3.25	3.52	3.80	4.11	4.44
10	1.11	1.22	1.34	1.48	1.63	1.79	1.97	2.16	2.37	2.59	2.84	3.11	3.40	3.71	4.05	4.41	4.81	5.23
11	1.12	1.24	1.38	1.54	1.71	1.90	2.11	2.33	2.58	2.85	3.15	3.48	3.84	4.23	4.65	5.12	5.62	6.18
12	1.13	1.27	1.43	1.60	1.80	2.01	2.25	2.52	2.81	3.14	3.50	3.90	4.34	4.82	5.35	5.94	6.58	7.29
13	1.14	1.29	1.47	1.67	1.89	2.13	2.41	2.72	3.07	3.45	3.88	4.36	4.90	5.49	6.15	6.89	7.70	8.60
14	1.15	1.32	1.51	1.73	1.98	2.26	2.58	2.94	3.34	3.80	4.31	4.89	5.54	6.26	7.08	7.99	9.01	10.15
15	1.16	1.35	1.56	1.80	2.08	2.40	2.76	3.17	3.64	4.18	4.79	5.47	6.25	7.14	8.14	9.27	10.54	11.97

Table 7-3: DIFFERENCE BETWEEN STOCKS AND BONDS

Stocks	Bonds
1. All corporations issue or offer to sell stock. That act is what makes them corporations.	1. Corporations are not required to issue bonds.
2. Stocks represent ownership.	2. Bonds represent debt.
3. Stocks do not have a fixed dividend rate (except preferred stocks).	3. Bonds pay a fixed rate of interest.
4. Dividends on stock are paid only if the corporation makes a profit.	4. Interest on bonds must always be paid, whether or not the corporation earns a profit.
5. Stocks do not have a maturity date. The corporation issuing the stock does not repay the stockholder.	5. Bonds have a maturity date. The bondholder is to be repaid the value of the bond.
6. Stockholders (except those with preferred stock) can elect a board of directors, who control the corporation.	6. Bondholders usually have no voice in or control over how the corporation is run.
7. Stockholders have a claim against the property and income of a corporation only after the claims of all creditors (including bondholders and holders of preferred stock) have been met.	7. Bondholders have a claim against the property and income of a corporation that must be met before the claims of any stockholders, including those holding preferred stock.

becomes part of the debt of the corporation or government, and the bondholder becomes a creditor. Table 7-3 lists some of the other differences between stocks and bonds.

Local and state governments also sell **tax-exempt bonds.** This means that the interest on this type of bond, unlike bonds issued by companies, is not taxed by the federal government. Interest that you earn on bonds issued by your own city or state is also exempt from city or state income taxes. Tax-exempt bonds are good investments for wealthier people who would otherwise pay high taxes on interest earned from investments.

The most common type of bond issued by the federal government is the United States savings bond. **Savings bonds** are sold for less than their stated value. When redeemed at maturity, they are worth their purchase price plus interest. If a bondholder does not cash in a bond at maturity, it will continue to earn interest. However, the rate may not be as high as for some CDs. The low price of savings bonds—as little as $25.00—is attractive to people with limited money to invest. In addition, the interest is exempt from state and local income taxes. You also put off paying federal income tax on the interest until the bonds are cashed in. The interest on savings accounts, on the other hand, is taxed each year.

The Treasury Department also sells several types of larger investments. **Treasury bills** mature in anywhere from three months to one year. The minimum amount of investment for Treasury bills is $10,000. **Treasury notes** have maturity dates of two to ten years, and **Treasury bonds** mature in ten or more years. Notes, bonds and bills are sold in minimums of $1,000 or $5,000. The interest on all three is exempt from state and local income taxes, but not from federal income tax.

STOCK AND BOND MARKETS

If you decide to buy stocks or bonds, you will have to use a broker. A broker is a person who acts as a go-between for buyers and sellers. There are thousands of brokerage firms throughout the country that buy and sell daily for ordinary investors.

Stocks are bought and sold on stock markets. The largest is the New York Stock Exchange (NYSE) in New York City. The second largest is the American Stock Exchange (AMEX), also in New York. The stocks listed on these two exchanges account for over 90 percent of the market value of all stocks listed on exchanges in the United States. In addition to the New York and American exchanges, there are supplemental stock exchanges and regional exchanges. For example, there is the Midwest Stock Exchange in Chicago. Another large exchange is a national exchange, the National Association of Securities Dealers Automated Quotations (NASDAQ) National Market. Stocks must be listed to be sold on all of these exchanges. That means that a corporation offering stocks for sale must prove to the exchange that it is in good financial condition and engaged in legal business. Most of the companies traded on stock exchanges are among the larger corporations.

Stocks can also be sold on the **over-the-counter market.** Unlike stock exchanges, there is no actual place where over-the-counter stocks are traded. Brokerage firms hold quantities of shares of stock that they buy and sell for investors. The stocks of smaller, lesser-known companies are traded in this way. For example, assume that XYZ Corporation is a small company that sells computers. If you wanted to buy stock in it, you would check the stock market listings in your local newspaper. In the table of over-the-counter stocks, you would find XYZ Corporation, the number of shares of stock sold the day before, and the price at which shares were bought and sold that day. You would then call a broker and tell him or her to buy so many shares. Usually stocks are sold in amounts of 100 shares. Some brokers will handle smaller amounts. The largest volume of over-the-counter transactions occur through NASDAQ, which publishes price lists for various types of stock.

The New York Stock Exchange Bond Market and the American Exchange Bond Market are the two largest exchanges. Bonds are also sold over-the-counter. United States government bonds are sold this way.

CAPITAL GAINS AND LOSSES

Suppose a person buys stock at $20 a share and sells it for $30. That profit of $10 per share is called a **capital gain.** The person has had an

Figure 7–2: AVERAGE YIELD ON STOCKS AND BONDS, 1976–1986

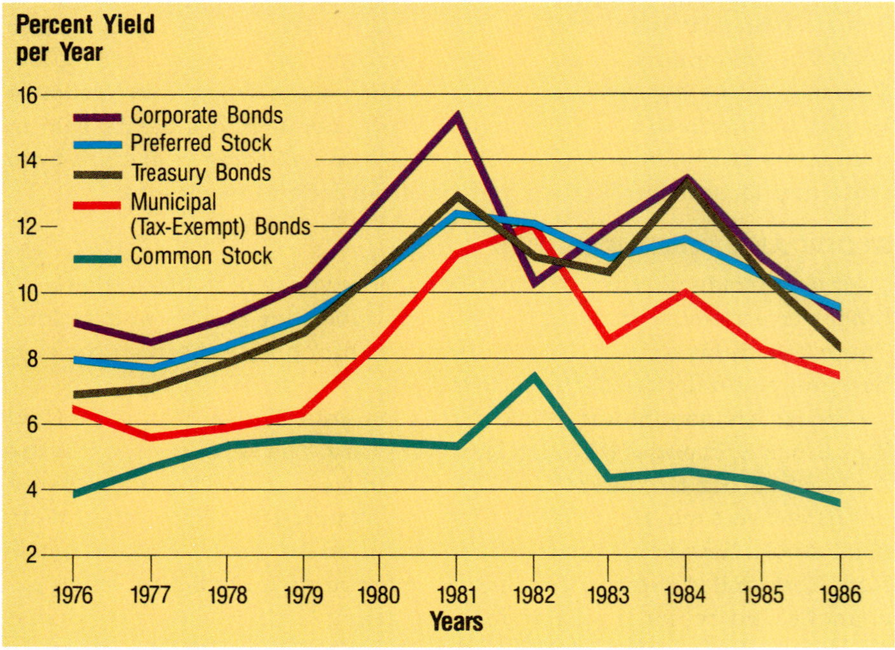

Source: Board of Governors of the Federal Reserve System

The term *average yield* means average return on investment. According to this graph, which type of investment has had the highest yield over the 10-year period shown? Which involves the highest risk?

increase in his or her capital, or wealth, of $10 a share. Of course, the value of stock may also fall. If a person decides to sell stock at a lower price than he or she paid for it, that person suffers a **capital loss.** Money may be made or lost on bonds in much the same way. Capital gains and losses are important. They tell you how wise your investment was, which may be useful information for future investing. Figure 7-2 shows the average annual yield for various types of stocks and bonds.

MUTUAL FUNDS: AN EASY WAY TO INVEST

One of the easiest ways to invest in stocks and bonds is to participate in a mutual fund. A **mutual fund** is an investment company that pools the money of many individuals to buy stocks or bonds or other investments. By putting savings into a mutual fund, an individual usually is able to purchase a little bit of a large number of stocks or bonds. Ordinarily, this would be difficult because most people have limited savings.

Mutual funds have several other important advantages for investors with only a small amount of money. One is that the risk of losing money from a poor investment is decreased. Most mutual funds hold a variety of stocks or bonds. Losses in one area are likely to be made up by gains in another. You do not have to try to outguess investors yourself. Professionals with experience in the stock or bond market make decisions about how to invest the fund's money. In addition, various mutual funds buy different types of investments. This allows you to choose the fund that best meets your needs. Some funds invest in stocks that are likely to increase rapidly in value, some in stocks and bonds that pay high dividends and interest, and some in tax-exempt bonds.

One type of mutual fund, called a **money market fund,** uses investors' money to make short-term loans to businesses and banks. Most money market funds allow investors to write checks against their money in the fund. Any check, however, must be above some minimum amount, usually $500. Of course, in writing a check against your account, the total value of your account is reduced. You then earn money only on the amount left in your account. As you read earlier in the chapter, banks, savings and loan associations, and savings banks now offer a similar service, called money market accounts. A major advantage of these accounts is that they are insured against loss by the federal government. Mutual funds and money market funds are not insured.

REGULATING SECURITIES AND EXCHANGES

The securities market is heavily regulated today, both at the state and federal levels. The Securities and Exchange Commission (SEC), created by the Securities Exchange Act of 1934, is responsible for administering all federal securities laws. It has regulatory authority over brokerage firms, stock exchanges, and most businesses that issue stock. It investigates any dealings between or among corporations, such as mergers, that affect the value of stocks.

securities: another name for stocks and bonds

The Securities Act of 1933 was passed to avoid another stock market crash like that of 1929. The act requires that all essential information concerning the issuing of stocks or bonds be made available to the investors. This is done through a registration statement filed with the federal government. A briefer description called a prospectus must be given to each potential buyer. It lists the amount offered, the price, and the use that the company plans to make of the money raised by the stock or bonds. Mutual funds must also distribute a prospectus describing the fund and the way in which the money will be invested.

Today states also have securities laws. These are designed mostly to prevent schemes that would take advantage of small investors.

REVIEWING ECONOMIC PRINCIPLES

1. Define these terms: **a.** stock, **b.** dividends, **c.** bond, **d.** tax-exempt bond, **e.** savings bond, **f.** Treasury bill, **g.** Treasury note, **h.** corporation, **i.** over-the-counter stock, **j.** capital gain, **k.** mutual fund, **l.** money market fund.
2. Why would some people prefer to save their money in a savings plan rather than invest it in stocks and bonds?
3. What are the advantages and disadvantages of mutual funds?
4. What is the job of the Securities and Exchange Commission?
5. **Critical Thinking: Expressing Opinions.** Based on the table on page 164, write a paragraph explaining why you would choose to either own stock in a company or the company's bonds.

Case Study

SAVINGS AND THE NATION'S ECONOMY

People save money for many different reasons—for their education, for retirement, for emergencies. There have been many incentives to save in recent years—lower tax rates, low inflation, and lower mortgage rates. Yet, in the early 1980s Americans' savings averaged only 5.3 percent of their disposable income, the lowest figure since the 1940s. The mid-1980s saw a slight increase with savings averaging around 7 percent. But most economists agree that these are very low rates and that the economy of the United States would benefit if more people saved more money. Why? What are the benefits of a high savings rate?

A country's savings are the ultimate source of its investment, and investment is the ultimate source of jobs, economic growth, and rising living standards. Americans' failure to save more of their income has meant that in the United States net investment in plant and equipment has fallen in real terms. And with the government's gigantic annual budget deficit, saving is even more important than ever. Without sufficient savings, the government must rely on attracting capital from overseas to finance the deficit. In fact, the Japanese hold around $100 billion in United States securities. The Japanese people also support their own government's spending with an incredible history of savings.

For years the Japanese people have saved at a rate nearly two times the United States' savings rate. They save for the same reasons that United States citizens do, but the Japanese also have greater incentives to save. In Japan individual tax rates are very low by international standards. This encourages workers to save, and they save heavily because most of them have no guaranteed pensions. Japan's famous "lifetime employment"

system often ends at age 55, when the worker retires and receives a modest lump-sum payment.

The major result of Japan's savings tradition is that Japan has become a world economic leader, with surplus funds to pour into overseas investments at an increasing rate.

Why do Americans save less than the Japanese and the people of other industrialized countries? Many hypotheses have been offered to explain this fact. These range from many Americans' need for instant gratification—which accounts in part for the high consumption rate in the United States—to the ease with which Americans can borrow money. Some economists point to Social Security as the cause. Because Americans can count on Social Security in retirement, they do not save as much for their retirement as people like the Japanese who have much more modest retirement plans.

What can or should be done to encourage increased savings? There are many answers but none that most economists agree would be effective. Government policy can, of course, make savings as attractive as possible. Thus, government can adopt policies such as tax reform that encourage savings. In the end, however, Americans will save at their own rate for their own reasons.

1. How do Americans compare with the Japanese in the rate at which they save?
2. Why are savings important to a nation's economy?

This woman is consulting a financial advisor to help her work out an investment plan. What are some investment choices she faces?

3 | SPECIAL SAVINGS PLANS

Ask yourself as you read:

- What kinds of pension plans are there for retirement?
- Are the purchase of life insurance and real estate wise choices for the future?

As you read earlier in this chapter, one of the reasons that people save is to have income to spend when they retire. In addition to their savings, most Americans have additional sources of income for the years after they stop work.

RETIREMENT PLANS

Many individuals have company retirement plans called **pension plans** that provide for retirement income. Also, most people are eligible for, or able to receive, Social Security payments when they reach retirement. Nevertheless, many people choose to save and invest in private retirement plans.

eligible (EL-uh-juh-buhl): qualified, having what is required

A major benefit of a private or personal pension plan is the tax saving. You do not have to pay federal income tax *immediately* on the earned income that you invest in one of these retirement plans, or on the interest that the plan earns as long as it does not exceed a certain amount. However, should you need to take money out of the plan early, you have to pay a tax penalty. Otherwise, you pay income tax only as you withdraw money from the plan at retirement. Because your income will in all probability be less then, your tax rate will be lower.

INDIVIDUAL PENSION PLANS

The Keogh (KEE-oh) Act of 1972 was passed to help self-employed people, such as small business owners, doctors, lawyers, and accountants, set up their own pension plans. The **Keogh Plan** allows a person to set aside a maximum of 15 percent of income up to $9,500 a year.

A newer approach to retirement plans is the **Individual Retirement Account** (IRA). A person can contribute up to $2,000 of his or her earnings per year to an IRA. Each year's contribution can be made in a lump sum or in installments. A married couple, if both husband and wife are working outside the home, can contribute up to $4,000 a year. If only one spouse is working outside the home, the amount allowed is $2,250. As in pension plans, you pay income tax only when you withdraw money from IRA and Keogh Plans at retirement. The Tax Reform Act of 1986 put some restrictions on IRA contributions. If you are already in a retirement plan, or if your income is over a certain amount, you may not be able to have an IRA.

LIFE INSURANCE AS A FORM OF SAVING

You have already read about buying insurance in Chapter 6. Besides providing benefits in case of the insured's death, straight life insurance can also provide a savings plan. The premiums for straight life are higher than those for the same amount of term insurance coverage. This is the savings aspect and is known as the policy's cash value.

The insurance company will pay the cash value if, at any time, the insured wants to cancel his or her policy. Many people cash in their straight life policies when they retire, taking the cash value either as a lump sum or in installments. These are the living benefits of a straight life policy because the policy holder, rather than his or her survivors, receives them. In any one year, more than 70 percent of all insurance payments are in the form of living benefits.

The rate of return on this type of savings plan is often less than what a person could get from savings institutions. That is, the interest rate paid on the cash value of a straight life policy is low. When buying life insurance, an individual might consider buying term insurance in the amount of coverage desired and then putting into savings the difference between the premiums for term insurance and for the same amount of straight life insurance. Remember that this is only a suggestion. The decision of what to save and how much is up to each individual.

REAL ESTATE AS AN INVESTMENT

Buying real estate, such as land and buildings, is another form of investing. For the past 20 years or so, an investment in one's own home, condominium, or co-op has often proven to be wise. Resale values have soared at times, especially during the late 1970s. Beginning in the early 1980s, however, the growth in the price of housing slowed in some areas. In some places real estate values fell for a few years. Buying raw, or undeveloped, land is a much riskier investment. There is no guarantee that there will be a demand in the future for a particular piece of land. This is true for housing, too, but most people do not buy housing to sell it.

Real estate, either as raw land or developed land, is not very easy to turn into cash on short notice. Sometimes property stays on the market for long periods of time. This is one of the trade-offs involved in investing in real estate. You cannot get your money as quickly as if you had invested in stocks, bonds, a CD, or other savings plans.

REVIEWING ECONOMIC PRINCIPLES

1. What are the tax benefits to owning a Keogh Plan or an IRA?
2. How do some people use straight life insurance as a form of savings?
3. **Critical Thinking: Evaluating Choices.** What are the disadvantages and advantages to investing in real estate?

4 | DECISION MAKING: PLANS, GOALS, AND PROBLEMS

Ask yourself as you read:
- What decisions does a person make in determining how much to save?
- Which investments involve the most risks?

At the beginning of this chapter, you read about the different reasons that people save. Saving involves a trade-off like every other activity. The more you save today means the more you can buy and consume a year from now, 10 years from now, or 30 years from now. However, you will have less to spend today. The decision about the percentage of income to save depends on the following factors:
- How much are your fixed expenses?
- What are your reasons for saving?
- How much interest can you earn on your savings and, therefore, how fast will they grow?
- How much income do you think you will be earning in the future?

Older Americans who have retired from their jobs have leisure time for sports and community affairs. How do their earlier investing and saving decisions affect their lives?

This last point is very important. There is less reason for a person to save a large percentage of today's income if he or she expects to make a much higher income tomorrow. In that case, it would be better to wait until the future to start a large savings plan. That does not mean that a person should not save at all until he or she has a large income.

Once you, or anyone, have decided to save part of your income, you must decide where to put your savings. But before you can make this decision, you must decide:

- How important is it that your savings be easily available in case you need immediate cash?
- What degree of risk are you willing to take?
- Will your standard of living at retirement depend largely on your accumulated savings?

AMOUNT OF RISK

These are difficult questions to answer because there are so many ways to save and invest, as this chapter points out. Perhaps the most important factor to consider is risk. The amount of risk that you are willing to take with your savings can determine your choice of investment.

Perhaps the most risk-free investment is an insured passbook savings account. Certainly, a Certificate of Deposit (CD) is relatively risk free. A slightly riskier investment is a mutual fund that invests in bonds issued by businesses. Why is this riskier? The market value of those bonds could fall. Some of the companies might go out of business and not be able to repay the bonds at maturity. In both cases, the value of your shares in the mutual fund would fall. You could also invest your savings in the stock or bond market directly. Here, you are taking the most risk. The market value of stocks can rise and fall dramatically and so, too, can the value of your investment. A possibility would be to spread risk among several types of investments, putting a lesser amount in the more risky methods. That way you would have some security with your savings and have some money available should you need cash in a hurry. You would also have a chance of making high returns. But the decision is up to each individual.

REVIEWING ECONOMIC PRINCIPLES

1. **a.** On what three factors does the decision about how much income to save depend? **b.** Which factor is the most important?
2. What is the most important factor to consider in deciding where to put one's savings?
3. **Critical Thinking: Applying Economic Principles.** Based on the text, how would you invest $20,000? Would you split it among several savings plans or put it all into one investment? Explain your reasons in a paragraph.

SUMMARY OF
IMPORTANT PRINCIPLES

1
- People save to have a source of money in case of emergencies and for retirement.
- Some savings plans allow immediate access to a saver's money, but pay low interest. Others pay a high rate of interest, but usually require that a saver's money be tied up for a long period of time. Others pay a higher rate of interest and allow immediate access to money, but require a large minimum balance.

2
- Simple interest is figured only on the original amount deposited, not on any interest earned. Compound interest is paid on the original amount plus any interest earned. The method used for figuring interest can make a significant difference in the amount of interest earned over a period of time or with large amounts of money.
- Stocks have the following characteristics: ownership of the corporation that issued the stock; no fixed dividend rate (except with preferred stock); payment of dividends only if the corporation makes a profit; no maturity date and, therefore, no payment in full of the cost of buying the stock; right to elect a board of directors (except with preferred stock); claim against property and income of the corporation after all creditors' claims have been met.
- Bonds have the following characteristics: ownership of a company's debt; payment of a fixed rate of interest; payment of interest regardless of whether a profit is made; maturity date and, therefore, repayment in full of the borrowed money; no voice in or control over how the corporation is run; claim against the property and income of the corporation that must be met before the claims of any stockholders.
- Stocks and bonds are sold on stock and bond exchanges.
- By putting savings into a mutual fund, an individual can purchase shares of a large number of stocks or bonds or other investments. Because of their number and variety, the risk of losing money from a poor investment is decreased.
- The Securities and Exchange Act of 1934 created the Securities and Exchange Commission. It regulates brokerage firms, stock exchanges, and businesses issuing stock. The Securities Act of 1933 requires essential information concerning the issuing of stocks or bonds be filed with the federal government. State securities laws are designed mostly to prevent schemes that would take advantage of small investors.

3
- Federal income tax is not paid immediately on the earned income that is invested in a Keogh Plan or IRA or on the interest they earn. A saver pays income tax when the money is withdrawn at retirement.
- The premiums for straight life insurance are significantly higher than for the same amount of term insurance coverage. This is the savings aspect and is known as the policy's cash value.

4
- In considering a savings plan, a person first has to decide about the percentage of income to save. Then a person has to decide where to put his or her savings. The amount of risk one is willing to take can determine the choice of investment.

Putting Economics to Work

DECISION MAKING: SAVINGS PLAN

Jamal Thomas is saving for college. Jamal has been working since his freshman year in high school and is now a senior. He had kept his savings in a passbook savings account that he had opened at a commercial bank located near his home. Then one day he noticed in the newspaper an advertisement for a Savings and Loan association. It was offering a higher passbook interest rate. That started him thinking that maybe he was making a mistake.

Jamal started checking. He found that Savings and Loan Associations (S & Ls) were paying higher interest rates on savings accounts. He also found that he could have put his savings in a one-year CD at his own bank and earned more than a percentage point higher than the interest rate he received on his passbook account.

After doing some more comparison shopping, Jamal decided to withdraw $2,000 from his savings and purchase a one-year CD from a local Savings and Loan association. He was almost certain that he would not need any of his savings for cash until he actually went to college. He calculated that at the end of the year he could save about $27 more for his college education fund with the CD than with the passbook account.

1. What other alternatives are available to Jamal for saving his money?
2. How much risk is involved in the alternatives?
3. Which seem best suited to Jamal's needs?

EIGHT REASONS TO SAVE
Skill: Organizing Information

 John Maynard Keynes, one of the most influential economists of all time, studied patterns of consumption and saving in the economy. In this reading from his book published in 1936, he lists the reasons why people save.

There are, in general, eight main motives or objects of a subjective character which lead individuals to refrain from spending out of their incomes:

1. To build up a reserve against unforeseen contingencies;
2. To provide for an anticipated future relation between the income and the need of the individual or his family different from that which exists in the present, as, for example, in relation to old age, family education, or the maintenance of dependents;
3. To enjoy interest and appreciation [increase in value], *i.e.* because a larger real consumption at a later date is preferred to a smaller immediate consumption;
4. To enjoy a gradually increasing expenditure, since it gratifies a common instinct to look forward to a gradually improving standard of life rather than the contrary, even though the capacity for enjoyment may be diminishing;
5. To enjoy a sense of independence and the power to do things, though without a clear idea or definite intention of specific action;
6. To secure a [fund] to carry out speculative or business projects;
7. To bequeath a fortune;
8. To satisfy pure miserliness, *i.e.* unreasonable but insistent inhibitions against acts of expenditure as such.

These eight motives might be called the motives of Precaution, Foresight, Calculation, Improvement, Independence, Enterprise, Pride, and Avarice; and we could also draw a corresponding list of motives to consumption such as Enjoyment, Shortsightedness, Generosity, Miscalculation, Ostentation, and Extravagance.

1. Savings has been defined as "delayed consumption." Which of the eight motives offered by Keynes relate to delayed consumption?
2. Keynes offers 8 motives for saving and 6 motives for consumption. Organize these motives into columns labeled SAVINGS and CONSUMPTION, with each pair of entries representing opposite motives. (*Hint:* After making 6 pairs, you will need to suggest two additional motives for consumption.)

John Maynard Keynes, *General Theory of Employment, Interest, and Money.*

HOW WALL STREET GREW IN IMPORTANCE
Skill: Drawing Conclusions

 Wall Street in New York City is immediately associated with America's largest stock exchange, the New York Stock Exchange. This reading tells some of the history of this famous American institution.

The new United States in 1789 was desperately short of money in any reliable or secured form. Accounts were still kept in pounds, shillings, and pence. But the creation of the national debt led to a money market. When Congress authorized the issue of $80 million worth of government bonds to fund that debt, those securities established a market.

In the beginning it was a haphazard one [market]. Brokers, or stockjobbers as they were first called, did their business out on the street, retiring to nearby coffee houses when the weather turned bad. They bid for and sold United States government bonds and the stocks offered by the new Bank of the United States. Speculation was feverish, and the marketability of securities was always questionable. . . .

On May 17, 1792, a band of twenty-four merchants and brokers met to bring some order into the market. They gathered under a buttonwood tree at a curbstone on Wall Street in New York City and signed a simple agreement written out on both sides of a single sheet of paper. It read: "We, the Subscribers, Brokers for the Purchase and Sale of Public Stocks, do hereby solemnly promise and pledge ourselves to each other that we will not buy or sell, from this day, for any person whatsoever, any kind of Public Stock at a less rate than one-quarter per cent Commission on the Special value, and that we will give preference to each other in our negotiations." It was negative and tentative in tone, but the "buttonwood compact" changed the securities market from a catch-as-catch-can auction, where real values were all but impossible to ascertain, into a nearly viable exchange.

The following year, the buttonwood signers moved indoors in the newly built Tontine Coffee House. Business did not increase for years. . . .

In 1817 the market became formalized with a constitution and the name "New York Stock & Exchange Board." There was an initiation fee of $25 and a penalty of expulsion for selling fictitious securities. . . .

The Stock Exchange moved in 1865 to new quarters at No. 11 Wall Street, only a few steps from where the buttonwood agreement had been signed, and completed its present Roman Renaissance building at the same location in 1903.

1. What effect did the "buttonwood compact" have on the stock market?
2. For more than eighty years the New York Stock Exchange has been located in the same building at 11 Wall Street in New York

City. What beneficial effect might this have on the public's image of the Stock Exchange?

REAL ESTATE—A UNIQUE INVESTMENT
Skill: Comparing and Contrasting Information

Several aspects of the real estate market make it very different from other investment markets. In this reading author Chris Mader describes how real estate investors have gotten by without the intense analysis that other investors use.

Real estate is the largest investment market, exceeding the value of stocks, bonds, commodities, or savings. Yet each property is unique, and comparable data on profitability and risk are sparse. Investors have had to rely heavily on experience, judgment, and intuition. They still do. But increasingly, professionals and part-timers are seeking a better approach to investment analysis. The successes of the past did not have to contend with the problems of today [1975]: 10 percent mortgage rates, 15 percent construction loan interest, inflation, shortages, environmental impact studies, changing population and transportation patterns.

Ironically, real estate investing has been the subject of surprisingly little research and analysis. Stock market investing, by contrast, has been statistically analyzed for decades. And since 1960, when the first large-scale, computer-readable, stock price files were compiled, thousands of comprehensive studies have enumerated its rate of return, risk, liquidity, diversification, and so on. . . .

In contrast with real estate, the market for stocks is centralized, publicized, and standardized. Three million investors own shares of A.T.&T. that are exactly identical. Their price and trading volume can be checked daily in the local newspaper. And financial disclosure of operating results, as mandated by law for any publicly owned company, is prompt and detailed.

In 1850 the New York Stock Exchange was a busy but still modest-sized market where shares of stock were traded.

Instead, real estate investors have enjoyed decades of unscrutinized, but profitable, anonymity—bringing to mind the story about the unspectacular student who returned to his class reunion as a very successful restauranteur. When asked how he had made out so well, he replied, "I buy steaks for $1 each and sell them for $3, so I make 2 percent on every one." Something had made his investment profitable, but it certainly wasn't his analysis. Real estate investors have often enjoyed a similar kind of success. Overall, their record can be described by the kid writing home from camp, who said, "We are all having fun here, but we don't know how much."

1. What are the similarities and differences between the real estate market and the stock market?
2. What is wrong with the restauranteurs's logic in relating his success at his class reunion?

Chris Mader, *The Dow Jones-Irwin Guide to Real Estate Investing*. Homewood, Illinois: Dow Jones-Irwin, © 1975.

WHO ARE THE FINANCIAL PLANNERS?

Skill: Drawing Conclusions

 **An increasing number of Americans are turning to financial planners for saving and investment advice. In the following reading, such financial services are evaluated. The conclusions are based on the findings of two *Consumer Reports* reporters who, posing as husband and wife, consulted with seven financial planning firms for financial advice.**

The growing field has gone virtually unregulated. The Council of Better Business Bureaus alleges that con artists operating under the guise of financial planners have defrauded consumers to the tune of $90 million in the last three years. Right now, anyone can hang out a shingle calling himself or herself a "financial planner." . . .

There are three kinds of planners: those who sell only financial plans and refer their clients to others who sell financial products; those who charge for their plans and also sell on commission some or all of the products they recommend; and those who don't charge for the plans but earn their living from commissions on the financial products the plans recommend.

Planners may be independent and work out of an office at home, or they may be affiliated with large, well-known companies and work out of a skyscraper on Wall Street. Some planners are lawyers or accountants who write financial plans as a sideline. They hope you'll also send your tax or legal business their way.

You can also buy financial plans from insurance companies or brokerage firms. In some cases, you sit down with a planner and chat face to face about your financial needs. In others, you fill out a questionnaire and get your plan back in the mail.

Just as there is no typical financial planner, there is no typical fee arrangement. Some planners charge for their time—anywhere from $50 to $200 an hour. Others charge fixed fees—so much to write the plan, so much to implement it, so much for an annual review. Still others are paid according to a percentage formula—a percentage of the client's earned income, for example. Financial plans can cost anywhere from a pittance to several thousand dollars. . . .

Though most of the plans we looked at contained some useful features, on balance we thought that none of the mass-marketed plans available for less than $500 represented a good value. People of moderate assets, we think, would usually be better off reading up on personal finance subjects and doing their own planning than using a plan from a mass-market financial services firm. Plans prepared by independent planners may well be better. However, since we didn't systematically evaluate them, we can't say. Perhaps in the future, as the number of planners increases, the quality of plans available for a moderate cost will improve. Meanwhile, we advise consumers to beware of salespeople in planners' clothing.

1. Differentiate among the three kinds of financial planners by the services they offer.
2. Explain why the financial-planning industry should be regulated.

Consumer Reports, January 1986, pp. 37–44.

PRACTICING YOUR COMMUNICATION SKILLS: DISCUSSION

During this course you have undoubtedly been participating in class discussions, as you probably have been since you first began school. You may not think about it, but any time you have a conversation with someone about a specific topic, you are taking part in a discussion, too. However, you may not be getting as much out of discussions or contributing as much as you might. Below are some tips to help you become an effective discussant (dis-KUHS-nt).

- If you are going to participate in a class discussion, be sure you are prepared. Read your assignment so that you have something to contribute.
- Be open-minded. Although you have probably formed some opinions ahead of time, you should not have made up your mind about the issue.
- Be willing to share your ideas and opinions. Everyone has something to contribute because everyone's viewpoint is unique.
- Respect the opinions of others. Everyone has a right to his or her ideas.
- Do not make disagreements personal. It is all right to disagree with another's ideas, but not with the person.
- Be clear in expressing your ideas when you speak.
- When listening, try to distinguish between the main argument and side issues. Concentrate on the main argument.
- If you agree with the person speaking, listen for additional information that will support your opinion.
- If you disagree with the person speaking, listen carefully to his or her point of view and the reasons used to support it. In that way, you will be able to argue against that view more effectively when it is your turn.

Activity: Practice these tips the next time you are part of a discussion, and see if you find that you contribute more ideas more effectively. If you have difficulty with one particular item on the list, concentrate on working on that in the next discussion.

VOCABULARY REVIEW

For each of the following terms, write a sentence using the term: maturity of a bond, preferred stock, over-the-counter market, compound interest, simple interest, common stock.

PRACTICING YOUR ECONOMIC SKILLS

1. **Analyzing Graphs.** The line graph below shows how $100 will grow at five different

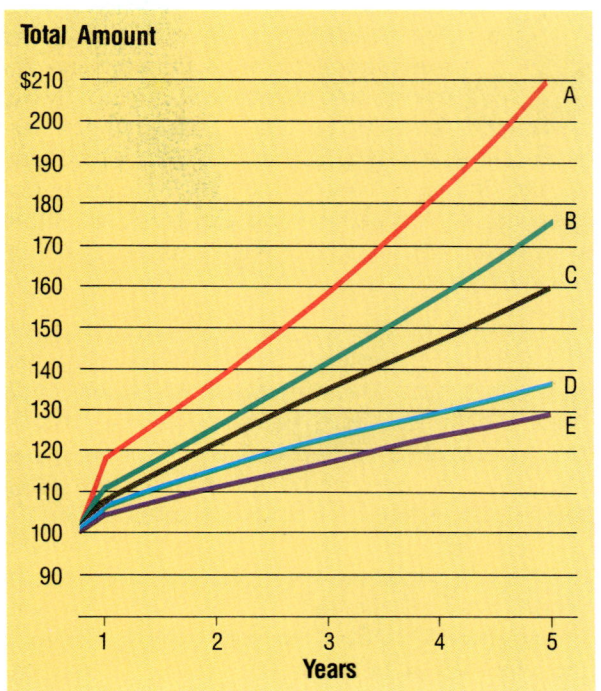

How $100 Grows at Various Rates of Interest

rates of annually compounded interest. Use the compound interest table on p. 163 to answer the following. **a.** Which curve represents an interest rate of 5 percent? **b.** Which curve represents an interest rate of 12 percent? **c.** Between which two curves would a curve based on 9 percent interest be drawn?

2. **Drawing Line Graphs.** Using the compound interest table on p. 163, create a line graph similar to the one on p. 178. Draw one line on the graph to show how $100 will grow over 15 years at 8 percent annually compounded interest. Draw another line to show how the same amount of money will grow during that period at 8 percent simple interest. a. What is the difference in the shape of the two curves? b. What causes this difference?

3. **Creating a Table.** Use the material in this chapter to create a table comparing these investments: passbook savings accounts, NOW accounts, Super NOW accounts, money market accounts, CDs, common stocks, bonds, tax-exempt bonds, U.S. savings bonds, mutual funds. Include the following information for each type of investment: possible return on investment (how much investors can expect to make); access to money (how easily investors can get their money); and amount of risk (how much chance is there of losing the original investment).

DISCUSSING ECONOMIC QUESTIONS

1. There are many different reasons why people save and many different savings plans they can use. What reasons would be best suited to short-term investments like savings accounts? What purposes would be best suited to longer-term methods such as CDs?

2. Most teenagers have a limited source of income. Should they nonetheless put a small amount of what they earn or are given in a savings account? Why or why not?

APPLYING CRITICAL THINKING SKILLS

1. **Researching Financial Services.** With your class, decide on several different types of financial institutions in your area and then divide into groups. Visit one of the institutions and find out about the services offered and rates of interest on the different savings plans. Use this information to make a table comparing services.

2. **Doing Research.** Using newspaper or magazine articles from 1980, research the provisions of the Depository Institutions Deregulation and Monetary Control Act. Then write a one-paragraph description of one way in which the act affects banks.

3. **Gathering and Analyzing Information.** Choose two stocks on the New York or American stock exchange, and follow their prices for two weeks in the financial pages of a newspaper. You will need to read only the last columns of figures. Note the daily closing prices, and then make a line graph showing the stocks' performance over the two weeks.

READINGS

Brown, Betty J., and Clow, John E. *General Business: Our Business and Economic World.* Boston: Houghton Mifflin, 1982. Savings accounts, insurance, and investing in stocks and bonds, real estate, and other investments.

Gupta, U. "How to Read the Financial Pages." *Black Enterprise*, April 1982, p. 27.

Heilbroner, Robert, and Thurow, Lester. *Economics Explained.* Englewood Cliffs, N.J.: Prentice-Hall, 1985. Chapter 6, "Savings and Investing."

Ruby, Linda. "How to Pick a Mutual Fund to Match Your Money Needs." *Woman's Day*, 1 September 1982, p. 14.

Thoryn, Michael. "Good News for the Economy: IRAs Are Off to a Running Start." *Nation's Business*, June 1982, pp. 49–52.

ISSUE 2

HOW MUCH CREDIT IS TOO MUCH?

After you study this Issue, you will be able to explain why Americans in general abuse the use of credit.

> bankruptcy
> asset
> inflation

The use of credit has long been a part of the American economy. The ability to borrow money to buy land, build homes, and create farms and factories helped the United States to expand. Credit continues to fuel the nation's economic growth. However, many economists, businesspeople, and private citizens believe that Americans are using too much credit.

Total personal debt in the United States has more than doubled since 1975. At the same time, many people who once considered themselves well off are filing for **bankruptcy.** They find themselves no longer able to pay their debts based on the amount of income they receive. Personal bankruptcies rose from 224,352 in 1975 to 338,213 in 1985. They rose at an even faster rate during 1986.

Why are so many Americans taking on too much debt? Economists list several reasons. Among them are the effects of inflation on the economy, the ease with which people can obtain credit, and Americans' habits of consumption.

THE EFFECTS OF INFLATION

During the 1970s, inflation began a rapid rise and it continued during the first part of the 1980s. **Inflation** is the prolonged increase in the general price level of goods and services. While inflation drove up prices, it also drove up the money value of goods and property. For example, a house that was worth $66,000 in 1978 was worth $80,000 a year later. Each year that inflation rose, Americans were able to borrow more against the increased value of their **assets**—all items of value such as housing, cars, jewelry, and so on.

Because the dollars used to make loan repayments were worth less and less as inflation rose, people were eager to borrow while inflation was high. They knew that the same amount of dollars today could not buy the same amount of goods as it had yesterday. For example, in 1978, $66,000 could buy a particular house. A year later, $66,000 would buy a smaller house. Inflation made the goods people purchased, whether home, car, or health club membership, seem like a great buy because their replacement cost kept rising year after year. Also, in a time of high inflation, people tend to go into debt because they pay back the debt with dollars that are worth less than they were when borrowed. The increase in prices also means that if an item such as a house can be sold at the inflated price, the sellers will receive a profit.

EASY CREDIT

In Chapter 4, you read about the steps in applying for credit. No doubt it seems difficult to you now to obtain a bank loan or credit card, and it is true that establishing a credit rating can be difficult. Creditors want to be reasonably sure that borrowers will be good credit risks.

For many Americans, the fastest way to attain luxuries, represented here by lobster dinners and diamonds, is through the use of credit cards and other means of borrowing. What problems might such over-use of credit cause?

Once a person has established credit, however, getting new credit is not very difficult. In fact, people receive applications for credit cards and charge accounts without asking for them. Most car dealers can arrange financing at the same time a person agrees to buy a car. Owners trying to sell their homes will often arrange special mortgage deals to help buyers finance the purchase.

These temptations can be difficult to resist. Part of the problem with the overuse of credit is the eagerness of lenders to extend credit. They may push customers into spending beyond their ability to pay by offering too easily available credit.

HABITS OF CONSUMPTION

Many of the people who find themselves in bankruptcy court would never have thought of themselves as poor. They are members of the middle class with good incomes. Often both husband and wife work outside the home. What may have once been considered luxuries have become necessities to them. Because such couples know they have good incomes and good credit ratings, they may carelessly assume more debt than they can afford. Sometimes people, especially those with many charge accounts and credit cards, lose track of just where their money is going and how much they owe. Suddenly, they find themselves with a high debt load.

IS CREDIT GOOD OR BAD?

Credit can be good for both borrower and lender. As you read in Chapter 4, by using credit a consumer has the immediate use of goods or services without having to wait to save enough to pay for them. Lenders—whether department stores, banks, or finance companies—profit by charging interest. Using credit to buy consumer goods benefits the economy because it stimulates the production of more goods. Increased production creates more jobs.

The overuse of credit, on the other hand, hurts both the individual and the national economy. Savings are necessary if the economy is to grow. Too much consumer credit puts a drain on personal savings. Banks use savings to finance loans to business and agriculture.

Individuals who find themselves in debt over their heads can get help from counseling services and from their banks. With care, they can limit their use of credit to buying the real necessities— food, shelter, and clothing—while working out repayment plans with their creditors. Prevention, however, is easier than the cure.

Discussing Economic Questions

1. Based on what you have read in this unit, what preventive measures can consumers take when planning their use of credit?
2. When inflation rises, creditors increase the interest rates. Why? Do you think that rising interest rates would put a brake on consumers' use of credit? Consider the influence of inflation on repaying debts.

UNIT 3

MARKETS, PRICES, AND BUSINESS COMPETITION

In Unit 1, you learned some of the basic principles of economics. Unit 2 showed you how those principles affect your decisions primarily as a consumer. In this unit, you will learn how consumer decisions fit into the market economy of the United States. Through a study of the topics of supply and demand, types of business organizations, and perfect and imperfect competition, you will learn more about the workings of the American economy. The Issue in this unit will help you understand the relation of free enterprise to big business.

CHAPTER 8

The supply of any product—the quantity available—and the demand for the product by consumers help determine its price. A surplus of wheat or factory goods, or a shortage of snow at a ski resort affect the market for these items.

SUPPLY AND DEMAND

Occasionally, you may hear a news report or read an article about the damage some storm or spell of cold weather has caused a particular crop, such as oranges. The report often says that this damage will result in higher prices to the consumer. This cause-and-effect relationship is an example of the way the laws of supply and demand operate in the real world. This chapter examines these principles and how they affect you as a producer and consumer. Learning Economic Skills describes demand and supply schedules and demand and supply curves. These are special types of tables and graphs.

CHAPTER OBJECTIVES After you study the sections of this chapter, you will be able to:

1 • describe how voluntary exchange is the basis of a market economy.
  • list three factors that affect price and quantity demanded.
  ★ explain what demand schedules and demand curves show.

2 • explain why there is an elastic demand for some goods and an inelastic demand for others.
  • contrast change in quantity demanded and change in demand.

3 • list three factors that cause a change in demand.

4 • describe the relationship between profit incentive and the quantity supplied.
  ★ explain what supply schedules and supply curves show.

5 • contrast change in quantity supplied and change in supply.
  • list three factors that cause a change in supply.

6 • determine how supply and demand operate in the real world.
  ★ explain why supply and demand curves are combined on one graph.

ECONOMICS VOCABULARY

voluntary exchange
law of demand
demand
utility
demand schedule
demand curve
law of diminishing marginal utility
real income
income effect on demand
substitution effect
price elasticity of demand
elastic demand
inelastic demand
supply
law of supply
supply schedule
supply curve
equilibrium price
surplus
shortage

When you buy something, do you ever wonder why it sells at that particular price? Perhaps you often feel that as an individual consumer you have no influence over the price that you pay for an item. To be sure, few individual consumers do. But in a market economy, all consumers collectively, or as a group, have a great influence on the price of all things that are bought and sold. Perhaps the best way to understand this is to look first at how people in the marketplace decide what to buy and at what price. This is demand. Then you need to examine how the people who want to sell those things decide how much to sell and at what price. This is supply.

collectively (kuh-LEK-tiv-lee): as a group

1 | DEMAND

Ask yourself as you read:
- What is demand?
- What causes demand to change?

What is the marketplace? As you read in Chapter 2, a market is the freely chosen action between buyers and sellers of goods and services. A market for a particular item can be local, national, and international. In a market economy, individuals decide for themselves the answers to the four basic economic questions through the interaction of individuals looking out for their own best interests.

THE MARKET AND VOLUNTARY EXCHANGE

The basis of activity in a market economy is this principle of **voluntary exchange.** A buyer and a seller exercise their economic freedoms by working out on their own the terms of an exchange. For example, the seller of a videocasette sets a price based on the market, and the buyer, through the act of buying, agrees to the product and the price. By definition, the two parties to a voluntary exchange are freely choosing to engage in that transaction, or business deal. Once the exchange has been made, both must feel they are better off—happier and richer.

transaction (tran-ZAK-shuhn): single act in a business process

It is through the principle of voluntary exchange that supply and demand enter into the activity of a market economy. Remember, as you read this chapter, that supply and demand are models of how buyers and sellers operate in the marketplace. They are a way of explaining cause and effect in relation to price. Other factors also influence what people will buy and what people will produce.

THE LAW OF DEMAND

The **law of demand** states the following: As the price of a good or service falls, a larger quantity will be bought. As the price of a good or service rises, a smaller quantity will be bought. **Demand** means the quantity that will be purchased at all possible prices. It includes willingness and the ability to pay. A person may say he or she wants a slice of pizza. However, until that person is both willing and able to buy it, no demand for pizza has been created by that person.

According to the law of demand, quantity demanded and price move in opposite directions. As price goes up, quantity demanded goes down. As price goes down, quantity demanded goes up. There is an inverse, or opposite, relationship between demand and price. There are several factors that affect how much people will buy of any item at a particular price. These are diminishing marginal utility, real income, and possible substitutes.

inverse (in-VERS): opposite

marginal (MAHR-juh-nuhl): additional

DIMINISHING MARGINAL UTILITY

Almost everything that people like, desire, use, think they would like to use, and so on, gives satisfaction. The term economists use for satisfaction is utility. **Utility** (yoo-TIL-uh-tee) is defined as the power that a good or service has to satisfy a want. People decide what to buy and how much they are willing and actually able to pay based on utility. That is, in deciding to make a purchase, they decide the amount of satisfaction, or use, they think they will get from a good or service. Consider the utility that can be derived from eating slices of pizza.

At $1.00 a slice, how many slices will you buy? Assuming that you have money and like pizza, you will buy at least one. Will you buy a second? a third? a fourth? That depends on the additional utility, or satisfaction, you expect to receive from buying and eating another slice. You will have a higher level of total, or overall, satisfaction from eating more slices of pizza. But, most likely, the satisfaction you receive from each additional slice will be less than for each previous slice. This example explains the **law of diminishing marginal utility.** Your total satisfaction will rise with each unit bought. But the amount of additional satisfaction, or marginal utility, will diminish, or lessen, with each additional unit until you find you are full.

At some point, you will stop buying additional slices. At that point, the satisfaction that you receive from eating pizza is less than the value you place on the $1.00 that you must pay for a slice. People stop buying an item when one event occurs—when the value that they place on additional satisfaction from the next unit of the same item becomes less than the price they must pay for it. Assume that at a price of $1.00 per slice you have had enough pizza after buying three slices. Thus, the value you place on additional satisfaction from a fourth slice would be less than $1.00. According to what will give you the most satisfaction, you will save or spend the $1.00 on something else.

But what if the price drops? Suppose the owner of the pizza parlor decided to have a special and sell pizza at $.75. Unless three slices were all you could eat, you would probably buy at least one additional slice.

If you look at the law of diminishing marginal utility again, the reason becomes clear. People will buy an item to the point where the value they place on the satisfaction from the last unit bought is equal to the

Learning Economic Skills

READING DEMAND CURVES

Economists use special types of tables and graphs to show the relationship between demand and price. A **demand schedule** is a table showing the quantity demanded at different prices. The following table, for example, shows how many slices of pizza might be sold in one year at prices ranging from $.50 to $2.00. By reading the demand schedule, you can see that as the price of pizza increases, fewer slices are sold. As price decreases, more slices are sold.

Demand Schedule for Slices of Pizza

Price per Slice	Quantity Bought per Year
$0.50	7 million
$0.75	6 million
$1.00	5 million
$1.25	4 million
$1.50	3 million
$1.75	2 million
$2.00	1 million

Demand can also be shown on a graph. The combinations of prices and quantities demanded are shown at points on a line called a **demand curve.** The curve is a visual representation of a demand schedule. The horizontal axis of the graph shows the quantity of goods. The vertical

Quantity of Pizza Demanded

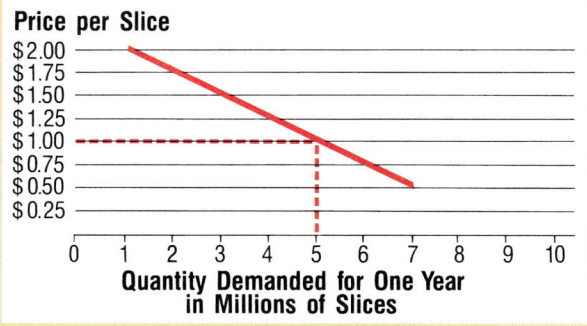

Increased Demand for Pizza After an Increase in Income

axis shows the price per item. The curve always slopes downward to show the opposite relationship between price and demand.

To find the demand for pizza at $1.00, read up the vertical axis to $1.00 and across until you meet the curve. Look down to the horizontal axis to see what quantity corresponds to that point.

Movement along the same demand curve shows a change in the quantity demanded because of a change in price. Factors other than price affect demand. These nonprice factors, such as an increase in income, result in a change in overall demand at each and every price for which the good might be sold. A change in demand is shown by shifting the entire demand curve to the right or left. If demand increases, the curve moves to the right. If demand decreases, the demand curve shifts to the left.

Practicing Your Skills

1. With all other factors remaining the same, how many slices of pizza will be bought at:
   a. $1.75? **b.** $.75? **c.** $1.25?
2. **a.** If everyone's income doubles, how many slices of pizza will be bought at $2.00?
   b. Which demand curve did you read to find the answer?
3. Using the information on the demand curve, make a demand schedule for slices of pizza bought if income doubles.

price. At that point, people will stop buying. If the price falls again, the lower price will attract people to buy more. This is true even though the satisfaction, or utility, from each additional unit is less. People will continue to buy to the point again where the satisfaction they receive falls below the price they must pay. This proves part of the law of demand. As the price of an item that people want decreases, they will generally buy more.

REAL INCOME EFFECT

The basis for the law of demand, however, does not rest only on diminishing marginal utility. As you read in Chapter 1, no one—not even the wealthiest person in the world—will ever be able to buy everything he or she wants to buy. There is a limit to what people can spend, and that limit is the amount of their incomes.

For example, suppose you buy seven slices of pizza every week at a $1.00 a slice. If the price rises by $.50, you would have to spend $10.50 instead of $7.00 to purchase the same number of slices. If the price of pizza continues to rise while your income does not, in time you would not be able to buy seven slices. This is true even if all other prices stay the same. Why? Because at some point, you will be reaching beyond the limit of your available income. The rise in the price of pizza has reduced your real income. **Real income** is the amount of goods and services you can actually buy with your income. It is your purchasing power.

People cannot keep buying the same quantity of a good if its price rises while their incomes do not. This is known as the **income effect on demand.** In order to keep buying the same amount of pizza, you would need to cut back on buying other items. Or you could cut back on the amount of pizza you buy. The income effect forces you to make a trade-off. You can see this in the real world in the housing and automobile markets. To keep up with car payments, a person often has to give up other things he or she may find equally satisfying, such as a vacation or new clothes.

The income effect works in the opposite direction as well. If you are already buying pizza and the price of pizza falls to $.75, your real income increases. You will have more purchasing power and will probably increase the amount of pizza that you buy.

SUBSTITUTION EFFECT

Suppose there are two goods that are not exactly the same but that satisfy basically the same need. Their cost is about the same. If the price of one falls, people will most likely substitute it in favor of the now higher-priced good. If the price of one of the items rises in relation to the price of the other, people will substitute the now lower-priced good. This is called the **substitution effect.**

Suppose, for example, you like both pizza and tacos and occasionally eat a taco instead of a slice of pizza. If the price of tacos drops from $1.00 to $.85, you would most likely buy more tacos and fewer slices of pizza.

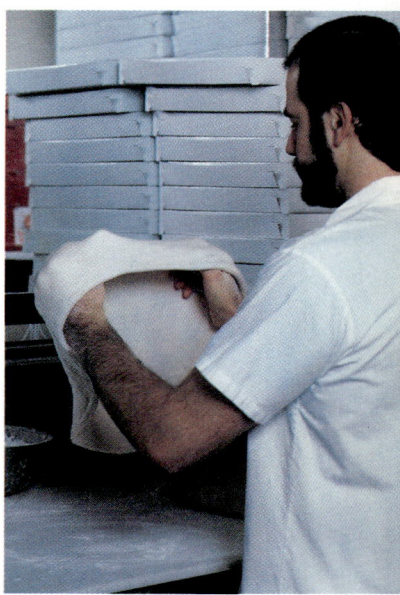

What factor would cause an increase in the number of competitors for this pizza shop?

In effect, you are substituting the lower-priced tacos for the now higher-priced pizza. If the price of tacos rises to $1.15, you would probably buy more slices of pizza and fewer tacos.

REVIEWING ECONOMIC PRINCIPLES

1. Define the following economic terms: **a.** voluntary exchange, **b.** law of demand, **c.** demand, **d.** utility, **e.** law of diminishing marginal utility **f.** real income, **g.** income effect on demand, **h.** substitution effect.
2. Using an example of your own, explain how the law of diminishing marginal utility affects the quantity demanded of a good.
3. How does income cause: **a.** an increase in quantity demanded? **b.** a decrease in quantity demanded?
4. **Critical Thinking: Applying Economic Principles. a.** How does the substitution effect operate on demand? **b.** What are two goods that you might substitute for one another?

2 | ELASTIC AND INELASTIC DEMAND

Ask yourself as you read:
- What are some examples of elastic demand?
- Why is the demand for some goods inelastic?

According to the law of demand, the quantity demanded depends on the price. When the price of an item changes, the quantity demanded will change, but in the opposite direction. For example, if the price goes up, the quantity demanded will go down. But by how much? If the price goes up by 1 percent, will quantity demanded fall by .5 percent, by 1 percent, or by 10 percent? The only way to answer the question is to examine how people in the real world respond to changing prices. Economists term this responsiveness **price elasticity of demand.** This means that demand varies according to changes in price.

elasticity (ih-las-TIS-uh-tee): ability to change, flexibility

ELASTIC DEMAND

There are some goods for which the rise or fall in the price greatly affects the amount of that product that people are willing to buy. The demand of these good is considered **elastic.** For example, the demand for a particular brand of frozen pizza is probably very elastic. After all, there may be many competing brands that are almost the same. A small rise in the price of one brand will cause consumers to shift their demand to the now cheaper substitute.

INELASTIC DEMAND

If a price change does not result in a substantial change in quantity demanded, that demand is considered **inelastic.** Sugar, salt, milk, and

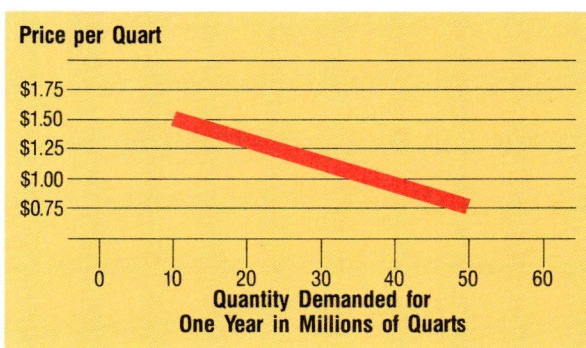

Figure 8-1: ELASTIC DEMAND FOR SELTZER WATER

Price per Quart

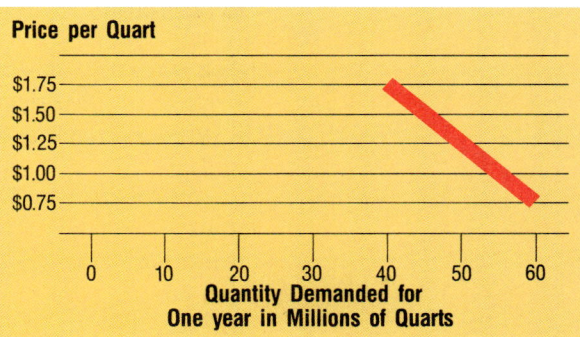

Figure 8-2: INELASTIC DEMAND FOR MILK

Price per Quart

The slope of a curve shows how responsive the item under study is to changes in price. The steeper the slope, the less responsive and more in elastic is demand for the item.

bread are some items whose demand is inelastic. So is the demand for medical care. Figures 8-1 and 8-2 show responsiveness to price changes for movie tickets and milk.

THE RESPONSIVENESS OF DEMAND

Three factors determine whether the quantity demanded of a good is elastic or inelastic: 1. whether it is a necessity or luxury, 2. its substitutability, and 3. the amount of income of an individual. Whether an item is considered a necessity or a luxury is one factor. Milk, for example, is considered a necessity, while ice-cream cake roll is not. A change in the price of milk probably will not greatly affect demand. The change in the price of ice-cream cake roll probably will affect demand.

Whether one item can be substituted for another can also determine whether demand is elastic or inelastic. There is no substitute for pepper. However, depending on the price, tacos could be substituted for pizza and vice versa.

The third factor is the amount of income a person spends on an item. If the amount of income spent is not very large, then an increase in price probably will not affect the quantity demanded very much. If a box of salt goes from $.70 to $.80, most people will probably continue to buy the same amount as before the price increase. Also, if a person does not buy an item often—a winter coat every four years—there will probably be little effect on the quantity demanded.

REVIEWING ECONOMIC PRINCIPLES

1. What is meant by each of the following terms: **a.** price elasticity of demand? **b.** elastic demand? **c.** inelastic demand?
2. What three factors determine whether the quantity demanded of a good is elastic or inelastic?
3. **Critical Thinking: Explaining Concepts.** Choose one factor from question 2 and write a paragraph describing how it affects the quantity demanded of an item. Be sure to use an example to illustrate your paragraph.

3 | CHANGES IN DEMAND

Ask yourself as you read:
- What nonprice factors cause demand to change?
- What causes demand curves to shift to the right and to the left?

So far you have been reading about changes in the quantity demanded. These changes come about because of changes in price. But other factors may affect how much of a product is bought. These factors can cause a change in the overall demand for the good at all the prices for which it might be sold. For example, when electronic calculators became widely available in the 1970s, the demand for all types of adding machines—whether they were expensive or inexpensive—dropped sharply.

A change in the quantity demanded of an item indicates movement along the same demand curve to a lower or higher price and quantity demanded. On the other hand, a change in the demand to buy more or less of an item at the same price indicates a shift in the entire demand curve to the right or left. A decrease in demand—less at a given price—will always shift the demand curve to the left. An increase in demand—more at a given price—will always shift the curve to the right. This shift shows the change not in the quantity of a good that will be bought at one price, but at all prices. The nonprice factors that can cause a change in demand are income, the tastes and preferences, or first choices, of buyers, and the prices of related goods.

INCOME

If people's salaries and wages increase, they will have more money income to spend, and they will spend more. They may save some of the money income, but they will also probably spend some, too. For most goods, an increase in income will lead to an increase in demand. For example, if a student takes a part-time job that triples her or his income, it is likely that she or he will spend more on goods such as cassettes. There are some goods and situations, however, in which demand will decrease as income increases. For example, as a nation's income increases, people may buy fewer potatoes and more meat regardless of the price.

TASTES AND PREFERENCES

Consumer tastes and preferences also account for shifts in demand curves. Some goods are more likely to be affected by this factor than others. Style in clothes, for example, changes quickly and often. If narrow-legged pants are in style, then the demand for them will increase. The demand curve will move to the right. When wide-legged pants come into style, the demand for narrow-legged pants will decrease. The demand curve for narrow-legged pants will move to the left.

preference (PREF-uhr-uhns): thing wanted above all others, first choice

These young consumers are purchasing food they enjoy. How might an increase in price affect their demand for this product?

Case Study

SNEAKERS, A BOOMING INDUSTRY

Until recently, the average American owned one pair of sneakers, or so-called tennis shoes. Sneakers were practical and were worn by gym students and by tennis players and basketball players, young and older do-it-yourselfers. For the serious athlete, the green-striped leather soccer shoes made by the Adidas company were about the fanciest footwear that money could buy. Then in the 1970s, the running and jogging craze and the growing popularity of many sports and physical activities, from racquet ball to aerobic dancing, caused a boom that created a new market for sports shoes. This boom produced many new competitors to the once-dominant Adidas company.

Nike is one of those competitors that vaulted from almost nowhere to a multimillion-dollar status in a remarkably short time. The company's early strategy was to build a new market in specialized shoes for jogging, taking advantage of the booming health fitness movement of the 1970s. This strategy paid off handsomely. Nike is now the United States leader in sales of athletic shoes, earning some $570 million in sales in a recent year.

A major reason for Nike's success, aside from its creative and enthusiastic management, has been its use of endorsements by star athletes. Nike spends large sums on athletes like John McEnroe and Michael Jordan to have them endorse and wear its shoes, and this has paid off handsomely in increased sales.

Nike has also expanded its range of products. As the jogging boom slowed down, Nike began to diversify into sports and leisure clothing as well as footwear for casual dress. As a result of its accurate forecasting of market trends, the company's growth has continued.

However, just when it seemed Nike's impressive market share was secure, a British company, Reebok, entered the American market. Widely known for its highly popular soft-leather aerobic shoes, Reebok quickly achieved enormous popularity, especially among those willing to pay a high price for a status symbol. Women especially seemed willing to spend $80 or more for Reebok athletic shoes. Says a major retailer, "They just don't think of them as sneakers any more." Nor did it hurt Reebok's fashion image, for example, when actress Cybil Shepherd showed up at an Emmy Awards broadcast in an evening gown wearing a pair of high-top Reeboks.

The sneaker industry has become one of the most competitive in the world. Korea, Japan, and many other nations also produce and sell all types of athletic shoes in the American market. From the days when kids had one pair of all purpose sneakers to today when many youngsters and adults have several shoes for various occasions, the sneaker has risen to star status. Athletic shoe companies saw a want and produced products to fill it.

1. What accounts for the popularity of athletic shoes?
2. What was the basis of Reebok's success?
3. If you were the advertising manager of an athletic shoe company, what would you stress in your ads to compete with industry leaders?

Figure 8-3: DECREASED DEMAND FOR BUTTER AFTER A DROP IN THE PRICE OF MARGARINE

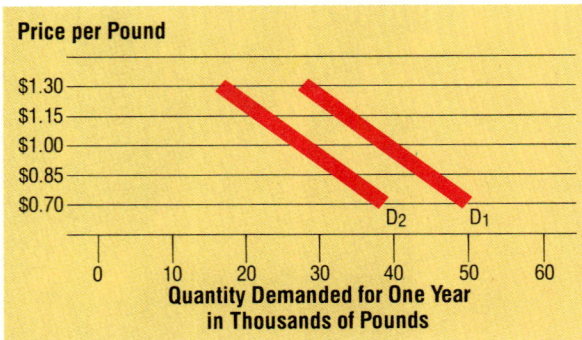

Price per Pound

Quantity Demanded for One Year in Thousands of Pounds

Figure 8-4: INCREASED DEMAND FOR BUTTER AFTER A DROP IN THE PRICE OF BREAD

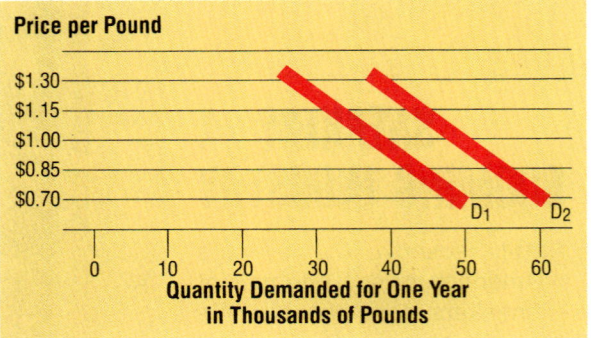

Price per Pound

Quantity Demanded for One Year in Thousands of Pounds

The subscript shows the direction in which the curve is shifting. The original curve is labeled with *1* and the new curve with *2*.

RELATED GOODS: SUBSTITUTES AND COMPLEMENTARY GOODS

Some goods that people buy, such as butter and margarine or bread and butter, are related. The change in the price of one will shift the demand for the other. There are two types of related goods: substitutes and complementary goods.

Generally, people think of butter and margarine as substitutes. Suppose that the price of butter remains the same and the price of margarine falls. People will buy more margarine and less butter at all prices. The demand curve for butter will shift to the left. In other words, as the price of the substitute (margarine) decreases, the demand for the item under study (butter) also decreases. You can see this relationship in Figure 8-3. However, if the price of margarine rises, people will buy less margarine and more butter at all prices. The demand curve for butter will shift to the right. As the price of the substitute (margarine) increases, the demand for the item under study (butter) also increases.

Although bread and butter can be used separately, they are often used together. Suppose the price of butter remains the same. If the price of bread drops, people will probably buy more bread. They will also probably buy more butter to use on the bread. Therefore, a decrease in the price of bread leads to an increase in the demand for its complementary good, butter. There will be a shift to the right for the demand curve for butter. Figure 8-4 shows this. However, if the price of bread increases, less bread will be bought and less butter. An increase in the price of bread leads to a decrease in the demand for butter. The demand curve for butter will shift to the left.

REVIEWING ECONOMIC PRINCIPLES

1. What is the difference between quantity demanded and change in demand?
2. Use examples to explain the two ways in which income can cause a change in demand.

3. Which two of the following goods would be most subject to a change in demand because of consumer tastes and preferences: car models, steak, records by a particular singing group, kitchen sinks, typewriters.
4. List one pair of each of the following: **a.** substitute goods, **b.** complementary goods.
5. **Critical Thinking: Applying Concepts.** The demand schedules that follow show the number of concert tickets that fans of a certain rock group will buy at various prices. The schedule on the left gives the quantity of tickets demanded just after the group has become known nationally. The schedule on the right is for one year later. Use the schedules to draw curves showing change in demand. Use the terms D1 and D2 to show the direction in which the demand curve shifted.

Price per Ticket	Quantity Demanded	Price per Ticket	Quantity Demanded
$5	5,000	$5	8,000
$10	4,000	$10	7,000
$15	3,000	$15	6,000
$20	2,000	$20	5,000
$25	1,000	$25	4,000

4 | THE LAW OF SUPPLY

Ask yourself as you read:
- What is the relationship between price and the quantity of goods and services produced?
- Why does the profit incentive affect supply?

The law of demand alone is not enough to explain what determines the price of things people buy. In order to understand fully how prices are set, you have to look, too, at the opposite side of demand. That side is concerned with the producers, or suppliers. The willingness and ability of producers to provide goods and services at different prices in the marketplace is called **supply.**

The **law of supply** states: At higher prices, a larger quantity will generally be supplied than at lower prices. At lower prices, a smaller quantity will generally be supplied than at higher prices. In other words, as the price rises for a good, the quantity supplied rises. As the price falls, the quantity supplied also falls. There is a price at which a supplier cannot sell a product and stay in business. Unlike demand, there is a direct relationship between the price and quantity supplied. With demand, price and demand move in opposite directions.

Learning Economic Skills | READING SUPPLY CURVES

Like the law of demand, the law of supply can be shown by special tables and graphs. The table for supply is called a **supply schedule**. It shows the quantity that suppliers are willing to supply at various prices. By comparing the supply schedule below with the demand schedule on p. 188, you can see the difference between supply and demand.

Supply Schedule For Slices of Pizza

Price per Slice	Quantity Supplied per Year
$2.00	7 million
$1.75	6 million
$1.50	5 million
$1.25	4 million
$1.00	3 million
$0.75	2 million
$0.50	1 million

At a price of $2.00, the largest quantity will be supplied, but the smallest quantity will be demanded. At $.50, the smallest quantity will be supplied, but the largest quantity will be demanded. If you recall, the law of demand shows an inverse relationship between price and demand. For supply, however, there is a direct relationship between price and quantity supplied. The higher the price, the greater the quantity supplied.

Quantity of Pizza Supplied

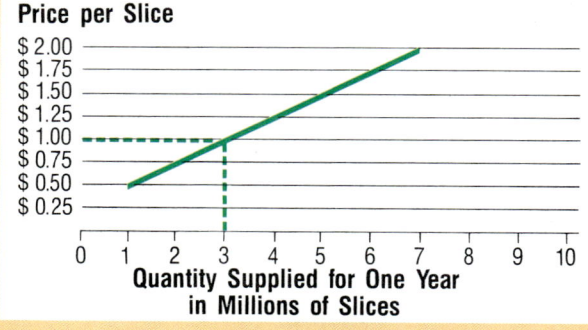

Increased Supply of Pizza After a Drop in Production Costs

Supply can also be shown as a graph. The **supply curve**, as it is called, shows the combinations of prices and quantities supplied. It is a visual representation of a supply schedule. The horizontal axis shows the quantity of goods. The vertical axis shows the price per item. A supply curve always slopes upward to show the direct relationship between price and quantity supplied.

Movement along the same supply curve shows a change in quantity supplied because of a change in the price charged. Other factors besides price affect supply, such as the cost of production. These nonprice factors result in a change in supply at each and every price for which the good might be sold. An increase in supply is shown as a shift of the supply curve to the right. A decrease in supply is shown as a shift to the left. The subscripts show the direction of the shift.

Practicing Your Skills

1. With all other factors remaining the same, how many slices of pizza will be supplied at: **a.** $1.75? **b.** $2.00? **c.** $.50?
2. **a.** If the cost of producing pizza drops by 50 percent, how many slices will be sold at $.50? **b.** Which supply curve did you read?
3. Using the information on the supply curve, make a supply schedule for slices of pizza if production costs are cut.

The willingness and the ability of a supplier to produce more goods affect the quantity supplied. Although producers may be willing, they may not be able. Increased costs and possibly a time lag affect a company's ability to respond to changes in price. A company needs time and money to change production methods to produce more of an item or to change what it produces. These changes can mean buying additional equipment, converting present equipment from one use to another, and hiring more workers.

THE INCENTIVE OF GREATER PROFIT

The higher the price of a good, the greater is the incentive for a producer to produce more. The producer will expect to make a higher profit because of the higher price. As you read in Chapter 2, profit incentive is one of the factors that motivates people in a market economy.

Suppose that instead of being a pizza customer, you own a pizza parlor. What costs are involved in supplying pizza to the people who are willing and able to buy it? First, there is either rent on the building that houses your restaurant or mortgage payments on the building and land. Next, there are the costs of the ingredients of the pizza as well as the costs of buying, repairing, and maintaining the equipment in your restaurant. You have to hire employees to make and serve the pizza, and there are also taxes and insurance to pay. These are all considered costs of production.

Suppose that the prices you are charging for your pizza cover all your costs and give you a small profit. Under what circumstances would you be willing to produce more slices of pizza? Remember that increasing output means expanding production. To take on the expense of expanding production, you would have to be able to charge a higher price for your pizza. In fact, if the price at which you could sell slices of pizza went up enough, you would probably be willing to hire more workers, buy more equipment, and even build more pizza parlors. In other words, at a higher price for each slice of pizza, you would be willing to supply—produce and sell—more than you would at the current lower price. Each slice of pizza would cost more to produce. However, at a higher price, you could afford to pay the additional costs of increasing the quantity sold. This fact is the basis of the law of supply.

The law of supply works not just for individual suppliers but for all suppliers who either are or could be in an industry. Consider the entire pizza industry. At a higher selling price, potential operators might be attracted into the business. At a higher price, they can see the opportunity to make larger profits than they could have made before the price of pizza went up. This example, of course, assumes that no other prices in the economy increase.

Why had the potential operators not already been in the business? They faced two problems that made owning a pizza parlor look unprofitable to them. One was the lower price they could charge. The second was the degree of efficiency they thought they would have in operating

A pizza shop is a popular place for young people to get together. How does this illustrate the fact that the price of pizza is determined by the forces *underlying* supply and demand?

efficiency (uh-FISH-uhn-see): ability to do something without wasting resources

197

a pizza parlor. That is, many potential producers would like to enter the pizza industry. However, they do not have the same skill and expert knowledge in operating a pizza parlor that current producers have. As a result, the potential producers would not be able to keep the cost per slice as low as it is for current producers. Only if the price goes up will these potential producers be able to cover their higher costs of production. But if the price of pizza goes up, they will enter the industry.

In summary, at higher prices, present suppliers will increase what they make or sell. At higher prices, potential suppliers will become actual suppliers because of the attraction of profits. Both will add to the total output.

REVIEWING ECONOMIC PRINCIPLES

1. What is the law of supply?
2. How does profit incentive affect the quantity supplied: **a.** by individual suppliers? **b.** by an industry as a whole?
3. **Critical Thinking: Making Inferences.** How does the ability of a company to respond to price changes affect quantity supplied? You will have to infer this from the text.

5 | CHANGES IN SUPPLY

Ask yourself as you read:
- What causes supply curves to shift to the right? to the left?
- What nonprice factors affect supply?

A change in price causes a change in the quantity supplied. This, in turn, causes movement up or down on the same supply curve. However, just as there are nonprice factors that affect demand, so there are nonprice factors that affect supply. These nonprice factors cause a change in the supply offered at every price for which the item is sold, not just a change in the quantity supplied at one price. With a change in supply, supply curves actually shift to the right or left. If there is a decrease in supply, the supply curve shifts to the left. If there is an increase in supply, the supply curve shifts to the right. Among the nonprice factors that can affect a change in supply are: 1. the costs of production, 2. the effects of technology, and 3. the entrance and exit of firms within an industry.

1. The costs of production are the costs of the resources—raw materials, labor, capital, and entrepreneurship—involved in producing a good. Suppose a very wet summer has caused much of the tomato crop to rot in the fields. As a result, there is a very small supply of tomatoes for sale. Producers of tomato paste as well as companies that use tomatoes for other products will drive up the price as they compete with one another to buy the available tomatoes. Because of the greatly increased

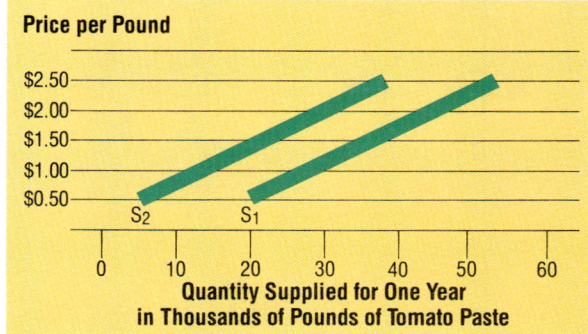

Figure 8-5: DECREASED SUPPLY OF TOMATO PASTE AFTER A RISE IN PRODUCTION COSTS

Price per Pound

Quantity Supplied for One Year
in Thousands of Pounds of Tomato Paste

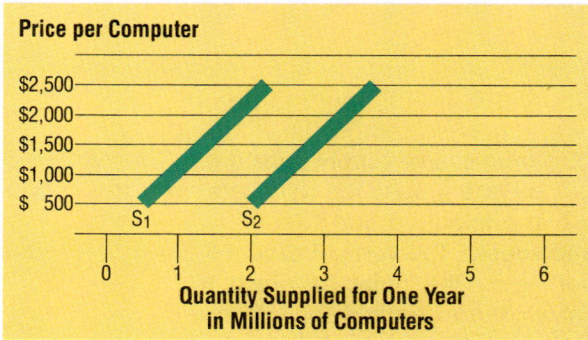

Figure 8-6: INCREASED SUPPLY OF COMPUTERS AFTER A CHANGE IN TECHNOLOGY

Price per Computer

Quantity Supplied for One Year
in Millions of Computers

What three factors cause supply curves to shift? What does a shift to the right indicate? What does a shift to the left indicate?

cost of the resources, the supply of tomato paste will fall dramatically at all prices. The supply curve for tomato paste will shift to the left. Figure 8-5 shows this shift. If, however, there were an overabundant tomato crop, the price of tomatoes would fall. The supply curve would shift to the right. More tomato paste would be supplied at each price.

2. Technology can also affect profit by increasing productivity. Introduction of new technology into an industry will increase supply. The supply curve will shift to the right. For example, improvements in the technology for manufacturing computer chips has made it possible to make smaller yet more powerful chips. This has, in turn, reduced the costs of producing computers. Figure 8-6 shows this shift.

3. As firms enter and exit an industry, supply also changes. As new firms enter a particular industry, supply will increase. In the last 15 years or so, the entrance of foreign automakers into the American market for subcompacts has greatly increased the number of small cars.

Firms also exit markets, often because of a decline in demand. For example, as the popularity of video games has increased in recent years, the demand for playing pinball has decreased. As a result, some companies that made pinball machines switched much of their production to video games. Others left the market completely. This resulted in a decrease in supply. Any supply curve for pinball machines would show a shift to the left.

REVIEWING ECONOMIC PRINCIPLES

1. What is the difference between a change in the quantity supplied and change in supply?
2. How do production costs cause a change in the supply of a good?
3. Using an example such as the mechanical reaper and the supply of wheat, explain how technology caused a change in the supply of a particular good or service.
4. **Critical Thinking: Categorizing Information. a.** List two industries that American businesses have been entering in recent years. **b.** List two industries that they have been exiting.

Learning Economic Skills

READING SUPPLY AND DEMAND CURVES TOGETHER

Demand and supply curves can be combined on one graph. The horizontal axis still shows the quantity, but it represents both demand and supply. The vertical axis still shows the price per item. The point at which the curves cross shows where demand and supply are in balance. It is the equilibrium price. The following graph combines the two previous graphs for quantity demanded and quantity supplied of pizza slices. On the graph, what is the equilibrium price?

Equilibrium Price for Pizza

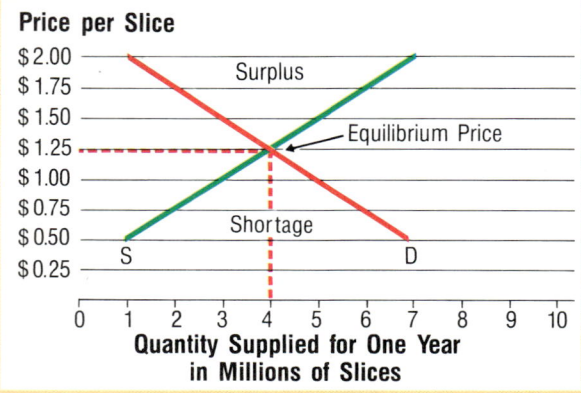

Only at a price of $1.25 is both demand and supply satisfied. The quantity demanded is 4 million slices and the quantity supplied is the same. Above that price a **surplus**—greater amount supplied than demanded—results. Below that price a **shortage**—more quantity demanded than supplied—results.

As you read earlier in the chapter, various factors other than price can affect both demand and supply. Suppose that the cost of a substitute for pizza such as tacos goes up. As a result, people are willing to buy fewer tacos and more pizza at all prices for which it is offered. The demand curve for pizza shifts to the right, and a new equilibrium price is reached. It is higher than the original one.

If the price for tacos drops while that of pizza stays the same, the demand for pizza will de-

Increased Demand for Pizza After a Rise in the Price of Tacos

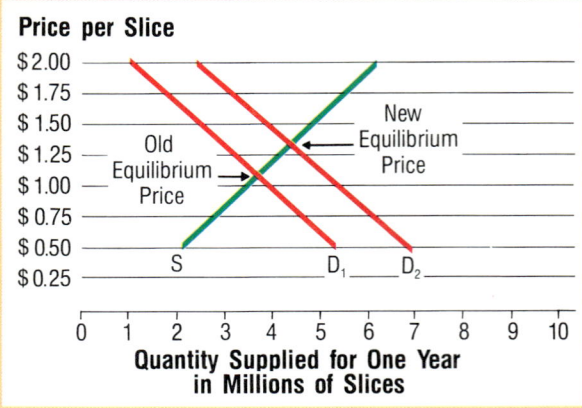

crease. The demand curve for pizza will shift to the left, and a new equilibrium price will be created. It will be lower than the original one.

The quantity that suppliers are willing to produce can also change. The supply curve may shift to the right or left depending on whether supply increases or decreases. Where supply and demand reach a balance, a new equilibrium price is created. It may be higher or lower than the original one.

Practicing Your Skills

1. Demand and supply curves can both shift at the same time. Suppose the cost of producing pizza drops at the same time the cost of tacos, a substitute, drops. **a.** Create your own prices and quantities and make two each of demand and supply schedules based on this situation. **b.** Draw a graph illustrating these demand and supply schedules.
2. **a.** In which direction will the supply curve for pizza shift? **b.** Why?
3. **a.** In which direction will the demand curve for pizza shift? **b.** Why?
4. **a.** Will the new equilibrium price be lower or higher than it was before the curve shifted? **b.** Why?

6 | SUPPLY AND DEMAND TOGETHER

Ask yourself as you read:
- How do supply and demand operate together?
- How does the market system eliminate shortages and surpluses?

Up to this point, you have read about price and demand and price and supply as though they were separate. But in the real world, they operate together. As the price of a good goes down, the quantity demanded rises, and the quantity supplied falls. As the price goes up, the quantity demanded falls, and the quantity supplied rises.

Is there a price at which the quantity demanded and the quantity supplied meet? Yes. This level is called the **equilibrium price.** It means that the price of any good or service will find the level at which the quantity demanded and the quantity supplied are balanced. There is enough of the good that satisfies suppliers. In other words, at the equilibrium price the plans of buyers and the plans of sellers are the same. Suppliers provide the amount that is demanded by consumers. One way to visualize equilibrium price is to put supply and demand curves on one graph. Where the two curves intersect is the equilibrium price.

intersect (in-tuhr-SEKT): to cross

Whenever the market price of a good falls below the equilibrium price, we say that a shortage has developed. Shortages occur when at the going price the quantity demanded is greater than the supply available. If the market is free, without government regulations or other restrictions, shortages put pressure on prices to rise. Consumers reduce their demand while suppliers increase the quantity they supply.

When the market price is higher than the equilibrium price, a surplus develops. At prices above the equilibrium price, suppliers produce more than consumers demand in the marketplace. As surpluses occur, suppliers end up with large inventories of goods, and this and other forces put pressure on the price to drop to the equilibrium price. When the price drops, suppliers have less incentive to supply as much as before, while consumers begin to demand a greater quantity. The drop in price toward the equilibrium price, therefore, eliminates the surplus.

One of the benefits of the market economy is that when it operates without restriction, it eliminates shortages and surpluses. Whenever there are shortages, the market ends up taking care of itself—the price goes up to eliminate the shortage. Whenever there are surpluses, the market again ends up taking care of itself—the price falls to eliminate the surplus. In command, or controlled, economies, such automatic market forces usually are not allowed to operate. It is not surprising, therefore, that in the Soviet Union people have to wait in lines to buy many goods, including food and clothes. In America also, consumers sometimes wait for goods and services. However, consistent shortages and rationing of goods. In the United States and other nations with mainly free enterprise systems, prices serve as signals to producers and con-

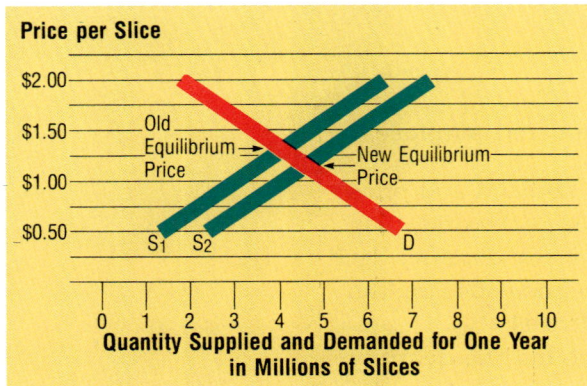

Figure 8-7: INCREASED SUPPLY OF PIZZA AFTER THE ENTRANCE OF A NEW CHAIN INTO THE MARKET

Price per Slice

Old Equilibrium Price
New Equilibrium Price

$2.00
$1.50
$1.00
$0.50

S₁ S₂   D

0 1 2 3 4 5 6 7 8 9 10
Quantity Supplied and Demanded for One Year
in Millions of Slices

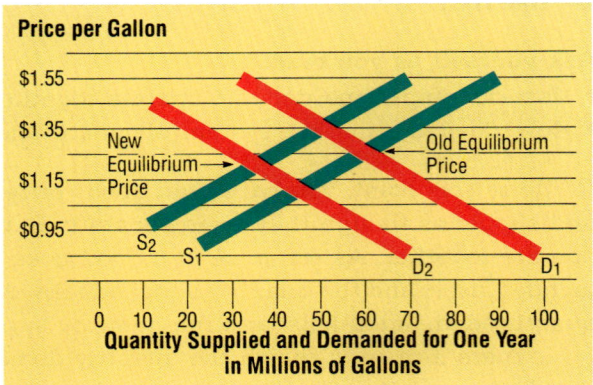

Figure 8-8: DECREASED DEMAND FOR GASOLINE ALONG WITH DECREASED SUPPLY

Price per Gallon

New Equilibrium Price
Old Equilibrium Price

$1.55
$1.35
$1.15
$0.95

S₂ S₁   D₂   D₁

0 10 20 30 40 50 60 70 80 90 100
Quantity Supplied and Demanded for One Year
in Millions of Gallons

By combining supply and demand curves, you can see how the interest of buyers and sellers work in opposite directions. What is the reason for the suppliers in each of these curves? What is the reason for the shortages?

sumers. Rising prices signal producers to supply more and consumers to demand less. Falling prices signal producers to produce less and consumers to demand more. This free changing of the price of goods and services is a major strength of the free enterprise system.

FORCES AND PRICES

Do supply and demand determine all prices? Yes and no. Supply and demand are important aspects of the economy, and they do affect prices. But prices are really determined by the forces that determine supply and demand. Many such forces operate in the economy. On the demand side, as you read in this chapter, are people's income and their tastes and preferences. On the supply side, among determining factors are the ability of suppliers to produce, the profit incentive, and costs of production. Price is really determined by the forces underlying supply and demand. *Underlying* is the important word.

Then, too, even these forces do not always determine price. Many prices in the United States, for example, are fixed by legislation or government regulations. For example, many states set the rates public utilities may charge for natural gas and electricity. You should also understand that the forces of supply and demand set prices only in a market system. In a command economy, such as that of the Soviet Union or the People's Republic of China, government planners set most prices.

REVIEWING ECONOMIC PRINCIPLES

1. What is an equilibrium price of a good?
2. Where would you find an equilibrium price on a supply and demand curve?
3. In the real world, how are prices determined?
4. **Critical Thinking: Explaining Ideas.** Why is the free changing of prices a strength of the free enterprise system?

SUMMARY OF
IMPORTANT PRINCIPLES

1
- In a voluntary exchange, a buyer and a seller exercise their economic freedoms by working out on their own the terms of the exchange. This principle of voluntary exchange is the basis of the market economy.
- Three factors that affect price and the quantity of a good demanded are diminishing marginal utility, the real income effect, and the substitution effect.
- A demand schedule is a table showing the quantity demanded at different prices. A demand curve is a graph showing the same information in a visual way.

2
- Three factors determine whether the quantity demanded of a good is elastic or inelastic: classification as a necessity or luxury, the presence of substitutes, and the amount of income a person spends on the item.
- Changes in the quantity demanded come about because of changes in price. This is shown on a demand curve by movement along the same curve. Change in demand means a change in the demand for a good at all prices for which it might be sold. With a change in demand, demand curves actually shift to the right if demand increases and to the left if it decreases.

3
- Three factors that cause a change in demand are income, buyers' tastes and preferences, and the prices of related substitute and complementary goods.

4
- A supply schedule is a table showing the quantity suppliers are willing to supply at various prices. A supply curve is a graph showing the same information in a visual way.
- At higher prices, present suppliers will increase what they make or sell. At higher prices, potential suppliers will become actual suppliers because of the attraction of profits.

5
- A change in price causes a change in the quantity supplied, which, in turn, causes movement up or down the same supply curve. Change in supply means a change in the supply offered at every price for which a good may be sold. With a change in supply, supply curves actually shift to the right if supply increases and to the left if supply decreases.
- Three factors that can cause a change in supply are the costs of production, the effects of technology, and the entrance or exit of firms from an industry.

6
- In the real world, prices are determined by the underlying forces that determine supply and demand.
- The point at which supply and demand curves intersect on the same graph indicates the equilibrium price. This is the price at which there is enough of the good to satisfy the demand and at a price that satisfies suppliers.

Putting Economics to Work

SURPLUS: SALE MERCHANDISE

It is the end of January, and Teresa Cintron is taking inventory—counting what she has—in her clothing store. Each summer and winter, Teresa holds a sale of the previous season's remaining items. In her latest end-of-season inventory, Teresa has found that she is left with 90 blouses and tops. The 90 items are divided almost equally among three price ranges. There are 40 blouses selling for $30 each, 30 tops for $20 each, and 20 tops for $15 each.

To sell these remaining winter items, Teresa lowers the prices on the 90 blouses and tops by 20 to 50 percent. To bring customers into her store, Teresa advertises the $15 tops at $7.50 each. This price is about what Teresa paid for the tops from her supplier. Teresa reduces the other items about 20 percent. Teresa will still be able to make a small profit on these items.

Teresa's January Sale Days are a success. She sells 80 of her 90 summer blouses and tops. The ten remaining tops she places on a rack marked "Reduced" and will sell at an even lower price. Teresa's spring and summer stock will fill the rest of the store.

1. How does Teresa's decision to hold a sale illustrate the law of demand?
2. How might the law of diminishing marginal utility work on customers in Teresa's store?
3. What might happen to Teresa's sale if another nearby clothing store reduced prices to less than Teresa's prices?
4. Is the demand for Teresa's tops and blouses elastic or inelastic? Why?

A LOW PRICE DRIVES MUSTANG SALES

Skill: Identifying Cause and Effect

Lee Iacocca, president of Chrysler Corporation, was responsible for the introduction of the new Ford Mustang in 1964 when he was vice president of Ford Motor Company. In this reading from his autobiography, he describes a lesson in the law of demand that he got before the Mustang hit the market.

Long before the car came out, we started doing market research. One of our final tests was especially encouraging. We invited a select group of 52 Detroit area couples to our styling showroom. Each of these couples already owned a standard-sized car and earned average incomes, which meant they were not prime candidates for a second car. We brought them in small groups into our styling studio to view the prototype of the Mustang, and we recorded their impressions on tape.

What we found was that white-collar couples were impressed by the car's styling, while blue-collar workers saw the Mustang as a symbol of status and prestige. When we asked them to estimate the price of the car, almost everybody guessed a figure that was at least $1,000 too high. When we asked if they would buy a Mustang, most said they wouldn't. They explained that it was too expensive, or too small, or too difficult to handle.

But when we told them the actual price of the car, a funny thing happened. Most people said: "The hell with my objections, I want it!" Suddenly their excuses vanished. They came up with all sorts of innovative reasons why this particular car made good sense after all. One fellow said: "If I parked that car in my driveway, all my neighbors would wonder what gravy train I fell into." Another one told us: "It doesn't look like an ordinary car—and at that price what you get is an ordinary car."

The lesson was clear. When it came time to market the Mustang, we had to make sure to emphasize its low price.

The final sticker price on the Mustang reflected our early decision to hold the price under $2,500. We ended up with a car that was an inch and a half longer than we had originally planned and 108 pounds heavier. But we held the line on price, and the Mustang sold for $2,368.

1. What things do most people consider when buying a new car?
2. What can you infer or guess about Ford's reasons for building their advertising campaign for the Mustang around price?

Lee Iacocca with William Novak, *Iacocca: An Autobiography.* New York: Bantam, 1984. pp. 75, 76.

THE DEMAND FOR CD'S

Skill: Predicting Outcomes

If the price of a good greatly affects the quantity demanded of that good, the demand for it is considered to be elastic. The declining price for compact disc players and compact discs and the consequent surge in demand for these items illustrate the elasticity of demand for CDs and CD players.

Home computers are in the doldrums, telephone makers are still in the throes of a shakeout and color-television sales are stagnant. Amid this wreckage, the consumer-electronics industry and

In the few years of their existence, compact discs (CD's) have become the preferred format for recorded music, despite the fact that they are more expensive than discs or cassettes.

gadget lovers have a new darling: the compact disc.

Using digital technology to create a sound far superior to that of traditional phonograph records, the compact disc, or CD, is rejuvenating the audio business and producing a generation of born-again music lovers.

By any yardstick, CDs were the buzzword at the Consumer Electronics Show in Chicago during early June [1985]. "Sales are phenomenal," exclaims Marc Finer of Sony, which co-developed the technology with Philips of the Netherlands. Confirms Walton Stinson of Listen Up, a two-store Colorado chain: "We've been selling CDs like gangbusters ever since they came out.". . .

At the electronics show, dozens of companies exhibited players in a growing variety of formats—tabletop models, car units, models inside "boom boxes" and as part of expensive audio-video systems.

One crowd drawer was a new $300 portable model from Technics. Touted as the world's smallest CD player, the unit measures 5 by 5 inches on the surface and is 1¼ inches thick.

The arrival of several $300 models, coming on the heels of Sony's larger $300 portable, already available, enhances the likelihood that CD players will soon become a mass-market product, much like video recorders.

In some areas, the players already have sold for under $200. When Pacific Stereo, a big chain based in Emoryville, California, dropped the price of a Sanyo model to $199 last Christmas, it sold 1,800 units in two weeks. One company, Symphonic Corporation, soon will ship a player priced at $180. Dealers predict prices on some models will hit $150 by Christmas. The first CD players in 1983 cost more than $1,000.

1. What happened to consumer demand for CD players when prices were lowered?

2. "In order to compete and survive in the marketplace, all a company has to do is reduce prices to consumers." Is this statement true or false? Explain your answer.

Manuel Schiffres, excerpted from *U.S. News & World Report*, June 17, 1985. Copyright 1985, U.S. News and World Report. Chapter 8, Reading 3

DEMAND CHANGES IN THE SIGNATURE MARKET

Skill: Drawing Conclusions

 **SECTION 3** Changing tastes and styles and fashions affect the demand for particular goods. This reading describes how demand changes for a rather unusual commodity—autographs.

Autograph collecting began as an out-growth of Romanticism; it was thought that a person's character could be analyzed by his handwriting. By the early Victorian period, in 19th-century England, it was a fashionable pasttime. People would ask one another to write sentiments, or just signatures, in an album.

But today, with the proliferation of word processors and automated pens, handwritten documents and signatures are becoming more scarce—and more valuable. "What price can you put on history?" asks Charles Sachs, the owner of Scriptorium, a Beverly Hills manuscript gallery. "Content is the name of the game." To determine an autograph's value, experts weigh the importance of the author, the substance of a document and its condition and rarity. . . .

Most experts agree that United States presidential autographs are always in demand, but demand for many other types can be mercurial [quickly changing]. James Lowe, a New York dealer attuned to autograph fashion, says early 20th-century composers—such as Bartok of Hungary and Prokofiev of Russia—now are in vogue among his clients. . . .

Hot autographs can cool. Consider John Galsworthy, the English novelist and playwright (1867–1933), who was avidly collected in the twenties. When his *Forsythe Saga* inspired a TV miniseries a few years ago, there was renewed interest in Galsworthy autographs, Mr. Lowe says, "but it didn't last." Mr. Lowe says Galsworthy speculators fared poorly. . . .

Autographs of the late astronauts on the space shuttle Challenger are in high demand now, says Herman Darvick, the president of the Universal Autograph Collectors Club, a Rockville Centre, N.Y., group whose ranks have mushroomed to

2,650 from 350 a decade ago. For instance, a handwritten letter by Christa McAuliffe—about how she looked forward to teaching in space—has sold at auction for $1,500 he says. (The original owner spent merely 22 cents, to send Mrs. McAuliffe a letter.) . . .

Historical anniversaries affect autograph fashions. The values of Founding Father autographs—such as John Hancock's, whose name has become synonymous with signature—soared during the 1976 bicentennial of American independence. A George Washington, which went for about $450 in 1970, now commands about $1,500.

Mr. Darvick, the club president, predicts that autographs of the signers of the Constitution will gain value because of the pending bicentennial of the document. And he advises collectors to start searching now for autographs of Queen Isabella I and King Ferdinand V of Spain, the patrons of Christopher Columbus; the 500th anniversary of Columbus's discovery of America is in 1992.

1. List the various factors that affect the value of an autograph and therefore consumer demand for an autograph.

2. What conclusions can you draw about the reasons collectors buy autographs?

A CHANGE IN DEMAND IN THE MUSIC INDUSTRY
Skill: Applying Information

Concert promoters were concerned about the number of empty seats at music concerts featuring top stars during the summer tour season of 1986. The following reading explores some of the possible reasons for this change in demand in the concert music industry.

The summer tour season, historically a lucrative time for the music industry, is turning out to be a bomb this year, with even the most successful acts failing to sell out in certain markets. Concert

Autographs are often sold at auctions like the one shown here. Other objects frequently sold at auctions include paintings, valuable pieces of furniture, and rare coins. In an auction, goods are sold to the highest bidders.

Readings in Economics

promoters are blaming a variety of factors for the slump, including the glut caused by the large number of mid-level bands on the road, acts demanding headliner status before they're ready for it, competition from other forms of summer entertainment and the unpredictable tastes of concert-goers. . . .

"We may finally have come to a point in the entertainment industry where bigger is no longer better," says promoter Rick Kay of Detroit's Brass Ring Productions. Kay cites "the graying of America" as the reason why he'll be trying in the future to "take a lot of the bigger acts who appeal to an older demographic and scale them into the Fox Theatre, which is our 5000-seater. I think that everyone wants to go to those places, as opposed to being forced to go to an arena.". . .

An additional problem for the concert industry, says Cooley, is that video has created a class of "instant headliners," acts whose video exposure allows them to demand top billing before they've become proven draws on the road. The video generation, says Cooley, "likes an act quicker and they drop them quicker. An act will come on MTV, get saturation play and become what they consider to be headliners. And sometimes before the act can actually get out and play, they're off heavy rotation on MTV and they're over." Stating that his own midsized outdoor shows—including Willie Nelson, Jackson Browne and Whitney Houston—have all done well with "the older, yuppie kind of crowd," Cooley also blames competition from "amusement parks, whitewater parks and beaches" for the overall slow box office this summer.

1. According to the article, what economic factors contributed to the decreased attendance at music concerts during the summer of 1986?
2. How is the music-industry market trying to make up for the decrease in demand among the traditional teen-ager market of summer concertgoers?

SUPPLY SHIFTS IN THE MARKET FOR DOCTORS
Skill: Predicting Outcomes

 **When the supply curve shifts to the right, more of a good is offered at any price, and the price will end up dropping if demand has not changed. Consider the "good" to be doctors and the "price" to be doctors' incomes when you read this article about the oversupply in the medical market.**

[College Course] Economics 101 says that prices rise when demand for a product exceeds the supply available at the old price. The higher price elicits additional production. Result: Either prices drop again or some production goes unsold. But does supply-and-demand economics apply to medicine? Apparently it does. After decades of almost limitless freedom to charge what they wished for as much health care as they wished to supply, the country's doctors are suddenly finding that there is more health care available than there are customers for it.

As a result, for many doctors, income growth is beginning to slow, or stop completely. According to the American Medical Association, United States physicians' mean income after expenses and before taxes was $108,400 in 1984 . . . a 2% increase over 1983, well below the rate of inflation. Some doctors—neurosurgeons and plastic surgeons, for example—fared better. But for most, the earnings trend is flat to somewhat down. . . .

What happened? In essence, this: High medical prices induced both a greater supply of doctors and a drive by medical entrepreneurs and their customers to reorganize health care delivery so as to cut costs.

From 1950 to 1965, when . . . doctors still drove Buicks, instead of Porsches and Mercedes, and made house calls, the doctors' ranks grew at less than 2% annually, while medical outlays were increasing 8% a year in the United States. Demand and ability to pay were clearly rising much faster than the number of doctors. Doctors' incomes took off: $16,017 in 1955, $28,960 in 1965, $58,440 in 1975, over $100,000 today, according to *Medical Economics* magazine. Rising incomes elicited additional supply. In 1965 there were 277,600 doctors in the U.S., 1 for every 697 Americans. . . . Today there are 506,000 practicing physicians, 1 doctor for every 471 Americans, with more doctors per capita every day. A recent . . . study warns there will be a surplus of between 70,000 and 185,000 physicians by 1990.

1. According to this article, how did the high prices for medical services affect the supply of medical care?
2. As doctors' incomes level off, what can you predict about enrollments in medical schools in the next few years?

Ellen Paris, 'Hippocrates Meets Adam Smith.' *Forbes*, February 10, 1986. Adapted by permission of *Forbes* magazine. © Forbes Inc., 1986.

SUPPLY AND DEMAND IN THE EARLY AUTO INDUSTRY
Skill: Drawing Conclusions

Since firms do not always know the exact supply and demand curves for their products, they may not know what the equilibrium price is. This reading discusses how early automobile makers tried to determine their supply and demand curves in setting their prices.

Willie Durant . . . decided it was time to move into cars after several months of driving a prototype containing David Buick's valve-in-head engine— the most powerful in the world for its size— through rural Michigan in 1904. Within four years, Durant was to parlay his sturdy Buick vehicle into domination of the automobile industry, with a 25 percent share of the market in 1908, the year he founded General Motors. . . .

Henry Ford made a portentous announcement: "I will build a motor car for the great multitude. . . ."

Ford fulfilled his boast with the Model T. . . .

Nonetheless, during the first year, at a selling price of $850, the Model T had lost money and market share to the dashing $900 Buick. To in-

crease his profits the next year, Ford raised his price by a full $100 to $950 and saw his sales more than double again as Buick, Oldsmobile, and other companies proceeded to underprice him. . . .

Focusing on the rising profits that followed his price hike, his [Ford's] advisers urged him to raise prices again in 1910 to take advantage of a market exploding beyond the ability of the firms to fulfill it. This was the course chosen by General Motors, which raised the price of Buick to $1,150, leaving Ford plenty of room to follow.

Indeed, in the usual accounting analysis, Ford had no plausible alternative to continuing the strategy that had worked for him in the past. Most analysts denied the existence of a large market for low-priced vehicles. . . .

Economists have long believed that inherent in most products is a set price, covering costs and making "reasonable" profits, which can be computed by accountants and toward which supply and demand will eventually settle. Willie Durant believed that autos had reached that point in 1910. . . .

Automotive history might have taken this course, at least for a while, if Ford had followed the GM example and raised his price. But rather than raising his price as Buick did, Ford dropped it by nearly one-fifth, to $780. At this price Ford could break even only if he vastly expanded sales, or lowered production costs. . . .

In effect, Ford set his price not on the basis of his existing costs or sales but on the basis of the much lower costs and much expanded sales that might become possible at the lower price. The effect in the case of Henry Ford in 1910 was a 60 percent surge in sales that swept the Model T far ahead of Buick.

1. Henry Ford's intent was to design a car for "the great multitude." What strategy allowed him to accomplish this objective?
2. What gamble did Ford take in lowering the price of his Model T to $780?

George Gilder, *The Spirit of Enterprise.* New York: Simon & Schuster. Copyright 1984 by George Gilder. Reprinted by permission of Simon & Shuster, Inc.

8 | CHAPTER REVIEW

PRACTICING YOUR WRITING SKILLS: PARAPHRASING

Paraphrasing is restating a quotation or a passage from a book or article in your own words. This skill is very useful in writing papers and book reports and in giving oral reports. It allows you to convey, or tell, the meaning of another's words in less space. However, you must give credit to the original author or speaker when you paraphrase. Using someone else's material as if it were your own is plagiarism.

Here are a few tips to remember when paraphrasing:

1. Use your own words throughout the paraphrase, not those of the original source.
2. Do not add your own ideas.
3. Include main ideas and their supporting details.
4. Name your source.
5. Generally, your paraphrase should be shorter than the original material.

Activity: Reread the passage under Real Income Effect, page 189. Paraphrase it following the tips just given.

VOCABULARY REVIEW

For each of the following terms, write a sentence using the term: utility, real income, inelastic demand, equilibrium price, surplus, voluntary exchange

PRACTICING YOUR ECONOMIC SKILLS

1. **Drawing a Demand Graph.** Plot the information contained in the demand schedules at the bottom left to show the relationship between the price of beef per pound and the quantity demanded.
2. **Drawing a Supply Graph.** Plot the information in the supply schedule at the bottom right to show the relationship between the price of beef per pound and the quantity supplied.
3. **Graphing the Equilibrium Price.** Combine the two curves to illustrate the concept of equilibrium price. Mark the following: Shortage, Surplus, Equilibrium Price.
4. **Graphing Increased Demand.** Suppose the supply of beef increased because of imports. The price dropped by 20 percent at each and every price for which it was being sold. As a result, the quantities demanded also increased by 20 percent. What would happen to the demand and supply curves?

DISCUSSING ECONOMIC QUESTIONS

1. The law of demand states that as the price of an item falls, the quantity of that item demanded will be larger. At times during the 1980s, United States automakers cut automobile prices. However, sales of new automobiles did not rise very much at those times. Was the law of demand not working? What nonprice factors were involved? Con-

Beef Price per Pound	Quantity Demanded in Thousands of Pounds
$1.89	5,000
$1.99	4,500
$2.09	3,500
$2.39	2,000
$2.69	1,000

Beef Price per Pound	Quantity Supplied in Thousands of Pounds
$1.89	1,000
$1.99	2,500
$2.09	3,500
$2.39	4,000
$2.69	6,000

sider imported cars, the level of the nation's economy activity, and so on.

2. When the number of word processors being used in offices increased in the 1980s, many jobs opened for people who could operate word processors. How does this illustrate the laws of supply and demand? What nonprice factors were involved for each? In this case, who represents the supply, and who, the demand? Consider those who own the word processors and those who operate them.

3. Based on what you have read in this chapter, do you think the laws of supply and demand favor entrepreneurs? Why or why not? Support your argument with examples from the real world.

4. In a command economy, prices are set by central planners. What effect do you think setting prices has on quantity demanded and quantity supplied? Will the laws of supply and demand ultimately affect the prices planners set? Why or why not?

APPLYING CRITICAL THINKING SKILLS

1. **Gathering Information.** Clip articles from newspapers or magazines that show the laws of supply and/or demand operating in the real world. Possibilities would be weather damage to crops and economic conditions affecting housing starts, retail sales—sales directly to the public—and so on. Use these as the basis for a class discussion.

2. **Explaining Ideas in Writing.** Choose one of the following topics, and write one paragraph explaining how the topic relates to supply and/or demand: rebates on cars, lower prices for day-old bread, higher prices for fresh vegetables and fruit in the winter, marked-down prices on slightly damaged clothing, sales on Christmas cards right after Christmas.

3. **Writing a Report.** In the early 1980s, the

United States suddenly had a greater supply of gasoline than it used. Research the oil glut, as it was called, and explain in one paragraph what caused the decrease in consumer demand and the resulting oversupply.

4. **Using an Interview to Gather Information.** Interview a local merchant to learn what effect, if any, a recent change in price for a popular item had on its sales. Using this information as the basis, write a paragraph that answers the following questions: Was the price change an increase or decrease? Does what happened with the sales of this product tend to support the theory of the law of demand? Why or why not? Ask the owner the reasons for the change in price. Do the reasons support what you learned about supply and demand in this chapter? If so, how? If not, why not?

READINGS

Brue, Stanley L., and Wentworth, Donald R. *Economic Scenes: Theory in Today's World.* 3rd ed. Englewood Cliffs, N.J.: Prentice-Hall, 1984. Chapter 4, "The Basic Elements of Supply and Demand," pp. 41–55; Chapter 5, "The Economics of Utility, Elasticity and Changes in Supply and Demand," pp. 59–77.

Friedman, Milton, and Friedman, Rose. *Free to Choose: A Personal Statement.* New York: Harcourt Brace Jovanovich, 1981. Chapter 1, "The Power of the Market," pp. 9–37.

Heilbroner, Robert L., and Thurow, Lester C. *Economics Explained.* Englewood Cliffs, N.J.: Prentice-Hall, 1985. Chapter 15, "How Markets Work," pp. 157–167; Chapter 16, "Where Markets Fail," pp. 168–178.

Levi, Maurice. *Economics Deciphered.* New York: Basic Books, 1981.

The Price System. Philadelphia: Federal Reserve Bank of Philadelphia.

CHAPTER 9

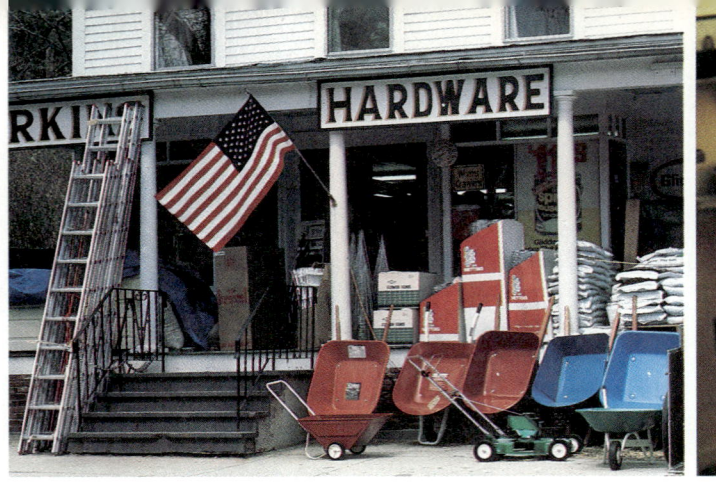

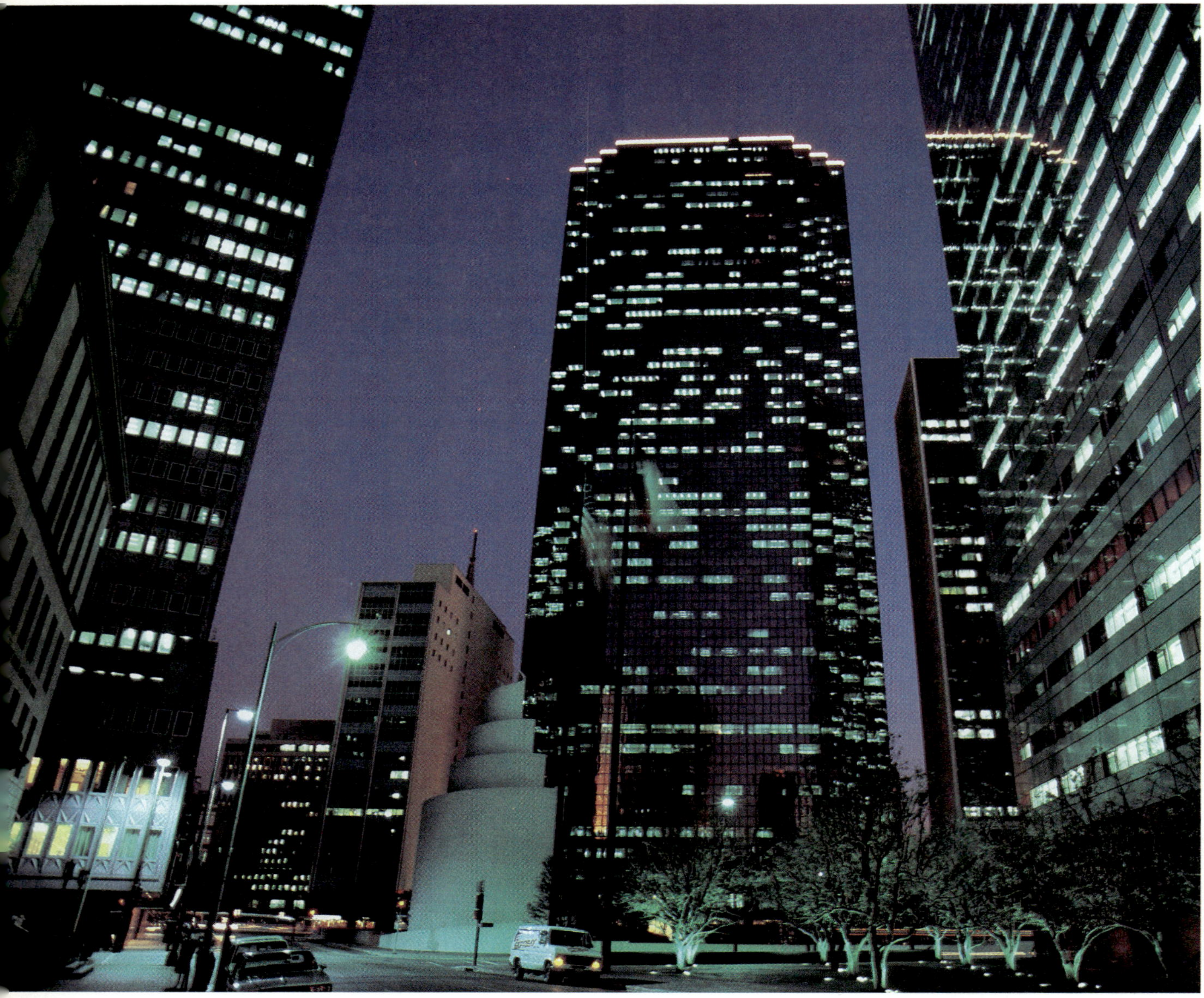

Large corporations with offices in city skyscrapers, sole proprietorships—often small business or professional offices—and partnerships are the three major types of business organizations.

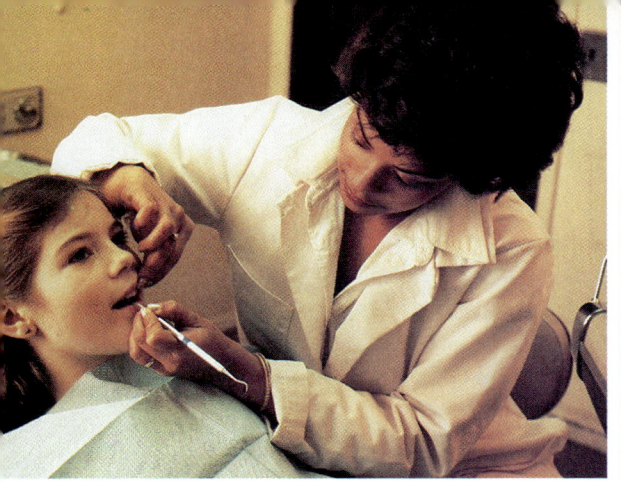

BUSINESS ORGANIZATIONS

There are three major types of business organizations: sole proprietorship, partnership, and corporation. This chapter describes in table form the advantages and disadvantages of each type of organization and asks you to compare and contrast them. You will also read about three less numerous, specialized forms of business organization: cooperative, nonprofit corporation, and franchise. Learning Economic Skills explains how to read the financial pages of newspapers.

CHAPTER OBJECTIVES After you study the sections of this chapter, you will be able to:

1 • list the five elements involved in setting up a business.

2 • state the advantages and disadvantages of sole proprietorships.

3 • state the advantages and disadvantages of partnerships.
   • compare and contrast sole proprietorships with partnerships.

4 ★ explain the information found on financial pages in newspapers.
   • state the advantages and disadvantages of corporations.
   • compare and contrast sole proprietorships and partnerships with corporations.

5 • describe a cooperative, a nonprofit corporation, and a franchise.

ECONOMICS VOCABULARY

inventory
sole proprietorship
unlimited liability
asset
partnership
index
revenue
articles of incorporation
corporate charter
nonprofit corporation
franchise

Suppose that you have been tinkering with electronic equipment since you were a child. By now you can take apart and reassemble radios, stereos, tape decks, videocassette recorders, and televisions without difficulty. In fact, you are so good at repairing this kind of equipment that you have been doing it for your friends and relatives for some time. Then an idea occurs to you: Why not charge people for your services? Why not go into business for yourself? As mentioned in Chapter 1, by starting your own business, you will become an entrepreneur.

1 | STARTING A BUSINESS

Ask yourself as you read:
- What are some of the risks of starting a business?
- What are some of the major steps in starting a business?

Every person who makes the decision to start a business is an entrepreneur because he or she is willing to take a risk. In fact, the first step in starting a business is to decide to start one. Usually people make such a decision because they hope to gain profits. However, there are many reasons for starting a business, including the desire to "do something on one's own" or to be one's own boss.

The next step for entrepreneurs is to gather the factors of production and to decide on the form of business organization that best suits their purposes. You will read about types of business organization later in the chapter. Methods of financing and managing businesses are discussed in Chapter 11. Anyone hoping to become an entrepreneur must also learn as much about the business they plan to start as possible. This includes learning about the laws, regulations, and tax codes that will apply to the business.

ELEMENTS OF BUSINESS OPERATION

Every business regardless of size involves five elements: 1. advertising, 2. expenses, 3. receipts, 4. record keeping, and 5. risk. To start a business, you must make potential customers aware that your services are available for a price. You could have one-page fliers printed to advertise your business and pass them out. You could also buy advertising space in the local newspaper. You will quickly find out that letting potential customers know that you are in business is costly. However, once you have customers, information about your business will spread by word of mouth.

flier: printed material, a small handbill

Because of the kinds of jobs you do, you will need replacement parts. At first, you might buy parts as you need them for a particular job. But in time, you will find it easier to have an **inventory.** This is a supply of whatever items are used in a business. As your business grows, you may decide you need more sophisticated equipment than what you began with. With the new equipment you could handle more complex

sophisticated (suh-FIS-tuh-kay-tid): complex, specialized

What factors do you think these men considered before they started their own shipping business? What risks are they taking? What rewards do you think they might expect?

problems and complete repairs more quickly. This would add to the income of your business. However, in both cases, the parts and equipment will probably take more capital than you have on hand. In Chapter 11 you will read about how businesses finance such expenses.

Because you could be working for someone else and making an income, you should pay yourself a wage equal to what you could earn elsewhere. It's important not to forget this opportunity cost when you figure out the profits and losses your new business is making. By adding your wages to your other expenses, including taxes, and then subtracting the total from your receipts, you will have your profit. From the very beginning, you will need to keep records of how much you owe and to whom, and of how much your business is taking in. You will need this information to do your taxes. At first, you may not make enough money to owe taxes. However, you will not know this unless you have records of your expenses and receipts.

As an entrepreneur, you are taking many risks, but the profit you expect to make is your incentive for taking those risks. The risks may not seem big, but they exist. For example, if you spend part of your savings to pay for advertising and equipment, you are taking a risk. You may not get enough business to cover these costs. Whenever you buy inventory, you are taking a risk. Your business could drop off so that you never use the parts. You could be forced to sell them at a loss if you go out of business. Whenever you buy a special part for a job, you are taking a risk. Suppose you do the work and your customer never pays you. Even if you are left with the compact disc player or stereo, you may not be able to sell it. Or you may not get enough money to cover your costs for all of the parts.

Case Study

THE STORY OF THE APPLE

The story of the Apple computer is one of the great success stories in modern American business. In creating the Apple Company, two young men, Steven Wozniak and Steven Jobs, combined their technical genius with marketing flair to start what became the multi-billion dollar personal computer industry. Apple's co-founders were self-taught electronic wizards, who introduced their first computer, the Apple I, in 1976. The account of their success is a present-day version of the classic rags-to-riches stories that were so familiar in the earlier days of America's industrial history. Andrew Carnegie, Henry Ford, Thomas Edison, and countless other business pioneers made fortunes for themselves and in the process changed the daily lives of all Americans.

Wozniak and Jobs first teamed up when Jobs was a high school student in Palo Alto, California. Their most successful early product was a device that enabled a caller to make free long-distance telephone calls! From this questionable start, the two moved on to more legitimate—and profitable—ventures.

Wozniak and Jobs designed what became Apple I in Jobs' bedroom and built the prototype in the family garage. Jobs was able to place an order for 25 of the computers with a local electronics retailer. In order to finance the production of their computer to fill orders, they sold two of their most valuable assets—Jobs's Volkswagen bus and Wozniak's scientific calculator. With this source of funds and more borrowed from friends in the electronic supply business, the Apple partners were off and running.

Six hundred Apple I computers were sold at a price of $666. The Apple II, selling for $1,350, followed soon after. It quickly set the industry standard for personal computers. Within three years, the Apple II earned $140 million. The success of the Apple Company was ensured when in 1980 it became a publicly owned company. With the sale of shares in the company to the public, Steven Wozniak and Steven Jobs became multi-millionaires.

Apple Computer, Inc. continued to be a pacesetter in the computer field, marketing new, more powerful and versatile machines like the Macintosh computers. But in 1986 the company experienced internal problems that led to the departure of both Wozniak and Jobs from Apple. The departure was painful for both of Apple's founders. However, Jobs organized a new company to develop education-oriented computer software. Some of Apple's key employees joined Jobs' company, leaving Apple with a potential "brain-drain." Fearing that they would use company secrets in their new position, the new president of Apple, Inc. won a lawsuit in which Jobs agreed to stop such hiring.

All of this has not dampened Jobs' enthusiasm for his latest business venture. He's doing what he likes best: planning a new enterprise with a group of bright, young, computer experts. It is similar to his first venture, but this time the investment money comes from the sale of his stock in Apple Computers, Inc. rather than from a used Volkswagon.

1. Two methods used to finance the Apple company are described. What were they?
2. In what ways does the success of the Apple company demonstrate the operation of a free enterprise economy?

You are even taking a risk with the time you spend setting up your business. That is, you are using time to think about what you will do, to write ads, to set up the bookkeeping, and so on. As you read in Chapter 1, your time has value. It has an opportunity cost. You could have used it to do something else, including work for someone for a wage. If you work for someone else, you take only the risk of not being paid, which is usually small. As an entrepreneur your risks are great, but so may be the rewards.

REVIEWING ECONOMIC PRINCIPLES

1. Define the following economic term: inventory
2. If you were setting up your own business, why would you need to advertise?
3. Name two types of expenses you as a business owner would have.
4. Why do businesses need to keep records of expenses and receipts?
5. Give one example each of the following risks involved in setting up a business: **a.** money, **b.** time.
6. **Critical Thinking: Explaining the Main Idea.** What is the incentive for taking risks to start a business?

2 | SOLE PROPRIETORSHIP

Ask yourself as you read:
- What is a sole proprietorship?
- What are some examples of sole proprietorship?

The type of business described in Section 1 is the most basic type of business organization—**sole proprietorship** (pruh-PRY-uh-tuhr-ship). This is a business owned by one person. It is the oldest form of business organization and also the most common. The colonies of Maryland and Pennsylvania were founded as sole proprietorships.

This small store, a sole proprietorship, is the most basic type of business organization. Why do you think this woman decided to start this business?

Table 9-1: ADVANTAGES AND DISADVANTAGES OF SOLE PROPRIETORSHIPS

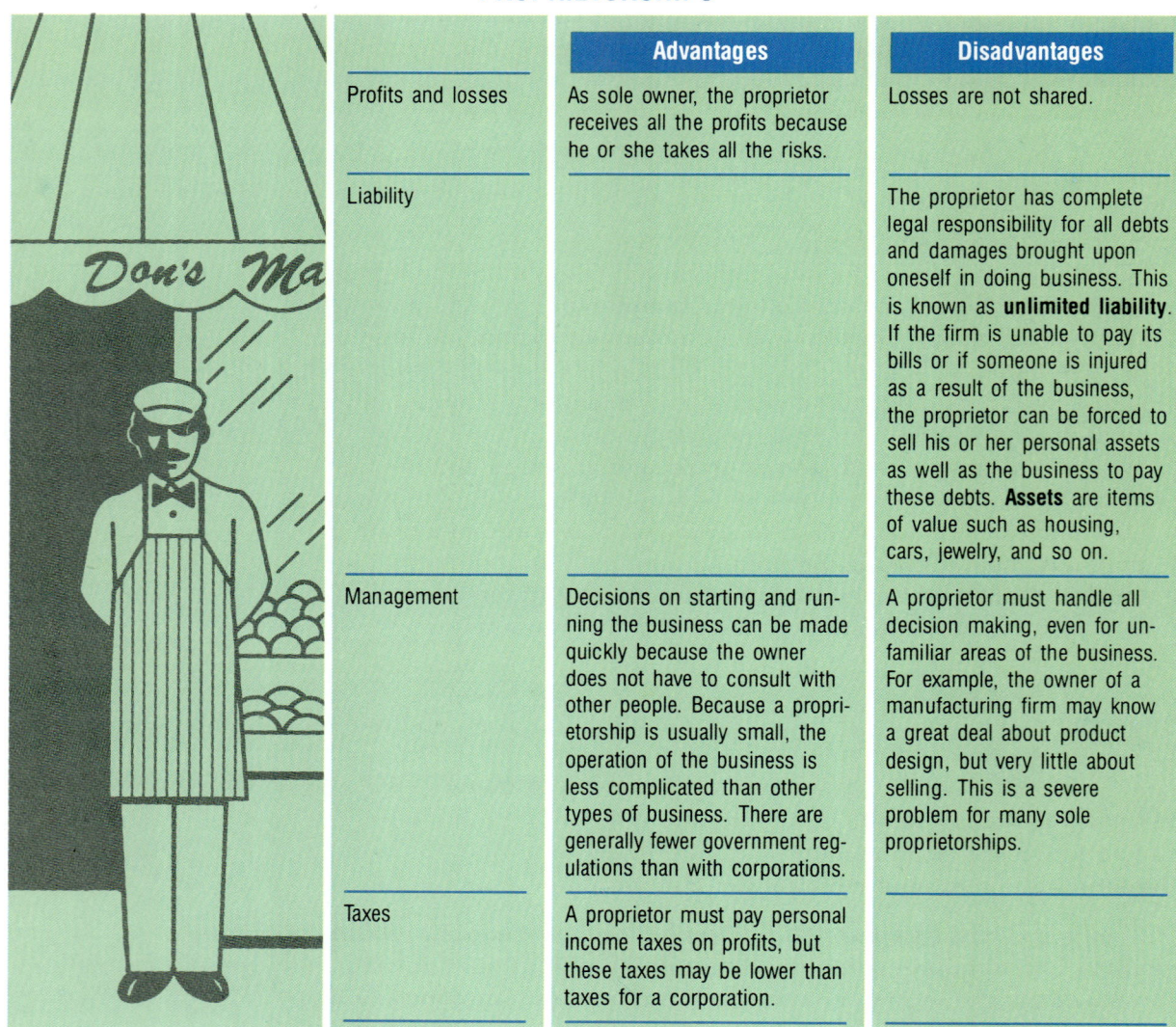

	Advantages	Disadvantages
Profits and losses	As sole owner, the proprietor receives all the profits because he or she takes all the risks.	Losses are not shared.
Liability		The proprietor has complete legal responsibility for all debts and damages brought upon oneself in doing business. This is known as **unlimited liability**. If the firm is unable to pay its bills or if someone is injured as a result of the business, the proprietor can be forced to sell his or her personal assets as well as the business to pay these debts. **Assets** are items of value such as housing, cars, jewelry, and so on.
Management	Decisions on starting and running the business can be made quickly because the owner does not have to consult with other people. Because a proprietorship is usually small, the operation of the business is less complicated than other types of business. There are generally fewer government regulations than with corporations.	A proprietor must handle all decision making, even for unfamiliar areas of the business. For example, the owner of a manufacturing firm may know a great deal about product design, but very little about selling. This is a severe problem for many sole proprietorships.
Taxes	A proprietor must pay personal income taxes on profits, but these taxes may be lower than taxes for a corporation.	

Today, there are more than 12 million such businesses the United States, and many of them are small businesses. For that reason, they usually are easier and less expensive to start, organize, and to run. You probably have contact with many sole proprietorships every day without realizing it. Fruit stands, corner grocery stores, drugstores, hobby shops, repair shops, dry cleaners, and so on, are often owned and operated by one person. Many doctors, dentists, lawyers, and accountants also practice as sole proprietors. In such industries as farming, construction, and contracting, they are the most numerous type of business organizations. Table 9-1 lists the advantages and disadvantages of operating a sole proprietorship.

Table 9-1: ADVANTAGES AND DISADVANTAGES OF SOLE PROPRIETORSHIPS *(continued)*

	Advantages	Disadvantages
Personal satisfaction	Because a proprietorship is owned by one individual, that person has full pride in owning it. The person is his or her own boss and makes the business whatever it is.	Running a sole proprietorship is demanding and time-consuming. If the proprietor does not enjoy such responsibility, he or she will find ownership a burden.
Financing growth	Because the proprietor has liability for all debts, it is occasionally easier for a proprietorship to obtain credit than for a corporation of the same size. Lenders are more willing to extend credit knowing that they can take over not only the assets of the business but also the assets of the proprietor if the loan is not paid back.	A sole proprietor must rely on his or her own funds plus money that can be borrowed from others. Borrowing small amounts may be easier for a sole proprietorship than for a coroporation of similar size, but borrowing large amounts can be difficult. Creditors are unlikely to lend more money than the value of the business and any personal assets of the proprietor.
Life of the business		A sole propietorship depends on one individual. If that person dies, goes bankrupt, or is unwilling or unable to work, the business will probably close. If a proprietorship is passed on to a family member, that person may not have the same dedication as the original owner. This uncertainty about the future increases the risk to both employees and creditors.

REVIEWING ECONOMIC PRINCIPLES

1. List the seven categories that are used on Table 9-1.
2. For a sole proprietorship, which categories clearly show: **a.** advantages? **b.** disadvantages?
3. Which categories give both advantages and disadvantages?
4. Rank the importance of each category. For example, is unlimited liability a more important factor than receiving all the profits?
5. **Critical Thinking: Drawing a Conclusion.** Based on your ranking of categories, do you think the advantages outweigh the disadvantages or vice versa? Explain your choice in a paragraph.

These women have formed a partnership to establish this specialty clothing store. What risks and benefits might they expect?

3 | PARTNERSHIP

Ask yourself as you read:
- Why do people form partnerships?
- What risks are involved in forming partnerships?

To take the example of your repair business a little further, suppose that your business is doing very well. It is doing so well that your work-load has increased to the point where you have little time for anything else. You have several alternatives open to you.

You could discourage business by charging higher prices, which might also affect your profits. Or you could expand your business by hiring an employee. However, you have also decided that you want to buy more equipment. You would also like to give up keeping the books so you could spend more time on the actual repair work. This is the part of the business you like best. You need financial capital, but would rather not take out a bank loan.

So you decide to look for someone who need not know much about repairing electronic equipment but who can keep books and handle customers. Equally important, this person must have money to invest in a business. When you find such a person, you offer to form a **partnership.** This is a business that two or more individuals own and operate for their own profit. The two of you sign a partnership agreement that is legally binding. It describes the duties of each partner, the division of profits, and the distribution of assets should the partners end the agreement.

You probably know of and deal with several partnerships. Many doctors, dentists, and lawyers work in partnerships. Small stores are often owned by two or more people. Sometimes they are members of the same family. Table 9-2 lists some of the major advantages and disadvantages of partnerships.

Table 9-2: ADVANTAGES AND DISADVANTAGES OF PARTNERSHIPS

	Advantages	Disadvantages
Profits and losses	Losses are shared. Several individuals can sometimes survive a loss that might bankrupt a sole proprietorship.	Because partners share the risks of the business, they also share the profits.
Liability		Partners as a group have unlimited liability for all debts and damages incurred in business. If a partner is unable to pay his or her share of a debt, the others must make up for the difference.
Management	Partnerships are usually more efficient than proprietorships. They allow each partner to work in areas of the business that he or she knows most about or is best at doing.	Decision making is often slow because of the need to reach agreement among several people. Disagreements can lead to severe problems in running the business.
Taxes	Partners must pay personal income taxes on their share of profits. These taxes are usually lower than those for a corporation.	
Personal satisfaction	Partners, like sole proprietors, often feel pride in owning and operating their own company. An individual who does not want responsibility for all decisions may especially enjoy working with others in the business.	If partners do not get along with each other, trying to work together can result in constant arguments. This can lessen the pleasure of owning and running the business.
Financing growth	A partnership combines the capital of two or more people. It makes more money available to operate a larger and perhaps more profitable business. Because the risk is shared, creditors are often willing to lend more money to a partnership than to a sole proprietorship.	Like sole proprietorships, partnerships can have trouble obtaining large amounts of capital. The amount that partnerships can borrow is usually limited by the combined value of the assets of the business and of the partners.
Life of the business		If one partner dies or leaves, the partnership must be ended and reorganized. The others may be unable or unwilling to continue operating, and the business may close. This uncertainty is a risk to employees and creditors.

1. On Table 9-2, which categories clearly show: **a.** advantages? **b.** disadvantages?
2. Which categories give both advantages and disadvantages?
3. **a.** Rank the seven categories on Table 9-2 in what you think is their order of importance for partnerships. **b.** Do you think the advantages outweigh the disadvantages or vice versa?
4. **Critical Thinking: Comparing and Contrasting Information.** Compare and contrast Tables 9-1 and 9-2. Would you rather be a sole proprietor or a member of a partnership? What was the most important factor in your decision? Explain your choice in a brief paragraph.

4 | THE CORPORATE WORLD

Ask yourself as you read:
- What is a corporation?
- How does a corporation raise capital?

Suppose your electronic repair business has grown. You now have several partners and have turned your garage into a shop. Still you are not satisfied. You think that you are more efficient than many similar businesses in your area and you want to expand further. In fact, you would like to rent a store so that your business would be more visible. You would like to buy the latest equipment, charge a little less than

The corporation is the most important form of business in terms of the amount of business done. What is the role of the shareholders who are attending this annual meeting?

Figure 9-1: TOP TEN INDUSTRIAL CORPORATIONS RANKED BY SALES

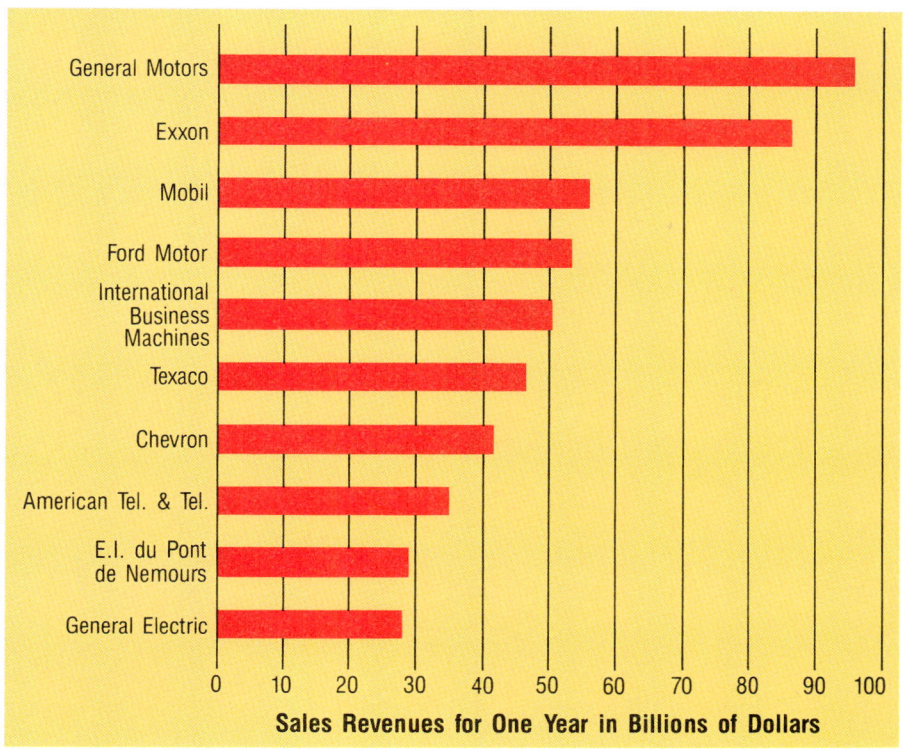

Sales Revenues for One Year in Billions of Dollars

Source: *Fortune* magazine, April 28, 1986

Corporations this large make up about .1 percent of all corporations in the United States. The majority are what is known as small corporations.

your competitors, and capture a larger share of the market for electronic repair work. (Remember the law of demand: At lower prices, more is demanded, and that will be true for electronic repairs that you offer.) But you do not have the needed capital.

You have decided that you do not want any more partners. You would have to consult with them about every detail of the business as you do now with your present partners. What you want is financial backers who will let you use their money while letting you run the business. What you are proposing is a corporation.

As you may recall from Chapter 7, a corporation is an organization owned by many people but treated by the law as though it were a person. It can own property, pay taxes, make contracts, sue and be sued, and so on. It has a separate and distinct existence from the stockholders who own the corporation's stock. Stock represents ownership rights to a certain portion of the profits and assets of the company that issues the stock. However, the stockholders do not have direct control over the operation of the business.

In terms of the amount of business done, the corporation is the most important type of business organization in the United States today. Figure 9-1 shows the sales of the 10 largest corporations in a recent year. The financial pages of most daily newspapers will give the latest stock

Table 9-3: ADVANTAGES AND DISADVANTAGES OF CORPORATIONS

	Advantages	Disadvantages
Profits and losses	Owners of the corporation—stockholders—do not have to devote time to the company to make money on their investment.	
Liability	The corporation, and not its stockholders, is legally responsible for its debts. If a corporation goes bankrupt or is sued, creditors cannot take personal property from stockholders to pay debts. This is known as limited liability, and many people consider it to be the major advantage of the corporate form of business.	
Management	Responsibility for running a corporation is divided among many people. Decisions are made at many levels by individuals trained in specific areas, such as sales, production, and so on. This allows a corporation to handle large and complicated operations and to carry on many types of business activity at the same time.	Decision making can be slow and complicated because so many levels of management are involved. Also, the interests of those running the corporation, who may not be stockholders, are not always the same as those of the stockholders, who often seek an immediate return on investment. In addition, corporations frequently must deal with more government regulations than partnerships or sole proprietorships.

prices for these corporations. Table 9-3 shows the advantages and disadvantages of corporations. Although corporations make up only about 15 percent of all business firms, corporations collect about 85 percent of all business **revenue**—money taken in.

In order to form a corporation, its founders must do three things. First, they must register their company with the government of the state in which it will be headquartered. Second, they must sell stock. Third, along with the stockholders, they must elect a board of directors.

REGISTERING THE CORPORATION

Every state has laws governing the formation of corporations, but most state laws are similar. Suppose that you and your partners decide to form a corporation. You will have to file an **articles of incorporation** application with the state in which you will run your corporation. In general, these articles include four items:

Table 9-3: ADVANTAGES AND DISADVANTAGES OF CORPORATIONS *(continued)*

	Advantages	Disadvantages
Taxes		The federal government and some state and local governments tax corporate profits. The profits that are paid to stockholders as dividends are again taxed as income to those individuals. Some states also tax corporate property or charge a fee for the right to carry on business within their borders.
Personal satisfaction	An individual may feel satisfaction simply in owning a part of a corporation.	Individual stockholders, except perhaps through voting at the annual stockholders' meeting, have little or no say in how a corporation is run.
Financing growth	Corporations draw on the resources of many investors. Corporations may issue stock at any time and can, therefore, raise capital at any time.	
Life of the business	Unlike the life of a sole proprietorship or partnership, the life of a corporation can continue indefinitely if it remains profitable. Its life is not affected by the death of stockholders. Stock can easily be transferred from one person to another.	

1. Name, address, and purpose of the corporation;
2. Names and addresses of the initial board of directors (these men and women will serve until the first stockholders' meeting, when a new board is elected);
3. Number of shares of stock to be issued;
4. Amount of capital to be raised through issuing stock.

initial (ih-NISH-uhl): first

If the articles are in agreement with state law, the state will grant you a **corporate charter.** This is a license to operate from that state.

SELLING STOCK

To continue the example of your electronic repair business, you could sell shares of either common or preferred stock in your new corporation. Common stock gives the holder part ownership in the corporation and voting rights at the annual stockholders' meeting. It does not guarantee a dividend—money return on the money invested in a company's stock. Preferred stock, on the other hand, does guarantee a cer-

Learning Economic Skills

READING THE FINANCIAL PAGE

Activity on the stock market, as well as on the bond and commodities markets, is considered a sign of the nation's economic health. Many people follow the market by listening to reports on radio or television and by reading the financial pages of the newspaper. At a glance, these pages may seem very confusing, but once you understand the keys, they become easy to read.

READING STOCK MARKET QUOTATIONS

At the beginning of each trading day, stocks open at the same prices they closed at on the day before. The price for a particular stock will move up or down throughout the day as people buy and sell shares of that stock. At the end of the day, each stock has a closing price. This is the information that newspapers report.

The example that follows of the stocks traded on the New York Stock Exchange is from a typical newspaper financial page. American Stock Exchange quotations are given as well in most papers. Some newspapers also carry regional or local stock exchange listings. In a listing, the name of each company is printed in an abbreviated form. In this listing, *TexInst* refers to Texas Instruments. Next to the name of a stock you will sometimes see other letters, such as *pf*. These letters are explained in the key to the stock table that appears on the newspaper page along with the table. For example, *pf* means the issue is a preferred stock. Prices are listed in dollars and fractions of a dollar. The figure *70½* means $70.50. The labels of the various columns are explained for you below.

Stocks traded over the counter are also listed on the financial page. The information varies slightly from that given for stocks traded on the New York and American exchanges. Over-the-counter quotations give information on the highest, lowest, and last price for the shares at the end of the day. The sample on p. 227 shows such listings, found in the financial sections of almost all major newspapers.

Quotations on the New York Stock Exchange

52-Week High	Low	Stock	Sales 100s	High	Low	Last	Chg.
56½	37	TexEst	115	54½	53¾	54¼	+ ⅞
22	19	TxEt pf	40	22¾	22¼	22¾	+ ¾
25¼	20¾	TxEt pf	13	24¾	24¼	24¼	− ¾
37¼	22¼	TexGT	77	31⅝	31	41⅝	+ ⅝
32⅛	18	TexInd	180	31⅝	30⅝	31½	+1
111½	70½	TexInst	1738	110	105⅝	110	+4⅛

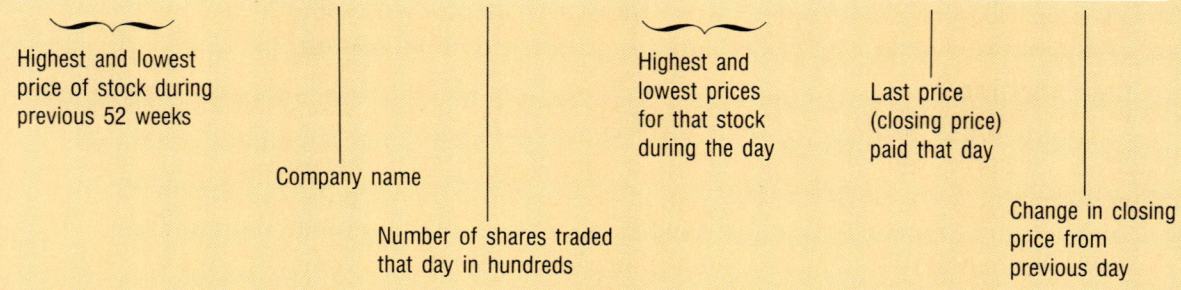

Highest and lowest price of stock during previous 52 weeks

Company name

Number of shares traded that day in hundreds

Highest and lowest prices for that stock during the day

Last price (closing price) paid that day

Change in closing price from previous day

Quotations for Over-the-Counter Stock

Stock	Div	Sales In 100s	High	Low	Last	Chg.
Filtrik $	.44	34	16¼	15¾	16	− ¼
Finalco	.20	12	2½	2½	2½	…
FinNws		779	9⅝	9⅜	9⅜	− ⅛
FnTrst	1.60	6	47	44	44	…
Fingmx		471	6⅜	6	6⅜	+ ⅛
Finigan		35	10¾	10½	10¾	− ¼

Company name

Annual dividend per share

Number of shares traded that day in hundreds

Highest price dealers are willing to pay (the price if you as a stock-holder want to sell)

Lowest price dealers are asking for stock they want to sell (the price if you want to buy)

Last price (closing price) paid that day

Change in bid price from previous day

Quotations for Mutual Funds

	N.A.V.	Buy	Chg.
Constel G	13.92	NL	−.13
Cont Mut	….	….	….
Copley	1.80	NL	….
Ctry Cap	14.10	15.24	−.12
Delaware Group:			
Decat	15.02	16.42	−.16
Delaw	19.96	21.81	−.19
Dech	7.54	8.24	−.07
Tx Fre	6.82	7.14	+.07
Delta	9.96	10.89	+.03

Specific mutual fund within the company (some companies offer several funds)

Company name

Price for buying a single share

Change in buy price from previous day

Net asset value: value per share

READING MUTUAL FUND QUOTATIONS

Mutual funds, including money market mutual funds, may also be listed on the financial page. Quotations for money market mutual funds usually give the total amount of assets in a fund and the rate of return that investors have been receiving. Listings for mutual funds include a column labeled *N.A.V.*, meaning net asset value. This is the value of each share in the fund expressed in dollars. The listing also shows the cost of buying into the fund and how much this buy price has changed since the previous day. If the letters *NL* appear instead of a buy price, it means no load, or no sales, charge. The buyer does not have to pay a fee for buying into the fund. The net asset value, then, is the same as the buy price. The sample that follows is a typical mutual fund listing.

READING BOND MARKET QUOTATIONS

Bonds, because of their fixed rate of interest, do not grow in value in the same way as stocks. However, their values do change depending on the return investors can get on other possible investments. If other investments such as money market funds are paying only low rates, bonds will be worth more to investors, and they will bid the price up. Bonds are rated by financial analysts such as Moody's Investor Service as excellent, good, or poor risks. These affect the amount that people will pay for them. Although bonds usually have a face value of $1,000, they may sell for more or less depending on how valuable they are to investors at the time. Prices for bonds are listed as a percentage of their face value. A figure of *70½* means a $1,000 bond is selling at $705.

Quotations on the New York Stock Exchange Bond Market

Bonds	Current Yield	Sales in $1,000	High	Low	Last	Net Chge.
Crane 10½94	13.0	20	81	81	81	−1
CrdF 8s92	10.8	10	73⅞	73⅞	73⅞	+4⅞
CrdF 15½91	14.5	3	107	107	107	+ ½
CrdF zr90s	. . .	5	32½	32½	32½	+ ½
CrwnZ 8⅞00	12.7	28	70	67⅛	70	+ ¼
CyprM 8¾85	9.1	5	96	95	96	+2¼

Company name

Interest rate paid on face value of bond

Date of maturity (last two digits of year)

Current yield: annual percentage return on investment based on the current price

Highest and lowest price of bond during the day

Last price (closing price) paid that day

Change in closing price from previous day

Sales of bonds expressed in thousands

The sample above is a typical listing from the New York Stock Exchange Bond Market. The majority of bonds, however, including all tax-exempt bonds, are traded over the counter. Over-the-counter listings include bid and asked prices instead of high, low, and closing prices. You will sometimes see two or more entries for bonds from a particular company. This means that the company has different bond offerings, each maturing at a different time.

INDEXES OF ACTIVITY

The financial pages of many newspapers also carry various summaries of stock activity. These indexes list leading stocks or the most actively traded stocks over a stated period of time. An **index** is a number that measures the change in a set of statistics over a period of time.

There are four separate Dow Jones stock averages; 30 industrial stocks, 20 transportation stocks, 15 utility stocks, and the average of all 65 stocks. The Dow Jones industrial average (DJIA) is perhaps the best known index, and it is often quoted in radio and television reports. It is supposed to show the trend of activity in the stock market as indicated by the largest, most financially sound companies. There are also five Standard and Poor's Indexes: 400 industrial stocks, 20 transportation stocks, 40 utility stocks, 40 financial stocks, and a composite (kuhm-PAHZ-it), or combined, index of all 500 stocks.

Both the New York and American exchanges publish their own indexes. The National Association of Securities Dealers Automatic Quotations Index (NASDAQ) has a combined index of 2,900 over-the-counter stocks. NASDAQ also publishes indexes by industry for such industries as insurance, utilities, banks, and transportation.

Practicing Your Skills

1. Find the listing for Texas Instruments (TexInst) in the sample from the New York Stock Exchange. **a.** What was the last closing price for this stock? **b.** How much of a change was this from the previous day?
2. **a.** What was the dividend for Financial Trust (FnTrst) stock listed in the sample of over-the-counter quotations? **b.** How many shares of this stock were sold?
3. **a.** How many separate mutual funds are offered by the Delaware Group? **b.** What is the net asset value of a share of Delaware's tax free fund (TxFre)?
4. **a.** What is the interest rate being paid on bonds maturing in 1991 for Credit Thrift Financial (CrdF)? **b.** What is the current yield?

tain amount of dividend each year. Preferred stock also guarantees to the stockholder first claim, after creditors have been paid, on whatever value is left in the corporation if it goes out of business. Holders of preferred stock usually do not have voting rights in the corporation, although they are part owners. As you will read under the heading Naming a Board of Directors, even voting stockholders do not have much control over how a corporation is run.

If your corporation were to become large, you might find its stock traded in the local stock market as over-the-counter stock. Over-the-counter means that individual brokerage firms hold quantities of shares of stocks that they buy and sell for investors. Should your corporation continue to grow, it would be traded on a regional stock exchange. Or it might be listed as an over-the-counter stock with the National Association of Securities Dealers Automated Quotation (NASDAQ) in one of their three lists discussed in Chapter 7.

Selling stock is not the only way a corporation can raise capital to develop or expand. It can also sell debt. That is, it can issue bonds. A bond promises to pay a stated rate of interest over a stated period of time and to repay the full amount borrowed at the end of that time. You might wish to review Tables 7-2 and 7-3 for a complete summary of the differences between common and preferred stocks and between stocks and bonds. In Chapter 11, you will be reading more about the ways that businesses have to finance their operations.

NAMING A BOARD OF DIRECTORS

To become incorporated, a company must have a board of directors. The first board for your corporation would be selected by you and your partners, as founders of the corporation. After that, the board would be elected by stockholders at their annual stockholders' meetings. This

Based on what you have read, how much power does the Board of Directors have over the way a corporation is run?

Figure 9-2: STRUCTURE OF A TYPICAL CORPORATION

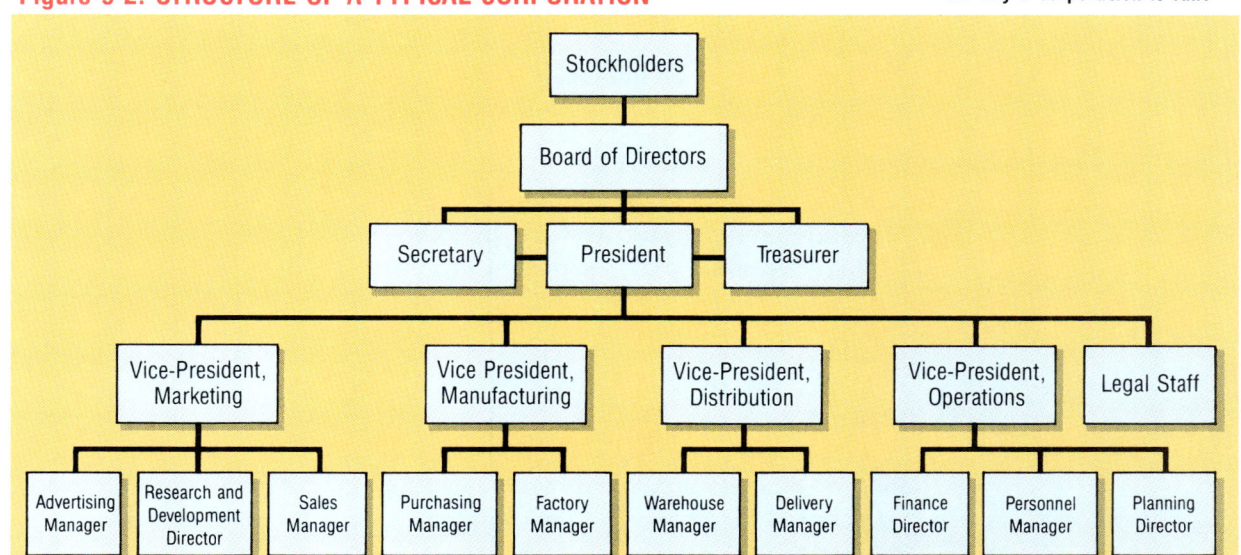

election is governed by the bylaws of the corporation. Bylaws are a set of rules describing how stock will be sold and dividends paid, with a list of the duties of the company's officers. They are written after the corporate charter has been granted.

The board is responsible for supervising and controlling the corporation. However, it does not run business operations on a day-to-day basis. Rather, it hires officers for the company—president, vice-president(s), secretary, and treasurer—to run the business and hire other employees. Figure 9-2 shows the typical structure of a corporation.

REVIEWING ECONOMIC PRINCIPLES

1. Define the following economic terms: **a.** revenue, **b.** articles of incorporation, **c.** corporate charter.
2. On Table 9-3, which categories clearly show: **a.** advantages? **b.** disadvantages?
3. Which categories give both advantages and disadvantages?
4. Based on what you have read on Tables 9-1 and 9-2, do you agree with the statement on the table that limited liability is the major advantage of the corporate form of business? Explain your answer in a sentence.
5. **a.** Rank the seven categories on Table 9-3 in what you think is their order of importance. **b.** Do you think the advantages of corporations outweigh their disadvantages, or vice versa?
6. What three things must the founders of a corporation do?
7. **Critical Thinking: Comparing and Contrasting Categories.** Compare and contrast your rankings of the categories of Table 9-3 with your answer for question 5 above. Would you rather be a sole proprietor, a member of a partnership, or a stockholder in a corporation? Why? What was the most important factor in your decision? Explain your choice in a paragraph.

5 | OTHER FORMS OF BUSINESS ORGANIZATIONS

Ask yourself as you read:
- What other types of business organizations are there besides sole proprietorships, partnerships, and corporations?
- What are some major nonprofit organizations?

There are several other types of specialized business organizations. One is the cooperative, a business owned and operated by its members. In Unit 2, you read about consumer co-ops in the form of credit unions, housing arrangements, and food stores. But there are also producer co-ops. These manufacture and market products or sell services to their members or the public. For example, many farmers belong to producer co-ops that help process, transport, and even advertise their members' products.

The association that supports an art museum often is nonprofit. How is a nonprofit corporation different from a corporation?

Churches and many cultural, educational, and charitable associations, such as a museum or opera association, Goodwill, and the National Wildlife Federation, are nonprofit organizations. A **nonprofit corporation** is legally incorporated by the state and has most of the characteristics of the corporations you have just read about. However, it does not pay taxes or issue stock.

Many hotel, motel, gas station, and fast-food chains are franchises. A **franchise** is a contract in which a franchisor (fran-chy-ZOR) sells to another business the right to use its name and sell its products. The person or business buying these rights, called the franchisee (fran-chy-ZEE), pays a fee that may include a percentage of all money taken in. In other words, if a person buys a motel franchise, that person agrees to pay the motel chain a certain fee plus a portion of the profits for as long as his or her motel stays in business. In return, the chain will help the franchisee set up the motel.

The chain will help in choosing a location for the building and in arranging credit. If necessary, it will train the new owner and his or her staff. Because the motel is part of the chain, the new owner benefits from the advertising campaigns that the chain runs. His or her motel will be identified by travelers with the national chain. Since most people value their time, they will decide to stay in a well-known motel chain in a strange city than to spend the time researching available lodging. The chances are that they will have stayed in a motel in this chain in another city. For that reason, once the motel is operating, the chain will oversee it to make sure that a certain quality of service is maintained.

REVIEWING ECONOMIC PRINCIPLES

1. Reread page 230 on the different types of cooperatives. Use that information plus the information on cooperatives in this chapter to make a table, listing type of co-op, characteristic(s) that make it a co-op, and services.
2. What is a franchise? Name three franchises in your area.
3. **Critical Thinking: Comparing and Contrasting. a.** Write one sentence describing how a nonprofit corporation is different from a regular corporation. **b.** Explain how they are alike.

SUMMARY OF
IMPORTANT PRINCIPLES

1
- Every business involves five elements: advertising, expenses, receipts, record keeping, and risk.
- A potential entrepreneur must also gather the factors of production and decide what type of business organization he or she wishes to form. Entrepreneurs must also learn about the laws, regulations, and tax codes that apply to the business.

2
- The advantages of sole proprietorships involve taxes. Disadvantages are unlimited liability and uncertainty about the life of the business. The following categories involve both advantages and disadvantages: profit and losses, management, personal satisfaction, and financing growth.

3
- The advantages of partnerships involve taxes. Disadvantages are unlimited liability and uncertainty about the life of the business. The following categories involve both advantages and disadvantages: profits and losses, management, personal satisfaction, and financing growth.
- Although some of the specific details vary, both sole proprietorships and partnerships have about the same advantages and disadvantages.

4
- The financial pages of newspapers carry the closing prices of stocks, bonds, mutual funds, commodities, and stock options. The key to each table explains the various column headings and other information on the table.
- The advantages of corporations involve profits, limited liability, financing growth, and continued life of the business. Disadvantages are taxes. The following categories involve both advantages and disadvantages: management and personal satisfaction.
- Compared to sole proprietorships and partnerships, corporations differ in advantages and disadvantages. The major differences in advantages are limited liability, financing growth, and continued life of the business. The major disadvantage is the amount of taxes a corporation must pay. All three types of business have both advantages and disadvantages in the categories of management and personal satisfaction.
- To form a corporation, the founders must register the business, sell stock, and name a board of directors. After this first board, stockholders elect members of the board.

5
- A cooperative is a business owned and operated by its members. A nonprofit corporation is similar to a corporation except that it pays no taxes and issues no stock. A franchise is a contract in which a franchisor sells to another business the right to use its name and sell its products.

Putting Economics to Work

TRADE-OFFS: GOING INTO A PARTNERSHIP

Sandy Harrigan has been a bicycle racer since she was 15. She also has great mechanical ability. During her last two years in high school, Sandy worked in Mike's Bicycle Shop. At first, she was a cashier. Then she began fixing flats. By the end of the first summer, she was overhauling sophisticated racing bikes. By the end of the second summer, Sandy had earned a citywide reputation as an expert bicycle mechanic.

Sandy is now a freshman business major at a local community college. However, Mike Lewicki, the bicycle store owner, has invited her to become a partner in the business. But Sandy does not want to leave college, so she has to find a compromise. She will switch from day to evening classes and work at the bicycle store during the day.

Sandy and Mike next make an appointment with an attorney to work out the details of the partnership agreement. Under the agreement, Sandy will receive a percentage of the shop's profits in return for an investment of $5,000. Part of this sum represents most of Sandy's savings and part of it, a bank loan. Sandy will share in current profits as well as in whatever additional value her being involved in the business might add to its income.

If the business is successful, Sandy can expect to face a difficult decision sometime in the future. She will have to decide whether to give more time to the bicycle store or more time to her studies.

1. What are the risks Sandy faces by becoming a partner in the shop?
2. If Mike and Sandy decide to form a corporation, what steps will they have to go through?

Readings in Economics

RAGS TO RICHES IN THE RAG TRADE

Skill: Drawing Conclusions

Sometimes even very young people who take the risk of starting a business can be successful. This reading tells of a hard-working brother and sister who went from humble beginnings to running Italy's largest clothing company in 1986.

Giuliana Benetton remembers the night 30 years ago when her elder brother Luciano made a frightening proposal. Why not combine her love of working with wool with his sales experience and go into business for themselves?

Giuliana, then 17, thought it was too much for "a little girl" and too large a commitment for such poor siblings. Luciano, who worked in a clothing store, pestered her for months until she agreed. Luciano sold his accordion for the down payment on a knitting machine and Giuliana quit her job and began producing sweaters at home that Luciano hustled to local shops after work.

Now the pair, together with younger brothers Gilberto and Carlo, run Italy's largest clothing company with more than 3,200 stores, most of which are privately owned, in 53 countries. . . .

Innovations, in the use of colors, stores and technology, have helped make the company successful. So has the Benettons' almost-fanatical dedication to their work. Luciano, whose father died when he was 10, and Giuliana set the pace from the beginning by going to work at early ages to help support the family.

The two paid for the first knitting machine in six months by working 18 to 20 hours a day, bought another machine and hired young women to keep up with the demand.

Even now Signora Giuliana, as her employees call her, works as if it never happened. The mother of four rarely takes vacations because "I'm always afraid that there will be something that doesn't work right."

By 1965 business was good enough to open up a small factory. In 1968 they opened their first retail store in the small town of Belluno. Ten years later, the company opened a store in Paris and in 1980 set up in the United States, now its largest market with more than 400 stores and nearly 14% of sales (they hope for 600 stores by the end of [1986]).

1. What resources did the Benettons need in order to start their business?
2. The Benettons were entrepreneurs who used a creative idea and took the risk of going into business. What qualities did they possess that helped them succeed in their business?

"Benetton: Rags to Riches in the Rag Trade," *The Wall Street Journal*, June 25, 1986. Reprinted by permission of *The Wall Street Journal*, © Dow Jones & Company, Inc., 1986. All Rights Reserved.

SOLE PROPRIETORSHIP: THE BEGINNING OF COLGATE

Skill: Sequencing Information

Some of America's best-known companies began as sole proprietorships. This reading describes one company that has been keeping the United States clean for over 180 years.

"Cleanliness is next to godliness," preached the Methodist John Wesley. It was the sort of lesson that the young religious nonconformist, William Colgate (1783—1857), took to heart as well as to

The clothes worn by this couple in a Benetton ad highlight the international appeal of the chain.

mind. He was only twelve years old when his father, Robert, fled with him from England to Maryland in 1795, after heading a list of dangerous Anabaptists destined for prison, or a worse fate.

William's father did poorly at farming and . . . moved to Baltimore to make soap and candles. When he took up farming again, he left William to run the business. The youth had little success, however, and in 1803 moved to New York City. He became an apprentice in a soap factory, and after three years struck off on his own.

To the business he established, he brought a concept of uniform quality that won a market for his products. He added a scent to his soap and cut the cakes into equal-sized bars of one-pound weight. The popularity of his pale soap and pearl starch, along with the fact that he delivered his products to people's homes, earned him a fast-growing clientele.

In 1807 Colgate took in a partner, who provided him with $700 of new capital. After six years he bought him out for $1,000. In 1817 he ran his first public ad: "Have for sale on best terms a constant supply of Soap, Mould, and Dipt Candles of first quality." He even bid for sales abroad in his advertisements—a step that eventually paid off handsomely.

The completion of the Erie Canal in 1825 opened a new sales territory in the West. Colgate's sons and nephews joined him in the thriving business. By 1835 exports of soap and candles from the United States totalled $534,476, and the American industry was on its way to becoming soap sellers to the world.

In 1872 the company that Colgate had founded introduced the brand-name soap Cashmere Bouquet, and the following year it brought out the first flavored toothpaste. By 1906 the firm was making 160 different kinds of toilet soaps, laundry soap, and 625 varieties of perfume. . . .

When in 1928 Colgate merged with the Palmolive-Peet Company, which had learned the virtues of combining palm and olive oils in soap, the new firm had assets of $63 million.

1. What did William Colgate offer his customers that earned him a fast-growing clientele?

2. What forms of business organization did Colgate's company have before it merged with the Palmolive-Peet Company in 1928? What can you infer about the kind of organization it probably became when it merged to form Colgate-Palmolive?

A PARTNERSHIP IS SEWN UP
Skill: Understanding Decision Making

 Business partnerships arise out of the partners' mutual need of each other. This reading describes the partnership that Isaac Merritt Singer entered so that he could develop his famous invention, the sewing machine.

Into Singer's life at this juncture, like a plump hen advancing confidently into a den of foxes, came a would-be capitalist of a commonplace sort. This innocent, a man called George Zieber, paid Singer some $3,000 for the Massachusetts rights to the type-carving device and rented space in a Boston machine shop at 19 Harvard Place, not far from the Old South Meeting House. Singer went along to demonstrate the machine to prospective buyers, but, these proving conspicuous by their scarcity, he found time to take notice of his surroundings.

The chief business of the machine shop, owned by Orson Phelps, was supposed to be the manufacture of sewing machines. Owing to some defect in their design, however, more time was spent in repairing the old than in making the new. This was a monotonously familiar complaint against all the early sewing machines, no matter by whom designed or manufactured. . . .

Singer thought the machine could be made to work. Phelps was skeptical. "If," he retorted, "you can make a really practical sewing machine, you will make more money in a year than you can in fifty with that carving affair."

Singer reflected. Theretofore he had considered that the manufacture of sewing machines was a paltry business; but maybe Phelps knew what he was talking about. If there was money in it, Singer was interested. . . .

He directed the full force of his considerable charm on Zieber, and, on September 18, 1850, the three men concluded an agreement, drawn up by Zieber. The capitalist was to "furnish the sum of Forty Dollars"; Singer was to "contribute his inventive genius"; Phelps was to provide "his best mechanical skill." The contract was, Zieber later maintained plaintively, "sufficient to secure to each the interest to which he was entitled, had all the other parties been honorably disposed." . . .

When Phelps suggested that, according to their agreement, his name should be linked to Singer's on the patent application, Singer peremptorily shouted him down. When Zieber attempted to mediate and pacify, Singer hectored [bullied] both men impartially while privately he urged Zieber to buy up Phelps' interest. When Zieber refused, Singer did the job himself, paying Phelps off from the money belonging to all three. In short, he behaved like a ruthless man of business whilst his partners behaved like gentle chuckleheads [well-meaning amateurs].

1. According to the article, how was the formation of the three-man partnership mutually beneficial to the partners?
2. What are some disadvantages of a partnership as a form of business?

Peter Lyon, "Isaac Singer and His Wonderful Sewing Machine." *American Heritage*, Vol. 9, #6, October 1958. Reprinted by permission of Roberta Pryor, Inc. Copyright © 1958 by Peter Lyon.

PAULINE ALKER IS MAKING IT IN THE CORPORATE WORLD

Skill: Applying Information

The computer industry is one that has attracted many new corporations willing to compete with some large established ones, such as Digital Equipment and International Business Machines. This reading is about a woman who, as president of a new corporation, is about to make her mark on the high-technology world.

On a flight from New York to San Francisco three years ago, James F. Riley, a computer industry consultant, found himself seated next to a petite Chinese woman named Pauline Lo Alker. Impressed with the "personal odyssey, imagination, and determination" of the woman who started life as a refugee in Hong Kong but had risen to marketing vice-president at Convergent Technologies Inc., the fast-growing computer startup, Riley asked Alker to keep him in mind if ever she decided to leave Convergent. A year later, she did. And now the two of them—Riley as chairman and Alker as president—are launching Counterpoint Computers Inc. to compete in the rapidly growing market for workstations used by engineers and scientists. . . .

Alker's grit is a product of her unsettled childhood. During China's Communist revolution, the Lo family fled to Hong Kong in 1949, leaving a banking fortune behind. They started over by selling souvenirs to tourists. At 17, Alker left to attend Arizona State University where she studied music and mathematics and took some computer programming courses. But in the early 1960s, breaking into the male-dominated industry was tough. She worked in the accounting department at Sears, Roebuck & Co., then landed a programming job as a technical typist. This circuitous route "taught me humility," says Alker. "But it also taught me persistence."

Since leaving GE in 1968, she has worked for some of the computer industry's biggest successes—Intel, Amdahl, and Four-Phase Systems. At Convergent, she honed her skills as a dealmaker while working with customers such as AT&T, Burroughs, and NCR. She also met up with hardware manager Fred Kiremidijian, a likeminded Bulgarian refugee and engineer, who later helped her found Counterpoint. When Convergent went public in 1982, stock options made Alker wealthy. But soon she felt her comrades were becoming more interested in personal gain and less committed to the company itself. Alker wanted a company that lived and breathed her personal philosophy.

. . . That company is Counterpoint. And her personal touch is apparent. Her motto, spelled out in Counterpoint literature, is: "EQUIP—Excellence, Quality, Unity, Integrity, and Profit."

1. What personal qualities did Pauline Lo Alker have that contributed to her success in the male-dominated computer industry?
2. How might her personal motto, EQUIP—Excellence, Quality, Unity, Integrity, and Profit—contribute to the company's success in a highly competitive market?

Deborah C. Wise, "IBM and Digital Equipment Don't Scare Pauline Alker." Reprinted from February 3, 1986, issue of *Business Week* by special permission, © 1986 by McGraw-Hill, Inc.

THE FRANCHISE THAT DOES IT ALL FOR YOU
Skill: Sequencing Information

A successful franchise requires a lot of hard work and planning from both the franchisee and the franchisor. Ray Kroc, the franchisor of McDonald's restaurants, describes in his 1977 autobiography what goes into preparing a new applicant for a McDonald's franchise.

What does it take to get a McDonald's franchise? A total commitment of personal time and energy is the most important thing. A person doesn't need to be super smart or have more than a high school education, but he or she must be willing to work hard and concentrate exclusively on the challenge of operating that store. The value of our franchises has increased greatly over the years. I started issuing them for $950 back in 1955. Ten years later, when we went public, the average investment was $81,500. These days it takes about $200,000 for the franchise and related expenses—equipment, furnishings, signs, etc.—not counting interest or finance charges on borrowed money.

In the initial interview, the applicant is told what we expect and what the corporation will contribute. If he's still interested after learning about the kind of personal and financial investment required, we put him to work in a McDonald's store near his home. He's assigned evening or weekend hours that won't conflict with his present job, and he learns firsthand what's involved in both crew work and management. If he's not really suited for our kind of restaurant operation, this is the time to find that out. . . .

The applicant is advised when a site comes up for him (usually less than two years after his registration), and if he's still interested after looking over the location, we begin getting him more involved in McDonald's. . . . We now ask him to spend another 500 hours working in a McDonald's restaurant. He's also invited to attend orientation and management classes. Then, about four to six months prior to the date his store is scheduled to open, the licensee attends our advanced operations course at Hamburger U. This adds polish to the management skills and operations know-how he'll need to greet his first customers. . . .

It's all interrelated—our development of the restaurant, the training, the marketing advice, the product development, the research that has gone into each element of our equipment package. Together with our national advertising and continuing supervisory assistance, it forms an invaluable support system. Individual operators pay 11.5 percent of their gross to the corporation for all of this, and I think it's a . . . bargain.

1. Trace the steps involved in obtaining a McDonald's franchise.
2. What might a franchisee need to consider when making a decision to purchase a McDonald's franchise?

Reprinted from *Grinding It Out*, © 1977 by Ray A. Kroc, used with permission of Contemporary Books, Inc., Chicago, IL. Permissions received 2/11/87 for Reading 1–2 (The Disual Scientists. . .)

Managers of fast-food restaurants rely on young people and others who work part time to staff their stores.

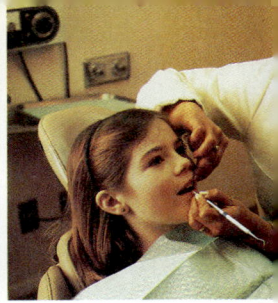

9 | CHAPTER REVIEW

PRACTICING YOUR READING SKILLS: POINT OF VIEW

Economists, like most people, have a point of view. That is, they have thoughts or feelings about an issue based on their values, experience, political attitudes, education, and beliefs. When you read the works of economists—or of any author—you must be able to identify the point of view in order to understand and evaluate the works. However, point of view is not always directly stated. Often you may have to infer it from the material you read.

Scan the textbook material suggested in each of the questions that follow. Use it to write a sentence stating point of view. Include details from the material to support your answer.

1. Under the heading "Starting a Business" in this chapter, what is the author's point of view on entrepreneurship?

2. According to Issue 2, do economists believe the amount of debt that Americans are carrying is good or bad for the nation's economy?

3. In Issue 1, what is the point of view toward government regulations held by: **a.** environmentalists? **b.** business groups?

VOCABULARY REVIEW

Write the letter of the definition in Column B that correctly defines each term in Column A.

Column A	Column B
1. inventory	a. item of value
2. revenue	b. supply of items that are used in a business
3. asset	c. sale by a business of the right to use its name to another business or individual
4. franchise	
5. unlimited liability	d. money taken in by a business or a government
	e. legal responsibility for all debts and damages incurred when doing business

PRACTICING YOUR ECONOMIC SKILLS

1. Using a Circle Graph. Use the circle graph on this page to answer the following questions. **a.** What percentage of businesses in the United States are sole proprietorships? partnerships? corporations? **b.** How many businesses does the percentage given represent for: sole proprietorships? for partnerships? for corporations?

2. Drawing a Pie Graph. Using the following percentages, draw a pie graph to show the percentage of total business receipts accounted for by: sole proprietorships, 8.4 percent; partnerships, 3.8 percent; corporations, 87.8 percent.

Number and Percentage of Businesses by Type

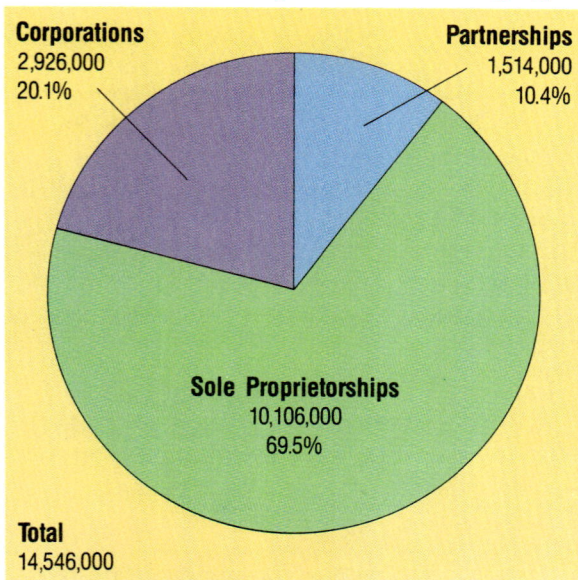

Corporations
2,926,000
20.1%

Partnerships
1,514,000
10.4%

Sole Proprietorships
10,106,000
69.5%

Total
14,546,000

Source: *Statistical Abstract of the U.S.*, Bureau of the Census

3. **Compiling a Table.** Transfer the information on the two graphs into a table, and then write a sentence comparing and contrasting the number of businesses and their receipts.

4. **Determining the Rate of Return.** Calculate the rate of return on each of the following exercises. To calculate the rate of return, divide the interest or dividend received by the amount saved or the purchase price of the stock.

interest/dividend − amount saved or the purchase price of stock = rate of return

    a. a savings account worth $1,000 that paid $40 interest during the past year
    b. a savings account worth $4,500 that paid $150 in interest during the past year
    c. a share of common stock that was purchased for $200 and that paid a dividend of $22 during the past year
    d. a share of common stock that was purchased for $750 and that paid a dividend of $80.00

DISCUSSING ECONOMIC QUESTIONS

1. One goal of business is to make as much profit as possible. What might some other goals be? Consider service to others, personal satisfaction, and social status.

2. Imagine that you are the head of a major corporation and need to obtain additional money. You believe that you need to build a new factory in order to keep up with the growing market. From the company's point of view, compare the advantages and disadvantages of borrowing money from a bank, selling common stock, or of selling bonds.

3. **a.** What are some of the possible advantages and disadvantages of playing the market, that is, of selling stock at higher prices than you paid for it and of buying stock when prices are low? **b.** What are some of the advantages and disadvantages of buying well-known and reliable stocks that you can keep for years and of buying reliable bonds?

ECONOMICS IN DEPTH

1. **Checking Information.** Figure 9-1 lists the top 10 industrial corporations in the United States in a recent year. Check the most recent May issue of *Fortune* magazine, and note any changes in the top 10 industrial companies. What companies have been dropped or added to the list?

2. **Gathering and Listing Information.** Using a local insurance agent as a resource, list the types of insurance that sole proprietorships and partnerships might have.

3. **Analyzing Financial Data.** Select a corporation listed in the financial pages of a newspaper. Then use business magazines and financial and annual reports, if possible, to determine the annual earnings, dividends, and stock prices of that corporation over the last year. Compare the corporation with those of classmates and discuss which stocks would have been the best investments during the past year.

4. Follow a bond issue from one company for a week. Plot the price on a line graph.

READINGS

Leftwich, Richard H., and Sharp, Ansel M. *Economics of Social Issues.* 6th ed. Plano, Texas: Business Publications, Inc., 1984.

Mauser, Ferdinand F., and Schwartz, David J. *American Business: An Introduction.* 5th ed. New York: Harcourt Brace Jovanovich, 1982.

Thoryn, M. "Small Business Speaks, Government Listens." *Nation's Business,* May 1982, pp. 38–40.

CHAPTER 10

The four ways American industries are organized range from the pure monopoly of local electric utilities to nearly perfect competition in agriculture. Some industries are oligopolies in which a few companies dominate, but most industries are engaged in monopolistic competition.

COMPETITION AND MONOPOLIES

In Chapter 8, you read about the model of supply and demand. Chapter 9 described various types of business organizations. This chapter explains how competition, regardless of the type of business organization, influences supply and demand and, therefore, price. Perfect competition and pure monopoly, the two extremes of business organization, are explained as well as the more moderate forms of oligopoly and monopolistic competition. You will also read about government regulation of business. Learning Economic Skills explains the information given in a corporation's annual report.

CHAPTER OBJECTIVES After you study the sections of this chapter, you will be able to:

1 • list the four conditions of a perfectly competitive market that together result in businesses' having no control over price.
 • describe supply and demand in a perfectly competitive market.
 • explain why agricultural markets seem perfectly competitive.

2 • list the three conditions of a pure monopoly that result in a business's having almost complete control over price.
 • identify the operations of supply and demand in a pure monopoly.
 • identify the relation between profit incentive and monopolies.

3 • list the four conditions of an oligopoly that result in businesses' having limited control over price.
 ★ state the types of information found in an annual report.

4 • list the four conditions of monopolistic competition that result in businesses' having some control over price.
 • describe supply and demand in monopolistic competition.
 • contrast types of competition found in the American economy.

5 • describe the purpose of federal legislation regarding business.

ECONOMICS VOCABULARY

perfect competition
imperfect competition
pure monopoly
barriers to entry
natural monopoly
geographic monopoly
technological monopoly
patent
government monopoly
cartel
oligopoly
annual report
product differentiation
monopolistic competition
antitrust legislation
interlocking directorate
merger
horizontal merger
vertical merger
conglomerate
conglomerate merger
deregulation

To continue the example from the last chapter, in running your electronic repair business, you know that yours is not the only such business in your area. You know that there are other people in the same business, and they are in competition with you. You want to attract as much business as you can, and so do they. In Chapter 2, you read that competition is one of the basic characteristics of a market economic system. Regardless of its form of organization, each business attempts to capture as large a share of its market as possible. After all, that is why your business went from a sole proprietorship to a corporation.

There are four ways that industries are organized in the American economy. In order from the most competitive to the least competitive, they are perfect competition, monopolistic competition, oligopoly, and pure monopoly. Markets that are either perfectly competitive or pure monopolies are rare. Most industries in the United States fit one of the two other forms.

1 | PERFECT COMPETITION

Ask yourself as you read:
- Why is perfect competition a special situation?
- Why is the agricultural industry a good example of perfect competition?

All businesses must engage in some form of competition as long as there are other businesses producing similar goods or services. When there are so many sellers of a particular good or service that each seller accounts for a very small part of the total market, a special situation exists. Economists term it **perfect competition.** Perfect competition has four conditions:

1. a large market. There are numerous sellers and buyers of the good or service.
2. similar product. The sellers are selling a good or service that is almost the same.
3. easy entry. There is no way for sellers already in the market to prevent competition, or entrance, into the market. In addition, the initial costs of investment are small, and the good or service is easy to learn to produce. This is more true of small businesses than of large ones. It is easier and less expensive to set up a retail store or dry cleaning service than to explore for oil.
4. easily obtainable information. Information about prices, quality, sources of supply, and so on, are easy for both buyers and sellers to obtain.

As a result, there is:

5. no control over price. In perfect competition, no single seller or buyer has any control over what the market price is. The market is controlled by the workings of supply and demand.

On the supply side, perfect competition requires a large number of suppliers of a similar product. On the demand side, perfect competition requires a large number of informed buyers who know exactly what the market price is for the good or service. The market price is the equilibrium price. In a perfectly competitive market, total supply and total demand are allowed to interact to reach the equilibrium price. That is the only price at which quantity demanded equals quantity supplied. In a world of perfect competition, each individual seller would accept that price. Because there are so many buyers and sellers, one person's charging a higher or lower price would not affect the market price.

Perfect competition is rarely seen in the real world. For one thing, information is not easily obtainable. There is only one way for the price of a good or service to be the same for all sellers at every moment in time. All buyers and sellers would have to know what is happening to prices for that good or service everywhere at every moment. Obviously, information is never that complete.

THE AGRICULTURAL INDUSTRY AS AN EXAMPLE

As you have just read there are few perfectly competitive industries in the United States. The stock market is an example. The one that perhaps comes closest is agriculture before 1930, when the federal government started to protect and regulate it. Since that time the government has sought to protect farmers by keeping the prices of some agricultural products high and by restricting the production of some products. Nonetheless, the agricultural market is often used as an example of perfect competition because individual farmers have almost no control over the market price of their goods.

The United States is one of the world's largest wheat producers. Why is the farm industry considered so close to the model of a perfectly competitive industry?

Consider the wheat market as an example. There are thousands of wheat farmers and thousands of wholesale buyers of wheat. Though there are different grades of wheat, all wheat is fairly similar. The costs of buying or renting farmland are low compared to starting a corporation, and farming methods can be learned. Because wheat is sold to wholesalers, information about prices is fairly easy to obtain. Each individual wheat farmer, however, contributes such a small part of the total amount put on the market each year that no one farmer has any great influence on price.

The price of wheat is determined by the interaction of supply and demand. The supply is the total supply produced by all farmers growing wheat. The demand is the total demand for all uses of wheat. The equilibrium price is the price where supply and demand meet.

Individual wheat farmers have to accept the market price. If the price is $5 per bushel, that is the price each and every farmer must accept. Farmers who attempt to raise their price above $5 will find that no one will buy their wheat. No farmer is going to sell his or her crop for less than $5 per bushel either. Why would any farmer be willing to take less than $5 when he or she can sell the entire harvest at that price?

The demand for wheat—and food in general—is somewhat different from the demand for many other products. People's demand for food is for the most part unresponsive to changes in price. As you read in Chapter 8, this demand would be considered inelastic. There are only so many uses for wheat, and people can eat only so much wheat.

The supply side of most agricultural markets is also unique. It is highly dependent on conditions over which farmers have little control. Variations in weather, a crop disease, or a crop-destroying insect can wipe out entire harvests. This means that farmers may have a good harvest one year and a poor one the next. As a result, you would expect widely fluctuating, or changing, supplies of goods in the agricultural market. In the absence of controls on price, you would also expect large fluctuations in prices. During the Great Depression of the 1930s, the federal government began a program to even out the prices of wheat, tobacco, and many other farm products. Where government controls operate, the resulting market price is not the same as in perfectly competitive industries.

fluctuating (FLUHK-choo-ayt-ing): changing

REVIEWING ECONOMIC PRINCIPLES

1. What is perfect competition?
2. List the four conditions of a perfectly competitive market that together result in businesses' having no control over price.
3. How do the laws of supply and demand operate in a perfectly competitive market?
4. **Critical Thinking: Summarizing a Main Idea.** Explain in a paragraph how supply and demand work in the agricultural market when government controls are not operating.

2 | PURE MONOPOLY

Ask yourself as you read:
• Why is pure monopoly an extreme form of imperfect competition?
• How many types of pure monopoly are there?

Most industries in the American economy are not perfectly competitive. Most are some form of imperfect competition. **Imperfect competition** exists when any one or a group buys or sells a good or service in large enough amounts to affect price. The most extreme form is a **pure monopoly.** Here a single seller controls the supply of the good or service and thus affects the price. A few such markets do exist in the real world. Local electric utilities are monopolies. The United States Postal Service's delivery of first-class mail is another example of a monopoly. The characteristics of a pure monopoly are:

1. a single seller. There is only one seller of the good or service.
2. no substitutes. There is no adequate substitute for the good or service that the monopolist is selling.

3. no entry. The market is protected by **barriers to entry.** These are obstacles to competition that prevent others from entering the market. The major barriers are government regulations, large initial investment, and ownership of raw materials.

These result in:

4. almost complete control of market price. The monopolist can control the market price by controlling the supply available.

In a pure monopoly, the supplier can raise the price without fear of losing all of his or her business to competitors. Unless buyers choose to pay the new price, they have nowhere else to buy the good or service. A monopolist, however, cannot charge outrageous prices. In a monopoly market, the law of demand is still operating. As the price of a good or service rises, consumers buy less. Profits, as a result, may decrease. For example, customers cut back on electricity when electric companies raised their rates after the increase in oil prices in 1970s and early 1980s.

BARRIERS TO ENTRY

The most obvious barriers to entry are legal ones. For example, state laws prevent a competing electric, gas, or water company from operating in an area where there already is a utility company. The reasoning against competition in utility industries is that too much competition will lead to wasteful duplication. For example, if there were two electric companies in your town, they would both have electric lines strung around the city. They would be duplicating efforts, and that would result in a wasteful use of resources. It would also probably result in higher rates to customers because of the lack of efficiency in operation.

Another barrier to entry is the cost of getting started. This barrier to entry is called excessive capital costs. It is found in industries, such as cars and steel, where initial investment is large because of the amount and cost of the equipment. The first company to make the investment will clearly have an advantage over later companies that want to enter the market.

Ownership of essential raw materials can also provide a barrier to entry. A good example is the diamond industry. The De Beers Company of the Republic of South Africa controls the marketing of nearly all the world's diamonds. An example from American history is the Aluminum Company of American (ALCOA). At the turn of the 20th century, it controlled almost all sources of bauxite (BAWK-zyt), the major ore used in aluminum. For many years, ALCOA was able to keep its near-monopoly in aluminum because it would not sell bauxite to potential competitors.

TYPES OF MONOPOLIES

Pure monopolies can be separated into four categories depending on why the monopoly exists. There are natural, geographic, technological, and government monopolies.

Most electric power in the United States is produced by private utilities. Why are these utilities considered monopolies?

Learning Economic Skills | HOW TO READ AN ANNUAL REPORT

Every year the management of a corporation puts together an **annual report**. This report summarizes for the corporation's stockholders—and for any interested outsiders—the facts about the company's revenues, costs, and profits.

Although annual reports vary, most begin with a letter from the corporation's president to its stockholders. This letter is usually positive in tone and may concentrate more on the successes of the corporation than on its problems. The rest of the report shows in figures what the president describes in words. Although the amount of detail varies, all annual reports include two major financial documents: an income statement and a balance sheet.

The income statement shows the company's receipts and expenses over the past year. The table that follows is a simplified version of a recent income statement for an American corporation. This income statement compares figures for the past year with those of the previous year. Revenues are listed first, followed by expenses. Subtracting expenses from revenues gives the figure listed as *Income before taxes*. The figure labeled *Net income* is the amount left after taxes have been subtracted. This is the profit for the year. *Net income per share* is the profit divided by the number of shares. Only a part of this profit is paid out as a cash dividend, the bottom line of the statement. The rest of the profit is re-invested in the company by its management.

The balance sheet shows a corporation's financial condition at a certain point in time. The left side of the sheet lists all the corporation's assets—the things of value it owns. The right side of the sheet lists its liabilities—the debts it owes—plus the amount of money invested by stockholders. Stockholders' investment is listed with liabilities because the corporation owes its owners whatever value is in the company after creditors have been paid. The balance sheet that follows is also adapted from an annual report.

Assets are always listed in order of their availability to pay debts. *Current assets* are those that are easily available. *Cash*, which can be used immediately, is listed first. Next come *marketable securities*, investments such as stocks and bonds that can be sold quickly. *Accounts receivable* is a term for the amount of money customers owe the company, and *inventories* are unsold items. *Property and equipment* are harder to turn into cash quickly. *Net property and equipment* is the total value of these assets after the costs of depreciation or wear and tear have been subtracted. The total for all types of assets is listed at the bottom of the left side.

Liabilities are arranged according to how soon they must be paid. *Current liabilities* are those

Income Statement (dollars in thousands)

	1987	1986
Revenues		
Broadcasting	$2,112,961	$1,972,922
Publishing	275,335	231,645
Other	55,417	75,813
Total revenues	2,443,713	2,280,380
Expenses		
Operating expenses and cost of sales	$1,599,337	$1,504,387
Selling, general and administrative	500,059	438,145
Interest	8,273	13,228
Other	38,884	30,104
Total expenses	2,146,553	1,985,864
Income before taxes	$ 297,160	$ 294,516
Taxes	150,847	148,212
Net income	$ 146,313	$ 146,304
Net income per share	$5.13	$5.18
Dividend per share	$1.60	$1.60

Balance Sheet (dollars in thousands)

Assets	1987	1986
Current assets		
Cash	$ 32,937	$ 26,265
Marketable securities	161,050	121,176
Accounts receivable	330,715	297,343
Inventories	24,210	21,816
Other current assets	414,582	348,026
Total current assets	963,494	814,626
Property and equipment		
Land	$ 29,905	$ 29,994
Buildings	203,477	199,601
Equipment	296,557	281,931
Leaseholds	36,380	34,393
Total	566,319	545,919
Less depreciation	181,994	168,131
Net property and equipment	384,325	377,788
Other assets	$ 240,530	$ 225,890
Total assets	$1,588,349	$1,418,304

Liabilities and Stockholders' Investment	1987	1986
Current liabilities		
Accounts payable	$ 36,258	$ 44,505
Accrued program costs	108,118	98,449
Accrued compensation	47,856	38,505
Taxes payable	75,227	39,639
Long-term debt payable within one year	7,992	9,206
Other current liabilities	91,156	75,374
Total current liabilities	366,607	305,678
Long-term liabilities		
Long-term debt	$ 179,691	$ 187,511
Other long-term liabilities	66,608	62,458
Total long-term liabilities	246,299	249,969
Total liabilities	$ 612,906	$ 555,647
Stockholders' investment		
Common stock	$ 190,193	$ 178,285
Retained earnings	785,250	684,372
Total stockholders' investment	975,443	862,657
Total liabilities and stockholders' investment	$1,588,349	$1,418,304

due within the next year. *Accounts payable* is the term used to designate bills owed to creditors. The next two lines list specific costs that have accrued, or built up, and have not yet been paid. *Other* is taxes and the portion of long-term debt that must be paid over the next year.

Long-term liabilities are debts such as loans and leases that must be paid off in the years to come.

The stockholder's investment comes next. *Retained earnings* is the amount of profit the company has earned over the years that was not paid as dividends, but re-invested in the company.

The last line is the total of liabilities and stockholders' investment. As the name implies, the bottom lines on the left and right side of a balance sheet will always balance exactly.

Practicing Your Skills

1. Using the income statement, find the following figures for 1986: **a.** total revenues. **b.** total expenses. **c.** net income.
2. **a.** What was the change in net income per share between 1986 and 1987? **b.** What was the change in cash dividend?
3. Using the balance sheet, find the following figures for 1986: **a.** total current assets. **b.** total current liabilities.
4. Between 1986 and 1987 did the amount of long-term liabilities rise or fall?

Natural monopolies are those that come about through natural circumstances. That is, any company that can produce a particular product for the lowest cost will eventually drive its competitors out of business. The company does this by underselling its competition. Natural monopolies are usually found in industries that require large amounts of money to get started and where efficiency in operation is best done by one company rather than by several. A good example is an electric company. A single large firm is typically able to sell electricity at a lower cost than could several smaller competing companies.

Geographic monopolies occur when an individual seller has control over the market because of the seller's location. Consider a small town that has only one camera store. Because it is the only camera store within 50 kilometers (31 miles), that store has a geographic monopoly. However, in today's world, where information is so easily available, geographic monopolies are becoming less important. For example, the geographic monopoly of this small-town camera store is probably very limited. Buyers could check ads in national magazines and find that the local store's prices are much higher than the national average. They could then buy their equipment by phone or mail order from discount stores in such cities as Los Angeles or Chicago. Or potential buyers could wait until they visited a town or city with more camera stores.

A **technological monopoly** occurs when a seller develops a product or production process for which it obtains a patent. A **patent** is the right granted to the inventor for the exclusive manufacture and sale of an invention for a specified number of years. In effect, a patent is a legal barrier to entry into a market. Using its potential technology, a company can sell products that are unique or better in some way than competing products. For example, the inventor of the patented self-developing film known as Polaroid film enjoys a technological monopoly.

Many technological monopolies today result from an employee's discovery, which is then patented by the company. The product or process usually belongs to the company, though the employee may receive some payment. Such patents have brought many companies monopoly power. It is the reward a company receives for investing in the research and development of new products and new technology.

Some important monopolies in the United States are owned by the federal government. Known as **government monopolies,** they are created by legal barriers to entry. For example, the United States Postal Service is a monopoly of the federal government, as is the Tennessee Valley Authority (TVA), which supplies power to several southern states.

Government—both state and federal—has other roles in regard to monopolies. State governments regulate the rates that public utilities may charge. The federal government, as you will read later in this chapter, regulates certain areas of business activity in an attempt to ensure competition.

Another type of monopoly is the cartel, which is an international form of monopoly. A **cartel** is an arrangement among groups of industrial businesses, often in different countries, to reduce international competition by controlling price, production, and the distribution of goods. Among the best-known cartels is the Organization of Petroleum Exporting Countries (OPEC), which was formed in 1960. Today OPEC includes several nations in the Middle East and North Africa, as well as Nigeria, Gabon, Venezuela, Ecuador, and Indonesia.

HOW IMPORTANT ARE MONOPOLIES?

Monopolies today are far less important than they once were. You have already read that geographic monopolies probably have little effect because of potential competition from mail-order businesses. You can also be fairly certain that a technological monopoly will not last much longer than the life of a patent. In fact, because of modern technology, slight variations in new products can be made quickly by competitors and patented. This is how the microcomputer revolution occurred in the early 1980s. One company copied another's product, making changes and adding features to obtain a patent of its own.

Whenever a monopoly exists because of government, it can exist for only as long as the government prevents competition. Consider the United States Postal Service. For many years, it was illegal to deliver any mail in competition with the Postal Service. By the late 1970s, however, it had become clear that the demand for the rapid delivery of urgent mail was greater than the Postal Service could meet. Private companies that wanted to provide this service began asking the federal government to give up part of its monopoly. Finally, in 1979, the Postal Service issued new regulations allowing competition in the delivery of urgent mail. Consumers willing to pay extra to have a letter or package delivered overnight can now choose from among a number of such services, including one offered by the Postal Service. The government still maintains a monopoly for normal first-class mail delivery.

The Postal Service, like many industries, has adopted automated work systems. Why is it the nation's largest government monopoly?

REVIEWING ECONOMIC PRINCIPLES

1. Define the following economic terms: **a.** imperfect competition, **b.** pure monopoly, **c.** barriers to entry, **d.** natural monopolies, **e.** geographic monopolies, **f.** technological monopoly, **g.** patent, **h.** government monopoly, **i.** cartel.
2. List the three conditions of a pure monopoly that result in a business's having control over price.
3. How does the law of demand work in a pure monopoly?
4. **a.** List the three barriers to entry in a pure monopoly. **b.** Choose one, and explain in a paragraph why it occurs.
5. **a.** List the four types of monopolies. **b.** Choose one, and explain in a paragraph why it occurs.
6. **Critical Thinking: Applying Concepts.** Explain why the free enterprise system works to break the power of monopolies.

3 | OLIGOPOLY

Ask yourself as you read:
- How do suppliers in an oligopoly control price?
- What are the major barriers to entry in an oligopoly?

An **oligopoly** (ahl-uh-GAHP-uh-lee) is an industry dominated by a few suppliers that exercise some control over price. The characteristics of an oligopoly are:

1. domination by a few sellers. Several large firms dominate the industry. They supply as much as 70 to 80 percent of the total output of the entire industry.
2. substantial barriers to entry. These include excessive capital costs and customer loyalty to particular brand names. A brand name is a word, picture, or logo on a product that helps customers distinguish it from similar products of competitors.
3. identical or slightly different products. In some industries, such as light bulbs, products are the same. In other industries, such as breakfast foods, the products vary even though they serve the same purpose.
4. nonprice competition. This is competition based on something other than price.

These result in:

5. limited control over price. The leading companies in an industry have some control over the price of a good or service in that any one company can raise or lower its prices. However, when one company changes its price, that company can expect a reaction by competitors.

logo (LOH-goh): trade-mark

THE AUTOMOBILE INDUSTRY AS AN EXAMPLE

The domestic automobile industry is a good example of an oligopoly. It is dominated by three large American companies known as the Big Three: General Motors (GM), Ford, and Chrysler. Because each company accounts for such a large portion of the total market, decisions made by any single company affect all three. This interdependence among suppliers is one of the main features of an oligopoly. Any change in one supplier's output or price influences the profits and sales of its competitors. Thus, a supplier will attempt to anticipate changes in the pricing and output policies of its competitors before changing its own policies.

Most competition in an oligopoly is not in the form of price changes because prices affect profits. If one automaker, for example, raises prices and none of the other Big Three do, that manufacturer will lose customers. If one lowers prices and the others follow, they will all suffer a similar drop in profits. In oligopolies, competition more often takes place in such nonprice areas as a product's image with the public. Man-

image: impression presented to others

Table 10-1: SELECTED OLIGOPOLIES

Industry	Percent of Industry Output Produced by Four Largest Firms
Primary lead	100.0%
Chewing gum	93.0
Motor vehicles and car bodies	93.4
Electric lamps (bulbs)	89.6
Household laundry equipment	89.0
Cereal breakfast foods	88.6
Batteries	86.8
Household sewing machines	83.5
Household vacuum cleaners	82.6
Household refrigerators and freezers	81.6

Source: *Census of Manufacturers,*
Bureau of the Census

ufacturers use special ingredients, service to customers, and differences in quality and minor features to try to differentiate among similar products, such as brands of cereal. Sometimes the difference is in the packaging, the use of a special logo or design or even a special type of box or container. This is known as **product differentiation** (dif-uh-ren-shee-AY-shuhn).

Advertising is an especially important tool in product differentiation. Advertising emphasizes minor differences and attempts to build customer loyalty for a product. For example, with some products, such as electronic equipment, tonic water, and some makes of automobiles, there may be very little difference among brands. The manufacturer, however, may attempt to build customer loyalty by giving its product an image distinct from those of its competitors. Advertising slogans such as "Schweppervescence" for Schweppes tonic water, "The Pride is back" for the Dodge automobile, and "full-color sound" for the Sony Walkman pocket-sized cassette player with headphones are an important way to do this.

ADVANTAGES OF OLIGOPOLIES

Table 10-1 shows a number of industries in which the four largest firms produce more than 80 percent of the total industry output. All these industries are oligopolies. Saying that an industry is an oligopoly does not necessarily mean that the situation should be changed. In fact, a surprising feature of the general criticism of oligopolies is that little proof is given that they are harmful. It is true that consumers may be paying more than if they were buying in a perfectly competitive market, where supply and demand would set the price. However, oligopolistic markets tend to have generally stable prices. They do not fluctuate much from year to year. They also offer consumers a wider variety of different products than would a perfectly competitive industry.

1. Write a sentence defining each of the following economic terms:
   a. oligopoly, **b.** annual report, **c.** product differentiation.
2. List the four conditions of an oligopoly that result in businesses' having limited control over price.
3. How does interdependence among suppliers affect price in an oligopoly?
4. Why is advertising important to suppliers in an oligopoly?
5. **Critical Thinking: Classifying Information.** Choose two categories from Table 10-1, and see if you can list two manufacturers in each category.

4 | MONOPOLISTIC COMPETITION

Ask yourself as you read:
- Why is monopolistic competition common in the United States?
- What are some examples of monopolistic competition?

In **monopolistic competition,** a large number of sellers offer similar but slightly different products. Obvious examples are such brand-name items as toothpaste, cosmetics, and designer clothes. Many industries in the United States are characterized by monopolistic competition. This type of industry has:

1. numerous sellers. There are so many sellers of the good or service that no one seller or no small group dominates the market.
2. relatively easy entry. Though not as easy as in perfect competition, entry is still easier than in other types of markets. One drawback is the high cost of advertising.
3. differentiated products. Each seller sells a slightly different product to attract customers.
4. nonprice competition. Businesses compete by product differentiation and by advertising.

These result in:

5. some control over price. Each firm has some control over the price it charges. Because of customer loyalty and product differentiation, competitors can charge a little more for their product and not lose all their customers.

COMPARISONS WITH OLIGOPOLIES AND PURE MONOPOLIES

Many of the characteristics of monopolistic competition are the same as those of an oligopoly. The major differences, however, are in the number of sellers of a product and in the product. In an oligopoly, a few companies dominate an industry, and control over price is interde-

In American cities and towns most businesses that consumers deal with are involved in monopolistic competition. Can you explain why?

pendent. The products may or may not be similar. In monopolistic competition, there are many firms and no real interdependence. There is some slight difference among products.

As you read earlier in this chapter, there are so many buyers and sellers in a perfectly competitive industry that no one has any control over price. Everyone must take the price as determined by the interaction of total demand and total supply. In monopolistic competition, however, each competitor has some control over the price of its product. A monopolistic competitor does not have as much control over price as a pure monopolist. This is because other monopolistic competitors are selling almost, but not quite, the same product. As you read in Chapter 8, the quantity demanded of a good or service will drop if the price is raised and there are cheaper substitutes available. In other words, if one monopolistic competitor raises the price too much, most customers will buy another brand, or substitute, of the same good.

NEIGHBORHOOD BUSINESSES

Neighborhood businesses such as cleaners and drugstores are also involved in monopolistic competition. Each business within the neighborhood has an identity of its own. This is true even though the differences between its good or service and those of its competitors may be small. This is product differentiation again. Nonetheless, each seller is a partial monopolist because he or she has some control over price.

COMPETITIVE ADVERTISING

Competitive advertising is especially important in monopolistic competition. As you may recall from Chapter 3, this is advertising that attempts to persuade consumers that the product being advertised is different from, and superior to, any other. Businesses also compete by gaining shelf space—space on store shelves for which companies compete in displaying their products and attracting buyers. A cosmetics company, for example, may produce several lines of cosmetics. Each is aimed at a different market segment, or section. By having three lines, the company competes in three areas with competitors. The differences in products attract different customers and add to the profits of the company.

REVIEWING ECONOMIC PRINCIPLES

1. What is monopolistic competition?
2. List the four conditions of monopolistic competition that result in businesses' having some control over price.
3. Why are the following important to sellers in monopolistic competition: **a.** advertising? **b.** shelf space?
4. How do supply and demand operate to set prices in monopolistic competition?
5. **Critical Thinking: Organizing Information.** Based on the lists of characteristics for each type of competition, make a table comparing and contrasting the four types. For any characteristic that applies only to one, make a category called *Other.*

5 | GOVERNMENT POLICIES TOWARD COMPETITION

Ask yourself as you read:
- How has the federal government tried to encourage competition in American business?
- What are the major antitrust laws in the United States?

Historically, one of the goals of government in the United States has been to encourage competition in the economy. Through the years, federal and state governments have passed laws and established regulatory agencies in an attempt to force monopolies to act more competitively. Known as **antitrust legislation,** these laws act to prevent new monopolies from forming and to break up those that already exist. *Trust* is another name for monopoly. One reason that many economists and legislators oppose monopolies and noncompetitive situations in general is that they normally result in higher prices for consumers. Table 10-2 summarizes major federal laws that affect attempts by business to reduce competition.

There are two terms from the table with which you should be familiar: interlocking directorate and merger. An **interlocking directorate** occurs when the majority of members of the boards of directors of competing corporations are the same. In effect, there is only one management for both companies. Because the same people control both companies, it is easy for them to make sure that the two companies do not compete with one another.

Table 10-2: ANTITRUST LEGISLATION

Federal Law	Function
Sherman Act (1890)	Outlawed agreements and conspiracies that restrain inter-state trade. Made it illegal to monopolize or even attempt to monopolize any part of interstate commerce.
Clayton Act (1914)	Restricted the practice of selling the same good to different buyers at different prices. Prohibited seller from requiring that a buyer not deal with a competitor. Outlawed interlocking directorates between competitors. Outlawed mergers that substantially lessen competition.
Federal Trade Commission Act (1914)	Established the Federal Trade Commission (FTC) as an independent antitrust agency. Gave the FTC power to bring court cases against private businesses engaging in unfair trade practices.
Robinson-Patman Act (1936)	Strengthened the law against charging different prices for the same product to different buyers. An amendment to the Clayton Act of 1914.
Celler-Kefauver Antimerger Act (1950)	Strengthened the law against firms joining together to control too large a part of the market. An amendment to the Clayton Act of 1914.
Hart-Scott-Rodino Antitrust Improvement Act (1980)	Restricted mergers that would lessen competition. It required big corporations planning to merge to notify the Federal Trade Commission (FTC) and the Department of Justice. They would then decide whether to challenge the merger under the terms of the Clayton Act of 1914.

SHERMAN ACT

CLAYTON ACT

The last point in the table under the Clayton Act refers to corporate mergers. A **merger** occurs when one corporation buys more than half of the stock in another corporation. When the two corporations are in the same business, this is called a **horizontal merger.** The buying out of an oil company by another oil company is an example of a horizontal merger because they produce the same product. When a business that is buying from or selling to another business merges with that business, a **vertical merger** takes place. For example, if a shoe manufacturer buys retail stores that are selling its shoes, a vertical merger takes place. Some corporations have become big by buying out other corporations dealing in totally unrelated activities. These expanded corporations are called **conglomerates.** The buying out of unrelated businesses is termed **conglomerate merger.** An oil company, for example, will buy oil and other energy companies to diversify and to raise total profits. There are other types of conglomerate merger also.

The Clayton Act forbids mergers when they tend to lessen competition substantially. However, the Clayton Act does not state what the term *substantially* means. As a result, it is up to the government to make a subjective decision as to whether the merging of two corpora-

Agency	Function
Interstate Commerce Commission (ICC) (1887)	Regulates interstate commerce, primarily railroads and trucking.
Federal Trade Commission (FTC) (1914)	Regulates product warranties, unfair methods of competition in interstate commerce, and fraud in advertising.
Food and Drug Administration (FDA) (1931)	Regulates purity and safety of foods, drugs, and cosmetics.
Federal Communications Commission (FCC) (1933)	Regulates television, radio, telegraph and telephone; grants licenses, creates and enforces rules of behavior for broadcasting; most recently, regulates satellite transmissions and cable TV.
Securities and Exchange Commission (SEC) (1934)	Regulates the sale of stocks, bonds, and other investments.
Environmental Protection Agency (EPA) (1970)	Regulates the amount of pollutants that business and industry may release into the environment.
Occupational Safety and Health Administration (OSHA) (1970)	Regulates the workplace environment; makes sure that businesses provide workers with safe and healthful working conditions.
Nuclear Regulatory Commission (NRC) (1975)	Regulates the nuclear power industry; licenses and oversees the design, construction, and operation of nuclear power plants.

tions would substantially lessen competition. This provision has been used to block horizontal mergers in which large corporations attempt to buy smaller corporations in the same industry. For example, in 1982 the Federal Trade Commission blocked the Mobil Corporation in its attempt to acquire Marathon Oil Company. The government maintained that the merger would have reduced competition in gasoline retailing in the Midwest.

REGULATORY AGENCIES

Besides the use of antitrust laws to create a competitive atmosphere, the government uses direct regulation of business pricing and product quality. The overseeing of these regulations is done by government regulatory agencies. These exist not only at the federal level, but also at the state level and even local levels. Table 10-3 shows some major federal regulatory agencies. Many states have similar agencies.

In spite of the fact that the aim of most government regulations is to promote efficiency and competition, recent evidence indicates something quite different. Many regulations, as a by-product of their goals to protect consumers and companies within industries from unfair prac-

Another Point of View: Joan Robinson (1903–1983)

Joan Robinson is considered one of the world's most important contemporary economists. She taught for more than 40 years and was professor of economics at Cambridge University. Robinson wrote and lectured widely on economic theory. Among her important books are *Introduction to the Theory of Employment*, *The Accumulation of Capital*, *Economic Philosophy*, and *Freedom and Necessity: An Introduction to the Study of Society*.

The underlying basis of most economic thought today is that "the pursuit of self-interest by each individual redounds to the benefit of all." This means that everyone can benefit if each person looks out for his or her own well-being in all activities in the marketplace. Even though Robinson accepts this as the basis for most economic thought, she does not believe it to be true.

Robinson is best known for developing the theory of monopolistic competition. She tried to make sense of the marketplace in an age when many large industries are dominated by relatively few corporations. She was not satisfied with the theories of perfect competition and pure monopoly. She first attempted to develop her alternative explanation of the behavior of large firms in her book *The Economics of Imperfect Competition*, published in 1933. She found that firms could obtain a partial monopoly simply by advertising a particular brand name of theirs. When enough consumers associate the product with each brand name, each company will have a partial monopoly. That means that each firm can raise its price a little and not lose all its customers because they exhibit brand-name loyalty.

Robinson's interest in monopolistic competition is also evident in much of her later work. In *Economic Heresies: Some Old-Fashioned Questions in Economic Theory* (1971), for example, she analyzes how monopolistic corporations grow by "continuously expanding capacity, conquering new markets, producing new commodities [products], and exploiting new techniques." She wrote that "the majority of businesses are either growing, being forced to close down because of the growth of other businesses, or being absorbed into some larger organization." In other words, businesses are getting larger and exercising greater power. Robinson believes that the growth of oligopolies has tended to reduce competition within individual countries, but that competition among the industries of different countries has increased.

Robinson criticized economists because they ignore social and moral issues. She disagreed with Adam Smith and those who accept his theory that morality will take care of itself. She thought that the worldwide Great Depression of the 1930s gave ample proof that morality does not take care of itself. Robinson believed that it showed that self-interest does not necessarily make everyone better off. She also believed that economists have a duty to enlighten the public about the economic aspects of such social and moral problems as the nuclear arms race and the destruction of the environment.

1. What was Robinson's theory about monopolistic competition?
2. Do you agree or disagree with Robinson's charge that economists ignore social and moral issues? Explain your answer.

The trucking industry is subject to the regulations of the ICC. What is the aim of such government controls, and how do they affect consumers?

tices, have actually decreased the amount of competition in the economy. The Interstate Commerce Commission (ICC), for example, has raised the prices that consumers pay for the shipment of goods by preventing entry into the trucking industry and restricting price competition. For many years the Federal Communications Commission (FCC), in an effort to help UHF stations, in effect prevented the entry of competitive pay-TV, cable, and satellite systems into the television market. Different researchers have also shown that while the Civil Aeronautics Board (CAB) regulated airfares, these fares were 20 to 50 percent higher than they would have been if competition had been allowed to set prices. The Federal Trade Commission has often prosecuted businesses because of complaints by businesses who are having difficulty competing in a particular industry. The Occupational Safety and Health Administration (OSHA) has been accused of creating thousands of regulations that have had little benefit but have been costly to enforce.

Because of findings such as these, the 1980s have been called the era of **deregulation.** This refers to a gradual reduction in government control over business activity. This does not mean there should or will be no government regulation. It just means there will be less than existed in the 1960s and 1970s. For example, the CAB no longer controls airfares or route selection by the nation's airlines. Additionally, the FCC is now allowing almost open competition in the cable and direct-satellite television transmission fields. The many regulations in the banking industry have been slowly decreased, allowing consumers to obtain competitive interest rates on savings for the first time in many years.

REVIEWING ECONOMIC PRINCIPLES

1. Define the following economic terms: **a.** interlocking directorate, **b.** merger, **c.** conglomerates, **d.** deregulation.
2. What is the purpose of each of the following: **a.** antitrust legislation? **b.** regulatory agencies?
3. Why is it difficult to enforce part of the Clayton Act?
4. **Critical Thinking: Making Predictions.** Based on recent studies, how effective do you think regulations about business practices will be in the future?

SUMMARY OF
IMPORTANT PRINCIPLES

1
- Perfect competition has four conditions that result in businesses' having no control over price: a large market, similar product, easy entry, and easily obtainable information.
- On the supply side, perfect competition requires a large number of suppliers of a similar product. On the demand side, perfect competition requires a large number of informed buyers who know exactly what the market price is for the good or service. The market price is the equilibrium price and is reached when the total supply and the total demand are allowed to interact.

2
- Pure monopoly has three conditions that result in a business's having almost complete control over the market price: a single seller, no adequate substitutes, and no entry.
- In a pure monopoly, a monopolist controls the supply available and, therefore, the market price. However, the law of demand still operates and, as the price of a good or service rises, consumers will buy less.
- The profit incentive works on potential competitors to find a way to break down a monopoly.

3
- An oligopoly is dominated by a few sellers and may have substantial barriers to entry, identical or slightly different products, and nonprice competition. These factors result in limited control over price.
- A corporation's annual report summarizes in words and financial data the facts about a company's revenues, costs, and profits.

4
- Monopolistic competition has numerous sellers, limited entry, differentiated products, and nonprice competition that results in some price control.
- In monopolistic competition, a business does not have complete control over price because other monopolistic competitors are selling almost, but not quite, the same product. The quantity demanded of a good or service will drop if the price is raised and there are cheaper substitutes available.
- Perfect competition has a large market; pure monopoly, a single seller; oligopoly, a market dominated by a few sellers; monopolistic competition, numerous sellers. Perfect competition has easy entry into the market; pure monopoly, no entry; oligopoly, substantial barriers to entry; monopolistic competition, relatively easy entry. In perfect competition, the product is similar; in a pure monopoly, there are no substitutes; in an oligopoly, products are identical or slightly different; in monopolistic competition, there are differentiated products. The conditions of perfect competition result in no control over price; pure monopoly, complete control of market price; oliogopoly, limited control over price; monopolistic competition, some control over price.

5
- The federal government has passed laws and established regulatory agencies to force monopolies to act more competitively, to prevent new monopolies, and to break up those that exist. Recent evidence suggests that such regulations have had an opposite effect.

Putting Economics to Work

COMPARISON SHOPPING: COMPETITION AND THE PHONE COMPANY

Sam and Betty Schultz and their family own and operate a hardware store in a large western city. Sam handles the store, and Betty keeps the books. As part of doing business with suppliers scattered across the country, the Schultzes make many long-distance telephone calls. In addition, Sam's parents live in the eastern United States, and he calls them once a week.

For years Betty has been concerned about the high cost of phone service, but there was, after all, only one phone company. However, she recently noticed an ad in a magazine for a long-distance telephone service that was not part of the Bell system. Then she saw a television ad for another, similar company. She began investigating and found that at least three nationwide phone services were available in her city. According to their advertising brochures, all three charged 10 to 50 percent less than the regular telephone company for long-distance calls to selected cities.

Sam and Betty next compared services and prices and then picked the company that served all the cities that they phoned regularly. After trying the service for a month, they found they had saved almost 20 percent.

1. Did the existence of one telephone company mean that consumers were necessarily paying higher rates? Why or why not?
2. What barrier(s) to entry might prevent a new long-distance telephone company from being formed?
3. According to the Schultz's experience, what form of competitive market situation now exists for long-distance telephone service?

THE THEORY OF PERFECT COMPETITION
Skill: Applying Information

 The theory of perfect competition and automatic price-making by the laws of supply and demand was a product of the era in which it first appeared, as economist Edwin G. Nourse makes clear in this reading.

The essence of automatic price-making is to be found in the process of individual bargaining. Economics got its start as a branch of formal learning at a time when the tide of individual freedom of productive effort and bargaining activity was just beginning to rise or to reassert itself. . . .

Money exchange was highly developed, but financial controls had not grown much beyond individual or family limits. . . . From top to bottom of society, the individual was released from old obligations and endowed with new rights and resources. . . . The new competition which emerged in the late eighteenth and early nineteenth centuries took on a more dynamic quality as increases in productive efficiency, derived from new explorations and techniques, became more and more available.

The times begot their relevant philosophy. Adam Smith gave it classic expression. The heart of his doctrine was that if the individual was left free to exert himself in the midst of opportunities and was given responsibility for his own well-being, self-interest would produce results better than could be achieved under any program of official direction. Prices, reflecting the actions of economically free men, could not be quarreled with any more than one could quarrel with the thermometer for registering the temperature. Moreover, this free price system would, like a thermostat, be not merely a recording device but also one of control. If prices went up sharply, production would be stimulated to reduce the shortage; if down, it would be checked until the glut was relieved. . . .

In this remote and somewhat idealized situation, prices will be registered automatically as the expression of the balance which spontaneous supplies and demands strike in the market. The "economic man," using only common sense in the pursuit of the individual interest or advantage . . . age . . . , may be relied upon to keep supplies constantly adjusting themselves to demands. . . .

While it was the professional economist who elaborated this theory of automatic price-making, the businessman has been quick to admire the picture and accept it for himself. He has indeed been prone to put it forward as an explanation of price movements even today, although conditions are quite different from those to which the original theory was applied. The major point of difference is that economic life is no longer dominated by the business operations of individual producers and traders. Great blocks of capital, management, and labor having crystallized in modern business, the flow of automatic price-making and its accompanying economic adjustments gives place to consciously previewed and purposely directed group operations.

1. In your own words, explain what Adam Smith meant by the "invisible hand."
2. Explain the analogy between a purely competitive market and a thermostat.

Edwin G. Nourse, "Price-Making, a Key to Economic Analysis." *Selected Readings in Modern Economics*. Ed. by Asher Isaacs, C. W. McKee, and R. E. Slesinger. New York: Dryden Press, 1952.

ROCKEFELLER AND THE STANDARD OIL TRUST
Skill: Identifying Cause and Effect

 The Standard Oil Company was a classic example of one firm monopolizing an entire American industry. Ida Tarbell, a leading muckraker and famous for her *History of the Standard Oil Company*, published in 1904, describes how this company got control over its market by controlling transportation lines.

The most brilliant illustration of the supremacy possible through a control of shipping rates was the practical monopoly of the petroleum industry which since 1872 had been developed by an oil-refining and marketing concern of Cleveland,

Readings in Economics

Ohio, known as the Standard Oil Company. Yet considering the remarkable abilities of John D. Rockefeller, who headed the Standard, it may well be asked whether the company had needed to resort to unfair methods of competition in order to gain preeminence in the field. . . . Rockefeller was a man who gave himself entirely to his business, saw it as a whole, its tiniest detail as well as its largest possible ramification [future development]. . . . He took deep satisfaction in economies, hated waste whether in small or great things. Combined with these qualities was a genius for organization. . . .

This dignified, formal portrait of oil magnate John D. Rockefeller shows him after he had made his Standard Oil Company the nation's No. 1 oil refiner by using questionable methods of suppressing competition.

Rockefeller detested and feared free competition and the disorder and uncertainties which attended it. It interfered with stable prices and profits; it glutted the crude and refined markets; it was wasteful. He had seen no way to bring order and stability into the industry but for him and those with him to take over the entire oil-refining and marketing business of the country. By this means it could be run economically, efficiently and profitably for those in the combination. This could be done most expeditiously [easily] by getting special rates from the railroads. It was fair to ask them, he held, because the Standard would be the biggest and the most regular shipper. Aided by these special advantages over competitors, the Rockefeller group had acquired . . . some 74 refining concerns, including many of the most successful in their districts. Contracts limiting the quantity of oil to be refined had also been made with certain firms strong enough to refuse to sell. In 1878 the Standard Oil Company was manufacturing over 90 per cent of the output of the country.

In securing mastery of the refining industry the Standard had been aided by its success in carrying out one of the most farsighted policies in its history, that of controlling the pipe lines which carried oil from the wells to the railway shipping points as well as to the tanks in which surplus was stored. . . .

The Rockefeller group took steps to consolidate their control of the various companies they had acquired in order to obviate [do away with] competition. To overcome the objections inherent in the pool, they devised a novel form of industrial organization: the trust.

1. What kind of barriers to entry into the oil-producing market did Standard Oil erect against other oil firms?
2. What kind of legislation resulted from the actions of John D. Rockefeller and Standard Oil? How might such legislation benefit consumers today?

Ida Tarbell, *The Nationalizing of Business*, Vol. IX of *A History of American Life*. Edited by Arthur M. Schlesinger and Dixon Ryan Fox. New York: Macmillan, 1936. pp. 74–76.

END OF AN OLIGOPOLY
Skill: Making Inferences

The American automobile industry has long been considered an oligopoly. According to this magazine article, however, that market structure has recently changed.

The most significant change in the market is the final end of the oligopoly. For a half-century economic reality created an oligopoly in the U.S. auto market, which was controlled, dominated or administered—whatever the word—by a handful of companies: General Motors as the key player, plus Ford and Chrysler.

Such were the economies of scale, finance and marketing that the smaller manufactures disappeared: good-sized ones, such as Packard, Studebaker, Hudson; lesser makers, such as Willys, Graham-Paige, Hupp. The United Auto Workers [UAW] helped the big three, forcing the struggling smaller producers to pay more for labor than the giants; pay or take a strike that would put you out of business. That was the successful union threat. The small firms yielded and went under anyhow.

Foreign competition? It was only a marginal threat until fairly well into the 1970s. The big three had the rich market pretty much to themselves. Profits were lush. They had 95% of the nation's sales in 1955. . . . But even within the big three, it was jump when the dominating partner, GM, said jump. At one point, GM decided to take out side vent windows in order to cut costs. Everybody had to take out side vent windows, like it or not, or look old-fashioned. GM decides to bury the windshield wipers under the hood, where it's hard to get them out when they freeze. Anyone with wipers showing looks old-fashioned. GM went up, down, sideways on prices? Everybody jumped.

But today that oligopoly is dead. In addition to the big three, the U.S. industry now includes three big Japanese companies, Toyota, Nissan and Honda. Call it six major companies. The smaller contenders, like Mercedes, Volkswagen, Mazda

and others, moreover, are a lot stronger than the U.S. auto independents who went under after World War II. They have strong home and world markets and are often supported by their governments. Nor are their dealers weak and ill financed, as so many dealers were for the old independents. Even the UAW gives lower-cost contracts to foreigners building plants here than it gives U.S. companies. . . .

Now? "Best car wins," says Lataif of Ford, talking about the new competitive environment. "Best car wins" doesn't mean that imports will disappear or that General Motors is a powerless giant. It means that the playing field is now more even and that a lot of market is up for grabs.

1. How did the United Auto Workers union help eliminate competition for the "big three" from smaller American automobile manufacturers?
2. Explain what Lataif of Ford Motor Company meant by his comment "best car wins" in today's market.

Jerry Flint, "Best Car Wins." *Forbes*, January 27, 1986. Adapted by permission of *Forbes* magazine. © Forbes Inc., 1986.

COMPETITION'S NOT ALWAYS PERFECT
Skill: Justifying an Answer

In a book published in 1938, Joan Robinson, a well-known British economist, studied the monopolistic nature of some competitive markets. In this excerpt, Robinson lists some reasons why the pure competition model is rarely a reality.

In actual markets the customer takes into account a great deal besides the prices at which rival producers offer him their goods. Quite apart from the inertia or ignorance which prevents him from moving instantly from one seller to another, as soon as a difference appears between the prices which they charge, he has a number of good reasons for preferring one seller to another. And these reasons will affect different individuals differently.

In the first place, the customer must take costs of transport into account. . . . Secondly, the different customers will be differently influenced by the guarantee of quality provided by a well-known name. Thirdly, they will be influenced in varying degrees by the difference between the facilities provided by different producers—quickness of service, good manners of salesmen, length of credit, and the attention paid to their individual wants. In some cases (most disconcertingly from the point of view of analysis) the customer will be influenced by the actual price, since he will sometimes take a high price to be a sign that the article in question is a good one, and reject a cheaper substitute because its very cheapness makes him suspect that it is inferior. Lastly, the customer will be influenced by the advertisement, which plays upon his mind with studied skill, and makes him prefer the goods of one producer to those of another because they are brought to his notice in a more pleasing or more forceful manner.

Thus there are many reasons why a customer buys from one producer rather than another besides the simple one of a difference in the prices which they charge, and since the rival producers make it their business to exploit all these influences upon the customer's choice, the very existence of competition, in the plain sense of the word, ensures that the market will not be perfect. Rival producers compete against each other in quality, in facilities, and in advertisement, as well as in price. And the very intensity of competition, by forcing them to attract customers in every possible way, itself breaks up the market and ensures that not all the customers, who are attached in varying degrees to a particular firm by the advantages which it offers them, will immediately forsake it for a rival who offers similar goods at an infinitesimally smaller price.

1. Name five factors besides price that influence a customer to choose one seller over others.

2. The "universal law of demand" states that at higher prices, consumers will buy less of a good. Why, then, do some consumers choose an item just because it is more expensive?

Joan Robinson, *The Economics of Imperfect Competition*. London: MacMillan, 1938. pp. 89, 90.

FLYING THE COMPETITIVE SKIES

Skill: Suggesting Outcomes

When the federal government stops regulating an industry, the result is often increased competition and greater efficiency within that industry. In this reading from a speech delivered in 1986, Donald D. Engen, Administrator of the Federal Aviation Administration, discusses the effects of deregulation on the airline industry.

The Airline Deregulation Act of 1978 was the first in a series of laws by which Congress deregulated several modes of transportation. In order to understand why we changed the economic regulations affecting air carriers, let's review the kinds of incidents that inspired deregulation.

During the forty years before 1978, the Civil Aeronautics Board received 79 applications from people who desired to establish "trunk" airlines. It approved none of them, in effect shutting the door of opportunity to people who might have contributed to aviation.

Regulations affecting routes and rates kept some air carriers flying unprofitable routes, and prevented others from establishing routes where people wanted to go. The system had little flexibility. As a result, carriers who had secured lucrative [profitable] routes operated very profitably, and even marginal carriers usually profited to some extent. . . .

As burdensome as this regularity system was, proponents could point to sustained safety progress in aviation to rationalize continued regulation. Throughout the industry, people recognized a common interest in air safety. . . .

When Congress agreed to deregulate rates and routes in 1978, it ordered the Secretary of Transportation to report on the effects of deregulation for air safety each year. Air safety progress continued under deregulation.

Long-term advocates of deregulation took special pride in the economic benefits that came with this sustained safety progress. As the General Accounting Office reported to Congress in a special study of deregulation based on data through 1984:

The ad at left illustrates the price war that airlines engaged in after deregulation. At right, in another highly competitive industry, cosmetics are offered for sale at a department store.

Increased competition has generally kept average fares lower and made them more cost-based than they would have been under regulation. . . . In addition, service is more widely available nationwide and more convenient, while profits have varied widely among airlines. These changes result in the industry operating more efficiently and offering more price/quality options than it did under regulation. Most, but not all, airline passengers benefited from industry changes. . . .

The report added a concluding caution, however, noting, "the industry is still adapting to deregulation, with a complete adjustment likely being years away.". . . .

Aviation is still adapting to the changes brought about by deregulation. The one constant in this atmosphere of change is the shared responsibility for aviation safety. . . .

Deregulation has resulted in changes in every form of transportation. It has yielded substantial benefits to the American people, both in terms of economic gains and improved service.

Changes in the aviation industry will affect the shape of the FAA in the future. We are a dynamically changing world. We will move forward, with aviation safety continuing to be the watchword. Thank you.

1. Before Congress passed the Airline Deregulation Act in 1978, what had been the main reason for continued federal regulation of the airline industry?
2. Why is it likely that safety standards for airlines will remain high after federal deregulation?

Donald D. Engen, "Deregulation: Seven Years Later," from a speech delivered Jan. 15, 1986, New York. *Vital Speeches of the Day*, March 15, 1986, Vol. LII, No. 11, pp. 335–57.

10 | CHAPTER REVIEW

PRACTICING YOUR STUDY SKILLS: READING CARTOONS

Political cartoons are one way to represent an opinion. They capture feelings and facts about issues or events. Cartoons that deal with historical and political topics may be difficult to understand if you are not familiar with the issue represented. That is because such cartoons often rely on symbols to express meaning. For example, Uncle Sam is one symbol for the United States; and the bald eagle, another.

Current cartoons also require special knowledge. To get their points across, cartoonists often use caricatures of famous people. A caricature is a drawing that emphasizes a person's features, such as the nose or ears. The cartoonist expresses attitudes about a person by the way he or she draws that person. To read a cartoon, you must answer three questions:

1. What is the topic of the cartoon?
2. Who or what do the caricatures and symbols represent?
3. What is the cartoonist's point of view about the topic?

Activity: Study the cartoon on p. 419 and answer the above three questions about it.

Bonds	Current Yield	Sales in $1,000	High	Low	Last	Net Chge.
AmMot 6s88	cv	50	69½	69⅜	69½	− ½
ASug 5.3s93	9.1	22	58½	56¾	58½	+ 3½
ATT 2⅞s87	2.9	55	98⅝	98⅝	98⅝	....
ATT 3⅞s90	4.2	71	92⅞	92½	92½	+ ⅛
ATT 8¾00	8.6	371	102⅝	102⅛	102¼	....
ATT 7s01	7.8	301	89¼	89	89¼	+ ⅜
ATT 7⅛03	8.0	273	89¼	89	89	+ ⅜
ATT 8.80s05	8.8	215	100¾	100⅜	100½	....
ATT 8⅝07	8.7	246	99¼	98½	99¼	+ ½

VOCABULARY REVIEW

Write the letter of the definition in Column B that correctly defines each term in Column A.

Column A	Column B
1. barriers to entry	a. large corporation made up of smaller corporations dealing in unrelated activities
2. annual report	
3. conglomerate	
4. interlocking directorate	b. the purchase by one corporation of more than half of the stock in another corporation
5. natural monopoly	
6. merger	c. obstacles to competition that prevents new companies from being formed
	d. summary of a corporation's receipts, costs, and profits
	e. production by one company rather than several due to efficient operation
	f. type of business organization in which the board of directors for competing companies are the same

PRACTICING YOUR ECONOMIC SKILLS

1. **Reading Bond Quotations.** Based on the sample from the New York Stock Exchange Bond Market on the left, answer the following: **a.** What was the high price for American Telephone and Telegraph (ATT) bonds maturing in 1990? **b.** What was the low price? **c.** What was the closing price?
2. **Reading Bond Quotations. a.** What is the interest rate on ATT bonds maturing in 2003? **b.** What is the current yield of ATT bonds maturing in 1987?

266

3. **Analyzing Information.** Determine in what kind of market each of the different products listed below is sold in your local area. Answers may vary depending on the size of your shopping area. Remember there are few perfect markets.

Milk
Automobiles
Football team
Restaurants
University Education
Television shows

4. **Understanding Concepts.** Decide whether each of the following would increase competition or decrease it.

a. the passage of a series of protective tariffs on imported goods by the Congress of the United States.

b. a merger among the top three advertising firms.

c. the discovery of an acceptable substitute for steel.

d. vigorous enforcement of antitrust laws by Congress.

DISCUSSING ECONOMIC QUESTIONS

1. With large corporations becoming ever larger through mergers, acquisitions, and expansion, is it possible and probable that in the future there will be only a few huge corporations in the United States controlling all types of industry? Consider the profit incentive as well as current government legislation and regulations.

2. Would it be in the public interest if pure monopoly existed in the automobile industry? Why or why not?

3. Identify an example of a monopoly in your area or a nearby area. What would happen if another firm successfully entered that monopolistic market?

APPLYING CRITICAL THINKING SKILLS

1. **Preparing a Research Report.** Research and prepare a report on the 1982 settlement of the Justice Department's antitrust suit against American Telephone and Telegraph. Be sure to explain what the settlement means for consumers.

2. **Gathering Information.** Clip pictures from newspapers and magazines to make a collage showing the types of industries that are in one of the following market situations: pure monopoly, oligopoly, or monopolistic competition. The table on p. 251 will help you to determine which companies in the United States are in oligopoly industries.

3. **Holding an Interview.** Interview an owner or manager in an industry in your area that can be considered as an example of monopolistic competition. Ask how the firm uses price and nonprice competition in retailing the product. Summarize the interview for the class, explaining any conclusion you reached.

4. **Writing a Research Report.** Choose one of the regulatory agencies mentioned in the chapter to write to for information about its functions. Use the information that it sends you to write a report summarizing the main functions of that agency.

READINGS

Brue, Stanley L., and Wentworth, Donald R. *Economic Scenes: Theory in Today's World,* 3rd ed. Englewood Cliffs, N.J.: Prentice-Hall, 1980.

Mauser, Ferdinand F., and Schwartz, David J. *American Business: An Introduction,* 5th ed. New York: Harcourt Brace Jovanovich, 1982.

Robinson, Joan. *The Economics of Imperfect Competition.* New York: St. Martin's, 1969.

Sampson, Anthony. *The Sovereign State of ITT.* Briarcliff Manor, New York: Stein & Day, 1980.

CAN BIG BUSINESS AND FREE ENTERPRISE EXIST IN THE SAME ECONOMY?

After you study this Issue, you will be able to explain the roles of free enterprise in relation to big business.

> gross national product
> economies of scale

General Motor's (GM) revenue of over $75 billion in a recent year was larger than the gross national product of at least a dozen nations. **Gross national product** (GNP) is the total value of all final goods and services produced by a nation during a given period. If corporations have become so large, you might wonder if it is possible for free enterprise to operate in the same economy.

DOES BIGNESS ALWAYS MEAN IMPERFECT COMPETITION?

Although people may think that big business always has power over prices, the truth is not so clear. If size alone meant imperfect competition, then bigger businesses should be making higher profits. Of course, the dollar amount of their profits are high because the largest firms take in large amounts of money. But the real question is whether bigger businesses earn higher rates of return on their investment than do small businesses? Rate of return is the ratio of a company's profit to the size of the investment of its owners. Measuring rate of return is the only true test of a business's ability to set monopoly prices.

Interestingly, the rates of return for large businesses are about the same as those of much smaller companies. In fact, the biggest companies in the world—the oil companies—make about the same average rate of return as the average of all other companies combined, which is about 5 percent. Also, some industries whose firms are small in size make much higher rates of return than the big industries. For example, some small companies that make computer chips have rates of return of 20 to 25 percent or higher.

CAN BIG BUSINESS HELP THE ECONOMY?

Many economists have observed that as companies become larger, they become more efficient. That happens because they are able to create **economies of scale.** This means that, because of their large size, these firms can take advantage of mass production techniques that result in lower production costs.

Today some economists believe that antitrust laws may actually be harming the national economy. First, laws that prevent horizontal mergers prevent companies from taking advantage of economies of scale. Instead, corporations that have capital and want to expand may become conglomerates. Because they acquire a variety of companies in different industries, productivity of the various companies may decrease. The managers and executives of the parent company cannot be familiar with the business activities of every subsidiary, or company, they own.

Second, millions of dollars are used in legal fights to break up big businesses that are considered monopolies. The Justice Department in 1974 filed an antitrust suit against American Telephone

Based on what you have read, do you think there is a conflict between big business, represented by this robot-run assembly line and a manager, and free enterprise?

and Telegraph (AT&T) in an attempt to break up the giant corporation. By the time the suit was settled in 1982, AT&T had spent around $360 million in defending itself. This is money that could have been used to produce more goods or for research and development. This does not include the costs to taxpayers for the Justice Department's work.

CAN FREE ENTERPRISE CONTROL BIG BUSINESS?

Adam Smith believed that some business people conspire to raise prices. But he also pointed out that other business people would try to break the power of very large businesses. It is, therefore, wrong to assume automatically that a small number of companies in one industry means less competition and consequently higher prices. There can be competition even among huge companies in industries having two or three large companies. In some industries, in fact, such as the personal computer industry, prices are actually decreasing every year. In addition, United States industries face competition from big companies in other countries. For example, GM's share of the auto market declined from 45 to 43 percent between 1981 and 1982, mostly because of competition.

Competition, of course, is what free enterprise is all about. Apparently, the Justice Department decided to drop its antitrust suit against IBM in 1982 because it decided that any potential gains to consumers were not worth the costs. At the time the suit was filed in 1969, IBM sold about two-thirds of all computers. However, strong competition from new American and Japanese firms began chipping away at IBM's share of the market in the 1970s. By 1982, IBM still sold the majority of large, general purpose computers, but its share of small business computers had fallen to less than 35 percent. It sold only about 3 percent of the new personal computers. Recently, though, IBM's share of the personal computer market has continued to increase. But even so, IBM cannot stop all of the imitations manufactured by other companies that are cheaper.

The computer industry is a good example of free enterprise. There are several success stories of people, some of them in their 20s, who started computer businesses and built them into multi-million dollar companies.

Discussing Economic Questions

1. Why are economies of scale considered beneficial?

2. What is the current point of view of some economists toward the formation of monopolies?

3. Consider carefully the characteristics of the American economy that are described on pp. 31–32, 34–35, and again on page 38. How might these characteristics be influenced by the growth of monopoly power in the United States?

4. Consider the goals for the American economy on pp. 39–40. How might monopolies influence the nation's ability to achieve these goals?

UNIT 4

AMERICAN BUSINESS IN ACTION

As a future—or current—member of the American labor force, or as a future business manager or owner, you should understand how business operates in the American economy. In this unit, you will learn about how businesses finance and manage their production activities and about how they then market and distribute the goods and services they produce. Labor, which is a major productive factor in business, is also discussed. The Issue in this unit deals with the important question of technological unemployment.

CHAPTER 11

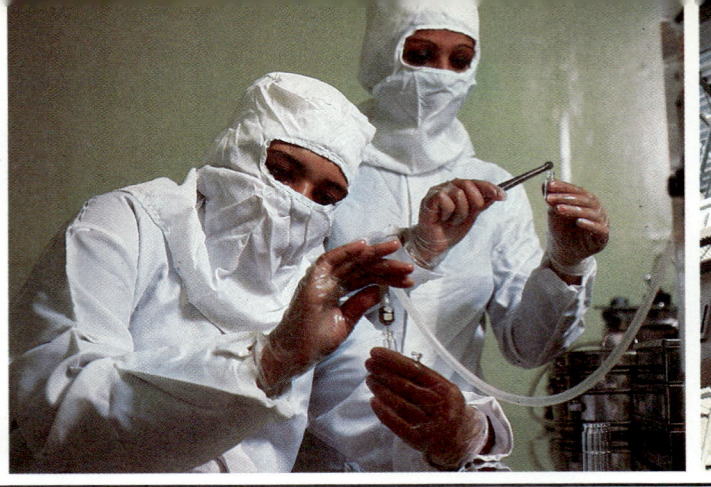

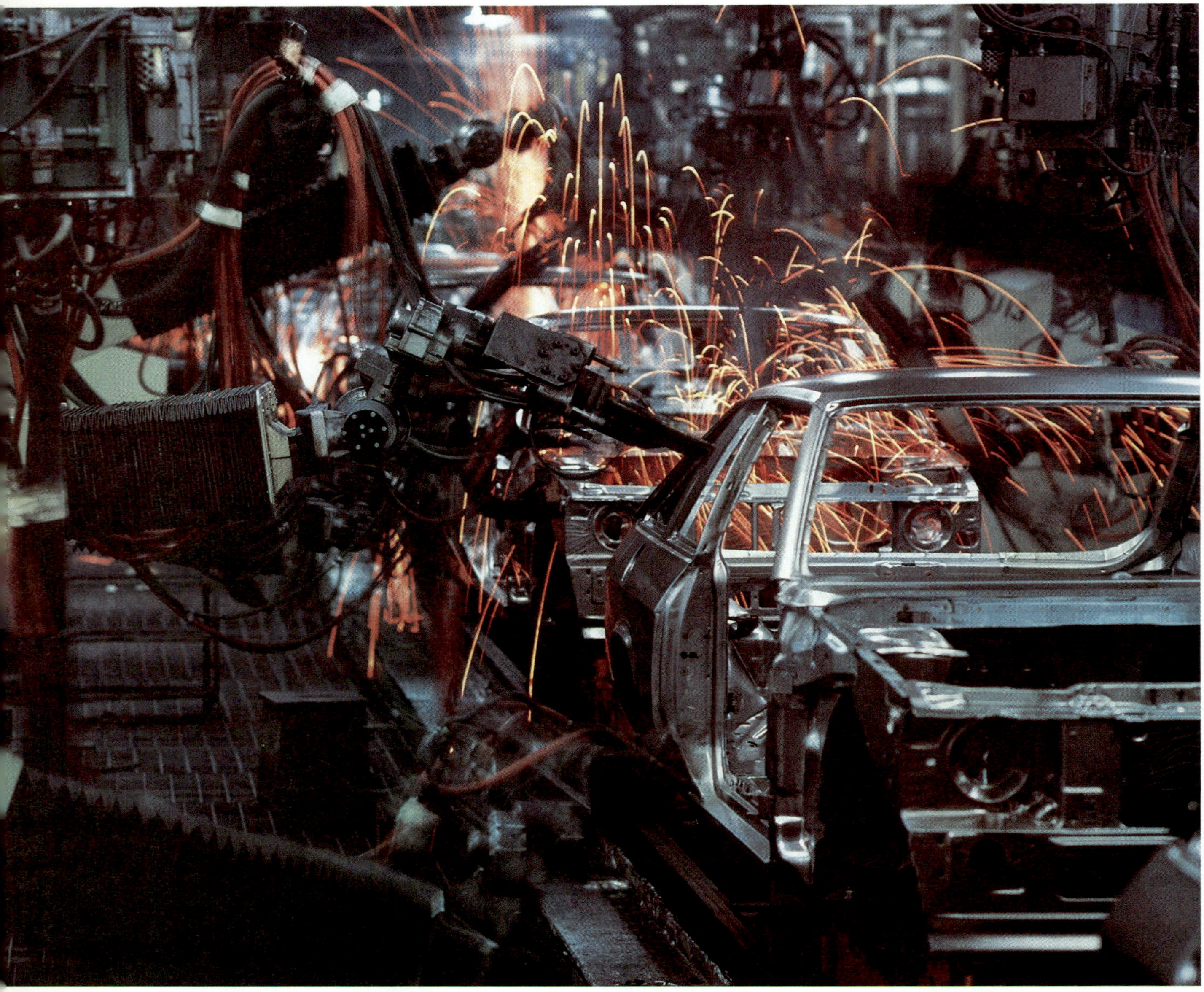

Manufacturing goods and producing services for profit is the purpose of business. Using the latest technology to manufacture products and sound financial planning is essential to the success of businesses.

FINANCING AND PRODUCING GOODS

The purpose of business is to produce and sell goods or services in order to make a profit. This chapter begins with a discussion of the role of management in business. It then discusses how businesses raise and use money to manufacture goods or offer services. You will also read about the production process and the effects of technology on production. Learning Economic Skills describes how businesses make financial planning decisions.

CHAPTER OBJECTIVES After you study the sections of this chapter, you will be able to:

1 • explain the effect of the law of diminishing returns on management decisions.

2 • state the different types of financing available to businesses.
 • identify the factors managers must consider in deciding on the best mix of debt and equity financing for business operations.
 ★ describe the trade-offs and opportunity costs involved in making financial planning decisions.
 • explain why Thorstein Veblen is considered a critic of big business.

3 • list the operations involved in the production process.

4 • explain the impact of technology on production methods since the industrial revolution

ECONOMICS VOCABULARY

management
law of diminishing returns
finance
debt financing
short-term financing
intermediate-term financing
long-term financing
trade credit
promissory note
accounts receivable
line of credit
equity financing
financial planning
market share
production
consumer goods
producer goods
mechanization
assembly line
division of labor
automation
robotics

When you buy an item in a store, you probably do not think about how that product reached the seller's shelf. But goods get into the marketplace because businessmen and businesswomen use the factors of production to produce the goods that consumers demand. Organizing and coordinating the factors of production—land, labor, capital—for maximum efficiency is known as **management.** Effective management is itself considered an important part of the factors of production.

1 | MANAGING BUSINESS OPERATIONS

Ask yourself as you read:

- What are the two major responsibilities of management?
- How do managers adapt to the marketplace?

Management methods follow the same basic principles whether a manager is concerned with a two-employee tailor shop or an automobile assembly plant. Managers' duties include deciding on a company's immediate activities, organizing and overseeing its day-to-day operation, and motivating employees to work harder. Managers also make long-range plans that will enable the company to adapt to future changes in the marketplace.

Adapting to the marketplace can mean adding to or laying off workers as well as buying more equipment or shutting down machinery. It can also mean shifting production from one style or product to another. At one time, for example, Xerox made only photocopiers. Today, it also makes word processors and small business computers. Because a business has limited resources, the more a firm uses of one of its resources, the more it must deal with the law of diminishing returns.

THE LAW OF DIMINISHING RETURNS

To return to the example of your electronic repair business, the business is growing and you decide to hire an employee. The output of the additional worker increases your weekly number of repair jobs by 10. Then you add a second worker. Your number of repair jobs increases to 22. However, when you add a third worker, you find that the number of repair jobs your business can do increases by only 8. Together the three workers are doing only 30 jobs. With the next worker you hire, the number of repair jobs increases by just 5, or 35 for all 4 workers. This is less output per worker than when you had only 3 employees.

Based on output, two workers seem able to use the equipment and work space most efficiently. After this point, each additional worker adds less and less to the total output of your business. This is an example of the **law of diminishing returns.** According to this law, after some point adding units of a factor of production—such as labor—to fixed factors of production—such as equipment—increases total output for a

Managers make long-range plans to allow their business to adapt to changes in the marketplace. How does the law of diminishing returns apply to their decisions?

time. However, after a certain point, the extra output per each additional unit will begin to decrease.

When the income from the employees' work is less than the wages paid to them, your business has reached the point where it no longer pays to hire more workers. A good manager has to know when to stop hiring additional workers or when to stop buying new equipment.

REVIEWING ECONOMIC PRINCIPLES

1. **a.** What is management? **b.** What duties do managers of businesses have regardless of the size of the business?
2. State the law of diminishing returns.
3. **Critical Thinking: Inferring the Main Idea.** Why is it important for a manager to understand the law of diminishing returns? You will have to infer the answer from the text.

2 | FINANCING BUSINESS OPERATIONS

Ask yourself as you read:
- What are the major forms of debt financing?
- What are the major duties of financial managers?

Finance is concerned with the sources and uses of money capital—how it can be obtained and how it should be spent. Before businesses can produce goods, such as frozen foods, or offer services, such as medical care, they must obtain capital. After they get their capital, businesses then have to decide how to spend it. How much of their money should they use to buy raw materials; to replace or modernize equipment; and to pay for rent, advertising, wages, and so on? Planning the best use of money capital is a major part of managing a business, regardless of its size.

275

Table 11-1: TYPES OF FINANCING

	Short-Term Financing
Trade credit	**Trade credit** is extended by a seller to a business buying goods. It allows a buyer to take possession of goods immediately and pay for them at some future date. With most trade credit, customers have from 30 to 90 days to pay a bill. Trade credit accounts for more than 85 percent of all transactions involving goods. By using trade credit, a business does not have to tie up its capital in inventory. At the same time, trade credit benefits the seller by increasing its sales. Trade credit, like other types of credit, involves a cost to the user. Often a buyer will receive a discount, for example, 2 percent, if a bill is paid within 10 days. If the buyer does not take advantage of the discount, he or she is in effect paying a 2 percent interest for the use of the trade credit.
Unsecured loans	Most short-term bank credit for businesses is in the form of unsecured bank loans. These are loans not guaranteed by anything other than the promise to repay them. The borrower must sign a **promissory** (PRAHM-uh-sor-ee) **note** to repay the money in full by a specified time and with a specified rate of interest. The usual repayment period is one year.
Secured loans	A bank may require a business to secure its loans after it has borrowed a certain limit or if it has a poor credit rating. Secured loans are backed by collateral—something of value that a borrower uses as a promise to repay a loan. Businesses offer as collateral property such as machinery, inventories, or **accounts receivable**—money owed to a business by its customers.
Line of credit	A **line of credit** is the maximum amount of money a company can borrow from a bank during a period of time, usually one year. Rather than apply each time for a loan, a company may automatically borrow up to the amount of the line of credit, for example, $100,000. Banks establish lines of credit for larger businesses with good credit ratings. Usually a line of credit must be renewed annually following an examination of the company's credit history and financial health.

For a business to succeed, revenue from operations—money taken in from the sale of goods or services—has to be sufficient for that business to pay its bills and make a profit. Usually, businesses can operate year after year on their revenues. However, sometimes businesses need more money than revenues provide. This may happen if a business decides to expand into a new market or to repair or replace its equipment.

Business borrowing is similar in many ways to borrowing by individuals, which was described in Chapter 4. A business that wants to borrow must show creditworthiness by undergoing a credit check. A credit rating of good, average, or poor is then assigned to the business. Like

Table 11-1: TYPES OF FINANCING *(continued)*

	Intermediate-Term Financing
Loans	Intermediate-term loans have repayment periods of from one to ten years and generally require collateral such as stocks, bonds, equipment or machinery. The loan is considered a mortgage if it is secured by property, such as the building in which the business is located. Sometimes large, financially sound companies may be able to get unsecured intermediate-term loans. Because the financial condition of a company can change dramatically over a long period of time, the risk for intermediate-term financing is greater than for short-term loans. As a result, the lender may demand special conditions. For example, the borrower may be required to keep its debts below a certain level or to ask permission of the lender before taking out another loan.
Leasing	Leasing means renting rather than buying equipment. One advantage of leasing is that the leasing company will often service the equipment at low cost. Another advantage is that the company may deduct a part of the money spent on a lease before figuring its income taxes. One disadvantage is that taking out a long-term lease often costs more than borrowing the money to buy the same equipment.
	Long-Term Financing
Bonds	Bonds promise to pay a stated rate of interest over a stated period of time and to repay the full amount borrowed at the end of that time.
Stock	Selling stock is call **equity** (EK-wuh-tee) **financing** because part of the ownership, or equity, of the company is being sold. Corporations may sell either preferred or common stock. Preferred stock guarantees the stockholder a certain amount of interest. However, it rarely carries with it voting rights in the company's affairs. If the company fails, preferred stockholders are paid before holders of common stock. Besides a share in the profits of the corporation, common stock entitles the shareholder to a vote in certain matters, such as electing the board of directors.

an individual who borrows money, a business must pay interest on its loan. It must also repay the loan within a stated period of time.

Raising money for a business through borrowing, or **debt financing** as it is called, can be divided into three categories—short term, intermediate-term, and long-term financing. **Short-term financing** involves borrowing money for any period of time less than a year. Borrowing money for one to ten years is considered **intermediate-term financing.** Borrowing for any longer period is called **long-term financing.** As Table 11-1 shows, the reasons for using one type of financing rather than another differ. There are also different sources for financing for each type of debt.

Learning Economic Skills

FINANCIAL PLANNING FOR THE USE OF CAPITAL

Financial managers, or business managers as they are also called, decide on how a business should use its money. Should it expand its already existing business? Or should it invest in a totally new field? An entrepreneur faces the same problems. Should he or she invest in this business venture or in that one? Once the business is started, should the entrepreneur invest more money in it now or wait? Should the new investment be made through reinvesting profits or by taking on new debt? Each decision involves an opportunity cost. Every dollar that is spent on a new product cannot be spent for something else.

All these questions can be answered through financial planning. In general, **financial planning** is predicting revenues and costs and then comparing the estimated profit with the cost of the investment.

ESTIMATING REVENUE

Financial planning involves a mystery—the mystery of figuring out the amount that people will buy of a product that a company wishes to sell. Imagine you are the financial officer of a company planning to sell a new camera. In your job, you will have to predict how many cameras will be sold. The number of cameras sold depends on the product itself—what sets it apart from similar items—and its price. Price, in turn, will depend on the costs of research and development, production, distribution, advertising, and promotion.

In estimating the number of cameras you will sell, you also have to consider your competitors. Because you will not know what your competitors will be selling by the time you bring out your new camera, you will have to make educated guesses. You can use information from competitors' ads, from discussions with other camera makers, and from trade shows where companies display new equipment. Taking all these factors into consideration, you must estimate your **market share**—the percentage of total sales—you might be able to capture with your camera.

Another important factor to consider in financial planning is the time line for expected revenues. Will it take six months, two years, or longer before revenues from the product will begin to come in regularly? This is an important question because if you must wait for a long period to receive revenue, your investment will be less attractive. After all, every month you wait for revenue is a month when you cannot use that money to pay off any loans you might have taken out for your original investment. It is also money you cannot use for new product research and development. If you are a financial manager of a corporation, it is also money that you cannot use to pay dividends to stockholders or help pay interest on bonds.

ESTIMATING COSTS

Your expected costs may be easier to determine than your expected revenues. For example, your engineers can tell you how much it will cost to produce the new camera. Your marketing department can tell you the cost of promotion and advertising campaigns. Distribution costs can also be estimated fairly accurately. You will be reading more about these last items in the next chapter.

The time line of your costs is important, but it differs from the time line for your revenues. Ideally, you would like your costs to occur far in the future. That way you would avoid borrowing money or using current revenue to pay for your costs. However, with a new product this is almost impossible. Research and development and the start-up costs of production occur before a saleable product can be manufactured. Advertising costs may also be high when a product is first introduced. However, once a product is firmly established in the market, these costs may become fairly fixed over the life of the product.

COMPARING REVENUES AND COSTS

Once you have estimated your revenues and costs for each year of expected production and sales, you can compare them and make a decision. Consider the following example. For the first year, you expect your costs to be $1 million. You expect $500,000 for the second year; and $300,000 for the third year. You expect your gross revenues to

Comparison of Costs and Revenues for First Three Years

Year	Expected Gross Revenue	Expected Costs*	Expected Net Income
1	$0	$1 million	−$1 million
2	$1 million	$500,000	$500,000
3	$1.5 million	$300,000	$1.2 million

*Research and development, production advertising, wages, and so on, including the cost of credit.

be $0 for the first year while you are developing the product, $1 million for the second year, and $1.5 million for the third. *Gross* means before costs are subtracted, and *net* means after costs are subtracted. You can see from the table that in the first year, not only will you make no profits, but you will lose $1 million. In the second year, your net income will be $500,000; and in the third year, $1.2 million.

MAKING THE DECISIONS

Should your company invest in producing this new camera? That depends on how much it will cost to obtain the capital needed to make the investment. Suppose that to borrow the $1 million for the first year, you are charged 20 percent interest on a bank loan. Your real total costs for the first year will be $1.2 million, while you receive no revenue.

During the second year, your net income of $500,000 could go toward paying off your loan. But you would still owe at least $700,000 ($1.2 million minus $500,000) at the end of the year. Actually, because you would not receive your net

revenue of $500,000 in a lump sum at the beginning of the year, you will owe more than $700,000 on the loan at the end of the year. The reason for owing this much is because you would be paying interest on the loan throughout the second year.

Through the third year, with net income of $1.2 million, you would just about be able to pay back the loan. It would only be in the fourth year that you could hope to come out ahead.

After the fourth year, if you want to expand your business, you might consider reinvesting some part of your net income rather than taking out a new loan. This is a possibility for a company that already has a heavy debt load. It is also possible for a company that has stockholders who are willing to give up some of their dividends in the short-run in return for the long-term growth for the company.

Obviously, a key factor in your decision to produce the new camera is how much you have to pay to raise the needed capital. If, for example, you used an interest rate of 10 percent in figuring your loan, your business venture would look like a much better investment. The interest rate, however, depends on the general price of money—credit—in the economy. You will be reading more about this in Chapter 16.

Practicing Your Skills

1. What four factors does a financial manager have to consider in predicting: **a.** revenues? **b.** costs?
2. Why is the cost of obtaining capital important in deciding whether to produce a new product or expand a business?
3. Besides borrowing, how else might a large corporation finance expansion?
4. Suppose you and a partner own a clothing store. You decide to buy the store next door in order to expand. What type of financing do you think you and your partner would want? Why?

SHORT-TERM FINANCING

A business may seek short-term financing for many reasons. Because most billing is done monthly, a company may do an excellent business during the month but not be paid until the beginning of the following month. In the meantime, the company needs money to pay salaries and its own bills. During a growing season, a farmer may have to borrow to buy seed, repair equipment, and pay workers. In both cases, it would be unwise for the business to take out a long-term loan for a short-term need.

INTERMEDIATE-TERM FINANCING

When a company wants to expand its business by buying more land, buildings, or equipment, short-term financing generally is not adequate. For example, if you decided to expand your electronic repair business by opening a second repair shop, you would not apply for a 90-day loan. In 90 days, you would not be able to take on enough repair jobs to make the additional revenue to repay the loan. As a result, you would look for intermediate-term financing.

LONG-TERM FINANCING

For financing debts of more than 10 or 15 years in length, corporations either sell bonds or issue stock. Long-term financing is used for major expansion, such as building a new plant or buying new machines to replace outdated ones. Long-term financing is used to match the length of the borrowing with the useful life of the building or the equipment being purchased. It is usually only large corporations that finance long-term debt through selling bonds. Unlike smaller companies, large corporations with their huge assets appear to be better risks to investors who are interested in buying bonds.

CHOOSING THE RIGHT FINANCING

In raising capital, financial managers try to obtain it at a minimum cost to the company. As a result, they try to choose the best mix of financing. The length of a loan that a company takes out or a corporation's decision regarding whether to sell bonds or issue stock depends on several factors: interest costs, market climate, control of the company, and the financial condition of the company itself.

When interest rates in general are high, a business may be reluctant to take out a loan. For example, a company wanting to buy new equipment may delay its expansion until it can borrow at better interest rates. Or a financial manager may decide to take out a series of short-term loans at high rates, hoping that interest rates will drop. When that happens, the company will take out a long-term loan. Interest rates also affect the decision to issue bonds. When rates are high, corporations must offer high rates of interest on their bonds to attract investors. When interest rates in general drop, corporations can offer lower rates of return on their bonds.

Critic of the Business System: Thorstein Veblen (1857–1929)

Thorstein Veblen has been called a radical son of the Midwest. During a time when the country's economy was expanding rapidly, Veblen was a harsh and usually unwelcome critic of American capitalism. Although Veblen was in many ways a brilliant thinker, his unpopular ideas and eccentric, or unusual, behavior kept him from being accepted by his fellow economists.

Veblen's major published work is *The Theory of the Leisure Class* (1899). In this book as well as in later works, he attacked the economists of his day for not understanding the dynamic, or changing, nature of society. Early in his thinking, Veblen was influenced by Charles Darwin's theory of evolution, or gradual change within nature. Veblen felt that a society, like a plant or animal species, undergoes constant change and conflict. As a result, a society should not be studied as if it remained static, or unchanging.

Part of the conflict that Veblen saw in society was a struggle between those trying to increase production for the good of all and those wishing merely to make money. He felt that human beings naturally take pride in their work and try to make more and better products—a tendency he called the "instinct of workmanship." Opposed to this, however, was what Veblen saw as wastefulness in the way business was organized. Veblen felt that in the pursuit of profits many capitalists purposely produced goods in an inefficient manner. They limited production and fixed prices at high levels so that they could make more profit. This, however, was at the expense of the general good of all society.

The most visible example of this wastefulness for Veblen was the spending habits of the rich, or leisure class. He coined, or made up, the term **conspicuous** (kuhn-SPIK-yoo-uhs) **consumption** to describe buying things for the purpose of impressing others rather than buying goods to satisfy personal needs. Veblen predicted that a society based on such waste, inefficiency, and misguided values would eventually break down.

Veblen's criticisms of the American business system—often ignored in his own time—eventually proved to be true in part. He died three months before the stock market crash in 1929 that marked the beginning of the Great Depression. In the prosperous years just before the crash, few had paid attention to Veblen's criticisms. They did not believe that the conflicts he had identified could lead to the economic breakdown he predicted. Today Veblen is also respected for his theory of the changing nature of society. Veblen's ideas have provided the basis for a number of theories in history and politics that have been developed by later social scientists.

1. Explain what Veblen meant by "conspicuous consumption."
2. Why did Veblen emphasize the struggle in our economy between those working to increase productivity and those working merely for profits?

Corporate financial managers are responsible for borrowing or the debt financing of their business. What types of financing can they use?

A second factor a corporate financial manager would consider is the market climate. That is, what do investors consider the nation's economic health to be? If there does not appear to be much economic growth, investors may prefer the fixed rate of return of bonds or preferred stock to the unknown return on common stock.

The third factor that corporate managers consider in deciding whether to sell bonds or to issue stock is control of the company. Bonds do not have voting rights attached to them. As a result, bondholders have no control over how the business is run. Most preferred stocks do not give voting rights to shareholders either. However, the owners of common stocks do have the right to vote in company elections.

Corporations as well as other types of businesses have to consider their financial conditions before taking on debt. If a company's or corporation's sales and profits are stable or are expected to increase, taking on more debt would probably be safe. However, just as an individual needs to examine current debt load, so does a business. If the debt load is too large, the business would be unwise to increase its debts.

REVIEWING ECONOMIC PRINCIPLES

1. Define the following economic terms: **a.** finance, **b.** trade credit, **c.** promissory note, **d.** accounts receivable, **e.** line of credit, **f.** equity financing, **g.** debt financing, **h.** financial planning.
2. How is borrowing by a business similar to borrowing by an individual?
3. **a.** Why would a company use short-term financing? **b.** Name four types of short-term financing.
4. **a.** Why would a company choose intermediate-term financing? **b.** List two types of intermediate-term financing.
5. **a.** When would a company choose long-term financing? **b.** Why is the sale of stock called equity financing? **c.** Why do large corporations rather than small companies finance debt through bonds?
6. **Critical Thinking: Summarizing the Main Idea.** Write a paragraph describing the four factors that financial managers consider in deciding on financing.

3 | OPERATIONS IN THE PRODUCTION PROCESS

Ask yourself as you read:

- What are the major steps in the production process?
- How do the costs of production affect price?

Once businesses have the necessary financing, they can begin **production.** This is the process of changing resources into goods that satisfy the needs and wants of individuals and other businesses. As you can infer from this definition, businesses may produce one of two kinds of goods. Goods that are produced for individuals are called **consumer goods.** They are sold directly to the public to be used as they are. Goods produced for businesses to use in making other goods are called **producer goods.** The machines used in an auto assembly line are examples of producer goods. Besides the actual manufacturing of a good, the production process for both types of goods involves several operations. They are product design, planning, purchasing, quality control, and inventory control. Each becomes a cost of production. You will read more about product design in Chapter 12.

PLANNING

Planning includes choosing a location for the business and scheduling production. Where a business is located is directly related to how successful the business will be. This is as true for a company that is opening its first factory or store as it is for an older business that is expanding into a new area. Among the factors to consider are nearness to markets, raw materials, labor supply, and transportation facilities. In the past, most cities have grown up near waterways. Today, with railroads, airlines, and pipelines, it is not so important to be located near waterways.

Here, officials of a corporation use gold-plated shovels in a ground-breaking ceremony. Why is choosing the right location for a business directly related to how successful it will be?

This chemist is working in a quality control lab. Quality control is an important part of the production process. What trade-off is involved in quality control?

Scheduling production operations involves setting beginning and ending times for each step in the production process. It includes planning and checking the use of labor, machinery, and materials so that production moves smoothly. Scheduling ensures that work will be finished on time whether it is manufacturing cars or books or dry cleaning a blouse or shirt.

PURCHASING

In order to do business, a company needs the raw materials to produce its goods or offer its services. It must also have machinery, office supplies, and any other supplies it uses. Obtaining raw materials, machines, and supplies is the purchasing function of the production process and involves getting the best deal for the company. The people who buy goods for a business have to decide what to buy, from whom, and at what price.

Price is just one factor, however. A business also has to consider the quality of the goods it needs as well as possible services offered by suppliers, such as repairs on office equipment. The delivery system of each supplier is also important. How much time lag is there between ordering and receiving goods? How are goods shipped? Who pays the shipping costs? Are minimum orders required or discounts given? Often a business will buy from several suppliers to encourage competition among them and, therefore, get the best deal.

QUALITY CONTROL

Quality control is checking the quality of the goods produced. It involves overseeing the grade or freshness of goods, their strength or workability, the workmanship or design, harmlessness, adherence to federal or industry standards, and many other factors. Quality control systems can be as simple as testing the 1,000th item produced or testing each product as it is finished. Every production manager faces a trade-off in the area of quality control. The more time spent in quality control, the higher are the production costs. This, of course, raises the price to consumers. Less quality control, however, may result in items of poor quality. This, in turn, can cause unhappy customers and declining sales. The decision usually depends on the product. For inexpensive goods such as ball-point pens, testing samples is usually considered adequate. However, for expensive items such as cars, every one that is produced is tested.

INVENTORY CONTROL

Almost all manufacturers and many service businesses such as dry cleaners need inventories, or stockpiles, of the materials they use in making their products or offering their services. Manufacturers and businesses such as supermarkets also keep inventories of finished goods on hand for sale. But inventories are costly. The more inventory a business has, the less capital it has for other activities. For example, it costs money to warehouse and insure goods against fire and theft. Some goods such as film and drugs spoil if kept beyond a certain period of time. Other goods such as cars and stylish clothes become obsolete, or out of date, in time.

obsolete (ahb-suh-LEET): out-of-date

In deciding how much inventory to keep on hand, however, those in charge of inventory control have other costs to consider. If the price of a raw material is expected to rise, a business may stockpile it to keep future costs down. Often a supplier will discount large orders. Some businesses may decide that the discounts outweigh the other costs of maintaining a large inventory.

REVIEWING ECONOMIC PRINCIPLES

1. What is the difference between consumer goods and producer goods?
2. **a.** What four factors should a business consider in choosing a location for a factory or store? **b.** What is the purpose of scheduling the steps in the production process?
3. **a.** What four factors should purchasing departments consider in buying raw materials and other supplies? **b.** Why would a company buy from several suppliers?
4. What is the trade-off involved in quality control?
5. What are four costs involved in maintaining an inventory of products or materials?
6. **Critical Thinking: Expressing Opinions.** Choose an operation in the production process that most interests you. Write a paragraph explaining why your choice is of vital importance to the production of goods.

4 | TECHNOLOGY AND METHODS OF PRODUCTION

Ask yourself as you read:
- How does technology affect production?
- What is the information revolution?

As you read in Chapter 1, technology is the use of science to develop new products and new methods for producing and distributing goods and services. Technology influences businesses in many ways.

The use of technology on a large scale began in the textile industry in England in the late 1700s. From there the machine-powered textile industry spread to the United States in the early 1800s. The industrial revolution, as the beginning of the factory system is called, came about through **mechanization,** which combines the labor of people and large power-driven machines. These machines could be operated by unskilled workers, and they began to replace skilled workers. Before that time, all the operations of cloth making—from spinning thread to weaving—were done in homes by skilled craftworkers. With the introduction of spinning and weaving machines, entrepreneurs put the machines into factories and hired unskilled workers to run them. As a result of replacing handwork with machines, the rate of output per labor hour increased greatly.

An outgrowth of mechanization is the **assembly line.** This is a production system in which the good being produced moves on a conveyor belt past workers who perform individual tasks in assembling it. The modern assembly-line process was developed by the Ford Motor Company at the beginning of the 20th century. Because of the assembly line, Ford was able to increase its annual production from less than 20,000 cars in 1910 to 700,000 in 1917. Because the assembly line results in the more efficient use of machines and labor, the costs of production drop. As a result, Ford was able to lower its price to consumers from $950.00 a car to $350.00. This would be about from $6,800 a car to about $2,450 in today's dollars.

THE ASSEMBLY LINE

Assembly-line production is only possible with interchangeable parts made in standard sizes and with **division of labor,** the breaking down of a job into small tasks. Each task is performed by a different worker. Division of labor is a general economic principle that is used in many businesses besides assembly-line operations. However, the assembly line process requires that each worker do a limited number of tasks or even just one task, no matter how monotonous, or dull. In an auto assembly plant, for example, one task might be tightening bolts.

monotonous (muh-NAHT-n-uhs): dull, routine

AUTOMATION

Mechanization combines the labor of people and machines. In **automation,** machines do the work and people oversee them. Except for

Robotics are a vital part in the automobile production process. What other roles do computers have in industry in the United States?

some supervisory people, machines in the form of computers control the machines that produce goods. For example, computers now run some steel mills and oil refineries and are widely used in offices and banks.

Some social scientists believe that computers are bringing about a new revolution. The first industrial revolution changed production processes. This new one is resulting in an information revolution—data that can be used to inform people of events, goods and services, and of other types of knowledge. It includes methods and processes, scientific formulas, and even the knowhow to send missiles into space.

In more and more industries, robotics are a key part of the production process. **Robotics** refers to sophisticated computer-controlled machinery that operates the assembly line. Soon computers will be keeping track of the entire production process from the arrival at the factory of raw materials and parts to the shipping of the finished product. Engineers are beginning to use computers to develop new products and new production techniques on video screens. In offices, computers are enabling office workers to store and retrieve vast amounts of information and send it instantly between cities. Using computers, managers are able to test the advantages of alternative plans and make better-informed decisions. You will read more about the information revolution in Chapter 19. As workers and consumers, everyone benefits from improved technology and the division of labor. This improvement allows firms to become more efficient. As a result, these firms are able not only to reduce the price of products, but also to pay higher wages.

REVIEWING ECONOMIC PRINCIPLES

1. Define the following production terms: **a.** mechanization, **b.** assembly line, **c.** division of labor, **d.** automation **e.** robotics
2. What effect did replacing skilled labor with machines have on output?
3. Write a paragraph explaining why an assembly line would not be possible without division of labor.
4. **Critical Thinking: Analyzing Concepts.** How is automation the next step after mechanization in the technological development of the production process?

SUMMARY OF
IMPORTANT PRINCIPLES

1
- According to the law of diminishing returns, after some point adding units of a factor of production, such as labor, to fixed factors of production, such as equipment, results in a smaller and smaller increase in output per each unit added. A good manager has to know when to stop hiring additional workers or when to stop buying new equipment for the business.

2
- Short-term financing involves borrowing money for any period of time less than a year. It may be one of several types: trade credit, secured or unsecured loans, and a line of credit. Borrowing money for one to ten years is considered intermediate-term financing and may be in the form of either loans or leasing. Financing for any longer period is called long-term financing and may be done through selling bonds or issuing stock. Selling stock is called equity financing because part of the equity, or ownership, of the corporation is being sold. Two types of stock are sold, preferred stock and common stock. Preferred stock guarantees stockholders interest but rarely gives voting rights in the company's affairs. Common stock usually gives the shareholder some interest and a vote in some company matters.
- In deciding on the best mix of debt and equity financing, managers consider interest costs, market climate, control of the company, and the financial condition of the company itself.
- Financial planning for the use of capital involves predicting revenues and costs and then comparing the estimated profit with the cost of the investment, including the cost of credit. Financial managers must consider how such factors as price, advertising and promotion costs, and competitors will affect the market share that a product can capture.

3
- The production process involves product design, planning, purchasing, quality control, and inventory control.

4
- In the production process, technology increases the productivity of people and machines. Mechanization, in which machines replaced skilled labor, was introduced in the late 1700s. With it began the industrial revolution. The assembly line was an outgrowth of mechanization and resulted in more efficient use of machines and labor. Automation, in which machines do the work and people oversee the machines, was the next step. Today, robots, which are computer-controlled machines, can operate the assembly line. Computers are also being used to develop new products and to store data in offices. Some think that a new information revolution is at hand with the use of computers.

Putting Economics to Work

SURPLUS OF INVENTORY: LAYOFFS

Roy Whitecloud arrived at work one Friday as he had just about every work morning for the last 20 years. But this was not to be an ordinary workday. On Friday, Roy joined the ranks of millions of Americans who found themselves unemployed in the 1980s. He was laid off from his supervisor's job at the Rupert Steel Mill.

Steel production in the United States had been falling for some time. As the American economy fought a slowdown in economic activity, the laws of supply and demand were at work. The recession, as it was called, had begun in the early 1980s and had especially hurt the major buyers of steel. Demand for steel by the auto and construction industries had declined steadily. Other users of steel had begun buying cheaper steel from other countries. To reduce supply to match demand, some steel companies closed their mills for several weeks at a time to give their workers unpaid holidays. Other mills laid off workers. Some of these workers would never be called back to their old jobs unless the demand for steel rose again.

Roy was one of the luckier workers. He was laid off for only a few weeks. The mill retrained him to operate a new computerized production system.

1. Many people worry that automation will cause unemployment. According to this case study, what other factors may cause unemployment?
2. How can businesses cut down on a surplus of inventory?

Readings in Economics

KEEPING SMALL AND SIMPLE MAY BRING EXCELLENT RETURNS

Skill: Applying Information

 One reason why large companies find they have diminishing output per worker, as predicted by the law of diminishing returns, is that as organizations get bigger, they become more complex. In addition, after a certain point, adding units to the factors of production can reduce the quality per unit. In the following excerpt, management consultants Thomas J. Peters and Robert H. Waterman, Jr., examine the best-managed companies in America. They also discuss the importance of keeping big organizations simple and keeping each operation small to maintain high quality.

Along with bigness comes complexity, unfortunately. And most big companies respond to complexity in kind, by designing complex systems and structures. They then hire more staff to keep track of all this complexity, and that's where the mistake begins. The solution just doesn't go well with the nature of people in an organization, in which things need to be kept reasonably simple if the unit is truly to pull together. The paradox is clear. On the one hand, size generates legitimate complexity, and a complex systems or structural response is perfectly reasonable. On the other hand, making an organization work has everything to do with keeping things understandable for the tens or hundreds of thousands who must make things happen. And that means keeping things simple. . . .

![The making of fine violins and other musical instruments is a craft that requires highly skilled hand labor.]

The making of fine violins and other musical instruments is a craft that requires highly skilled hand labor. Many economists now believe that small-scale operation has certain advantages over bigness.

[In excellent companies] the efficiency/effectiveness contradiction dissolves into thin air. Things of quality are produced by craftsmen, generally requiring small-scale enterprise, we are told. Activities that achieve cost efficiencies, on the other hand, are reputably best done in large facilities, to achieve economies of scale. Except that that is not the way it works in the excellent companies. In the excellent companies, small *in almost every case* is beautiful. The small facility turns out to be the most efficient; its turned-on, motivated, highly productive worker, in communication (and competition) with his peers, outproduces the worker in the big facilities time and again. It holds for plants, for project teams, for divisions—for the entire company. So we find that in this most vital area, there really is no conflict. Small, quality, excitement, autonomy—and efficiency—are all words that belong on the same side of the coin. Cost and efficiency, over the long run, follow from the emphasis on quality, service, innovativeness, result sharing, participation, excitement, and an external problem-solving focus that is tailored to the customer. The revenue line does come first. But once the ball gets rolling, cost control and innovation effectiveness become fully achievable, parallel goals.

1. According to Peters and Waterman, how do excellent companies benefit from understanding the theory of the "law of diminishing returns"?

2. What action might Peters and Waterman suggest that a large corporation take in a "search for excellence"?

Two specified excerpts from pp. 306, 321 of IN SEARCH OF EXCELLENCE by Thomas J. Peters and Robert H. Waterman Jr. Copyright © 1982 by Thomas J. Peters and Robert H. Waterman, Jr. Reprinted by permission of Harper & Row, Publishers, Inc.

FINDING FUNDS FOR BUSINESS
Skill: Organizing Information

Different types of financing are needed by businesses for different purposes. John M. Chapman, research associate of the National Association of Manufacturers, describes some of the methods of financing in this reading.

Business enterprises, if properly financed, need or require various types of funds which may be classified as follows: (1) short-term [loans], (2) term loans or working capital or intermediate capital, and (3) permanent funds including equity funds or long-term bonds.

(1) Short-term loans are those which are obtained by business and usually run from three to six months but in some cases may extend for much longer periods. Trade credit granted by suppliers usually runs for 30 to 90 days. The funds obtained from short-term loans are generally used to meet payrolls or discounting of bills, re-stocking or maintaining of inventories or financing other current operations.

(2) Term loans are needed to improve the plant, to expand inventories, to add machinery and equipment and in some cases to expand the business by extending it into new territories or by the taking on of a new line. Such loans usually run from one to three years, but in some cases term loans are extended for five years or longer. In general the terms of repayment for each loan agreement are fixed to meet the individual needs of the borrower with special reference to his prospective earning power and ability to pay the loan at maturity.

(3) Permanent funds are essentially of two kinds: (a) equity funds (venture or risk capital) and (b) long-term mortgage or bonds. Equity funds . . . represent the original contribution or investments by enterprisers and other stockholders. Additions may be made through the same sources, but most future additions from the owners will come through the plowing back of earnings. Long-term loans are sometimes obtained by small businesses. This type of funds is frequently referred to as "loan capital" to distinguish it from the permanent capital supplied by the shareholders. The distinction between this type of financing and term loans is not always easily fixed. Neither is there a clear line of distinction between the uses of equity funds and long-term credit funds. . . .

Taking small business as a whole, the commercial banks are the most important source of short-term commercial and term loans. Banks offer a variety of loans which have been designed to meet the needs of . . . businessmen. . . . For the country as a whole it is likely that banks will . . . be the primary source of short-term and term loans for small business in the years ahead. . . .

A fairly substantial group of businessmen holds that business practices have been changing so rapidly and fundamentally in recent years that new methods of financing are required to meet new developments. Another argument that has been advanced is that commercial banks have not provided sufficient funds to meet the essential needs of small business, consequently new institutions should be established to finance properly business under these new conditions.

1. Organize the information on different types of financing in a chart. Use the headings "Type of Loan," "Term of Loan," and "Purpose of Loan."
2. Why have new types of financing been needed in recent years?

John M. Chapman, "The Need and Source of Funds." *Selected Readings in Modern Economics*. Ed. by Asher Isaacs, C. W. McKee and R. E. Slesinger. New York: Dryden Press, 1952.

PLANNING STEP BY STEP

Skill: Understanding Decision Making

Author Peter F. Drucker has written many books on business management. In this reading Drucker discusses some of the steps involved in planning for businesses.

Planning starts with the objectives of the business. In each area of objectives, the question needs to be asked, *What do we have to do now* to attain our objectives *tomorrow?*" The first thing to do to attain tomorrow is always to be sloughing off yesterday. Most plans concern themselves only with the new and additional things that have to be done—new products, new processes, new markets, and so on. But the key to doing something different tomorrow is getting rid of the no-longer-productive, the obsolescent, the obsolete.

The first step in planning is to ask of any activity, any product, any process or market, "If we were not committed to this today, would we go into it?" If the answer is no, one says, "How can we get out—fast?" . . .

The next step in the planning process is to ask, "What *new* and different things do we have to do, and when?"

In every plan there will be areas where all that is needed—or appears to be needed—is to do more of what we already do. It is prudent, however, to assume that what we already do is never adequate to the needs of the future. But, "What do we need?" is only half the question. Equally important is "When do we need it?" for it fixes the time for beginning work on the new tasks.

There is indeed a "short" range and a "long" range to every decision. The time between the commitment to a course of action, . . . [for example,] to building a steel mill, and the earliest possible moment for results, . . . [that is,] getting

Planning is a key to the success of any business. These company executives use computer printouts to help make decisions about their company's future.

finished steel, is the short range of a decision. And the twenty-plus years it takes before, at the earliest, we get back with compound interest the money invested in the steel mill is the long range. The long range is the time during which the initial decision must remain reasonably valid—as to markets, process, technology, plant location, etc.—to have been the right decision originally.

1. In planning for a business, what is the importance of yesterday in planning for tomorrow?
2. Contrast short- and long-range planning. Give examples of each.

Two specified excerpts from pp. 126, 127 of *MANAGEMENT: Tasks, Responsibilities, Practices* by Peter F. Drucker. Copyright © 1973, 1974 by Peter F. Drucker. Reprinted by permission of Harper & Row, Publishers, Inc.

THE HARSHNESS OF FACTORY LIFE
Skill: Making Inferences

English novelist Charles Dickens, who had his first factory job at the age of 11 and spent his childhood in poverty, wrote about the harshness of factory life during the Industrial Revolution. In his 1854 novel *Hard Times*, Dickens describes the fictional industrial city of Coketown. In describing the city he dramatizes for his readers the monotony of life in a mechanized world.

Let us strike the keynote, Coketown, before pursuing our tune.

It was a town of red brick, or of brick that would have been red if the smoke and ashes had allowed it; but as matters stood it was a town of unnatural red and black like the painted face of a savage. It was a town of machinery and tall chimneys, out of which interminable serpents of smoke trailed themselves forever and ever, and never got uncoiled. It had a black canal in it, and a river that ran purple with ill-smelling dye, and vast piles of buildings full of windows where there was a rattling and a trembling all day long, and where the piston of the steam-engine worked monotonously up and down like the head of an elephant in a state of melancholy madness. It contained several large streets all very like one another, and many small streets still more like one another, inhabited by people equally like one another, who all went in and out at the same hours, with the same sound upon the same pavements, to do the same work, and to whom every day was the same as yesterday and tomorrow, and every year the counterpart of the last and the next. . . .

These attributes of Coketown were in the main inseparable from the work by which it was sustained; against them were to be set off comforts of life which found their way all over the world, and elegancies of life which made, we will not ask how much of the fine lady, who could scarcely bear to hear the place mentioned. The rest of its features were voluntary, and they were these.

You saw nothing in Coketown but what was severely workful. . . . All the public inscriptions in the town were painted alike, in severe characters of black and white. The jail might have been the infirmary, the infirmary might have been the jail, the townhall might have been either, or both, or anything else, for anything that appeared to the contrary in the graces of their construction. Fact, fact, fact, everywhere in the material aspect of the town; fact, fact, fact, everywhere in the immaterial. The McChoakumchild school was all fact, and the school of design was all fact, and the relations between master and man were all fact, everything was fact between the lying-in hospital and the cemetery, and what you couldn't state in figures, or show to be purchaseable in the cheapest market and saleable in the dearest, was not, and never should be, world without end, Amen.

1. Charles Dickens is known for his descriptive skills as a writer and for his crusades against abuses in society. List some phrases from this article that vividly describe the effects of industrialization on the lives of workers in this imaginary town in England in the 19th century.
2. What is the significance of the sentence "You saw nothing in Coketown but what was severely workful"?

From *Hard Times* by Charles Dickens, 1854.

11 | CHAPTER REVIEW

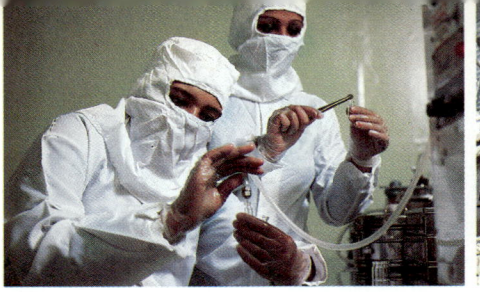

PRACTICING YOUR STUDY SKILLS: SUMMARIZING

The ability to summarize data is useful in studying new material, reviewing information for a test, and writing research papers and reports. To summarize material means to restate it in more general terms and with fewer details than the original material had. A summary should be much shorter than the original because it includes only the main ideas and most important details of a passage, chapter, or article. Choosing the most important details to include is an important part of summarizing. You can also summarize information that you read on tables, graphs, and charts. Following are some tips:

1. Read carefully the material to be summarized. If you are summarizing visual data, read the labels and figures, and look closely at the way the data are arranged. Make this information the basis for your written description.
2. Take notes in your own words. Do not copy sentences from the original material.
3. Choose the main ideas and their most important supporting details.
4. Do not add your own ideas.
5. After writing your notes in paragraph form, check that your summary is brief, complete, and accurate.

Activity: Read the section under the heading "Technology and the Methods of Production," pp. 286–87, and summarize it in a paragraph.

VOCABULARY REVIEW

For each of the following terms, write a sentence using the term:

promissory note   line of credit

market share   accounts receivable

law of diminishing returns

PRACTICING YOUR ECONOMIC SKILLS

1. **Using a Table.** Use the income statement that follows to answer these questions:
a. What is the company's net income expressed as a percentage of its total revenues?
b. What is the net income per share if there are 200,000 shares of stock? c. If the company's total expenses remained the same and its total revenues increased 5 percent, what would the company's income before taxes be?

Income Statement	
Revenues	
Sales	$13,000,000
Income from securities	200,000
Total revenues	$13,200,000
Expenses	
Cost of goods	$ 9,690,000
Selling and administrative costs	1,610,000
Other expenses	1,260,000
Total expenses	$12,560,000
Income before taxes	$ 640,000
Taxes	276,000
Net income	$ 364,000

2. **Analyzing a Line Graph.** The graph on page 295 shows the amount of steel produced between 1880 to 1910 using two different types of technology: the Bessemer process and the open hearth process. Use the graph to answer the following: a. About what percentage of total steel output in 1885 was produced using the Bessemer process? b. About what percentage of total steel output in 1910 was produced using the Bessemer process? c. What can you infer abut the efficiency of the open hearth process compared to the Bessemer process?

Raw Steel Production in the U.S., 1880-1910

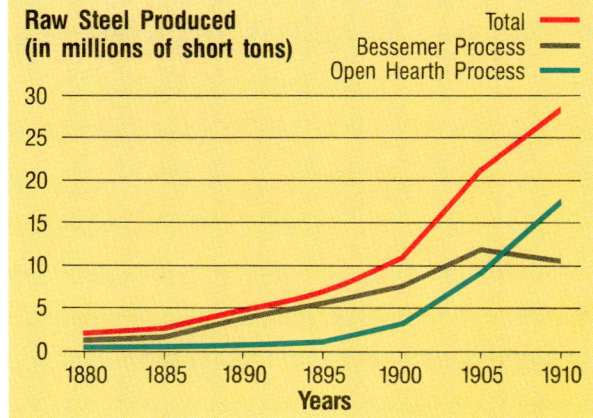

Raw Steel Produced (in millions of short tons)	Total — Bessemer Process — Open Hearth Process —

Source: *Historical Statistics of the United States*, Bureau of the Census

DISCUSSING ECONOMIC QUESTIONS

1. Based on what this chapter says about managing a business, what kinds of things would a sole proprietor need to keep in mind? Refer to Table 9-1. If you did not like to do all the things involved in running a business, would that be enough to keep you from owning your own business? Consider also the rewards of running your own business.
2. For quality control, do you think it necessary to inspect every item that is produced? Why would the type and cost of a product be used as criteria in deciding whether to test every item or only a sampling? Consider the attitude of a customer who is having problems with a faulty product. Would the price paid for the item affect his or her attitude?
3. Do you agree with the idea that the late 20th century is the era of the computer? Consider what you know about computers and what you may have read or heard about them.
4. The author says that the monotony of assembly-line work creates problems. What kinds of problems do you think would occur?

APPLYING CRITICAL THINKING SKILLS

1. **Writing a Report.** The Small Business Administration (SBA) helps small businesses with short-term financing. Research and write a one-paragraph report describing the functions of the SBA.
2. **Gathering Information.** Visit your guidance counselor, or write to several colleges that give degrees in business, to find out what courses are needed for an undergraduate degree in business administration. Make a list to share with your classmates.
3. **Writing a Research Report.** Research and write a short report on one of the following: the use of robots, technological unemployment, or the use of computers.
4. **Writing a Research Report.** One discovery that made assembly-line work possible was the use of interchangeable parts by Eli Whitney. Research and write a short report explaining the importance of interchangeable parts to the manufacturing process.
5. **Gathering and Graphing Information.** Check in the *Reader's Guide to Periodical Literature* entries under "Computer Industry" for the past year and then for 5, 10, and 15 years ago. Make a line graph to show the increase in the number of articles.

READINGS

Heilbroner, Robert L. *The Worldly Philosophers*, rev. ed. New York: Simon & Schuster, 1980. Chapter 8, "The Savage World of Thorstein Veblen," pp. 181–213.

Masuda, Yoneji, *The Information Society as Post-Industrial Society*. Washington, D.C.: World Future Society, 1981.

Schumacher, E.F. *Small is Beautiful: Economics as if People Mattered*. New York: Harper & Row, 1976. Critique of assembly-line production.

Terkel, Studs. *Working*. New York: Avon, 1982.

CHAPTER 12

Marketing goods to consumers involves moving these products through channels of distribution as well as researching what consumers want in a product and how price and advertising can affect consumer buying decisions.

MARKETING AND DISTRIBUTION

Have you ever seen a new product in a store or an ad and wondered why the manufacturer decided to make that product? Most likely, the company spent a great deal of money over a number of years on market research to produce that particular product with those particular features. Market research is just one part of marketing, which includes all the activities needed to get goods from producers to consumers. This chapter describes how the idea and purpose of marketing has changed as American productivity has increased. You will read about market research and about the "four *P*s" of marketing—product, price, place, and promotion. The ways that goods are distributed are also explained. Learning Economic Skills describes how a market survey is done.

CHAPTER OBJECTIVES After you study the sections of this chapter, you will be able to:

1 • describe the four stages of development that marketing has undergone in the United States.
  • summarize the way market research is carried out.
  • describe the purpose of a market survey and how it is carried out.

2 • describe the "four *P*s" of the marketing mix.
  ★ describe the purpose of a market survey and how it is carried out.

3 • summarize the various channels of distribution that businesses use.

ECONOMICS VOCABULARY

marketing
market research
test marketing
price leadership
penetration pricing
promotion
channels of distribution
wholesaler
retailer

promote (pruh-MOHT): to further the sale of something

sovereignty (SAHV-ruhn-tee): power, control

In addition to financing and producing a product, businesses must promote and eventually sell the products and services they produce. **Marketing** involves all of the activities needed to move goods and services from the producer to the consumer. These activities include market research, advertising and promotion, and the actual distribution of goods and services from the producer to the consumer. Some economists estimate that about 50 percent of the price people pay for an item is for the cost of marketing. The idea and importance of marketing in the United States has changed considerably since the beginning of this century. Marketing has developed through four stages: production, sales, marketing (production and sales), and consumer sovereignty.

1 | THE CHANGING ROLE OF MARKETING

Ask yourself as you read:
- What is marketing?
- Why has market research become an increasingly important part of marketing?

In the early 1900s, marketing dealt with getting goods to the consumers who wanted them. Demand was great, but supply was often unable to satisfy demand. During this period, companies emphasized the production of goods. By the 1920s and 1930s, however, many consumers had most of the necessities and some of the luxuries of American life. Technology was increasing productivity. Companies found that to increase sales they had to stimulate demand by actively selling their products. They began to use advertising to promote, or further the sale of, their goods and to attract customers.

CREATING A DEMAND FOR GOODS

The 1950s saw the rise of marketing as a combining of the production and sales functions. Through technology, businesses were now able to produce more than consumers' normal demand would use. There was also a greater variety of goods available to satisfy the same needs. As a result, businesses began actively to create demand for the goods and services that they sold. Advertising became even more important as the number of competitors increased.

CONSUMER SOVEREIGNTY

By the late 1950s and early 1960s, marketing had changed again. Producers began researching consumer tastes and preferences and then designing goods to meet those tastes and preferences. Instead of just creating demand, businesses found they could take a larger share of the consumer dollar by designing products that matched what consumers wanted. As a result, the consumer became the most important element in product development. Consumer sovereignty had arrived.

MARKET RESEARCH

Finding out what consumers want can be a difficult job. However, it is crucial because so many markets are nationwide. Therefore, before a product is produced or a service is offered, businesses research their market. Market in this sense means the people who are potential buyers of the good or service. From cosmetics companies to automakers to textbook publishers and frozen food processors, all major companies and many smaller ones do market research. Through **market research** a company gathers, records, and analyzes data about the types of goods and services that people want. A market research department attempts to discover the quality, features, and style that consumers find desirable in a particular kind of product. Market researchers also ask questions about the type of packaging that will attract consumers and the price that will get them to buy. How well competitors' products are selling is another part of the research.

During the market survey, researchers gather information about who might be possible users of the product. Such characteristics as age, sex, income, education, and location—urban, suburban, rural—are important to a producer in deciding the market at which to aim a product. For example, the concern of Americans in the late 1970s and 1980s with physical fitness and good health led many cereal companies to test and then market bran and granola cereals. Though there had been some "adult" cereals before this, most cereals had been presweetened and aimed at children.

survey (SER-vay): study of attitudes

Market research typically involves a series of carefully worded questions. The questions may be administered in the form of a written questionnaire, which is mailed to consumers. Or market researchers may conduct personal interviews. These may be as brief as answering five or six questions on the telephone or while leaving a store. Or an interview may take several hours. Manufacturers of such small appliances as hair dryers and microwave ovens often put a questionnaire on the back of the warranty card that purchasers are to return.

WHEN SHOULD MARKET RESEARCH BE DONE?

Market research may be done at several stages of product development. It can be done at the very beginning when the first ideas about a new product are being developed. It can be done again to test sample

Many companies use market research to obtain information about their product from consumers. This market research staff is applying this information in taste testing a new frozen dinner. Why do firms need such market research?

products and alternative packaging designs. Early market research has several purposes. It helps producers determine whether there is a market for their good or service and what that market is. It can also indicate any changes in quality, features, or design that should be made before a product is offered for sale.

To investigate initial consumer response, market research is often done immediately after a product is released for sale. Some companies even test their advertising to make sure it is attracting the market for which the product was designed. Information can also be gathered about a product that has been on the market for a while. Market researchers then attempt to discover what should be done to maintain the current level of sales or increase it.

TESTING NEW PRODUCTS

As a final step before offering a product for national distribution, market researchers will often test market a product such as a detergent or a toothpaste. **Test marketing** means offering a product for sale in a small area, perhaps several cities, for anywhere from two months to two years to see how well it sells before offering it nationally. For example, before attempting to market its new granola cereal, a company might sell it in several selected areas. Those are areas where the product is most likely to attract the market that the company is seeking. Researchers keep track of the units sold and test different prices and ad campaigns within the test markets. If the cereal is successful, the company will offer it nationally. If sales are disappointing, the company has two choices. It can make changes based on the data collected in the test market. Or, rather than spend more money redesigning the product, the company can abandon the idea.

The majority of new products introduced every year in the United States are not profitable and do not survive in the marketplace. But it is the continued lure of developing a high-profit item that motivates companies to continue developing new products.

REVIEWING ECONOMIC PRINCIPLES

1. Define the following marketing terms: **a.** marketing, **b.** market research, **c.** test marketing.
2. What stages of development has marketing in the United States undergone?
3. Why has the consumer become so important in marketing?
4. What kinds of information does a market research department attempt to discover about: **a.** possible products? **b.** possible consumers of that product?
5. **Critical Thinking: Summarizing the Main Idea.** Summarize in a paragraph the stages of product development at which market research may be done. Be sure to include the reasons for doing research at each stage.

Spokesperson of Classical Economics: John Stuart Mill (1806–1873)

John Stuart Mill was a brilliant man whose ideas are still studied and admired today. His writings on politics, philosophy, and economics clearly show his genius, and helped to shape our knowledge in all these fields. Mill's *Principles of Political Economy* remains today as the outstanding work in classical economic thought.

Mill was a child prodigy. At the age of three, he was learning Greek, and he had mastered both Greek and Latin by the time he was eight. By the time he was 12, he had studied the writings of the classic Greek philosophers. He mastered geometry, algebra and calculus, and wrote a history of Rome. At the age of 12, Mill immersed himself in studying logic, and just one year later he read nearly everything ever written in the field of economics, then called political economy.

In 1823, when he was 17, Mill followed in his father's footsteps by serving in the British East India Company, where he remained until his retirement in 1858. However, Mill suffered severe mental depression for many years starting in 1826. During this period in his life he came to value poetry and art and he developed a new appreciation of people. He also met Harriet Taylor, who was to have a profound impact on his theories of economics, the rights of women, and individual liberty. However, Harriet Taylor was married, and not until 20 years later when her husband died were they able to marry.

Through his early studies of the classic Greek philosophers, Mill developed a deep belief in the key importance of individual liberty and freedom. Mill's theories of economics argued for a free market or free enterprise system. He saw little purpose in government involvement in a nation's economy. In his *Principles of Political Economy*, he stressed the central role of liberty and freedom in the lives of people everywhere. Mill asserted that government itself by its action could become a threat to individual freedom. The government's role was to enable individuals to pursue their interests more effectively.

In his writings, Mill made a distinction between the laws of production and distribution. Mill argued that once goods were produced, they were available for people "individually or collectively, to do with them as they pleased." His theory therefore tended to focus on production and the inputs in the production process. He recognized that scarcity of resources forces us to make choices about how we use resources. This was a startling idea in the late 1800s when people were more concerned about the distribution of goods than with the resources used to produce them.

Mill wrote considerably about individual liberty. In his autobiography, he attributed much of his humanitarian philosophy to his wife, Harriet. In fact, his essay "Subjection of Women," written in 1869, is regarded as one of the most important early writings in support of women's rights.

1. How did Mill's theories support a free market economic system?
2. Explain how Mill's deep belief in individual liberty was reflected in his writings.

2 | THE MARKETING MIX

Ask yourself as you read:
- What does planning a marketing strategy involve?
- How are goods and services promoted?

strategy (STRAT-uh-jee): plan

After a company's marketing department has determined the best product, the company has to produce it. Chapter 11 described the production process. But in today's highly competitive world, simply producing a product and offering it for sale is not enough. Companies through their marketing departments plan a marketing strategy, which details how the company will sell the product effectively. The marketing strategy, or plan, combines the "four *P*s" of marketing: product, price, place, and promotion. Decisions about each topic are based on the data collected through the company's market research.

PRODUCT

Besides deciding on the actual product, market research helps a company determine what services to offer with the product, how to package it, and what kind of product identification to use.

As you read in Chapter 5, warranties have similarities, but some manufacturers offer special services free or for a small charge. For example, if you buy a camera, you may be able to purchase from the manufacturer a two-year extended warranty in addition to the one-year warranty given by the company. Automakers used to offer one-year or 12,000-mile warranties on new cars. In 1981 Chrysler began offering 5-year or 50,000-mile warranties to persuade people to buy its cars.

Packaging is also an important factor in selling a product. The "right" packaging will combine size, design, and color in such a way as to attract potential consumers. Often producers introduce otherwise saleable products only to discover that consumers do not like the packaging. Record albums, book covers, and food are especially dependent on packaging. Colorful pictures of steaming hot, fresh-looking vegetables on frozen food packages are supposed to convince people to buy that product. Such words as *New and Improved* or *Economy Size* are also used to attract customers. For economy-minded shoppers, manufacturers add cents-off coupons and rebate offers to their packages. Cents-off coupons are used to persuade consumers to make a repeat purchase and, therefore, develop the habit of buying the product.

rebate (REE-bayt): money returned, refund

Once a product is offered for sale, product identification becomes important. Product identification can involve the use of a logo or of certain colors on a package. It can also involve a certain type of packaging, a particular slogan, or anything that can be associated with and identify a product. Product identification is meant to attract consumers to look at, buy, and remember a particular product. The red and white labels of Campbell Soup cans are a good example of packaging to achieve prod-

uct identification. So is the egg-shaped container for L'eggs panty hose. The Jolly Green Giant, Tony the Tiger, and such slogans as "the Uncola" are other successful examples of product identification.

PRICE

As you may recall from Chapter 8, supply and demand play a large part in determining the price of a good or service. According to the law of supply, at higher prices, a larger quantity of a product will generally be supplied than at lower prices. The law of demand states that as the price of a good or service falls, a larger quantity will be bought. Conversely, as the price rises, a smaller quantity will be bought.

Because of the laws of supply and demand, the price at which a product sells may determine whether it is successful in attracting buyers and profitable to its maker. In setting a price, a company has to consider the costs of producing, advertising, selling, and distributing the product, and the amount of profit it hopes to make. It also needs to find out the price at which its competitors are selling similar products. Often companies sell similar goods at similar prices. This is especially true in oligopolies and is known as **price leadership.** For example, Ford and Chrysler usually set their prices close to those of GM. In monopolistic competition, a company may claim that its product is of higher quality than those of its competitors and sell it at a slightly higher price.

Selling a new product at a low price is another marketing strategy. This is called **penetration pricing.** The low price is meant to attract customers away from an established product. The manufacturer hopes to make up in the quantity of goods sold what it loses in potential profits. With this strategy, the difference between costs and profit is usually very small. Once the product is successful, the company may raise the price to create a larger profit.

PLACE TO SELL

Where the product should be sold is another decision of the marketing department. Should it be sold through the mail, by telephone, in department stores, in specialty shops, in supermarkets, in discount stores, or door-to-door? Usually, the answer is obvious because of past experience with similar products. A cereal company, for example,

Learning Economic Skills

TAKING A MARKET SURVEY

Most industries must be constantly aware of the needs of consumers. This is true of industries as different as manufacturers of large appliances and publishers of science fiction. This is why market research is important. Market research can provide businesses with information about the demand for a new product or changes that must be made in an existing product to keep it profitable.

Market researchers collect, analyze, and interpret data from consumers and about competitors to help businesses plan marketing strategies. These strategies are known as the marketing mix, or "four *P*s": product, price, place, promotion. The process of analyzing the right marketing mix is shown in the following flow chart. To read the chart, begin at the top and follow the direction of the arrows.

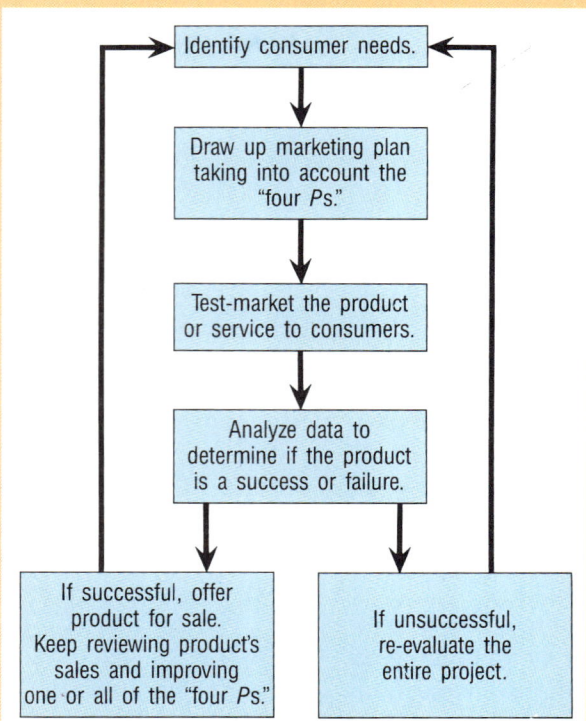

Please answer the following questions by placing a check in the appropriate box.

Sex □ Male □ Female

Marital Status
□ Single, never married
□ Single, divorced or widowed
□ Married

Children □ None □ 2-3
□ 1 □ more than 3

Occupation _____

Annual Income
□ Less than $10,000
□ $10-25,000
□ $25-40,000
□ $40-55,000
□ More than $55,000

Education
□ High school
□ College (2-yr.)
□ College (4-yr.)
□ Graduate school

Leisure Activities
□ Team sports
□ Individual sports
□ Reading, writing
□ Camping, hiking
□ Sewing, crafts
□ Collecting
□ Other _____

Where did you obtain this item?
□ Retail store
□ Wholesale outlet
□ Gift
□ Other _____

THE MAIL SURVEY

Determining consumer needs and evaluating the success of a product requires the use of market, or consumer, surveys. A typical consumer survey would be similar to the questionnaire above. It asks questions about the individual who bought a particular item and would be used in a test market or after a product has been selling for a while. Surveys such as this one may be mailed to magazine subscribers, printed on the back of warranty cards, or slipped into a product's package.

A manufacturer may also send a questionnaire to a random sample of users of its product. A random sample is a group chosen by chance from a larger population to ensure a cross-section of age, occupation, and so on. For example, before the publisher of a textbook begins to work on a second edition, it sends questionnaires to a sample of teachers throughout the nation who have used the first edition. The excerpt below is taken from such a survey.

1. What grade levels do you teach using this text? (Please circle one)

    Grade: 7   8   9   10   11   12

2. Do you use this text in your class:
    ☐ as the primary or main text?
    ☐ as a supplement to another text?

3. How long have you been using this text to teach economics?
    ☐ less than 1 year   ☐ 3-4 years
    ☐ 1-2 years   ☐ 4-5 years
    ☐ 2-3 years   ☐ 5 or more years

4. What is the average size of the economics classes you teach?
    ☐ less than 10   ☐ 30-39 students
       students   ☐ 40-49 students
    ☐ 10-19 students   ☐ 50 or more
    ☐ 20-29 students   students

5. Is your economics course:
    ☐ a half year/one semester?
    ☐ a full year/two semesters?
    ☐ other? (please specify) _____

PERSONAL INTERVIEWS

Personal interviews are another source of consumer information. Although they are the most costly type of market survey, they are done quite often. Companies believe that a personal interview yields more complete information than a card the consumer fills out and returns to the manufacturer. In a personal interview, a researcher can ask more detailed questions about a consumer's reaction to a product.

Personal interviews may be conducted at the place of purchase, such as outside a supermarket, or over the phone. Phone numbers are chosen at random by a computer to avoid favoring one group of consumers.

USING THE RESULTS

After the company has taken its market survey, its marketing department evaluates and analyzes the data. It determines if people are interested in a potential product or whether they are satisfied with existing products. The data are then put to use to create, change, or improve a product. For example, the editors of this textbook used information gathered from questionnaires to design the skill features in this book.

The results of market surveys are also used to decide on pricing, to forecast sales for products, and to decide on the market at which to aim promotion. In effect, market surveys enable producers to predict the demand for their products.

Practicing Your Skills

Imagine you are a market researcher. You have been asked by a restaurant chain to find out what changes need to be made to increase profits.

1. Write a paragraph explaining: **a.** how you will select your sample. **b.** the techniques you will use to survey the market. **c.** the kinds of information you will need to gather.
2. Using the last information as the base, design a set of questions to use in your survey.

would most likely market a new cereal in supermarkets. However, when convenience stores opened, cereal companies began to sell a small number of their cereals in these stores. They did not market their entire lines. Instead, they chose several cereals that would appeal to the different kinds of people who shopped in convenience stores. In another example, a company might decide that its goods would appeal to a limited market only and choose, therefore, to sell their goods only in specialty shops. Many often and commonly used items such as cosmetics, health care, dental hygiene, and hair care are often sold in discount stores, where bargain hunters look for the best buys for frequently purchased sundry goods.

PROMOTION

Promotion is the use of advertising and other methods to inform consumers that a new or improved product or service is available. Promotion also attempts to persuade consumers to purchase that product or service. As Figure 12-1 shows, businesses spend billions of dollars each year to advertise through direct-mail pieces and in newspapers, magazines, radio, and television. You might wish to review Chapter 3 for the different types of advertising. Other promotional efforts include free samples, cents-off coupons, gifts, and rebates. Where and how a product is displayed are also important. Paperbacks and magazines are often placed on racks next to checkout lines where people wait.

What type of advertising had the largest increase between 1975 and 1985? Why do you think advertising expenditures have increased so greatly?

Figure 12-1: ADVERTISING EXPENDITURES IN THE UNITED STATES, 1945-1986

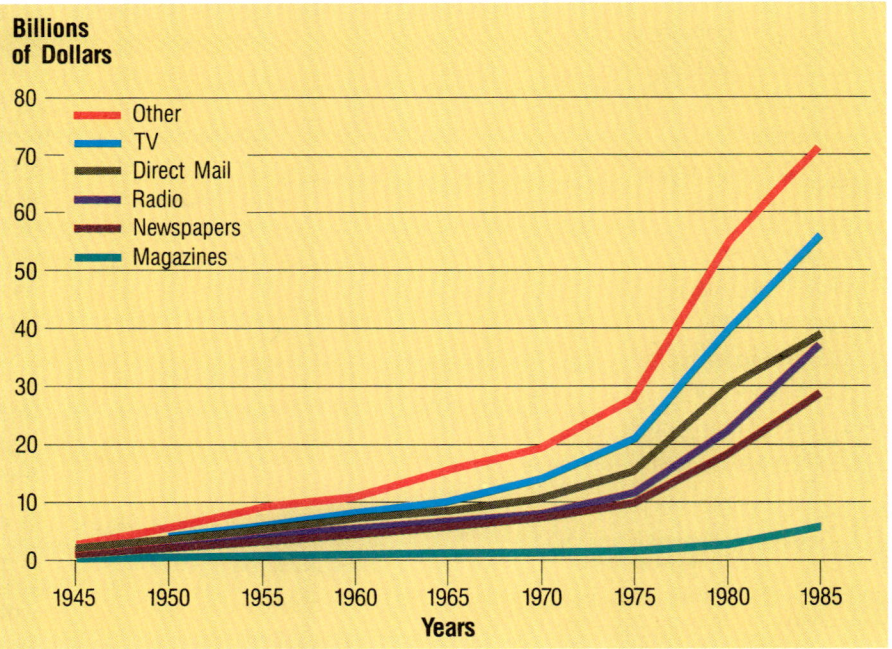

Source: *Statistical Abstract of the U.S., Historical Statistics of the U.S.,* Bureau of the Census 1986 Data are estimates.

306

The particular types of promotion that a producer uses depend on three factors. These are: 1. the product, 2. the type of consumer that the company wants to attract, and 3. the amount of money it plans to spend. Magazines, credit card companies, and insurance companies often use direct-mail advertising. The mailer usually includes a letter describing the product or service and an order blank or application form.

As you may recall from Chapter 1, all resources, including money for promotion, are limited. As a result, companies aim their ads and other promotional efforts at certain groups. A company selling books about economic theory might advertise in a journal that only economists read. To advertise on television stations that the general public watches would not be the most efficient use of the company's limited promotional budget. On the other hand, producers of more general goods, such as cereal, mix their use of radio, television, newspaper, and magazine advertising to get the most for their promotional dollars.

REVIEWING ECONOMIC PRINCIPLES

1. In Chapter 10, you read about product differentiation in monopolistic competition. How does product identification relate to product differentiation? You will have to infer the answer from your reading.
2. **a.** What five factors does a business have to consider in deciding price? **b.** What is price leadership? **c.** What is penetration pricing?
3. In the marketing mix, to what does *place* refer?
4. **a.** In deciding on the type of promotion to use, what three factors should a business consider? **b.** Why do companies aim their promotion at specific groups?
5. **Critical Thinking: Applying Concepts.** Choose a product or service such as peanut butter, dry cleaning, a car, or a personal computer, and decide how you would market it. Write a paragraph to answer: To whom would you aim it? How would you price it? Where would you sell it? How would you promote it?

3 | DISTRIBUTION CHANNELS

Ask yourself as you read:
- What are distribution channels?
- What are the major types of wholesalers?

Distribution, moving goods from where they are produced to the people who will buy them, is another function of marketing. The routes by which goods are moved are called **channels of distribution.** There are several types of goods, and Figure 12-2 shows their various distribution channels.

Figure 12-2: CHANNELS OF DISTRIBUTION

Consumer Goods

Manufacturer → Consumer

Manufacturer → Retailer → Consumer

Manufacturer → Wholesaler → Retailer → Consumer

Raw Materials and Producer Goods

Producer (Manufacturer or producer of raw material) → Business

Producer (Manufacturer or producer of raw material) → Wholesaler → Business

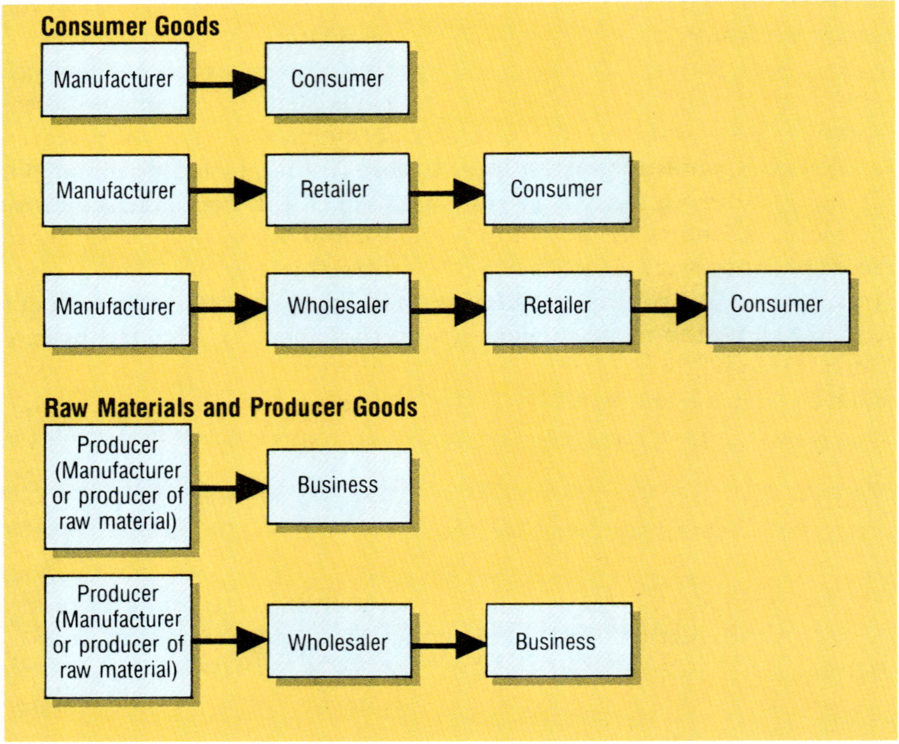

This flow chart shows typical channels of distribution for goods. From raw materials to finished product, how do you think a pizza gets to consumers?

Some consumer goods, such as clothing, are usually sold by a producer to a wholesaler and then to a retailer, who sells them to consumers. Other consumer goods, such as automobiles, are sold by the producer directly to a retailer and then to consumers. Some goods, such as vegetables sold at a farmer's roadside stand, go directly from producer to consumer. With each transaction, or business deal, the price increases.

WHOLESALERS

Wholesalers are businesses that purchase large quantities of goods from producers for resale to other businesses. They may buy goods from manufacturers and sell them to retail stores that then deal directly with consumers. Or they may buy and sell raw materials or producer goods to manufacturers. There are various types of wholesalers.

Full-service wholesalers warehouse goods and deliver them once they are bought. They may also extend trade credit. Wholesalers known as drop shippers, on the other hand, never take possession of goods. They buy merchandise with the agreement that the producer will store it. After the drop shipper sells the goods, the producer must deliver them. A cash-and-carry wholesaler has inventory and sells merchandise, but the buyer must ship it. A truck wholesaler sells and delivers at the same time. Goods such as dairy products are often sold this way.

RETAILERS

Retailers sell consumer goods directly to the public. There are hundreds of thousands of retailers that sell all types of goods. You are probably familiar with many of them: department stores; specialty stores such as bookshops, record stores, and clothing stores; discount stores; supermarkets; door-to-door or at-home selling such as Avon and Tupperware; mail-order houses; and so on.

Of particular interest today are mail-order retailers. They use catalogs and advertisements to promote and sell their goods. The consumer either calls a toll-free number and places an order using a credit card or mails an order form with a check or money order. Montgomery Ward was the first mail-order house in the United States. But today there are many mail-order houses, including such specialty houses as L. L. Bean for outdoor clothing and New York's Metropolitan Museum of Art, which sells reproductions of objects from its collections. One reason for the growth in mail-order sales is state sales taxes. In most states, residents who purchase goods from out of state by mail avoid paying any sales tax. Retailers also similarly advertise on television.

STORAGE AND TRANSPORTATION

Part of the distribution process is warehousing goods for future sales. The producer, wholesaler, or retailer may perform this function. For example, a book company may ship finished books to its own warehouse to await shipment to bookstores. Or it may pay the printer to warehouse the books. Most retailers keep some inventory on hand for immediate sale. Many have a two-to three-month's supply, depending on the type of merchandise. There is less need, for example, to keep several months' supply of seasonal goods such as wool coats.

Transportation involves the physical movement of goods from producers and/or sellers to buyers. Various means of transportation, such as airlines, railroads, trucks, and automobiles, can be used. Some goods, such as petroleum and natural gas, are often transported by pipeline. In deciding on the method of transportation to use, business people must consider the type of good, such as perishable food. But the size and weight of the good are also important. Airfreighting tons of wheat is impractical, but airfreighting small machine parts is not. To fulfill a sale or to get fruit to a food plant are two instances where speed is important. The cost of the different types of transportation is also a factor.

REVIEWING ECONOMIC PRINCIPLES

1. What is the major difference between wholesalers and retailers?
2. Who may perform the storage function of distribution?
3. What five factors should businesses consider in choosing a method of shipping goods?
4. **Critical Thinking: Interpreting Information.** Write a summary of the information on channels of distribution found in Figure 12-2.

SUMMARY OF IMPORTANT PRINCIPLES

1
- Marketing in the United States has developed through the following four stages: production, sales, marketing (production and sales), and consumer sovereignty.
- Since the 1950s, businesses in the United States have begun actively to create demand for their goods and services. An important part of this strategy has been the use of advertising to increase interest in goods and services, hoping thereby to increase sales.
- Through a series of predesigned questions, market research attempts to discover the quality, features, and style that consumers find desirable in a product, the type of packaging that will attract consumers, and the price that will get them to buy. Researchers gather information about the age, sex, income, education, and location of possible users. Market research can be done at the very beginning, immediately after a product is released, and after a product has been on the market a while.
- A market survey collects information from consumers either about the demand for a new product or about changes that should be made in an existing product. Market surveys may be conducted by mail or through personal interviews.

2
- The "four *P*s" of the marketing mix are product, price, place, and promotion. Included under product are the product itself, its packaging, and product identification. In setting price, a company has to consider the costs of producing, advertising, selling, and distributing the product; the amount of profit it wishes to make; and the price of its competition. Place refers to where a product should be sold. Promotion is the use of advertising and other methods to inform consumers about products and services.

3
- Raw materials and producer goods are sold by the producers to businesses or to wholesalers, who sell them to other businesses. Consumer goods may be sold by a manufacturer to a wholesaler and then to a retailer, who sells them to the consumer; by the manufacturer to a retailer and then to the consumer; or by the manufacturer directly to the consumer.
- Wholesalers purchase large quantities of goods from producers for resale to other businesses. Retailers sell consumer goods directly to the public.
- As part of the distribution process, goods may be warehoused by the producer, wholesaler, or retailer for future sales. Transportation involves the movement of goods. In deciding on method, businesspeople should consider the type of good, size, weight, speed of delivery, and costs.

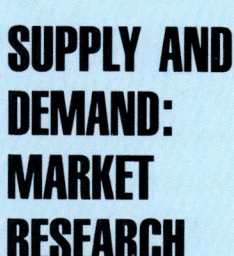

Putting Economics to Work

SUPPLY AND DEMAND: MARKET RESEARCH

The Freeland family is working on their budget when the telephone rings. The father, Earl, answers. The caller identifies herself as a market researcher for a large corporation that specializes in household cleaning products. She asks to speak to whoever does the family food shopping. Earl answers that he does. The market researcher asks what dishwashing detergent Earl buys and why. He replies that he buys the store brand because it is the cheapest.

The market researcher then asks whether Earl has seen a new detergent called *Whistle*. Earl recalls seeing the new product on the shelf, next to some old, familiar brands. The market researcher asks if Earl remembers the detergent's packaging. What was the bottle's shape and color and the colors of its label? Earl does recall most features of the product's packaging. But he tells the researcher that the new detergent is too expensive. It is 30 cents more than the brand he buys.

To persuade Earl to try *Whistle*, the market researcher offers to send a coupon for 50 cents off the purchase price. In a few weeks, the market researcher will call again to see how the Freedlands like the new detergent.

After he hangs up, Earl discusses the call with his family. His son Tom says that although the store-brand detergent is cheaper, it does not last long. His daughters Jane and Arlene agree. They say that if there are a lot of pans to wash, they have to refill the sink with clean water and more detergent.

1. Why do you think the market researcher asked about the product's packaging?
2. Do you think the Freedlands live in a test market for the new detergent? Why or why not?
3. How do you think the corporation that makes *Whistle* will use the information from phone interviews like this one?

Readings in Economics

ADS FOR WOMEN
Skill: Contrasting Information

 As marketing agencies increasingly attempt to tailor their ads to the needs and desires of consumers, they have dropped former stereotypes of women from their ads. In the following reading, Bernice Kanner, senior editor at *New York* magazine, discusses this change in advertising.

Advertising has been humoring women for years, not just in hiring them but in talking or "pitching" to them. But recently—and I may be overly optimistic—it seems that advertising is beginning to reflect the way women really are. Before, by and large, advertising depicted women the way advertisers wanted them to be, the better to sell to them.

Before 1970, most ads portrayed women as helpless, dependent on men not just for approval but for solutions to everyday problems. But as the women's movement rippled through Adland, more and more advertisers attempted to placate the activists by showing reasonably independent women. . . .

Those commercials substituted one cliché for another and alienated stay-at-home women, who complained that the spots romanticized the role of work in a woman's life and made them feel inferior. That kind of advertising may have also alienated the very group it attempted to reach: working women. Showing a female executive in a conference room wowing a board of directors with her brilliance seems too forced and contrived, and women sensed advertising's clumsy efforts to stereotype them, to "buy" their favor.

Now it seems the force-feeding and obviousness have ceased. American Express shows a woman confidently treating her guest to a meal, not humiliating him by picking up the tab. In the Luvs commercials, Daddy knows how to diaper Junior. And instead of flaunting her independence, the Harvey's Bristol Cream woman reaches out for companionship. . . .

Ad campaigns often are scrapped when they fail to reach their prime audience. . . .

It seems that advertisers are finally getting the message to scrap the old stereotypes of women. And it's about time.

1. Contrast the image of women presented in today's advertisments with the image portrayed before 1970.
2. How did consumers indicate to advertisers that it was time to drop the old stereotypes of women?

Kanner, Bernice, "Comment: Ad Pitches." *Working Woman*, September 1984. Reprinted with permission from WORKING WOMAN magazine. Copyright © 1987 by Working Woman, Inc.

MARKETERS RECOGNIZE SENIOR CITIZENS
Skill: Predicting Outcomes

 As companies try to design products that match consumer tastes, they must carefully watch the American consumer. A big change now occurring is the aging of America as a large part of the population gets older. This reading describes how marketers are selling to older consumers.

Consumers aged 50 and older account for half, or $130 billion, of the country's discretionary income, according to the Conference Board, a New York business-research organization. Moreover, the 50-plus age group is expected to grow 23% by the year 2000, compared with 14% for the rest of the population.

"Retailers and suppliers better take heed," warns Kurt Banard, publisher of Retail Marketing Report newsletter, "Something is happening right under their noses." . . .

Last year Great Factory Stores of Reading, Pa., changed the illustrated model in its newspaper ads after store managers began to notice that customers were older than they once were. The company gradually aged the schoolgirl-looking model by changing her makeup and adding an older, more mature haircut. Says Jim Oswell, the sales-promotion director: "We changed with the market." . . .

But marketing to older consumers can also be risky. When [Johnson & Johnson] introduced Affinity shampoo, the product initially stumbled because the advertising overemphasized age. . . .

The shampoo "didn't totally flop, but it didn't get the attention we thought it would get," says a company spokesman. The new ad is more upbeat and features a perky, middle-aged woman saying things like, "When my hair looks good, I feel great." Adds an announcer: "Affinity is made for hair that time has changed."

1. What advice would you offer to an advertising agency preparing an ad campaign for a product used by older consumers?
2. What do you predict will happen regarding the number of television ads focusing on products for older consumers? Explain.

Hank Gilman, "Marketers Court Older Consumers as Balance of Buying Power Shifts." *The Wall Street Journal*, April 23, 1986. Reprinted by permission of *The Wall Street Journal*, © Dow Jones & Company, Inc. (1986). All Rights Reserved.

"THE GOODS WILL BE PROMPTLY SENT"

Skill: Contrasting Information

Today's specialized mail-order retailers developed long after mail-order sales were made popular in the 1800s. This reading discusses one of the most famous mail-order retailers in history, Sears, Roebuck & Co.

To hundreds of thousands of Americans, particularly in rural areas, the annual Sears, Roebuck catalogues were exciting links to an outside world where everything was up to date and dreams came true. From thin sales brochures they grew into "the Great Wish Book," with more than 1,000 pages crammed with illustrations and text, much of it written by Richard W. Sears himself in a manner calculated to bring in money for stoves, saddles, buggies, fishing tackle, and clothing.

Sears, Roebuck's newspaper and magazine advertising was aimed primarily at getting readers to order the catalogue, which then did its best to hook people on the mail-ordering habit. . . .

The store worked hard at convincing its readers that the company really existed in Chicago and would honor mail orders. Catalogues contained pictures of mammoth warehouses, bank testimonials attesting to the vast assets and reliability of the firm, and even offerings for sale of stereopti-con views of Sears, Roebuck's headquarters. Instructions for ordering, aimed at immigrants, were run in German and Swedish: "Tell us what you want in your own way, written in any language, no matter whether good or poor writing, and the goods will be promptly sent to you."

Sears imparted economic maxims on almost every page. "The gold cure for poverty can only be effected with the aid of economy," he wrote. "Take regular doses from this catalogue and be well healed." . . . In 1897 [Sears] claimed that "we are doing more for the farmer and the laborer than all the political demagogues in the country. . . . Our factory-to-consumer system brings about a revolution in profits, and is in reality a profit-sharing enterprise, as the consumer benefits by the middleman's profits which are cut off by our methods of merchandising." . . .

The company recognized that it sold to the trade as well as to individual consumers, and to protect those who bought for resale it did not put its name and address on any package or piece of merchandise. To get people to order, it used the lure of loss leaders [items which lose money for the company but attract customers], especially in yellow pages in the back of the catalogue. In 1908 such bargains, at two cents each, included iron quilting-frame clips, a set of cloth-covered elastic sleeve holders, door springs, and brass balls to cover the ends of an oxen's horns. . . .

Sears built its business when people could not easily get to central sources of massed consumer products. It was aided by the introduction of rural free delivery in 1896 and by the start of parcel post in 1913. But even with the coming of automobiles, highways, supermarkets, and shopping centers, the Sears catalogues—and mail order—have continued to flourish, accepted and necessary American institutions.

1. Why has the Sears, Roebuck mail-order business continued to flourish today?
2. Contrast Sears' marketing strategy and merchandise in the late 19th century with that of today.

Alex Croner and the editors of *American Heritage* and *Business Week*, *The History of American Business and Industry*. New York: American Heritage, 1972. p. 243.

12 | CHAPTER REVIEW

PRACTICING YOUR STUDY SKILLS: OUTLINING

An outline is a useful way to organize information. It can help you to organize your thoughts before you begin writing a paper or preparing an oral report. Outlining is also useful in taking notes from lectures or your reading. An outline allows you to see relationships among topics and subtopics. Textbooks are already partially outlined for you. Chapter, section, and subsection heads present the main topics and subtopics to you. The best headings are those using full sentences or enough of a phrase to identify main ideas clearly.

In all outlines, the material under each topic should be arranged from the most general kinds of information to the most specific ones. You should have at least two topics in your outline and two subtopics under each topic. Use brief, clear phrases. It is not necessary to use sentences. To arrange information in an outline, follow the form below:

I. Topic: Use a Roman numeral for topics, and begin the first word of each topic with a capital letter.
  A. First subtopic: Use capital letters for the first subtopics, and begin the first word with a capital letter.
    1. second subtopic: Use Arabic numerals, and begin the first word of each second subtopic with a small letter.
    2. second subtopic
  B. First subtopic
II. Topic
  A. First subtopic
    1. second subtopic
    2. second subtopic
    3. second subtopic
  B. First subtopic
III. Topic

Activity: To help you study this chapter, reread it, and organize the information in outline form.

VOCABULARY REVIEW

Write the letter of the definition in Column B that correctly defines each term in Column A.

Column A	Column B
1. test marketing	a. use of advertising to inform consumers about a product and to persuade them to purchase it.
2. wholesaler	b. business that sells goods directly to the public
3. penetration pricing	c. business that purchases large quantities of goods from producers for resale to other businesses
4. price leadership	d. selling a new product at a low price to attract new customers away from an established product
5. retailer	e. offering a product in a small area for a limited time to see how well it sells
6. promotion	f. setting prices close to those of competing companies

PRACTICING YOUR ECONOMIC SKILLS

1. **Preparing a Market Survey.** Chip McElroy is preparing a market survey for a new type of modeling clay. It has some advantages over existing products, but the main competitor has been in business for 40 years. Chip knows from previous research done on the types of modeling clay on the market that most modeling clay is bought by parents with young children. He has to decide what strategy to use.

a. If the money available for the survey is limited, do you think it would be better to conduct personal interviews or a mail survey? Why?

b. Give two questions Chip is likely to ask on his survey.

2. **Using Tables.** Use the table below to do the following exercises.

a. Which two groups of products had the greatest increase in spending?

b. What changes in the American way of life might help to explain the increase in spending for these two groups?

Magazine Advertising: Spending For Selected Product Groups (in millions of dollars)

Product Groups	1975	1984
Apparel, footware, and accessories	47	240
Automobile, related accessories and equipment	102	473
Computers, office equipment and stationery	29	321
Food and Food Products	87	89
Travel, hotels and resorts	65	212

DISCUSSING ECONOMIC QUESTIONS

1. Do you think that market research fulfills a real need? Should a company be concerned with matching its products to the needs of consumers? What alternatives besides market research does a company have in deciding on criteria for designing, pricing, and promoting a product?

2. How do the major electronic equipment companies try to make their products appear to be better or different from one another? Use examples from actual ads in your discussion.

APPLYING CRITICAL THINKING SKILLS

1. **Explaining Decisions.** Suppose you are about to try a new product such as cereal or soap. In your decision to try the new product, how important is each of the "four Ps"? Rank them in their order of importance to you, and write a paragraph explaining why you chose this ranking.

2. **Explaining Decisions.** When you make a repeat purchase of a product, how important is each of the "four Ps" in your decision? Rank them in their order of importance to you, and write a paragraph explaining why you chose this ranking.

3. **Explaining Advertising Strategies.** Choose three brands of similar products such as cereal, cars, or jeans, and write a paragraph describing how each manufacturer has used the concept of product differentiation to make its product appear different from and better than its competitors'.

4. **Holding a Class Discussion.** Organize a round-table discussion on the ways in which technology and automation have changed the role that transportation plays in marketing.

5. **Gathering Information.** From magazine and other ads, create a bulletin board display that illustrates the functions of marketing in your community.

READINGS

Advertising Code of American Business, The. Washington, D.C.: American Advertising Federation.

Eckardt, W. Von. "Heraldry for the Industrial Age." *Time*, 18 October 1982, pp. 84–85.

Flax, S. "Wholesalers." *Forbes*, 4 January 1982, pp. 222–23.

Mauser, Ferdinand F., and Schwartz, David J. *American Business: An Introduction*, 5th ed. New York: Harcourt Brace Jovanovich, 1982.

CHAPTER 13

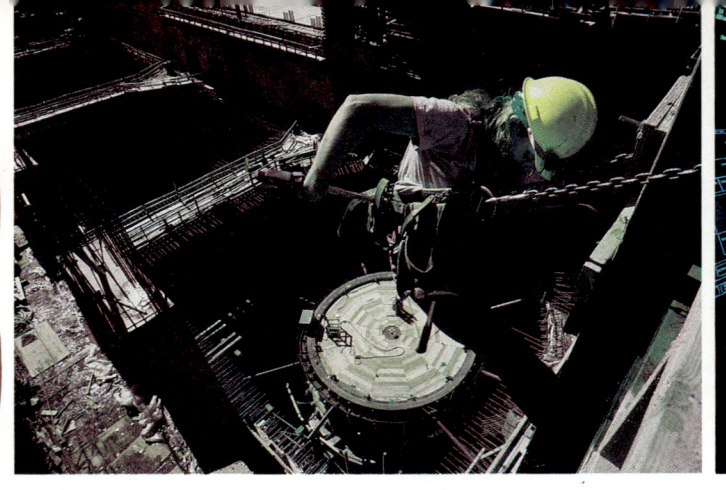

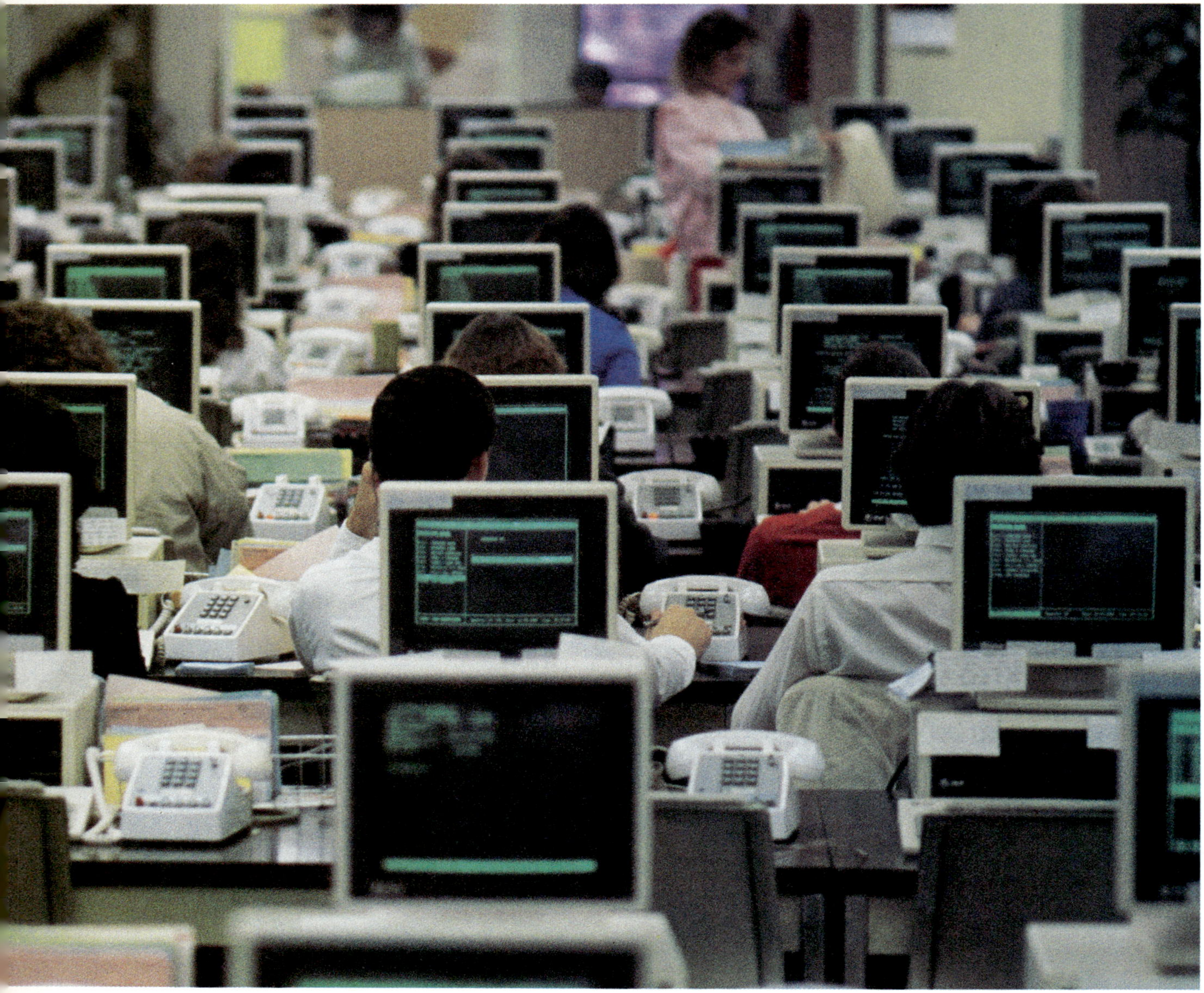

The American labor force is comprised of over 100 million men and women who work at an amazing variety of occupations in businesses and industries. Unions have made important contributions to many workers, but union membership has declined in recent years.

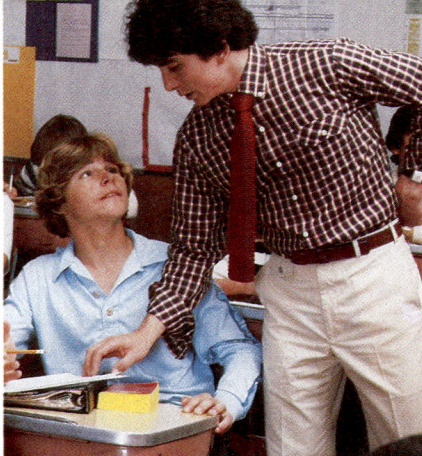

THE AMERICAN LABOR FORCE

You may already be working, but if not, you probably will be joining the American labor force sometime in the future. What kinds of jobs exist for you? What kind of training will you need for them? Which jobs are growing the fastest? How are wages determined? This chapter will help you answer these important questions. The chapter also presents a time line of the labor movement in the United States and describes how unions and management arrive at contract agreements. You will also read about the possible future of unions as technology changes the workplace. Learning Economic Skills discusses job possibilities for your future.

CHAPTER OBJECTIVES After you have studied this chapter, you will be able to:

1 • identify jobs by the type of work performed and by the education and/or training needed.

2 • describe the workings of supply and demand in the labor market.
   ★ use information from the *Bureau of Labor Statistics* to determine the future of some jobs.

3 • summarize the history of organized labor in the United States.
   • describe union organization in the United States.

4 • list the major issues involved in collective bargaining.

5 • describe the possible future of unionism in the United States.

ECONOMICS VOCABULARY

civilian labor force
blue-collar
white-collar
service worker
unskilled worker
semiskilled worker
skilled worker
professional
minimum wage law
labor union
craft union
industrial union
local union
closed shop
union shop
agency shop
right-to-work law
collective bargaining
mediation
arbitration
strike
picketing
cost-of-living adjustment
boycott
lockout
injunction

A factory worker on an assembly line, the vice-president of a corporation, and a police officer all belong to the productive resource known as labor. In discussing labor, economists use the term *labor force* in a specific way. The **civilian labor force** is the total number of people 16 years of age or older who are either employed or actively seeking work. Individuals not able to work, such as disabled people or those in prisons or mental institutions, are not included in the civilian labor force. Nor are people in the armed forces or those not looking for a paying job, such as full-time students and homemakers. Figure 13-1 shows the civilian labor force in comparison to the total working-age population. By 1987 about 120 million workers were in the United States civilian labor force. Of these, about 54 percent were women. In 1900, women made up only about 17 percent of the labor force.

1 | WHO IS THE LABOR FORCE?

Ask yourself as you read:
- What percentage of Americans are in the civilian labor force?
- What are the main categories of workers?

The size and makeup of the American labor force have changed greatly since the nation's birth. Two hundred years ago, more than 95 percent of the nation's workers were involved in agriculture. Even though farm production has increased dramatically because of technology, only about 3 percent of America's workers are still employed in agriculture, either as farmers or as laborers. This decrease in the number of farm jobs has been accompanied by an increase in manufacturing and service jobs.

CATEGORIES OF WORKERS

During the latter part of the 19th century, large numbers of farm workers moved to cities. This migration occurred in part because of the higher wages paid workers in the growing industries of the cities. As you read in Chapter 8, higher wages also increased the number of workers since they attracted more people to enter the labor force. The migration to the cities also occurred because of the increased use of machinery on farms. Fewer farm workers were required. These people found work in what are now called blue-collar jobs. **Blue-collar** is a category that includes craftworkers, workers in manufacturing, and nonfarm laborers. About 25 percent of the labor force are blue-collar workers.

The largest sector of the labor force is white-collar workers. **White-collar** refers to office workers, salespeople, and professionals—highly trained individuals such as doctors, accountants, engineers, and so on. This sector has experienced steady growth throughout the 20th century and now accounts for about 54 percent of the labor force.

Figure 13-1: EMPLOYMENT STATUS OF UNITED STATES POPULATION 16 YEARS OLD AND OLDER*

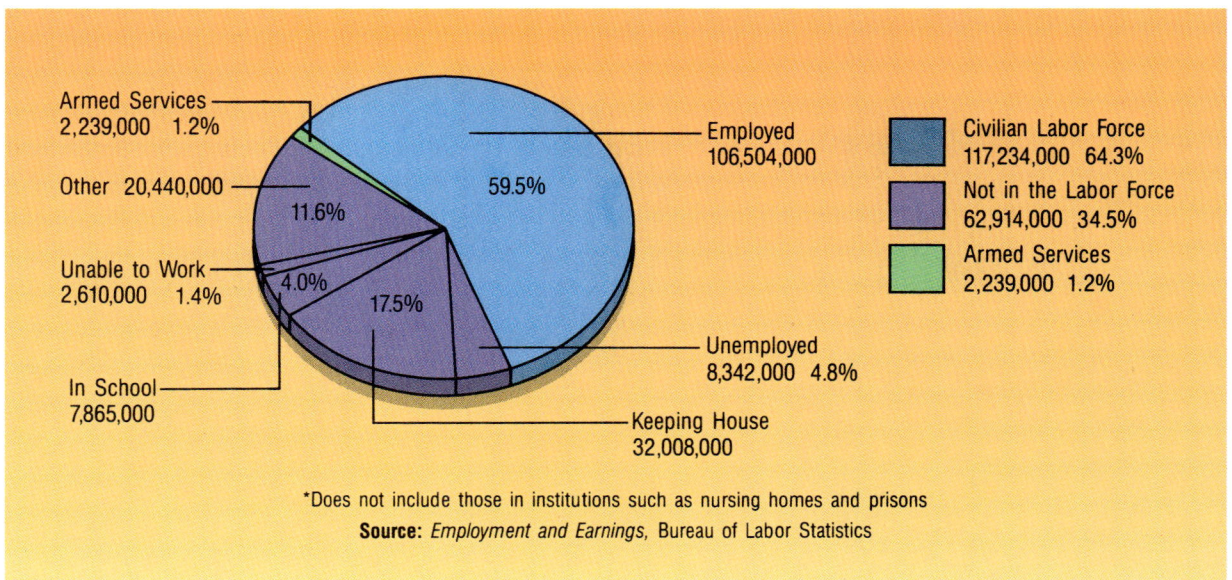

Armed Services 2,239,000 1.2%

Other 20,440,000

11.6%

Unable to Work 2,610,000 1.4%

4.0%

17.5%

In School 7,865,000

Employed 106,504,000

59.5%

Unemployed 8,342,000 4.8%

Keeping House 32,008,000

Civilian Labor Force 117,234,000 64.3%

Not in the Labor Force 62,914,000 34.5%

Armed Services 2,239,000 1.2%

*Does not include those in institutions such as nursing homes and prisons

Source: *Employment and Earnings,* Bureau of Labor Statistics

In recent years, there has been a steady shift away from farm work and blue-collar jobs to the service sector of the economy. **Service workers** are those who provide services directly to individuals. Cooks, piano tuners, health-care aides, and barbers are all service workers. The service sector now makes up about 75 percent of all non-farm jobs.

Classifying jobs as white-collar, blue-collar, service, or farm work is one way of describing the labor force. Another way is to group workers by the level of training or education their jobs require. **Unskilled workers** are those whose jobs require no specialized training. Such jobs as assembly-line worker and general farm labor are considered unskilled, although obviously such work requires skills such as patience and the ability to pace oneself or to work according to a schedule. Such jobs may also demand the ability to work well with people, and so on. **Semiskilled workers** work in jobs that need some training, often using modern technology. Telephone operators, typists, and factory-production inspectors are examples of semiskilled workers. Someone who has learned a trade or craft, either through a vocational school or as an apprentice to an experienced worker, is considered a **skilled worker.** Plumbers, carpenters, and computer programmers are classified as skilled. **Professionals** are those with college degrees and usually additional education or training, such as doctors, lawyers, teachers, and business executives.

THE PROBLEM WITH CATEGORIES

Although terms such as semiskilled are helpful in picturing different areas of the labor force, individuals do not always fall into a single cate-

The percentage of unemployed among those 16 and older is not the same as the nation's unemployment rate. Why? Using the data on this graph, determine the unemployment rate.

gory. A college student, for example, may work at an unskilled job such as cook at a fast-food restaurant while he or she is going to college. Workers may move from one job to another as they gain training and experience. The vice-president of a department store chain, for example, may have begun as a sales clerk. Also, the definitions of technician and professional have become increasingly vague. Some technicians today require considerable training in very difficult and demanding jobs. Moreover, the line between some technicians and scientists, who are professionals, is often very thin.

REVIEWING ECONOMIC PRINCIPLES

1. What is the civilian labor force?
2. Why has the farm sector lost so many workers?
3. Make a table with four columns: Farm, Blue-Collar, White-Collar, and Service. Under each, list whether that type of work involves unskilled, semiskilled, skilled, or professional workers. More than one type of worker may be listed under each heading.
4. Use the statistics under the heading "Who is the Labor Force?" to draw a graph of the makeup of the civilian labor force.
5. **Critical Thinking: Forming Opinions.** Based on what you read in Chapter 12, why do you think blue-collar jobs are declining?

2 | SUPPLY AND DEMAND IN THE LABOR MARKET

Ask yourself as you read:
- What determines wages in the labor market?
- What prevents wages from constantly shifting in response to supply and demand?

In Chapter 8, you read about supply and demand in terms of products and services that businesses produce. But supply and demand work in the labor market, too. There, suppliers are the workers who offer their services, while the demand comes from employers who require workers. Three major factors underlie how supply and demand affect prices, or, in this case, wages in the labor market. These are: 1. skill, 2. type of job, and 3. location.

The first factor, skill, is the ability a person brings to a job. It may come from talent, initiative, education and/or training, or experience. For example, a brain surgeon and a major-league home-run hitter will be paid large sums of money, even though their educational backgrounds may be quite different. Employers wishing to hire skilled workers must usually pay high wages to bid them away from other potential employers. Part of the ability that a worker brings to a job is his or her attitude toward work. Some individuals take their jobs seriously and work very hard. Others do not. Generally, those who are serious about their work have the "right" attitude—that is, the attitude that will help them to succeed in the workplace.

The type of job also affects the amount an employer is willing to pay and a potential employee is willing to take. Jobs that are unpleasant or dangerous, such as coal mining, often pay high wages compared to other jobs requiring equal levels of skill. On the other hand, some jobs are enjoyable or prestigious or valued enough that people are willing to take them even at low wages. Many young people take lower-paying jobs in industries such as filmmaking and publishing for these reasons.

prestigious (pre-STIJ-uhs): important

The location of both jobs and workers is the third factor in determining wages. If workers are relatively scarce in an area, companies may have to pay high wages to attract workers to move. Alaska, for example, has the highest wages per person in the country. However, if there are many unemployed in an area and a company needs only a few workers, it can often hire enough people even at relatively low wages.

RESTRICTIONS ON WAGES

Demand for a product also affects wages. A person may be a highly skilled tailor. However, his or her wages will probably not be very high even though the price of services is high because the demand for handmade clothing is low today. As another example, someone might be an extremely talented portrait artist, but he or she will not earn much if that style of painting is not in demand.

If the labor market were perfectly competitive, the changing supply and demand for labor would result in constantly shifting wage rates. But the labor market is not perfectly competitive. For one thing, the flow of information about jobs is imperfect. Workers cannot know exactly what all other employers will pay for their services. Employers for their part do not know what all workers are willing to accept.

In the real world, two other factors affect wages. One is the federal—and sometimes state or city—**minimum wage law,** which sets the lowest legal hourly wage rate that may be paid to certain types of workers. The other is the process of wage negotiations between organized labor and management. Supply and demand have less influence on negotiations than do such things as seniority, or length of time on the job, the company's ability to pay higher wages, and the length of the contract.

seniority (see-NYOR-uh-tee): length of time on the job

REVIEWING ECONOMIC PRINCIPLES

1. What is the minimum wage law?
2. In the labor market, who creates: **a.** supply? **b.** demand?
3. **a.** What three factors underlying supply and demand affect wages in the labor market? **b.** Which factor seems to benefit workers most?
4. **Critical Thinking: Interpreting Information.** What are the disadvantages of imperfect competition in the labor market?

Learning Economic Skills | CHOOSING A CAREER

Your choice of career will be one of the most important decisions you make. A career should supply more than income. It should also be satisfying. After all, you will spend much of your time working once you have finished your education.

Some experts believe that workers in the future may actually make decisions about career choice several times. Rapidly changing technology will cause expanding and contracting job markets in certain fields. As a result, workers may need to retrain several times during their work lives.

OCCUPATIONAL OUTLOOK

The Bureau of Labor Statistics forecasts how people will be employed in the future. The Bureau publishes this information in various bulletins of labor statistics. Such statistics may also be found in the *Monthly Labor Review.* Some examples of these occupations are listed in the table on the next page.

As you can see, certain kinds of occupations are expected to increase greatly in the 1980s, while others will decline. In general, the number of jobs that relate to computer technology and the sciences, such as electrical and mechanical engineering, will increase. Jobs in industries that provide services, such as auto repair and health care, are also expected to increase.

The number of jobs related to the needs of older people will also increase. This results from the steady increase in the median age of the United States population. The number of people 65 years of age or older will have increased 40 percent between 1985 and 2000, while the population of those 14 years of age or younger will have increased only slightly. This is because the birth rate has been declining since the late 1960s.

On the other hand, there will be less demand for certain workers. Among these are teachers, telephone operators, and farm workers. Some of the declines will be because of automation; and some, because of the changing age of the population.

MAKING A CAREER CHOICE

Many factors influence a person's choice of career. These factors may include interests and abilities, education and/or training, place of residence, and the amount of time a person wants to spend at a workplace. The actual hours that a person can work also can be important. For example, some people have two jobs, have young or sick children, or are taking courses that make it impossible for them to work during the day or during regular nine-to-five working hours.

Knowing your interests and abilities is extremely important when deciding on a career. It should be your first step before you spend time and money on education and/or training or begin looking for your first job. Guidance counselors have tests that can help you to identify your abilities in different fields. For example, these tests can identify skills in areas as different as written communication, oral communication, mathematics, science, muscular coordination, spatial relationships, ability to do detail work, or interest in such various fields as human services, archeology, marine life, meteorology, or the synthesis of sounds.

Your interests may not, however, match the area where you have the most ability. In that case, you might consider a second or third area of ability. You may be very unhappy later if you make a career choice that you do not enjoy.

A second factor to consider is education and/or training. How much preparation does a particular occupation require? Do you want to spend the time and money? As a rule, the time and money spent for advanced education for a profession, such as law or nursing, or for training for a craft, such as carpentry or plumbing, generally results in a higher paying job. In addition, economists predict that there will be fewer and fewer jobs

Percentage Growth of Selected Occupations from 1984 to 1995

Occupation	Percent
Accountants and auditors	34.8
Aircraft pilots and flight engineers	17.0
Announcers and newscasters (radio/television)	11.0
Artists and commercial artists	29.0
Auto mechanics	20.1
Bricklayers and stonemasons	11.0
Bus drivers	17.0
Carpenters	10.7
Computer operators	46.1
Computer programmers	71.7
Economists	19.0
Electrical and electronic engineers	52.8
Electricians	13.6
Farm workers	−11.2
Lawyers	35.5
Mechanical engineers	34.0
Medical assistants	62.0
Physicians and surgeons	23.0
Postal clerks	−08.5
Psychologists	22.0
Registered nurses	32.8
Salespersons	12.6
Teachers	
College and university	−11.0
Kindergarten and elementary	20.3
Secondary school	05.0
Truck drivers	17.2

Source: *Monthly Labor Review*

available for unskilled workers in the future, as the industry of the United States becomes more highly specialized and automated.

Where you live or choose to live can also influence your career choice. For example, if you want to be a book editor, you may find that you have to move to a city such as New York, Chicago, or San Francisco where there are many publishing companies. If you do not want to leave your home-town, you would need to adapt your career choice to occupations available there. You could use similar writing and editing skills on a local newspaper or a company newsletter, or writing advertising copy for an ad agency.

Today more and more people are finding different ways to divide the time spent at home and at work. Having flexible work hours is one way. Some people also choose to work only part time. Sometimes two people share the same job. That is, each one works half the hours and receives half the pay of the full-time job. Others, such as artists and architects, work at home. Some people such as insurance agents and sales representatives work from their home rather than from central offices. Futurists, those who study the future, predict that with more sophisticated computers people will be able to work at home but stay in touch with their offices and other business contacts.

Practicing Your Skills

1. What other factors besides the four mentioned above do you think might influence a career choice?
2. Based on what you have read in this chapter and in Chapter 11, why do you think the number of farm workers and postal clerks will decline?
3. What kinds of jobs do you think the needs of the aging population will create? Use the table as well as you own ideas.
4. Imagine you are choosing a career. Use the information presented earlier in making your choice. First, list a set of interests and abilities and the possible education needed for various jobs using these interests and abilities. Consider where you would like to live, whether you would need to move, and how much time you would like to spend at your job. Describe your decision-making process in a paragraph. You may find it helpful to review the decision-making model in Chapter 1.

Ask yourself as you read:

- What are the major kinds of labor unions?
- What dates and events in the history of American unionism are of special importance?

To have some control over the wages they receive as well as over other working conditions, American workers have formed labor unions. A **labor union** is an association of workers organized to improve wages and working conditions for its members. Unions are based on the idea that workers as a group will have more influence on management than will individual workers acting alone. In discussing labor-management relations, the term *management* refers to those in charge of a company—the executives and managers.

The working conditions of the 19th century were very different from those of today. Men, women, and children as young as five labored from 12 to 14 hours a day, sometimes six days a week, often in unsanitary and unsafe factories. The buildings were sometimes poorly lighted and ventilated, and the machinery was sometimes dangerous to operate. When business slumped, factory owners fired employees. When business improved, new employees were hired. There was no unemployment insurance to help those out of work until they found new jobs. Health-care benefits, sick leave, and paid vacations and holidays did not exist. Unions offered a way to force employers to improve working conditions, shorten the workday, and end child labor.

Unionism, however, met strong resistance. For much of the 19th century, state legislatures influenced by business interests passed laws against unions, and state courts upheld those laws. Many businesses refused to hire union members or to deal with unions. Workers who were found trying to organize unions were fired and blacklisted—kept from being employed. Strikes during the late 1800s and early 1900s often resulted in violence between strikers and police. It was not until the mid-1930s that Congress began passing laws to regulate labor-management relations.

The time line on pages 326–327 shows the major dates in the development of the American labor movement. As you can see, for much of its history, organized labor in the United States has been split into two groups: craft unions and industrial unions. A **craft union** is made up of skilled workers in a specific trade or industry, such as carpentry or printing. For many years, craft unions dominated the labor movement. The first permanent federation, or organization of national labor unions, was the American Federation of Labor (AFL), composed of craft unions.

An **industrial union** is made up of all the workers in an industry regardless of job or level of skill. Attempts to organize industrial unions date back to the late 1800s. However, the major effort to unionize unskilled and semiskilled workers did not begin until the formation of the

This worker was employed at a weapons factory in World War I. How do you think her working conditions would compare with those of today's workers?

blacklist: to keep a person from being employed

Congress of Industrial Organizations (CIO) in 1938. Because they employ large numbers of unskilled and semiskilled workers, the automobile and steel industries were among the first to be organized.

During the late 1930s and early 1940s, both the AFL and the CIO launched organizing campaigns in which the lines between industrial and craft unions became less clear. AFL unions began recruiting semiskilled and unskilled workers, while the CIO began organizing workers in the skilled trades. The resulting rivalry was costly in both time and effort. By the mid-1950s union leaders realized that the labor movement would make greater gains if craft and industrial unions worked together. As a result, the two federations merged in 1955 to form the present AFL-CIO. Today, many unions are affiliated, or joined, with the AFL-CIO. There are several independent unions, however, including the United Mine Workers of America (UMW), the United Electrical Workers (UE), and the International Longshoremen's & Warehousemen's Union (ILWU).

affiliate (uh-FIL-eee-ayt): to join with

UNION ORGANIZATION

Today, organized labor operates at three levels: the local union, the national or international union, and the federation. A **local union** consists of all the members of a union in a particular manufacturing plant, company, or geographic area. The local deals directly with a company or management council by first negotiating a contract and then making sure the terms of the contract are kept.

negotiate (ni-GOH-shee-ayt): discuss and reach an agreement

The influence that a local has often depends on the membership policy it has been able to negotiate with management. In the past, a number of locals were set up as **closed shops.** The companies in which these locals operated were allowed to hire only union workers. This arrangement, however, was outlawed by the Taft-Hartley Act. Today, many locals are **union shops.** A new employee must join the union after a certain period of time, usually three months. There are also **agency shops.** In an agency shop, employees are not required to join the union, but they must pay union dues.

Supporters of union and agency shops argue that all employees in a bargaining unit should be required to pay union dues because they benefit from contracts the union negotiates. Opponents believe that a person should not be required against his or her will to join a union. Since 1947 a number of states have passed **right-to-work laws** that forbid union shops and closed shops. These laws protect the right of workers to continue working in a particular job without joining a union. The employee benefits negotiated by the union must be made available to the workers who do not join the union. The power of unions in states with right-to-work laws is less than in other states. At present, 20 states, mostly in the South and West, have right-to-work laws.

bargaining unit: all non-supervisory workers in a company eligible to belong to a union

Above the locals are the national unions. These are the individual craft or industrial unions that represent locals nationwide. Those unions which also have members in Canada or Mexico are often called

Figure 13-1: TIME LINE OF AMERICAN UNIONISM

1790s	Local groups of skilled workers in a particular craft join to fight division of labor and unfair hiring practices. To save money, employers are dividing skilled workers into teams to do only parts of jobs and hiring women and children at low wages to do some jobs. Most associations disband after demands are met.
1820s-1850s	Skilled workers such as carpenters and printers form citywide craft unions. Some local unions are able to form nationwide associations. Because of poor economic conditions in the nation, many unions disappear in the late 1830s, but reappear in the 1840s and 1850s as the economy improves. Blacks and women are not included in these craft unions.
1866	National Labor Union (NLU) becomes first nationwide federation of craft unions, but disbands in 1872 after it fails to improve conditions.
1869	National Colored Labor Union formed to avoid hostility of white members of NLU.
	Knights of Labor set up by group of Philadelphia clothing workers as an industrial union. Members include skilled and unskilled workers as well as farmers and merchants—black and white. Knights support an eight-hour workday, health and safety regulations, and child labor laws.
1877	Baltimore & Ohio Railroad Workers strike after wages are cut during economic depression. Federal troops break up strike after rails are torn up, stations burned, and freight cars smashed.
mid-1880s	Knights of Labor claims 700,000 members. Series of violent strikes result in decline in membership and end of group by early 1900s.
1886	American Federation of Labor (AFL) is formed to bring independent craft unions together into a national federation. Membership is limited to white male skilled workers. Haymarket Riots in Chicago begin as a protest against police action against strikers at a local factory. A bomb is thrown into a crowd and seven police are killed. Eight labor leaders are sentenced to death and four actually are hanged for the bombing although no evidence is found.
1892	Amalgamated Association of Iron, Steel and Tin Workers strike the Homestead plant of Carnegie Steel after management demands a wage cut and a 70-hour work week. Armed guards are called in and several strikers as well as guards are killed. The state militia breaks up the strike.
1894	Pullman factory workers and American Railway Unions strike the Pullman car company after a wage cut and a union leader is fired by management. The strike halts all rail traffic in and out of Chicago for two months and interrupts rail service in 27 states. Federal troops are sent in and 22 workers are killed.
early 1900s	AFL concentrates on improving wages and working conditions and claims over 2 million members by 1914 and over 4 million by 1920.
1911	Triangle Shirtwaist Factory fire claims 143 lives, mostly young women clothing workers. They were trapped on the top floors of a tenement factory that had no fire escapes.

Figure 13-1: TIME LINE OF AMERICAN UNIONISM *(continued)*

1920s	Opposition by business, unfavorable court rulings, and rising anti-labor and anti-immigration feelings cause decline in union membership.
1929	The Depression begins. Sympathy grows among the general public for concerns of organized labor.
1932	Congress passes Norris-LaGuardia Act, the first major pro-labor legislation. Act limits power of the courts to stop picketing and boycotts* and makes yellow-dog contracts illegal. This is the practice whereby employers require that employees pledge not to join a union.
1935	National Labor Relations Act (Wagner Act) guarantees labor's right to organize and bargain collectively.* Act sets up National Labor Relations Board (NLRB) to oversee the establishment and operation of unions.
1938	In an effort to organize unskilled workers in such assembly-line industries as automobile, steel, and chemicals some leaders of the AFL form the Congress of Industrial Organizations (CIO). CIO encourages membership of blacks and women.
1945-47	Wave of strikes to improve wages and working conditions follow end of World War II and contribute to growing anti-union feelings.
1947	Congress passes Labor-Management Act (Taft-Hartley Act) over strong objections of labor. Act outlaws certain strike tactics, permits states to pass laws making union shops* illegal, and allows the President to delay a strike if it will threaten the nation's health and safety.
1955	AFL and CIO unite into a single union, AFL-CIO.
1959	Congress passes Labor Management Reporting and Disclosure Act (Landrum-Griffin Act). Act increases government control over unions and guarantees union members certain rights, such as freedom of speech and control over union dues.
1962	President John Kennedy signs into law an order giving federal employees the right to organize into unions, but not the right to strike. Union membership among workers at all levels of government grows rapidly during the 1960s and 1970s.
mid-1960s-1970s	Union membership among blacks, women, Hispanics, and agricultural workers increases.
1981	President Ronald Reagan fires 11,400 federal air traffic controllers for striking illegally.
	AFL-CIO warns of growing anti-union feelings as economy worsens. As the economy weakens, some large unions such as the United Auto Workers negotiate contracts that give back some of their earlier gains.
	United Auto Workers rejoin AFL-CIO.
1982-1986	Some unions have to accept pay cuts and many did not receive wage increases.

*You will read more about this topic later in this chapter.

international unions. To help in negotiating a contract between a local and a particular company, plant, or group of businesses, the nationals make available lawyers, professional negotiators, and other staff members. In certain industries such as steel and mining, the national union negotiates the contract for the entire industry. Once it is accepted by the majority of union members, all the locals within the industry must work under that one contract. National unions also send in organizers to help employees with organizing campaigns to set up locals. Some of the largest unions are the International Brotherhood of Teamsters; United Automobile Workers (UAW); United Steelworkers of America (USW); and the American Federation of State, County and Municipal Employees.

At the federation level is the AFL-CIO, which is made up of national and international unions. Over 100 unions with about 16 million members are associated with the AFL-CIO. Representing its member unions, the AFL-CIO lobbies for pro-labor legislation at the state and federal level. It also offers training and advice to the leadership of member unions and promotes the causes of organized labor to the public.

lobby: use influence to try to get a bill passed

REVIEWING ECONOMIC PRINCIPLES

1. Define the following economic terms: **a.** labor union, **b.** craft union, **c.** industrial union, **d.** local union, **e.** closed shops, **f.** union shops, **g.** agency shops, **h.** right-to-work laws.
2. **a.** Why did labor unions appeal to workers in the 19th century? **b.** What did business do to fight unionism? **c.** Why do you think business was opposed to unions? You have to infer the answer.
3. **a.** What was the split in organized labor for much of its history? **b.** How was this split finally ended? **c.** Why?
4. Read the time line and list: **a.** four incidents involving unions that would have turned public opinion against organized labor. **b.** three laws that have helped the cause of labor.
5. **Critical Thinking: Interpreting Information.** Draw a diagram showing the structure of union organization in the United States.

 **4 | COLLECTIVE BARGAINING**

Ask yourself as you read:
• What is collective bargaining?
• What methods have unions used to achieve their goals?

Collective bargaining is the process by which unions and employers negotiate the conditions of employment. At the center of the collective bargaining process is compromise. The company wants to keep wages and benefits low to hold its labor costs down and remain com-

Table 13-1: UNION CONTRACT ISSUES

Issue	Description
Wages	Most contracts provide for wage increases of a certain percentage for each worker during each year of the contract. Some contracts also provide for an additional increase each year if the general level of prices in the economy rises beyond a certain amount. This provision is known as a **cost-of-living adjustment** (COLA).
Working hours	The contract establishes the number of hours a day that employees must work. Employees who work longer hours must usually be paid extra wages, called overtime pay.
Fringe benefits	Fringe benefits are payments other than wages made to employees. These can include health and life insurance, a retirement plan, and time off for vacations and holidays.
Working conditions	Contracts often provide for a joint union and management committee to ensure that safe and pleasant working conditions exist. Working conditions are a particularly important issue to employees in industries that deal with poisonous substances or dangerous machinery.
Job security	At issue under job security is protection against layoffs because of technological change or a slowdown in business. Most contracts do not forbid layoffs, but rather set up rules that the employer must follow in laying off workers. For example, those with the least seniority—amount of time spent with the company—are usually laid off first.
Grievance procedures	Grievance procedures are a set of formal rules used to resolve a dispute between union members and management. A grievance, or complaint, may be filed if one side feels that the other is not living up to the terms of the contract. If the union and the company cannot settle the grievance, a third party will often be asked to judge the matter objectively.

petitive in the market. The union wants to increase wages and benefits for its members as much as possible. Obviously, both sides must be prepared to give and take a little.

NEGOTIATIONS

Negotiations take place when labor and management sit down on either side of a table to discuss in detail a wide range of contract issues. Table 13-1 lists a number of the most important issues that labor and management may negotiate. In most cases negotiations are friendly and result in an agreement that satisfies all parties. In the case of a deadlock, however, the two sides may agree to try mediation. **Mediation** (mee-dee-AY-shuhn) occurs when a neutral, or disinterested, person steps in and tries to get both sides to reach an agreement. The mediator suggests solutions and works to keep the two sides talking with each other.

neutral (NOO-truhl): disinterested

The federal government, through the Federal Mediation and Conciliation Service (FMCS), provides a mediator free of charge upon request of either union or management. In a typical year, FMCS mediators were involved in about 20,000 negotiations. Recently, FMCS helped settle contracts involving petroleum workers, nurses, and television and film directors. There are also a number of state and private mediators. A private mediator helped players and owners reach an agreement in the National Football League strike in 1982.

If mediation fails, the negotiation process may go one step further to arbitration. In **arbitration** (ahr-buh-TRAY-shuhn), the two sides submit the issues they cannot agree on to a third party for a final decision. Both sides agree in advance to accept the arbitrator's decision, though one or both sides may not be completely happy with the outcome. The FMCS often helps in these cases by providing labor and management with a list of private arbitrators in their area.

STRIKES

Most contracts are settled at the bargaining table. Sometimes, though, the negotiation breaks down and a strike results. A **strike** is a deliberate work stoppage by workers to force an employer to give in to their demands. Workers on strike usually walk up and down in front of the company carrying picket signs that state their disagreement with the company. **Picketing** is meant to discourage all actual or potential workers from crossing the picket line to work for the employer. It is also aimed at embarrassing the company and building support among the public for the strike. Often, members of other unions, such as truck drivers, will not cross a picket line. This further handicaps the business being struck.

Striking unions may also use a boycott to exert or create economic pressure. In a **boycott,** unions urge the public not to purchase the goods or services produced by the company. Unions may also ask local or national politicians to push management for a settlement or to support the union's demands publicly. A strike is settled when management and labor eventually return to the negotiating table and work out an agreement acceptable to both sides. Strikes can, however, drag on for months and even years. After a long period of time, striking union members sometimes become discouraged. Either individually or as a group, they may decide to go back to work without gaining what they wanted.

MANAGEMENT RESPONSE TO STRIKES

When faced with a strike, management has several methods of its own that it can use against strikers. One is the **lockout.** This occurs when management closes the doors to a business and prevents workers from returning until they agree to the contract. Another tactic, or plan of action, is to bring in strikebreakers, called scabs by strikers. These are individuals willing to cross a picket line to work for the terms offered by the company.

Union members sometimes go on strike when their union and management cannot agree on a work contract. What trade-offs are involved when workers strike?

tactic (TAK-tic): plan of action

330

Case Study

BLUE-COLLAR STAR: BRUCE SPRINGSTEEN

In the 1984 Presidential election, both Democrats and Republicans tried to associate themselves with rock and roll star Bruce Springsteen. Lee Iacocca, it is rumored, offered $12 million for the use of the song "Born in the USA" for a Chrysler commercial. In 1985, some 236,000 tickets for four Springsteen concerts in New Jersey were sold in less than a day. In November 1986, lines formed at record stores across the United States as people waited to purchase for more than $30 the just released collection of Springsteen's biggest hits.

Even in the rock-and-roll business the success of Bruce Springsteen is phenomenal. Yet he is a simple man who expresses in his songs deep affection for home and family. Like Bob Dylan before him, Bruce Springsteen seems to address, in warm, direct songs ideas that many Americans are thinking about. In the words to his music set mainly in blue-collar towns, Springsteen suggests that the working class is uncertain and even disillusioned about what's happening to the nation and its economy. Although his songs appeal to blue-collar workers' concerns and sometimes seem filled with powerful images of despair, there is always hope and compassion in his music.

Bruce Springsteen has become the champion of blue-collar, working class Americans, even though his concerts are attended by everyone from preteens and teenagers, to young business-people and blue-collar workers. But it is the blue-collar workers who seem to find the greatest "truth" and perhaps the greatest comfort in his songs. "The River" tells the story of a young working-class man trapped in a bad marriage. "Johnny 99" tells of a laid-off auto worker who turns to crime due to overwhelming financial prob-

lems. The words to "My Hometown" somberly tell of the slow death of a town and workers losing jobs as the town's major employer, a textile plant, closes. Springsteen's lyrics tell a story painfully familiar to jobless workers, and the music which Springsteen uses to tell the story captures deep emotions. The result is that this rock-and-roll star has become a cult figure to many blue-collar Americans.

Springsteen has achieved his great success not only because of his songs but because of his personality and generosity. He is concerned and compassionate, and during his concerts he urges people to support food banks and groups that help the homeless. He also helps publicize the plight of small farmers, Vietnam veterans, and the unemployed. And he has donated significant sums of money to charity and community groups. To his audiences, he is basically a decent, caring person—as well as a star rock musician.

Springsteen believes that his music means something—that properly used, rock and roll can heal or at least ease the pain of the hard times. With the huge following he has attracted, it may well be that he is right.

1. What are some reasons that make Bruce Springsteen a popular blue-collar "hero"?
2. Why have blue-collar workers needed a hero in recent times?

Management sometimes requests a court injunction to limit picketing or to prevent a strike from continuing or even occurring. An **injunction** is a legal order of a court preventing some activity. Under the Taft-Hartley Act of 1947, the President of the United States can obtain a court order to delay or halt a strike for up to 80 days if the strike will endanger the nation's safety or health. During this cooling-off period, the two sides must try to reach a settlement.

REVIEWING ECONOMIC PRINCIPLES

1. **a.** What are the six major issues that are usually considered in collective bargaining? **b.** Choose one and explain it.
2. During a strike, what is the purpose of: **a.** picketing? **b.** a boycott?
3. What three methods might management use against a strike?
4. **Critical Thinking: Comparing and Contrasting.** In a paragraph compare and contrast mediation and arbitration.

5 | THE FUTURE OF UNIONS

Ask yourself as you read:
- What goals has organized labor realized?
- What problems face labor unions today?

The establishment of the AFL in 1886 is considered the beginning of the modern union era. Since that time, unions have been successful in achieving their goals. Supporters of organized labor list among union accomplishments better wages and working conditions for all employees—union and nonunion. They point out that many workers now enjoy a sense of belonging and self-respect that goes along with joining together to maintain some control over their jobs and lives. Union sup-

It is at the local level that most union members are involved. They elect union officers and vote on union contracts, as these workers are doing.

porters also note that the collective bargaining process has brought more order and fairness to the workplace. It has made clear the rights and responsibilities of both management and labor.

During this 100 years, unions have changed from small groups of workers with no real power to large, powerful institutions that play a major role in American political life. Along with this success, however, have come problems. Because working conditions have improved so dramatically over the years, nonunion workers often see little to gain from joining a union. Therefore, many union members no longer feel the same commitment to organized labor that earlier union members did.

The labor movement also has its critics. Some opponents charge that unions have grown so large and bureaucratic that they are out of touch with their members' needs. Others claim that increased wages to union members are passed on to consumers in the form of higher prices. Employers often argue that union rules decrease productivity. They point to rules that slow the introduction of new technology or require more employees than necessary to do a job, such as keeping five or six workers on to run a new automated printing press that requires only two operators. In addition, corruption and misuse of union dues among some labor leaders have damaged the reputation of organized labor with the public.

bureaucratic (byoor-uh-KRAT-ik): operating through rigid routine, complicated

Despite its past successes, the labor movement today faces many problems. The percentage of union members among the civilian labor force reached a high of about 26 percent in the mid-1950s and has been declining since. Today the more than 21 million union members in the United States represent only about 18 percent of the civilian labor force. The chart on page 336 shows the declining union membership.

One reason for this decline is the changing nature of the economy. More jobs are opening in the white-collar and service sectors, while because of automation blue-collar jobs are decreasing. Service firms typically employ small numbers of employees. For this reason, it is difficult and expensive for unions to organize workers. In addition, many service workers and white-collar employees see themselves as individuals working on their own. They often do not identify with large groups of their fellow employees in the same way as an assembly-line worker might. As you read in Chapter 11, technology is changing the workplace. With technology comes the potential loss of manufacturing jobs. This may result in a further decline in union membership and a weakening of the role of unions in the future unless unions find ways to meet these challenges.

REVIEWING ECONOMIC PRINCIPLES

1. What are three factors that supporters list in favor of unions?
2. What are three criticisms that opponents of unions have?
3. **Critical Thinking: Making Predictions.** What are two factors that may cause a decline in union membership in the future?

SUMMARY OF IMPORTANT PRINCIPLES

1
- Work can be divided into the following four categories: farm; blue-collar such as crafts, manufacturing, and nonfarm labor; white-collar such as office, sales, and professional; service, with services provided directly to individuals. Work can also be divided into four categories depending on the education and/or training needed: unskilled workers have no special training or education; semiskilled workers have limited training in job-related skills and can perform specific routine tasks, often using modern technology; skilled workers have learned a trade or craft; professional workers have a college degree and usually additional education or training.

2
- In the labor market, suppliers are the workers who offer their services, while the demand comes from employers who need workers. Three factors underlie how supply and demand affect prices, or in this case, wages: skill, type of job, and location. Certain restrictions in the labor market, such as minimum wage laws and union contracts, also influence wages.

3
- Working conditions in the 19th century were very different from those of today. Hours were long; workplaces were often unsanitary and unsafe. Unemployment insurance, health-care benefits, sick leave, and paid vacations and holidays did not exist. Unions appealed to working people because they seemed to offer a way to force employers to improve working conditions, shorten the workday, and end child labor. Unionism, however, met strong resistance for much of the 19th century and early 20th century. Federal laws to regulate labor-management relations were not passed until the 1930s.
- Organized labor operates at three levels: the local union, the national or international union, and the federation. All locals belong to some national or international union. Most, but not all, national or international unions belong to a federation, which is the AFL-CIO. There are other independent unions as well.
- Career decision depends on interest and abilities, education and/or training, choice of location, and the amount of time a person chooses to spend in the workplace.

4
- The major issues in collective bargaining usually are wages, working hours, fringe benefits, working conditions, job security, and grievance procedures.

5
- Since the late 19th century, unions have been so successful in achieving their goals that nonunion workers often see little to gain from joining a union. Today the more than 21 million union members in the United States represent only about 18 percent of the civilian labor force. One reason for this decline is the changing nature of the economy. More jobs are opening in the white-collar and service sectors, while blue-collar jobs are decreasing. With technology comes the potential loss of manufacturing jobs. This will result in a further decline in union membership and a weakening of the role of unions.

THE JOB MARKET: BECOMING AN APPRENTICE

Dot Kenneck has helped her parents in their business from the time she was a teenager. The Kennecks own and operate a plumbing business. In the beginning, Dot did not think about the work as a job. She was just helping her parents. Eventually, she began to like the work.

At the end of her senior year in high school, Dot faces a problem. Though she wants to go to college and her parents want her to go, they cannot afford it. Dot decides she has two alternatives. She can get a part-time job and work her way through college. Or she can work for a year or two and save enough to be able to attend college full time. Dot decides she would rather work for a couple of years and then go to college full time.

Her parents do not have a full-time job available in their business. However, a friend of theirs, Sam DeLucia, has an opening—for a plumber's apprentice. He explains that because Dot is going to become a paid, full-time employee of the plumbing company, she will have to join the plumber's local. As an apprentice, at first she will be allowed to do only certain jobs such as carrying tools and supplies and cleaning up at a job. Dot will also be paid an apprentice's wages. This is somewhat less an hour than what a journeyman plumber receives. A journeyman plumber is one who has completed training as an apprentice and is now qualified to do all types of plumbing jobs. Dot is not happy with this news. She has been performing many different kinds of jobs for three years under her family's supervision.

After doing some research, Dot finds that Mr. DeLucia is correct. She will have to join the plumbers' union and work as an apprentice for one year. Dot does not think this is fair. But the union agent explained that this is one way unions have of ensuring workers of high quality.

1. What are some disadvantages of union membership for Dot?
2. What are some benefits Dot might receive as a union member?

Readings in Economics

THE ORIGINS OF THE "PINK COLLAR" WORKER

Skill: Interpreting Information

 In the late 1980s much attention has been focused on discrimination against women in the work force. The following reading gives some insight into why and how such discrimination began.

As machines and assembly-line production reduced the need for skilled workers, employers cut wage costs by hiring more women and children. Between 1880 and 1900, the numbers of employed women grew from 2.6 million to 8.6 million, and their employment patterns underwent major changes. First, the proportion of working women engaged in domestic and personal service jobs (maids, cooks, laundresses), traditionally the most common form of female employment, dropped dramatically as jobs opened in other economic sectors. Some new jobs were in manufacturing—usually menial positions in textile mills and food-processing plants that paid women as little as $1.56 a week for seventy hours of labor. But though the number of female factory hands tripled, the proportion of women workers in these jobs remained about the same.

Second and more important, a major shift was occurring that set the trend among female workers for much of the twentieth century. The numbers and percentages of women in clerical jobs—clerks, typists, bookkeepers, salespersons—skyrocketed. These workers served the new needs of retail marketing and corporate record-keeping. From the late nineteenth century onward, the invention of numerous machines, such as the typewriter, cash register, adding machine, and others, greatly simplified office and sales work. Firms could now increase efficiency by hiring more clerks to operate machines and to replace more expensive managers. . . .

By 1920 nearly half of all clerical workers were women; only 4 percent had been women in 1880. Analysts often explain the transformation of the clerical sector by asserting that women would work for lower wages than men would and that women's nimble fingers and toleration of boring work suited them for office and sales-floor labor.

A more likely explanation, however, is that machines reduced the skills needed for clerical jobs, and companies were willing to hire large numbers of women streaming into the labor market who needed little training for these jobs. . . .

1. Over the past 100 years, what kind of jobs have generally been available to women?
2. During the 20th century, what major shift took place in the kinds of jobs women performed?

From *A People and a Nation: A History of the United States* by Mary Beth Norton. Copyright © 1986 by Mary Beth Norton. Reprinted by permission of Houghton Mifflin Co.

THE REWARDS OF LABOR

Skill: Applying Information

 One of the factors that affects the wage a worker receives is the kind of job he or she does. Adam Smith discusses wages in the 18th century from this point of view in this reading.

The wages of labor vary with the ease or hardship, the cleanliness or dirtiness, the honorableness or dishonorableness of the employment. Thus in most places, take the year round, a journeyman tailor earns less than a journeyman weaver. His work is much easier. A journeyman weaver earns less than a journeyman smith. His work is not always easier, but it is much cleanlier. A journeyman blacksmith, though an artificer [skilled craftworker], seldom earns so much in twelve hours as a collier [coal miner], who is only a laborer, does in eight. His work is not quite so dirty, is less dangerous, and is carried on in daylight, and above ground. Honor makes a great part of the reward of all honorable professions. In point of pecuniary [financial] gain, all things considered, they are generally under-recompensed, as I shall endeavor to show by and by. Disgrace has the contrary effect. The trade of a butcher is a brutal and an odious business; but it is in most places more profitable than the greater part of common trades. The most detestable of all employments, that of public executioner, is, in proportion to the quantity of work done, better paid than any common trade whatever.

Hunting and fishing, the most important employments of mankind in the rude state of society, become in its advanced state their most agreeable amusements, and they pursue for pleasure what they once followed from necessity. In the advanced state of society, therefore, they are all very poor people who follow as a trade what other people pursue as a pastime. . . .

Disagreeableness and disgrace affect the profits of stock in the same manner as the wages of labor. The keeper of an inn or tavern, who is never master of his own house, and who is exposed to the brutality of every drunkard, exercises neither a very agreeable nor a very creditable business. But there is scarce any common trade in which a small stock yields so great a profit.

1. According to Adam Smith, what factors determined wages in the 18th century?
2. Applying this logic, what can you predict about wages today for such occupations as nuclear waste-disposal workers, trash collectors, high-rise construction workers, and so on?

Adam Smith, *The Wealth of Nations*, pp. 100, 101.

UNIONS PUSH FOR A SHORTER DAY
Skill: Interpreting Information

Before the emergence of labor unions, American workers often had poor working conditions and long working days. This reading by Ida Tarbell, a leading muckraker known particularly for her investigation of the Standard Oil Company in 1904, describes efforts of the American Federation of Labor, led by Samuel Gompers, to reduce the working day to eight hours.

In 1884 the Federation called upon its affiliated bodies to direct their energies toward the establishment of an eight-hour day by May 1, 1886. The long day was one of the oldest grievances of American labor. The first call for eight hours seems to have been in Maine where a slogan, "Eight hours for work, eight hours for sleep, and eight hours for God and the brethren," was sounded as early as 1844; but it had come to

Picket lines like the one shown here are used by strikers to keep the public aware of their demands.

nothing. . . . After the Civil War the eight-hour demand was included in most labor programs, and Eight Hour Leagues sprang up in various states to promote the cause. Though some states took favorable action, the laws always left loopholes by which employers could escape their obligations. Nevertheless, conditions in the course of half a century had in some respects improved. Thus, in 1830, four out of five wage-earners had worked more than ten hours a day; in 1880 only about one in four. The eight-hour day, however, was virtually nonexistent.

The Federation had allowed two years in which to educate the public as to the need of the shorter day. Reluctant employers it expected to whip into line through the strike. Its most important ally should have been the Knights of Labor, but after considerable hesitation Powderly [leader of the Knights] refused to cooperate. . . . He saw more clearly than Gompers that most industries at that day were too badly managed to stand a change to shorter hours. Gompers himself wrote thirty-nine years later that in 1886 there were "hardly twelve industries in the United States sufficiently organized to establish an eight-hour day," but that he considered the campaign valuable as an "educational influence."

The approach to employers was carefully planned, conferences were sought, and many employers promised to cooperate. While most of them were doubtless actuated by fear of the consequences of refusal, others, more enlightened, believed that a shorter day would make the workers more productive. Labor was so convinced of this that it had a slogan.

> Whether you work by the hour or work by the day,
> Decreasing the hour increases the pay.

1. Why were most businesses in the late 1800s not able to maintain production with a labor force working only eight hours a day?
2. Why did some employers cooperate with the union in establishing an eight-hour day?

Ida M. Tarbell, *The Nationalizing of Business*, Vol. IX of *A History of American Life.* Ed. by Arthur M. Schlesinger and Dixon Ryan Fox. New York: Macmillan, 1936. pp. 157, 158.

GM AND UAW—A WORKING PARTNERSHIP

Skill: Interpreting Information

 **Most industries try to work with unions peacefully and productively. In a 1984 speech, Roger B. Smith, chairman of General Motors Corporation, discusses GM's relationship with the United Auto Workers (UAW).**

GM and the UAW went into the labor talks last July sharing at least one common thought, and that was this: We knew that the central challenge today for business and labor is managing change. With the growth of the world market, the technical revolution confronting us, and the changing dynamics of the workplace, we knew that we must change or die. There's just no question about that—especially when a company is faced, as we are, with aggressive global competitors who pay significantly lower labor rates.

We knew that corporations like GM—however successful they are today—must be different in the future if they are to survive. The adage, "if it ain't broke, don't fix it," just doesn't apply. The solutions to yesterday's problems are no longer relevant—not when today's problems are different than yesterday's, and tomorrow's will be vastly so.

So change was inevitable. The central question was how best to manage change to benefit both the business and our employees.

The answer provided in our 1984 agreement was that we would not try to find immediate solutions to every problem; rather we would establish a structure to allow us to manage future changes together. We produced a win-win situation for both parties. The framework we built would allow us to leave the negotiating table and get back to the business of making cars. But at the same time it would provide further points of contact between management and the union so we would become better partners in the business.

In fact, if I were to choose one word to characterize this GM-UAW contract it would be "partnership." This document—in so many of its provisions and paragraphs—emphasizes that the company, the union, and our employees are partners in the business. When the business is successful, our employees stand to gain. Our success is their success. . . .

Union-management partnership is a new concept for most American businesses. And we have to change the way both managers and employees see their roles and their relationship, if we are to succeed.

It's a big job. But with this new contract at General Motors, we feel we have . . . the drive, dedication, and determination to carry it off. After all, what we're building is not just a labor contract or a working relationship. We're building a future—a better future for everyone.

1. What changes have occurred in the automobile industry that have led to cooperation between management and labor?
2. What do you think Smith means when he refers to the "changing dynamics of the workplace"?

Roger B. Smith, "A Working Partnership for Managing Change." From a speech delivered Oct. 31, 1984, Milwaukee. *Vital Speeches of the Day,* Dec. 15, 1984, Vol. LI, No. 5., pp. 146–148.

A "LABOR" PROBLEM OR A NATIONAL ONE?
Skill: Supporting Evidence

5

AFL-CIO president Lane Kirkland sees the decrease in the number of industrial workers in the United States as a serious national problem. In this speech delivered to his union's convention in October 1985, he discusses this problem and its effects on the union.

Since 1955, not counting growth by merger, 15 of our unions have at least doubled their membership, growing from a combined total of 1½ million in 1955 to 4.8 million in 1985. Six unions have more than tripled their size, from a total of 435,000 in 1955 to over 2½ million in 1985. Two unions have multiplied their membership by ten times or more, from a total of 140,000 in 1955 to 1,480,000 in 1985.

We have more than 11 times as many teachers, 10 times as many state, county, and municipal workers, 4 times as many pilots, 3½ times as many service employees, 3 times as many postal workers, fire fighters and communications workers as we did in 1955.

But we have fewer steelworkers, fewer garment and textile workers, fewer railroad workers, and, alas, many fewer deep sea sailors than we did then.

We have fewer of them because there are fewer of them—not because trade unionism has lost its appeal, nor its necessity, nor because of any delinquency of leadership. I can testify from long and close experience that the leadership of the trade unions in these sectors today is every bit as able, every bit as vigorous, every bit as dedicated, and every bit as creative as in 1955.

What has happened to these unions is a measure of what has happened to America. Let those who revel in their distress consider that the consequences will not be confined to their members only, but will extend across society to the shopkeeper, the landlord and mortgage banker, the farmer and ultimately, I trust, to the most hidebound politician. This is not just an AFL-CIO problem or a "labor" problem. It is a profound national

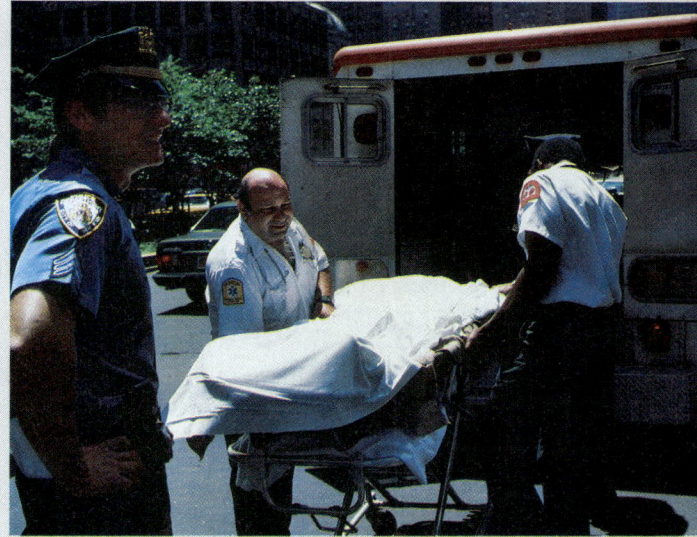

As the number of blue-collar workers declines, unions of hospital employees and other service workers grow in size.

problem and must be addressed as such.

Thirty years ago, a third of the workforce was directly engaged in manufacturing; today only a fifth are. Twelve percent were in service jobs; today, that's up to 22 percent.

In 1955, there were 3,324 American flag merchant ships afloat; now there are but 488.

We fully understand that some degree of that trend is irreversible. The ever-accelerating pace of technological change assures us of that.

But much of it is not benign progress, much of it is deeply damaging to the strength and promise of American society and much of it is approaching an ominous point of no return.

1. How can you explain the decreasing membership in labor unions since 1955 when Kirkland's statistics in the first two paragraphs of the reading indicate a growth in union membership?

2. What evidence is there that the United States is shifting from a manufacturing economy to a service economy?

Lane Kirkland, "Meeting the Challenge of the Future." From a speech delivered October 28, 1985, Anaheim, California. *Vital Speeches of the Day*, Vol, LII, No. 5., Dec. 15, 1985, pp. 133, 134.

PRACTICING YOUR THINKING SKILLS: PREDICTING ALTERNATIVE FUTURES

Economists, market researchers, and financial planners all depend on their ability to predict alternative futures. That is, they have to be able to make predictions about possible outcomes in the future based on events from the past and present.

First, you would try to identify the trends in your field of interest. You would take into account past and present trends, their duration, and the nature of the most recent changes in the field. You might also ask yourself whether any changes that you find were the result of a temporary situation, or whether they were due to a fundamental shift such as a new technological breakthrough. Suppose, for example, that very few secretaries were hired last year. Was it because business was slow or was it because new roboticized office machinery made secretaries obsolete? Could there be other causes? Economic changes also can be caused by political events, such as treaties and changes in long-standing practices. Look for as many causes as you can. It is important to understand what is happening in the present to predict the future.

In predicting alternative futures, you would try to consider all the possible solutions to a problem. You would not settle on the most obvious one. To do this, you have to learn to be flexible in your thinking. Developing the ability to be flexible will help you to prepare for the unexpected events and changes that may happen in your life.

Once you have made some predictions for alternative futures, read what leading economists, newspaper magazine writers, and other commentators are saying about your field of interest. Consider surveys and use economic models whenever you can.

Activity: Based on the table in Learning Economic Skills, what kind of job future would you have if you became a: **a.** carpenter? **b.** medical secretary? **c.** secondary teacher?

VOCABULARY REVIEW

Write the letter of the definition in Column B correctly defines each term in Column A.

Column A	Column B
1. unskilled workers	a. employees are not required to join a union but must pay union dues
2. agency shop	
3. arbitration	b. refusal to purchase the goods and services of a company
4. injunction	
5. right-to-work law	c. court order preventing some activity, often a strike
6. closed shop	
7. boycott	d. no special training in job-related skills
	e. undecided issues between labor and management are given to a third party for a final decision
	f. company in which only union members can be hired
	g. forbids contracts that require employees to join a union

PRACTICING YOUR ECONOMIC SKILLS

1. **Analyzing a Graph.** According to the graph on page 341: **a.** when did union membership as a percentage of the labor force begin its first decline? **b.** about when did union membership begin to grow again?
2. **Analyzing Information.** Has the actual number of union members declined in the last 20 years? Explain.
3. **Comparing Graphs.** Compare the information on the graph on page 341 with the information given in Figure 13-1. About how many people in the labor force today are union members?

Union Membership as a Percentage of Civilian Labor Force, 1910-1990

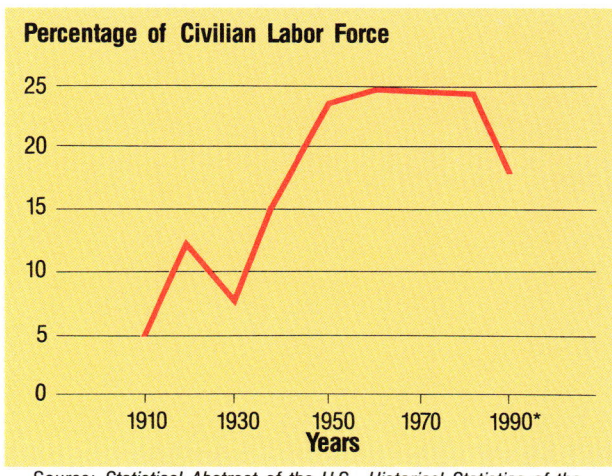

Percentage of Civilian Labor Force

Years

Source: *Statistical Abstract of the U.S., Historical Statistics of the U.S.*, Bureau of the Census.   *Estimate

DISCUSSING ECONOMIC QUESTIONS

1. Do you agree or disagree with arguments in favor of union and agency shops?
2. According to the table "Percentage Growth of Selected Occupations From 1984 to 1995," the number of college and university teachers needed will decline, but the number of kindergarten and elementary teachers needed will increase. Why do you think this will happen? Why do you think computer programming jobs will increase while farm jobs will decrease? Consider the influence of automation on the types of jobs available and the amount of productivity per worker.

APPLYING CRITICAL THINKING SKILLS

1. **Writing a Research Report.** Research and write a brief report about either one of the strikes listed on the time line or one of the laws.
2. **Writing a Research Report.** Some of the first strikes were organized in Lowell, Massachu-
setts, by women textile workers. Research and write a short report on the conditions that led to the Lowell Female Labor Reform Association.
3. **Gathering Information.** Consult the guidance counselor in your school to find out what kinds of tests are available for people who wish to find out about their aptitudes, special skills, and abilities. Share your findings with the class.

READINGS

Carrell, Michael R., and Christina Heavrin. *Collective Bargaining and Labor Relations*: Columbus, Ohio: Charles E. Merrill, 1985.

Friedman, Milton, and Friedman, Rose. *Free to Choose: A Personal Statement*. New York: Harcourt Brace Jovanovich, 1981.

Green, James R. *The World of the Worker, Labor in Twentieth Century America*. New York: Hill & Wang, 1980.

Rima, Ingrid. *Labor Markets, Wages, and Employment*. New York: W.W. Norton, 1980.

WILL TECHNOLOGY CAUSE WIDESPREAD UNEMPLOYMENT

After you have studied this Issue, you will be able to describe possible alternatives to technological unemployment.

technological unemployment

Mechanization has been a very necessary factor in the growth of the United States. For example, the invention of the mechanical reaper in 1834 helped farmers increase the productivity of their land. Before that time, American farmers had used sickles—curved metal blades—to harvest grain as had farmers for thousands of years.

The mechanical reaper along with other new machinery, such as the steel plow, opened the Midwest to farming. The increased production of food made it possible to feed more Americans and to export more agricultural products. To carry these raw materials, railroads were built. These new railroads also carried settlers to the Midwest, many of whom were immigrants attracted by the idea of owning their own land. New businesses grew up to sell goods to the settlers. As a result of the invention of a few farm machines, the entire nation was greatly changed.

TECHNOLOGY AND THE MODERN WORKPLACE

Mechanization and its more sophisticated form—automation—continue to bring changes to the American workplace. An example is the use of computerized robots to replace human workers on the assembly line. Robots are used to perform dangerous jobs such as coating parts with hazardous chemicals, thereby sparing human workers certain risks. Robots can also perform repetitive tasks more efficiently than humans and with less error. The use of robots ensures that all the products coming off an assembly line will be of the same quality.

Today computers play a large role in changing the workplace. As you read in Chapter 11, computers program the robots that work on assembly lines and run operations in oil refineries and steel mills. Computers send interoffice messages as well as information between cities. In time, most business correspondence will be sent by electronic mail. Wherever large amounts of data must be handled rapidly, computers can be used.

TECHNOLOGICAL UNEMPLOYMENT

Of course, when a robot takes the place of an assembly-line worker or electronic mail replaces the mail-room clerk, people lose their jobs. This is often called **technological unemployment,** unemployment resulting from the increased use of labor-saving machines. For example, government economists predict that by the year 2000 computer technology could eliminate 5 million jobs or 18 percent of the work force in the manufacturing sector.

Technological unemployment is not new. The looms invented during the industrial revolution displaced many craftworkers. Handweavers, for example, lost the market for their skills. In frustration, they sometimes wrecked and burned the new looms. At the same time, the new textile mills cre-

American agriculture, using such machines as the rice harvester, above left, the hay raker, above, and the wheat harvester, left, is the most highly mechanized in the world.

ated a demand for unskilled workers. Often these were women and children who were paid less than the skilled workers that they replaced.

Some economists believe that technological unemployment can be relieved by shortening the work week. Employees would receive less in wages per week because they would be working fewer hours. However, employers would hire more workers so their businesses could produce as much as they did with a 40-hour work week.

Other economists believe the federal government should either help industry to finance new jobs or should create jobs directly through public-works projects. Often, however, these government jobs are short-term jobs like road repair and do

not prepare workers for better opportunities in the future. Still a third group of economists believes that displaced workers will be able to find new jobs in the changing workplace.

RETRAINING FOR NEW OPPORTUNITIES

The automation of an existing job frequently creates new job categories. Obviously, people are needed to design and build computers and other machines. People are also needed to operate and maintain them. Beginning in the late 1960s, the increasing dependence on computers created a great demand for computer programmers. Similarly, the increase in types of office equipment such as photocopiers, word processors, and computer workstations that are now used in offices has created a demand for office-equipment repairers.

Computer programming and machine repair are two examples of service occupations. The number of jobs in this category has grown steadily since the 1940s. In fact, between 1969 and 1976, 90 percent of all new jobs were in service occupations. This trend has continued.

One thing service jobs have in common is that they require training. The demand for unskilled labor is falling sharply. More and more, economists are predicting that retraining will be needed to provide workers with future jobs. In many cases, workers who are laid off are able to retrain to learn new skills or to adapt old skills that will make them attractive to potential employers.

However, this brings up an important question: Who should pay for retraining—the individual in need of retraining, private industry in need of skilled workers, or the federal government? People answer this question based on their point of view about economic freedom and the nation's goals.

Discussing Economic Questions

1. How will the growth of service occupations affect the educational level of the average American worker?
2. Who do you think should pay for retraining? Why?
3. Which national goals are in agreement with your answer to number 2? With which goals does your viewpoint conflict?

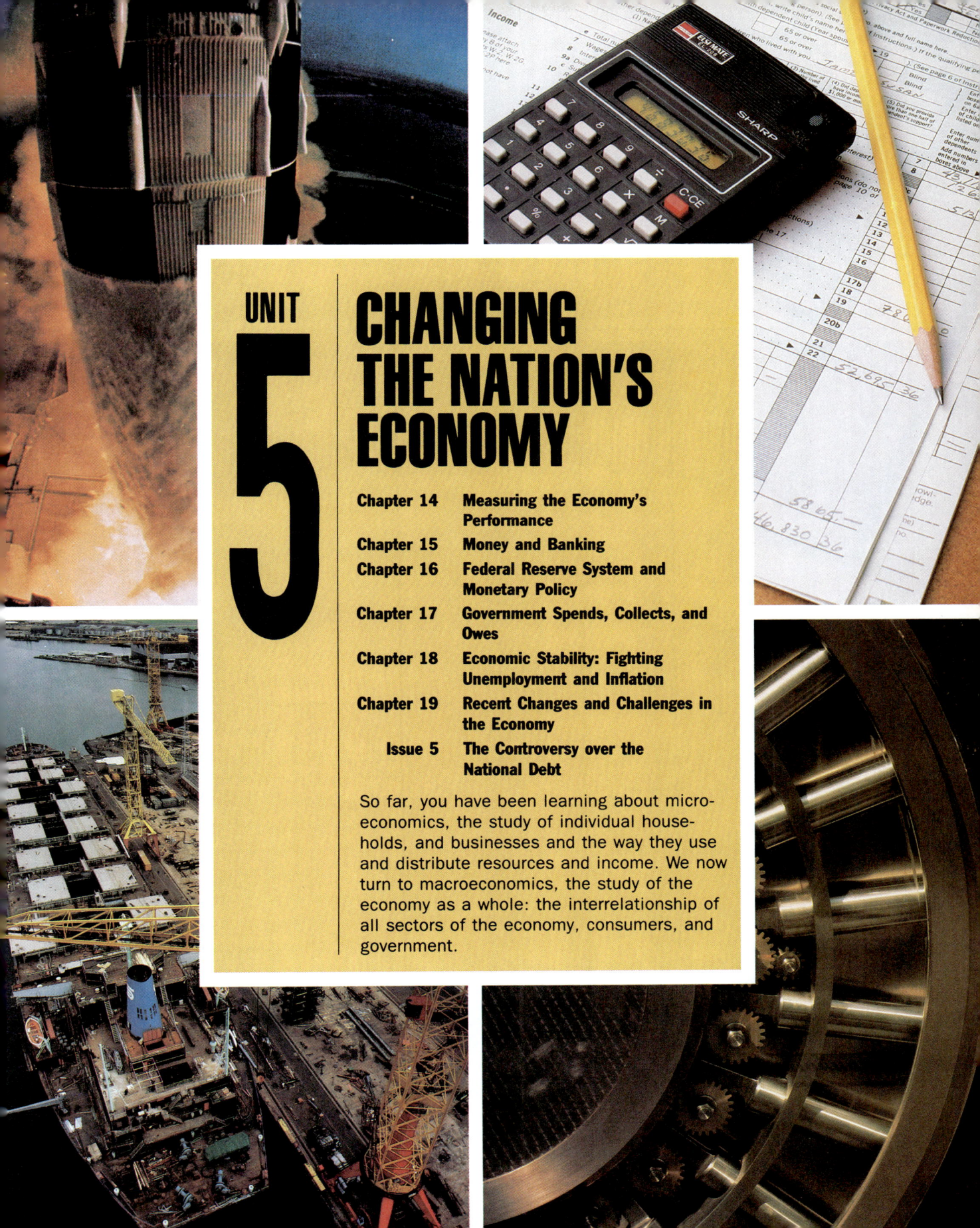

UNIT 5

CHANGING THE NATION'S ECONOMY

So far, you have been learning about microeconomics, the study of individual households, and businesses and the way they use and distribute resources and income. We now turn to macroeconomics, the study of the economy as a whole: the interrelationship of all sectors of the economy, consumers, and government.

CHAPTER 14

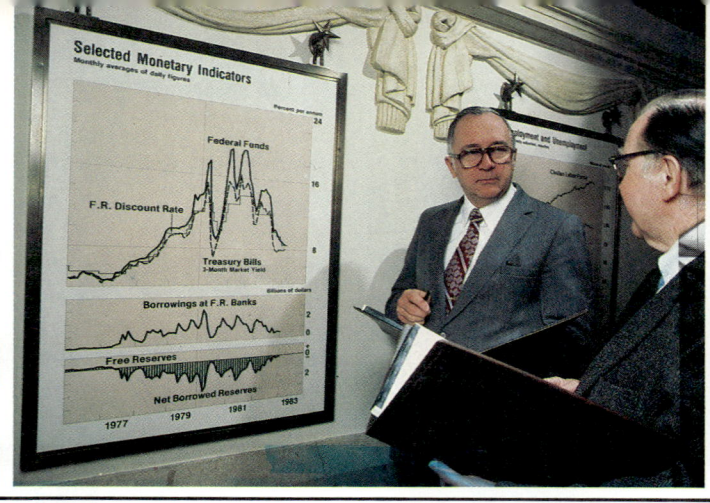

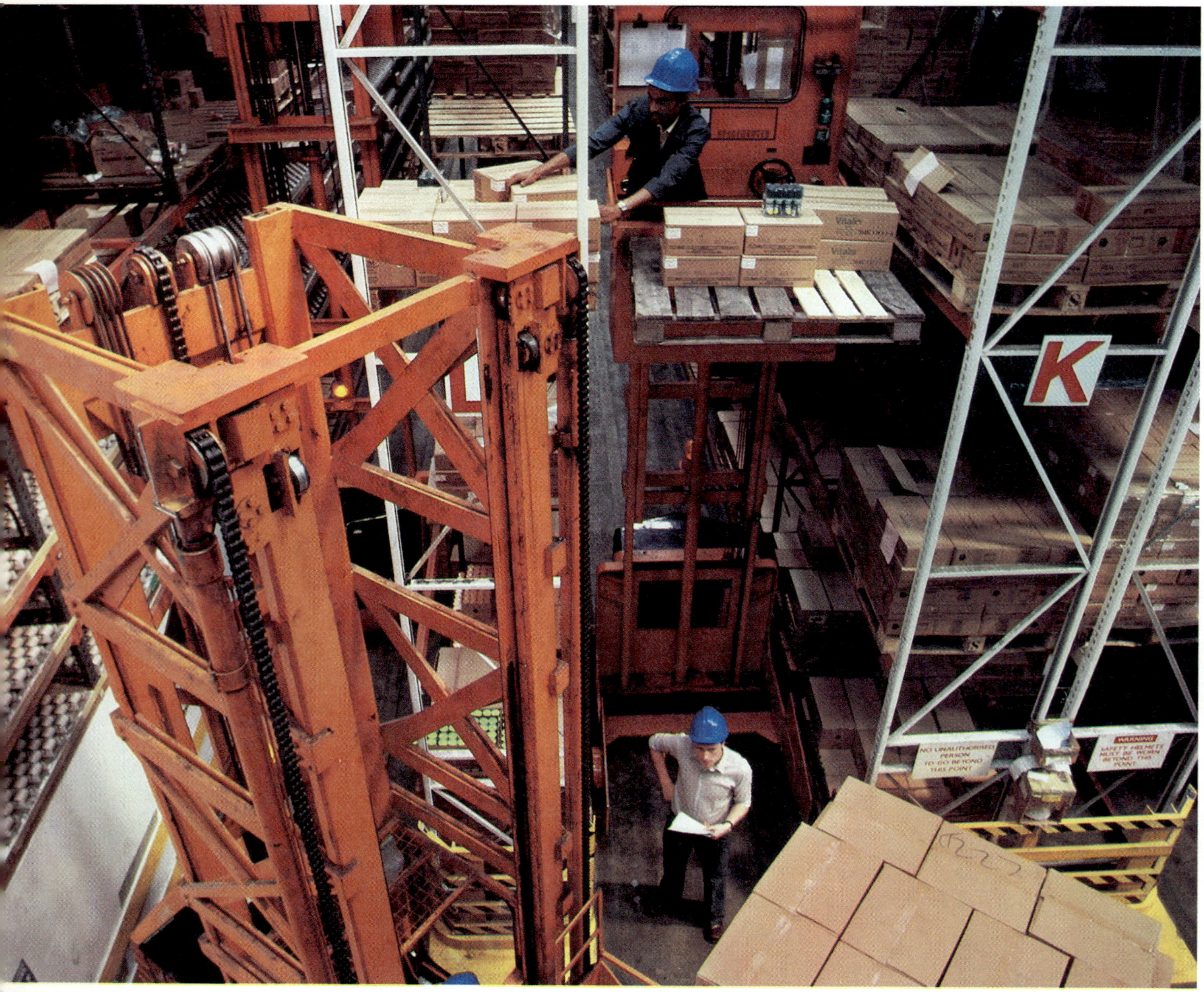

The health and wealth of the nation's economy can be measured by the amount of building and other economic statistics and indicators, as well as by the employment rate.

MEASURING THE ECONOMY'S PERFORMANCE

In Chapter 2 you learned a little about what statistics are and how they can be used. This chapter describes how economists use statistics to measure the health and wealth of the nation's economy. You will read about various measures of the nation's income and ways to correct these measures for the effects of inflation. The business cycle, some possible causes for it, and three economic indicators used in describing its phases are also discussed. Learning Economic Skills describes how to use consumer price indexes to determine your own cost of living.

CHAPTER OBJECTIVES After you study this chapter, you will be able to:

1 • list two reasons why the use of economic statistics is important.

2 • contrast the five major measurements of national income accounting.

3 • explain why and how economic statistics are corrected for inflation.
   ★ use price indexes to determine cost of living.

4 • describe the phases of the business cycle model.

5 • identify four possible causes of the business cycle.

6 • explain the relationship between economic forecasts and economic indicators.

ECONOMICS VOCABULARY

national income accounting
gross national product (GNP)
net national product (NNP)
personal income (PI)
transfer payment
disposable personal income (DI)
inflation
national income (NI)
consumer price index (CPI)
base year
producer price index (PPI)
implicit GNP price deflator
real GNP
business cycle
peak
boom
contraction
recession
depression
trough
expansion
recovery
economic indicator
leading indicator
coincident indicator
lagging indicator

From an economic standpoint, people can measure how successful they are by the size of their incomes. The higher the income, the more successful people can say they are. Each individual wants his or her spendable income to grow each year in order to buy more goods and services and to improve his or her standard of living. If you have a job, you can probably tell if your standard of living is improving. If there is no rapidly rising inflation, you can compare the amount of goods and services you can buy this year with what you could buy last year.

The well-being of the overall economy is measured in a similar way. Economists constantly measure and record such factors as the amount of goods and services produced by the nation and the amount of money individuals have to spend. In doing so, they take the vast number of activities that make up the economy and translate it into the more manageable form of statistics.

1 | THE IMPORTANCE OF ECONOMIC STATISTICS

Ask yourself as you read:
- What are economic statistics?
- How do statistics help people to make educated predictions?

It may seem at times that economics suffers from too many statistics. The annual *Statistical Abstract of the United States* has hundreds of pages of closely set statistics on almost every imaginable area of economic activity. As you read this chapter, you will gain an understanding of these statistics. What at first may seem like a flood of meaningless numbers will take shape as a carefully controlled flow of information. Knowing how to use this information to predict future trends is important to businesses; federal, state, and local governments; and to individuals. Economic statistics help people avoid costly mistakes and make informed decisions about the future. Statistics are the difference between a hunch and an educated guess.

A BASIS FOR DECISION MAKING

Statistics help people plan for the future. For example, business executives are faced each year with thousands of decisions about steps to take next. Should the company build a new plant this year or put it off for a year? Are inventories sufficient to meet demand or should they be increased? Because the future is uncertain, the full answer to these questions can never be known in advance. However, a business executive can study the economy's past performance, its current condition, and its prospects for the future. With this information in hand, the executive can then make an informed prediction on which the company would be willing to risk a large investment.

As you will read in Chapters 17 and 18, the federal government often designs its taxing and spending policies to achieve a certain economic goal, such as low unemployment. Government officials must be able to evaluate the results of past and present policies to decide what action is needed for the future. Statistics provide the basis for their decision-making.

Economic statistics can also be useful to individuals. For instance, you are probably aware from reading the newspaper or hearing the news that most prices rise some each year. To decide how satisfied you are with your current wage, you need to know how much prices rose on average in the past year. Other useful statistics are those measuring the ups and downs in the economy. If you know that many people are out of work, you may be less willing to quit your job before you have another. Individuals also use measures of the economy's performance in deciding for whom to vote and where to place their savings.

REVIEWING ECONOMIC PRINCIPLES

1. What are two reasons why using statistics is important to businesses, governments, and individuals?
2. **Critical Thinking: Summarizing the Main Idea.** In a paragraph, explain how economic statistics might be of use to you. Consider the examples given in the text.

2 | NATIONAL INCOME AND PRODUCT ACCOUNTING

Ask yourself as you read:
- What is national income accounting?
- What does GNP measure?

The measurement of the national economy's performance is called **national income accounting.** This area of economics deals with the overall economy's income and output. It also measures the interaction of consumers, businesses, and governments. The major measurements used for the nation's income and production are gross national product,

Businesses, government, and individuals all find economic statistics useful in their decision making and planning. What are the major measurements of the nation's economic performance?

Figure 14-1: GNP AND ITS COMPONENTS IN A RECENT YEAR

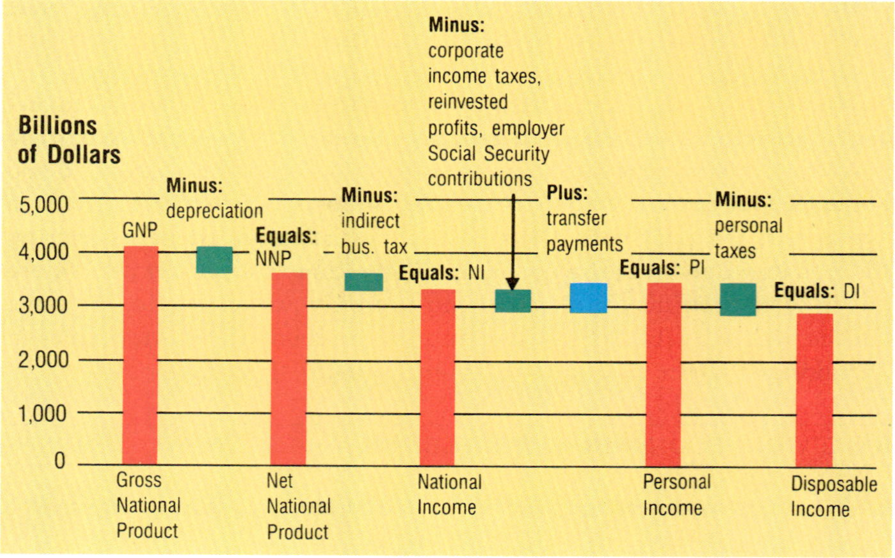

Billions of Dollars

Minus: corporate income taxes, reinvested profits, employer Social Security contributions

Minus: depreciation

Minus: indirect bus. tax

Plus: transfer payments

Minus: personal taxes

GNP

Equals: NNP

Equals: NI

Equals: PI

Equals: DI

5,000 — 4,000 — 3,000 — 2,000 — 1,000 — 0

Gross National Product | Net National Product | National Income | Personal Income | Disposable Income

According to this graph, what is the difference in dollars between gross national product and disposable personal income? Which is the better measure of the economy's health.

net national product, national income, personal income, and disposable personal income. While all of these terms are related, each measures an increasingly smaller portion of the overall economy. Figure 14-1 shows gross national product and its components in descending order of value.

GROSS NATIONAL PRODUCT

The broadest measure of the economy's health is **gross national product (GNP).** This is the total dollar value of all final goods and services produced in the nation during a single year. This figure tells how much American workers have produced in that year and how much is available for people to purchase. GNP is one way to measure the nation's material standard of living. It also provides a way of comparing what has been produced in one year with what was produced in another year.

Note the word *value* in the definition. Simply adding up the quantities of millions of different things produced, such as shoes and cars, would not mean much. How can we measure the strength of the economy, for example, if we know that 3 billion safety pins were produced and two space shuttles? What needs to be totaled is the value of the items, using some common measure. Economists use the dollar as this common measure of value. As a result, GNP is always expressed in dollar terms. For example, in 1986 GNP totaled more than $4 trillion.

The word *final* is also important. To measure the economy's performance accurately, economists add up only the value of final goods and services. This avoids double counting. To add the price of transistors to the price of a transistor radio is not realistic. The final price to the buyer already includes the price of the transistors.

Also, only new goods are counted in GNP. The sale of a used car or a secondhand refrigerator is not counted as part of GNP. Such a sale does not add to the production of the nation but only transfers a product from one person to another. That is, if you sell your car, all you've done is transfer something that already exists. However, if a new battery is put in an old car, that new battery is counted as part of GNP.

GNP CATEGORIES

In computing GNP, economists measure economic activity in four areas. These are:

1. consumer goods—goods and services bought by consumers for their direct use;
2. business, or producer, goods—money spent by businesses on the tools, machines, buildings, and so on, used to produce goods; this figure also includes money spent on business inventories;
3. government goods—the goods and services, ranging from paper clips and road graders to jet planes, that are bought by federal, state, and local governments;
4. net exports—the difference between what the nation sells to other countries (exports) and what it buys from other countries (imports). This net export figure may be a plus or minus. It will depend on whether the nation buys more from other countries than it sells or sells more than it buys. (International trade is discussed in Chapter 20.)

The percentage of GNP that each economic activity makes up is shown in Figure 14-2.

Figure 14-2: FOUR AREAS OF ECONOMIC ACTIVITY AS PERCENTAGE OF GNP IN A RECENT YEAR

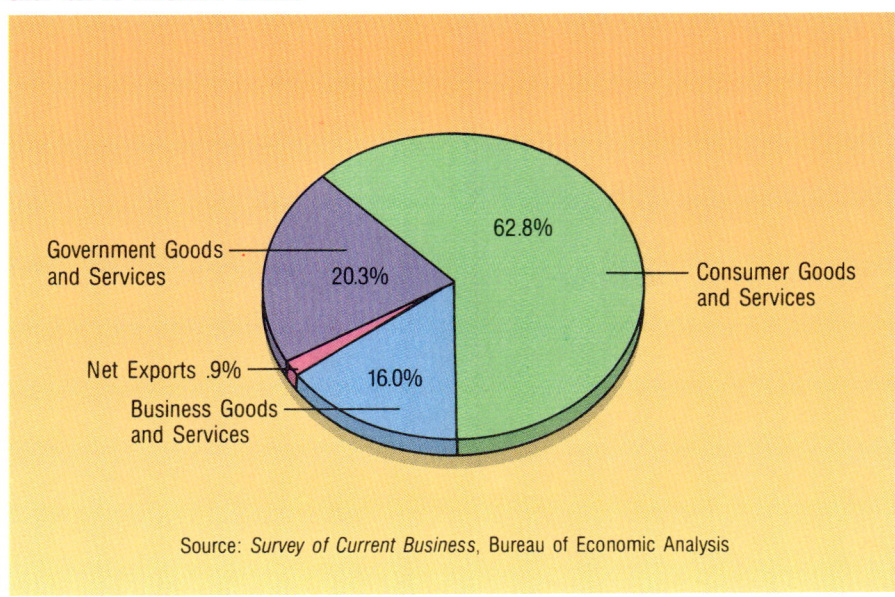

Government Goods and Services 20.3%

Net Exports .9%

Business Goods and Services 16.0%

62.8%

Consumer Goods and Services

Source: *Survey of Current Business*, Bureau of Economic Analysis

Based on GNP in Figure 14-1 and on this graph, what is the dollar value of consumer goods and services? of government goods and services? of net exports? of business goods and services?

It is important to remember that the statistics used in computing GNP are accurate only to a point. Statistics about easily quantifiable things, such as government purchases, are reliable. But some statistics can only be estimated and therefore are less reliable. For example, some workers are given food, fuel, or housing in place of or as supplements or additions to wages. An apartment building superintendent, for example, sometimes gets his or her apartment at reduced rent. GNP includes an estimate of the value of such goods and services. Moreover, GNP omits certain areas of economic activity. Unpaid work done by individuals for themselves or their families are not counted as part of GNP, even though it adds to the nation's output. This includes maintenance work on a home, baby-sitting, lawn mowing, and so on. If you baby-sit for your neighbor or mow your neighbor's lawn and they pay you, this payment is included in GNP. On the other hand, if you perform these services for your parents and you are not paid, there is no addition to the gross national product.

ANOTHER WAY OF ESTIMATING GNP

What you have just read is the expenditure approach to GNP. In this method, gross national product is measured by what is spent on consumer goods, government goods, business goods, and net exports. However, there is another way to measure GNP, and that is to measure income. When gross national product is measured this way, four categories of income are measured. They are:

1. wages, including all forms of labor income;
2. interest received by households;
3. rent that is earned by individuals for use of their farms, houses, and stores;
4. profits earned by corporations, partnerships, and proprietorships.

Deducting sales and business property taxes that were paid as well as the cost of machines and equipment that deteriorated throughout the year from the income gives us the gross national product:

$$\text{GNP} = \text{wages} + \text{rents} + \text{interest} + \text{profit} + \text{adjustments}.$$

The income approach to GNP gives about the same figure as the expenditure approach.

NET NATIONAL PRODUCT

As you may recall from Chapter 6, the loss of value because of wear and tear to consumer durables, such as cars, is called depreciation. The same concept applies to producer goods—machines and equipment. GNP disregards this factor. It does not take into account that some output is used merely to keep machines and equipment in working order and to replace them when they wear out.

Net national product (NNP) accounts for this loss of value. It measures GNP minus the total loss in value of producer goods through depreciation. In recent years, the amount used by economists to account for depreciation has been a little more than 10 percent of GNP. In 1986, for example, GNP was a little more than $4 trillion. After subtracting $470 billion for depreciation, the NNP was about $3.6 trillion. Because NNP accounts for depreciation, it can be a better measure than GNP of the economy's actual productivity.

NATIONAL INCOME

National income (NI) is a measure of the total income earned by everyone in the economy. NI includes those who use their own labor to earn an income as well as those who make money through the ownership of the other factors of production. National income is equal to NNP minus indirect business taxes, such as sales and property taxes, and license fees.

As GNP is divided into four areas of economic activity, NI is divided into five types of income. These are:

1. wages and salaries paid to employees;
2. income earned by self-employed individuals, including farmers and owners of sole proprietorships and partnerships;
3. rental incomes of property owners;
4. corporate profits;
5. interest on savings and investments received by individuals. NI is equal to the sum of all income in these five areas. However, wages and salaries make up about three-fourths of NI.

PERSONAL INCOME

Personal income (PI) is the total income received by individuals before personal taxes are paid. PI can be derived from NI through a two-step process. First, corporate income taxes, profits that businesses put back into their businesses to expand, and Social Security contributions made by employers are subtracted from NI. These are subtracted because they represent money that is not available for individuals to spend. Then, transfer payments are added to NI. **Transfer payments** are welfare payments and other supplementary payments, such as unemployment compensation, Social Security, and Medicaid, that are made to individuals by a state or the federal government. These transfer payments add to an individual's income. However, they are not in exchange for any current productive activity that has been done by an individual.

DISPOSABLE PERSONAL INCOME

In Chapter 3 you read that the income people have left after taxes, including Social Security contributions, have been paid is called disposable income. It is the income available to an individual for the immediate purchase of goods and services and for savings. It is also known as **disposable personal income (DI).** DI equals PI minus personal taxes. DI is an important indicator of the economy's health because it measures the actual amount of money income people have to spend.

Like most Americans, this young couple enjoys shopping for souvenirs on their vacation. Why is this an example of how disposable personal income is sometimes spent?

1. Define the following economic terms: **a.** national income accounting, **b.** gross national product (GNP), **c.** net national product (NNP), **d.** national income (NI).
2. **a.** What four areas of economic activity make up gross national product? **b.** How is double counting avoided in determining GNP? **c.** Why is GNP accurate only up to a certain point?
3. How does the net national product differ from GNP?
4. **a.** What five types of income make up national income? **b.** How does national income differ from net national product?
5. **a.** How is personal income derived? **b.** Why do you think that transfer payments are added to personal income but not to national income?
6. **Critical Thinking: Making a Judgment.** Which do you think would be a better measure of a person's standard of living—disposable personal income or personal income? Explain.

3 | CORRECTING ECONOMIC STATISTICS FOR INFLATION

Ask yourself as you read:
- What are the most commonly used measures of inflation?
- How does GNP differ from real GNP?

The dollar value of GNP is affected by ever-rising prices. Such prolonged rise in the general price level of goods and services is called **inflation.** For example, last year a hamburger may have cost $2.50. This year it may cost $3.00. The physical output—the hamburger—has not changed, only its money value. The higher GNP figures that result from inflation do not represent any increase in output. To get a true measure of the nation's output in a given year, inflation must be taken into account. The dollar value of GNP is also affected by **deflation,** a prolonged decline in the general price level. But deflation rarely happens.

If all prices rose at the same rate, only one measure of inflation would be needed. However, prices in different sectors of the economy rise at different rates. As a result, the government uses several measures of inflation. The three most commonly used are the consumer price index, the producer price index, and the implicit GNP price deflator.

CONSUMER PRICE INDEX

The **consumer price index (CPI)** measures the change in price over time of a specific group of goods and services used by the average household. This group of items, called a market basket, includes about 400 goods and services in the areas of food, housing, transportation, clothing, entertainment, medical care, and personal care. It is the price index that you are probably most familiar with from the news media.

The CPI is compiled monthly by the federal Bureau of Labor Statistics. In compiling the CPI, the base year is set at 1967 and given a value of 100. A **base year** is a year used as a point of comparison for other years in a series of statistics. CPI numbers for later years indicate the percentage that the market basket price has risen since the base year. For example, the 1986 CPI of 328 means the cost of living has risen 228 percent since 1967: 328 − 100 = 228. The CPI also can be used to compare inflation from year to year. At the end of 1984, the CPI was 316.1; at the end of 1985, it was 327.9, which is a difference of 11.8 points:

$$327.9 - 316.1 = 11.8.$$

Now if we use 1984 as the base year, we can find out by what percentage consumer prices on average rose from 1984 to 1985. We do this by dividing 11.8 by 316.1, which gives us 3.7 percent:

$$11.8 \div 316.1 = 3.7 \text{ percent.}$$

PRODUCER PRICE INDEX

Another important measure of inflation reported monthly by the Bureau of Labor Statistics is the **producer price index (PPI).** Formerly called the wholesale price index, it measures the change in price over time of about 2,800 goods used by businesses. These include farm products, rubber and plastic products, and transportation equipment. Like the CPI, the PPI also uses 1967 as a base year.

By comparing the CPI and the PPI, economists can see how inflation has affected different areas of the economy. During the late 1960s, for example, consumer prices were rising faster than producer prices. That situation reversed in about 1973, but changed again in 1978 and 1979, when inflation rose again. Beginning in 1981 the percentage increases in both consumer and producer prices declined steadily.

IMPLICIT GNP PRICE DEFLATOR

The federal government also issues a measure of price changes in GNP, called the **implicit GNP price deflator.** Every year the government publishes a number that is the GNP price deflator for the year before. The federal government uses the year 1982 as the base year for the implicit price deflator for gross national product. That means that in 1982 the price deflator was 100. By the beginning of 1986 it was 113.5. The price deflator removes the effects of inflation from the measurement of the value of the nation's total output. Using the price indicator to correct GNP for price-level changes gives **real GNP:** money GNP ÷ Price Index (as decimal) = real GNP.

Real GNP makes it possible to compare figures over time to see if the economy is growing or if the changes have occurred because of inflation. Figure 14-3 gives both GNP and real GNP for the years 1975 to 1986. Notice that the two lines cross at the year 1982, where GNP and real GNP are equal. As you can see from the graph, real GNP has grown for most of the years shown, though at a slower rate than GNP.

These picture tubes being inspected by this worker are a major component of TV sets. Why is the cost of these tubes included in the PPI?

USING INDEXES OF CONSUMER PRICES

The consumer price index (CPI) is the measure of inflation with which you are probably most familiar. It is the one most often quoted in news reports and articles. This index, however, is just one of many measures of consumer prices published by the Bureau of Labor Statistics. Although the CPI indicates the average rise in prices, it is not necessarily the best guide to how much your own cost-of-living has gone up.

As you read earlier in this chapter, the CPI is based on the price of all items in a market basket of goods and services. The Bureau also publishes separate price indexes for each of the ten major groups making up the market basket. These are: food, residential rent, home ownership, home purchase, fuel oil and coal, gas and electricity, clothing, private transportation, public transportation, and medical care.

Price Indexes for Selected Consumer Groups*

	Food	Rent	Home-owning	Fuel	Clothes	All Items
1965	94.4	96.9	92.7	94.6	93.7	94.5
1970	114.9	110.1	128.5	110.1	116.1	116.3
1975	175.4	137.3	181.7	235.3	142.3	161.2
1980	254.6	191.6	314.0	556.0	178.4	246.8
1981	274.6	208.2	352.7	675.9	186.9	272.4
1982	285.7	224.0	376.8	667.9	191.8	289.1
1983	291.7	236.9	334.8	628	196.5	298.4
1984	307.2	249.3	336.5	641.8	200.2	315.5
1985	315.2	264.6	349.9	619.5	206.0	327.4
1986	318.4	281.7	362.4	521.4	206.9	329.0

*1967=100

Source: *Statistical Abstract of the U.S.*, Bureau of the Census

The table here shows price indexes for several of these categories over a 21-year period. Figures given are averages for the year. As you can see, prices have risen faster for certain consumer products than for others. Clothing, for example, has increased in price about 110 percent since 1967. But prices for fuel oil and coal have gone up about 410 percent over the same period. Although clothing is more expensive now than it was in 1967, the cost of clothing compared to most products on the market has actually decreased.

The rise in your own cost of living will depend on which consumer goods and services you use most. For example, if you live in a rented apartment and walk to work or school, your daily costs have probably gone up less than they have for a homeowner who drives to work. Rent increased an average of 172 percent between 1967 and 1986. However, during the same period, the cost of homeownership went up 236 percent. The cost of owning a car has also gone up considerably. The prices of automobiles, gasoline, garages, automobile insurance, as well as of highway and bridge tolls, have all increased.

Your own cost of living also depends on the mix of products you buy. To remain consistent, the market basket that the Bureau uses to compute the CPI is always the same. In reality, however, individuals vary the products and services they buy based on price. For example, if the price of beef increased steeply, you might buy less beef and more chicken. Because of careful shopping and substitution of goods, your own cost might go up less than the consumer price index would show.

Practicing Your Skills

1. What was the rate of inflation for food between 1985 and 1986?
2. **a.** For which group listed in the table did the price index go down in the last year? **b.** What was the annual percent change for this group between 1985 and 1986?
3. Suppose a person had an income of $12,000 in 1985. What would his or her 1986 income have to be to keep purchasing power even with inflation as indicated by the CPI for all items?

1. Write a sentence defining each of the following economic terms: **a.** inflation, **b.** consumer price index (CPI), **c.** base year, **d.** producer price index (PPI), **e.** implicit GNP price deflator, **f.** real GNP.
2. Why must inflation be taken into account in measuring the nation's output in a given year?
3. How are each of the following compiled: **a.** consumer price index? **b.** producer price index?
4. **Critical Thinking: Analyzing Information.** Why is knowing real GNP useful to businesses, governments, and individuals?

4 | PHASES OF THE BUSINESS CYCLE

Ask yourself as you read:
- What are the main phases of a business cycle?
- How does the model of the business cycle differ from reality?

When you read the changes in real GNP in Figure 14-3, you can see that there are periods when the economy is growing. You can also see that there are periods when the economy is not. Ups and downs in economic activity are associated with what are called the **business**

Figure 14-3: GNP AND REAL GNP, 1975-1986

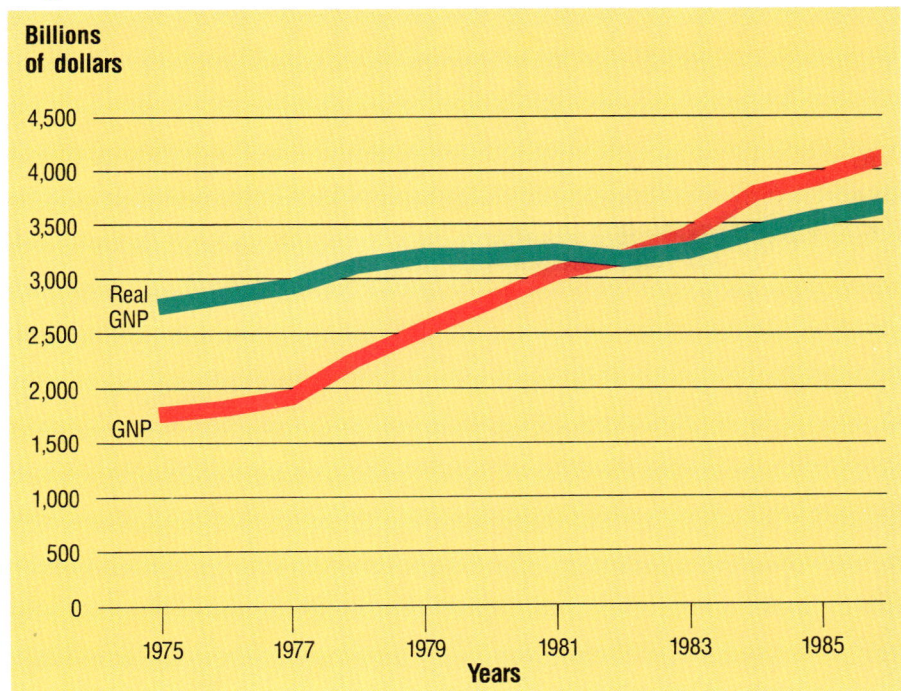

Source: *Statistical Abstract of the U.S.*, Bureau of the Census; Bureau of Economic Analysis
Base year for Real GNP is 1982.

To change a given year's GNP into real GNP, divide GNP by the implicit GNP price deflator and multiply by 100. If GNP in 1984 was $3 750 billion and the GNP price deflator was 223.4, what was real GNP?

Figure 14-4: A MODEL OF THE BUSINESS CYCLE

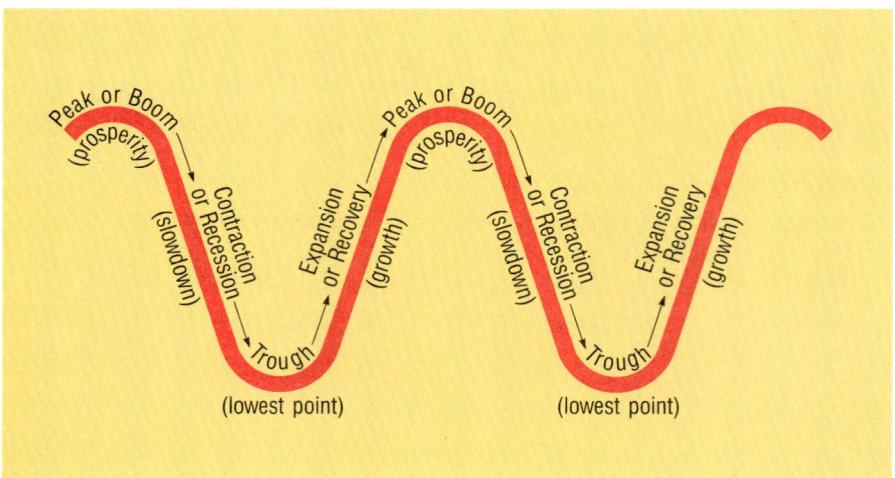

What does the word *model* tell you about the business cycle?

cycle. This means that there are changes in the level of total output measured in real GNP. The term *business cycle* is somewhat misleading, however. *Cycle* usually refers to a regular series of changes. Changes in business activity in the United States show no such regularity, as you will see.

MODEL OF THE BUSINESS CYCLE

Figure 14-4 shows an idealized business cycle. According to this model, the phases of a business cycle begin with an economic **peak** or **boom.** This is a period of prosperity. New businesses open, factories are producing at full capacity, and everyone who wants work can find a job.

Eventually, however, real GNP levels off and begins to decline. During this part of the cycle, a **contraction** of the economy occurs. Business activity begins to slow down. If the contraction lasts long enough and is deep enough, the economy can continue downward until it slips into a recession. A **recession** is any period during which the real GNP does not grow for at least two quarters—six months—in a row. In a recession, business activity starts to fall at an alarming rate. Factories begin cutting back on production and laying off workers. Consumers, with less income, cut back on purchases. With less money being spent, factories may reduce production further, laying off even more workers. Faced with a worsening economy, fewer new businesses open and many existing ones may fail. If a recession becomes extremely bad, it deepens into a **depression.** Then millions are out of work, many businesses fail, and the economy operates at far below capacity.

At some point, this downward spiral of the economy levels off in a trough. A **trough** is the lowest point in the business cycle. It occurs when real GNP stops going down, levels off, and begins increasing. The increase in economic activity that follows is called an **expansion** or a **recovery.** Consumer spending picks up, signaling factories to hire

Changing the Face of Economics: John Maynard Keynes (1883–1946)

Perhaps the most influential economist of the twentieth century is John Maynard Keynes (kaynz). Like Adam Smith and Karl Marx, Keynes helped to shape the thinking of future generations of economists. In fact, one modern school of economic thought is called Keynesian economics.

The son of an economist, Keynes was born in Cambridge, England, and was educated at Cambridge University. He originally studied mathematics, but later switched to economics. Keynes was a highly successful businessman as well as a scholar. He involved himself in investments, insurance, and publishing. Keynes became a financial advisor to a number of businesses and chairman of the board of directors of a large insurance company. He built a fortune in the stock market.

During World War I, he served as an economic advisor to the British Treasury and was appointed chief economic counsel for the British representatives negotiating the Treaty of Versailles. The harsh settlement imposed on the Germans inspired his book *The Economic Consequences of the Peace* in 1920. In it he predicted the collapse of the European economy. His prediction unfortunately proved to be accurate.

Keynes's most influential publication is *The General Theory of Employment, Interest, and Money* published in 1936. It was written during the Great Depression when not only millions of Americans were unemployed, but Europeans were also suffering a prolonged economic depression. Economists were at a loss to explain how such a situation could continue year after year. Where was Adam Smith's "invisible hand"?

During this period, Keynes became convinced that the marketplace was not self-regulating. When a depression occurs, people save more than businesses want to invest. So the demand for goods and services among people who have the money to spend must be maintained. To bring the economy out of a depression, some force is needed to stimulate investment and capital expansion. This, in turn, would reduce unemployment. Keynes believed the government was this force. Government can avoid recessions by using a combination of deficit spending—spending more than the government receives in revenue—and of regulation of tax rates and the supply of money in the economy.

The Keynesian view of the world differs markedly from that of Adam Smith. Keynes believed that government must involve itself in attempting to smooth out the low periods of business activity. He argued that there must be increases in government spending whenever unemployment gets too high. Keynes's theories were met with a mixture of enthusiasm, confusion, and opposition among economists at the time. However, despite economists who believed otherwise, from Roosevelt to Carter, American Presidents to some degree have used Keynesian economics as the basis for their economic policies.

1. What was Keynes's view of the role of government in the economy?
2. Compare and contrast Keynes's theories with those of Adam Smith.

workers and increase production to meet demand. As more people are hired, the public has more income to spend, which further encourages growth. New businesses begin to open, and factory production climbs back toward full capacity. The recovery continues until the economy hits another peak, and a new cycle begins.

UPS AND DOWNS OF BUSINESS IN THE UNITED STATES

Remember that what you have just read is a description of the business cycle model. In the real world, as you can see from Figure 14-5, the cycles are not that regular. However, the peaks and troughs are clear. The largest drop immediately followed the stock market crash in October 1929. The preceding years had been a time of widespread prosperity. The twenties had been a decade in which Americans began buying increasing numbers of radios, refrigerators, stoves, and automobiles. During these years, prices remained stable, and the standard of living grew at about 3 percent per year. By October 1929, heavy speculation had driven stock prices to an all-time peak. Then the stock market began to collapse. Stock prices started falling in early October and continued through the month. Suddenly, on October 28, there was a nationwide stampede to unload stocks. In one day the total value of all stocks fell by $14 billion. The next day was even worse.

Not long after the stock market crash, the United States fell into a serious recession. Factories shut down, laying off millions of workers. Businesses and banks failed by the thousands. Real GNP fell sharply over the next few years, pushing the nation into the depths of the Great Depression. Then began a gradual recovery, with some short slips downward until about 1936, when another steep downturn occurred. A gradual upward rise climaxed in the boom period of World War II.

After the war and throughout the 1950s, there were small ups and downs. However, recessions were short and mild, and the economy was generally prosperous. From 1960 through 1969 there were no re-

Figure 14-5: BUSINESS ACTIVITY IN THE UNITED STATES, 1863-1987

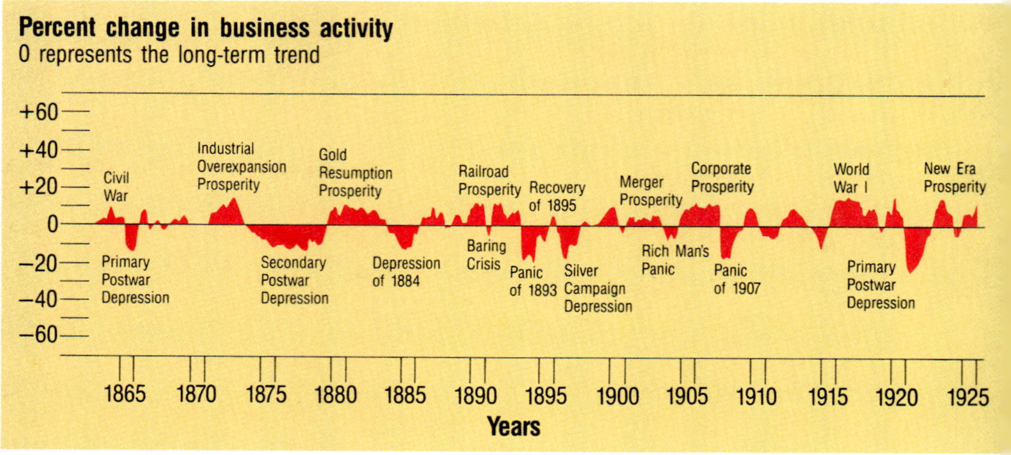

Percent change in business activity
0 represents the long-term trend

Source: AmeriTrust, Cleveland, Ohio

cessionary periods. In the 1970s and the 1980s, the American economy suffered recurring recessions. The 1980s started off with a small recession that developed into the most serious economic downturn by some measurements since World War II. This downturn ended in 1982 and was followed by relative prosperity.

REVIEWING ECONOMIC PRINCIPLES

1. Define the following economic terms: **a.** business cycle, **b.** peak or boom, **c.** contraction, **d.** recession, **e.** depression, **f.** trough, **g.** expansion or recovery.
2. Choose one phase of the business cycle model and explain how the economy would act during this phase.
3. **Critical Thinking: Explaining the Main Idea.** Using Figure 14-4 and the text, choose one business cycle and describe its phases in a paragraph.

5 | CAUSES OF THE BUSINESS CYCLE

Ask yourself as you read:
- What might cause the ups and downs in the business cycle?
- How might psychological factors affect the business cycle?

For as long as booms and recessions have existed, economists have tried to explain why the business cycle occurs. If they could understand the causes, economists could take actions to smooth out the business cycle. However, no one theory seems to explain past cycles or to serve as an adequate measure to predict future ones. It seems that at any one time several factors are working together to create a business cycle.

Figure 14-5: BUSINESS ACTIVITY IN THE UNITED STATES, 1863-1987* (continued)

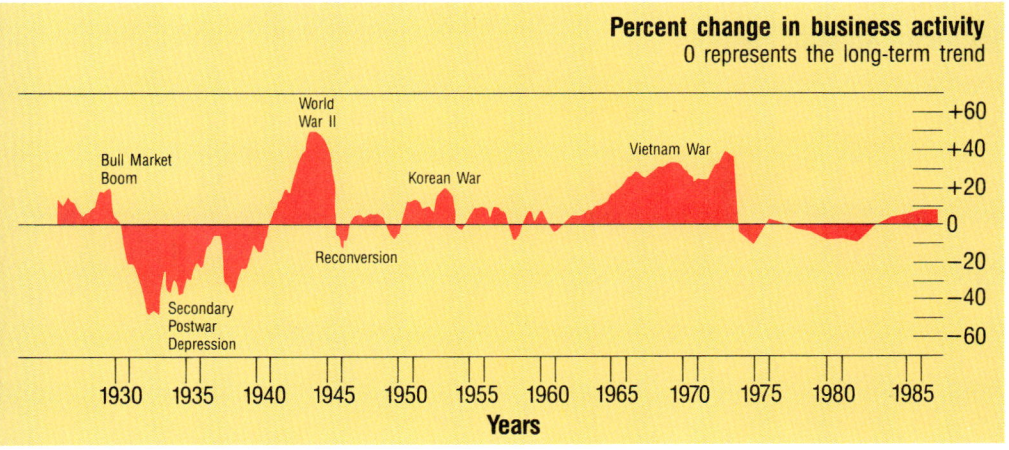

This graph shows business cycles since the Civil War. How many cycles have there been?

Source: AmeriTrust, Cleveland, Ohio
*1987 data are estimates.

BUSINESS INVESTMENT

Some economists believe that the decisions businesses make are the keys to the ups and downs in the business cycle. Suppose a firm believes that prospects for future sales are good. It will most likely increase its capital investment. That is, it will buy new machines, build new factories, expand old ones, and so on. This expansion will create new jobs and more money for consumer spending. This, in turn, will contribute to expansion. After a time, businesses no longer need to expand. The increased demand for their goods has been met or some other factor in the economy has slowed. When businesses stop purchasing new producer goods, a contraction of the economy may occur.

Innovations—inventions and new production techniques—can have a similar effect on the economy. When one firm begins to use an innovation, others will follow. As you read in Chapters 2 and 9, technological innovations give a business an advantage over competitors. To become competitive again, the other businesses must duplicate the product or production method. All this takes capital. Eventually, however, investment will drop off because no additional capital for the innovation is needed. This is an example of the law of diminishing returns that you read about in Chapter 11.

If businesses anticipate a downturn in the economy, they will cut back on their inventories. Producers, in turn, will have to cut back on production to prevent a surplus. Enough inventory cutbacks could lead to a recession. On the other hand, if they feel consumer orders are going to rise, businesses will invest in larger inventories. This will stimulate production and increase employment.

GOVERNMENT ACTIVITY

A number of economists believe that the changing policies of the federal government are a major reason for business cycles. The government affects business activity in two ways: through its policies on taxing and spending and through its control over the supply of money available in the economy. You will be reading in detail about the effect that government has on the economy in Chapters 16 to 18.

EXTERNAL FACTORS

Factors outside a nation's economy can also influence the business cycle. As you can see from Figure 14-5, wars in particular have an important impact. This results from the huge increase in government spending during wartime. Discoveries of new sources of raw materials such as oil may have a favorable effect on the economy by lowering operating costs for certain industries. However, the sudden loss of raw materials and the resulting higher price can have the opposite effect. The recession of 1974–1975 was caused in part by the huge increase in oil prices in late 1973 by the Organization of Petroleum Exporting Countries (OPEC). The return to prosperity in the mid-1980s was caused in part by the sharp decline in world oil prices.

PSYCHOLOGICAL FACTORS

Finally, it is possible that people's psychological reactions to events also cause changes in business activity. The prospects of peace in the Middle East or the discovery of a new oil field off the coast of California can lead to feelings of confidence and optimism. War or the overthrow of the government of an important trading partner can cause pessimism about the future. As people ride these ups and downs of attitude, so does the economy to some degree.

Psychology is a factor in each of the possible causes of the business cycle. Business executives, for example, make decisions based on what they think will happen in the future. Even though these decisions can be based on objective facts, psychological factors such as personal optimism can also influence them. An optimistic executive may predict rising sales, for example, although past performance has been slow.

REVIEWING ECONOMIC PRINCIPLES

1. Why is there no single cause given for business cycles?
2. List the three areas of business investment that may affect business cycles.
3. What two aspects of government activity affect business cycles?
4. Think of an example of an external factor and write a paragraph explaining how it might affect the economy. Consider such factors as an increase in immigration and the introduction of low-priced foreign goods.
5. **Critical Thinking: Making Predictions.** How might people's attitudes about the future affect the economy? Choose an example and write a paragraph describing it.

6 | INDICATORS OF THE BUSINESS CYCLE

Ask yourself as you read:

• What are the most important economic indicators?

• Why are economic indicators essential for making economic forecasts?

Every day, business and government leaders are faced with the dilemma of trying to predict what will happen to the economy in the coming months and years. As you read earlier in the chapter, businesspeople base their decisions on such questions as when to build a new plant or what they feel will happen in the future. Government officials also need information about the future in planning taxing and spending policies. To aid these decision-makers, government and private economists constantly create and update economic forecasts. These indicate what is likely to happen in the economy as it moves through the various phases of the business cycle. Although GNP is an important measure of the economy's performance, it is not very helpful in preparing these forecasts. GNP shows what *has* happened in the economy, but it is not a good predictor of what *might* happen. It is too broad a measure to show detail about activity in the various sectors of the economy.

For these reasons, economists study a number of other economic indicators to learn about the current and possible future state of the economy. **Economic indicators** are statistics that measure variables in the economy, such as stock prices or the dollar amount of loans to be repaid. Each month the Department of Commerce publishes statistics for 300 economic indicators covering all aspects of the economy.

variable (VER-ee-uh-buhl): something that changes

Those statistics that point to what will happen in the economy are called **leading indicators.** Their activity seems to lead to a change in overall business activity—whether it is an upward or a downward trend. Economists can use leading indicators to predict which phase of the business cycle the economy is moving into. For example, a few months before a reduction in the growth rate of GNP, the number of hours worked per week in manufacturing industries declines. On the other hand, if the economy is about to take an upswing, layoffs will be reduced and employees recalled to work. Although the Commerce Department keeps track of dozens of leading indicators, those listed in Table 14-1 are the ones with which economists are most concerned.

There are other economic indicators whose changes in activity seem to coincide with, or happen at the same time as, changes in overall business activity. When these **coincident** (koh-IN-suh-duhnt) **indicators** begin a downswing, they indicate that the economy is slowing down and that a contraction in the business cycle has begun. If they begin an upswing, they indicate the economy is picking up and a recovery is underway.

coincide (koh-in-SYD): occur at the same time

A third set of indicators seems to lag behind changes in overall business activity. For example, it may be six months after the start of a downturn before businesses begin to reduce their borrowing noticeably. The amount of change in these **lagging indicators,** whether up or down, gives economists clues as to the size and timing of the phases of the business cycle. The four major coincident indicators and the six major lagging indicators are also listed in Table 14-1. The federal government publishes composite indexes, or averages, of all three sets of indicators.

Although economic indicators are essential in making economic forecasts, they are far from perfect predictors. Often different indicators within each group will move in opposite directions. During a recession some leading indicators may point to an upturn in the economy, while others are predicting a continued decline. Also, the economy does not always behave in the way predicted by the indicators. In recent years, all recessions have been preceded by a downturn in the composite index of leading economic indicators. However, the leading indicators frequently predicted turning points that did not occur.

Table 14-1: MAJOR ECONOMIC INDICATORS

Leading indicators
1. Average workweek for production workers in manufacturing
2. Layoff rate in manufacturing
3. New orders for consumer goods
4. Speed with which companies make deliveries (the busier a company, the longer it will take to fill orders)
5. Number of new businesses formed
6. Number of contracts and orders for plants and equipment
7. Number of building permits issued for private housing units
8. Change in the inventories on hand and on order
9. Change in the PPI for certain non-agricultural raw materials
10. Change in total liquid assets (securities such as Treasury bills and bonds that can easily be turned into currency)
11. Stock prices
12. Supply of money in the economy

Coincident indicators
1. Number of nonagricultural workers who are employed
2. Personal income minus transfer payments
3. Rate of industrial production
4. Sales of manufacturers, wholesalers, and retailers

Lagging indicators
1. Average length of unemployment
2. Size of manufacturing and trade inventories
3. Labor cost per unit of output in manufacturing
4. Average interest rate charged by banks to their best business customers
5. Number of commercial and industrial loans to be repaid
6. Ratio of consumer installment debt to personal income

Another problem is the variation in lead or lag time between a change in an indicator and a change in the overall economy. Some leading indicators, for example, change an average of six months before a predicted change in the economy. Others have an average lead time of more than a year. It is difficult, therefore, to know when, or even if, a predicted economic change will occur. This is why you will often hear or read about predictions from private or government economists that turn out to be wrong about the timing or predictions that do not occur at all. Economic forecasting, despite its importance, remains an uncertain and often frustrating job.

REVIEWING ECONOMIC PRINCIPLES

1. Define the following economic terms: **a.** economic indicators, **b.** leading indicators, **c.** coincident indicators, **d.** lagging indicators.
2. Why is GNP not very useful in making economic forecasts?
3. Choose one of the leading indicators from Table 14-1 and describe how it might indicate: **a.** an upward trend in the economy, **b.** a downward trend.
4. Choose one of the coincident indicators and describe how it might show that the economy is: **a.** slowing down, **b.** picking up.
5. **Critical Thinking: Explaining Main Ideas.** Explain why economic indicators are "far from perfect predictors of the future." Include an example that uses specific indicators.

SUMMARY OF
IMPORTANT PRINCIPLES

1 • Knowing how to use economic statistics to predict the future enables businesses, individuals, and federal, state, and local governments to make informed decisions and avoid costly mistakes.

2 • Gross national product (GNP), the broadest measure of the economy's health, measures the total value of all final goods and services produced in the nation during a given year, or, alternatively, measures the total value of all income produced. Net national product (NNP) measures GNP minus the total loss in value of producer goods through depreciation. Because NNP takes into consideration depreciation, it can be a better measure than GNP of the economy's actual productivity. National income (NI) is a measure of all the income earned by everyone in the economy. Personal income (PI) is equal to all money income received by individuals before personal taxes are paid. PI is derived from NI first by subtracting corporate income taxes, profits that businesses choose to reinvest, and Social Security contributions made by employers, and then adding transfer payments. Disposable personal income (DI) measures the actual amount of money people have to spend and is found by subtracting personal taxes from personal income.

3 • The higher GNP figures that result from inflation do not represent any increase in output. To get a true measure of the nation's output in a given year, any measurement must take inflation into account. To do this, the federal government publishes several different measures of inflation, such as the consumer price index, the producer price index, and the implicit GNP price deflator.
  • The consumer price index is based on the prices of all items in the market basket of goods and services. Because a person's cost of living depends on the type and mix of goods and services bought, using separate price indexes can be a better guide to individual cost of living.

4 • The business cycle is measured from one period of prosperity to another. It begins with a peak, or boom, period. As the economy begins to contract, a recession may occur, which may turn into a depression. At the lowest point, or trough, the economy levels off and begins a period of expansion, or recovery, which may lead to another peak.

5 • Four possible causes of business cycles are business investment decisions involving capital investment, innovations, and inventories; government taxing and spending policies and control over the supply of money; external factors; and psychological factors.

6 • Economic forecasts indicate what is likely to happen in the economy in the future. Economists use leading, coincident, and lagging indicators to measure the activity of certain variables in the economy. This information helps them learn about the current and possible future state of the economy.

Putting Economics to Work

BUSINESS DECISION MAKING: USING ECONOMIC INDICATORS

Peter Lopez is the owner of a small wood-working company that makes cabinets. Most of his cabinets go to home builders to install in new houses. Some of the more expensive, hand-made units he sells to interior designers for use in remodeling old homes in the area.

After a few years of only moderate success, Peter's business is now doing quite well. He has no trouble selling all the cabinets he and his workers can produce. In fact, he often cannot meet the demand for cabinets because his workshop is too small for any more employees. For this reason, Peter is considering opening a second shop. Although his rent would more than double, the additional shop would give Peter plenty of room to expand production.

Before making any final decisions about opening the new shop, Peter decides to look at some monthly and quarterly government statistics about the economy. He finds the following: the number of building permits for new housing has dropped steadily over the last five months. Sales of consumer goods are down. As a result, manufacturing industries have been laying off increased numbers of workers during the last year. The change in the composite index of leading economic indicators had been either zero or negative for the last seven months. Real GNP has been level for two quarters in a row.

Peter must decide if now is a good time to expand his business or if he should wait and see what happens to the economy.

1. If you were Peter, what decision would you make about opening a second shop? On what did you base your answer?
2. What other costs—aside from increased rent—would Peter face if he decided to expand production?
3. Suppose Peter decided against opening the new shop now. What signs in the economy might he look for in the future to indicate that it would be a good time to expand his business?

Readings in Economics

ECONOMIC STATISTICS CAN'T TELL IT ALL
Skill: Justifying an Opinion

 Economic statistics are important and useful, yet there are many things they cannot measure. A. A. Berle, Jr., a well-known expert on corporations, addressed the drawbacks of the Gross National Product as an index of economic well-being.

It is nice to know that at current estimate the Gross National Product [GNP] of the United States in 1968 will be above 850 billions of dollars. It would be still nicer to know if the United States will be better or worse off as a result. If better, in what respects? If worse, could not some of this production and effort be steered into providing more useful "goods and services"?

Unfortunately, whether the work was sham or useful, the goods noxious [harmful], evanescent [short-lived], or of permanent value will have no place in the record. Individuals, corporations, or government want, buy, and pay for stuff and work—so it is "product." The labor of the Boston Symphony Orchestra is "product" along with that of the band in a honky-tonk. The compensated services of a quack fortune teller are "product" just as much as the work of developing the Salk vaccine. Restyling automobiles or ice chests by adding tail fins or pink handles adds to "product" just as much as money paid for slum clearance or medical care. They are all "goods" or "services"—the only test is whether someone wanted them badly enough to pay the shot [price].

This blanket tabulation raises specific complaints against economists and their uncritical aggregated [total] figures and their acceptance of production as "progress." The economists bridle, "We," they reply, "are economists, not priests. Economics deals with satisfaction of human wants by things or services. The want is sufficiently evidenced by the fact that human beings, individually or collectively, paid for them. It is not for us to pass on what people ought to have wanted—that question is for St. Peter. . . ."

What they are saying—and as far as it goes, they are quite right—is that nobody has given economics a mandate to set up a social-value system for the country. Fair enough—but one wonders. Closer thinking suggests that even on their own plane, economists could perhaps contribute a little to the subject, although, . . . we must get ourselves some philosophy, too.

1. According to the article, what do economists not tell us when reporting the GNP?
2. In your opinion, should economists be given a mandate to set up a "social-value system for the country"? Justify your opinion.

A. A. Berle, Jr., "What GNP Doesn't Tell Us." *Is Economics Relevant?* Ed. by Robert L. Heilbroner and Arthur M. Ford. © 1968 *Saturday Review* magazine. Reprinted by permission.

A NEW WAY TO EVALUATE THE ECONOMY
Skill: Contrasting and Comparing Information

 There have been criticisms of GNP as a measure of economic health because it includes all products and services produced annually, including harmful as well as helpful products. In this reading, economist Paul Samuelson describes an alternative measure.

What is new? Net Economic Welfare (or NEW) is a key motif, and high time.

Net Economic Welfare is the *corrected* version of GNP—corrected to subtract out from the conventional calculation those *non-material disamenities* [disadvantages] *that have been accruing* [growing] *as costs to our economy* whether or not they have been recognized and charged against the industries and activities that cause them.

I refer to effluents [outflows] that pollute our rivers and lakes: the mercury from industry and the phosphates from home washers. Included are the hydrocarbons that darken our skies: carbon monoxide, sulphur; nitrogen compounds. . . .

Included too are the disamenities of modern urban life. If you must pay a messenger to ride for two hours, then your trip to and from work is really a cost that must be subtracted from your cushy income that goes into the GNP. . . .

To go from GNP to NEW, you not only have to *subtract* items. You also have to *add in* items—

items such as the value of work of housewives, which for no logical reason never got into the conventional GNP. But, when all's said and done, what does the record show about NEW?

NEW has been growing in America. But it has been growing at a considerably lower rate than GNP. What is more important, by my extrapolations [predictions based on] the Nordhause-Tobin data, NEW will fall behind GNP's growth increasingly in the future.

But all this is not inevitable. Modern economics teaches us that we can trade off some GNP growth for more healthy NEW growth. It's up to the public.

Modern economics, in the age after Keynes, knows how to limit GNP's material growth in the good cause of healthier welfare growth. . . .

In short, modern political economy is the calculus of *quality* of life, and not merely that of national *quantity*.

1. Contrast and compare Net Economic Welfare (NEW) and the Gross National Product (GNP).
2. Since Net Economic Welfare (NEW) attempts to measure the quality of life as reflected in the goods and services produced, what problems might there be in using NEW as a measure of economic growth?

Paul Samuelson, *The Samuelson Sampler.* Glen Ridge, New Jersey: Thomas Horton and Co., 1973. pp. 180–183.

ADJUSTING TO AND ADJUSTING FOR INFLATION
Skill: Interpreting Information

Correcting numbers for inflation is important not only to the government in computing GNP. Business managers use the measures of inflation discussed in this section as well. In this reading, author Peter Drucker discusses the importance of adjusting business statistics for inflation.

Before one can manage successfully, it is necessary to know precisely what one is managing. But executives today—both in business and in non-business public service institutions—do not know the facts. What they think are facts are largely illusions and half-truths. The reality of their enterprise is hidden, distorted and deformed by inflation. Executives today have available to them many times the reports, information, and figures their predecessors had; they have become dependent on these figures and are thus endangered if the figures lie to them. During inflation, however, the figures lie. Money still tends to be considered the standard of value and to be a value in itself, but in inflation this is a delusion. Before the fundamentals can be managed, the facts about any business—its sales, its financial position, its assets and liabilities, and its earnings—must be adjusted for inflation. . . .

We need to adjust sales, prices, inventory, receivables, fixed assets and their depreciation, and earnings to inflation—not with total precision but within a reasonable range of probability. Until this is done, even the most knowledgeable executive will remain the victim of the illusions inflation creates. He may know that the figures he gets are grossly misleading; but as long as these are the figures he has in front of him, he will act on them rather than on his own better knowledge. And he will act foolishly, wrongly, irresponsibly. . . .

Not to adjust for inflation is slothful and irresponsible. Managing in turbulent times must begin with the adjustment of the enterprise's figures to inflation, roughly yet within a realistic range of probabilities. The executive who fails to do so tries to deceive others. He only deceives himself.

1. What happens when the manager of a business fails to take inflation into consideration when figuring costs and profits?
2. When inflation is rising, why might it be a good idea to build a plant this year rather than next year?

Three specified excerpts from pp. 10, 11, 13 of *Managing in Turbulent Times* by Peter F. Drucker. Copyright © 1980 by Peter F. Drucker. Reprinted by permission of Harper & Row, Publishers, Inc.

CONDITIONS LEADING TO THE GREAT FALL
Skill: Making Inferences

The most serious recession in American history, the Great Depression, began with the stock market crash of October 1929. Economist John Kenneth Galbraith describes some of the economic conditions of the 1920s that led to the crash.

Readings in Economics

The decade of the twenties, or precisely the eight years between the postwar depression of 1920–21 and the stock market crash in October of 1929, were prosperous ones in the United States. . . .

These years were also remarkable in another respect, for as time passed it became increasingly evident that the prosperity could not last. Contained within it were seeds of its own destruction. The country was heading into the gravest kind of trouble. Herein lies the peculiar fascination of the period for the study in the problem of leadership. For almost no steps were taken during these years to arrest the tendencies which were obviously leading, and did lead, to disaster.

At least four things were seriously wrong, and they worsened as the decade passed. A knowledge of them does not depend on the always brilliant assistance of hindsight. At least three of these flaws were highly visible and widely discussed. In ascending order, not of importance but of visibility, they were as follows:

First, income in these prosperous years was being distributed with marked inequality. . . .

This was the least visible flaw. . . .

But the other three flaws in the economy were far less subtle. During World War I the United States ceased to be the world's greatest debtor country and became its greatest creditor. . . . A debtor country could export a greater value of goods than it imported and use the difference for interest and debt repayment. This was what we did before the war. But a creditor must import a greater value than it exports if those who owe it money are to have the wherewithal [ability] to pay interest and principal. Otherwise the creditor must either forgive the debts or make new loans to pay off the old. . . .

The second weakness of the economy was the large-scale corporate thimblerigging [sleight-of-hand tricks] that was going on. This took a variety of forms, of which by far the most common was the organization of corporations to hold stock in yet other corporations, which in turn held stock in yet other corporations. . . .

Finally, and most evident of all, there was the stock market boom. Month after month and year after year the great bull market of the twenties roared on. Sometimes there were setbacks, but more often there were fantastic forward surges. . . .

Down it went with a thunderous crash in October of 1929. In a series of terrible days, of which Thursday, October 24, and Tuesday, October 29, were the most terrifying, billions in values were lost, and thousands of speculators—they had been called investors—were utterly . . . ruined.

1. Why must a creditor nation import more goods than it exports?
2. What are the dangers when a corporation holds stock in other corporations, which in turn hold stock in other corporations and one or more experience huge losses?

John Kenneth Galbraith, "The Days of Boom and Bust." *American Heritage*, Vol. IX, No. 5., August 1958, pp. 28–33, 101, 102.

THE DYNAMICS OF BOOMS AND RECESSIONS
Skill: Sequencing Information

The business cycle is a phenomenon that has been studied and explained by many economists. Economists Robert L. Heilbroner and Lester C. Thurow present one explanation for it in this reading.

Generally when we speak of business cycles we refer to a wavelike movement that lasts, on the average, about seven to eleven years. . . .

What lies behind this more or less regular alternation of good and bad times?

Economists no longer seek a single explanation of the phenomenon. Rather, they tend to see cycles as variations in the rate of growth that are . . . induced by the dynamics of growth itself.

Let us, for example, assume that some stimulus—such as an important industry-building invention—has begun to increase investment expenditures. We can easily see how such an initial impetus can generate a cumulative and self-feeding boom. The first burst of investment stimulates additional consumption, the additional consumption induces more investment, and this in turn reinvigorates consumption. Meanwhile, this process of mutual stimulation serves to lift business expectations and to encourage still further expansionary spending. Inventories are built up in anticipation of larger sales. Prices firm up, and the stock market rises. Optimism reigns. A boom is on.

What happens to end such a boom? There are many possible reasons why it may peter out or come to an abrupt halt. It may simply be that the new industry will get built and thereafter an important stimulus to investment will be lacking. Or even before it is completed, wages and prices may have begun to rise as full employment is neared, and the climate of [people's] expectations may become wary. . . .

It is impossible to know in advance what particular cause will retard spending—a credit shortage, a very tight labor market, a saturation of demand for a key industry's products. . . . Whatever the initial motivation, what follows thereafter is much like the preceding expansion, only in reverse. Downward revisions of expectations reduce rather than enhance the attractiveness of investment projects. As consumption decreases, unemployment begins to rise. Inventories are worked off. Bankruptcies become more common. . . .

But just as there is a natural ceiling to a boom, so there is a more or less natural floor to recessions. . . . Sooner or later, in other words, expenditure will cease falling, and the economy will tend to bottom out.

1. List some of the events that occur at the top of a business cycle.
2. What role does investment play in the wave-like movement of the business cycle?

From *Five Economic Challenges* by Robert L. Heilbroner and Lester C. Thurow. © 1981. Used by permission of the publisher, Prentice-Hall, Inc., Englewood Cliffs, N.J.

FORECASTING THE ECONOMIC CLIMATE
Skill: Interpreting Information

SECTION 6

Although economic forecasts are far from perfect, they are important to business and government policy makers. Here, economic forecaster Murray Weidenbaum discusses the outlook for 1986.

A cynic once said that economic forecasting is neither an art nor a science—it is a hazard. . . . The harsh reality is that economists are not good at estimating the economy's performance for very short time periods, such as the next month or quarter. However, the record for forecasts of year-to-year changes is much better.

For example, each month a group of 50 professional economic forecasters provides a consensus estimate for the year ahead. The result is called Blue Chip Economic Indicators. The forecasts made by this panel in October of each year is especially important, because that month is the typical starting point for the annual company planning cycle.

Over the past eight years, the Blue Chip panel's October estimates of real growth for the next year have turned out to be within 1.2 percentage points of the actual figure. The record on inflation is about the same, with the Blue Chip panel averaging within 1.1 percentage points. That record will not qualify for the Guinness Book of World Records, but it suggests why government and business executives continue to rely on economic forecasts.

When we step back from the details of econometric models, we can spot some basic trends [for 1986]. . . . The economy will continue to grow, by between 2 and 3 percent. . . . The basic reason for the slowdown [in growth] is that domestic production is much weaker than domestic consumption. The difference, of course, is due to the rising tide of imports. For a while, consumer credit can finance the gap between income earned and money spent. But most people's spending ultimately reflects their income. Thus, the more modest pace of domestic production and income generation is slowing down the purchases of American consumers.

1. Give evidence to support or refute the statement "economic forecasting is neither an art nor a science—it is a hazard."
2. Why do government and business executives continue to rely on the economic forecasts of the Blue Chip panel?

Murray L. Weidenbaum, "Economic Prospects for 1986." From a speech delivered Nov. 14, 1985, St. Louis. *Vital Speeches of the Day*, Vol. LII, No. 8., Feb. 1, 1986.

14 | CHAPTER REVIEW

PRACTICING YOUR STUDY SKILLS: TAKING NOTES FROM YOUR READING

To prepare an oral report or to write a research paper, you need to be able to take accurate notes from your reading. These notes are the raw material of your final work. The following tips will help you in your note taking:

- Before you begin taking any notes on a book or article, record all the information about your source: author, title, publisher, date of publication, any volume number, and any other information. You will need all of this information to acknowledge the source in the footnotes or bibliography.
- Record data on index cards, using one card per topic per source. Cards will save you time in arranging your notes when you begin writing the outline for your paper or report.
- On each card record the author, title, and page number of that particular note. You can design a code for each source to save time.
- Scan your source for main ideas and supporting details. Paraphrase the main ideas of important paragraphs or sections and any supporting details that you might need. If you find something that you might wish to quote in your paper or report, be sure to copy the quotation accurately.
- Keep your topic in mind as you skim material for information. Avoid being distracted by interesting but unnecessary information.
- Write clearly and, preferably, in ink. Be brief, but not so brief that you do not provide yourself with enough information for your report or paper.
- If there are graphs or other complicated kinds of background information that you might use to substantiate your report, make a photocopy of each piece, if possible. Note on each copy all the source information you will need to locate it again.

Activity: Practice note taking by taking notes for a paper on GNP as a factor in determining the nation's economic health. Use library books.

VOCABULARY REVIEW

Write the letter of the definition in Column B that correctly defines each term in Column A.

Column A	Column B
1. base year	a. economic activity is at its lowest point
2. trough	b. figures for the nation's productivity that have been corrected for inflation
3. economic indicator	c. measurement of specific aspects of the economy such as stock prices
4. expansion	d. used as a point of comparison for other years in a series of statistics
5. real GNP	e. periodic ups and downs in the nation's economic activity
6. business cycle	f. business recovery period, when economic activity increases

PRACTICING YOUR ECONOMIC SKILLS

1. **Analyzing Data.** The following table gives gross national product and the implicit GNP

Year	GNP (in billions)	Implicit GNP Price Deflator
1980	$3187.1	85.7
1981	$3282.8	94.0
1982	$3166.0	100
1983	$3277.7	103.8
1984	$3492.0	108.1
1985	$3573.5	111.7

price deflator for five recent years. Use it to answer the following questions:

a. What was the percent rate of increase in GNP between 1980 and 1981? **b.** in real GNP for the same period? **c.** Suppose GNP for 1985 is $3573.5 billion and the implicit GNP price deflator is 111.7. What would real GNP be for 1985?

2. Circle the letters before each of the activities below that would add to the nation's Gross National Product.

a. Mr. Perès purchases a cake at the bakery.

b. Mrs. Chan, after learning that some relatives are coming to visit her, rushes to her neighbor to "borrow" a chicken. Mrs. Chan insists on paying her neighbor.

c. Jonas Donahue uses his earnings to purchase a government bond.

d. Susan Halek receives a $50 check for a graduation present.

e. Susan Halek spends the money she received as a gift to purchase a new handbag.

f. The Smith family buys a car from a neighbor who is moving.

3. Use the statistics given in the table below to calculate the following: **a.** gross national product, **b.** net national product, **c.** national income, **d.** personal income, e. disposable income.

Consumer spending	$960 billion
Government purchases	$400 billion
Depreciation	$ 80 billion
Purchases of capital goods	$240 billion
Change in business inventories	$ 40 billion
Government transfers	$160 billion
Undistributed profits	$ 60 billion
Personal taxes	$120 billion
Wages	$700 billion
Indirect business taxes	$ 20 billion
Net exports	$ 40 billion

DISCUSSING ECONOMIC QUESTIONS

1. Which measure of the economy appears to be the most important to you as an individual? Why?

2. Do you think the amount and types of natural resources that a nation possesses affects its gross national product? How? Use specific natural resources in your answer.

3. Some economists believe that the federal budget should be balanced in boom times, but that hard times might require it to become unbalanced. Explain why they believe this.

APPLYING CRITICAL THINKING SKILLS

1. **Researching Data for a Graph.** Go to the library and find the latest edition of the *Statistical Abstract of the United States*. Locate the tables in the "Prices" section that give price indexes for consumer goods for selected cities and metropolitan areas. Make a line graph showing the rise in the index for "all items" in a city or area near you over the last six years. Draw on the same graph a line indicating the "city average" index for "all items" over the same period of time.

2. **Gathering Information.** Consult recent articles about the nation's major indicators in newspapers and magazines. Summarize their description of the economy's performance.

READINGS

Bagby, Wesley M. *Contemporary American Economic and Political Problems*. Chicago: Nelson Hall, 1981.

Bartlett, Bruce R. *Reaganomics: Supply Side Economics in Action*. Westport, Conn.: Arlington House, 1982.

Brue, Stanley L., and Wentworth, Donald R. *Economic Scenes: Theory in Today's World*. 3rd ed. Englewood Cliffs, N.J.: Prentice-Hall, 1984.

CHAPTER 15

U.S. BULLION DEPOSITORY
FORT KNOX KY.

Money and banking are a vital part of the nation's economy. The use of paper money and checks as well as banking services benefits businesses and individuals alike.

MONEY AND BANKING

What money is, why the United States uses paper money, how much money there is in the country—these are probably ideas you take for granted. This chapter describes money: its functions, different types, and characteristics. Because the history of money and banking is so important to the growth of the United States, the chapter presents a time line showing the interrelated development of the nation's money and banking systems. You will also read about money in the United States today as well as a description of modern banking services. Learning Economic Skills describes the use of a checking account.

CHAPTER OBJECTIVES After you study this chapter, you will be able to:

1 • list the three functions of money.

2 • contrast the three types of money.
   • describe the six characteristics of money.

3 • summarize the history of the development of money and banking in the United States.

4 • explain the three types of money in use in the United States today.
   • define the money supply in the United States.

5 • list modern banking services available from many banking institutions.
   ★ describe how to write and endorse a check correctly and how to balance a checkbook.

ECONOMICS VOCABULARY

money
medium of exchange
barter
double coincidence of wants
unit of accounting
store of value
commodity money
representative money
fiat money
legal tender
monetary standard
checking account
demand deposit
near monies
M1
M2
electronic funds transfer
overdraft checking
endorse
blank endorsement
restrictive endorsement
special endorsement

Consumers at this outdoor market in Mexico City use Mexican pesos, their nation's medium of exchange, to purchase what they want.

In Unit IV, you read about how American businesses produce, market, and distribute their goods and services. But what makes it possible for businesses to obtain what they need from suppliers and for consumers to obtain finished goods? Money is the answer. **Money** is defined as anything customarily used as a medium of exchange, a unit of accounting, and a store of value. As you read in Chapter 8, the basis of the market economy is voluntary exchange. In the American economy, the exchange usually involves money in return for a good or service.

1 | THE FUNCTIONS OF MONEY

Ask yourself as you read:
- What is money?
- Why is using money preferable to bartering?

Though most Americans think of money as bills, coins, and checks, in other economies money might be shells, gold, or even goods such as sheep. Economists identify money by the presence or absence of certain functions. Anything is considered money that is used as a medium of exchange, a unit of accounting, and a store of value.

MEDIUM OF EXCHANGE

To say that money is a **medium of exchange** simply means that a seller will accept it in exchange for a good or service. Most people are paid for their work in money, which they then can use to buy whatever they need or want. Without money people would have to **barter**—exchange goods and services for other goods and services.

Suppose you worked in a grocery store and were paid in groceries because money did not exist. To get whatever else you needed, such as clothes and housing, you would have to find people who have the goods or could perform the services that you want. In addition, those people would have to want the exact goods or services—in this case, groceries—that you have. Barter requires what economists call a **double coincidence of wants.** Each party to a transaction must want exactly what the other person has to offer. This situation is rare. As a result, people in societies that barter for goods spend great amounts of time and effort making trades with one another. They waste much of their own potential for making goods or services in bartering for what they cannot make. Bartering can only work in small societies with fairly simple economic systems.

UNIT OF ACCOUNTING

Money is the yardstick that allows people to compare the values of goods and services in relation to one another. Money that is a measure of value functions in this way as a **unit of accounting.** Each nation uses a basic unit to measure the value of goods, as it uses the foot or meter to measure distance. In the United States, this basis unit of value is the dollar. In Germany, it is the mark; in France, the franc. An item for sale is marked with a price that indicates its value in terms of that unit— $.50, $5.00, and so on.

Using money as the single unit of accounting provides a simple and convenient way to compare the values of various items. By using money prices as a factor in comparing goods, people can determine whether one item is a better buy than another. A single unit of accounting also allows people to keep accurate financial records—records of debts owed, income saved, and so on. Business men and women can better calculate their profits and losses over the years by using a single money unit of accounting.

STORE OF VALUE

Money also serves as a **store of value.** In other words, you can sell something, such as your labor, and store the purchasing power that results from the sale in the form of money for later use. People usually receive their money income once a week, once every two weeks, or once a month. However, they usually spend their income at different times during a pay period. To be able to buy things between paydays, a person can store some of his or her income in cash and some in a checking account. It is important to note that in periods of rapid and unpredictable inflation, money is less able to act as a store of value.

REVIEWING ECONOMIC PRINCIPLES

1. Define the following economic terms: **a.** money, **b.** medium of exchange, **c.** barter, **d.** double coincidence of wants, **e.** unit of accounting, **f.** store of value.
2. What are the three functions that must be present for an item to be considered money?
3. **Critical Thinking: Explaining the Main Idea.** Choose one function of money and explain it.

2 | TYPES AND CHARACTERISTICS OF MONEY

Ask yourself as you read:
• What are the most important types of money?
• What is the most common type of money used today?

Anything that people are willing to accept in exchange for goods can serve as money. At various times in history, cattle, salt, animal hides, gems, and tobacco have been used as mediums of exchange. Each of these items has certain characteristics that make it better or worse than others for use as money. Cattle, for example, are difficult to transport,

Every American recognizes and accepts money issued by the nation's government. How does the dollar serve as this nation's unit of accounting?

Table 15-1: CHARACTERISTICS OF MONEY

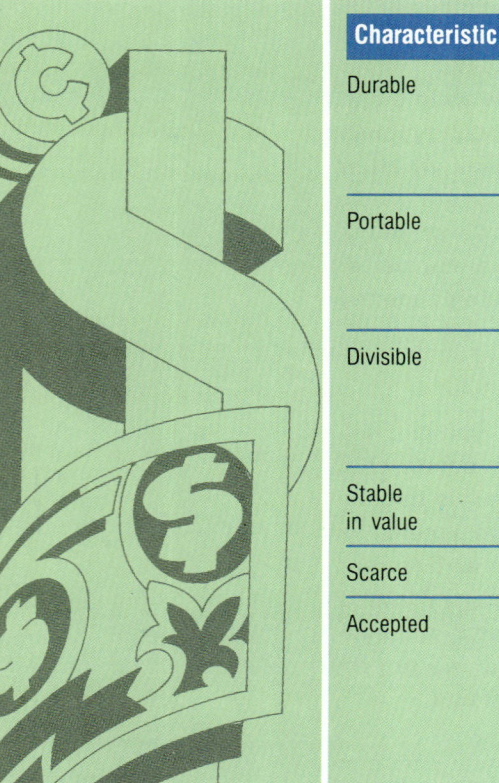

Characteristic	Description
Durable	The material that is used as money must be able to withstand the wear and tear of being passed from person to person. Paper money lasts on the average of only one year, but old bills can be easily replaced. Coins, on the other hand, last for years.
Portable	People need a medium of exchange that they can carry around easily so they can buy things whenever and wherever they want. Though paper money is not very durable, it is very portable. People can easily carry large sums of paper money.
Divisible	It must be possible to divide money into small parts so that purchases of any price can be made. Carrying large amounts of coins and small bills is not handy, but these make it possible to make purchases of any amount.
Stable in value	Money must be stable in value. Its value cannot change rapidly or its usefulness as a store of value will decrease.*
Scarce	Whatever is used as money must be scarce. That is what gives it value.*
Accepted	Whatever is used as money must be accepted as a medium of exchange by those who use it. They must be willing to accept it in payment for debts and to pass it on to others. In the United States, that acceptance is based on the knowledge that others will continue to accept paper money, coins, and checks in exchange for desired goods and services.

*You will read more about the changing value of money in Chapters 16 and 18.

but they are durable. Gems are easy to carry, but they are not easy to split into small pieces to use.

Mediums of exchange such as cattle and gems are considered **commodity money.** That is, they have a value as a commodity, or good, aside from their value as money. Cattle are used for food and transportation. Gems are used for jewelry. Salt, for another example, was used as a seasoning as well as money.

Representative money, though not in itself valuable for nonmoney uses, can be exchanged for some valuable item. Money of this sort is said to be backed by—exchangeable for—some commodity, such as gold or silver. Like commodity money, the amount of representative money in circulation, or in use by people, is limited. This is because it is linked to some scarce good, such as gold. At one time, the United States government issued representative money in the form of silver and gold certificates. In addition, private banks accepted deposits of gold or silver and issued paper money, called bank notes. These were a promise to convert the note into coin or bullion on demand. These banks were supposed to keep enough gold or silver in reserve-on hand-to redeem their bank notes. As you will read in this chapter, they often did not.

in circulation: passing from person to person

bullion (BUL-yuhn): gold or silver in the form of bars

378

Today all United States money is **fiat** (FEE-aht) **money.** Its face value occurs through government fiat, or order. It is in this way declared **legal tender.** This means that by law the money must be accepted for payment of public and private debts. In reality, fiat money is accepted because we all have faith that others will accept this money from us when we use it to buy things.

Table 15-1 lists the major characteristics that to some degree all items used as money must have. Almost any item that meets most of these criteria can be and probably has been used as money. However, precious metals, particularly gold and silver, are especially well-suited as mediums of exchange and have often been used as such throughout history. It is only in more recent times that paper money has been used as a medium of exchange.

REVIEWING ECONOMIC PRINCIPLES

1. What is the difference between commodity and representative money?
2. What is the difference between commodity and fiat money?
3. What type of money does the United States use?
4. What is legal tender?
5. **Critical Thinking: Summarizing Main Ideas.** Write a paragraph describing the six characteristics that any item used as money must have to some degree.

These bills of credit were issued by the Continental Congress to help finance the Revolutionary War. Were they an effective form of money?

3 | HISTORY OF AMERICAN MONEY AND BANKING

Ask yourself as you read:
• When did Congress gain the sole power to mint coins?
• When was the First Bank of the United States founded?

During the colonial period, the English colonies were for the most part forbidden to print or mint their own money. Bartering was common. Colonists used various goods in place of coins and paper money. In Massachusetts Bay for a time, colonists used Native American wampum—beads made from shells and strung on thread—as a medium of exchange. In the Virginia Colony, tobacco became commodity money. Though scarce, some European gold and silver coins also circulated in the colonies. The Spanish doubloon, later called the dolár by colonists, was one of the more common. It could be cut into equal parts, such as halves, quarters, and eighths. Because Spanish dolárs could actually be cut into eight pieces, they came to be called "pieces of eight."

The Revolutionary War brought even more confusion to this already haphazard system. To help pay for the war, the Continental Congress

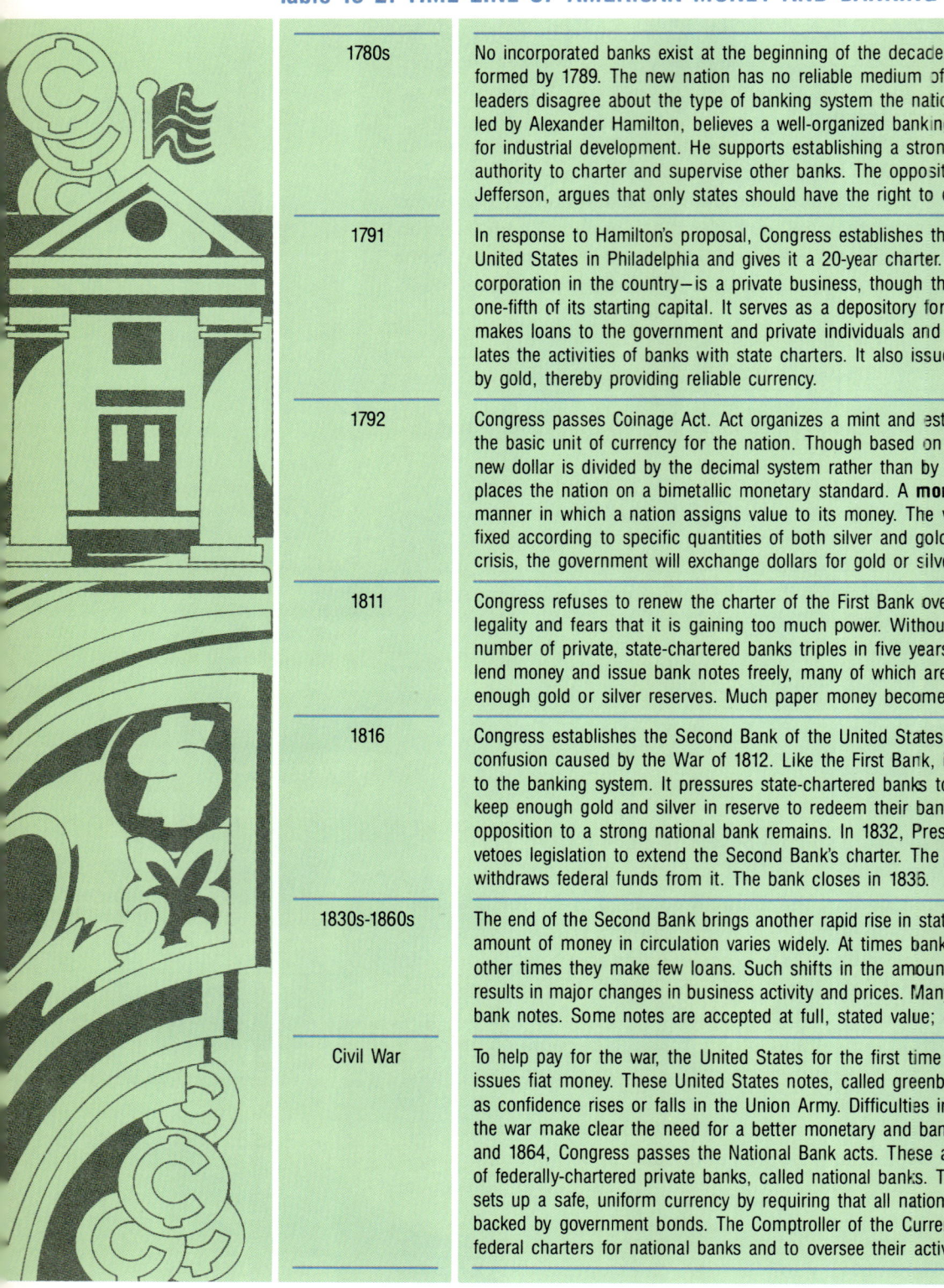

Table 15-2: TIME LINE OF AMERICAN MONEY AND BANKING

1780s	No incorporated banks exist at the beginning of the decade, and only three are formed by 1789. The new nation has no reliable medium of exchange. National leaders disagree about the type of banking system the nation needs. One group, led by Alexander Hamilton, believes a well-organized banking system is necessary for industrial development. He supports establishing a strong national bank with authority to charter and supervise other banks. The opposition, led by Thomas Jefferson, argues that only states should have the right to charter banks.
1791	In response to Hamilton's proposal, Congress establishes the First Bank of the United States in Philadelphia and gives it a 20-year charter. The bank—the largest corporation in the country—is a private business, though the government supplies one-fifth of its starting capital. It serves as a depository for government funds, makes loans to the government and private individuals and businesses, and regulates the activities of banks with state charters. It also issues bank notes backed by gold, thereby providing reliable currency.
1792	Congress passes Coinage Act. Act organizes a mint and establishes the dollar as the basic unit of currency for the nation. Though based on the Spanish dólar, the new dollar is divided by the decimal system rather than by eights. The act also places the nation on a bimetallic monetary standard. A **monetary standard** is the manner in which a nation assigns value to its money. The value of the dollar is fixed according to specific quantities of both silver and gold. Except for times of crisis, the government will exchange dollars for gold or silver in these ratios.
1811	Congress refuses to renew the charter of the First Bank over questions of its legality and fears that it is gaining too much power. Without federal controls, the number of private, state-chartered banks triples in five years. Dozens of banks lend money and issue bank notes freely, many of which are not backed by enough gold or silver reserves. Much paper money becomes worthless.
1816	Congress establishes the Second Bank of the United States after the financial confusion caused by the War of 1812. Like the First Bank, it brings some order to the banking system. It pressures state-chartered banks to limit lending and to keep enough gold and silver in reserve to redeem their bank notes. However, opposition to a strong national bank remains. In 1832, President Andrew Jackson vetoes legislation to extend the Second Bank's charter. The following year he withdraws federal funds from it. The bank closes in 1836.
1830s-1860s	The end of the Second Bank brings another rapid rise in state-chartered banks. The amount of money in circulation varies widely. At times banks lend freely and at other times they make few loans. Such shifts in the amount of money available results in major changes in business activity and prices. Many banks issue their own bank notes. Some notes are accepted at full, stated value; others are worthless.
Civil War	To help pay for the war, the United States for the first time since the Revolution issues fiat money. These United States notes, called greenbacks, change in value as confidence rises or falls in the Union Army. Difficulties in raising money for the war make clear the need for a better monetary and banking system. In 1863 and 1864, Congress passes the National Bank acts. These acts establish a system of federally-chartered private banks, called national banks. The government also sets up a safe, uniform currency by requiring that all national bank notes be fully backed by government bonds. The Comptroller of the Currency is created to grant federal charters for national banks and to oversee their activities.

Table 15-2: TIME LINE OF AMERICAN MONEY AND BANKING *(continued)*

Late 1860s-early 1900s	The nation shifts to a gold monetary standard in 1879. Federal government begins redeeming early 1900s greenbacks for gold coins. Despite the new banking system, problems remain. There is no simple way to regulate the amount of national bank notes in circulation so periodic shortages of money occur. On occasion, many people rush to exchange currency for gold. Financial panics occcur in 1873, 1884, 1893, and 1907. Many banks with low reserves are forced to close.
1913	To control the amount of money in circulation, Congress establishes the Federal Reserve System. It serves as the nation's central bank with power to regulate reserves in state and national banks, make loans to member banks, and control the growth of the money supply. In 1914, the system begins issuing fiat money, called Federal Reserve notes. Though national bank notes, greenbacks, and gold and silver coins and certificates remain in circulation, Federal Reserve notes soon become the major form of money in circulation.
1929	The Great Depression begins. Stocks and other investments owned by banks lose much of their value. Bankrupt businesses and individuals are unable to repay their loans. Many banks come under severe financial stain.
1929-1933	A financial panic causes thousands of banks to collapse. When President Franklin Roosevelt takes office on March 4, 1933, four-fifths of the states have stopped all banking operations. The next day Roosevelt declares a "bank holiday," closing all banks. Each bank is allowed to reopen only after it proves it is financially sound. Congress passes the Glass-Steagall Banking Act in June, establishing the Federal Deposit Insurance Corporation (FDIC). The new agency helps restore public confidence in banks by insuring funds of individual depositors in case of a bank failure. Nation switches from gold standard to a fiat monetary standard. Government stops converting greenbacks into gold, calls in all gold coins and certificates, and prohibits private ownership of gold. Silver coins and certificates remain in circulation until the mid-1960s.
1930s-1960s	Banking reforms of the 1930s allow banks to enter a period of long-term stability, in which few banks fail. Because of the public's trust in the FDIC, banks are no longer subject to panics or runs on deposits.
Late 1960s-1970s	Congress passes series of laws to protect consumers in dealing with banks and other depository institutions. Truth in Lending Act of 1968, Equal Credit Opportunity Act of 1974, and Community Reinvestment Act of 1977 make clear the rights and responsibilities of banks and consumers. They also provide individuals with procedures to file complaints if treated unfairly. Banks begin using computers to transfer money electronically and to handle many banking activities. Congress passes Electronic Funds Transfer Act of 1978 to protect consumers using these new services.
1980s	As part of the general move toward deregulation of business, Congress passes Depository Institutions Deregulation and Monetary Control Act in 1980. Act gradually removes ceilings on interest that financial institutions can pay on savings and permits interest payments on checking accounts. Act also allows savings and loan associations and savings banks to compete more directly with commercial banks. It gives the Federal Reserve System the power to set reserve requirements on *all* financial institutions—not just banks that are members in the Federal Reserve System.

Case Study

DELAWARE AS A BANKING CENTER

In 1981, the state of Delaware adopted the Financial Center Development Act. This law provides that out-of-state banks can open offices in Delaware. They cannot serve Delaware customers, but they can do just about everything else! Delaware was able to pass this measure as a result of a quirk in federal law. Congress allows states to bypass the ban on interstate banking by deciding for themselves if they wish to permit out-of-state bank holding companies. A bank holding company, like a corporate holding company, is set up to run one or several banks. One of the major advantages of establishing a holding company is that it may engage in other financial activities as well as banking.

In passing its 1981 law, Delaware opened itself up for amazing economic growth. Since the state passed this measure, many of the nation's largest bank holding companies have legally incorporated in Delaware. As a result, the state, which was economically depressed eight years ago, is thriving today. How did Delaware accomplish this feat?

First, Delaware offers banks and business is a strategic location. The state lies halfway between New York City and Washington, D.C. A third of the United States' population lives within 350 miles of Wilmington, the state's largest city. This makes Wilmington an attractive corporate site.

In addition the Financial Center Development Act has lured banks by offering them liberal tax breaks. The law abolishes usury limits for banks and provides a regressive tax structure. Banks are required to pay 8.7 percent on the first $20 million of their annual income. For annual income above that amount, the tax rate drops, in stages to 2.7 percent on income over $30 million. In this way, the tax structure, too, encourages large banks to establish in Delaware. At the same time, it discourages small banks from locating in Delaware by requiring that out-of-state banks start with at least $25 million in capital and have 100 employees within a year.

Since 1981, some of the biggest New York bank holding companies have moved their headquarters to Delaware. Morgan Bank opened in Wilmington in December, 1981, with $200 million in capital. By the end of 1982, the bank's assets there had grown to $1.65 billion! Chemical Bank, Manufacturers Hanover, Citibank, and Chase Manhatten all have made the move. In addition, Maryland's four largest banks have shifted their credit card operations to Delaware. Maryland lost nearly 1,000 jobs when these operations moved.

In general, the results for Delaware's economy have been phenomenal. The big-bank subsidiaries there have added employees. Two years after the Financial Center Development Act was passed, Delaware's economy saw an increase of 6,800 jobs in retailing, construction, and manufacturing. Employment rose at a time when neighboring states were experiencing declines.

The only criticism to Delaware's liberal banking laws comes from those who accuse the state of "raiding"—attracting business at the expense of neighboring states. However, former Governor Pierre S. DuPont, who was, in large part, responsible for Delaware's turnaround, states flatly, "We are not raiders, we are creating jobs." And indeed Delaware has. Soon other states may follow Delaware's lead.

1. How has Delaware benefited from the Financial Center Development Act?
2. What have been the advantages to out-of-state bank holding companies moving their headquarters to Delaware?

382

issued bills of credit, called Continentals, that could be used to pay debts. So many of these notes were issued that people often refused to accept them. The money became so worthless that the phrase "not worth a Continental" came to mean something of little value.

After the war, establishing a reliable medium of exchange became a major concern of the new nation. The Constitution, ratified in 1788, gave Congress the sole power to mint coins. Private banks were still allowed to print bank notes representing gold and silver on deposit. Because the history of money in the United States is so closely tied to the development of the banking system, the time line on pp. 312–313 describes both.

mint: to make coins out of metal

REVIEWING ECONOMIC PRINCIPLES

---

1. In a paragraph summarize the history of money in the colonies before and during the Revolutionary War.
2. According to the time line, what was the controversy over establishing a banking system in the new nation? Answer in a paragraph.
3. **a.** What is a monetary standard? **b.** Read the time line and list the dates on which the United States changed its monetary standard.
4. **Critical Thinking: Analyzing Information.** From the time line, list two events that would have shown legislators in the early 1900s that some central banking authority was needed.

4 | TYPES OF MONEY IN THE UNITED STATES

Ask yourself as you read:
- What types of money are in use today?
- What are federal reserve notes? demand deposits?

Money in use today consists of more than just currency. It also includes money deposited in checking and savings accounts in banks and savings institutions, plus certain other investments.

CURRENCY

All United States coins in use today are token coins. That is, the value of the metal in each coin is less than its exchange value. A quarter, for example, consists of a mixture of copper and nickel. If you melted down a quarter—which is illegal—the value of the resulting metal would be less than 25 cents. All coins are made by the Bureau of the Mint, which is part of the Treasury Department. The government produces coins in six denominations: 1¢, 5¢, 10¢, 25¢, 50¢, and $1. Of the currency in circulation in the United States today, about 9 percent is in coins.

Most of the nation's currency is in the form of Federal Reserve notes. These notes are issued by the Federal Reserve Banks, which you will read about in Chapter 16. All Federal Reserve notes are printed by the Bureau of Printing and Engraving, also part of the Treasury Department. They are issued in denominations of $1, $5, $10, $20, $50, and $100. Bills of higher denominations were once issued, but have since been recalled by the Federal Reserve.

The Treasury Department has also issued United States notes in $100 denominations only. These bills have the words *United States Note* printed across the top and can be distinguished from Federal Reserve Notes by the red Treasury seal on the right side of the note's face. These make up less than 1 percent of the paper money in circulation. Both Federal Reserve notes and United States notes are fiat money or legal tender.

CHECKS

A **checking account** is money deposited in a bank that a person can withdraw at any time by writing a check. The bank must pay the amount of the check when it is presented for payment, that is, on demand. For this reason, such accounts are called **demand deposits.** In the United States, most purchases and debts are paid with checks that are written on checking accounts. Checking-account and checking-type-account balances are considered a form of money. They serve all the functions of money. They are a medium of exchange and provide a convenient unit of accounting and store of value.

Until the 1970s, only commercial banks could legally offer checking accounts. Since then, regulatory changes and new laws have altered the concept of demand deposits and increased the types of accounts that offer check-writing privileges. Beginning in 1974, savings and loan associations, savings banks, and commercial banks in a few northeastern states were allowed by the federal government to offer checking-type accounts that paid interest. Permission for the service was extended to similar banking institutions nationwide on December 31, 1980. Credit unions can also offer checking-type accounts called share drafts.

NEAR MONIES

There are numerous other assets that are almost but not exactly like money. These are called **near monies.** Their values are stated in terms of money, and they have high liquidity in comparison to other investments, such as stocks. That is, near monies can be turned into currency or into a means of payment such as a check relatively easily and without the risk of loss of value. For example, if you have a bank savings account, you cannot write a check on it. But you can go to the bank and withdraw some or all of your funds. You can then redeposit it in your checking account or take it in cash to buy what you want.

Figure 15–2: GROWTH IN THE MONEY SUPPLY, 1977–1986

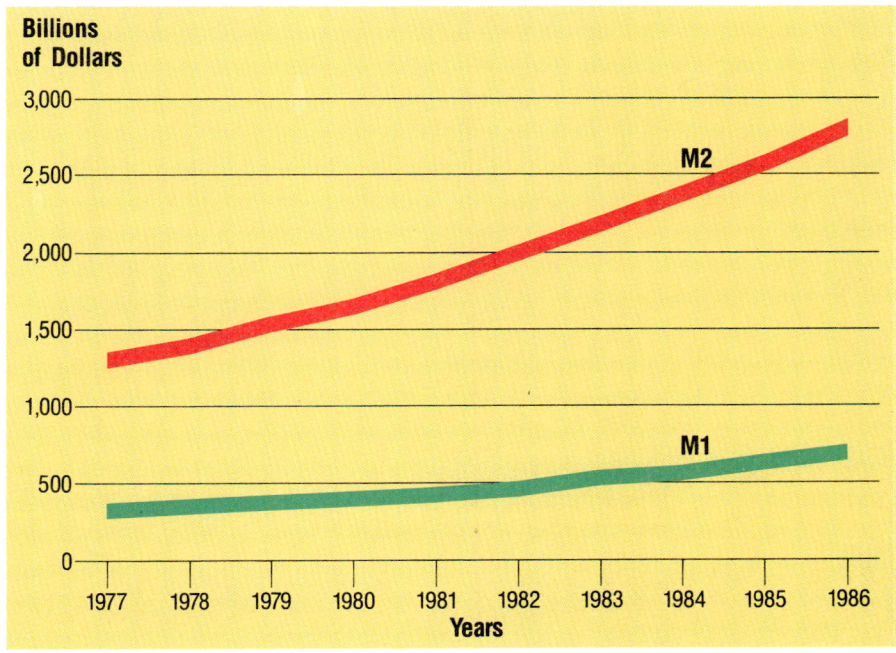

Billions of Dollars

Years

Source: *Federal Reserve Bulletin,* Board of Governors of the Federal Reserve System

With the deregulation of banking services in the early 1980s, the definition of the money supply was enlarged to include the new types of accounts.

Time deposits are near monies as are savings-account balances. Both pay interest, and neither can be withdrawn by check. They require that a depositor notify the financial institution within a certain period of time, often 10 days, before withdrawing any money. However, with savings accounts, this practice is usually waived.

waive: to give up a right

THE MONEY SUPPLY

How much money is there in the United States today? That question is not so easy to answer. First, the money supply must be defined and agreed upon. Currently, two basic definitions are used, although there are others. The first is called M1 and the second M2. Both definitions include all the paper bills and coins in circulation. The difference lies in what checking-type accounts are included.

M1, the narrowest definition of the money supply, consists of monies that can be spent immediately and against which checks can be written. It includes currency, traveler's checks, demand deposits and other checking-type deposits in commercial banks, savings institutions, and credit unions. A broader definition of the money supply, **M2,** includes all of M1, plus such near monies as overnight repurchase agreements and Euro dollars, money market mutual fund balances, money market deposit accounts (MMDAs), and savings in small time deposits. Figure 15-1 shows the growth of M1 and M2 over a 10-year period. As you will read in Chapter 16, measuring M1 or M2 exactly is difficult.

Table 15-3: BANKING SERVICES

Service	Description
Checking accounts	A checking account offers a safe and convenient way to transfer money from one person to another. If a check is lost or stolen, a stop-payment order can be placed on it for a small fee and the customer will not lose his or her money. Canceled checks returned with the monthly bank statement are also proof that bills have been paid.
Interest on checking	Both NOW and Super NOW accounts combine the benefits of checking and savings accounts. They offer check-writing privileges and interest on any unused money in the account. NOW accounts, however, offer a low rate of interest compared to other savings plans. Super NOW accounts pay higher rates of interest, but typically require a minimum balance of at least $2,500 in order to earn that high rate of interest.
Automatic deposit and payment	Many financial institutions now allow their customers to have their paychecks automatically deposited by their employer. Social Security checks may also be deposited automatically. Some institutions also offer automatic payment of major recurring bills, such as mortgage payments or utility bills. Often these services are tied in with an EFT system, which allows a customer to pay bills or transfer funds over the phone.
Storage of valuables	A bank usually sets aside a part of its vault space to store valuables such as stock certificates, real estate deeds, and jewelry for an annual fee. A safe deposit box is kept under dual lock and key. Both the customer's key and the bank's key must be used at the same time to open the box.

REVIEWING ECONOMIC PRINCIPLES

1. Why are checking-account and checking-type account balances considered a form of money?
2. Explain what is meant by the term *near monies.*
3. **Critical Thinking: Comparing. a.** State the two definitions of the money supply. **b.** What is the difference between the two?

5 | BANKING SERVICES

Ask yourself as you read:
- What is EFT?
- What important services do banks provide?

Banks and savings institutions today offer a wide variety of services. You have already read about some of them—credit services in Chapter 4 and savings plans in Chapter 7. In general, the types of services are

Table 15-3: BANKING SERVICES *(continued)*

Service	Description
Transfer of money	Banks and savings institutions offer several other services that transfer money from one person to another. **1.** A certified check is a personal check that a bank has guaranteed will be honored when it is cashed. A bank does this by taking out of a customer's account enough money to cover the check as soon as it is written. A small fee is usually charged for this service. **2.** A cashier's check enables a person without a checking account to send a guaranteed check. To obtain a cashier's check, a person must give the amount of the check to the bank in cash, plus a fee. The bank then issues a check payable to whomever the purchaser requests. **3.** A money order is essentially the same as a cashier's check, but is usually used for small amounts—less than $1,000. **4.** Traveler's checks, like the guaranteed checks above, are paid for when they are bought. They are issued in denominations of $10, $20, $50, $100, $500, and $1,000. A small fee is charged for every $100 of checks bought.
Overdraft checking	**Overdraft checking** allows a customer to borrow money by writing checks for more money than is in his or her account. The overdraft is the extra money for which the check is written. Instead of refusing payment, the bank automatically deposits the extra money into the customer's account. This is a loan, but the customer does not have to fill out a loan application. Repayment of the principal plus interest is made in regular amounts over a period of time. Customers may write new overdrafts while paying off old ones. The interest rates that banks charge for this convenient use of credit are high.

the same across the country. But the exact conditions of the services vary from state to state according to each state's banking laws. Table 15-3 describes checking-type accounts and additional banking services.

In choosing a bank or savings institution for a checking-type account, you should consider the service charges. Service charges on checking accounts vary from bank to bank and with the type of account. You may be charged from $.25 to $.50 for each check you write. Or you may be charged a flat fee of $4 to $6 per month if your account balance for the month drops below a minimum amount. The minimum ranges from $100 to $500. Some institutions offer "free checking"—no per check fee or monthly fee—providing the balance in the account remains above a minimum. If it drops below this minimum, a service charge is collected.

ELECTRONIC BANKING

One of the most important changes in banking began in the late 1970s with the introduction of the computer. With it came **electronic funds transfer** (EFT), a system of putting onto computers all the various banking functions that in the past had to be handled on paper.

Learning Economic Skills

KEEPING A CHECKING ACCOUNT

The easiest way to pay bills and keep track of your money is with a checking account. Writing and endorsing a check correctly are fairly easy to do. Keeping an accurate record of your checking account requires more skill.

WRITING A CHECK

Before writing a check, you should always fill out your check stub or check register. In this way you will have an accurate record of the checks you write, including the check number, date, amount, payee, and balance. The illustration on p. 389 shows a typical page from a checkbook register.

For your own protection always fill out checks in ink, clearly and completely, so that your check cannot be altered. When writing a check, follow these steps:

1. Enter the date when the check is actually being written. Postdating, or writing a check now but dating it later, is not wise. A check should not be cashed until the date that appears on it. If you postdate a check in the hopes of having sufficient funds later to cover it, you may find yourself with an overdraft because the bank mistakenly cashed it.
2. Spell the payee's name correctly. Be careful about making out checks to *cash.* If you lose such a check, anyone can cash it.
3. Enter the amount in numerals as close as possible to the dollar sign. This is to prevent anyone else from increasing the amount.
4. Write the amount on the line below the name of the payee. Start as far to the left as possible and draw a line through any inused space. By doing this, you prevent anyone else from adding words that would raise the amount.
5. Sign the check on the signature line as your signature appears in your bank's records.

Many banks print their checks with a line to the left of the signature where you can indicate what the check is for, such as rent or groceries.

At the bottom of each check are a series of numerals and symbols. The first nine numerals help route the check through the Federal Reserve's check-clearing system. You will read more about how checks are cleared in Chapter 16. The next group of numerals is your account number, and the last set of numerals is the number of the particular check you are writing. These numerals are the same as the check number at the top right of the check. Business checks have a slightly different arrangement of symbols, but the information they show is the same.

ENDORSING A CHECK

Besides writing checks, you will also probably be depositing checks, such as your paycheck, in your checking account. To deposit a check, you must **endorse** it. This means to sign your name on the back of the check so that it can be cleared and the money transferred from the account of the person who wrote the check to your account. In endorsing a check, you should sign your name exactly as it is written on the front, with or without initials and with any misspellings.

There are three types of endorsements. To use a **blank endorsement,** you simply write your name on the back of the check. With this method, whoever has the check may deposit or cash it. This means that if the check is lost or stolen, anyone can cash it by endorsing the check below your name.

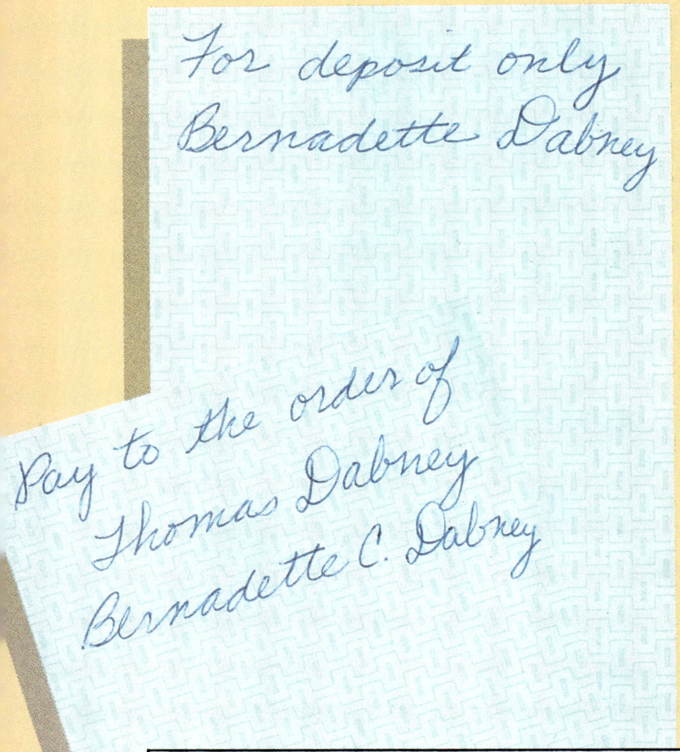

A **restrictive endorsement** uses the words *For deposit only* and your signature. With this type of endorsement, no one else can deposit the check to his or her account or cash it.

A **special endorsement** is used if you want to transfer a check written to you to someone else without having to deposit it in your account and write a new check. The person to whom you endorse the check signs his or her name below yours and deposits or cashes the check.

BALANCING YOUR CHECKBOOK

Every month the bank will send you your canceled checks and a statement of your account. It is important to check your bank balance against your checkbook balance so that you know exactly how much money you have in your account. You can also discover any mistakes the bank might have made and find out if someone has not cashed a check that you wrote.

Rarely will your checkbook balance agree with the balance on your bank statement. If you wrote checks immediately before the closing date on your bank statement, they probably will not have

For deposit only
Bernadette Dabney

Pay to the order of
Thomas Dabney
Bernadette C. Dabney

NUMBER	DATE	DESCRIPTION OF TRANSACTION	PAYMENT/DEBIT (-)	√ T	FEE (IF ANY) (-)	DEPOSIT/CREDIT (+)	BALANCE
		RECORD ALL CHARGES OR CREDITS THAT AFFECT YOUR ACCOUNT					$ 827 91
132	10/25	The Fashion Shop (dress)	$ 33 00	√	$	$	794 91
133	11/1	Rent	462 50	√			332 41
134	11/7	Phone Company	62 00	√			270 41
135	11/14	Cash	50 00	√			220 41
136	11/15	J. W. Little (chorus dues)	10 00				210 41
137	11/15	National Geographic (subscription)	21 00	√			189 41
—	11/22	John's check				4 00	193 41
—	11/23	Paycheck				500 61	694 02
138	11/29	Walk-A-Boot (shoes)	40 16				653 86
139	12/1	Rent	462 50				191 36

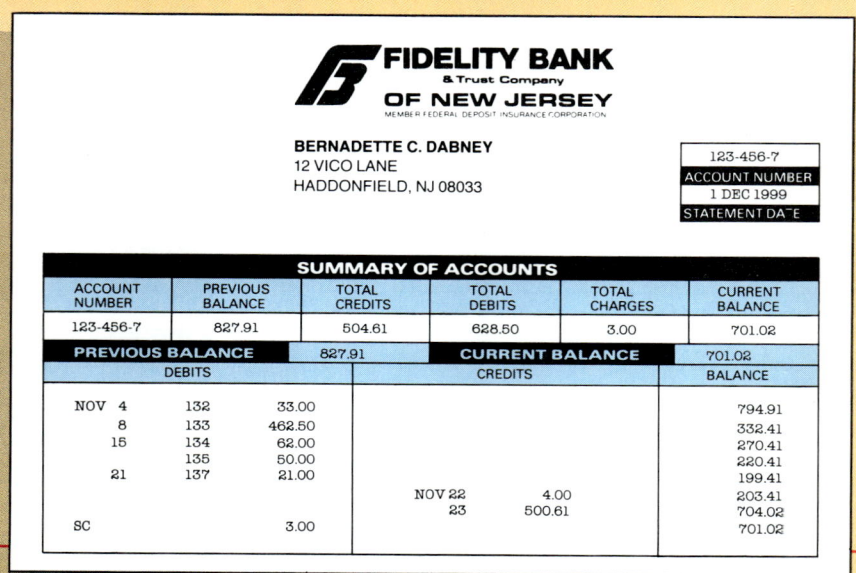

BERNADETTE C. DABNEY
12 VICO LANE
HADDONFIELD, NJ 08033

205

December 31, 19 _99_   55-255
312

PAY TO THE ORDER OF _cash_ $ _100_

One hundred _____ DOLLARS

FIDELITY BANK & TRUST COMPANY
OF NEW JERSEY
322 HIGH ST.
BURLINGTON, N. J. 08016

MEMO _Visa bill_   _Bernadette C. Dabney_

⑈:031202563⑈: ⑈123⑈456 7⑈ 0205

---

been paid by the bank yet. Depending on the type of account you have, you may have a monthly service charge and/or per check charges subtracted from your account balance. These will appear on your bank statement but not in your checkbook register. To check your balance, follow these steps:

1. Sort your checks by check number. You can then check them off in your checkbook register to determine which checks have not yet cleared.
2. Sort your deposit slips and check them off.
3. Deduct from your checkbook balance any service charges and/or per check fees.
4. Add to the balance on the bank statement any deposits that have not cleared.
5. Add up the amount of checks that have not yet cleared. Subtract the total of these checks from the amount on your bank state-

ment. The result should be the same as your checkbook balance minus the service charge and/or per check fees.

Keep your canceled checks and bank statements. They may be your only proof that you have paid a bill or made a deposit. Also, for income tax purposes, it is important to keep bank statements and canceled checks for at least three years.

Practicing Your Skills

1. Read the check made out below, and list the errors made in writing it.
2. According to the checkbook register on p. 389, you have a running total of $191.36 in your account. Balance this total against the statement below for the month of November. Follow the steps outlined above.
3. Why is there a difference between your running balance and the statement balance?

FIDELITY BANK
& Trust Company
OF NEW JERSEY
MEMBER FEDERAL DEPOSIT INSURANCE CORPORATION

BERNADETTE C. DABNEY
12 VICO LANE
HADDONFIELD, NJ 08033

123-456-7
ACCOUNT NUMBER
1 DEC 1999
STATEMENT DATE

SUMMARY OF ACCOUNTS

ACCOUNT NUMBER	PREVIOUS BALANCE	TOTAL CREDITS	TOTAL DEBITS	TOTAL CHARGES	CURRENT BALANCE
123-456-7	827.91	504.61	628.50	3.00	701.02

PREVIOUS BALANCE		827.91	CURRENT BALANCE		701.02

DEBITS			CREDITS		BALANCE
NOV 4	132	33.00			794.91
8	133	462.50			332.41
15	134	62.00			270.41
	135	50.00			220.41
21	137	21.00			199.41
			NOV 22	4.00	203.41
			23	500.61	704.02
SC		3.00			701.02

One of the most common features of EFT is automated teller machines (ATMs). These units let consumers do their banking without the help of a teller. ATMs receive deposits, give out funds from checking or savings accounts, transfer funds from one account to another, verify balances, and accept payments. To use an ATM, the customer inserts an encoded plastic card into the machine and enters a personal identification number on a keyboard. This is to make sure that the person is authorized to use that card. Most ATMs are available 24 hours a day.

Point-of-sale terminals are a less common but growing part of EFT. Such systems allow the consumer to make purchases through direct transfer of funds to a merchant. This is done through terminals located at check-out counters in the merchant's store. The customer's card is inserted into the terminal to verify that there is enough money in the customer's account. The amount of the purchase is then subtracted from the customer's account and transferred to the merchant's.

A few banks have authorized customers with home computers to use them for banking transactions. If problems with security can be solved, many people may one day bank by computer from home.

Although EFT can save time, trouble, and costs in making transactions, it does have some drawbacks. The possibility of tampering and lack of privacy is increased because all records are stored in a computer. A person on a computer terminal could call up and read or even alter the account files of a bank customer in any city if he or she knew how to get around the safeguards built into the system. Another problem for customers—but a benefit for banking institutions—is the loss of "float," or the time between when you write a check and when the sum of the check is deducted from your account.

In response to these and other concerns, the Electronic Funds Transfer Act of 1978 describes the rights and responsibilities of participants in EFT systems. For example, EFT customers are responsible for only $50 in losses if someone illegally uses their card, if they report the card missing within two days. If they wait more than two days, they could be responsible for as much as $500. Users are also protected against computer foulups. If the balance appearing on a person's statement or given out by an automatic or human teller is less than the customer believes it to be, the bank must investigate and straighten out the problem within a certain period of time.

REVIEWING ECONOMIC PRINCIPLES

1. Define the following economic terms: **a.** electronic funds transfer, **b.** overdraft checking.
2. In choosing a banking institution for a checking-type account, what is one factor to consider?
3. What are three uses of the electronic funds transfer system?
4. **Critical Thinking: Expressing Opinions.** Write a paragraph explaining what you think is the main drawback to EFT.

SUMMARY OF
IMPORTANT PRINCIPLES

1
- Anything is considered money that is used as a medium of exchange, a unit of accounting, and a store of value.

2
- Commodity money has a value as a commodity, or good, aside from its value as money. Representative money, though not in itself valuable for nonmoney uses, can be exchanged for some valuable item. Fiat money has value because a government fiat, or order, has established it as legal tender. That is, by law it must be accepted for payment of public and private debts.
- Anything that is used as money must meet most of these criteria to some degree: durable, portable, divisible, stable in value, scarce, and accepted.

3
- The history of the nation's money and banks has been a process of gradually bringing order to a disordered system. Congress took the first step in this direction in 1792 when it established the dollar as the basic unit of currency and set up the first mint. For two 20-year periods between 1791 and the Civil War, the nation's banking system was kept in order by a strong central bank. At other times, state-chartered banks often caused economic chaos by over issuing bank notes and lending too much money. Despite a national banking system set up by Congress in 1863 and 1864, financial panics continued to occur because banks were unable to meet sudden demands for money. To end the panics, Congress in 1913 established the Federal Reserve System. It was given power to control bank reserves and the money supply. The FDIC, set up in 1933 in response to many bank failures, restored consumer confidence in banks by providing deposit insurance. As a result, the banking industry entered a period of long-term stability. Recent bank changes have included new consumer protection laws, a move toward electronic banking, and deregulation of much of the industry.

4
- United States money today is in the form of currency (coins and paper money), checking-account and checking-type-account balances, and near monies.
- The money supply in the United States may be defined as M1 or M2. M1 equals money that can be spent immediately and against which checks can be written. It includes currency, traveler's checks, plus checking accounts and checking-type accounts in commercial banks and savings institutions. M2 includes all of M1, plus certain near monies—savings accounts, money market accounts, time deposits, and money market funds.

5
- Modern banking services include: electronic banking; checking accounts; interest on checking in the form of NOW and Super NOW accounts; overdraft checking; automatic deposit and payment; transfer of money through certified checks, cashier's checks, money orders, and traveler's checks; and storage of valuables.
- There are several steps that can be followed to write and endorse checks correctly and balance one's checkbook.

Putting Economics to Work

COMPARISON SHOPPING: BANKING

Celia Mason is finally out on her own. She has a job, an apartment, and a fairly new used car. Before she receives her first paycheck, she begins to shop for a bank. Her main concern is a checking account. But she finds that many banks offer many more services than just checking. After several days of using her lunch hour for comparison shopping, Celia decides to open an account at the First National Bank, two blocks from where she works.

At First National, Celia opens a NOW account. The account not only pays interest on her money but also gives her an automatic teller card and the ability to pay bills by phone. She has no passbook in which to record transactions. Instead, each month Celia receives a statement of all the transactions related to her account—interest, deposits, withdrawals, checks presented for payment, and bills paid by phone—all on one or two sheets of paper. In this way, Celia can easily keep a record of all her financial transactions. In return for these services, Celia has to keep a minimum balance of $500.00 in her account or pay a monthly fee of $4.00. Because Celia has over $700.00 saved, she has no problem in meeting the balance.

After several months, Celia finds that she often uses checks for purchases such as car repairs and groceries, and the pay-by-phone system to pay utility and department store bills, and the ATM card on evenings and weekends. Celia is pleased with the services her account at First National gives her.

1. Based on what you read in Chapter 7, what other alternatives does Celia have for saving her money?
2. What trade-offs would Celia have to make if she chose a regular checking account with a minimum balance requirement of $200?

Readings in Economics

OXEN FOR ARMOR

Skill: Applying Information

 The use of money arose out of the needs for a medium of exchange, unit of accounting, and store of value. In 1776, Adam Smith discussed the early origins of the use of money.

Many different commodities, it is probable, were successively both thought of and employed for this purpose [exchanging]. In the rude [early] ages of society, cattle are said to have been the common instrument of commerce; and, though they must have been a most inconvenient one, yet in old times we find things were frequently valued according to the number of cattle which had been given in exchange for them. . . . Salt is said to be the common instrument of commerce in some parts of the coast of India; dried cod at Newfoundland; tobacco in Virginia; sugar in some of our West Indian colonies; hides or dressed leather in some other countries; and there is at this day a village in Scotland where it is not uncommon, I am told, for a workman to carry nails instead of money to the baker's shop or the ale-house.

In all countries, however, men seem at last to have been determined by irresistible reasons to give the preference, for this employment [use], to metals above every other commodity. Metals can not only be kept with as little loss as any other commodity, . . . but they can likewise, without any loss, be divided into any number of parts, as by fusion those parts can easily be reunited again; a quality which no other equally durable commodities possess, and which more than any other quality renders them fit to be the instruments of commerce and circulation.

The man who wanted to buy salt, for example, and had nothing but cattle to give in exchange for it, must have been obliged to buy salt to the value of a whole ox, or a whole sheep, at a time. He could seldom buy less than this, because what he was to give for it could seldom be divided without loss; and if he had a mind to buy more, he must, for the same reasons, have been obliged to buy double or triple the quantity, the value, to wit, of two or three oxen, or of two or three sheep. If, on the contrary, instead of sheep or oxen, he had metals to give in exchange for it, he could easily proportion the quantity of the metal to the precise quantity of the commodity which he had immediate occasion for.

1. The characteristics of money include durability, divisibility, portability, stability in value, scarcity, and acceptability. Select three of the commodities listed in the article and describe why each was unsuitable as money. Why were metals more suitable?
2. One of the functions of money is to serve as a unit of accounting. Why do the commodities described in the reading not fulfill this important function?

Adam Smith, *The Wealth of Nations*, pp. 23, 24.

THE VALUE OF GREEN PAPER

Skill: Predicting Outcomes

 Since U.S. money is fiat money, it cannot be redeemed for gold, silver, or even cattle. Economist Milton Friedman, a Nobel laureate, explains why we value these strange pieces of paper.

Compare two rectangles of paper of about the same size. One is mostly green on the back side and has a picture of Abraham Lincoln on the front side, which also has the number 5 on each of its corners and some printing. You can exchange this piece of paper for some quantity of food, clothing, or other goods. People will willingly make the trade.

The other piece of paper, perhaps cut from a glossy magazine, may also have a picture, some numbers, and some printing on its face. It also may be colored green on its back. Yet it is fit only to light the fire.

Whence the difference? The printing on the $5 bill gives no answer. It simply says, "FEDERAL RESERVE NOTE / THE UNITED STATES OF AMERICA / FIVE DOLLARS" and, in smaller print, "THIS NOTE IS LEGAL TENDER FOR ALL DEBTS, PUBLIC AND PRIVATE." Until not very many years ago, the words "WILL PROMISE TO PAY" were included between "THE UNITED STATES OF AMERICA" and "FIVE DOLLARS." That seemed to explain the difference between the two pieces of paper. But it meant only that if you had gone to a Federal Reserve Bank and asked a teller to redeem the promise, he would have given you five identical pieces of paper except that the number 1 took the place of the number 5 and George Washington's picture the place of Abraham Lincoln's. If you had then asked the teller to pay the $1 promised by one of those pieces of paper, he would have given you coins which, if you had melted them down (despite its being illegal to do so), would have sold for less than $1 as metal. The present wording is at least more candid if equally unrevealing. The legal-tender quality means that the government will accept the pieces of paper in discharge of debts and taxes due to itself, and that the courts will regard them as discharging debts stated in dollars. Why should they also be accepted by private persons in private transactions in exchange for goods and services?

The short answer is that each person accepts them because he is confident that others will. The pieces of green paper have value because everybody thinks they have value. Everybody thinks they have value because in his experience they have had value. The United States could not operate at more than a small fraction of its present level of productivity without a common and widely accepted medium of exchange.

1. What do you predict would happen to the value of United States paper money if people refused to accept it in exchange for goods and services? What effect might this have in exchanges between buyers and sellers?
2. What would happen to productivity in the United States if there were no common and widely accepted medium of exchange?

From *Free to Choose* by Milton and Rose Friedman. © 1980 Milton Friedman and Rose D. Friedman. Reprinted by permission of Harcourt Brace Jovanovich.

A MOST ROMANTIC FORM OF MONEY
Skill: Identifying Main Ideas

 **When trading with American Indians, early colonial settlers did not use the same kind of money that they had used in Europe. Author Noble Foster Hoggson describes an unusual form of money that colonists did find useful.**

Quite the most romantic form of money ever employed by a civilized people was wampum, or, as it was sometimes called, peage. This unique currency descended to the first colonials along the Atlantic seabord as a heritage from the Indians of that region. It was not long, however, before the English and French settlers, as well as the Dutch traders who introduced it, were using it extensively.

From time immemorial the Indians had wrought [made] into various shapes bits of bright-colored clam shells which they dug along their native shores. In the beginning these trinkets were chiefly prized for personal adornment. Because they were sought for their own sake, however, they soon came roughly to exercise the function of currency, though the natives continued to use them for other purposes, such, for example, as the sending of ceremonial messages.

The periwinkle and the quahog, two varieties of hard-shelled mollusk common to the waters of the Atlantic coast, provided the chief source of raw material for the manufacture of wampum. It was made by breaking off the thin parts of the shell, clamping the remaining thick section into a stick, and grinding until the required shape and thickness were secured. The resultant bead was then

American paper money and coins have value because people accept them in payment for goods and services.

drilled with a crude flint rotated by the hands. Later a steel drill introduced by the Europeans was employed for a like service. While the shell was being drilled it was kept wet to avoid overheating and cracking. The artisan bored from one side until the drill was half through, then turned the shell and worked from the other side. Once pierced, the beads were rubbed to a high polish and strung.

With some slight variations this practice of making, we might say minting, wampum prevailed all along the Atlantic coast. . . .

Gold and silver, even had the early explorers possessed an adequate supply, would have been altogether useless in trading with the Indians. . . .

Under such peculiar circumstances wampum provided a convenient medium of exchange. . . . Captain John Smith had hardly completed his stockade and lit the fires upon his new hearth before a glass factory intended to manufacture imitation wampum was being built under his direction. The first imitation wampum was made in 1608. The next year Smith returned to England and the enterprise was abandoned.

1. Why were gold and silver useless in trading with the Indians during the colonial period?
2. How would widespread counterfeiting of wampum have affected its value as a medium of exchange?

Noble Foster Hoggson, *Epochs in American Banking.* New York: The John Day Company, 1929. pp. 21–23.

THE BIRTH OF 10,000 FISHSTICKS

Skill: Sequencing Information and Making Predictions

How lending money can create money is the subject of the following excerpt by Elbert V. Bowden. The scene below takes place on a small island where fishsticks are used as currency.

Suppose the eastsiders want to buy a plot of land from the westsiders, but they don't have enough money in their account. The eastside chief goes to see the northside chief who . . . is operating as the island's banker. The eastside chief asks if he can borrow 10,000 fishsticks (FS 10,000) to buy some land from the westsiders. The northside chief realizes that the eastside chief doesn't want cash—he only wants the amount added to his checking account so he can write a check to buy the land. Then the westsiders will deposit the check to their account, and the "loaned money" (FS 10,000) will be subtracted from the eastsiders' account and added to the westsiders' account.

The northside chief, knowing the eastside chief's credit is good, says, "Certainly. We will lend you as much as you would like." The northside chief adds FS 10,000 to the account of the eastside chief, and the eastside chief signs a note promising to repay the money, plus interest.

What has happened to the supply of money on the island? It's FS 10,000 bigger than before! The eastside family now has FS 10,000 which it did not have before. Nobody had it before. It didn't exist! The northside chief, acting as the banker, simply created that FS 10,000 when he added that amount to the eastsiders' account. Is it really money that has been *created*? Yes! It really is.

Look at it this way. Suppose *before* the FS 10,000 loan, you went around the island and found out how much money each person had (in cash and in his checking account). If you added up all these figures, what would you come out with? The total size of the island's money supply? Of course! Then *after* the FS 10,000 loan, suppose you did it again. You would come up with a larger total than before. How much larger? FS 10,000 larger. Where did the extra FS 10,000 come from? It was *created!* Right?

1. a. Where do you think the 10,000 fishsticks came from that is on deposit with the northside chief, the island's banker? b. How did the northside chief lend the money to the eastside chief? c. How did the eastsiders pay the westsiders for the land?
2. What if the northside bank had only 10,000 fishsticks to begin with and the westsiders cash their check for the 10,000 fishsticks?

What would happen if some of the depositors in the northside bank decide to withdraw some of their fishsticks?

3. What could the northside banker have done to prevent this situation from occurring? (HINT: What do banks do today to prevent a "run on the bank"?)

Elbert V. Bowden, "Lending Money Sometimes Creates Money." *Economics: The Science of Common Sense,* pages 168–169. South-Western Publishing Co., Cincinnati, OH.

TIME TO CHANGE OLD BANKING HABITS

Skill: Drawing Conclusions

Electronic funds transfer did not become widely accepted until the early 1980s. Authors Elbert Bowden and Judith Holbert describe some reasons for consumer reluctance in this reading.

Perhaps the single most important factor in the slow-down of the introduction of EFT [Electronic Funds Transfer] systems was the lack of widespread customer acceptance of the EFT terminals. Early in the 1970s, the extent of customer resistance to these new banking machines was not foreseen. In fact, some banks and thrifts that introduced remote terminals seemed to assume the customers would be attracted to the use of the terminals automatically. But it soon became clear that this was not going to happen, and that only through concerted and effective marketing efforts could the banks and thrifts achieve the widespread use of the EFT terminals required to justify the costs.

Consumers have been reluctant to use the electronic banking machines for several reasons. For one thing, people were already satisfied with the present banking system. They had no objection to making purchases by check, paying their bills by check, and then receiving their cancelled checks as proof of their expenditures. Bank customers have become accustomed to being in complete charge of their deposits and withdrawals—deciding their own timing and writing their checks accordingly. . . .

Apparently, customers in general are not eager to give up any of the control over their money. And they may also be concerned about questions of security and privacy. . . .

Perhaps another impediment to customer use of EFT services resulted from customer apprehensiveness about using these "strange new devices" which in the beginning were totally unfamiliar. But regardless of the reasons, the fact is that customer acceptance came only slowly, and at first, only in those places in which these services were aggressively promoted.

1. What are some of the reasons why bank customers were reluctant to use electronic banking machines?
2. What marketing strategies would you suggest to persuade customers to use the new banking machines?

Elbert V. Bowden and Judith L. Holbert, *Revolution in Banking,* Second Ed. Reston, Va.: Reston, 1984. pp. 186, 187.

The banking public now accepts automatic teller machines, as shown by the long lines at many of these machines. In fact, many people prefer banking by machine to dealing with bank tellers.

15 | CHAPTER REVIEW

PRACTICING YOUR WRITING SKILLS: WRITING AN ESSAY

You may already be familiar with writing essays from taking tests or preparing term papers. The following tips, however, will help improve your ability to write a well-organized essay.

- In deciding upon the topic, or thesis, of your essay, do not make it too broad. Keep the topic in mind as you write so that you do not include unnecessary information.
- Remember that most essays are shorter than term papers or research reports. Therefore, it is important to be sure of your main ideas and subtopics. They will need to be closely structured, with cause and effect relationships clearly stated.
- Use an outline. Even when answering essay questions on tests, take a minute to write a quick outline on scrap paper or on a blank page. You will be able to answer the question more quickly if you organize your ideas.
- Make your introduction interesting to catch the reader's attention. Starting with a quotation or question is a good technique. Do not begin with, "This essay is about. . .," but your thesis should be obvious after a few sentences.
- Do not assume knowledge on the part of the listeners or readers. Identify all books, people, places, and historical periods.
- Make your thoughts flow from paragraph to paragraph. You can do this by repeating a key word from the preceding paragraph or by using connecting words and phrases. Words and phrases such as *likewise*, *furthermore*, and *on the other hand* show how your ideas are related and make your essay read more smoothly.
- In the conclusion, bring together the main ideas.

Activity: Using the information you researched in the Activity for Practicing Your Study Skills in Chapter 14, write a brief essay on the use of GNP in determining the nation's economic health.

VOCABULARY REVIEW

Write the letter of the definition in Column B that correctly defines each term in Column A.

Column A	Column B
1. fiat money	a. money that by law must be accepted for payment of debts
2. demand deposit	
3. M1	
4. commodity money	b. paper money and coins in circulation, plus checking-type deposits
5. near money	
6. legal tender	
7. electronic funds transfer (EFT)	c. money in a bank that can be withdrawn at any time
	d. money that has value because the government has established it as acceptable payment for debts
	e. computerized banking functions that previously were handled on paper
	f. assets that can be turned into money fairly easily
	g. money that has value aside from its value as money

PRACTICING YOUR ECONOMIC SKILLS

1. **Drawing a Bar Graph.** Based on the table, make a bar graph showing the growth of the money supply between 1981 and 1986.
2. **Figuring Percentages.** Between 1985 and 1986 by what percentage did: **a.** M1 grow? **b.** M2 grow?
3. **Calculating Rate of Growth.** What was the average yearly rate of growth of M2 between 1981 and 1986?

Year	M1	M2
1981	440.9	1822.7
1982	477.7	1999.0
1983	525.4	2196.3
1984	545.5	2376.3
1985	626.6	2565.8
1986	675.9	2714.8

DISCUSSING ECONOMIC QUESTIONS

1. The banking industy has been undergoing deregulation since 1980. Part of this change allows banks to pay higher interest on most types of savings accounts. This benefits savers, but it raises costs to banks. Banks will either have to accept lower profits or pass the cost on as higher rates of interest on loans. Do you think the public is better off or worse off because of banking deregulation?

2. Many Americans today use ATMs. Discuss whether using them makes it easier or more difficult for you to balance your checkbook and to keep track of your expenses.

3. One of the three functions attributed to money is "store of value." Why might money be a better store of value than valuable goods such as art works, jewelry, and other precious items?

4. What effect does inflation have on the value of money? How does inflation affect your spending power?

APPLYING CRITICAL THINKING SKILLS

1. **Writing a Research Report.** Research and write a report on one of the following: the Greenback Party, Sherman Silver Purchase Act, William Jennings Bryan, and the gold standard.

2. **Gathering Information.** With several classmates, check local depository institutions to see what types of services and service charges they offer. Write a short summary of your findings.

3. **Researching Oral History.** Interview people who were young adults during the Great Depression. Ask them what happened to prices during the worst time of the depression, about the difficulty of finding jobs, and the bank failures. Report your findings to the class.

4. **Analyzing Issues.** Some economists argue that the United States should return to the gold standard. Do you think this is a good idea? Explain why or why not.

5. **Analyzing a Trend.** Direct deposits of paychecks, social security checks, and bill-paying by phone are three ways described in the text in which electronic banking has begun to become part of everyday life. Some banks also allow owners of personal computers to hook up to the bank so that customers can conduct many transactions at home. Research the trend toward computer banking. Go to a bank in your area which offers this feature. Gather information on costs, ease of access, possibility of outside tampering, confidentiality, and on subscription trends by customers over the past three years. Decide based on your information whether you think computer banking will become commonplace in the coming years, what effect you think this will have on the way Americans do their banking, and how banks may change as a resullt. Report your findings to the class.

READINGS

Brue, Stanley L, and Wentworth, Donald R. *Economic Scenes: Theory in Today's World*. 3rd ed. Englewood Cliffs, N.J.: Prentice-Hall, 1984.

Hartbarger, Neil. *Your Career in Banking*. New York: Arco, 1980.

Kadzis, P. "Here Come Those Financial Supermarkets." *Money*, July 1982, pp. 108-10.

Klein, John J. *Money in the Economy*. 5th ed. New York: Harcourt Brace Jovanovich, 1982.

CHAPTER 16

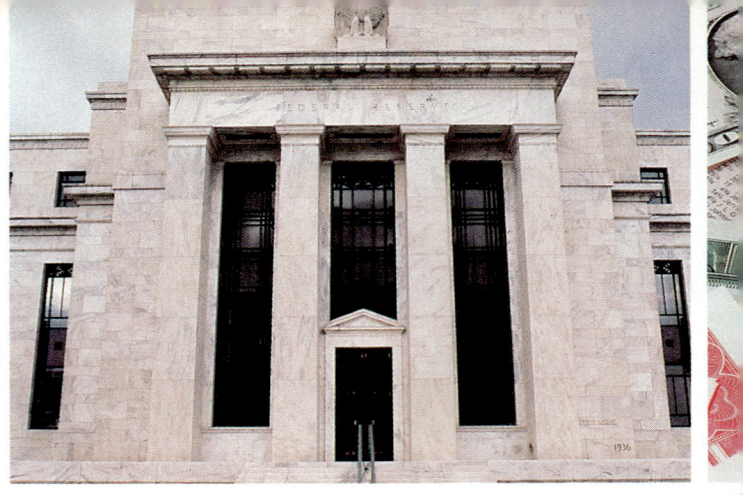

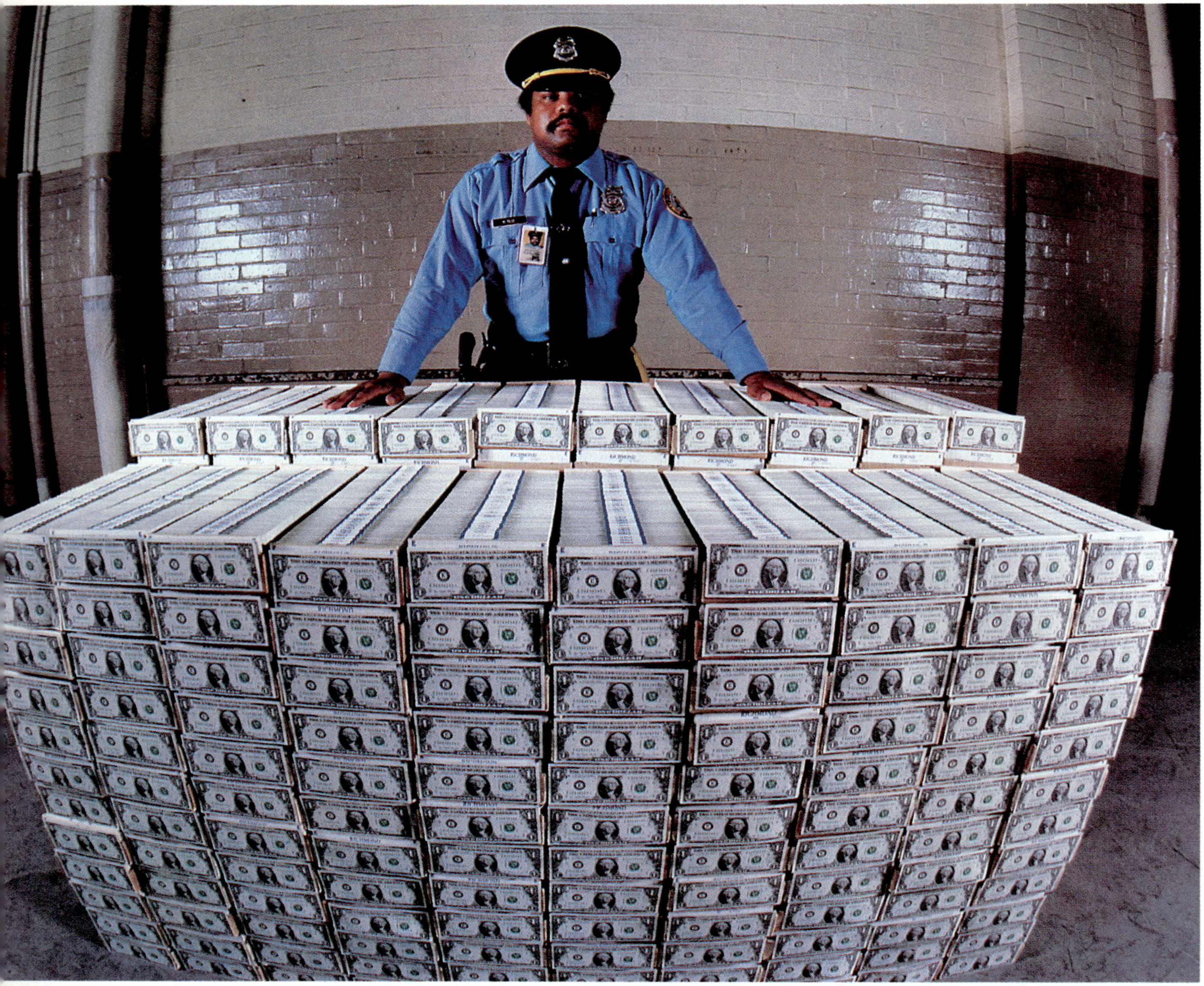

The nation's money supply and banking system are regulated by the Federal Reserve System. The Fed uses various methods to control the nation's monetary policy.

THE FEDERAL RESERVE SYSTEM AND MONETARY POLICY

In the last chapter, you read about the banking system and the types of money in use in the United States today. This chapter describes in detail how the supply of that money is regulated and why. You will read about the differences between tight money and loose money policies and the importance of finding the right balance between the two. Fractional reserve banking, the basis of the country's banking system, and money creation are also discussed. Then the organization and functions of the Federal Reserve System are described. This material details the Fed's regulation of the money supply and the problems involved in this kind of economic activity. Learning Economic Skills describes methods for interpreting news reports about economic events and ideas.

CHAPTER OBJECTIVES After you study this chapter, you will be able to:

1 • contrast loose money and tight money policies.
  • describe fractional reserve banking.
  • use an example describing how banks create money.

2 • describe the organization of the Federal Reserve System.
  ★ explain the steps in interpreting a news article.

3 • list the functions of the Federal Reserve System.

4 • explain the tools the Fed uses to regulate the money supply.

5 • describe the problems involved in using monetary policy to regulate the economy.

ECONOMICS VOCABULARY

monetary policy
loose-money policy
tight-money policy
fractional reserve banking
reserve requirement
check clearing
discount rate
prime rate
open-market operations

As you read in the last chapter, Congress created the Federal Reserve System in 1913 as the central banking organization in the United States. Its major purpose was to end the periodic financial panics that had occurred during the 1800s and into the early 1900s. Over the years, many other responsibilities have been added to the Federal Reserve System, or the Fed, as it is called. The jobs of the Fed today range from processing checks to serving as the government's banker. Its most important function, however, involves control over the rate of growth of the money supply.

1 | MONEY SUPPLY AND THE ECONOMY

Ask yourself as you read:
- What does the term *monetary policy* mean?
- What is fractional reserve banking?

You may have read or heard a news report in which a business executive or public official complained that money is "too tight." Or you may have run across a story about an economist warning that money is "too loose." In these cases, the terms *tight* and *loose* are referring to the monetary policy of the Federal Reserve System. **Monetary policy** involves changing the rate of growth of the supply of money to affect the amount of credit and, therefore, business activity in the economy.

Credit, like any good or service, is subject to the laws of supply and demand. Also, like any good or service, credit has a cost. The cost of credit is the interest that must be paid to borrow it. As the cost of credit increases, the quantity demanded decreases. On the other hand, if the cost of borrowing drops, the quantity of credit demanded rises.

If a country has a **loose money policy,** credit is inexpensive to borrow and abundant. People will usually be willing to borrow more. Consumers will take out loans to buy new cars and homes and other desired items. Businesses will borrow to expand or start new plants and hire more workers. These workers will have more money income to spend, which, in turn, will stimulate further production. If, on the other hand, a country has a **tight money policy,** credit is expensive to borrow and in short supply. Consumers may not buy as many new cars and homes. Business executives may postpone or cancel plans for expansion. Workers unemployed because of the slowdown will have less money income to spend. As a result, businesses may cut back even more on production. A contraction of the economy and possibly a recession may follow.

If this is the case, why would any nation want a tight money policy? The answer is inflation. If money becomes too plentiful too quickly, the result could be inflation. Prices would increase and the purchasing power of the dollar would decrease dramatically. As you read in the last chapter, this occurred during the Revolutionary War. The supply of continental currency grew so rapidly that notes became almost worthless.

The goal of monetary policy is to strike a balance between tight and loose money. As you will read later in this chapter, it is the Fed's responsibility to ensure that money and credit are plentiful enough to allow expansion of the economy. However, the Fed cannot let the money supply become so plentiful that rapid inflation results.

FRACTIONAL RESERVE BANKING

Before you understand how the Fed regulates the money supply, you need to understand the basis of the United States banking system and the way money is created. The banking system is based on what is called **fractional reserve banking.** Under this system, only a fraction of the deposits in a bank are kept on hand, or in reserve, in the form of cash or deposits. The rest are lent to borrowers or otherwise invested, for example, in Treasury bills.

Since 1913, the Fed has set specific **reserve requirements** for many banks. They must hold a certain percentage of their total deposits either as cash in their own vaults or as deposits in their district Federal Reserve bank. Currently, reserve requirements can be varied from between 3 percent and 14 percent for demand deposits—checking-type accounts—and between 0 percent and 9 percent for time deposits such as Certificates of Deposit (CDs).

MONEY EXPANSION

Currency makes up only a small part of the money supply. A much larger portion consists of bank deposits owned by the general public. Because banks are not required to keep 100 percent of their deposits in reserve, they can use their deposits to create what is in effect new money.

Suppose you sell a federal government bond back to the Federal Reserve and receive $1,000. This is $1,000 in ''new'' money because the Federal Reserve simply creates it by writing you a check on itself. You deposit the $1,000 in a bank. If a 10 percent reserve requirement is in effect, $100 of that money must be held in reserve. However, the bank is free to lend the remaining $900.

Suppose another customer asks the same bank for a $900 loan. The bank creates $900 of money simply by transferring the $900 to the customer's checking account. The bank must keep in reserve 10 percent of this new deposit—$90, but now it can lend the remaining $810. This $810 is in turn treated as a new deposit. Ninety percent of it—$729—can again be lent. The original $1,000 has become $3,439. So it goes—each new deposit gives the bank new funds to continue lending.

Of course, a bank is not likely to continue lending and receiving back the same money. Its customers will most likely withdraw money and spend it or deposit it in another bank. However, this does not stop the creation of money. As the money finds its way into a second, third, and fourth bank, and so on, each bank can use the nonrequired reserve portion of the money to make more loans.

Banks are able to create "new" money because of the reserve requirements of the Fed on total deposits. What are the reserve requirements on demand deposits? On time deposits?

Table 16-1: MULTIPLE EXPANSION OF THE MONEY SUPPLY

Round	Deposited by	Amount of Deposit	Required Reserves (20%)	Excess Reserves (80%)	Loaned to	Paid to
1	Student (you) (Bank A)	$1,000	$ 200.00	$800.00	John Jones	Jackson's Machine Supply
2	Jackson's (Bank B)	800	160.00	640.00	Ms. Wang	Mr. Días
3	Mr. Días (Bank C)	640	128.00	512.00	Mrs. Fontana	Mrs. Powers
4	Mrs. Powers	512	102.40	409.60	. . .	. . .
5	Mr. F. Santana	. . .	. . .	. . .	. . .	. . .
6	. . .	. . .	. . .	. . .	. . .	. . .
Eventual Totals		$5,000	$1,000	. . .	. . .	. . .

HOW THE MONEY SUPPLY INCREASES

Confusing? Let's look at another example, step by step. **Round I:** Suppose you are digging in your backyard and discover $1,000. Now suppose that after you check with the police and are allowed to keep the money, you take this money to your bank (Bank A) and deposit it in your checking account. Assume that your bank is required by the Federal Reserve to keep 20 percent of its total deposits on reserve. That means that your bank must hold $200 of your deposit on reserve. That means that your bank now has $800 of excess reserves, which is not earning interest.

Round 2: Bank A decides to loan out $800 in order to earn interest. John Jones has just applied to the bank for an $800 loan. Bank A finds him creditworthy and therefore credits his account with $800. (If he doesn't have an account with the bank, it will have him open one.) Mr. Jones borrowed the money in order to buy a machine for his business from Jackson's Machine Supply Company. Jackson's has its account at Bank B, which will credit $800 to Jackson's account balance. Bank B's reserves increase by $800. Of this amount, $160 (20 percent of $800) are required reserves, and the remaining $640 are excess reserves.

Round 3: To earn profits, Bank B loans out its excess reserves to Ms. Wang, who wants to borrow $640. She, in turn, buys something from Mr. Días, who does his banking at Bank C. He deposits the money from Ms. Wang. Bank C now has $640 in new deposits, of which $128 are required reserves. Bank C now loans out $512 of excess reserves to Mrs. Fontana, who buys something from Mrs. Powers, and so on. The end result is that a deposit of $1,000 in new money that was outside of the banking system has caused the money supply to increase to $5,000. This is called the multiple expansion of the money supply.

REVIEWING ECONOMIC PRINCIPLES

1. **a.** Explain the differences between a loose-money and a tight-money policy. **b.** Why is the goal of monetary policy to strike a balance between the two?
2. What is fractional reserve banking? reserve requirements?
3. Why do banks need to keep money in reserve?
4. **Critical Thinking: Interpreting Information.** Draw a flow chart to show how a bank creates money.

2 | ORGANIZATION OF THE FEDERAL RESERVE SYSTEM

Ask yourself as you read:
- What is the Federal Reserve System?
- What kinds of banks are in the Federal Reserve System?

Figure 16-1 shows the organization of the Federal Reserve System. As its name states, the Fed is a system, or network, of banks. Power is not concentrated in a single central bank but is shared by a governing board and 12 district banks. The Fed is made up of the Board of Governors assisted by the Federal Advisory Council, the Federal Open Market Committee, 12 Federal Reserve banks, and about 5,600 member banks.

BOARD OF GOVERNORS

The Board of Governors directs the operations of the Federal Reserve System. It establishes policies regarding such things as reserve requirements and discount rates. The board also supervises the 12 district Federal Reserve banks and regulates certain activities of member banks and all other depository institutions.

Figure 16-1: ORGANIZATION OF THE FEDERAL RESERVE SYSTEM

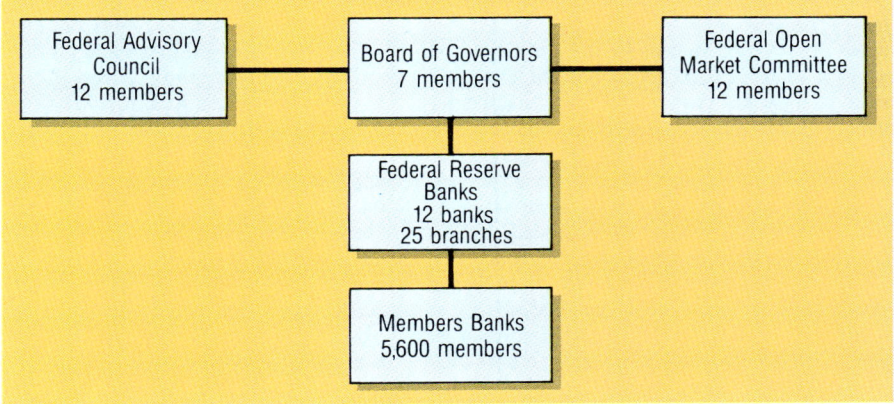

Since the change in banking regulations in the early 1980s, what are the differences between being a member bank and a nonmember bank of the Federal Reserve System?

Newspapers and business magazines are some of the easiest sources of economic information to use. Because so much news of the economy is reported every day, it is important that you be able to identify the issues raised and the economic concepts involved.

To begin your analysis of an article, note the source, author, date of publication, type of article, and purpose. Editorials are usually clearly marked as such and so are columns. They are meant to state a problem and possibly persuade the reader to a point of view. Straight news stories are factual or descriptive and are meant to inform. News articles occasionally express the personal opinions of the reporter. This is usually more true in news magazines than newspapers. The Practicing Your Reading Skills, p. 422, discusses bias and will help you in learning to detect it in what you read.

The headline of a news article is meant to catch the reader's attention, but it may not always inform you about its contents. Information is usually presented in order of importance. The most important information is at the beginning so that readers will find it quickly. The information becomes less important as you read to the end of the story. News articles usually deal with the 5 Ws and the H—who, what, where, when, why, and how. The who, what, where, and when are often treated in the first paragraph. The rest of the article describes the why and how.

As you read, circle the important facts or make notes about them. Skim the article for statistics and dates. Consider what economic concepts are behind the event, for example, supply and demand. Also consider the issues that the article may raise. What is the purpose of the article? Is it simply descriptive or does it suggest the need for new policies or action?

Practicing Your Skills

Read the article reproduced on this page, and then answer the following questions.

1. **a.** What type of news piece is it? **b.** What is its purpose?
2. **a.** What is the topic of the piece? **b.** What economic concepts does it present?
3. Summarize the news article in a brief paragraph.

Mergers in the Banking Industry

Nationwide banking is becoming a fact of American life. Responding to the great increase in mergers, banks in the Northeast, Midwest, Southeast, and West have been merging to create a new breed of "superregionals." These huge banking giants operate across state lines. As many as 8 or even 12 banks have been acquired by some financial holding companies to form national financial institutions that do business in about 20 percent of households in the United States. Some banks have persuaded state legislators to allow them to pass through loopholes in a federal law meant to prevent the formation of long-distance bank branches by joining them via computer to electronic-teller networks stretching from the Atlantic to Pacific coast. Also, some laws allow the operation of mortgage-banking firms and commercial loan offices in distant areas.

Response by the Public

Many Americans support the establishment of out-of-state banks. Small companies are in favor of out-of-state banks because it means that they might be able to get better interest on their savings, better loan terms, and more services. The disadvantage to businesses and individual consumers is that these customers might have to deal with longer delays and more impersonal service.

One of the reasons that some state legislators are in favor of out-of-state banking is that recessions have caused some banks to suffer losses in energy, farm, and real-estate loans. Also, some of the superregionals have been willing to buy state banks and savings and loan associations that are in trouble.

The trend to form superregional banks can be traced back to 1984 when a New York bank was allowed to open a "nonbank bank" in Florida by the Federal Reserve. The bank escaped the ban on interstate banks by not offering checking accounts or commercial loans. Soon, dozens of banks followed suit, but lawsuits have prevented further action until the suits are settled or the banks find other loopholes in the interstate banking ban.

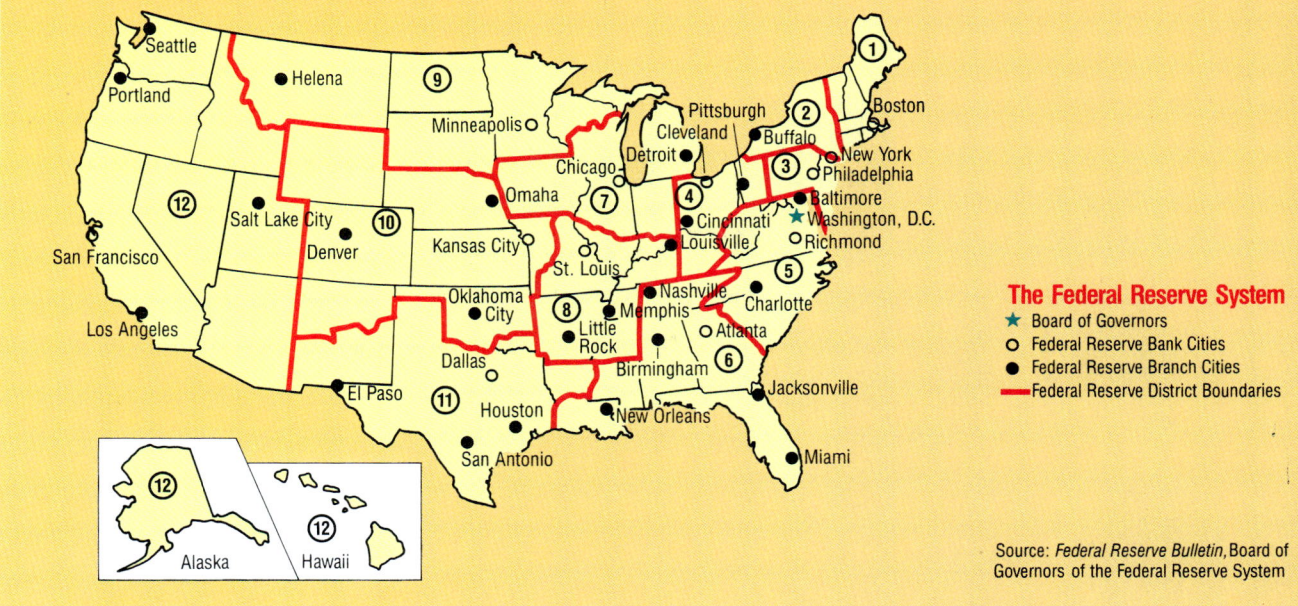

The Federal Reserve System
★ Board of Governors
○ Federal Reserve Bank Cities
● Federal Reserve Branch Cities
— Federal Reserve District Boundaries

Source: *Federal Reserve Bulletin*, Board of Governors of the Federal Reserve System

Which district do you live in? Where is the closest branch bank?

The board is made up of seven full-time members appointed by the President of the United States with the approval of the Senate. The President chooses one member as a chairperson. Each member of the board serves for 14 years. The terms are arranged so that an opening occurs every two years. Members cannot be reappointed, and their decisions are not subject to the approval of the President or Congress. Their length of term, manner of selection, and independence in working frees members from political pressures. Members do not have to fear that their sometimes-unpopular decisions will cause them to lose their jobs at election time.

The Board of Governors is assisted by the Federal Advisory Council (FAC). It consists of 12 members elected by the directors of each Federal Reserve bank. It meets at least four times each year and reports to the Board of Governors on general business conditions in the nation.

FEDERAL OPEN MARKET COMMITTEE

The Federal Open Market Committee (FOMC) meets approximately 13 times a year to decide the course of action that the Fed should take to control the money supply. This committee is made up of the members of the Board of Governors plus the presidents or vice-presidents of five of the Federal Reserve banks. Of these five, one is always from the Federal Reserve bank in New York City. The other four rotate periodically from the other district banks for one-year terms.

FEDERAL RESERVE BANKS

Each of the 12 Federal Reserve banks is set up as a corporation owned by its member banks. A nine-person board of directors made up of bankers and businesspeople supervises each Federal Reserve bank. Each one carries out for its member banks in its district the functions of the Federal Reserve System, described later in this chapter. There are

Table 16-2: FUNCTIONS OF THE FEDERAL RESERVE

Responsibility	Description
Clearing checks	**Check clearing** is the method by which a check that has been deposited in one depository institution is transferred to the depository institution on which it was written. Figure 16-2 explains this process.
Acting as the federal government's fiscal agent	The federal government collects large sums of money through taxation and spends and distributes equally large sums. It deposits some of this money in the Federal Reserve and distributes the rest among thousands of commercial banks. As the federal government's fiscal, or financial agent, the Fed keeps track of these deposits and holds a checking account for the United States Treasury. Checks for such payments as Social Security, tax refunds, and veterans' benefits are drawn on this account. The Fed also lends money to the Treasury and acts as a financial adviser to the federal government.
Supervising member banks	The Fed along with the Comptroller of the Currency and the Federal Deposit Insurance Corporation (FDIC) supervises and regulates member commercial banks. Nonmember commercial and savings banks as well as savings and loan associations and credit unions are regulated by other agencies. Because the comptroller supervises national banks, the Fed oversees state-chartered member banks. Among the Fed's duties are setting limits for loans and investments by member banks, approving bank mergers, and examining the books of member banks.
Holding and setting reserve requirements	Each of the 12 Federal Reserve banks holds the reserve requirements of member and nonmember depository institutions in its district. As you have just read, all depository institutions are required by law to keep a certain percentage of their deposits in reserve. By raising or lowering the percentage required, but within the limits set by Congress, the Fed can change the amount of money in circulation.
Supplying paper currency	Since 1914, the Federal Reserve System has been responsible for printing and maintaining much of the nation's paper money. All Federal Reserve notes are printed in Washington, D.C., at the Bureau of Printing and Engraving. However, each note has a code number indicating which of the 12 Federal Reserve banks issued it. The money is shipped from the bureau to the appropriate bank to be put into circulation. Much of this money simply replaces old bills. However, each Federal Reserve bank must have on hand a sufficient amount of cash to meet the demands for paper currency during different times of the year. For example, during the Christmas season commercial banks find that their depositors withdraw large amounts of cash. The banks then must turn to the Federal Reserve banks to replace it. After Christmas, depositors redeposit their money. The banks can then return what they borrowed to their district Federal Reserve bank.
Regulating the money supply	The major responsibility of the Federal Reserve is determining the amount of money in circulation, which, in turn, affects the amount of credit and business activity in the economy.

also 25 Federal Reserve branch banks. These smaller banks act as branch offices and aid the district banks in carrying out their duties.

MEMBER BANKS

All national banks—those chartered by the federal government—are required to become members of the Federal Reserve System. Banks chartered by the states may join if they choose. Currently, member banks include all of the approximately 4,600 national banks and about 1,000 of the 10,000 or so state banks. To become a member bank, a national or state bank buys stock in its district's Federal Reserve bank.

In the past, only member banks were required to meet regulations, such as those setting specific reserve requirements. Nonmember banks operated under less strict state laws but were not allowed to use such Fed services as its check-clearing facilities and its computerized funds transfer system. In 1980 Congress did away with most of the distinctions between member and nonmember banks. Now all institutions that accept deposits must keep reserves in their district Federal Reserve bank. Federal Reserve services are also available to all depository institutions—member or nonmember—for a fee. The only real advantage of membership now is that member banks, as stockholders in their district bank, are able to vote for six of its nine board members. Member banks also receive dividends on their stock in the district bank.

REVIEWING ECONOMIC PRINCIPLES

1. In separate paragraphs, summarize the duties of each of these:
   a. Board of Governors. **b.** Federal Open Market Committee.
2. **Critical Thinking: Comparing and Contrasting.** What is the advantage to Federal Reserve membership today? How does this differ from the past?

3 | FUNCTIONS OF THE FEDERAL RESERVE

Ask yourself as you read:
- What are the major responsibilities of the Federal Reserve?
- Why is it important for the Federal Reserve to determine the amount of money in circulation?

The Federal Reserve has a number of functions. Among them are clearing checks, acting as the federal government's fiscal agent, supervising member banks, holding and setting reserve requirements, supplying paper currency, and regulating the money supply. Table 16-2 lists these functions and how the Fed accomplishes them. The most important function of the Fed is regulating the money supply.

The Federal Reserve also sets standards for certain types of consumer legislation, mainly truth-in-lending legislation. By law, sellers of

Figure 16-2: CLEARING A CHECK

José Rodríguez in Dallas orders camping equipment by mail from a sporting goods store in Minneapolis. He sends a $25.00 check drawn on his account in Dallas bank.

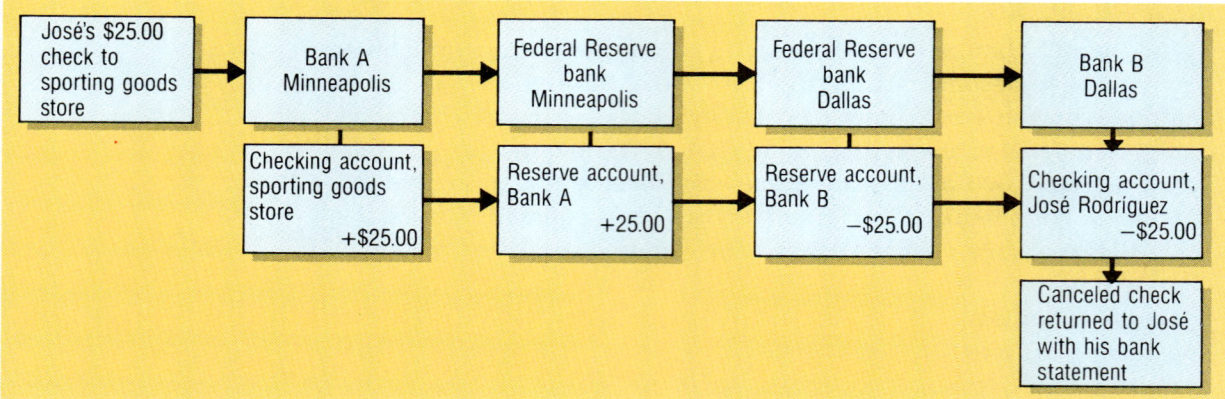

All depository institutions may use the Federal Reserve's check-clearing system. *Reserve account* refers to a bank's account in its Federal Reserve district bank.

goods and services must make some kinds of information available to people who buy on credit. This information includes the amount of interest and size of the monthly payment to be paid. It is the Federal Reserve that decides what type of credit information must be supplied.

REVIEWING ECONOMIC PRINCIPLES

1. What four responsibilities does the Fed have as fiscal agent for the federal government?
2. What does the Fed do in its role as overseer of state-chartered member banks?
3. How does each of its district banks help the Federal Reserve System fulfill its responsibility to supply paper currency?
4. **Critical Thinking: Interpreting Information.** Summarize in a paragraph how the Federal Reserve System's check-clearing process works. Use Figure 16-2 as the basis for your paragraph.

4 | TOOLS FOR REGULATING THE MONEY SUPPLY

Ask yourself as you read:

- How does the Federal Reserve increase the money supply? lower it?
- What tool does the Federal Reserve most often use to regulate the money supply?

The Fed has as its goal maintaining enough money to keep the money supply growing steadily and the economy running smoothly without inflation. To accomplish this, it has three major tools: 1. reserve requirements, 2. the discount rate, and 3. open-market operations.

CHANGING RESERVE REQUIREMENTS

The Federal Reserve can choose to control the money supply by changing the reserve requirements of member banks. Suppose a bank has $1 million in deposits and the reserve requirement is 10 percent. The bank must keep at least $100,000 in reserves. If the Fed wanted to increase the money supply, it could lower the reserve requirement to 5 percent, for example. The bank would then need to keep only $50,000 in reserve. It could lend out the other $50,000. This $50,000 would expand the money supply many times over as it was lent and redeposited. Of course, it would not be just one bank but every bank that could now lend its newly freed reserves. The money supply would expand dramatically. This could help to pull the economy out of a recession.

Suppose instead that the Fed wanted to decrease the money supply, or at least slow down its rate of growth. It could do this by increasing the reserve requirement from 10 percent to 15 percent. The bank in the example above would then need to keep $150,000 on reserve—$50,000 more than before. To build up its reserves to meet the new requirement, the bank has several possibilities. It can call in some loans, sell off securities or other investments that it owns, or borrow from another bank or the Federal Reserve. Obviously, because all banks would have to increase their reserves, this action by the Fed would greatly decrease the amount of money in the economy. This could be used to help slow the economy if it were expanding too rapidly.

Even small changes in the reserve requirement can have major effects on the money supply. As a result, some believe that this tool is not precise enough to make frequent small adjustments to the money supply. In recent years, changing the reserve requirement has not been used often to regulate the money supply.

CHANGING THE DISCOUNT RATE

Sometimes a depository institution will find itself without enough reserves to meet its reserve requirement. This may happen if customers unexpectedly borrow a great deal of money or if depositors suddenly withdraw large amounts. The bank must then borrow what it needs to meet the reserve requirement, at least temporarily. One of the ways it can do this is to ask its district Federal Reserve bank for a loan. The district bank, like any other bank, will charge interest. The rate of interest charged by the Fed is called the **discount rate.**

A bank, like a consumer, follows the law of demand. At higher discount rates, a bank may decide to borrow less reserves from the Fed or none at all. It could meet its reserve requirement by borrowing from another bank. This money would then be taken out of circulation and would not be available for lending to individuals or businesses. If a bank does decide to borrow at a high discount rate, it will need to pass its increased costs on to customers in the form of higher interest rates on loans. For example, it might raise its **prime rate**—the rate it charges its best business customers. These high rates, by discouraging borrowing, will also keep down the growth of the money supply. On the other hand, if the discount rate is low, even a bank with sufficient reserves might borrow money. This will raise the bank's reserves and increase its ability to make loans. Thus, a reduction in the discount rate also affects the total money supply.

OPEN-MARKET OPERATIONS

Buying and selling United States securities, called **open-market operations,** is the tool most often used by the Fed. This affects the money supply by changing depository institution reserves or by putting money into or taking it out of circulation. The term *open market* comes from the fact that the trading of these securities is done in the open market, that is, through regular dealers in securities. An open market is one that is open to almost all private businesses and one that the government does not own or control.

When the government buys securities such as Treasury bills, it pumps new money into the economy. Suppose you sell a $10,000 Treasury bill to the Federal Reserve and receive that amount of money in the form of a Federal Reserve check. This is "new" money because the Fed created it simply by writing the check on itself. When you deposit the $10,000 in a bank, that bank will keep part in reserves and lend the rest. The process of money creation is begun.

When the Fed wants to decrease the money supply, it sells securities on the open market. This takes money out of the economy. Suppose you decide to buy a Treasury bill and to use cash for the transaction. Turning the cash over to the Fed removes the money from circulation.

Of course, most open-market transactions are not carried out by individuals using cash. Most are made by financial institutions and large investors such as mutual funds. If a bank purchases Treasury securities from the Fed, the purchase amount will be deducted from the bank's reserve account. The bank then has less money to lend, and the money supply eventually will be smaller. If a bank sells its government securities, the Fed will credit the money to the bank's reserve account. The bank can then make additional loans, and the money supply will grow.

HOW THE FED MAKES MONEY-SUPPLY DECISIONS

As you read earlier in the chapter, the Federal Open Market Committee (FOMC) meets periodically to decide on how best to control the money supply through open-market operations. At the beginning of each meeting, staff economists present data about what has happened to the money supply in the past, what current credit conditions are like, and what is likely to happen to the economy in the future. Statistics on unemployment, retail sales, gross national product, and so on, are presented. The information is discussed, and at the end of the meeting the committee votes on a course of action. The FOMC's decision summarizes current economic conditions and outlines the Fed's long-term goals for its monetary policy. To help meet these goals, the FOMC also sets objectives for the rate of growth of the money supply or the cost of credit for the next month or so.

Federal Reserve Policy: Andrew F. Brimmer (1926–   )

Andrew F. Brimmer was appointed to the Board of Governors of the Federal Reserve System by President Lyndon Johnson in 1966. At the time of his appointment, *Business Week* termed Brimmer "the most prominent and controversial black economist in the country."

Prior to his term as a Governor of the Federal Reserve, Brimmer had worked in the Department of Commerce, taught at the University of Pennsylvania and Michigan State University, and been a staff economist in the New York Federal Reserve Bank. In 1963 President John Kennedy had appointed him Deputy Assistant Secretary in the Department of Commerce. In 1965 Johnson had advanced him to the rank of Assistant Secretary for Economic Affairs in the same department. In these positions, one of Brimmer's major efforts was the search for ways to control the flow of private capital out of the country. Businesses were investing much of their money overseas. This was endangering the United States balance of payments—the difference between total payments to other nations and the receipts from these nations.

When Brimmer was appointed to the Federal Reserve Board, inflation was on the rise. Board members agreed that interest rates had to be raised in an attempt to tighten the money supply and force inflation down. When this measure did not seem to work, Brimmer called for a tax increase. He said the Fed was being expected to do things with monetary policy in the fight against inflation that it simply could not do.

After leaving his governorship of the Federal Reserve System in 1974, Brimmer became a visiting professor at the Graduate School of Business at Harvard University. In a letter to President Gerald Ford in 1974, Brimmer suggested a 10 percent rebate of 1974 personal income taxes to stimulate the economy and to help end the recession. Congress later adopted this proposal.

In 1976 Brimmer started Brimmer and Company, Economic and Financial Consultants. Part of the work that his firm does involves the analysis of trends in interest rates and prices in the economy. Monitoring the Federal Reserve's monetary policy is part of this analysis. From Brimmer's point of view, understanding what is happening in the banking system is crucial to understanding not only what happens in the economy as a whole, but to individual industries and firms within that economy.

In addition to overseeing the activities of his consulting firm, Brimmer serves on the board of directors of several financial institutions, including Bank of America, and industrial corporations. He lectures and writes frequently on general economic developments and monetary policy. Brimmer also makes periodic studies of the economic condition of black Americans and often reports his findings in his column "Economic Perspective" in the magazine *Black Enterprise*.

1. Identify two proposals that Brimmer made regarding federal monetary policies.
2. Describe how Brimmer applied his experience in the Federal Reserve in the consulting firm he started.

The committee's decision is then passed to the trading desk at the Federal Reserve Bank of New York. There almost all of the Fed's buying and selling of securities takes place. For example, suppose the FOMC decides that the money supply should grow at a faster rate. The head of the trading desk at the New York Fed will carry out this policy by buying more United States securities in the open market. On the other hand, if the FOMC decides that the money supply should grow at a slower rate, this person will instead sell more securities.

REVIEWING ECONOMIC PRINCIPLES

1. Define the following economic terms: **a.** discount rate, **b.** prime rate, **c.** open-market operations.
2. Describe in a paragraph how increasing the reserve requirement can reduce the money supply.
3. **a.** What does it mean to say that the Fed has raised the discount rate? **b.** How does the law of demand operate on banks when the discount rate is lowered?
4. **a.** Why will the money supply grow if a bank sells its government securities to the Fed? **b.** Why will the money supply decrease if a bank buys government securities from the Fed?
5. **Critical Thinking: Summarizing Information. a.** How does the Fed reach its decision on the type of monetary policy to follow? **b.** How is this decision put into action?

5 | THE DIFFICULTIES OF MONETARY POLICY

Ask yourself as you read:
- Why is it difficult for the Fed to change the money supply quickly?
- Does the Federal Reserve actually have much control over the money supply?

Economists sometimes describe the Fed's control over the money supply as similar to a driver's control over a car. Like a driver, the Fed can accelerate or brake, depending on what phase of the business cycle the economy is in. Remember, though, that this is only a model and, therefore, simplified. In reality, the Fed cannot control the money supply as quickly and as surely as a driver can a car.

One problem is the difficulty in gathering and evaluating information about M1 and M2. As you read in Chapter 15, the money supply is measured in terms of M1—currency, traveler's checks, demand deposits, and other deposits against which checks can be written—and M2—M1 plus certain near monies. In recent years, new savings and investment opportunities have appeared. Keeping track of the growth of M1 and M2 becomes more difficult as money is shifted from savings accounts into NOW accounts or from checking accounts into money mar-

Figure 16-3: CHANGING THE MONEY SUPPLY

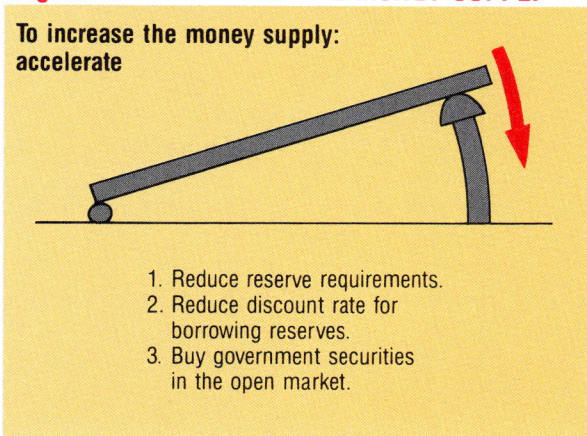

To increase the money supply: accelerate

1. Reduce reserve requirements.
2. Reduce discount rate for borrowing reserves.
3. Buy government securities in the open market.

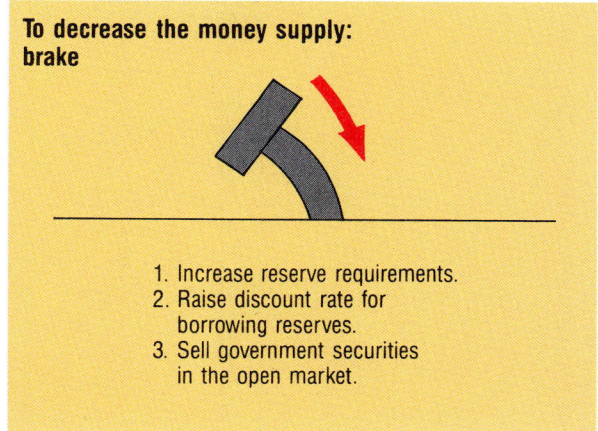

To decrease the money supply: brake

1. Increase reserve requirements.
2. Raise discount rate for borrowing reserves.
3. Sell government securities in the open market.

The brake/accelerator model is one way to remember how the Fed can regulate the money supply. Explain how the model works.

ket deposit accounts (MMDAs). The increased use of credit cards and electronic funds transfer have also changed the way money circulates through the economy.

Throughout its history, the Federal Reserve's monetary policies have been criticized. There have been many instances when during periods of rising inflation, the Federal Reserve increased the amount of money in circulation, thereby worsening the inflation. During other periods when the economy was slowing down and going into recession, the Federal Reserve decreased the money supply. This made the recession worse. To prevent such misjudgments, some critics of the Federal Reserve have requested that the money supply simply be increased at the same rate every year. In other words, they recommend that the Fed *not* engage in monetary policy.

As you read earlier in the chapter, the Fed's Board of Governors is protected from direct political pressure. However, it still receives conflicting advice from many directions. The President could suggest one course of action—lower interest rates, for example—while members of Congress may be urging a different course. Private business may call for one policy, while organized labor asks for the opposite. Finally, the Fed is not the only force working to affect the economy. As you will read in the next chapter, the spending and taxing policies of the federal government are also at work. The Fed's task is to consider all these factors as it plots a course for the growth of the economy.

REVIEWING ECONOMIC QUESTIONS

1. Compare the model of the accelerator and the brake in an automobile to the Fed's role in regulating the money supply.
2. Why has keeping track of the growth of M1 and M2 become more difficult in recent years?
3. Why is the advice that the Board of Governors receives sometimes a problem?

SUMMARY OF
IMPORTANT PRINCIPLES

1
- A loose money policy means that the growth of the money supply is increased and money is inexpensive to borrow and abundant. With a tight money policy, the opposite occurs.
- With the system of fractional reserve banking, only a fraction of the deposits in a bank are kept on hand. The rest are lent to borrowers or otherwise invested.
- Because banks are not required to keep 100 percent of their deposits in reserve, they can use their deposits to create what is, in effect, new money. Suppose a person sells a government bond back to the Federal Reserve and receives a $1,000 check written on the Fed. The person deposits the $1,000 in a bank. If a 10 percent reserve requirement is in effect, $100 of that money must be held in reserve. The bank, however, may lend the remaining $900. When the $900 is spent and deposited in the bank, the process of money creation continues. Each time part of the $1,000 is deposited in the bank, the money supply expands.

2
- The Board of Governors of the Federal Reserve System directs the operations of the Federal Reserve System and establishes policies regarding such things as reserve requirements and discount rates. The board is assisted by the Federal Advisory Council (FAC), which reports on general business conditions in the nation. The Federal Open Market Committee (FOMC) decides the course of action that the Fed should take to control the money supply. Federal Reserve banks carry out for its member banks the functions of the Federal Reserve System. Member banks are all banks chartered by the federal government and any state-chartered banks that wish to join. Congress removed many of the distinctions between member and nonmember banks of the Federal Reserve System in 1980.

3
- The functions of the Federal Reserve System include clearing checks for banks, acting as the federal government's fiscal agent, supervising member banks, holding reserve requirements of depository institutions, supplying paper money, and regulating the money supply.

4
- To regulate the money supply, the Fed uses changes in the reserve requirements, the discount rate, and open-market operations.

5
- There are several problems involved in using monetary policy. One is the difficulty involved in gathering and evaluating information about the growth of M1 and M2. Second, the Fed receives conflicting advice from various sources, which it must balance in deciding on policy. Finally, the Fed is not the only force working to affect the economy.

Putting Economics to Work

T he following is a story that happened again and again in the late 1970s and early 1980s. It is one that is repeated whenever inflation drives up interest rates.

Helen and Ray Lemperes had been saving for several years to buy a house. While they had been saving, they had watched the interest rates climb. The prime rate for a time was over 20 percent. Although the prime rate affects only business borrowers, a rise in the prime rate usually is an indication that interest rates for individual customers are also increasing. The prime rate is sometimes tied to the Federal Reserve's discount rate.

In periods of high inflation when the demand for loans is usually great, the Fed raises the discount rate. In response, member banks raise their interest rates on loans to business and personal borrowers to pay for the reserves they borrow from their district Federal Reserve bank. By raising the discount rate, the Fed tightens the money supply and attempts to discourage borrowing. During the late 1970s and early 1980s, inflation was running at more than 10 percent annually. This was about double what it had been in the early 1970s.

Because the discount rate was high, the Lempereses' bank decided to raise interest rates on its loans. At its highest rate, Helen and Ray's bank was charging 18 percent for a 30-year, fixed rate mortgage. The Lempereses had seen several houses they would have bought during these years. However, they believed that the rates were too high for them to take out a long-term loan. They believed from looking at the history of the American economy that interest rates would go down again, so they decided to wait before buying a home.

The Lempereses continued to save and watch the interest rates. By late 1983 interest rates in general were falling, and by 1987 mortgage rates had declined to under 10 percent for long-term fixed-rate mortgages.

Driving home from work one evening, Helen heard a radio report that the Fed's discount rate had fallen to 5.5 percent. The prime rate was somewhat higher. Ray called several banks and asked about mortgage rates. Within a week, he had found a bank that would give them a 9 percent, 30-year, fixed rate mortgage. The Lempereses were very happy. A house of their own—their dream for so long—was now within their reach.

SUPPLY AND DEMAND: INTEREST RATES

1. What policies could the Federal Reserve Bank use to tighten the money supply again?
2. In addition to mortgage loans, how are individual borrowers affected by increases in the federal discount rate and the prime rate?
3. How are businesses affected by increases in the federal discount rate and the prime rate?

Readings in Economics

THE FED DOES NOT HAVE ABSOLUTE CONTROL

Skill: Making Inferences

 There are many disagreements about how easily the Federal Reserve can change the money supply and how effective its policies are. Economist Ralph C. Bryant discusses some misconceptions about the Fed's control over the money supply in this reading.

It is widely believed that the money stock [supply] of the United States, somehow defined, should play a central role in the conduct of Federal Reserve monetary policy. In particular, it is believed that the Federal Reserve should publicly announce a target time path for the money stock and then try to make the actual stock follow that path closely. The analytical basis for this approach to monetary policy, however, is seriously deficient. Debate about the approach seldom focuses on the important controversial issues about which views can justifiably differ; instead, the debate often becomes mired in confusion and spurious [false] issues.

One source of confusion is an inadequate analysis of the operating procedures through which the Federal Reserve implements its policy from one short-run period to the next. In principle, the Federal Reserve can choose among several alternatives when selecting its operating procedures. The Federal Reserve did in fact change its operating procedures in October 1979. Both in theory and in practice the differences among alternative operating procedures and their implications for the money stock and for the economy tend to be poorly understood. Disagreement about the subject is rife [widespread], yet the participants in the controversy often fail to communicate effectively with each other.

Another source of confusion is a widespread misperception of the economic processes determining the money stock. Most non-economists, and even many economists, seem to believe that the Federal Reserve can straightforwardly cause the money stock to follow a target path closely—month by month—provided only that the Federal Reserve conscientiously tries to do so. In fact, however, the *nonpolicy* factors helping to determine the month-to-month changes in the money stock are much more important than is generally understood.

1. How would a public announcement of a target time path for a decrease in the money supply affect the actions and expectations of consumers?
2. Based on this reading and your study of the chapter, explain why the Federal Reserve has not been more successful and effective in its efforts to control the money supply in the economy.

Ralph C. Bryant, *Controlling Money: The Federal Reserve and Its Critics*. Washington, D.C.: The Brookings Institution, 1983.

FED GOVERNORS CAN VOTE AGAINST THEIR CHIEF OFFICER

Skill: Understanding Decision Making

 The head of the Federal Reserve Board of Governors is rarely outvoted. Therefore, when the majority of the board did vote against him in March 1986, many analysts and journalists were shocked. Herbert Stein, economist and former chairman of the Council of Economic Advisors, explains why such an occurrence should not be unusual or cause alarm, due to the structure of the board and the Federal Open Market Committe.

I cannot understand the common feeling of shock at the spectacle of the chairman being outvoted. One must ask why Congress established a seven-member Board of Governors and a 12-member Federal Open Market Committee. The answer is that Congress gave the Federal Reserve much power but was unable or unwilling to give the Fed any guidance on how to use the power. So, it sought safety in numbers and diversity as a protection against bias, idiosyncrasy and faddishness. It not only established a seven-member board but also provided for staggering 14-year terms, which made it unlikely that one President would have named a majority. It provided that no more than one member should be from one Federal Reserve District, as a further assurance of diversity. Congress also gave the major power to a 12-person group, the Open Market Committee, including five presidents of Federal Reserve Banks, serving on rotating terms, as a still further assurance of diversity.

Congress created diversity and the Federal Reserve exploits it. If the President asks the chairman to do something, the chairman can say, "Yes, Mr. President, I agree, but there are those other six or 11 people to contend with." If you ask any member why the board cannot commit itself to some policy or goals for the future, you will probably be reminded that they are a diverse, shifting group. And when the chairman testifies before a congressional committee he . . . is the spokesman for a group of . . . people who are free to disagree and capable of doing so but [who] in fact do not. . . .

Congress intended diversity, and the Federal Reserve establishment benefits from the appearance that diversity is at least possible. I doubt that any chairman would like to be rid of the board and bear sole responsibility for monetary policy. In these circumstances, to find the chairman outvoted should not be a surprise or a shock.

The surprise is that, as far as outsiders know, the chairman is outvoted so seldom, and there are rarely even any close votes. One possible explanation is that the objective case for a particular monetary policy is generally so strong that all reasonable people are compelled to agree. Merely to state this hypothesis is to show how incredible it is. A more believable hypothesis is that the opinions of most board and Open Market Committee members about monetary policy are so loosely held that they are quite prepared to subordinate any differences for the comfort of solidarity.

1. What are some of the "checks and balances" that Congress created when the Fed was established so that no one individual would exert complete control over monetary policy?
2. According to the article, what are two reasons why the chairman of the Federal Reserve is seldom outvoted?

Herbert Stein, "Backstage at the Fed." *The Wall Street Journal*, April 4, 1986.

WHAT DOES THE FED DO?
Skill: Applying Information

Many Americans know little more about the Federal Reserve than the fact that its name appears on U.S. currency. Author and television host Louis Rukeyser clarifies the subject in this reading.

Many an American mother dreams that her child will grow up to become President. Millions of dads fantasize about their sons becoming bonus babies or football heroes. . . . But no sensible parent ever looked at a newborn babe gurgling in the maternity ward, and said wistfully: "Perhaps it's too much to hope, but maybe someday my child could be chairman of the Federal Reserve Board."

The reason for this conspicuous exception are several. Many Americans are not quite sure precisely what a Federal Reserve chairman does. . . . Those who are aware that the Fed chairman is, in fact, the nation's chief monetary-

How did the banks in this cartoon react to President Woodrow Wilson's plan to establish the Federal Reserve System?

"Reading the Death Warrant" shows Wilson announcing his bank-control plans.

Readings in Economics

The Board of Governors of the Federal Reserve System set the Fed's policies. The chairman and one other member of the Board are shown here.

policy officer are likely to remain unentranced. . . .

It might be useful at this point to lower both the heat level and the bewilderment level where monetary policy is concerned. First, what is it? Monetary policy refers to the regulation of money and credit in an economy, as opposed to fiscal policy, which is concerned with the budget and taxes. . . . The present setup, in which Congress delegates specific powers to a board appointed by the President, traces to the Federal Reserve Act signed into law by Woodrow Wilson at 6 P.M., December 23, 1913. . . . The Fed, as it quickly became known to its friends, has three mighty powers for affecting the course of short-term interest rates: (1) In its "open market" operations, it can choose to buy or sell Government securities. When it sells such securities, it removes money from the private economy, thereby contracting the available supply of credit. When it buys such securities, it writes what for you or me would be a rubber check: it creates the funds out of thin air, thus in effect "printing" money at will. . . . (2) The Fed can raise or lower the "discount rate" at which it lends to the banks in its system, thus sending a

loud and clear signal of its overall policy intentions. (3) It can change the "reserve requirements" governing the amount of money banks must keep in relation to their deposits; higher reserve requirements mean "tighter" money, since the banks then will have less available for loans.

1. What are the three tools the Federal Reserve can use in regulating monetary policy? Explain the use of each of these powers.
2. Examine the powers of the Federal Reserve and explain how the Fed's actions affect consumers.

Louis Rukeyser, *What's Ahead for the Economy?* New York: Simon and Schuster, 1983. pp. 103–105.

THE INEQUALITIES OF MONETARY RESTRAINT
Skill: Predicting Outcomes

Economist John Kenneth Galbraith is one of many critics who have found faults with monetary policy. He explains how a tight money policy affects large firms and small firms differently in this reading.

If the central bank tightens up sufficiently on the commercial banks so that it affects decisively the money they have to lend and forces them to lend what they do lend at high interest rates, there will obviously be less spending, less demand in the economy. . . .

The effect of this restraint will always be highly unequal. It works, let me repeat, through restricting the aggregate [total] of spending in the economy, restricting what economists call aggregate demand. When this restriction in demand hits General Motors, Exxon, Philips, Shell or the other large corporations, it doesn't force them to stop raising prices. They first cut back on sales and production. We've already seen that they have the power to resist price reductions. It's one of the reasons they want to be big. And if their wage costs are going up or there is other justification for raising prices, they will do so. They will only be forced to stop raising prices and forced to resist wage increases when there is a lot of idle capacity. By then there will be a good deal of unemployment. And this will also help restrain union demands. So, for these large firms, monetary policy works by creating unemployment. And that, of course, has been the highly visible consequence of its recent use.

It has another effect—what amounts to another favor for the strong and against the weak. The large corporation, we saw, has a source of capital independent of the banks. That is from its own earnings, and resort to this source is not affected by central-bank restrictions on lending by the commercial banks. In any case, the big firms are the favorite customers of the banks, the first to be served if there is money to be lent. Since they control their prices, they can also pass higher interest rates on to their customers. So they are very well protected against adverse effects of monetary policy. In contrast, the farmer, the small [trader] who needs money to carry . . . inventories and, above all, firms in industries like housing which operate on borrowed money and depend on customers who borrow money are highly vulnerable to monetary policy. So you see how it works—by creating unemployment, by exempting the big and strong corporations and by putting the squeeze on the small and the weak.

1. According to Galbraith, how does a tight monetary policy lead to a rise in unemployment?
2. Why is a tight monetary policy particularly hard on small businesses?

John Kenneth Galbraith, *Almost Everyone's Guide to Economics.* Boston: Houghton Mifflin Company, 1978. pp. 84–86.

MAINTAINING STABLE MONETARY GROWTH
Skill: Drawing Conclusions

SECTION 5

The way that the Federal Reserve uses its control over the money supply to influence the economy has often been criticized. In this reading, one of the Fed's leading critics, Milton Friedman, discusses the importance of steadiness in monetary policy, the Fed's failure to set consistent targets for money-supply growth, and the Fed's failure to state its targets precisely.

The present monetary structure is not producing satisfactory results. Indeed, in my opinion, no major institution in the United States has so poor a record of performance over so long a period yet so high a public reputation as the Federal Reserve.

The conduct of monetary policy is of major importance; monetary instability breeds economic instability. A monetary structure that fosters steadiness and predictability in the general price level is an essential precondition for healthy non-inflationary growth. . . .

The Fed has vacillated between using one or more interest rates or one or more monetary aggregates as its intermediate targets. . . .

In my opinion, the selection of a target or of a target path is not and has not been the problem. If the Fed had consistently achieved the targets it specified to Congress, monetary growth would have been highly stable instead of highly variable, inflation would never have become the menace it did, and the United States would have been spared the worst parts of the punishing recession (or recessions) from 1979 to 1982. . . .

The use of multiple intermediate targets is undesirable. The Fed has one major instrument of monetary control: control over the quantity of high-powered money. With one instrument, it cannot independently control several aggregates. Its other instruments—primarily the discount rate and reserve requirements—are highly defective as instruments for monetary control and of questionable effectiveness in enabling it to control separately more than one aggregate.

It makes far less difference which aggregate the Fed selects than that it selects one and only one.

1. According to Friedman, what has been the effect of the Fed's inability to achieve stable monetary growth?
2. Explain the difference between the various tools the Fed uses to control monetary growth and the effectiveness of each.

Milton Friedman, "The Case for Overhauling the Federal Reserve." *Challenge*, July-August 1985, pp.4-12.

PRACTICING YOUR READING SKILLS: RECOGNIZING BIAS

Bias is a strong feeling for or against a person or idea by misuse of facts or without sufficient facts to support the feeling. Bias is based on opinion. You may think that economic data would not be biased because statistics are facts. But how data are interpreted and presented can reflect an author's bias—whether it is the author of a book, an article, or an economic theory.

An author, for example, may select only those facts that support his or her view. An author might also select too narrow a sample on which to base conclusions. Finally, an author might oversimplify a complex issue or problem so that his or her solution seems logical and reasonable. News stories about and news analyses of economic trends may also reflect bias. It may be the bias of the author or reporter or of the editors of the magazine or newspaper.

The following tips will help you to recognize bias in the writings or speeches of others.

- Look for words that reflect positive and negative feelings. They include such words as *rightfully*, *depressing*, *looked-for*, *glowing*, *unheard of*, and *astronomically high*. Ask yourself what feelings are touched by such words.
- Notice whether the facts are truly facts or whether they are only assumptions. Clues are words such as *may be*, *I have heard*, *thought to be*, and *commonly believed to be*.
- Check to see if the speaker or writer gives the source of the facts or statistics. The sources may not be reliable.

Activity: Choose an economic issue that is receiving frequent news coverage, such as the defense budget, aid to education, or Social Security. Look for articles about your topic from different publications. You might also listen to radio and television news accounts. What bias can you detect? Why do you think the author, reporter, or editors might be biased about this topic?

VOCABULARY REVIEW

Write the letter of the definition in Column B that correctly defines each term in Column A.

Column A	Column B
1. check clearing	a. method by which a check deposited in the bank is transferred to the bank on which it was written
2. prime rate	b. means of changing the rate of supply of money in the economy
3. discount rate	c. purchases and sales of United States securities by the Federal Reserve Bank
4. reserve requirement	d. interest rate that banks charge on loans to their best business customers
5. monetary policy	e. interest rate that the Federal Reserve charges banks for loans
6. open-market operations	f. requires banks to keep a certain percent of their deposits as cash on account with the Federal Reserve

PRACTICING YOUR ECONOMIC SKILLS

1. **Detecting Bias.** Each of the statements on p. 423 quotes statistics that are true, but uses them in a misleading way. After each statement is a text reference to help you recognize the bias. Explain how each statement slants the facts to support a certain viewpoint.

a. "I don't know why everyone is so worried about the economy. Even with a recession, GNP between 1981 and 1982 grew 4.1 percent." (See Figure 14–3, page 357.)

b. "Inflation is out of control. Prices for fuel oil alone have increased almost 400 percent since 1970." (See Learning Economic Skills for Chapter 14, p. 356.)

c. "During the past 100 years, unions have changed from small groups of workers with no real power to large powerful institutions that play a major role in American political life. That proves organized labor is stronger than ever." (See p. 333.)

2. **Calculating Money Supply.** A banking system that has excess reserves can use them to make new loans and thereby create more money. Calculate the amount of money that can be used for loans for each deposit in the following table.

Deposit	Reserve Requirement
a. $ 2,000	25%
b. 10,500	10%
c. 15,000	20%
d. 20,000	12.5%
e. 30,000	15%

3. **Checking Understanding.** Suppose the Federal Reserve wishes to increase the money supply. It has several choices. It can change the reserve requirement or the discount rate, or it can buy or sell government securities. Explain what the Fed will have to do for each of these choices if it wishes to increase the money supply.

4. Now suppose the Federal Reserve wishes to decrease the money supply. a. Should it raise or lower the reserve requirement? b. Should it raise or lower the discount rate? c. Should it raise or lower the buy or sell government securities?

DISCUSSING ECONOMIC QUESTIONS

1. Do you think a government agency such as the Federal Reserve System should have so much power in regulating the money supply? Why or why not? What other methods can you think of for regulating the money supply?

2. Is the Federal Reserve requirement that banks hold reserves a sound one? Why or why not? Is it necessary for the Federal Reserve to regulate the money supply?

3. If you were a banker, would you follow a policy of lending out your excess reserves? Why or why not? If not, what other policies might you follow to keep your bank profitable?

APPLYING CRITICAL THINKING SKILLS

1. **Analyzing Information.** In your local library, check the most recent issue of the *Federal Reserve Bulletin* for the current reserve requirements and discount rate. Check the same month's issue for the last four years to see how often they have changed and how much. Use this data as the basis for a discussion of the Fed's monetary policy.

2. **Gathering Data.** Ask five friends or relatives to look at the paper money they have and to find out which of the 12 Federal Reserve Banks issued it. The name of the bank will be in the black seal on the left side of each bill's face. If you find bills from banks in other areas, be prepared to discuss how the money may have found its way into your area.

READINGS

The Federal Reserve System—Purposes and Functions. Board of Governors: Federal Reserve System, 1982.

Historical Beginnings of the Federal Reserve. Boston: Federal Reserve Bank, 1977.

"Pressures That Drive the Fed to Loosen Up." *Business Week*, 16 August 1982, pp. 24-25.

CHAPTER 17

The federal, state, and local governments spends vast amounts of money to pay for the functions of government. Education, national defense, health and human services are among the programs financed by taxes on business and individuals, and by borrowing.

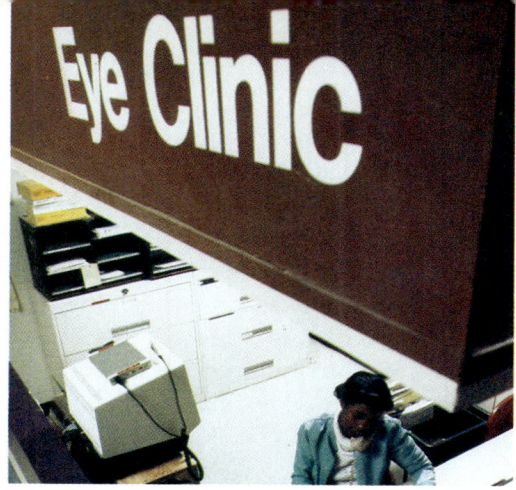

GOVERNMENT SPENDS, COLLECTS, AND OWES

Government is the biggest business in the nation. At all levels—federal, state, and local—it employs more workers than any other business. Government collects more revenue and spends more. It also owes more. This chapter describes the activities that governments finance and the taxes they levy to pay for these activities. You will also read about the effect of taxation on the economy. The chapter ends with a discussion of the nation's public debt. Learning Economic Skills explains the records to keep and the steps to follow in figuring personal income tax.

CHAPTER OBJECTIVES After you study this chapter, you will be able to:

1 • describe the growth in the size of government.

2 • explain the four functions that government finances.

3 • explain the need for compromise in the federal budget-making process.
  • describe the steps in the federal budget-making process.

4 • contrast the two principles upon which most taxes are levied.
  • contrast the three forms of taxation.
  • identify two ways taxes regulate economic activity in the nation.
  ★ list the records to keep and the steps to follow in figuring personal income tax.

5 • explain why government uses deficit financing.

ECONOMICS VOCABULARY

public goods
income redistribution
social insurance programs
Social Security
workers' compensation
public-assistance programs
welfare
Medicaid
fiscal year
benefits-received principle
ability-to-pay principle
progressive tax
regressive tax
proportional tax
deficit financing
national debt

As you read in Chapter 2, every economic system attempts to answer four basic questions. They are: What and how much should be produced? Who should produce what? How should goods and services be produced? Who should share in what is produced? In the United States, the forces of supply and demand operating in the marketplace affect many of the decisions that answer these questions. But, as you also learned in Chapter 2, the United States is not a pure market economy. In addition to the market forces, there are other forces that affect the distribution of resources throughout the economy. One of the most important of these forces is government on all levels—local, state, and federal.

When you travel a turnpike, you are using a resource that was financed by federal and state monies. You probably attend a school that receives some form of aid from the local, state, or, possibly, federal government. Many of the goods that you buy have been produced in accordance with local, state, and federal regulations. If you have a job, your working conditions are often determined by government safety and other regulations. If you earn money income, buy goods, or own property, you probably pay taxes that help pay for the many government activities. In fact, government at every level—federal, state, or local—is involved in almost every aspect of the United States economy.

Not only has government spending increased since 1930, but it also has accounted for a larger percentage of the GNP? Why do you think this has happened?

Figure 17-1: GOVERNMENT SPENDING AS A PERCENTAGE OF GROSS NATIONAL PRODUCT, 1930-1984

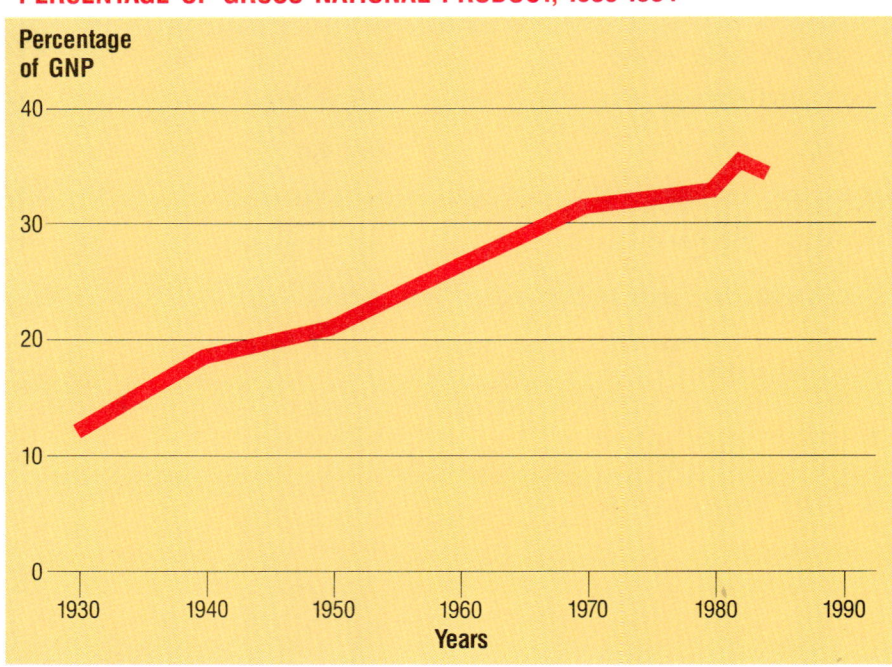

Source: *Facts and Figures on Government Finance,* New York Tax Foundation, *Economic Indicators*

1 GROWTH IN THE SIZE OF GOVERNMENT

Ask yourself as you read:

- In what ways has government grown during the last 50 or so years?
- When did the biggest jump in federal spending occur?

Government has grown considerably in the last 50 or so years. In 1929, just before the beginning of the Great Depression, government at all levels employed a little more than 3 million civilian workers. Today, slightly less than 3 million people work for the federal government alone. If you add local and state employees, government employs over 16 million civilian workers. This is a growth of more than 400 percent during the nearly 60-year period in which the population grew less than 90 percent.

As the functions of government, such as providing health care, have grown, so has government spending. Figures 17-1 and 17-2 show two ways of looking at the growth of government spending. The first graph shows total government expenditures, including Social Security and other welfare payments, as well as interest payments, expressed as a percentage of GNP from 1930 to the present. The second graph shows the amount of government purchases of goods and services (including

Figure 17–2: GOVERNMENT PURCHASES OF GOODS AND SERVICES, 1935–1986*

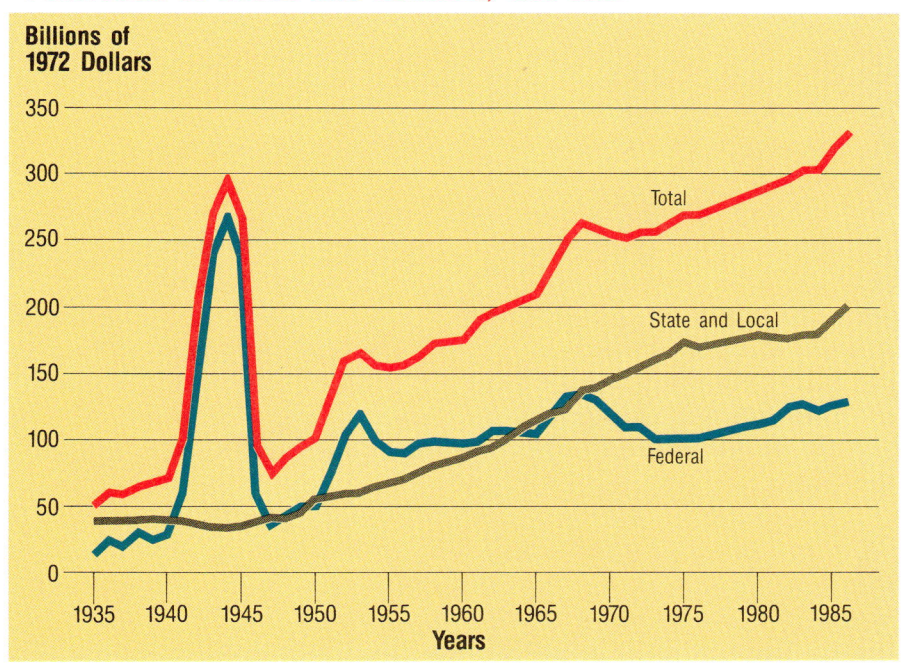

Why did government spending rise so dramatically in the early 1940's? What kinds of goods and services would the federal government be buying? state and local governments?

Source: *Historical Statistics of the U.S., Statistical Abstract of the U.S.,* Bureau of the Census

*The figure for 1986 is an estimate.

Social Security and other welfare payments and interest) corrected for inflation.

As you can see from the graphs, the different levels of government have grown at different rates. During the early 1930s, state and local governments spent far more than the federal government. Up until that time, the federal government paid for little more than national defense, a few public-works projects, and the salaries of members of Congress, federal judges, and the employees of executive departments such as the Post Office.

This distribution of spending changed during the 1930s. In an attempt to help pull the nation out of the Great Depression, the federal government began to establish public assistance and other aid programs. As a result, Federal spending more than tripled in ten years. Meanwhile, state and local spending remained about the same. The biggest jump in federal spending did not occur until World War II. Even though federal spending dropped steeply after the war, it generally remained higher than state and local spending. This situation continued until the late 1960s. Then, state and local government spending for such items as sewers, roads, schools, and public assistance increased rapidly.

WHY HAS GOVERNMENT GROWN?

Economists have often tried to find an explanation for the huge growth in government spending since the Great Depression. One theory is that as the nation became richer, especially in the late 1960s and early 1970s, people demanded more government services to even out certain inequities. This goal relates to the economic question of who should share in what is produced. More aid was demanded for education, medical care, welfare, and so on. The economy was booming, and many believed that taxpayers could afford higher government spending.

inequity (in-EK-wuh-tee): unfairness

However, the economy suffered a series of recessions in the late 1970s and early 1980s. Americans began to feel that maintaining all the programs they wanted was too costly. At some point, Americans—voters and politicians alike—had lost sight of the economic principle of scarcity. To remedy the situation, politicians began to think of ways to cut back on government spending. In doing so, they had to decide on the trade-offs Americans would be willing to accept: fewer services and less money for research, education, public assistance, and health care, for example.

Today total government purchases represent over 20 percent of GNP. However, this figure does not include such items as interest payments on the national debt and transfer payments such as welfare programs. Total government outlays exceed one-third of GNP. Moreover, the size of government cannot be measured only by the cost of government spending. Any discussion of government's size must include what government spends this money on.

1. Figure 17-2 shows that total government purchases have been increasing since the 1950s. According to Figure 17-1, however, total government purchases as a percentage of GNP have remained fairly even since the 1950s. How do you explain this apparent difference between the two graphs, Figure 17-1 and Figure 17-2?
2. According to the text, what caused the increase in state and local spending in the late 1960s?
3. **Critical Thinking: Testing Hypotheses. a.** According to some economists, what is the explanation for the growth of government since the Great Depression? **b.** Does the answer to question 2 seem to support or disprove this explanation of government growth? Explain.

2 | THE FUNCTIONS OF GOVERNMENT

Ask yourself as you read:
- What are the main economic functions of government?
- Which economic responsibilities are shared by the federal, state, and local governments?

Government in the United States secures four important economic functions: providing public goods, providing for the public well-being, regulating economic activity, and ensuring economic stability. Federal, state, and local governments share responsibilities for the first three functions. The fourth responsibility, ensuring economic stability, is handled almost entirely by the federal government.

Providing for the nation's defense is one of the most important functions of government. Why is this function the responsibility of the federal government?

PROVIDING PUBLIC GOODS

Public goods are goods or services that are supplied to all its citizens by government. These goods can be used by many individuals at the same time, without reducing the benefit each person receives. Public goods include education, national defense, and certain types of health care.

National defense is one of the few public goods provided only by the federal government. Usually, different levels of government share responsibilities. The legal system, which is a type of public good, for example, involves all three levels. Federal, state, and local governments maintain separate systems of courts, correctional institutions, and law-enforcement agencies.

REDISTRIBUTING INCOME

Another function of government is to provide for the public well-being by giving assistance to specific groups such as the aged, the ill, and the poor. Americans, through their elected representatives, have chosen to see that everyone in the nation is provided with a certain minimum level of income. This is done primarily through **income redistribution.** That is, income is taken from some people through taxation and then given to others. Government programs that redistribute this income can be classified into two areas: social insurance and public assistance.

Social insurance programs pay benefits to retired and disabled workers and their families. The benefits are financed by taxes that workers and their employers have paid into the programs. **Social Security,** a federal program, provides monthly payments to millions of people who are retired or unable to work. **Workers' compensation,** a state-run program, extends payments for medical care to workers injured on the job. Both programs also pay benefits to dependents of workers who have died. Workers who have lost their jobs can receive payments through unemployment insurance. This is also a state-run program that is financed by taxes on employers. Another state program, Medicare, provides low-cost health care for the aged and disabled.

Public-assistance programs make payments based on need regardless of whether an individual or his or her employer has paid taxes. Federal programs in this area include foods stamps, veterans' benefits, and payments to the aged, blind, and disabled, called Supplemental Security Income. Aid to families with dependent children, often called **welfare,** is a major state-run program. It provides money to needy parents raising small children. **Medicaid,** another state program, provides free health care for people with low incomes.

The formula for determining benefits under federal programs is the same for each person regardless of the state in which the individual lives. Payments for state programs, however, differ from state to state. Both social-insurance and public-assistance programs belong to the category of transfer payments that you read about in Chapter 14.

Politics and Economics: John Kenneth Galbraith (1908–)

John Kenneth Galbraith is one of the more controversial of modern American economists. His economic views are widely read and followed by the public, politicians, and economists alike, even though they may not agree with him. Galbraith has had a distinguished career as a professor of economics, a journalist, and public official. He has published numerous works including *The Affluent Society* (1958), *The New Industrial State* (1967), *Economics and the Public Purpose* (1973), *The Age of Uncertainty* (1977), and *A Life In Our Times: Memoirs* (1981), *A View from the Stands,* (1986).

One of Galbraith's themes is the nonexistence of a competitive market economy in the United States. He believes that giant corporations dominate large parts of the marketplace. These firms decide what is to be produced in the economy and then channel consumers by persuasive advertising to buy what they have produced. To Galbraith, large corporations have also become too influential in politics. By arguing for protection during bad economic times, corporations have been able to limit competition from manufacturers abroad who can produce a cheaper or better product.

Galbraith has argued that the federal government should take over many of the nation's largest corporations. He is not asking for more antitrust legislation or more enforcement of it but for the nationalization of these corporations. This means that the federal government would actually own and run the companies. It is not the great size of these corporations that worries Galbraith. Rather he sees the problem to be in their ability to control the social purpose of many of the nation's activities. For example, resources are used for video games rather than for the development of new medical equipment. He wants the larger interests of society put ahead of the interests of individual corporations.

In the early 1980s, Galbraith was an outspoken critic of President Ronald Reagan's economic policies. He believed that supply-side economics would expand the economy by giving poorer Americans less and wealthier Americans more. According to Galbraith, Reagan's emphasis on the private business sector would seriously reduce government benefits to the needy. Galbraith wants permanent price controls placed on the top 2,000 corporations. He believes that this is the only way to control inflation. Few economists today agree with this radical proposal.

Galbraith has been less interested in strict scientific research than in giving his readers a view of what he believes are the wrongs of society. Not surprisingly, not all economists regard Galbraith and his work highly. He, on the other hand, calls on his critics to confront the real issues of the day—inequality, the domination of the economy by giant corporations, and the destruction of the environment.

1. What criticisms does Galbraith make about the role of giant corporations in the nation's economy?
2. Why do you think many economists disagree with Galbraith's ideas?

REGULATING ECONOMIC ACTIVITY

In Chapters 3, 10, and 13 you read about three ways that government regulates economic activity. It protects the consumer, promotes competition, and supervises labor and management relations. A fourth way is through regulating the negative byproducts that often occur in the production of goods in our economy. When a steel mill produces steel, for example, the resulting pollution from the smokestacks may cause health problems in the surrounding area, not to mention dirtier clothes, cars, and buildings. The steel mill does not have to correct these negative byproducts, though it may do so. Therefore, the federal government has often stepped in to require the installation in plants of equipment that will reduce pollution. Local and state governments also have pollution laws. These include everything from city laws against littering to state laws regulating the dumping of toxic wastes in rivers.

toxic (TAHK-sik): poisonous

PROMOTING ECONOMIC STABILITY

Encouraging and promoting economic stability means smoothing out the ups and downs in the nation's overall business activity. This function is the responsibility only of the federal government. As you read in Chapter 16, it is one goal of the Federal Reserve System. However, the federal government has another tool besides monetary policy to even out the business cycle. It can also use fiscal policy, which is the government's set of financial policies on taxation and spending. You will read in detail about fiscal policy in the next chapter.

Figure 17-3 shows total government spending in a recent year. Why do you think that the percentage spent on interest is so high. What might be included in the category *Other*?

Figure 17-3: SPENDING BY THE FEDERAL GOVERNMENT IN A RECENT YEAR (in billions of dollars)

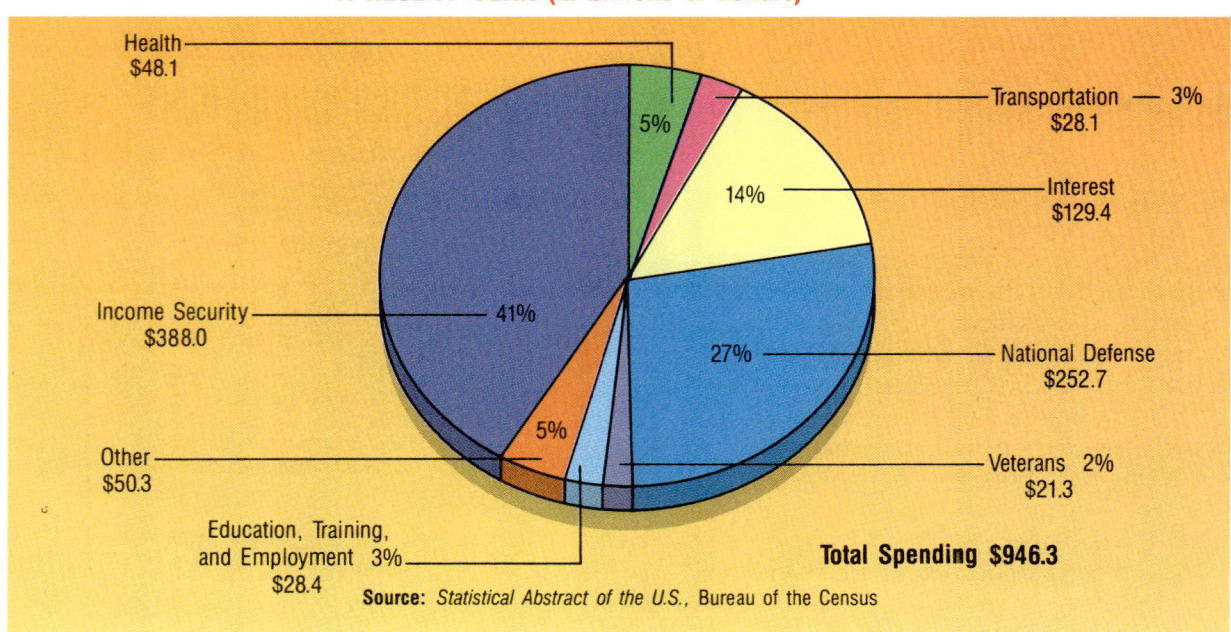

Health $48.1

Transportation — 3% $28.1

5%

14%

Interest $129.4

Income Security $388.0

41%

27%

National Defense $252.7

Other $50.3

5%

Veterans 2% $21.3

Education, Training, and Employment 3% $28.4

Total Spending $946.3

Source: *Statistical Abstract of the U.S.*, Bureau of the Census

1. Define the following economic terms: **a.** public goods, **b.** grants-in-aid, **c.** income redistribution, **d.** social-insurance programs, **e.** Social Security, **f.** workers' compensation, **g.** public-assistance programs, **h.** fiscal policy.

2. **a.** What two types of programs provide for the public well-being? **b.** List two programs in each category and state whether they are federal or state programs.

3. In what four ways does government regulate economic activity?

4. By what two methods does the federal government ensure economic stability?

5. **Critical Thinking: Summarizing the Main Idea.** In a paragraph, explain how the three levels of government share the responsibilities for providing public goods.

3 | THE FEDERAL BUDGET

Ask yourself as you read:

• Why is it important for the federal budget to be balanced?
• What are the largest categories of federal government spending?

To carry out all of its functions, government must spend large sums of money. As a result, the federal budget is huge and has numerous categories. Figure 17-3 shows the major areas of spending. Note that the federal budget is based on a fiscal, rather than a calendar, year. That is, spending is calculated from the beginning of the budget year on October 1 of one year to September 30 of the next year, which is the federal government's **fiscal year.**

Considerable debate and compromise is necessary in preparing an annual budget. As you read in Chapter 1, all resources are scarce. As a result, an increase in spending in one area will cause a decrease in spending in some other area. In other words, every spending action by the government has its own opportunity cost. There is always a trade-off between types of spending, even for the government. As you read earlier in this chapter, this fact was overlooked in some years when the economy was booming and government was collecting large revenues. However, today all levels of government are aware of the dangers of overspending and are trying harder to keep within their budgets.

THE BUDGET-MAKING PROCESS

A complicated budget-making process goes on every year not only in Washington, D.C., but in every state and local government unit. Eighteen months before the fiscal year begins on October 1st, the Executive Branch of the government begins to prepare a budget. The Office of Management and Budget (OMB) starts the process, with the advice of the Council of Economic Advisers (CEA) and the Treasury Department. The OMB makes an outline of a tentative budget for the next fiscal year. The various departments and agencies receive this outline and usually start bargaining with the OMB for a larger allocation of money.

The President submits his budget to Congress by January. Then its committees and subcommittees examine the budget's proposals, while the Congressional Budget Office (CBO) advises the committees and subcommittees about different aspects of the budget. Throughout the summer each subcommittee then holds a series of discussions about the budget.

Congress is supposed to pass a second budget resolution setting binding limits on spending and taxes for the upcoming fiscal year. In practice, however, the required budget resolutions often do not get passed on time. Moreover, when they are passed, the resolutions are not always treated as binding. As a result, the fiscal year sometimes starts without a budget, and the agencies must operate on the basis of a continuing resolution. This means they can continue spending as they spent the year before.

In spite of the budget process, federal government revenues have not been equal to government expenditures. For years, the federal government has spent more than it has taken in. The interest on the debt alone is staggering. You will read more about this national debt in Sec-

Figure 17-2 shows a higher total for state and local purchases than for federal. Why is the total for federal government spending greater than for state and local? What does *spending* include that *purchases* does not?

Figure 17-4: SPENDING BY STATE AND LOCAL GOVERNMENTS IN A RECENT YEAR (in billions of dollars)

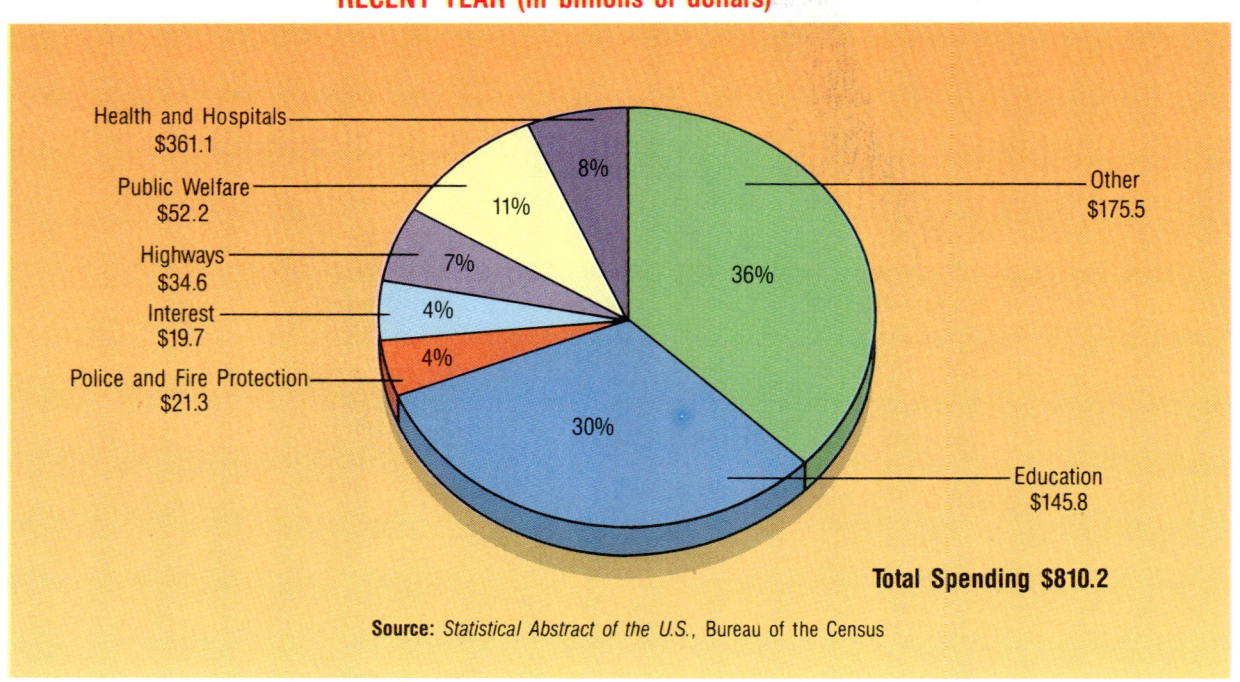

Health and Hospitals $361.1
Public Welfare $52.2
Highways $34.6
Interest $19.7
Police and Fire Protection $21.3

Other $175.5
Education $145.8

8% 11% 7% 4% 4% 36% 30%

Total Spending $810.2

Source: *Statistical Abstract of the U.S.*, Bureau of the Census

tion 5. To try to end the ever-rising debt, the Gramm-Rudman-Hollings Act was passed in 1983. The act requires Congress to reduce the deficit to zero by the year 1991 and provides the schedule Congress is to follow to insure that it happens.

STATE AND LOCAL BUDGETS

Figure 17-4 shows how state and local governments spend the revenues they collect. By far the largest single category in state and local expenditures is education. This is not surprising, since most elementary and secondary education, as well as a considerable portion of higher education, is provided by state and local funds. Other large expenses are for public assistance (welfare), hospitals, health maintenance, and highways. The "other" general expenditure also is large and includes parks and recreation, public housing, and other goods and services provided at the state and local levels.

REVIEWING ECONOMIC PRINCIPLES

1. Summarize in a paragraph how the federal budget is made.
2. Why are debate and compromise necessary in making a governmental budget?
3. **Critical Thinking: Inferring Similarities.** List two similarities between making a budget for the federal government and one for a family. You will have to infer your answer from the material in this chapter and in Learning Economic Skills in Chapter 4.

4 | TAXATION

Ask yourself as you read:
• What are the principal taxes used by government to raise revenue?
• What are the main reasons that governments levy taxes?

So far, you have read about how government spends its money, but from what is the source of this money? Most of it comes from you, the American taxpayer. About 85 percent of federal, state, and local government revenue comes from taxation. Table 17-1 lists the major taxes that the various levels of government use to raise revenue.

PRINCIPLES OF TAXATION

Taxes can be justified according to one of two major principles. Under the **benefits-received principle,** those who use a particular government service support it with taxes in proportion to the benefit they receive. Those who do not use a service do not pay taxes for it. For example, a gasoline tax to pay for highway construction and repair is based on this principle. Those who use the highways often buy more gasoline and, therefore, pay more in gasoline taxes.

Table 17-1: MAJOR TAXES

Tax	Description	Type
Personal income	Tax paid is a percentage of income. This is the major source of revenue for the federal government. Many states and some local governments also levy personal income taxes.	Progressive at the federal level, but is sometimes proportional at the state level.
Social insurance	Taxes covered by the Federal Insurance Contributions Act (FICA). This is the second largest source of federal government revenue.	Proportional up to $42,000 in 1987, regressive above that.
Corporate income	Tax paid to the federal government as a percentage of corporate profits. Some states also levy corporate income taxes.	At the federal level, progressive up to $100,000; proportional above that.
Excise	Tax paid by the consumer on the manufacture, use, and consumption of certain goods. The major federal excise taxes are on alcohol, tobacco, and gasoline. Some states also levy excise taxes.	Regressive if people with higher incomes spend a lower proportion of income on taxed items.
Estate	Federal tax on the property of someone who has died. Some states also levy an estate tax.	Progressive; percentage increases with the value of the estate.
Inheritance	Tax paid by those who inherit property from someone who has died. This is a state tax only.	Varies by state.
Gift	Tax paid by the person who gives the gift. This is a federal tax only.	Progressive; percentage increases with the value of the gift.
Sales	Tax paid on purchases. Almost all states as well as many local governments levy a sales tax. The rate varies from state to state and within states. Items that are taxed also vary from state to state. Some tax clothes, but many states do not.	Regressive if people with higher incomes spend a lower proportion of income on taxed items.
Property	State and local taxation of the value of property. Both real property, such as buildings and land, and personal property, such as stocks, bonds, and home furnishings, may be taxed.	Proportional; percentage is set by state and local governments.
Custom duties*	Tax on imports that is paid by the importer.	Proportional.

*You will be reading more about customs duties in Chapter 20.

A tax based on the benefits-received principle is useful in raising money to pay for a service used by only certain individuals. However, many government services—national defense, for example—benefit everyone equally. Also, those who most need services, such as assistance for the aged and poor, are the ones least able to pay taxes.

Under the **ability-to-pay principle,** those with higher incomes pay more in taxes than those with lower incomes. This is regardless of the number of government services they use. For example, in most cities all property owners, even those without school-age children, must pay property taxes to support the local school system.

FORMS OF TAXATION

Actual taxes are classified according to the effect they have on those who are taxed. A **progressive tax,** for example, has been justified on the basis of the ability-to-pay principle. It takes a larger percentage of higher incomes than of lower incomes. The federal personal income tax is an example of a progressive tax. As an individual earns more income, a larger percentage of that income is taken for federal taxes. Those who make less than a certain minimum—$3,560 for single people with no dependents in 1987—pay no federal income tax. This occurred because Congress passed a new tax law in 1986 to make the tax code fairer. It eliminated many of the deductions and tax shelters that had seemed to favor the wealthy. The new tax code lowered the top tax rates for individuals gradually from 50 percent to 33 percent. It also shifted some of the tax burden from individuals by raising corporate taxes.

A **regressive tax** is one that falls hardest on those with the least amount of income. It takes a larger percentage of lower incomes than of higher incomes. A state sales tax on food is a regressive tax. Because low-income families spend a larger percentage of their income on food than middle- or high-income families, they also spend a larger portion of their income on taxes on food.

The third form of tax distribution is the **proportional tax.** This is a tax that takes the same percentage of all incomes. As income rises, the amount of tax paid also rises. However, the percentage of income represented by that tax remains the same. Some government officials have suggested that the federal income tax be set at a flat 18 percent.

TAXES AS A WAY OF DIRECTING ECONOMIC ACTIVITY

Taxation is more than a way for government to raise money. It is also a way in which government can direct the use of resources by businesses and individuals and also a way to regulate economic activity.

Taxes are commonly used to encourage certain activities by businesses and individuals. Often cities and states will temporarily reduce or exempt taxes for a company as a way of persuading it to locate in a particular area. Governments at all levels encourage investment in their bonds by offering tax-free interest. Taxes are also used to direct re-

Filing an individual income tax return is the responsibility of every person who receives an income from a job or other sources. The 1986 tax reform law lowered the tax rate for most Americans.

Learning Economic Skills

PREPARING YOUR FEDERAL INCOME TAX

If you as a single person earn over a certain amount in income—$3,560 in 1987—you have to report that income and pay federal income tax on it. If you earn less than that, you do not have to file a federal income tax form unless you will receive a refund. You must also file if you have taxable interest, dividends, or other unearned income of $1,000 or more. You must file even though you are still claimed as a dependent on a parent's tax return.

Most states and a number of cities also have personal income taxes. Tax rates and income limits vary from state to state and community to community. Knowing what records to keep and which forms to fill out can save you money and problems in filing your tax returns.

RECORD KEEPING

If you are employed by a company, your federal income tax as well as any state and city income taxes are withheld—deducted automatically from each paycheck. Self-employed people who expect to pay more than a certain amount in taxes—$1,000 in 1987—must file an estimate of their taxes each year. They then pay their income tax in quarterly installments since it is not withheld from a paycheck. They still must file a tax return every year.

The stub on your paycheck shows the amount of taxes withheld during the pay period and also the amount withheld from the beginning of the year to that date. If your income includes tips, you have to report your tips to your employer. Your employer then records them as part of your income and withholds taxes for them.

By January 31 of each year, your employer must give you a tax form showing all taxes withheld during the previous year. You need this form to use when figuring your tax return. The withholding form is actually several sheets. You have to attach one sheet to your federal tax form, and one copy is yours. The others are for use with city or state tax forms if you have to file these, too.

Besides taxes on income, you must also pay federal income taxes on interest from savings accounts or other securities. Your bank or investment company will send you a statement of the income you earned from these sources during the past year. These statements should arrive at about the same time as your withholding form. Keep these statements because you will need them in figuring your taxes.

You should have records for all medical expenses including medical and dental insurance premiums, business expenses not covered by your company, finance charges, taxes paid, and so on. In other words, you should have records for everything that might reduce the amount of taxes you pay. Among deductions allowed are interest payments on loans, contributions to charity, finance charges on credit purchases, and expenses for child care if both parents work outside the home.

If you use a room of your home as a place of business, you will need records of such items as rental payments, utility bills, and telephone bills. Without these, you will not be able to deduct a part of these costs as business expenses.

The best way to keep records is to pay by check and keep your canceled checks. It is wise to keep records regularly. When you balance your bank statement each month, sort your checks and file them in envelopes marked *medical expenses*, *business expenses*, and so on.

FIGURING YOUR TAXES

There are three things you must know before figuring your income tax: your filing status, your exemptions, and the size of your income.

Whether on December 31 you are single or married determines your filing status for the entire year. If you are married, you may file a joint return with your husband or wife or file separately. In most cases, it is usually to the taxpayers' benefit to file jointly. Another filing status is called *head of household.* This usually applies to a single person who has one or more dependents.

Samples from Tax Table

If total taxable income is		And you are:			
At least	But less than	Single	Married filing jointly	Married filing separately	Head of a household
		Your tax is—			
3,250	3,300	117	0	200	117
3,300	3,350	123	0	207	123
3,350	3,400	129	0	214	129
3,400	3,450	136	3	221	135
3,450	3,500	143	9	228	141
7,500	7,550	782	536	916	710
7,550	7,500	791	543	926	718
7,600	7,650	799	550	935	726
7,650	7,700	808	558	945	734
7,700	7,750	816	566	954	742
11,750	1,800	1,600	1,214	1,887	1,513
11,800	11,850	1,611	1,222	1,900	1,524
11,850	11,900	1,622	1,230	1,912	1,535
11,900	11,950	1,633	1,239	1,925	1,546
11,950	12,000	1,644	1,248	1,937	1,557
15,000	15,050	2,337	1,828	2,812	2,228
15,050	15,100	2,350	1,837	2,828	2,239
15,100	15,150	2,364	1,847	2,845	2,251
15,150	15,200	2,377	1,856	2,861	2,262
15,200	15,250	2,391	1,866	2,878	2,274

Then figure your taxes using the standard deduction shown in the tax tables. If you would pay less tax by itemizing, then you should fill out that section of the tax return that itemizes deductions. A young, single person with no interest payments on a mortgage or real estate taxes to pay will usually find that the standard deduction results in a smaller tax payment than itemizing deductions.

Depending on your income and your number of exemptions, you may owe the federal government additional money. Or, as is frequently true for young people who are just beginning to work, the federal government may owe you money. This money is repaid to you from the taxes that were automatically deducted from your wages throughout the previous year.

Filling out state and city tax forms is similar to the procedure for filling out your federal form. You need to keep the same records for all three.

Practicing Your Skills

1. What records should you keep for tax reasons?
2. According to the tax table, how much tax would a person with a taxable income of $15,125 pay as: **a.** a single taxpayer? **b.** married filing jointly? **c.** married filing separately? **d.** head of a household?
3. According to the answer to number 2, who pays the most tax?
4. How much is the difference in number 2 between married filing separately and married filing jointly?
5. How much tax would a single person pay on the following taxable income: **a.** $3,445? **b.** $7,651? **c.** $11,864? **d.** $15,200?
6. What percentage of total taxable income is the tax paid on each of the amounts in number 5?
7. Based on your answer to number 6, is the federal personal income tax proportional, regressive, or progressive? Explain.

Federal tax laws allow you to take one exemption for yourself and one for every person who depends on you for 50 percent or more of his or her income. People who are blind are allowed an additional exemption as are people 65 or older.

If you have a great many deductions, you should itemize them on the worksheet provided in the tax booklet and see what your tax would be.

sources toward investments that are desirable but costly. For example, many states encourage homeowners to insulate their homes by allowing the cost to be deducted from their state income taxes.

On the other hand, taxes can also be used to discourage certain activities. Excise taxes, for example, are supposed to discourage the use of such items as cigarettes and gasoline. Customs duties are supposed to reduce sales of imported goods. Other taxes are used as penalties for certain actions. For example, a person withdrawing money from an Individual Retirement Account (IRA) before age 59½ must pay 10 percent of it as a federal tax penalty.

Taxes can also be used to control the nature and growth of economic activity. This is done by adjusting tax rates and the distribution of taxes—that is, who pays which taxes. However, government officials must keep it in mind that individuals and businesses may react to these changes. For example, raising taxes for a state or city can actually decrease revenues if businesses and homeowners move away to escape high taxes. On the other hand, a city can find itself short of funds if it grants too many tax reductions to try to attract businesses.

REVIEWING ECONOMIC PRINCIPLES

1. What is the benefits-received principle?
2. Why do some people think that most government revenue should be raised by taxation based on the ability-to-pay principle?
3. **a.** What is the difference between progressive and regressive taxes? **b.** How does a proportional tax differ from both?
4. **Critical Thinking: Analyzing Information.** How does the government use taxes to: **a.** direct the use of resources? **b.** control the nature and growth of economic activity?

5 | THE NATION'S PUBLIC DEBT

Ask yourself as you read:
• Why does the government use deficit financing?
• How does the government borrow money?

When government spends more than it collects through taxation, it must raise the extra money through borrowing. This is similar to an individual's overspending income and using credit. The government's spending more money than it takes in is called **deficit financing.** The federal government routinely spends more than it receives. From 1940 through 1987, the federal government had a deficit in 40 out of the 48 years. According to some estimates, federal, state, and local government spending will average 23 percent of GNP through the late 1980s. Government revenues, however, will be roughly 20 percent of GNP. The difference must be made up by borrowing.

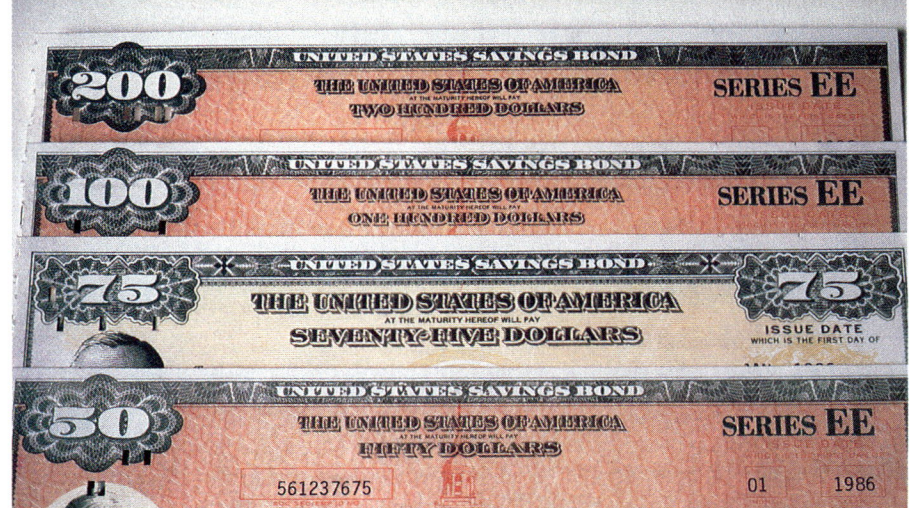

These United States savings bonds are securities sold mainly to individuals by the federal government. Why are they considered part of the nation's public debt?

GOVERNMENT BORROWING

Government borrows by selling securities to individuals and businesses. As you read in Chapter 7, securities sold by the federal government are Treasury bonds, notes, and bills. When you buy United States savings bonds, you are also lending money to the federal government. In addition, individual agencies of the federal government, such as the Tennessee Valley Authority, are authorized to sell bonds. State and local governments can borrow by selling municipal bonds to finance some of their activities.

Each year the federal government creates new debt by issuing new securities. At the same time, it retires old debt by paying off bonds, notes, and bills as they come due. The total amount of debt outstanding for the federal government is called the **national debt** or public debt. As you can see from Figure 17-3, the interest paid each year on the national debt makes up a sizeable portion of federal spending.

In recent years the dollar amount of the national debt has been growing at a steep rate. This has caused concern among many public officials and private citizens that the government is living too far beyond its means. Others, however, have pointed out that the national debt expressed as a percentage of GNP has actually decreased steadily since World War II until the last few years. They believe that federal borrowing, if controlled, is not necessarily a reason for alarm. You will read more about the controversy over the national debt in the Issue for this unit.

REVIEWING ECONOMIC PRINCIPLES

1. Define the following economic terms: **a.** deficit financing, **b.** national debt.
2. How do governments make up the difference between what they take in as revenue and what they spend?
3. **Critical Thinking: Analyzing Both Sides of an Issue.** What is the controversy over the national debt?

SUMMARY OF IMPORTANT PRINCIPLES

1 • Government has grown from 3 million employees in 1929 to about 16 million. Its spending on goods and services has also greatly increased. Some economists believe the government has grown so much because as the nation became richer, people demanded more government services to redistribute some of the nation's wealth to the needy.

2 • Federal, state, and local governments share the responsibilities for providing public goods; providing for public well-being through social-insurance and public-assistance programs; and regulating economic activity by protecting consumers, promoting competition, supervising labor and management, and regulating social costs. The federal government works to promote economic stability by adjusting tax rates and/or its spending policies.

3 • Debate and compromise are necessary in preparing an annual budget—whether federal, state, or local—because all resources are scarce. An increase in spending in one area will result in a decrease in spending in some other area.

• The federal budget-making process begins when the OMB prepares an outline of a tentative budget for the next fiscal year. Then the various federal departments and agencies bargain for their share of the budget's allocations. The President submits his budget to Congress by January. There, it is examined by the various Congressional committees and subcommittees. Because of the failure to reach an agreement about the budget on time, the fiscal year sometimes starts without a budget.

4 • Under the benefits-received principle, those who use a particular government service support it with taxes in proportion to the benefit they receive. Those who do not use a service do not pay for it. Under the ability-to-pay principle, those with higher incomes, regardless of the number of government services they use, pay more in taxes than those with lower incomes.
• A progressive tax takes a larger percentage of higher incomes than of lower ones. A regressive tax takes a larger percentage of lower incomes than of higher ones. A proportional tax takes the same percentage of all incomes; as income rises, the amount of tax paid also rises, but the percentage of income represented by the tax remains the same.
• Taxation can be used to direct the use of resources by individuals and businesses and to regulate economic activity.

5 • Government uses deficit financing when it spends more than it takes in and must borrow to make up the difference.
• To figure one's income tax, a person needs to keep the form sent by the employer; any statements of interest from banks or investment companies; and records for all medical expenses, finance charges, taxes paid, and so on, that might reduce the amount of tax to be paid.

Putting Economics to Work

SCARCITY: TUITION TAX CREDITS

In 1982 President Ronald Reagan had announced his support for tuition tax credits for parents who send their children to private schools. These tax credits would allow these families to deduct some of the tuition costs from their federal income taxes. The idea has been debated for years. This conversation is typical.

Nancy Lager and Hilary Walters were having a disagreement. Nancy, who attends a private high school, says the system used for financing public schools is unfair. She points out that her parents pay property taxes that support public schools. They also pay tuition to her private high school. For this reason, Nancy supports a system of tuition tax credits. Nancy feels it is a good way to help families that, in effect, are paying twice for education.

Hilary disagrees. She believes that parents should have the right to send their children to private school if they choose. However, she feels it is their duty as citizens to support public education as well. Hilary argues that the nation needs a strong public school system to ensure that everyone receives an education, regardless of income. Tuition tax credits would endanger public education by encouraging parents to enroll their children in private schools. Hilary also feels the credits would drain large amounts of income from the federal government. This is at a time when budget deficits are already huge.

1. Do you agree with Nancy or Hilary on the issue of tuition tax credits? Explain.
2. How might tuition tax credits eventually reduce the amount of money going to local schools? Consider what a community might do with property taxes if many parents removed their children from public schools.
3. Suppose the tax credit law was passed. What could public schools do to convince parents to keep their children in public schools?

Readings in Economics

GOVERNMENT—A COMPUTERIZED MONSTER?

Skill: Predicting Outcomes

In the following reading, Kenneth C. Laudon expresses concern about the growth of the power of the executive branch of government by means of the files and data at its disposal. Laudon is a professor of information systems at New York University and the author of *Dossier Society*.

The federal government is creating a computer-driven . . . monster in which the individual is going to be ground up.

I'm talking about what's in the 3 billion files that the government maintains on citizens. The 1974 Privacy Act contains a prohibition against combining data from different sources without congressional approval, but the government is already chipping away at that limit.

For example, to identify persons eligible for the draft, data from the Social Security Administration, Defense Department, Internal Revenue Service and Selective Service were matched to create a momentary national data center. Actions such as that concentrate too much power in the federal executive branch—something the framers of the Constitution wanted to avoid.

New systems the government is installing could have the potential for widespread social surveillance. . . .

These computerized files of the federal government contain information about millions of American citizens.

A major problem is that files in the data base may be incomplete, inaccurate or ambiguous. I examined FBI records of state criminal cases and found mistakes in up to 75 percent of them. The error rates in three states I checked ranged from 50 percent in Minnesota to 60 percent in California to 70 percent in North Carolina.

The most common error is showing an arrest but no disposition of the case. In other cases, people are arrested on several charges and the computer shows they were found guilty—but it doesn't say of what. And some data are plain wrong.

Another problem is that state policies differ. California jaywalkers may be fingerprinted and have their records go into the national system. But in Minnesota and other states, only felonies are recorded, so you can get into a drunken brawl and not be entered.

The potential for abuse is frightening. Within several years, the FBI will have arrest records on 40 million people—about a third of the labor force. And research shows that an employee whose criminal record becomes known is usually fired.

What's sad is that we tolerate such records.

1. According to Laudon, what are some of the problems in the government's use of computers to gather, store, and analyze information on United States citizens?
2. What can you predict might be the consequences of the continued use of government data files on individuals?

Kenneth C. Laudon, "Into a Kafkaesque Society." *U.S. News & World Report,* July 21, 1986. p. 67.

ECONOMIC INTERVENTION

Skill: Making and Testing Hypotheses

There is much disagreement among economists about the role that the government should play in the economy. In this reading, economists Robert L. Heilbroner and Lester C. Thurow present their views on the subject.

Is providing jobs a responsibility of government? Economists disagree about the answer to this question.

Government dominates our economic life. Or does it? Many of those who most deplore the presence of government in economic affairs are also the first to tell you that government in fact is powerless to exert its puny efforts against the pressures of the market system. To many conservatives, government can't accomplish anything. At best—or rather, at worst—it prevents the free enterprise system from accomplishing things. Government regulates industries that would serve the nation better if they were unregulated. It interferes with the system of rewards and incentives and thereby inhibits economic growth. It encourages the poor to remain poor. It spreads urban blight. It saddles us with debt. It is the worm in the apple, the root cause of every economic problem.

That is obviously not our view of the government. For better or worse, we see the public sector as the only mechanism by which a citizenry can intervene into the economic process when that process does not seem to work properly. *When problems arise from the market process itself,* there is no—we repeat, no—way of coping with those problems other than by government. When the business system fails to distribute incomes to the old, the ill, the unemployed, what redress is there other than government? When industries dump waste into rivers or into the air, what means does the public possess to stop pollution other than the restraining hand of government? When corporations sell products that contain risks of which the buyer cannot possibly be aware, . . . what guardian of the public interest can there be save government?

That most emphatically does not mean that we look with favor on government meddling everywhere, on the proliferation [rapid increase] of bureaucratic rules and regulations, on the inviolability [sanctity] of government secrets, on the police state, waste and extravagance, or centralized planning. There are as many ways to misuse government as there are ways to use it. *Our point, rather, is that government has become a central challenge because we have lost all perspective on it.* The issue, then, is not so much that government dominates our economic life—it is that government dominates our *thinking* about economic life. What government can and can't do are difficult questions to answer with certitude, but we cannot even begin to think about them as long as we perceive the role of government through lenses that distort its size and shape beyond all recognition.

1. According to the authors, there is no way of coping with some problems other than by the government, that is, by the public sector. What evidence do they use to support their view?
2. According to Heilbroner and Thurow, our view of the economic role of government has become distorted. Why do you think this is so?

From *Five Economic Challenges* by Robert L. Heilbroner and Lester C. Thurow. © 1981. Used by permission of the publisher, Prentice-Hall, Inc., Englewood Cliffs, N.J.

COPING WITH BUDGETARY COMPLEXITY
Skill: Making Comparisons

Planning the federal budget is an incredibly complicated process. In this reading, author Aaron Wildavsky describes some methods that Congress uses to deal with the complexities.

Budgeting is complex, largely because of the complexity of modern life. Suppose that you were a Congressman or a Budget Bureau official interested in the leukemia research program and you wondered how the money was being spent. By looking at the National Cancer Institute's budgetary presentation you would discover that $42,012 is being spent on a project studying "factors and

Readings in Economics

mechanisms concerned in hemopoiesis," and that $5,095 is being spent for "a study of the relationship of neutralizing antibodies for the Rous sarcoma virus to resistance and susceptibility for visceral lymphomatosis." Could you tell whether too much money is being spent on hemopoiesis in comparison to lymphomatosis or whether either project is relevant for any useful purpose? . . .

Aside from the complexity of individual budgetary programs, there remains the imposing problem of making comparisons among different programs that have different values for different people. This involves deciding such questions as how much highways are worth as compared to recreation facilities, national defense, schools, and so on down the range of governmental functions. No common denominator among these functions has been developed. No matter how hard they try, therefore, officials in places like the Bureau of the Budget discover that they cannot find any objective method of judging priorities among programs. How, then, do budget officials go about meeting their staggering burden of calculation? . . .

Budgeting is experiential. One way of dealing with a problem of huge magnitude is to make only the roughest guesses while letting experience accumulate. Then, when the consequences of the various actions become apparent, it is possible to make modifications to avoid the difficulties. . . .

Budgeting is simplified. Another way of handling complexity is to use actions on simpler items as indices of more complicated ones. . . .

Budgeting officials "satisfice." Calculations may be simplified by lowering one's sights. Although they do not use Herbert Simon's vocabulary, budget officials do not try to maximize, but instead, they "satisfice" (satisfy and suffice). . . .

Budgeting is incremental. The largest determining factor of the size and content of this year's budget is last year's budget. Most of the budget is a product of previous decisions. As former Budget Director Stans put it, "There is very little flexibility in the budget because of the tremendous number of commitments that are made years ahead."

1. Give at least two reasons to explain why the process of setting the federal budget is so difficult.

2. How is the federal budgetary process similar to the process you might use in preparing your personal budget?

Excerpted from Aaron Wildavsky, *The Politics of the Budgetary Process*, pp. 8—13. Copyright © 1964 by Boston: Little, Brown, and Co., (Inc.). Reprinted by permission.

IS THERE A NEED FOR TAX REFORM?

Skill: Comparing and Contrasting Information

SECTION 4

Before the historic tax-reform bill was passed in October 1986, the federal tax system had become complicated and often unfair. In a 1985 speech, President Ronald Reagan presented the American people with his views on the need for tax reform.

For the sake of fairness, simplicity and growth we must radically change the structure of a tax system that still treats our earnings as the personal property of the I.R.S. [Internal Revenue Service]; radically change a system that still treats people earning similar incomes much differently regarding the tax they pay and, yes, radically change a system that still causes some to invest their money, not to make a better mousetrap but simply to avoid a tax trap.

Over the course of this century our tax system has been modified dozens of times and in hundreds of ways. Yet most of those changes didn't improve the system; they made it more like Washington itself: complicated, unfair, cluttered with gobbledygook [meaningless words] and loopholes designed for those with the power and influence to hire high-priced legal and tax advisors.

But there is more to it than that.

Some years ago someone—a historian I believe—said that every time in the past when a Government began taxing above a certain level of the people's earnings, trust in Government began to erode. He said it would begin with efforts to avoid paying the full tax. This would become outright cheating, and eventually a distrust and contempt of Government itself, until there would be a breakdown in law and order.

Well, how many times have we heard people brag about clever schemes to avoid paying taxes, or watched luxuries casually written off to be paid for by somebody else—that somebody being you.

I believe that in both spirit and substance our [present] tax system has come to be un-American.

Death and taxes may be inevitable, but unjust taxes are not. The first American Revolution was sparked by an unshakable conviction: Taxation without representation is tyranny. Two centuries later a second American Revolution for hope and opportunity is gathering force again, a peaceful revolution but born of popular resentment against a tax system that is unwise, unwanted and unfair.

1. What justification does President Reagan offer for tax reform?
2. Describe the similarities and differences between the first American Revolution and the "second American Revolution" that Reagan refers to.

Ronald Reagan, "Overhauling the Tax System." From a speech delivered May 28, 1985, Washington, D.C. *Vital Speeches of the Day*, Vol. LI, No. 17, June 15, 1985.

WORRY OVER THE NATIONAL DEBT

Skill: Understanding Cause and Effect

 **Although there is considerable controversy over how burdensome the national debt in the United States really is, there is no disagreement over the fact that the debt situation in much of Latin America may lead to a crisis. In this reading, American business leader Francis X. Stankard, chairman of Chase Manhattan Capital Markets Corporation, compares the debt situation in the United States with that of Latin America.**

The factors in the world now appear to point toward a bright economic future. . . .

But, I have one great gnawing doubt that I'm afraid just might throw the whole world into a tailspin. That doubt, I am sorry to say, is about our own country and the other developed nations of the free world.

Let's go back over the four reasons for the Latin American problems. I submit that we in the United States appear to have three of the same symptoms:

First, *import substitution*—other words for the protectionism that is rearing its ugly head in the United States.

Second, an *overvalued exchange rate* policy; a consequence of our large persistent federal deficits.

Third, *heavy borrowing*. At the end of 1982, the United States had net assets abroad of $147 BB [billions]. In April 1985 the U.S. became a net debtor nation for the first time since World War I. Indeed, in the first nine months of 1985 we borrowed $93 billion—more than twelve times what we invested abroad. Therefore, sometime in 1986, the United States will surpass Brazil as the biggest foreign debtor country in the world.

The only thing we don't have is the 100 plus years' history of financial mismanagement, continuous deficits and ever increasing debt. But time is passing rapidly.

These cancers are gradually, but persistently, infecting our society also. . . . Perhaps we should take heed before it is too late.

Whether or not we can empirically prove it, I submit that we all know the basic problem. It is the enormous federal deficit. The tax cuts, combined with the increase in military spending, raised interest rates, which in turn created a huge inflow of capital, pushed up the dollar and resulted in painless growth and a free ride for the American consumer for the past four years.

It has also caused unprecedented foreign trade deficits and the further impoverishment of basic American manufacturing industry. And here, parenthetically, I think we will find that a simple righting of the exchange rate will not rapidly make the problem disappear. If this bleeding artery is not sutured, all the bandaging with various protectionist devices, central bank interventions in the exchange markets and the like, will not cure the patient.

1. What similarities between the causes of the debt problems in the United States and the debt problems of Latin America are listed by the author?
2. What does the author state are the causes of our growing national debt?

Francis X. Stankard, "Et Tu America?" From a speech delivered March 14, 1986, Cincinnati. *Vital Speeches of the Day*, June 1, 1986. Vol. LII, No. 16, pp. 491, 492.

PRACTICING YOUR COMMUNICATION SKILLS: GIVING AN ORAL REPORT

Being able to give an interesting, well-reasoned oral report in a relaxed manner is a useful skill not only for school but for your future job and community roles. Besides being able to stand in front of an audience and present your report, preparation is an important part of a good speech. The skills of paraphrasing, summarizing, note taking, and outlining that you learned previously in this book will help in your preparation. Below are some other tips.

- Read about and take notes on the topic you are speaking about.
- Organize your notes into an outline, and write only your outline on note cards. When you give your speech, do not read from the cards. Glance at them from time to time.
- Practice in front of your family or friends. In addition to practicing how to stand and look relaxed, you might also want to consider the body language that you use. Do not use your hands too much and keep them around waist level or a little above. Also, don't look up at the ceiling or down at the floor too often. Be watchful of gestures such as pulling an ear, rubbing your forehead, or scratching your head. Remain poised.
- Look at your audience and speak loudly and clearly in a normal, relaxed tone. Smile. Avoid *you know*, *um*, *er*, *like*, and so on.
- If you are using visual aids, such as posters, be sure they can be read from the back of the room. When you practice your talk, practice using the visual aids, too.

Activity: Prepare an oral report on one of the following topics. Use charts, graphs, or tables if possible.

1. Pros and cons of using property taxes to fund education

2. Guns vs. butter and the federal budget

VOCABULARY REVIEW

Write the letter of the definition in Column B that correctly defines each term in Column A.

Column A	Column B
1. benefits received	a. government's policy of spending and taxation
2. public goods	b. the taking of money from some to give to others
3. ability to pay	c. system by which those with higher incomes pay higher taxes
4. income redistribution	d. payment for a particular government service by those who use the service
5. national debt	e. goods and services supplied to all citizens by the government
6. fiscal policy	f. amount of money the government owes

PRACTICING YOUR ECONOMIC SKILLS

One deduction you may take if you itemize on your tax return is state sales tax. The federal income tax booklet has tax tables for those states that levy a sales tax. The following excerpt is from the sales tax table for Alabama.

Your Family Is

Income	1	2	3	4	5	More
$14,001-$16,000	152	174	194	209	225	248
$16,001-$18,000	164	186	210	226	242	266
$18,001-$20,000	176	197	225	242	259	284
$20,001-$22,000	188	208	239	257	275	301

1. **Figuring Tax Deductions. a.** If your income is $16,542 and you have three exemptions, what is your sales tax deduction? **b.** If you are single and your income is $18,790, what is your sales tax deduction?
2. **Calculating Taxes.** Social Security tax is determined by wage bases set for various levels of income. For each level, no tax is paid on the income above the wage base, up to the next level. Use the table below to calculate the amount of Social Security tax paid by the workers in each of the following exercises: **a. a worker who earned $17,750 in 1978. b.** a worker who earned $25,000 in 1979. **c.** a worker who earned $30,000 in 1981.

Year	Tax rate	Taxable Wage Base
1977	5.8%	$16,500
1978	6.05%	17,700
1979	6.12%	22,900
1980	6.13%	25,900
1981	6.65%	29,700

DISCUSSING ECONOMIC QUESTIONS

1. The amount of money spent on each function of government is one indicator of the nation's commitment to the goal or goals represented by that function. Based on Figures 17–3 and 17–4 and the material on national goals in Chapter 2, rank the nation's goals in order of importance. Do you agree or disagree?
2. Do you think government should be involved in the functions described in this chapter? Why or why not?
3. Discuss what you think would be the effect of a tax rate of 10% for everyone in the United States. Include financial and psychological considerations in your discussion.

APPLYING CRITICAL THINKING SKILLS

1. **Writing a Research Report.** A number of states have laws that require a balanced state budget. Check your state constitution and see if your state has such a requirement. Research and write a brief report explaining why the amendment was passed, when, and whether it makes the budget process more difficult.
2. **Making a Flow Chart.** Check with your local community's chief financial official to see how the budget is made and approved in your community. Make a flow chart to show the process.
3. **Comparing and Contrasting Information.** From newspapers and business magazines, gather information about the tax reforms that are part of the Tax Reform Act of 1986. Compare the reformed tax codes with those discussed in the chapter.
4. **Analyzing Issues.** In 1985 Congress passed the Gramm-Rudman Law requiring the federal government to balance the federal budget by 1991. It required cuts in the national deficit on a year-by-year basis. Find a copy of the law in the library and study it. Then gather newspaper and magazine articles discussing the law. Write a report explaining the major sides in the controversy over the need to balance the national budget.

READINGS

Boskin, Michael J., and Wildarsky, Aaron., eds. *The Federal Budget: Economics and Politics.* New York: Manhattan Institute for Policy Research, 1982.

Laffer, Arthur B., and Seymour, Jan., eds. *The Economics of the Tax Revolt.* New York: Harcourt Brace Jovanovich, 1979.

Leftwich, Richard H., and Sharp, Ansel M. *Economics of Social Issues.* 6th ed. Plano, Tex.: Business Publications, Inc., 1984.

CHAPTER 18

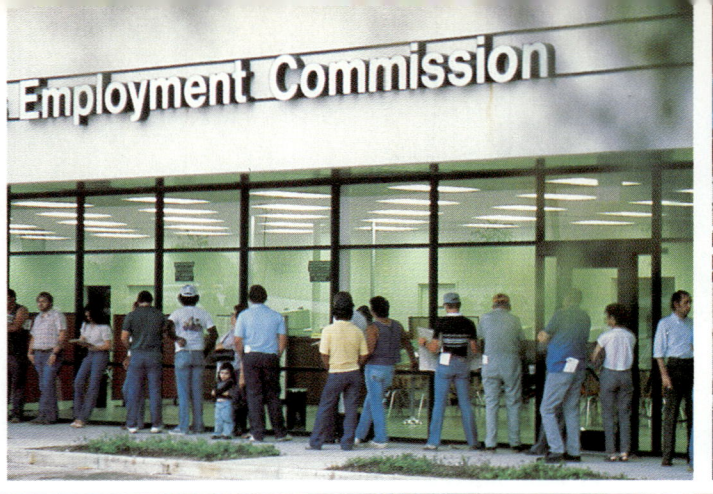

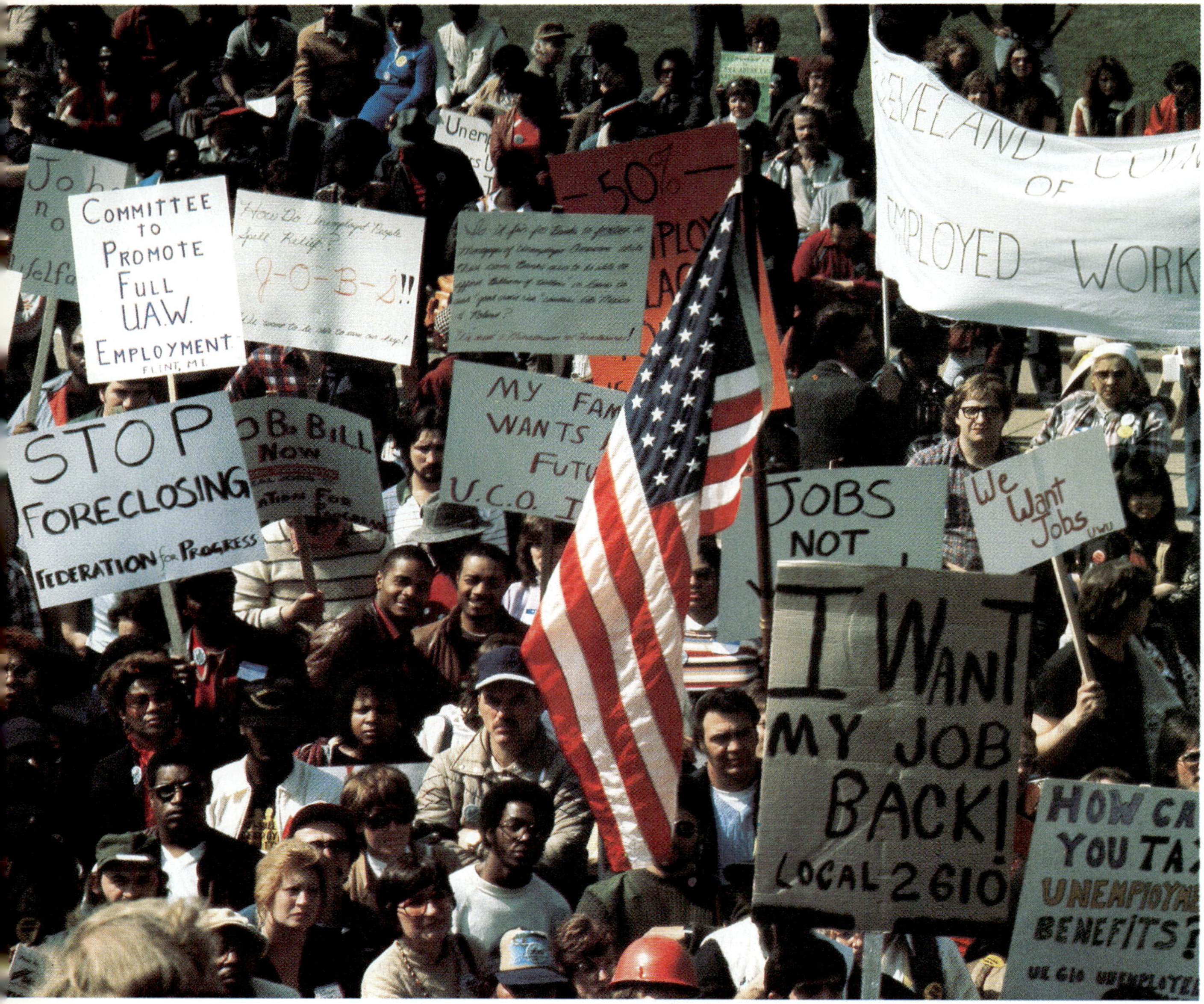

Unemployment and inflation have been major problems in the national economy. Economists do not agree on their causes on the most effective policies to achieve economic stability.

ECONOMIC STABILITY: FIGHTING UNEMPLOYMENT AND INFLATION

Economic Stability: Fighting Unemployment and Inflation

Unemployment and inflation are two major problems that affect the stability of the American economy. Different schools of economic thought have different explanations for the causes and solutions of these problems. This chapter begins with a description of the types of unemployment and of inflation. You will then read about the Keynesian and monetarist theories of dealing with these problems. Examples of recent government responses to unemployment and inflation are also given. Learning Economic Skills will help you in finding research materials that deal with topics in economics.

CHAPTER OBJECTIVES After you study this chapter, you will be able to:

1 • describe the four types of unemployment.

2 • contrast the theories of demand-pull and cost-push inflation.

3 • explain the model of the circular flow of income.
  • explain how Keynesians would use fiscal policy to solve the problem of unemployment.
  • explain how Keynesians would use fiscal policy to solve the problem of inflation.

4 • explain how monetarists would control growth of the money supply to solve the problems of unemployment and inflation.
  ★ locate different types of economic research materials.

5 • describe how supply-side economics was tried as an alternate approach to Keynesian economics and monetarism.

ECONOMICS VOCABULARY

stabilization policy
unemployment rate
full employment
demand-pull inflation
stagflation
cost-push inflation
aggregate demand
circular flow of income
monetarism
supply-side economics
Say's Law

In Chapter 14, you read that the American economy experiences ups and downs in its overall business activity—booms, recessions, and even depressions. In an attempt to keep the economy healthy and to make the future more predictable for planning, saving, and investing, the federal government uses what are called **stabilization** (stay-buh-luh-ZAY-shuhn) **policies.** The two most important are monetary policy and fiscal policy. Unfortunately, neither type of policy is always successful in solving the complex problems of the economy. Economists have developed various theories to explain how the economy works, but none adequately explains it. Economists disagree about both the causes and the cures of the economic problems that periodically face the nation. This chapter takes a closer look at two of the biggest threats to the nation's economic stability: unemployment and inflation.

1 | TYPES OF UNEMPLOYMENT

Ask yourself as you read:
- Why is unemployment a serious economic problem?
- Why can't unemployment be eliminated?

High unemployment is usually a sign that all is not well with the economy. Moreover, the waste of human resources caused by unemployment is an extremely serious problem. Unemployment can reduce living standards, disrupt families, and take from an individual his or her feeling of self-respect. It is the human cost of economic contractions, or slowdowns, during the business cycle. As a result, maintaining a low unemployment rate is one of the major goals in stabilizing the economy. The **unemployment rate** is the percentage of the civilian labor force that is without jobs but that is actively looking for work.

There are many types of unemployment. As you can see from the causes given in Table 18-1, some people work in seasonal jobs or those sensitive to technological advances or changes in the marketplace. As a result, not all unemployment can be eliminated. Moreover, economists disagree over what the level of full employment should be. In the 1960s, some economists thought the unemployment rate should be 4 percent. This figure was raised to 5 to 6 percent in the 1970s. After much careful study, economists now generally have come to consider the economy at **full employment** when the unemployment rate is less than 6½ percent. It is important to remember that the unemployment rate is only an estimate. The unemployment rate does not include people who are out of work and have stopped looking for work. It also does not include people who work in family businesses without pay.

Economists classify unemployment into four broad categories: cyclical (SIK-luh-kuhl), structural, seasonal, and frictional. As you will see as you study Table 18-1, most of the people who are in these unemployment categories are out of work because of forces beyond their control.

Table 18-1: TYPES OF UNEMPLOYMENT

Type	Definition	Characteristics
Cyclical	Unemployment associated with fluctuations up or down in the business cycle.	Rises during recessions and depressions; falls during recoveries and booms.
Structural	Unemployment caused by changes in the economy because of such factors as technological advances or discoveries of natural resources.	Can result when workers are replaced by computers or other machines or when cheaper natural resources are found elsewhere; often affects less skilled workers.
Seasonal	Unemployment caused by changes in the seasons or weather.	Affects construction workers, particularly in the Northeast and Midwest; also affects farm workers who are needed in certain areas only during certain months of the growing season.
Frictional	Temporary unemployment between jobs because of firings, layoffs, voluntary searches for new jobs, or retraining.	Always exists to some degree because of the time needed between jobs to find new work and the imperfect match between openings and applicants.

REVIEWING ECONOMIC PRINCIPLES

1. Write a sentence defining each of the following economic terms: **a.** stabilization policies, **b.** unemployment rate, **c.** full employment.
2. Define and give examples of the four types of unemployment.
3. **Critical Thinking: Explaining the Main Idea.** Why is an unemployment rate of no more than 6½ percent considered full employment?

2 | INFLATION AND ITS CAUSES

Ask yourself as you read:

- What are the two main theories about the causes of inflation?
- What is the difference between the demand-pull and cost-push theories of inflation?

A second major problem that faces the nation is inflation. The economy can usually adapt to gradually rising prices. However, unpredictable inflation has a destabilizing effect on the economy. That is, consumers and businesses act differently than they would if the economy were growing at a stable rate. For example, during periods of high inflation, consumers may borrow and spend more. They realize that the dollars they use to make loan payments will be worth less and less as inflation rises. As a result, creditors will eventually raise interest rates to maintain the level of profit they had before inflation began to rise rapidly. This, in turn, may eventually tend to have a slowing effect on the economy's growth. In the long-run in a time of high inflation, consumers and businesses often borrow less because of the high interest rates.

Consumers' living standards can also be affected by inflation. Suppose you receive a 5 percent raise in a year in which inflation has risen 8 percent. You have actually lost purchasing power. This is a particularly serious problem for people, such as those who are retired, who live on *fixed* incomes. Each year a little of the purchasing power of that income is eaten away by inflation.

Unfortunately, there is no single answer to why inflation occurs. Two competing ideas have developed, however: the demand-pull theory and the cost-push theory.

Inflation in the economy affects consumers' living standards. Why is inflation often an especially serious problem for retired persons?

DEMAND-PULL THEORY OF INFLATION

According to the theory of **demand-pull inflation,** prices rise as the result of excessive demand by businesses and consumers. If demand increases faster than total supply, the resulting shortage will lead to the bidding up of prices.

Demand-pull inflation can occur for several reasons. As you read in Chapter 16, inflation can occur if the Federal Reserve causes the money supply to grow too rapidly. Individuals, in their attempt to spend the additional dollars, will compete for the limited supply of goods and services. As you read in Chapter 8, this increased demand will cause prices to rise. Increases in government spending and in business investments for expansion can also increase overall demand. It can also increase if taxes are reduced or consumers begin saving less. Either results in more money being spent.

COST-PUSH THEORY OF INFLATION

The demand-pull theory, on the other hand, says that inflation usually happens only when there is full employment in the economy. Before full employment is reached, increased demand will increase output and reduce unemployment. Experience, however, has shown that rising prices and unemployment can occur at the same time. This combination of inflation and low economic activity is sometimes called **stagflation.** The United States for the first time experienced this type of inflation during the 1969 to 1970 recession, and it remained a problem through much of the 1970s and in 1982.

According to some economists, stagflation is a result of cost-push inflation at work in the economy. The theory of **cost-push inflation** states that prices are pushed up by the wage demands of labor unions and the excessive profit motive of large corporations.

excessive: too much

According to this theory, large unions have the power to demand and receive wage increases that are not necessarily justified by the productivity of workers. When businesses have to pay higher wages, their costs increase. In order to maintain their profit level, businesses must then raise prices. Each time this happens, it causes the cost of living to go up. Workers then demand higher wages to balance the decline in their purchasing power. This, in turn, gives corporations an excuse to raise prices again. So goes the cycle of wage and price increases. Some people, however, believe that giant corporations raise their prices whenever they want to increase their profits.

During periods of cost-push inflation, unemployment can remain high. This is because prices are rising because of the pressure for higher wages and profits and not because of increased aggregate demand. Without additional aggregate demand, producers will have no reason to increase output by hiring new workers. As a result, unemployment will continue.

REVIEWING ECONOMIC PRINCIPLES

1. How does rapid inflation have a destabilizing effect on the economy?
2. State two situations that result in demand-pull inflation.
3. According to the theory of cost-push inflation, what causes inflation?
4. What is stagflation?
5. **Critical Thinking: Making Generalizations.** How is employment affected by the two theories of inflation?

3 | THE KEYNESIAN APPROACH TO STABILIZATION

Ask yourself as you read:

- What did John Maynard Keynes contribute to the theory of economics?
- What did Keynes believe government should do in a serious recession?

Most economists fall into one of two groups on the question of economic stabilization. Both groups share some of the same ideas and theories. However, they take different approaches toward controlling unemployment and inflation. One group, about which you will read later in this chapter, emphasizes the role of monetary policy and of the Federal Reserve in stabilizing the economy. The other group concentrates more on the use of fiscal policy. As you read in Chapter 17, fiscal policy is the federal government's use of taxation and spending policies to affect overall business activity. The use of fiscal policy is associated with John Maynard Keynes, who, as you may recall from Chapter 14, developed his major theories during the Great Depression.

Up until the Depression, economists generally believed that recessions were a time of temporary surplus of goods and workers. As the forces of supply and demand reached a new equilibrium point, the economy would correct itself. The surpluses would be eliminated. Keynes believed that supply and demand operated too slowly. Therefore, he believed that in a serious recession, government should step in to stimulate aggregate demand. **Aggregate** (AG-ruh-git) **demand** is the total demand for goods and services from all sections of the economy—consumer, government, business, and foreign. In examining the government's effect on aggregate demand, Keynes and his supporters paid particular attention to how income moves through the economy.

THE CIRCULAR FLOW OF INCOME

Many economists use what is known as the **circular flow of income** in explaining their theories. In Chapter 2 you studied a simplified model of this circular flow. This model pictured income as flowing continually between businesses and consumers. Income flows from businesses to consumers as wages, rent, interest, and profits. These are payments for the use of the factors of production controlled by consumers—their labor, land, capital, and entrepreneurship. Income flows from consumers to businesses as payments for consumer goods and services.

Not all income, however, follows this circular flow. Some of it is removed from the economy through consumer saving and government taxation. Economists use the term *leakage* to refer to this removal of money. Figure 18-1 shows these leakages.

Offsetting these leakages are injections of income into the economy. Injections occur through business investment and government spending. The term *investment*, in this sense, means the purchase of new

Figure 18–1: THE CIRCULAR FLOW OF INCOME

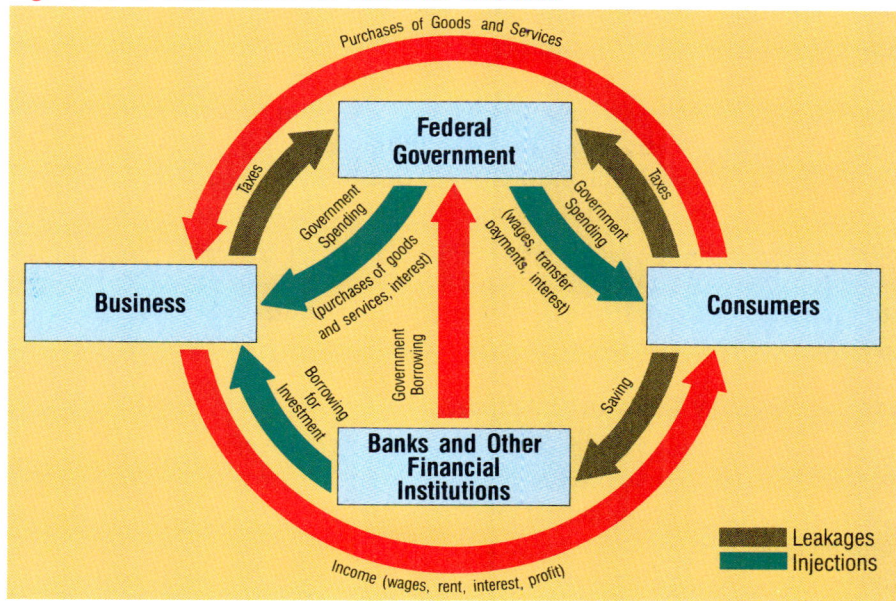

This flow chart is a model of the way income circulates through the economy. Beginning with the role of consumers, explain how income flows through the economy.

plants and equipment and increases in inventories. Much of the money for investment comes from saving—a part of the leakage from circular flow. Government spending benefits both businesses and consumers. Businesses sell goods and services to government agencies, while consumers receive wages and transfer payments. Interest payments on government borrowing flow to both sectors.

In Keynesian theory, both leakages and injections of income have an effect on aggregate demand. Leakages reduce aggregate demand by removing income from the economy. This is income that consumers could have used to purchase goods and services or that businesses could have used to invest, pay wages, purchase land, and pay interest on borrowed capital. Injections increase aggregate demand by placing more dollars in the hands of consumers and businesses. Ideally, leakages and injections balance each other. In this state of equilibrium, the income that consumers save is reinjected through business investment. Income taken out through taxes is returned through government spending. A helpful analogy to remember is that of a basin filled to the brim with water. As long as the water that is drained from the basin equals the water poured into it, the water level remains the same.

analogy (uh-NAL-uh-jee): similar example

But what happens if leakages of income are greater than injections? If more water is drained from a basin than is poured into it, the water level will fall. If saving and taxes are greater than business investment and government spending, economic activity will decrease. Aggregate demand will drop, and because businesses will not be able to sell all of their goods, they will lay off workers. Unemployment will increase.

On the other hand, if more water is poured into a basin than drained, the water level will rise and eventually overflow. If more income is injected than leaked, the economy will eventually expand too rapidly and cause inflation. This view supports the demand-pull theory of inflation. If business invests heavily and/or government spends large amounts of money, more income will be injected into the economy. The same will happen if consumers reduce their level of saving or government cuts taxes. In all cases, aggregate demand increases.

As you can see from Figure 18-1, government occupies a central position in the circular flow of income. Keynesian economists believe government should actively use this position to smooth out the ups and downs in the economy. By using fiscal policy, the federal government could control leakages and injections. This, in turn, would control the overall level of economic activity.

FISCAL POLICY AND UNEMPLOYMENT

Keynesian economists feel that the Great Depression resulted from a serious imbalance in leakages and injections. They point out that during the 1920s, the public engaged in a higher level of saving than usual. As long as businesses continued to invest, injections balanced leakages. In the months following the stock market crash of 1929, however, the desire and ability of businesses to invest also collapsed. Capital investment fell steeply, reducing output and causing a high rate of unemployment. Unemployment eventually reached almost 25 percent, as you can see from Figure 18-2.

According to Keynesian theory, at the beginning of the Depression, government should have filled the gap created when businesses began limiting their investments. The government could have increased injections of government spending or cut taxes to reduce its own leakages. Either would have given businesses and consumers more spendable income. Either would have brought leakages and injections back into equilibrium.

During the 1930s, the federal government did create a number of jobs programs to hire unemployed workers. These new jobs reduced some unemployment and injected more wages into the economy. However, these were not enough to make up for the large drop in consumer demand. It was not until World War II that the nation moved out of the Great Depression. After the war, the government cut back its spending. However, the economy was strong enough by then to continue operating without the extra government aid.

Since the Great Depression, many public officials and labor leaders have suggested starting jobs programs to reduce unemployment and stimulate the economy. Several suggestions for forming new government-sponsored jobs programs to bring down unemployment rates were made in the early 1980s. As you can see from Figure 18-2, increased unemployment in 1982 and 1983 was the highest since the 1930s. These programs were not enacted. Employment nevertheless increased as the recession ended in 1983.

Cuts in federal taxes are another way in which fiscal policy has been used in an attempt to speed up economic activity and fight unemploy-

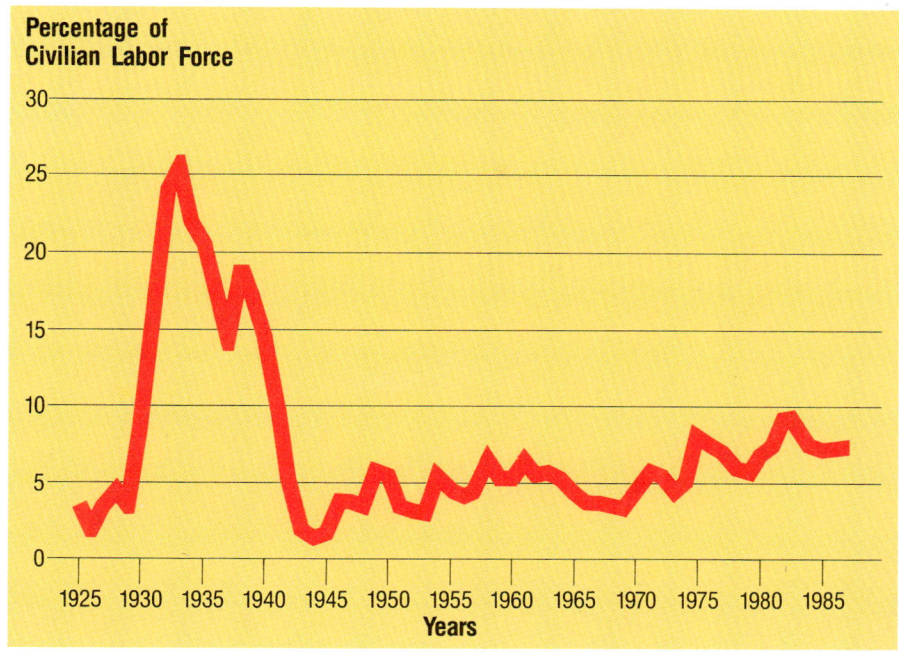

Figure 18-2: UNEMPLOYED AS A PERCENTAGE OF THE CIVILIAN LABOR FORCE, 1925-1987

Source: *Historical Statistics of the U.S., Statistical Abstract of the U.S.,* Bureau of the Census
*1987 percentage is an estimate

Using this graph and Figure 14-3, explain the relationship between unemployment and GNP.

ment. For example, when President John F. Kennedy took office in 1961, the nation was slowly pulling itself out of a recession that had started in 1958. To help the recovery, Kennedy convinced Congress to pass a law giving businesses tax credits on investments. Businesses could deduct from their taxes some of the costs of new capital equipment. The goal was to encourage businesses to expand production and hire more workers. In 1964, President Lyndon Johnson asked for and received from Congress a tax cut of about $11 billion. Keynesian economists believe that as a result, unemployment fell from 5.2 percent in 1964 to 4.5 percent in 1965. This stimulated investment and consumer spending.

FISCAL POLICY AND INFLATION

Fiscal-policy supporters also believe that inflation as well as unemployment can be reduced by increasing taxes and/or reducing government spending. They argue that either action will reduce the aggregate demand for goods and services. For example, because people are paying higher taxes, they are taking home less spendable income. They will, therefore, have to cut back on their purchases. As purchases decline, businesses will cut back on production. This reduction in demand will cause businesses to reconsider raising prices. Often, as inflation falls, unemployment rises slightly because of less business activity. The same pattern would occur if government spending were cut.

459

Fiscal policy as a means of reducing inflation has not been used frequently in the last several decades. One example of its use, however, occurred in 1968. Government spending was increasing rapidly to finance both the Vietnam War and new social programs, such as Medicare. President Lyndon Johnson persuaded Congress to pass a tax increase that he said was necessary to slow inflation. The tax increase did not, however, have the desired effect.

REVIEWING ECONOMIC PRINCIPLES

1. What is aggregate demand?
2. **a.** According to the circular flow model, how does income leak from the economy? **b.** How is income injected into the economy?
3. According to Keynes, what effect do leakages and injections have on the economy: **a.** if the two are balanced? **b.** if leakages are greater than injections? **c.** if injections are greater than leakages?
4. What did Keynes believe the government should have done at the beginning of the Great Depression to bring leakages and injections into equilibrium?
5. **Critical Thinking: Determining Cause and Effect.** Why would unemployment rise if fiscal policy were used to control inflation?

4 | MONETARISM AND THE ECONOMY

Ask yourself as you read:
- What is monetarism?
- What is the monetarist view of the Great Depression?

Monetarism is the theory that deals with the relation between the amount of money placed in circulation by the Federal Reserve and the level of activity in the economy. Just as fiscal policy is associated with one person—Keynes—monetarism is often linked with another economist—Milton Friedman, whose biography is on p. 463. Much of the discussion of monetary policy in Chapter 16 is based on monetarist theory. As you may recall from that chapter, the Fed can use reserve requirements, the discount rate, and open-market operations to change the growth of the money supply.

Friedman and his supporters are most concerned with the way the Fed's decisions act directly on the aggregate demand for goods and services. Stated simply, they believe that when the amount of money in circulation expands, people spend more. This increases the aggregate demand for goods and services. If the economy for some reason is operating below capacity, this extra demand will lead to a rise in output. To produce more, businesses will have to hire more workers, and unemployment will decrease. If there is already full employment, this increased demand will lead to a rise in prices—inflation.

Free Enterprise and Monetarist Champion: Milton Friedman (1912–   )

Milton Friedman is one of the nation's leading supporters of monetarism. Monetarism is the theory that the rate of growth of the money supply plays a significant part in keeping the economy stable. Friedman has argued persistently over the last three decades that the key to a healthy and noninflationary economy is a constant rate of growth in the money supply.

According to Friedman, the Federal Reserve Board's policy of tightening money during booms and loosening money during recessions is ineffective because of the time lag involved. For example, policies to tighten or loosen the money supply may take months to work. By then, such policies might not be necessary. Instead, the Fed should increase the supply of money at a steady rate of between 3 and 5 percent per year.

Friedman has often been termed a modern Adam Smith. Like Smith, he praises competition and the free market and criticizes government intervention in the economy at, what he terms, every opportunity. He argues that competitive capitalism can do almost anything governments can do more efficiently. Like Smith, Friedman argues that by pursuing their self-interest in earning profits, business leaders are performing their social responsibility most efficiently. Moreover, capitalism does not present the threat of tyrannical, if well-meant, trespassing into private lives.

An opponent of Keynesian economics, Friedman blames government policy for the Great Depression. Keynes's theories state that government intervention is necessary to keep the economy running smoothly. Friedman claims in his most important work, *A Monetary History of the United States, 1867–1960,* written in 1963 with Anna J. Schwartz, that it was the bungling of the Fed that in-

creased the length and depth of the Great Depression.

In line with these views on capitalism and government, Friedman advocates the end of price supports to farmers, subsidies to business, protective tariffs, regulatory agencies, welfare programs, and Social Security. In *Capitalism and Freedom,* coauthored with his wife Rose in 1962, Friedman proposed a negative income tax. The government would make cash payments to families whose income was lower than a certain level. This would do away with the need for any social welfare programs.

Friedman won the Nobel Prize for economics in 1976 for his monetary theories. Now retired from the University of Chicago, he and his wife coauthored *Free to Choose* in 1980. It is about the problems of government intervention and the benefits of a less controlled society. He appeared in a series of the same name for public television.

1. According to Friedman, what monetarist policy should the Federal Reserve Board follow? Why?
2. Describe some of Friedman's views on capitalism and government's role in the economy.

On the other hand, a decrease in the rate of growth of the money supply results in less aggregate demand. This reduction in aggregate demand, in turn, causes a surplus of goods. Faced with a surplus, businesses will lower prices and reduce inflation. Businesses may also cut production and lay off workers. Unemployment may increase.

MONETARIST VIEWS OF THE GREAT DEPRESSION

Friedman views much of what happened during the Great Depression differently from the supporters of Keynes. Monetarists do not deny the importance of decisions made by businesses about investments in the early 1930s. However, Friedman places more emphasis on the drop in the amount of money in circulation as a cause for the drop in aggregate demand. This, in turn, caused businesses to reduce their investment. Despite the Fed's stated goal of stimulating the economy, the money supply decreased one-third from the start of the recession in 1929 to the depths of the Great Depression in 1933 and 1934. To monetarists, the reduction in the amount of money in circulation could mean only one thing. It could mean only a reduction in the aggregate demand for goods and services. With less demand, fewer workers were needed and unemployment increased.

The monetarists claim that what would have been just another recession became the Great Depression because of the Fed's actions. During the period, the Fed claimed it wanted banks to loosen their money. However, at the same time, the Fed continued to sell government securities. As you may recall from Chapter 16, this reduces the money supply. The money supply was also reduced as the Fed increased reserve requirements. These actions, in turn, reduced credit and aggregate demand. The monetarists believe that the Fed should have increased greatly the amount of money in circulation. As a result, people would have started spending more, and businesses would have been able to invest more.

GOVERNMENT POLICY ACCORDING TO MONETARISTS

Friedman and his monetarist followers believe the economy is so complex and so little understood that government only does more harm than good in trying to second-guess businesspeople and consumers. As a result, monetarists are generally against the government's use of fiscal policy to stimulate or slow the economy. For example, they do not believe the government should operate with budget deficits each year in an attempt to stimulate the economy. Instead, monetarists believe that the government should balance the federal budget. This would keep government from competing with private business to borrow money in the credit market. It would also reduce the amount of interest that the government must pay each year.

The Fed, according to monetarists, should also stop trying to smooth out the ups and downs in the economy. Rather the Fed should allow the money supply to grow at a rate of perhaps 3 to 5 percent per year.

Monetarists believe that a steady growth in the money supply within strict guidelines, or targets, as they are called, is the best way to provide businesses and consumers with more certainty about the future. According to monetarism, this policy would result in a controlled expansion of the economy without rapid inflation or high unemployment.

Monetarist theory has had a major influence on Federal Reserve policies in the 1980s. Throughout much of the 1970s, the Fed concentrated on keeping interest rates at a certain level. It paid less attention to the growth of the money supply. In October 1979, following a period of high inflation, the Fed announced a shift in emphasis. It said it would follow the monetarist policy of keeping the rate of growth of the money supply within specific targets. In doing this, the Fed would ignore any resulting changes in interest rates.

The result was a dramatic drop in inflation. The annual rate of increase in the Consumer Price Index dropped from 13.3 percent in 1979 to 3.8 percent in early 1983. The cost of success, however, was high unemployment. The temporary high interest rates that resulted from the Fed's tight money policy caused consumers and businesses to cut back on borrowing. As output dropped, unemployment increased. Between 1980 and late 1982, the unemployment rate rose from 7.1 percent to a temporary high of about 10.8 percent.

With inflation finally under control, the Fed began loosening up its control of the money supply. By late 1982 it was allowing the money supply to grow at a rate faster than it had originally planned. In February 1983, the Fed announced that it would again look at other factors besides the growth of the money supply in determining policy. It would also look at the growth in total debt by businesses, households, and government. These changes indicated the Fed was again moving away from strict monetarism. It was adopting a looser policy of allowing the money supply to grow at faster or slower rates, depending on activity within the economy. It has continued this policy throughout the later 1980s.

REVIEWING ECONOMIC PRINCIPLES

1. According to monetarists, how do the Fed's decisions affect:
   a. aggregate demand and inflation? **b.** aggregate demand and unemployment?
2. During the Great Depression, how did the Fed's actions contradict what it said was its goal?
3. Why are monetarists against the government's use of fiscal policy to stimulate or slow the economy?
4. **a.** What do monetarists believe the Fed should do to control the money supply? **b.** According to their theories, what effect would this policy have on rapid inflation and high unemployment?
5. **Critical Thinking: Summarizing Main Ideas.** Summarize the policies of the Fed during the late 1970s and early 1980s.

Learning Economic Skills | USING ECONOMIC RESEARCH MATERIALS

Hearing about what is happening to the economy is relatively easy because the state of the national economy is a daily topic in the news. Radio and television reports, however, are seldom complete or in depth. Also, they rarely give information on the history of the economy. If you need to know more about the economy or some aspect of it, you will usually need to go to your school or community library. There you will find monthly, quarterly, and annual reports compiled by government agencies as well as economics and business publications.

LOCATING LIBRARY SOURCES

For books, the first place to look is the card catalogue. This will tell you what is available in the reference section and in the stacks. There are three types of cards for every book: author, title, and subject. You can tell the type of card by what is written at the top of the card. For example, if the phrase "Economics—National Income" is at the top, you are looking at a subject card. The call number is on the left side of the card and starts with a number or letter. The shelves in the library are arranged in alphabetical or numerical order. By looking at the top number or letter, you can determine which shelf the book will be on. The numbers or letters that follow indicate the location of the book on the shelf. All books are arranged numerically and alphabetically on the shelves. If the book is kept in the reference section of the library, the card will be marked *Reference*.

Depending on your topic, there are special types of reference books that might be helpful. Look for books that have *dictionary, handbook,* or *encyclopedia* in their names such as the *Dictionary of Economics, Handbook of Modern Marketing,* and *Encyclopedia of Advertising.* The *Encyclopedia Britannica* as well as other encyclopedias publishes a *Yearbook* annually that summarizes economic topics of the previous year.

If you need information about a specific economist, there are biographical collections such as *Ten Great Economists from Marx to Keynes* and *Ideas of the Great Economists.* These may be in the stacks or in the reference section. If you are looking for periodicals, check not only the *Reader's Guide to Periodical Literature* but also the *Business Periodicals Index.*

In small libraries, periodicals are in the reference section. In larger libraries, they are kept in a special periodicals section. Newspapers are also in this section as are government publications. The actual newspapers are kept on file for a month or so. Older copies are on microfilm.

330.9
PET   Peters, Thomas J.
      In search of excellence. New York:
Harper & Row, 1982.

     Includes index.

    1. Economic condition
Robert H., Jr. II. Title.

330.9
PET   ECONOMIC CONDITIONS

Peters, Thomas J.
    In search of excellence. New York:
Harper & Row, 1982.

330.9
PET   In search of excellence

    Peters, Thomas J.
      In search of excellence. New York:
Harper & Row, 1982.

ANNUAL STATISTICAL DATA

For a summary of economic conditions, the *Economic Report of the President*, compiled by the Council of Economic Advisors is the best source. The *Statistical Abstract of the United States* is published annually by the Bureau of the Census. It has tables of statistical data on thousands of subjects from population to federal finances. It is a good source for summaries of statistical data from various government agencies. Information contained in the *Economic Report of the President* can also be found in the *Statistical Abstract*.

For statistical data of a historical nature, the *Historical Statistics of the United States, Colonial Times to 1970* is useful. It covers many of the same topics as the yearly *Statistical Abstract* but concentrates on the nation's early economy.

FINDING MONTHLY STATISTICAL DATA

If you need data that has been compiled on a monthly basis, there are several periodicals that you should check. The *Business Conditions Digest* and the *Survey of Current Business* are both published by the Department of Commerce. The *Monthly Labor Review* is issued by the Department of Labor. In addition to monthly data on GNP, unemployment, prices, and so on, these publications contain articles about current conditions in the economy.

The Board of Governors of the Federal Reserve publishes the monthly *Federal Reserve Bulletin.* This contains data on banking, business, and the economy as well as the latest data on the money supply.

BUSINESS AND ECONOMIC NEWS

If you are interested in reviews of economic affairs, there are numerous periodicals and newspapers that specialize in news about the economy. Their articles are often accompanied by charts, graphs, and tables. The periodicals listed below can be found in most libraries:

WEEKLY

Business Week relates news affecting business. *Newsweek, Time,* and *U.S. News & World Report* contain sections on the economy, business news, and financial information.

MONTHLY

Forbes is particularly good for investment news. *Fortune* and *Nation's Business* report economic and business events.

BIMONTHLY

Challenge contains articles by leading economists on various economic problems.

NEWSPAPERS

Barron's, which is a weekly, reports on current industry trends. The *Wall Street Journal* is the nation's daily business paper.

Practicing Your Skills

1. Where would you check if you were looking for: **a.** the latest copy of *Business Week?* **b.** a particular copy of the *New York Times* that is six-months old? **c.** information on the economic policies of the Truman administration? **d.** information on Alexander Hamilton's views on banking? **e.** magazine sources for trends in consumer borrowing in 1987?
2. What government publications might you check for information on: **a.** population in the 19th century? **b.** GNP figures for the previous year? **c.** GNP figures for this year? **d.** latest data on the money supply? **e.** current conditions in the economy?
3. **a.** What do you think are the disadvantages of relying on newspapers and weekly newsmagazines for your information about the economy? **b.** What do you think are the advantages? **c.** If you were to do a report on some aspect of the economy, do you think these sources would be adequate? Explain.

5 | RECENT GOVERNMENT POLICIES

Ask yourself as you read:

- What stabilization policy did the federal government follow in the early 1980s?
- Why will the debate continue over the best type of economic policies the government should follow?

This chapter has discussed only the two major approaches to economic stabilization. In reality, many economists belong to neither group. Rather, they borrow ideas and theories from both Keynesians and monetarists. Given this variety of opinion, it is not surprising that government stabilization policy is often a changing mix of several approaches. Nevertheless, at any one time, one viewpoint may dominate.

For much of the time since the 1930s, Keynesian economics was the guiding theory for government policy. Government spending was encouraged for two reasons. It was seen both as a way to achieve national goals, such as better nutrition for the poor, and to ensure a strong economy. However, by the late 1970s and early 1980s, many economists and politicians were rethinking this view. Persistent, or lasting, high inflation and a series of recessions were problems that Keynesian economics seemed unable to solve. The dilemma of stagflation became the center of debates over the economy during the 1980 presidential election. With the election of Ronald Reagan, the set of policies called supply-side economics gained national attention.

Supply-side economics, though supposedly a new theory, has in fact been around since the early 1800s. The French economist Jean Baptiste Say, in **Say's Law,** stated that supply creates its own demand. That is, production, or supply, creates income that will be used by consumers to purchase, or demand, goods and services. Since production involves the use of resources—and those resources are paid for in wages, rents, interest, or profits—those incomes can then be spent. In other words, the process of production stimulates the economy. Growth, then, depends on increasing the economy's ability to produce. Modern supply-side theory argues that individuals will respond to incentives. If the government taxes less, then individuals and businesses will receive more discretionary money income. As a result, people will work more, save more, and invest more.

The supply-side economic package that President Reagan presented to Congress in 1981 had three major parts: 1. tax cuts for businesses and individuals, 2. reductions in federal spending, and 3. the removal of many federal regulations on business. According to Reaganomics, as President Reagan's policy came to be called, cutting taxes and business regulations would cause businesses to expand production rapidly. Because people would work harder and longer and be willing to invest more of their income, the output of goods and services would increase. The result would be reduced inflation and decreased unemployment.

persistent (puhr-SIS-thunt): lasting

466

As a consequence of the powerful arguments presented by supply-side economists, Congress approved the President's program for fiscal 1982. Despite hopes for a quick recovery, the economy worsened. Production and investment continued to drop while unemployment rose sharply. Inflation was reduced significantly, but this was generally credited to the Fed's tight money policy. By the middle of 1982, supply-side economics was not as strongly supported by many economists and officials. Even the President and his advisers had begun to reconsider his program. The administration supported a tax increase in certain areas that was approved by Congress for fiscal 1983 and reduced plans to cut deeply into the federal budget in areas of public service. Supply-side arguments were nonetheless used to justify a revision of the tax system in 1986. One goal of the revision was to simplify taxes and to eliminate many of the deductions that had allowed some taxpayers to reduce their taxes.

The Tax Reform Act of 1986 was the first complete overhaul of the federal tax system of the United States since 1954. It set two basic tax rates: 15 percent and 28 percent. Supply-side economists praised the reduction in tax rates. Besides reducing the number of tax brackets, the new law increased the standard deduction and personal exemption to provide a tax cut for the majority of taxpayers earning less than $20,000 a year. Tax cuts notwithstanding, middle-class taxpayers worried about their ability to plan for the future. Under the new law, many Americans no longer will be able to deduct the contributions they make to an Individual Retirement Account (IRA), or they can deduct only part ot it, depending on their income. Also, the amount that can be placed in 401 (K) salary-reduction plans was reduced. Sales tax and the interest paid on loans no longer were deductable.

The experience of the Reagan administration shows that there are no simple or immediate solutions to the complex problems of the economy. Nonetheless, the recent experiments with monetarism and supply-side economics have pointed to the need for new ideas to replace policies that are no longer adequate. Perhaps a new theory for both monetary and fiscal policy will arise that represents a compromise between Keynesian economics and monetarism. Such a policy could involve a moderate rate of increase in the money supply and a balanced federal budget most of the time. In any case, the debate on which policies the government should follow is sure to continue.

REVIEWING ECONOMIC PRINCIPLES

1. Why did many economists begin to rethink Keynesian economic theory in the late 1970s and early 1980s?
2. **a.** What is supply-side economics? **b.** How was the supply-side economic program supposed to help the economy?
3. **Critical Thinking: Making Generalizations.** What actually happened to the economy under supply-side economics?

SUMMARY OF
IMPORTANT PRINCIPLES

1
- Four types of unemployment are: cyclical, associated with fluctuations in the business cycle; structural, caused by such changes in the economy as technological advances or discoveries of natural resources; seasonal, caused by changes in the seasons or weather; frictional, temporary unemployment between jobs

2
- The theory of demand-pull inflation states that prices rise as the result of excess demand on the part of businesses and consumers and generally happens in times of full employment. The theory of cost-push inflation states that prices are pushed up by the wage demands of labor unions and the excessive profit motive of large corporations and occurs when both inflation and unemployment are high.

3
- According to the circular flow model of income, income flows continually between businesses and consumers. It flows from businesses to consumers in the form of wages, rent, interest, and profits. Income flows in the opposite direction, from consumers to businesses, as payments for consumer goods and services. Some income leaks from the economy through consumer saving and government taxation. Injections of income occur through business investment and government spending.
- Keynesian economists believe government should actively use its central position in the circular flow of income to smooth out the ups and downs in the economy. By changing its taxation and spending policies, the federal government could control leakages and injections and, therefore, the overall level of economic activity.
- Supporters of Keynes argue that increasing taxes and/or reducing government spending will reduce aggregate demand for goods and services.

4
- Monetarists believe that the Fed should allow the money supply to grow at a steady rate. They feel this policy would provide more certainty about the future than a constantly changing monetary policy. The result would be a controlled expansion of the economy without rapid inflation or high unemployment.
- To locate economic research materials in the library, look in the card catalogue, *Reader's Guide to Periodical Literature*, and the *Business Periodicals Index*. The federal government publishes statistical data annually as well as monthly. Many weekly, monthly, and bi-monthly magazines as well as newspapers provide coverage of current business.

5
- According to supply-side theory, cutting taxes and business regulations would cause businesses to expand production rapidly. Because people would work harder and longer and be willing to invest more of their income, the nation's output of goods and services would increase. The result would be reduced inflation along with a decrease in unemployment.

TRADE-OFFS: FEDERAL TAX CUTS

Jim and Jane Yokono are reading a news report about the impact of the 1986 Tax Reform Act. Jim thinks tax reform is a step in the right direction. His family will be able to use the extra money he will receive now that his federal personal income tax rate is lower. Although Jim has a fairly good salary as a lab technician, paying for a new home and taking care of two small children is not easy.

Jane does not share Jim's enthusiasm. She knows from reading the newspaper and listening to news reports that the national debt has been growing because of federal budget deficits. She believes that the 1986 Tax Reform Act lowering tax rates will only increase the deficit. This will mean more government borrowing, which may drive up interest rates. If rates rise, she and Jim will have to pay more interest on their mortgage.

Jane also has done some calculations and found that the reduction in tax rates is only going to give Jim an extra $9 a week in take-home pay. She does not think their standard of living will increase much. Jim is also disappointed to learn how little the tax cut will mean to them. However, over a period of a year, the extra money will come to almost $500. That $500 will make paying bills a little easier for the Yokonos.

1. Do you agree with Jim or with Jane's reasoning? Explain your answer.
2. Based on what you read in this chapter, what positive effects will a tax cut have on the economy?
3. If the economy were at full employment, what negative effects will a tax cut have on the economy?

Readings in Economics

THE STAGES OF UNEMPLOYMENT
Skill: Drawing Conclusions

 Unemployment can be disastrous for an individual, especially a young person trying to make a start in life. This reading from a book by Terry M. Williams and William Kornblum describes the tragic effects of unemployment on one teenage mother.

When young people experience long periods, often three or more months, of fruitless job search, their behavior tends to be quite similar to that of adults under the same conditions. They spend a great deal of time thinking about looking for work, somewhat less time actually tracking down leads, and increasing amounts of time doing household chores and watching television. Carol J. of Meridian, an enterprising teenage mother with an extensive work history, has provided a thumbnail sketch of the emotional cycle that teenagers go through when they want and expect to work but no jobs are to be found.

I have done all types of jobs to earn money. I worked as a babysitter for my cousin every weekend. I have cleaned homes and painted to make extra money. My stepfather was in the [lawn] sodding business. I started out by stacking grass, making about $25.00. To me that was big money. Then I moved up to planting grass, making about $75.00 a week. I did that type of work until I was 14. Then I started working at a nursery.
After being laid off, I went through the following stages:

Active. When I first got laid off, I found everything to do. My time slots were all filled.

Less Active. My activities slowed down, until I was finding things to do around the house.

Bored. After I had done everything that could be done, there was nothing to do.

Depressed. With an income of $20.00 a week, when I was used to making about $90 to $100.00 a week, it made me sick. I had lost weight and had no appetite. Having to save every penny, in order to get your bills paid.

Worried. I was worried about how . . . 20 . . . dollars would take care of two people. So when I got my money it all went towards things for my son. I bought nothing for myself, except health goods.

Tried to Find Work. After making out my budget, I soon realized that I needed a job, but none were to be found.

1. If Carol stopped actively seeking a job, would she still be included in the unemployment statistics?
2. Given this example, what can you conclude about the accuracy of the national unemployment statistics?

Reprinted by permission of the publisher, from *Growing Up Poor* by Terry Williams and William Kornblum (Lexington, Mass.: Lexington Books, D. C. Heath and Co., copyright 1985, D. C. Heath and Co.).

WHAT'S THE CHIEF CAUSE OF OUR INFLATIONARY ECONOMY?
Skill: Interpreting Information

 Economists offer varying explanations for the causes of "stagflation"—the combination of high inflation and low economic activity—experienced in the United States in the 1970s. In this reading, Robert L. Heilbroner and Lester C. Thurow, two leading American economists, discuss some of the conflicting views.

What has caused this new condition of chronic inflation accompanied by recession? There is no shortage of proffered explanations. . . .

One that is frequently heard is that chronic inflation is the result of concentrated private economic power. Often the power is deemed to be held by labor, which keeps demanding wage hikes larger than the system can afford. This jacks up prices and also boosts costs of production: result—inflation plus a drag on output. Economists on the other side of the fence agree about the concentration of power, but place it in the hands of big business, where it is used to hold up prices even when business is slack, and to restrict output in monopolistic fashion.

Power certainly is involved in inflation, but whose power? For every economist pointing the finger at the private sector, there are two pointing at government. Sometimes the problem is government regulation, saddling the economy with ex-

Even in periods of economic downturn there are jobs to be filled, as the help-wanted ads above show. But for those without jobs, unemployment insurance provides benefits that lessen the problems of joblessness.

cessive costs of regulation, anti-pollution activities, and the like. Sometimes the problem with government is deemed to be just plain excessive spending, although there is a debate whether the excess shows up in a swollen military budget or a swollen welfare budget. Very often the culprit is the federal deficit, a favorite target of political candidates. And not infrequently the trouble is located in some other government, in particular those that set the price of OPEC oil.

Even that does not exhaust the possibilities. There is much blame on sagging productivity as the cause for chronic inflation coupled with recession. Or there is an explanation that links America's difficulties with its role in the world economy. There is yet another account that lays the initial blame on the inflationary effects of the Vietnam War and the subsequent persistence of inflation on the particular institution known as indexing—the fact that we tie more and more payments, such as Social Security or wages, directly to the consumer price index, so that when the index

goes up, we automatically get a higher Social Security check or a cost-of-living adjustment in our pay. And there is talk that inflation simply reflects our state of mind—a desire to have more than we can afford, an appetite that exceeds our capacity to satisfy it.

Which of these explanations is correct? All—or nearly all—of them have something to contribute to our understanding of inflation. What is lacking is a coherent framework to put them in, an overarching account that will enable us to think about the subject without feeling that we have to single out one crucial element, or keep a dozen in our heads at the same time.

1. List the causes of inflation as presented in this article by Heilbroner and Thurow.
2. With so many explanations offered about the causes of inflation, what do the authors suggest is needed in considering the problem?

Robert L. Heilbroner and Lester C. Thurow, *Five Economic Challenges.* Englewood Cliffs, New Jersey: Prentice-Hall, 1981. pp. 4—6.

Readings in Economics

DEMAND AWAITS SUPPLY IN THE CIRCULAR FLOW
Skill: Making Inferences

 The concept of a circular flow is important in understanding Keynesian theory. In this reading from a book published two years before Keynes' *General Theory* appeared, economist Joseph A. Schumpeter discusses this concept.

All businessmen are . . . at the same time buyers—for the purposes of their production and consumption—and sellers. In this analysis the workers may be similarly conceived, that is, their services may be included in the same category with other marketable things. Now since everyone of these businessmen, taken by himself, produces his products and finds his buyers on the basis of his experience, . . . the same must be true for all taken together. . . .

Let us drive this home. How much meat the butcher disposes of depends upon how much his customer the tailor will buy and at what price. That depends, however, upon the proceeds from the latter's business, these proceeds again upon the needs and the purchasing power of the shoemaker, whose purchasing power again depends upon the needs and the purchasing power of the people for whom he produces; and so forth, until we finally strike someone whose income derives from the sale of his goods to the butcher. . . .

Our picture will be more complete if we represent the act of consuming otherwise than is customary. Everyone, for instance, considers himself a consumer of bread, but not of land, services, iron, and so forth. If we consider people as consumers of these other things, however, we can see still more clearly the way taken by individual goods in the circular flow. Now it is obvious that every unit of every commodity does not always travel the same road to the consumer that its predecessor in the process of production travelled in the preceding economic period. But we may suppose that this *does* happen without altering anything essential. We can imagine that, year in and year out, every recurring employment of permanent sources of productive power endeavors to reach the same consumer. The result of the proc-

ess is in any case the same as if this happened. Hence it follows that somewhere in the economic system a demand is, so to say, ready awaiting every supply, and nowhere in the system are there commodities without complements, that is other commodities in the possession of people who will exchange them under empirically determined conditions for the former goods. It follows, again from the fact that all goods find a market, that the circular flow of economic life is closed, in other words that the sellers of all commodities appear again as buyers in sufficient measure to acquire those goods which will maintain their consumption and their productive equipment in the next economic period at the level so far attained, and vice versa.

1. In the circular flow of economic activity in the marketplace, what can you infer about the roles of buyers and sellers and their interrelationship?
2. Explain what the author means when he states that "demand awaits supply."

Joseph A. Schumpeter, *The Theory of Economic Development.* Cambridge, Mass.: Harvard University Press, 1934. Copyright © 1934 by the President and Fellows of Harvard College; © 1962 by Redvers Opie. Reprinted by permission.

GALBRAITH DISAGREES WITH FRIEDMAN
Skill: Distinguishing Fact and Opinion

 Many economists disagree with monetarism, the theory that involves regulating the supply of money to affect the amount of credit and business activity in the economy. In this reading, John Kenneth Galbraith presents his view of the monetarist ideas of Milton Friedman.

There has always been a certain fascination among economists with the mechanics of central-bank policy. It's our profession's special form of magic. This has led some to overlook its highly discriminatory effect. But, in general, and quite rightly, it is the favored measure of very conservative people. . . .

Professor Friedman is a very attractive and persuasive man, but he is an avowed conservative, and it is not a function of a conservative to worry about policies that favor big business over small business. Or about unemployment. He does not, and it is his privilege to ignore these adverse effects. However, I don't want to make Friedman sound altogether heartless, and this takes us back to an earlier point. More than most, Milton Friedman has a vision of an economy that is made up of competitive firms ruled by the market. For him the market still lives, and the great and powerful corporation has never been important in his thinking. If you grant him his view of economic life—competition in a still effective market—although it does take some understanding and tolerance, you see how monetary policy can be imagined to spread itself more or less uniformly over an economy of competitive firms. It can be supposed to treat all more or less alike, and, since the firms are competitive and subject to the impersonal forces of the market, a curtailment of bank lending and aggregate demand forces all to reduce prices or forego price increases. This, not unemployment, is the first effect. And from this we get Friedman's central recommendation, which is that you limit lending and money creation so that the supply of money and the resulting demand increase only as the supply of goods and services increases or can be increased. Any tendency toward a greater increase in lending, money creation and demand is sternly controlled. The result is an economy of stable prices. . . .

We live in the real world. Monetary restriction doesn't stop the people who have escaped the discipline of the market and got control of their prices and incomes from shoving up those prices and incomes. They are stopped only when there is a lot of unemployment. Meanwhile it does work, in a rather punishing way, for those who are still subject to the market.

1. According to Galbraith, how does Friedman recommend that we achieve an economy of stable prices?
2. What does Galbraith suggest Friedman fails to take into account in his monetary policies?

John Kenneth Galbraith and Nicole Salinger, *Almost Everyone's Guide to Economics.* Boston: Houghton Mifflin Company, 1978. pp. 86, 87.

THE GOALS OF REAGAN'S ECONOMIC POLICIES
Skill: Understanding Decision Making

 **In this reading from a 1983 speech, economist Paul W. McCracken attempts to explain the basis for the changes in economic policy instituted by President Reagan in 1981.**

What were the basic elements of the strategy for economic policy deployed by the incoming Administration at the beginning of 1981? While those in or close to the Administration in the early stages of framing its program might not agree precisely with this formulation, there seemed to be about five basic building blocks in this new strategy. First, the high and even accelerating rate of inflation could be brought down to more traditional levels (to, say, the 2 percent per year annual average that prevailed from 1900 to 1967) with small adverse effects on employment, output, and real income. Second, the key to a more stable economy is a more stable management of monetary policy. Third, a liberal international economic order is urgently important for the United States and the rest of the Free World. Fourth, a reduction in tax rates would so energize incentives and activate the economy that the lower rates would also produce even larger revenues than would otherwise occur. And, finally, the scope of government, both through direct regulation and through its fiscal operations, had expanded too rapidly. . . .

"Central to the new policy," said the Administration, "is the view that expectations play an important role in determining economic activity, inflation, and interest rates."

1. According to the article, what concerns formed the basis for the Reagan administration's economic policies?
2. Explain how individuals who have an increase in income can actually experience a decline in their purchasing power during a period of inflation.

Paul W. McCracken, "Reaganomics: A Midterm Examination." *Reaganomics: Meaning, Means, and Ends.*, Vol. 24 of the Charles C. Moskowitz Memorial Lectures. New York: The Free Press, 1983. pp. 45, 61, 62, 66.

PRACTICING YOUR WRITING SKILLS: WRITING A RESEARCH PAPER

The first and perhaps most important step in writing a research paper is choosing a topic. It should be a topic that interests you and is not so broad or so obscure that finding information will take many hours of your time. Remember that your time is scarce. A topic such as "The Prime Interest Rate" is too broad, but "How the Federal Reserve Board Controls Interest Rates" would be an easier subject to research. In writing research papers, you will need many of the reading, study, and writing skills you have learned previously in this textbook. Here are some tips to help you:

- In doing your research, use the steps for taking notes on p. 372. Sort your note cards into two groups: important facts, ideas, statistics, and details in the first group and less important ones in the second.
- To outline your paper, use the steps on p. 314.
- Review the steps for writing an essay on p. 398, and write the first version, or draft, of your paper.
- Read your first draft carefully. Does it make sense? Is it clear and interesting? Do your ideas flow from paragraph to paragraph? The use of words such as *likewise*, *however*, *in addition*, *on the other hand*, *first*, *second*, *finally*, can help your reader recognize and understand comparison/contrast, cause/effect, and the classifying of information.
- Be sure to summarize your main points in the conclusion to your paper. You might review the steps for summarizing on p. 294. Compare your conclusion with your thesis. Does your conclusion reflect the purpose of your paper?
- Edit and rewrite until you are satisfied with your draft. Use any data from your second group of note cards if it adds interest to your paper or helps explain some idea.
- When you write out your final draft, be sure to use footnotes for any quotations or statistics.

Activity: Choose a topic from this chapter and write a four-page research paper about it.

VOCABULARY REVIEW

For each of the following terms, write a sentence using the term: demand-pull inflation, stagflation, supply-side economics, cost-push inflation, stabilization policy.

PRACTICING YOUR ECONOMIC SKILLS

1. **Making Calculations.** Use the table showing the Consumer Price Index on p. 356 to calculate any loss of purchasing power.

   a. Bob Kingsley put $1,000 cash in his safe deposit box in 1981. What was his loss in purchasing power on the money by 1982?

   b. In 1980, Catherine McNamara deposited $1,000 in a credit union savings account paying 7 percent interest compounded annually. She did not remove any of the money until she closed the account 5 years later. (1) How much was in the account when she closed it? (2) By what percentage had consumer prices increased during this time? (3) Was the purchasing power of the account more or less than in 1980?

Producer Price Indexes for Selected Commodity Groups, 1979-1985*

	Farm Products	Fuels	Furniture Household Durables	Lumber Wood Products	All Commodities
1979	241.4	408.1	171.3	300.4	235.6
1980	249.4	574.0	187.0	288.9	268.8
1981	254.9	694.5	198.5	292.8	293.4
1982	252.7	677.4	206.6	288.7	299.4
1983	248.2	664.7	214.0	307.1	303.1
1984	255.8	656.8	218.7	307.4	310.3
1985	231.4	644.3	223.4	314.2	308.1

*1967 = 100

Source: *Statistical Abstract of the U.S.*, Bureau of the Census

2. **Analyzing Data on a Table.** Use the table on producer price indexes on p. 474 to answer the following: **a.** Which index increased the most during the period shown? **b.** Which increased the least? **c.** What were the percentages of increase for these two indexes? **d.** Which index decreased by the largest percentage in a single year? **e.** What was the percentage of decrease and in which year did it occur?

DISCUSSING ECONOMIC QUESTIONS

1. There are several types of unemployment. People often choose to enter occupations that have occasional layoffs. Why do people enter such occupations? What alternatives do these workers have?
2. The theories of John Maynard Keynes and Milton Friedman are the major tools used for stabilizing the economy. Which do you think is a better solution for controlling recessions or overexpansion of the economy? Why?
3. Based on what you have read in this chapter, what do you think should be done to control or prevent inflation?

APPLYING CRITICAL THINKING SKILLS

1. **Doing Research.** Using the *Statistical Abstract*, research the Consumer Price Index since 1960. Write a paragraph describing how the rate of current inflation compares with that of the 1960s or the 1970s.
2. **Writing a Research Paper.** Write a research paper on what the Great Depression meant to the American people. Narrow your topic before you begin your research.
3. **Writing a Report.** Some states ran out of unemployment benefits during the high unemployment of the early 1980s. Research and write a short report on the unemployment benefits available in your state, time limit and qualifications for receiving them, scale of payments, and whether your state had to borrow from the federal government to pay benefits during the early 1980s.
4. **Drawing a Graph.** Using the *Statistical Abstract*, research and draw a graph showing unemployment rates for the past ten years for various groups of workers by age, occupations, race, and sex. Use this information for the basis of a discussion on unemployment in the United States.

READINGS

Bartlett, Bruce. *Reaganomics: Supply-Side Economics in Action.* Westport, Conn.: Arlington House, 1982.

Friedman, Milton, and Friedman, Rose. *Free to Choose: A Personal Statement.* New York: Harcourt Brace Jovanovich, 1981.

Hailstones, Thomas J. *A Guide to Supply-Side Economics,* Richmond, Va.: Robert F. Dame, 1983.

Leftwich, Richard H., and Sharp, Ansel M. *Economics of Social Issues.* 6th ed. Plano, Tex.: Business Publications, 1984.

Lekachman, Robert. *Inflation: The Permanent Problem of Boom and Bust.* New York: Vintage Books, 1973.

Lerner, Abba P., and Colander, David C. *MAP: A Market Anti-Inflation Plan.* New York: Harcourt Brace Jovanovich, 1980.

Solomon, Ezra. *Beyond the Turning Point: The U.S. Economy in the 1980s.* San Francisco: W.H. Freeman, 1982.

Swartz, Thomas R., and Bonello, Frank J. *Taking Sides: Clashing Views on Controversial Economic Issues.* Guilford, Conn.: Dushkin, 1984. Taxes, production, employment.

Tobias, Andrew. "A Talk With Paul Volcker." *The New York Times Magazine,* 19 September 1982, pp. 34.

CHAPTER 19

Changes in industry and agriculture have led to new technology and new products as well as important changes in the makeup of the labor force. The expansion of service industries and the growth of an information society are challenges being met in our market economy.

RECENT CHANGES AND CHALLENGES IN THE ECONOMY

The United States has one of the world's most productive and dynamic economies. For many decades, our free enterprise economy has made it possible for Americans to enjoy the highest standard of living of any nation. American business and industries have led the way in developing new technology and new products. In the process, they also have been transforming our nation's economy. This chapter surveys recent changes in the American economy and examines the challenges and opportunities they pose. Among the most important changes are the expansion of the service sector, the growth of an information society, rapid development in technology, and changing patterns in the work force. The chapter concludes by examining the role of government in this changing American economy.

CHAPTER OBJECTIVES After you study this chapter, you will be able to:

1 • explain what is meant by a service economy.
  • describe the changes in the work force.
  • understand the reasons for the rise of the two-income family.
  • explain the effects of consolidation in American agriculture.
  • locate the regions of the nation where the greatest growth is taking place.

2 • describe the growth of the information society.
  • identify several new scientific advances in the computer and telecommunications industries.
  • explain several effects of growth in these industries.

3 • define deregulation and understand its effects.
  • explain the trade-offs involved in setting national goals.
  • explain the tax reform legislation of 1986.
  • describe the wave of business mergers and takeovers.

ECONOMICS VOCABULARY

heavy industry
smokestack industries
service sector
service economy
organized labor
robotics
agribusiness
satellites
deregulation
merger
takeover

Two hundred years ago, nearly all Americans made a living from the land. The United States was an agricultural society, dependent on the steady cycle of planting and harvesting that still dominates life in many developing countries. Then, in the 19th century, the industrial revolution brought about the first great transformation, or basic change, of the American economy. The change began in the red-brick factories of New England and moved slowly west and then south. Over the next 100 years, a growing number of Americans left their farms to take manufacturing jobs in towns and cities. The ranks of labor in the factories were enlarged by thousands of immigrants who poured into the nation.

This shift from an agricultural to a manufacturing economy was the counterpart of the industrial revolution that was taking place in Western Europe at about the same time. In the United States, the industrial revolution led to the growth of **heavy industries** which manufacture steel, coal, and other materials that are used to make other goods. Economists sometimes group manufacturers of heavy goods into a single category, that of **smokestack industries.** These industries contributed to making the United States the world's economic leader by the mid-1900s.

1 | CHANGES IN INDUSTRY AND AGRICULTURE

Ask yourself as you read:
- What major changes have taken place in American industry recently?
- In which segment of the economy do most Americans now work?

In recent years another key economic transformation has been under way, one that promises to be as far-reaching as the industrial revolution. This change is sometimes called the post-industrial revolution. It has affected not only manufacturing but agriculture and other industries as well. Fewer and fewer American workers are now engaged in manufacturing and farming. Whereas in 1920 about 40 percent of America's workers were engaged in manufacturing, today 80 percent of them have jobs in non-manufacturing and non-farm business. Most of these workers are in the **service sector** of the economy, which is made up of workers who provide services, help, or information. Service workers include lawyers, accountants, physicians, sales persons, wholesalers, transportation workers, teachers, repairpersons, office personnel, computer programmers, and data processors. Because the overwhelming number of Americans hold these and similar jobs, economists say that the United States has now become a **service economy.**

The post-industrial economy has been characterized by a number of important developments. Among them have been the rapid growth of white-collar and service workers, the increase in the number of women in the work force, and the emphasis on higher education and vocational

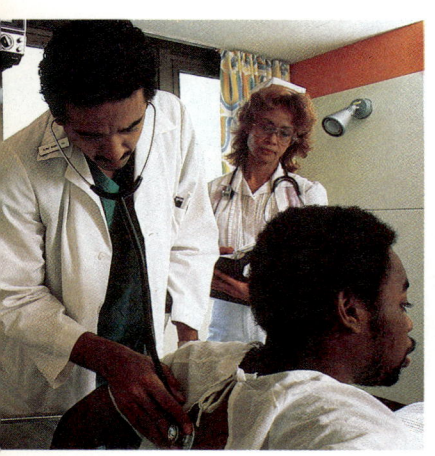

Americans receive health care. This physician is giving his patient a thorough physical examination. Why are doctors included in the service sector of the labor force?

and specialized training. Also, population has shifted to the West and South, and farms have become larger and more mechanized.

THE SHIFT TO A SERVICE ECONOMY

As you read in Chapter 13, economists have traditionally divided American workers into two broad categories, blue-collar workers and white-collar workers. Blue-collar workers are those who are directly involved in mining, manufacturing, and non-farm labor. Some of them work on assembly lines at auto plants. Some operate machinery in textile plants and other types of factories. Others dig coal, and operate oil rigs. Some drive buses and trucks. Blue-collar workers usually are paid by the hour. White-collar workers, on the other hand, serve as office workers, salespersons, managers, and professionals—accountants, lawyers, engineers, teachers, physicians, nurses, and so on. They work in business offices, retail shops, classrooms, laboratories, hospitals, classrooms, and industrial parks. They usually receive a weekly or monthly salary instead of an hourly wage.

After the end of World War II in 1945, the size of the white-collar work force in the United States began a rapid growth. In 1956, the number of white-collar jobs overtook the number of blue-collar jobs for the first time. Since then, the size of the white-collar work force has continued to grow 3 to 4 percent a year.

Accompanying this shift has been a decline in labor union membership, or **organized labor.** Unions, once dominated by blue-collar workers, reached their peak in 1960, when 1 out of every 3 American workers belonged to a labor union. By 1985 that number had dwindled to less than 1 in 5. Of those Americans still belonging to unions, moreover, a majority now work in white-collar jobs, including positions as postal workers, police officers, and fire fighters, employed by local, state, and federal governments. By and large, however, white-collar workers and service workers are hard to organize into unions. Most of them regard themselves as more independent economically and in less need of the protection of unions than blue-collar workers. Further, wages in the service sector have been going up more rapidly than in other sectors, so workers there feel less need for unions.

Two further factors other than the growth of the service sector account for the decline in the size of the blue-collar work force. One is that in many industries human workers are being replaced by computer-operated machinery. In automobile assembly plants, for example, robots, or mechanical workers, weld body parts and paint car bodies. In electronics factories robots assemble electronic circuits. Although the investment in robots is expensive, in the long run businesses find it worthwhile to purchase robot systems because of the great savings in labor costs they make possible. The science and technology of the development and use of robots is called **robotics.**

Another reason for the reduction in the blue-collar labor force is competition from imported products. Automobiles, electronic equipment, textiles, clothing, steel, and countless other items imported from Japan, Korea, China, Taiwan, countries of Latin America, and countries allied to the Soviet Union, where wage scales are lower than in the United States have meant the loss of American blue-collar jobs. And not only do foreign countries send their goods to the United States, but also many American businesses have moved their manufacturing and assembly operations to countries with low-paid workers, further limiting the number of available jobs in this country.

For many Americans, therefore, the opportunities for certain blue-collar jobs have narrowed considerably. As a result, many younger blue-collar workers are training for new careers in vocational and technical schools. However, many older workers replaced by the decline of smokestack industries face continued unemployment. In fact, many economists believe that for this reason unemployment in the United States for some years to come will remain at a higher rate than in the past no matter how prosperous the nation as a whole may be.

WOMEN IN THE WORK FORCE

With the growth of a service economy, where training often counts more than muscle, there has been a great increase in the number of women who have entered the labor market. Today they make up 44 percent of the American work force. In 1965 they represented a little more than 35 percent. Further, no longer are women limited to traditional jobs such as secretaries, receptionists, salespersons, and employees doing light work in factories. Increasingly, they have entered professions such as law and medicine, the building trades, managerial jobs, and other once male-dominated fields.

Why has the percentage of women in the work force risen so dramatically in recent years? One important reason for this change was the influence of changing social attitudes, which encouraged women to enter the American work force and to break down the barriers that had limited the kinds of work women could engage in. But for many women economic necessity rather than intellectual conviction was the motivation that impelled them to enter the work force. During the 1970s the United States suffered very high inflation. Between 1970 and 1980 the Consumer Price Index rose, on average, by 7.5 percent each year. As prices rose, the average family's purchasing power declined. In the decade beginning in 1973, for example, the purchasing power of a typical family headed by a person aged 25 to 34 fell by 11.5 percent. Such families found they could no longer maintain their standard of living with one income. For that reason, many families decided they needed two breadwinners instead of one.

Today in many American homes, both husbands and wives work. This is especially true of young families. In two thirds of all households occupied by married couples aged 25 to 34, husbands and wives both have jobs. These couples tend to have smaller families than their parents did. Births per 1,000 people have declined from 25 in 1955 to less

The women factory workers are performing a traditional job long held by women. What new fields of work are increasing numbers of women also now engaged in?

than 17 today. Smaller families are one of several factors that have also made life easier for working couples. Microwave ovens, automatic dishwashers, washing machines, and similar conveniences have reduced the time required for cooking, cleaning, and maintaining the home. Frozen foods and fast food restaurants are increasingly popular among working families, who are often busy or tired.

Of course, single women as well as wives have joined the work force in large numbers. Whereas in the past many young women took jobs only until they were married, by 1987 over 82 percent of single women between the ages of 25 and 44 were in the labor force. However, despite the fact that large numbers of women now work, women's earnings are far lower than men's. For example, in 1985, average earnings of women in all categories of work were 22 percent less than those of men.

HIGHER EDUCATION AND VOCATIONAL TRAINING

As the American economy has grown steadily more technologically advanced and more service-oriented, it has required an ever more highly skilled work force. The need for better educated workers has been especially profound in technical fields and in the professions.

Ever since early in the 19th century, Americans have responded to this need in growing numbers. In 1900, only 4 percent of college-age Americans were enrolled in institutions of higher learning. In 1960, a full 40 percent were, and that percentage rose another 10 percent within three years. As college graduates became more common, the economic value of their degrees declined. Thus, a growing number of graduates sought advanced degrees as well.

With increasing specialization in industry the number of persons seeking vocational and technical training has also risen sharply. It is estimated that almost 4 million students or over 20 percent of the total attending school beyond the high school level, are enrolled in vocational and technical courses. They take such courses in a variety of institutions, including community colleges and private technical institutes.

Figure 19-1 shows the increase in the percentage of high school and college graduates among all persons over the age of 25.

Figure 19-1: EDUCATIONAL ATTAINMENT IN THE UNITED STATES

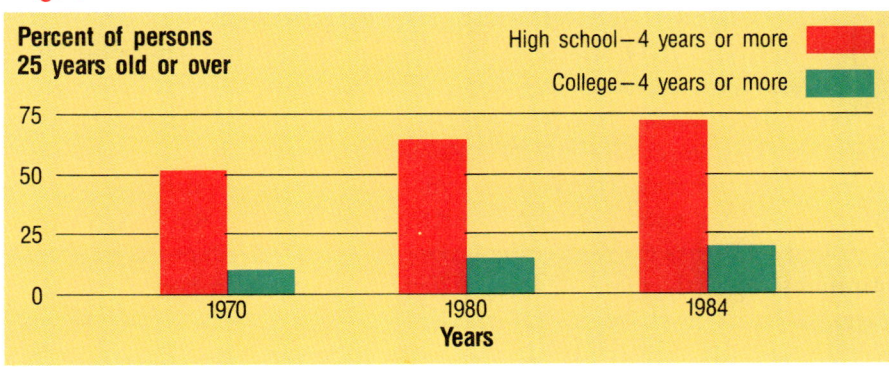

As this graph shows, an increasing number of Americans have graduated from high school and college in recent years. In the years shown, which group of graduates showed the largest increase?

481

CONSOLIDATION IN AGRICULTURE

As more and more Americans have entered the service sector of the economy, the percentage of the nation's population who work in agriculture has continued to decline. In 1950, about 14 percent of the nation's work force was engaged in agriculture. Today 3 percent are engaged in agricultural pursuits. Behind the decline in farm population lies a more remarkable story—that of changing technology.

In the past half century, the nation's farmers and farm businesses have poured billions of dollars into making farms more productive. This research and development has changed the face of agriculture in the United States. Today's farms use new and improved seeds to produce more robust strains of corn, wheat, soybeans, and other basic foods. They employ machines to harvest almost every kind of crop. Extensive use of pesticides and fertilizers increase crop yields.

robust (ROW-buhst): healthy, or strongly formed

With this technology, farm output has increased dramatically. But so has the need for farm investment. Farm machinery is expensive, as are fertilizers and pesticides, so farmers have needed more money to keep their operations going. Tragically, many family farmers have found that they are no longer able to keep their farms and have had to sell them. Increasingly, large corporations, with larger resources than independent farmers can call on, have been drawn into agricultural operations. For example, Tenneco, the oil and energy conglomerate, has become the largest "farmer" in the United States today.

Experts refer to such a large farm corporation as an **agribusiness.** Between 1970 and 1987, the nation lost over 680,000 farms, and farm population declined from 9.7 million to 5.8 million Americans. Yet crop production rose rapidly in the same years. Corn production, for example, increased by over 80 percent, wheat by 92 percent, and soybeans by 19 percent. In other words, fewer and fewer farms and farmers have been needed to meet the world's growing demand for food. The average farm today is 425 acres and produces enough food to feed 77 people.

FROM FROSTBELT TO SUNBELT

Along with other major economic changes has come a shift in population from one region of the country to another. In general, this shift has taken Americans from the North and East to the West and South. Between 1980 and 1984, the Northeast—that is, New England, plus New York, Pennsylvania, and New Jersey—grew in population by only 1.2 percent. By contrast, the South—the states from Maryland and Delaware through West Virginia and Kentucky to Oklahoma and Texas—grew by 6.9 percent. The West—from Colorado to California, including Hawaii, Alaska, and the Pacific Northwest—grew by 8.3 percent.

What accounts for the regional population shifts? Experts who have studied the matter point to several factors. First, a number of manufacturing industries followed the lead of textile manufacturers in relocating in the South in search of a stable and less expensive labor force.

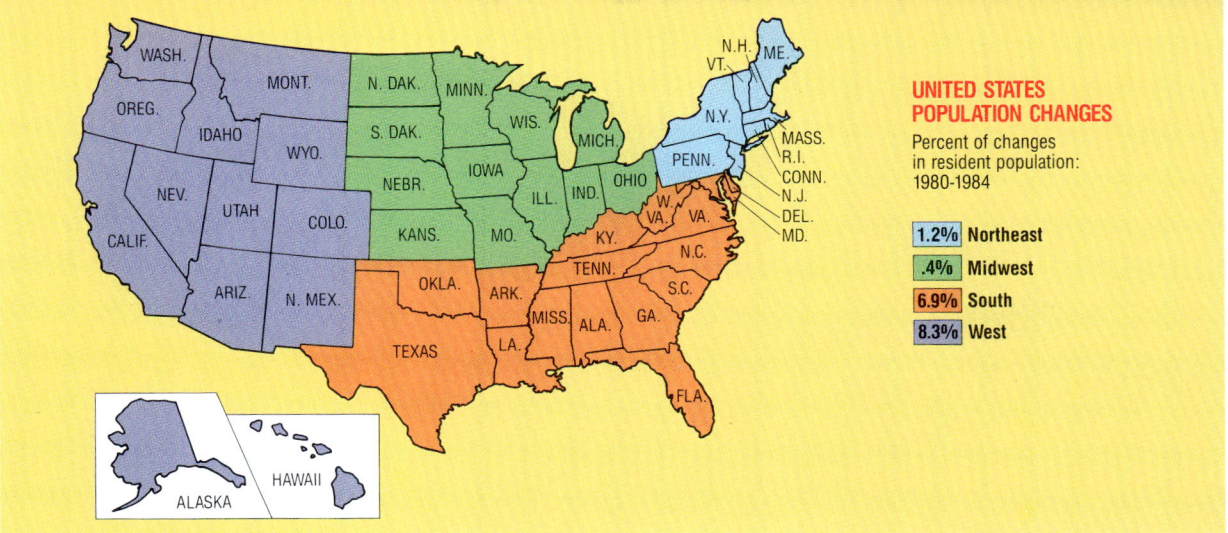

UNITED STATES
POPULATION CHANGES

Percent of changes
in resident population:
1980-1984

1.2% Northeast
.4% Midwest
6.9% South
8.3% West

The population of the sections of the United States grew at unequal rates between 1980 and 1984. Which section had the greatest gain of population?

Second, many people of retirement age have moved from the Frostbelt—the Northeast and the Midwest—to the Sunbelt—the South and the Southwest—in search of warmer climates. Third, many American workers have been attracted to the South and Southwest by the regions' job opportunities in expanding industries—oil and petrochemicals in Texas, for example, and aviation and electronics in California. Fourth, many workers in the smokestack industries of the North have found they had no work and had to move. They have simply gone where they can find jobs. However, as proof of the fact that population follows economic conditions, when the economics in the Sunbelt states of Texas, Oklahoma, and Louisiana worsened in the period beginning 1986, these states lost thousands of workers who had come there in search of jobs.

Nevertheless, these population shifts brought an expanding work force to these areas. The 14 states of the West now turn out 13 percent of the nation's GNP. Even so, limited water resources in parts of the West and Southwest pose problems for their future growth.

The map above shows percentages of growth in the four regions defined by the United States Bureau of the Census.

REVIEWING ECONOMIC PRINCIPLES

1. Write sentences defining each of these economic terms: **a.** service sector, **b.** service economy, **c.** organized labor, **d.** robotics, **e.** agribusiness
2. Name three developments that characterize the post-industrial economy.
3. What accounts for the decline in the size of the blue-collar work force?
4. Give two examples of the use of robots in manufacturing.
5. What are two reasons why the number of women in the work force has grown?
6. **Critical Thinking: Analyzing.** What advantages do large corporations engaged in agriculture have over family farmers?

HONDA—AN AMERICAN SUCCESS STORY

General Motors, Ford, and Chrysler are the three leading American car manufacturers. Which company do you think is the fourth largest producer of cars in this country? Would you be surprised to learn that the answer to that question is Honda? This Japanese company now produces more cars in the United States than American Motors, the company that it replaced in the number four position. In 1987, Honda planned to produce 320,000 cars at its American plant in Marysville, Ohio. Combined with its 400,000 cars imported from Japan, Honda now has surpassed its main Japanese competitors, Nissan and Toyota, in U. S. auto sales.

Why has Honda been so successful in capturing such a large share of the American car market? Initially, the success of the Honda was due to the fact that it was much cheaper than comparable American cars. But then, as Japanese wage scales rose, the price differential became less important than the consistently high quality of Honda cars. Lists of the world's best-made cars almost always now include a Honda. The pride in the quality of its product that characterizes its Japanese-made cars prompted Honda to make sure that quality would also be given high priority when it set up its American plant in 1979. Many American workers at the Marysville plant were sent to Japan to observe and work side by side with Japanese Honda workers, and they now teach their co-workers what they learned there. Workers at the Marysville plant are given responsibilities such as inspecting their own work that American auto workers traditionally did not have.

Vigorous and aggressive marketing has also helped Honda secure a strong presence in the car market. Honda spends about $60 million a year in advertising in the United States alone, and aims its ads at younger, upwardly mobile customers.

In 1986, Honda moved into the luxury car market with a new line of automobiles called Acuras. Honda was careful to distinguish its Acura line from other Hondas. It set up a complete new dealer network for the new car. Acuras are not sold in Honda showrooms. Honda believes a separate Acura marketing organization helps build the "snob appeal" needed to sell luxury cars—those that sell for $18,000 and more—in the United States. Luxury cars are the most profitable segment of the American automobile market, and their sales are expected to increase 28 percent, to a total of 1.5 million cars, by 1990.

Despite its record of success in the United States, Honda has not enjoyed a completely hospitable welcome in this country. American auto workers blame Honda and the other Japanese manufacturers for high unemployment in the American car industry. They also resent the fact that Honda does not have a union at its Marysville plant. American car manufacturers and unions worked hard in the effort to force the Japanese government to limit the export of Hondas and other cars to the United States. On the other hand, even American manufacturers admit that competition from Japanese cars has helped to improve the quality of American automobiles.

1. What has been the key to Honda's success in the American car market?
2. Why did Honda decide to make a luxury car?
3. What factors do you believe will determine whether Japanese cars continue to have a large share of the American market?

2 | GROWTH OF THE INFORMATION SOCIETY

Ask yourself as you read:

• What are the features of the information society?

• What effect has the information revolution had on American life?

Perhaps the most profound change in the American economy in recent years has been its transformation into an **information society.** In such a society, not only is more information available to more Americans than ever before, but it is faster and easier to obtain. With the flick of a television switch, Americans can watch events in distant parts of the world, carried via satellite relays, unfold before their eyes. With the turn of a knob on a microfilm reader, they can locate an account of events from the distant past. With the press of a photocopier button, they can obtain reproductions of almost any document they need. By using computer software, business managers can get printouts of up-to-date information on their inventories, payrolls, and profit margins. In fact, computer software and videotapes now provide Americans with tips on everything from nutrition and health care to home maintenance and auto repair.

The main reason for the information revolution, of course, is rapidly expanding technology in the computer and telecommunications fields. The computer revolution occurred because of the coming of the microchip. Microchips are tiny devices that can store vast amounts of information in an area smaller than a thumbnail. Their use in data processing has reduced powerful mainframe computers that can handle millions of complex calculations from the size of a large room to the size of a gasoline pump. Other smaller but still powerful computers the size of a typewriter have become widely used in offices, schools, and homes.

THE COMMUNICATION REVOLUTION

In the telecommunications industry, many new advances stand out. One is the development of fiber optics, the field that deals with the transmission of light through slender strands of special glass. These strands can relay data and information at much greater speeds than could be done with electricity or radio waves. A second advance is in **satellites,** structures that orbit the earth relaying signals to and from earth stations. As more of these satellites go into orbit, experts expect the cost of sending messages to be greatly reduced. A third advance is in the development of videodiscs, small discs about the size of records for storing visual and printed data. When videodiscs are connected to computers, they allow information to be retrieved more easily. Videocassettes have become one of the most popular means of providing information. A whole new industry has been created to provide videocassettes showing people how to do things and providing self-help and self-awareness information. This is in addition to the thousands of motion pictures that are available on videocassettes and the TV programs

retrieved (ree-TREEVD): to get back again

485

that viewers tape with videocassette recorders (VCRs) for their own use. The very ease of reproduction has brought its own problems to the industry. Producers have been trying to find ways to prevent their works from being copied and sold without permission and payment.

IMPACT OF THE INFORMATION SOCIETY

Not surprisingly, the growth of the information society has meant vital changes in the lives of the nation's people. When Americans need cash, they often obtain it from electronically operated automatic-teller machines at their bank or at other conveniently located facilities. When businesses pay their salaried employees, they usually do so with checks drawn up by a data processor. When advertisers use direct mail, their messages are sent to names on computerized lists of persons most likely to be interested in their products. When Americans buy groceries in a supermarket, at the checkout counter their purchases are passed across computer-connected laser. These scanners record the cost of their purchases, keep track of all items sold, and, in some cases, actually order stock to keep store inventories up to date. Americans in the information society are presented with a bewildering array of numbers— Social Security numbers, taxpayer codes, checking and savings account numbers, and other figures computers use to identify people in computer-managed recordkeeping.

The growth of the information society has required a great many people to learn to master the new technology. Business executives, designers, medical specialists, editors, dentists, and secretaries have taken special courses to learn to use computers in their work. The computers enable them to work accurately and with remarkable speed, using constantly changing data and information. The modern computer also makes it possible for more and more people to do all or some of their work at home through work stations connected to their offices.

coordinate (coh-OR-duhn-ayt): to put in order

Computers also play a major role in financial markets, in the buying and selling of stocks and bonds of the nation's corporations. Brokerage firms that represent major financial institutions and pension funds are able to trade larger and larger blocks of shares in shorter and shorter periods of time, sometimes in only a matter of minutes. Further, decisions about when to sell or buy shares are based on computer programs that coordinate information on current stock prices, various indices, and other sophisticated practices. Some critics believe that such programmed trading has made the stock market much more subject to sharp price increases and declines. As a result, they maintain, small investors who buy stocks and bonds as long-term investments are at a disadvantage.

Most economists predict that we have just begun to witness many of the changes created by the information society. They say, for example, that cellular telephone and radio communication and satellite television transmission will soon be greatly expanded. Such developments will broaden contact among the world's people, these observers believe. Some even maintain that this new information technology will facilitate the spread of democracy into lands where it does not now exist.

Microchips are the key component in computers. In what ways has the use of computers contributed to the growth of the information society?

REVIEWING ECONOMIC PRINCIPLES

1. Write sentences defining each of the following economic terms: **a.** information society, **b.** satellites
2. What justification is there for calling the United States an information society?
3. Describe three ways in which the information society has affected Americans' lives.
4. Describe one advantage and one disadvantage of the use of computers in the buying and selling of stocks and bonds.
5. **Critical Thinking: Identifying the Main Idea.** What is the main idea of Section 2?

3 | THE CHANGING ROLE OF GOVERNMENT

Ask yourself as you read:

• What has been the effect on business of government deregulation?
• What were the objectives of the 1986 federal income tax revision?

In recent years, the growth of the service economy and the information society has occurred against the backdrop of inflation and recession, which have become harder and harder to solve. The nation's political leaders and economists have grappled with these problems by experimenting with new theories such as supply-side economics (see Chapter 18). Other governmental activities on the economic front include limiting government regulation of businesses and reforming the tax code.

DEREGULATION OF BUSINESS

Both supply-side and demand-side economists have favored expanding the nation's business output by easing government regulation of business. This plan has become known as **deregulation.** Proposals for deregulation began during the administration of Richard Nixon in the early 1970s and continued under Gerald Ford and Jimmy Carter. Carter focused his attention on three industries—energy, airlines, and trucking. Ronald Reagan applied deregulation policy in other fields, including banking and financial services.

Deregulation brought benefits to some parts of the economy and hardship to others, as the experience of the nation's airlines shows. For many years, federal agencies had regulated interstate air fares and limited the number of carriers in the market. After deregulation, new car-

Learning Economic Skills

EVALUATING NATIONAL GOALS

Throughout the textbook you have learned skills that will help you to evaluate economic data. Economists use such data to help them establish financial policies for business and government. However, many policies help one group at the expense of others. Farm supports help farmers but increase prices for consumers. Protective tariffs help workers in protected industries but raise prices.

How do decision makers evaluate issues when presented with many conflicting reactions and responses? While assessing data, business leaders and government officials work within a very important framework—that of furthering the nation's goals. These goals include:

1. *Economic freedom:* the freedom of consumers in the marketplace to spend, save, invest, work, strike, and start a business.
2. *Economic efficiency:* the wise use of resources to obtain the largest output of goods at the best possible cost.
3. *Equity:* the fair application of policies to all.
4. *Stability:* full employment without inflation.
5. *Security:* protection from economic risks—unemployment, destitution in old age, bank failures, and other economic ills.
6. *Growth:* the desire on every level—individual, corporate, and governmental—for increased income, profit, and gross national product.

MAKING TRADE-OFFS

Economic decisions require the assessment of alternatives and making trade-offs. The chart on this page will help you evaluate national goals and decide on the minimum wage.

As you can see, the social goal promoted is equity, in this case that all workers receive a fair wage. The trade-off is that fewer individuals will be employed, which adversely affects stability and growth. The government's justification for promoting a minimum wage is that the relatively small number of jobs involved will not severely affect employment and the GNP. Meanwhile, workers at low-paying jobs will have some protection from exploitation. Finding out which groups in the nation support or oppose the issue will help you to decide how to promote your goal.

Practicing Your Skills

1. Use the chart on this page to help you analyze the following issues from the chapter:
   tax reform and income redistribution
   government deregulation
   equal pay for women
   government farm supports
2. Explain why it is important to analyze economic policy from the viewpoint of national goals.

Decision-Making Chart For National Goals

Policy Decision	National Goal(s)	Goal(s) Traded off	Justification for Trade-off	Groups Supporting the Policy	Groups Opposing the Policy
Establishment of a minimum wage	Equity	Stability Growth	Minimum wage will not seriously affect employment and GNP Protects workers in low-paying jobs	Parents Unions	Businesses who use mainly workers with few skills and young people

riers entered the airline industry, and intense price competition resulted in lower fares for passengers on many routes. Although lower fares enabled travelers to fly greater distances for less money, lower fares also meant smaller profits for some airlines. Saddled with higher costs than newcomers to the business, some of the established carriers could not compete and went out of business or were forced to merge with other carriers. Others had to reduce wages and other costs and lay off workers. Meanwhile, some consumer groups raised doubts about the effect of deregulation on air safety. They argued that carriers were cutting costs in areas like airplane maintenance, a charge that the carriers strongly denied.

The effects of deregulation went beyond those experienced in these and other industries. The Reagan administration reduced the role of the federal government in such fields as consumer and environmental protection. In some cases, these policies left state and local governments freer to enact their own rules. Administration officials applauded this objective since they believed that local regulators knew the needs in their communities better than federal regulators did. Critics complained, however, that such deregulation was misguided because its effects went beyond state boundaries and that state governments were not always willing or able to set up effective regulations.

TAX REFORM AND INCOME REDISTRIBUTION

Perhaps the most significant change in government economic strategy in recent years came in taxation policy. President Ronald Reagan took office promising the nation reduced individual income taxes. In 1981, Reagan sponsored a law passed by Congress, cutting personal income tax rates by 25 percent over the next three years. The Reagan administration believed that these cuts would spur the nation's economic growth. Such growth did occur, ending the economic slump of the early 1980s, but at a slower rate than originally forecast.

Reagan's tax cuts did not change the tax structure, however. For years critics had complained about the maze of tax shelters and deductions in the federal tax code that generally favored the wealthy at the expense of the middle and lower classes. Such complaints had grown louder as inflation in the 1970s pushed many taxpayers into higher tax brackets, requiring them to pay larger percentages of their income in taxes. Finally, in 1986 Reagan administration officials and Congressional leaders from both parties joined to enact a sweeping revision of the tax code.

The federal tax law of 1986 included several reforms. First, it lowered the top individual tax rate, in stages, from 50 percent of income to 33 percent. Second, it shifted the tax burden from individuals to businesses by increasing corporate tax rates. Third, it eliminated many of the deductions and tax shelters that had made the nation's system seem unfair to many taxpayers. Fourth, the working poor, with incomes less than $7,000, no longer had to pay any tax.

curtail (ker-TAYL):
to make less

Most economists agreed that the new code amounted, in part, to a redistribution of income for the nation's taxpayers. However, some economists were concerned that the new tax code might discourage saving and investment in business and thus curtail the future growth of the nation's economy. Others argued that future Congresses could enact modifications in the tax law if such problems arose.

BUSINESS MERGERS AND TAKEOVERS

Should the federal government take steps to regulate the circumstances under which one publicly-held company may buy another one? This question intensified in the second half of the 1980s as a result of the large number of corporate mergers and takeovers that took place in this period. As you read in Chapter 10, a corporate merger occurs when one corporation buys another corporation. Often these corporate mergers are **friendly mergers.** That is, the management of the company being bought agrees that the merger will be beneficial to the company. When the management of the corporation being bought does not want the merger, however, economists and journalists refer to the situation as an unfriendly or hostile takeover, or simply a **takeover.**

THE BENEFITS OF CORPORATE TAKEOVERS

Investors who are interested in corporate takeovers look for companies whose stock seems to be selling at a lower price than the value of the company would justify. That is, these investors look for companies that they believe are worth more than the public is valuing them, in terms of the price of their stock. They attempt to buy enough of the outstanding stock to be able to take control of the corporation and to vote out the current board of directors and install their own directors. Then the new board of directors often dismiss the current managers, or top executives, who they believe have not been performing their jobs effectively. And if the investors who take over the corporation are correct, their new management team will produce higher profits. The value of the shares of the company will then rise. Thus, the ultimate beneficiaries of the takeover are therefore the shareholders—the owners of the company—if everything goes as planned.

PROBLEMS INVOLVED IN MERGERS AND TAKEOVERS

But not all takeovers work out as planned, nor do all mergers work out well, even when both companies favor the arrangement and work to make the merger successful. Many mergers are decided upon because management thinks that combining two companies will lead to greater efficiency, lower costs, and more profits. The evidence shows that at least a third of the time, mergers between big corporations have not led to the planned efficiencies and higher profits.

In the case of unfriendly takeovers, the evidence shows that the risks are even greater. The management of the corporation that is the target of the takeover often spends much of its time and large amounts of money to fight off the so-called corporate raider. By the time the raider gets control of the company, its struggle to prevent the merger may have left it weaker than before and thus unable to perform as well as the raider hoped. As a result, both companies may lose out. Often, too, in a takeover, the new management sells off parts of the company it has bought in order to repay the loans it assumed to buy the company in the first place. Sometimes this results in a more streamlined, profitable company. Sometimes it does not.

SCANDALS IN THE TAKEOVER FIELD

The "merger mania" of the 1980s also resulted in a scandal on Wall Street—the financial heart of America. The Securities and Exchange Commission (SEC) discovered that many of the individuals who were involved in unfriendly takeovers were also using secret, insider information about unannounced but planned takeovers and mergers. They used this information for their own benefit by buying the shares of stock in companies that were going to be bought by other companies. Often, they found that when the public announcement of the takeover or merger was made, the stock of the company being bought went up sharply. The result was that certain members of brokerage firms as well as takeover investors who knew about the takeover, and who bought the stock before the public announcement when it was cheaper, often made enormous profits. The SEC investigated many of these cases in 1986 and 1987. Since using inside information in this way is unlawful, some of the individuals involved were prosecuted, fined, and jailed.

Many businesspeople in the financial world fear that the dishonest dealings that were revealed in the 1980s put all of Wall Street in an unfavorable light and discouraged Americans from investing in securities. Some legislators and administrators believe that tighter regulations of mergers and takeovers are needed to restore public confidence in Wall Street.

REVIEWING ECONOMIC PRINCIPLES

---

1. Write sentences defining each of the following economic terms:
   a. deregulation; b. friendly merger; c. takeover
2. Explain why the airline industry is a good example of the benefits and hardships brought about by the easing of government regulation of business.
3. What was the effect of the 1981 tax cuts sponsored by the Reagan administration?
4. What are the major provisions of the tax reform legislation of 1986?
5. In what way were some of the stock dealings of the 1980s a "scandal?"
6. **Critical Thinking: Summarizing Information.** Explain in a paragraph how an unfriendly merger is carried out.

SUMMARY OF
IMPORTANT PRINCIPLES

1

- Eighty percent of American workers are now engaged in the service sector of the American economy. Because so many Americans hold jobs in the service sector, the United States now has a service economy.
- Among the recent changes in the American economy have been the rapid growth of the number of white-collar and service workers, the increase in the number of women in the work force, and the emphasis on higher education and vocational and specialized training.
- With the growth in the size of the white-collar work force has come a decline in labor union membership. Only 1 out of 5 American workers now belong to labor unions, and, of these, a majority work at white-collar jobs.
- One reason for the decline in the size of the blue-collar work force is that human workers are being replaced by robots, or mechanical workers, in many industries. Another reason is the increase in the amount of goods imported from countries where labor costs are lower and the practice of many American businesses of moving their manufacturing and assembly operations to such countries.
- Women now make up 44 percent of the American work force, and they work in an increasing number of fields that were until recently almost entirely dominated by men.
- Because of the need for better educated workers, more and more Americans are attending college, seeking advanced degrees, and receiving vocational and technical training.
- In agriculture, farm output has increased enormously in recent years, and large corporations are becoming involved in agricultural operation. The practice of large corporations operating farms has become known as agribusiness.
- In recent years, many manufacturing and other industries have moved their operations from the Frostbelt of the Northeast and Midwest to the Sunbelt of the South and Southwest.

2

- With more information available and faster and easier to obtain, the United States has been transformed into an information society. The rapidly expanding technology in the computer and telecommunications fields is the main reason for the information revolution.

3

- Since the 1970s the federal government has been carrying out a policy of deregulation under which government regulation of industry has been eased. Deregulation has brought benefits to some parts of the economy and hardship to others.
- The Reagan administration sponsored a series of cuts in the federal income tax rates to spur the country's economic growth. Such growth did occur, but at a slower rate than forecast.
- In 1986, a major change was made in the income tax structure that redistributed income for the nation's taxpayers and eliminated many tax benefits.
- The 1980s saw a large number of corporate mergers and takeovers, by which publicly held companies obtained control of other companies.

Putting Economics to Work

SUPPLY AND DEMAND: SERVICE WORKERS

Charles Matthews is the owner of a convenience store in Concord, California, a suburb of Oakland and San Francisco. His store does a brisk business, but like many others in service industries, Charles has a major problem filling entry-level positions. Charles cannot find enough workers willing to take a low-paying job requiring few skills. The minimum wage has been frozen at $3.35 an hour since 1981. After that time inflation has caused the real value of the dollar to decline 18%. As a result, teens, women and others who are looking for jobs are exploring other options like staying in school longer or returning to school.

Charles has begun to research possible solutions to his problem. He has decided that he has several options that will help solve his worker scarcity problem. He realizes that he may have to raise wages in order to attract workers. He is fearful of getting into a "bidding war" with competitors, but believes higher wages will solve his problem.

Charles has also contacted local retirement groups in the hopes of attracting capable retirees who may want to work part-time and who are less likely to leave for a better job.

In addition, Charles is considering hiring mothers with young children who would like to work but cannot pay for child care. He would reimberse them for a portion of their day-care costs.

Each of these options involves costs higher than he presently has, but Charles must fill positions soon or his store will begin to lose money.

1. What do you think Charles should do to solve his worker scarcity problem?
2. What are other possible solutions to Charles' problem would you recommend?
3. Why do you think scarcity for such jobs exists and what do you predict for the future in service industries?

Readings in Economics

A RUST BELT CITY SHINES AGAIN
Skill: Applying Information

The shift in America from a manufacturing to a service economy has created a "rust belt" of once-prosperous industrial cities that are now facing hard times because of factory shutdowns and high unemployment levels. The following reading discusses the successful efforts of one such city, Fort Wayne, Indiana, to survive and prosper.

Even among Rust Belt cities devastated by the recession and the decline of heavy manufacturing, Fort Wayne, Indiana, seemed in 1982 to be down on its luck. In March, a once-in-a-century flood swept the city's downtown, which in any case had pretty well fallen apart. In the fall, International Harvester, Fort Wayne's biggest employer and the company generations of Fort Wayners had counted on for permanent and well-paid employment, announced it was shutting down its truck-building operations. . . . By February 1983, unemployment in Fort Wayne peaked at 14.5%, vs. a U.S. average of 11.3%.

Since those dismal days, Fort Wayne, whose metropolitan area comprises three counties with a population of 350,000, has mounted such a strong economic recovery that unemployment, now 5.7%, is 1.3 percentage points below the national average. Fort Wayne has proved that being an industrial city in the Rust Belt is not an incurable disease. . . .

In December, Fort Wayne will crown its job-hunting campaign when General Motors starts making pickup trucks at a new $500 million plant. The highly automated plant, GM's most modern for the moment, will employ 3,000 people, mostly workers brought in from GM sites elsewhere. Their paychecks will add fuel to the local economy, creating an estimated 3,500 additional jobs. Burlington Air Express, the second-largest air freight service in the U.S., last year made Fort Wayne its national hub. The city has also persuaded companies long established in the area, such as GE, ITT, and Magnavox, to expand rather than cut their work forces to pull out.

Instead of letting Fort Wayne lie down and die in 1982, politicians, businessmen, labor leaders, philanthopists, and many ordinary citizens responded with a single-minded drive to make the city well again. . . .

Winfield Moses, Jr., a pudgy, cheerful young homebuilder with a rich mop of dark hair, became the city's chief cheerleader and salesman after he was elected mayor in 1979. Says Moses: "Essentially, we buy jobs, just as you buy any product." Fort Wayne buys jobs with low- interest financing, tax abatements, grants, gifts, job training, and city amenities. . . . Other cities pitch such attractions, but Fort Wayne does it so wholeheartedly, and with such close cooperation between city officials and business, that the results are spectacular. . . .

1. What actions were taken that changed Fort Wayne, Indiana, from a city of despair to one of prosperity?
2. Imagine that you serve on an Industrial Development Committee of the Chamber of Commerce in a city similar to Fort Wayne, Indiana. What steps would you propose to avoid a severe economic downturn in the city? What steps would you take if one should occur?

Main, Jeremy, "A Rust Belt City Takes on a Shine." *Fortune*, November 10, 1986, pp. 116-128.

THE COMPUTER REVOLUTION
Skill: Sequencing Information

The communications revolution and the growth of our "information society" in the 20th century would have been inconceivable without the development of a singular piece of equipment: the computer. This reading gives a brief history of the computer.

Most Americans encountered the computer only in the 1970s and 1980s, but some of its basic principles date back to the seventeenth century when the great French philosopher, Pascal, devised the first machine that could multiply as well as add. At about the same time a mathematician, John

Napier, invented logarithms that allowed complex figures to be adapted easily to computer machines. The next key step occurred two centuries later when an eccentric British inventor, Charles Babbage . . . spent forty years building a huge . . . machine that contained nearly all the main features of the modern computer. It could even be programmed.

Americans then stepped in. . . .

Important scientific innovations began in the 1940s and were spurred on by U.S. military needs in the early Cold War years. . . . Sperry-Rand Corporation's UNIVAC of 1951 first used modern programming, including magnetic tape instead of punched cards. . . .

American scientists were now making breathtaking discoveries. In 1947 researchers at Bell Telephone Laboratories had developed the transistor. . . . Within a decade transistors were being printed on silicon pieces to become "microchips," or integrated circuits for computers. In the early 1970s engineers succeeded in putting the machine's entire processing unit on a single silicon chip. The chip thus became a "microprocessor." . . .

In the early 1980s small, pioneering businesses, led by Apple, Hewlett-Packard, and only later by IBM, developed desk-top-size computers that cost under $1000 and could be used in the home or office. Experts estimated that by 1990 offices would have more computers than typewriters. The American industrial revolution had thus come full circle. The single craftsman in his eighteenth-century cottage had become the centralized giant corporation producing iron, steel, and automobiles in the early 1900s. But now, as the twentieth century came to a close, the "electronic cottage" . . . created new possibilities for decentralization and individual enterprise.

1. Prepare a time line showing the historical development of the computer.
2. What effect do you predict the computer revolution will have on American society?

From *The American Century: A History of the United States Since the 1890s*, 3rd Edition, by Walter LaFeber, Richard Polenberg, and Nancy Woloch. Copyright © 1975, 1979, 1986 by Newbery Award Records, Inc. Reprinted by permission of Alfred A. Knopf, Inc.

THE "PRIVATIZATION" OF PUBLIC SERVICES

Skill: Explaining Information

 **The following reading discusses a proposal to allow private firms to administer public services as one way to cut federal spending.**

There has been talk lately that the U.S. Postal Service, the Federal Housing Administration, the Veterans Administration hospital system and the federal power marketing administrations might be better sent off into the private sector. But . . . this is mostly talk so far as Washington, D.C., is concerned. . . .

Horner [director of the Office of Personnel Management] says that there are about 600,000 federal jobs—in data processing, laundry, loan processing and vehicle maintenance, to name a few—that are "purely commercial in nature."

Horner would like to eliminate these federal jobs and hire out the services privately, at a net savings, she says, of around $4 billion a year. As a step in that direction, in August Horner unveiled her Federal Employment Direct Corporate Ownership Opportunity Plan [Fed Co-op]. . . .

Under Fed Co-op, . . . separate companies would be created by private firms to undertake many services now provided by public employees. . . . The firms would be required to offer jobs to displaced federal workers and offer them equity interest of up to 49%. . . .

As an incentive, the private firms would receive three-year . . . contracts, at the government's current cost to perform the service. . . .

But don't hold your breath for Fed Co-op. Among the . . . barriers are laws proscribing various levels of federal government from contracting out services. Veterans Administration hospitals... cannot by law contract out custodial services.

1. What government services might be provided more economically by the private sector?
2. What obstacles exist that may prevent a shift from the public to the private sector?

Heins, John, "Government Is on the Defensive." Excerpted by permission of *Forbes* magazine, December 15, 1986. © Forbes Inc., 1986.

PRACTICING YOUR SPEAKING SKILLS: DEBATING

While using this textbook, you have practiced analyzing issues, summarizing ideas, classifying information, and the reaching of conclusions, among other skills. Another important skill, and one that you might not consider, is debating. The ability to focus upon a topic and defend a point of view related to that topic is central to the thinking process. Debating allows you to use research skills, analytical skills, speaking, and listening skills while exploring an economic issue. You may not realize it, but everytime you put together arguments to convince parents and friends of something point-by-point, you are using debating skills. A formal debate, however, is highly structured. The format below is one that is widely accepted.

- The First Affirmative Speech: This opening speech introduces the topic, states what the affirmative side intends to prove, and presents information to support their point of view. All points should be presented clearly and in an orderly fashion.

- The First Negative Speech: The opposing side refutes the major issues raised by the Affirmative. It then states its own position and tries to prove its points.

- Second Affirmative: Another member of the Affirmative team restates the main points presented by his or her partner, answers the Negative attack, and clearly states and explains details of the Affirmative plan. The speaker summarizes all points.

- Second Negative Speech: Another member of the opposition restates the main points presented by the partner, addresses the Affirmative attack, and summarizes the Negative case.

- Rebuttals: Both sides zero in on specific arguments of the opposition and attempt to disprove them, using evidence and logic. Each ends by summarizing their case.

Activity: Select a topic related to the chapter, and then form two-person debate teams. Research the topic with your partner. It might help you to practice before holding the debate. After the debate, listen to classroom evaluation.

VOCABULARY REVIEW

Write the definition in Column B that correctly defines each term in Column A.

Column A	Column B
1. satellites	a. workers belonging to labor unions
2. organized labor	b. large farm corporations
3. agribusiness	c. unwanted purchase of a corporation by another corporation or individual
4. takeover	d. manufacturers of heavy goods
5. smokestack industries	e. structures that orbit the earth relaying signals
6. service sector	f. part of the economy that provides services, help, and information
7. heavy industry	g. steel, coal, and other industries that make goods to be used by industries

PRACTICING YOUR ECONOMIC SKILLS

1. **Analyzing a Table.** The table on the next page shows whether employment has increased or decreased in 9 metropolitan areas during the past few years. Use the table to do the following exercise. **a.** In which of the two types of areas listed was the change in employment the greatest? **b.** the least?

Employment Changes in 9 Metropolitan Areas

Employment changes in central cities and surrounding suburban counties of nine metropolitan areas

	City	Suburbs
Atlanta	+10.2%	+22.6%
Chicago	+ 4.0%	+20.0%
Detroit	+ 2.1%	+14.4%
Washington	+ 3.4%	+17.1%
St. Louis	− 4.1%	+14.8%
San Francisco	+ 2.1%	+ 9.7%
Baltimore	+ 0.1%	+ 8.9%
Philadelphia	+ 0.2%	+ 8.5%
New York	+ 3.5%	+ 5.5%

Source: U.S. Dept. of Labor

2. **Applying Information.** Based on information in the text, what might possibly account for the changes in employment reflected in the table?

3. **Making a Policy-Decision Chart.** Suppose you are the mayor of one of the cities in the chart. You wish to attract new industries to the city in order to increase the population of the city. Decide what policy you would like to follow. Then draw a chart like the one on page 488 to help you decide what the trade-offs would be for that policy. **a.** What was your policy decision? **b.** What goal or goals does your policy promote? **c.** What goals were traded-off? **e.** What was the justification for the trade-off?

DISCUSSING ECONOMICS QUESTIONS

1. Many colleges and universities have changed their courses of study. Do you think the United States educational system is doing enough to meet the changes and challenges of the American economy? What other changes should be made?

2. Every year the number of women entering the work force increases. What has been the economic impact of this trend?

3. Several American industries are in the process of being deregulated. What are the economic goals of deregulation?

APPLYING CRITICAL THINKING SKILLS

1. **Doing Research.** Go to the library and read newspaper and business magazine reports of the AT&T break-up. Write a report explaining whether the American consumer did or did not benefit from the government intervention.

2. **Drawing Conclusions.** Obtain copies of an old IRS tax return form and a new one created by the Tax Reform Act of 1986. Compare the similarities and differences in the two forms. Then write a paragraph explaining what you think the long term effects of the changes will be.

3. **Gathering Information.** Go to the local Chamber of Commerce and find out which companies or institutions have job retraining programs. Ask what kinds of job retraining programs these are, how long most of them are for, and whether they are successful. Summarize your findings to share with the class.

4. **Preparing a Bulletin-Board Display.** From newspapers and magazines, collect illustrations that show aspects of the United States as an information society. Arrange your displays into groups for a bulletin-board display.

READINGS

Bagsby, Wesley. *Contemporary American Economic and Political Problems.* Chicago: Nelson-Hall, 1981.

Baily, Martin, and Okun, Arthur M. *Battle Against Unemployment and Inflation,* 3rd ed. New York: W.W. Norton and Co., 1983.

Swartz, Thomas R., and Bonello, Frank J. *Taking Sides: Clashing Views on Controversial Economic Issues.* Guilford, Conn: Dushkin, 1984.

Weiss, L.W., and Strickland, A.D. *Regulation: A Case Approach,* 2nd ed. New York: McGraw-Hill, 1982.

THE CONTROVERSY OVER THE NATIONAL DEBT

After you study this Issue, you will be able to evaluate the controversy surrounding the size of the national debt.

The size of the national debt has recently been an issue of growing concern to many Americans. Many individuals and public officials warn that the government is living far beyond its means. They point to large yearly budget deficits and a national debt of over $2 trillion as signs that something is terribly wrong with the way the country is being run. Such concern reached a high point in the early 1980s. At that time, many state legislatures, public officials, and private citizens began calling for a Constitutional amendment requiring a balanced federal budget. Many states already had laws requiring balanced annual budgets.

But is there really cause for such widespread alarm? Although there are good reasons for keeping government borrowing under control, much of the concern over the national debt comes from a number of myths, or misleading beliefs. These have to do with the risk of government bankruptcy, with the supposed burden the debt places on future generations, and with the growing size of the debt.

CAN THE GOVERNMENT GO BANKRUPT?

Opponents of a large public debt often worry that more and more deficit financing must in the end lead to financial disaster. After all, if an individual continues to spend more than he or she takes in as income, then bankruptcy is likely to be the eventual result.

The problem here is that what are good financial principles for an individual or business do not necessarily apply to government. The federal government is in a unique position. Unlike an individual or business, it has the ability to raise money through taxes. It can use these taxes to pay as much interest on its debt as necessary each year. The government will go bankrupt only when it loses its revenue-raising powers.

A second important difference between government and private borrowing involves paying off the debt. Most individuals dislike being in debt. They look forward to the day when they can pay back their creditors. The national debt, however, never has to be paid off. It can be, and indeed is, refinanced as it comes due. That is, when a bond reaches maturity, it is retired with money raised by selling another bond. In this way, the debt can be carried from year to year, forever.

MAKING FUTURE GENERATIONS PAY

Another argument against the national debt is that deficit financing places the burden of current spending onto future generations. Actually, the debt that is passed to future generations is matched, for the most part, by federal securities that go with the debt. Future generations owe the national debt, but they owe it to themselves.

Even the interest paid on the national debt is not in itself a burden. It is true that interest on the debt must eventually be paid by taxation. But the taxes are paid by some Americans, and the interest is received by others. The interest on the debt then can be considered a redistribution of money and not a burden on all of society.

The Gross National Debt, 1940-1987

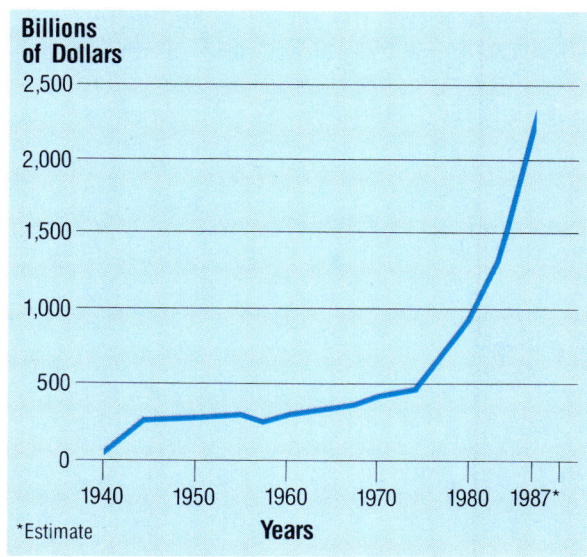

Billions of Dollars

*Estimate
Years

Source: *Historical Statistics of the U.S., Statistical Abstract of the U.S.,* Bureau of the Census

HOW BIG IS THE DEBT?

Finally, even the size of the debt is not as frightening as it seems at first glance. As shown in the first graph, the dollar amount of the national debt has indeed grown rapidly in recent years. The second graph, however, gives a different picture. Measured as a percentage of GNP, the national debt has in fact been decreasing since World War II until the early 1980s, when it started rising. The national debt has grown, but the economy has expanded at a more rapid rate. This should relieve much of the concern over what is sometimes called the nation's staggering debt load.

POSSIBLE REAL BURDENS OF THE DEBT

Does all this mean that Americans should not be concerned about the national debt? Not exactly.

Not all the national debt is owed to Americans. A small but growing portion is owed to individuals and businesses in other nations. Interest payments made on this portion of the debt are drained out of the economy. Nevertheless, when the federal government borrows resources from abroad, it increases the resources available to Americans at home. If these resources are invested wisely in such projects as dams and highways, future generations of Americans may still be better off.

A second and possibly more serious problem is the effect government borrowing can have on interest rates. As you learned in Chapter 16, the cost of credit is subject to the laws of supply and demand. The increased demand for credit that is caused by the government's borrowing can drive up interest rates. High interest rates can in turn slow the economy by discouraging consumer and

Gross National Debt as a Percentage of GNP, 1940-1987

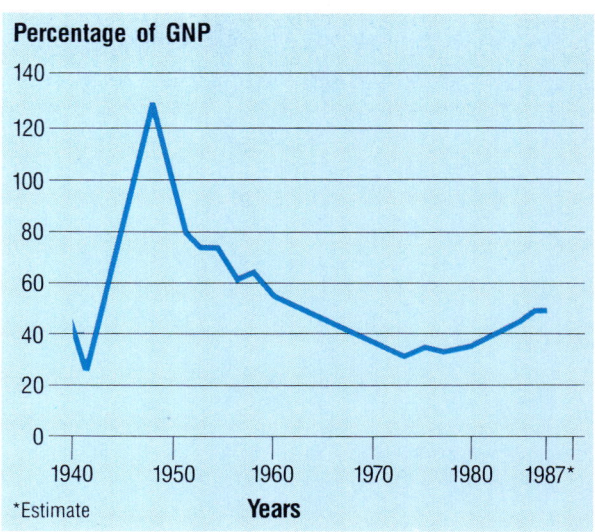

Percentage of GNP

*Estimate
Years

Source: *Historical Statistics of the U.S., Statistical Abstract of the U.S.,* Bureau of the Census

business borrowing. Less money spent on business expansion, the creation of new businesses, and on research for new techniques, inventions, or processes hamper the industrial development of the nation. It may also affect the nation's health since cuts in spending may mean fewer medicines, medical techniques, and medical services.

For these reasons, government officials do have reason to keep the federal government's deficit spending under control. At the same time, however, much of the alarm over the federal deficit grows out of a misunderstanding of what the national debt is and how it affects the economy.

Discussing Economic Questions

1. What possible steps could the Congress of the United States take to balance the federal budget and to reduce the national debt?
2. Why do you think Congress has found it difficult in recent years to take the steps needed to balance the federal budget and cut the national debt?
3. What do you think would happen to the economy of the United States if the federal government suddenly paid off all its debt? Do you think the federal government could pay off its high debt, already over $2 trillion by the middle of the 1980s?

UNIT 6

THE INTERNATIONAL SCENE

The United States economy does not operate in a vacuum. It has commercial and trade dealings with almost every other country in the world, and our economy depends to a great extent on our international trade. For this reason, what happens to economies other than our own has an impact on this nation. Such changes also affect you in your roles as employee, employer, consumer, saver, investor, and citizen. This unit describes world trade, economic systems other than market economies, and the problems and successes of developing countries in many parts of the world.

CHAPTER 20

The United States and all nations benefit from world trade. International trade makes it possible for businesses in many nations to sell those goods they can produce most efficiently.

IBM Argentina S A

TRADING WITH OTHER NATIONS

A discussion of the American economy would not be complete without describing the trading relations of the United States with other nations. This chapter describes why nations trade with each other, and how this trade is financed. For various reasons, nations sometimes restrict trade with all or some other countries. You will read about the arguments for and against free trade. The possible future of international trade is also explored. Learning Economic Skills describes how you would exchange currency on the foreign exchange market as a businessperson or a traveler.

CHAPTER OBJECTIVES After you study the sections of this chapter, you will be able to:

1 • explain why nations benefit from world trade.
  • describe how absolute advantage can result in specialization.
  • explain why a country would choose to produce a good in which it has only a comparative advantage in production.

2 • contrast fixed exchange rates with flexible exchange rates.
  ★ compute the prices of currencies on the foreign exchange market.

3 • identify four types of legal restrictions on world trade.

4 • state the arguments for and against free trade.
  • describe the possible future of world trade.

ECONOMICS VOCABULARY

import
export
absolute advantage
specialization
comparative advantage
foreign exchange market
fixed rate of exchange
devaluation
flexible rate of exchange
depreciation
balance of trade
tariff
revenue tariff
protective tariff
import quota
embargo
protectionist

What would happen if the United States could no longer buy goods from other countries or sell goods in return? Before you answer, you should be aware that the value of **imports**—goods bought from other countries for domestic, or one's own country's, use—is less than 10 percent of GNP in the United States. That seems small. However, there would be many inconveniences. For example, there would be no coffee, chocolate, or pepper. Consider also that over 60 percent of the radios, television sets, and motorcycles sold in the United States are imported. Many raw materials also come from foreign sources. More than 90 percent of the bauxite, from which aluminum is made, is imported.

But imports tell only half the story. Many American workers are employed in industries that export their products overseas. **Exports** are goods sold to other countries. For example, more than 11 percent of the nation's trucks and buses, and 40 percent of its engineering and scientific instruments are sold overseas. In addition, about one-third of the corn, half of the cotton, and almost two-thirds of the wheat produced in the United States are shipped abroad.

1 | THE BENEFITS FROM WORLD TRADE

Ask yourself as you read:
- Why do nations engage in world trade?
- What is the difference between absolute and comparative advantage?

Why does trade occur among nations? As you read in Chapter 8, a voluntary exchange among individuals is a transaction that benefits both parties. Trade among nations is based on this same concept of voluntary exchange.

DIFFERENCES AMONG NATIONS

Nations benefit through world trade because each differs in the type and amount of the factors of production it has available for use. The availability of natural resources is one of the most important of these differences. Some nations contain large amounts of a particular metal or mineral. For example, Zaïre contains two-thirds of the world's cobalt. Many Middle Eastern nations have abundant supplies of oil. Climate and location are other important natural factors determining a nation's output. Canada, because of its cold climate and heavy rainfall, has vast forests that can provide lumber for export. Being near rich fishing grounds makes fishing an important export industry for such countries as Norway and Peru.

The type and amount of labor and capital available to a nation are equally important. For example, much of the economy of the United States is based on high-technology production—the production of complex machinery such as computers and electronic equipment. Only the existence of a highly skilled labor force and of large amounts of capital—in the form of advanced equipment and machinery—makes this possible. Another nation having the same natural resources as the United States could have a very different economy.

ABSOLUTE ADVANTAGE AND SPECIALIZATION

The particular distribution of resources in a nation often gives it an absolute advantage in the production of one or more products. **Absolute advantage** is the ability of a country, using the same amount of resources as another country, to produce a particular product at less cost than the other country. For example, its tropical climate and inexpensive labor make Brazil ideally suited to growing bananas. Even using the same amount of land, labor, and capital, a country with a moderate climate, such as France, would produce far fewer bananas. Brazil, therefore, has an absolute advantage in banana production over France.

A nation often finds it profitable to produce and export a limited number of goods for which it is particularly suited. This is known as **specialization** (spesh-uhl-uh-ZAY-shuhn). It is because of specialization that certain countries are widely known for certain goods. For example, many people associate compact and subcompact cars with Japan.

COMPARATIVE ADVANTAGE

A nation does not have to have an absolute advantage in the production of a certain good to find it profitable to specialize and then to trade with other countries. As an example, consider two imaginary na-

What is the difference in dollars between the amount of goods the United States exports and the amount it imports? What makes up the largest percentage of exported goods? of imported goods?

Figure 20-1: UNITED STATES EXPORTS AND IMPORTS IN A RECENT YEAR (in billions of dollars)

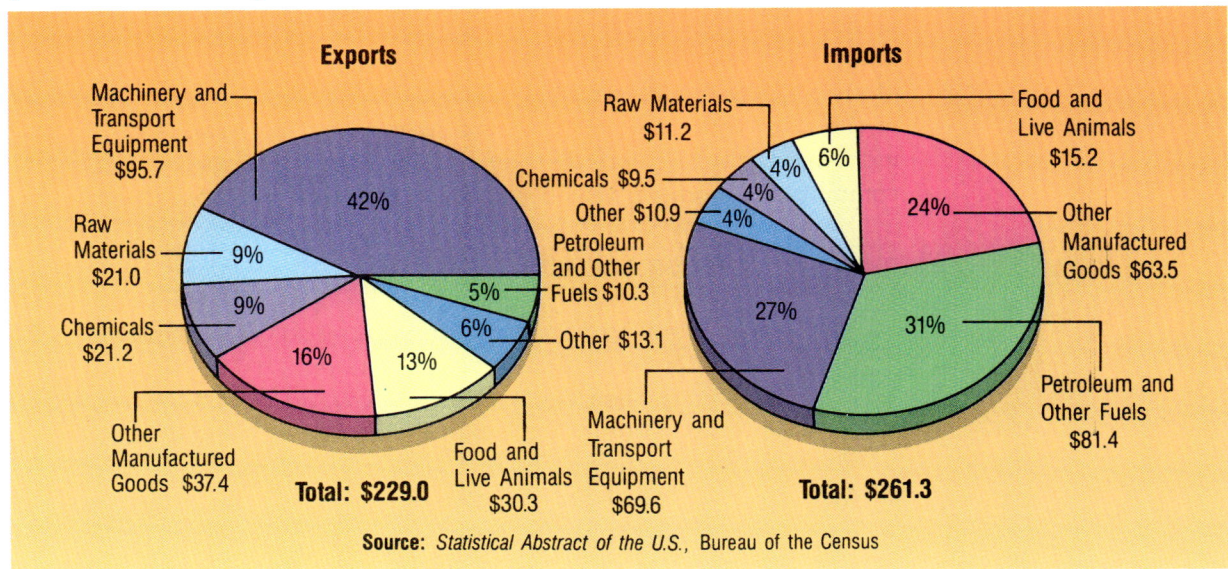

Source: *Statistical Abstract of the U.S.*, Bureau of the Census

tions, Country A and Country B. Assume that each country produces only soybeans and corn. Suppose that for some reason both countries one year decide to use all their resources to grow only soybeans. Country A produces 10 million bushels, while Country B produces only 8 million. The next year, suppose the two countries decide to grow only corn. Country A produces 50 million bushels, while Country B produces 25 million. According to this example, Country A has an absolute advantage in the production of both soybeans and corn. That is, with the same amount of input, Country A can produce more of either crop than Country B.

Does this mean that Country A will produce both crops and, therefore, have no reason to trade with Country B? No. Country A can produce slightly more soybeans than Country B. However, it can produce a great deal more corn. It would make little sense for Country A to take land, labor, and capital resources away from the efficient production of corn and use them for the less efficient production of soybeans. Country A's opportunity cost—what it gives up to get something else—would be less if it invested all its resources in the production of corn. It could export its surplus corn and use the money it receives to import soybeans from Country B.

Country A, then, is said to have a comparative advantage in corn production. **Comparative advantage** is the ability of a country to produce a product at a lower opportunity cost than another country. Despite Country A's absolute advantage in both areas, Country B still has a comparative advantage in soybean production. That is, Country B can produce about the same amount of soybeans as Country A, but only half as much corn. By using its resources to grow soybeans only, Country B is only giving up the relatively inefficient production of corn. Country B, then, has a lower opportunity cost for soybean production than does Country A. The best course for Country B is to produce the maximum amount of soybeans possible. It can then export soybeans to Country A and import corn. Both countries are best off because each concentrates on that production for which it is relatively the most efficient. Of course, in the real world, most trade is not carried out by nations or governments, but through private companies. Exceptions are nations with command economies, which you will read more about in Chapter 21.

REVIEWING ECONOMIC PRINCIPLES

1. Define the following economic terms: **a.** absolute advantage, **b.** specialization, **c.** comparative advantage.
2. Why do nations need and benefit from world trade?
3. Why do nations often find it profitable to produce and export goods for which they have an absolute advantage in production?
4. **Critical Thinking: Applying Concepts.** Invent a hypothetical, or imaginary, situation about the production capacities of two countries and use it to explain comparative advantage.

Champion of the World's Poor: Barbara Ward (1914–1981)

Born in England and educated in France, Germany, and England, Barbara Ward became one of the leading champions of the world's poor. She was an economist, lecturer, and writer who saw the growing gap between rich nations and poor nations as a basic problem of the mid 20th century. After World War II, the end of colonial rule made the problem most serious. The poorer nations that had been colonies of such countries as Great Britain and France were not prepared to govern themselves. In terms of their economies, their growth rates were much slower than those of the rich, or industrialized, nations.

Many of Ward's books are about the problems a nation faces in improving its standard of living. This is called economic development. She looked at the ways that industrialized nations such as the United States could help these poorer nations to develop their economies. Among her books are *The West at Bay* (1948), *Policy for the West* (1951), *Faith and Freedom* (1954), *The Interplay of East and West* (1957), *Five Ideas that Change the World* (1959), *India and the West* (1961), *Nationalism and Ideology* (1966), and *The Rich Nations and the Poor Nations* (1962).

Ward saw the world as one in which international trade is critical for the well-being of developing nations. Only by being able to export their products can they have the ability to import needed technology. But she always believed that international trade should be fair. She believed that unrestrained free enterprise allowed powerful rich nations to take advantage of poorer nations. As a result, Ward wanted a spirit of cooperation rather than competition in trading relationships. By cooperation, she meant giving better prices to poorer nations than would happen under a system of free enterprise. This is one way industrialized nations can help poorer nations with their economic development. Without a better balance of wealth between rich and poor nations, she believed that world peace was threatened.

In more recent years her concerns about developing nations widened to include a general concern for the environment. Her books on this topic include *Spaceship Earth* (1966), *The Lopsided World* (1968), and *Progress for a Small Planet* (1979). Ward coauthored *Only One Earth* (1972) with microbiologist Rene Dubois. In it, she stated that if energy use, food consumption, urbanization, and population growth continue at their present rates "the natural system of the planet upon which biological survival depends" will be changed "dangerously and perhaps irreversibly."

Ward called for a new vision of unity based on the realization that all nations and all people are interdependent. Such unity, she believed, is necessary for human survival. For her work, Ward was made a baroness by the British government in 1976.

1. Why did Ward believe that international trade was so crucial for developing nations?

2. What kind of international trade relationship did Ward favor? Why?

2 | FINANCING WORLD TRADE

Ask yourself as you read:
- What is a fixed rate of exchange?
- What is a flexible rate of exchange?

As you read in Chapter 15, the United States uses the dollar as its medium of exchange. But France uses francs; Great Britain, pounds; and Japan, yen. To engage in world trade, countries must have a way of exchanging one type of currency for another. After all, a Japanese bicycle manufacturer who exports bicycles to the United States probably does not want American dollars in payment. The firm needs Japanese currency to pay its workers and suppliers. Fortunately, international trade is so organized that individuals and businesses can easily and quickly convert one currency to another. This is done through **foreign exchange markets.** These are markets that deal in buying and selling foreign currency for businesses that want to import goods from other countries. Most of the trading of currency takes place through banks.

FIXED EXCHANGE RATE

From 1944 to the early 1970s, the foreign exchange market operated with a **fixed rate of exchange.** Under this system, a national government sets the value of its currency in relation to a single standard. Then, a government can establish equivalents between its currency and that of other countries.

equivalent (ih-KWIV-uh-luhnt): same in value, but in a different form

A fixed rate of exchange had some advantages for world trade. Importers and exporters knew exactly how much of a foreign currency they could purchase with their own nation's money. Also, the system allowed central banks to affect the level of exports and imports in their country by devaluing the currency. **Devaluation** means lowering a currency's value in relation to other currencies by government order.

Let's take a Japanese stereo system as an example. Suppose the stereo costs 20,000 yen. If the exchange rate is 200 yen to United States $1, an American wishing to buy a Japanese stereo would have to pay 20,000 yen divided by 200 yen, which is United States $100. If the dollar is devalued by one-half, $1 will only buy 100 yen worth. Therefore, the Japanese stereo costing 20,000 yen will now cost an American $200 (20,000 yen divided by 100 yen = $200.)

However, fixed exchange rates eventually proved impractical. The basic problem was the difficulty of fixing exchange rates in an international economic climate that was constantly changing. Suppose one nation such as the United States suffered from high inflation and a trading partner such as Japan did not. Then American goods would become very costly for the Japanese to buy. Since the price of Japanese goods would not be rising, Americans could use their inflated or "cheaper," dollars to buy more Japanese products. The United States would be importing huge quantities of goods but exporting little to Japan.

FLEXIBLE EXCHANGE RATE

The solution arrived at by most of the world's nations was the **flexible rate of exchange.** Under this arrangement, the forces of supply and demand are allowed to set the price of various currencies. With flexible rates, a currency's price may change, or float, up or down a little each day. For example, Japanese currency might be trading at 179.2 yen to the dollar on one day and 180.3 yen to the dollar on the next.

The forces actually determining exchange rates are the supply and demand of goods and services that can be bought with a particular currency. For example, suppose the amount of dollars wanted by Japanese exporters is greater than the supply of dollars provided by Americans who want to buy Japanese goods. Because the quantity demanded exceeds that supplied, the American dollar will become more expensive in relation to the yen. It will take more yen to equal $1. If the quantity of dollars supplied by American importers is more than the quantity demanded by Japanese exporters, the price of a dollar will become cheaper in relation to the yen. Fewer yen will equal $1.

When the price of a currency falls through the action of supply and demand, it is termed **depreciation.** As with devaluation, depreciation of a country's currency improves its competitive edge in trade. Suppose a pair of jeans costs $10 in the United States. If the exchange rate is five francs per $1, a French citizen must pay 50 francs for those jeans. But suppose the price of the dollar falls so that only 4 francs purchase $1. The French citizen would have to pay only 40 francs for the pair of American-made jeans.

Besides import-export transactions, political or economic instability within a country may encourage people to exchange their currency for a more stable currency. This is often the United States dollar. In that case, the value of the dollar would rise in relation to the other nation's currency. A country that is experiencing rapid inflation will find its currency falling in value in relation to other currencies. This happened to Brazil's and Mexico's money during the 1980s.

EXCHANGE RATES AND THE BALANCE OF TRADE

The rate at which a currency is being exchanged can have an important effect on a nation's balance of trade. The **balance of trade** is the difference between the value of a nation's exports and its imports. If a nation's currency depreciates, the nation will likely export more goods as its products become cheaper to other nations. If a nation's currency increases in value, or price, the amount of its exports will drop.

When the value of goods leaving a nation exceeds the value of those coming in, a positive balance of trade is said to exist. In this case, the nation is bringing in more money as payments for goods than it is paying out. A negative balance of trade exists when the value of goods coming into a country is greater than the value of those going out. This is also called a trade deficit. As you can see from Figure 20-2, the United States often has had a negative balance of trade.

Businesses and individuals can buy and sell the currencies they need to import goods from other countries. How are these exchange rates determined?

Learning Economic Skills | EXCHANGING FOREIGN CURRENCY

As transportation costs decrease and communications systems become better, people are finding it easier to travel to and trade with other nations. What may have seemed exotic, or unusual, a few years ago—a business trip to Saudi Arabia, for example—is now routine for a growing number of people. If you have not already traveled to other nations, you may sometime in the future. When you do, you will need to exchange your dollars for the currency of other nations.

Foreign currencies, like other items, have a price. At a foreign exchange market such as a bank, you will find posted the quotation, or rate of exchange, between the dollar and most other currencies. You can also find quotations for many foreign currencies in the *Wall Street Journal* and in other major daily newspapers. Each exchange rate is expressed in two ways—the dollar value per unit of foreign currency and the units of currency per dollar. The following table shows a typical day's quotations. On Wednesday, for example, a West German deutsche mark was worth a little more than 50 cents. If you wanted 500 marks, you would have to pay $253.55 (.5067 × 500 = 205.75). Expressed the other way, each dollar is worth 1.97 West German deutsche marks. If a West German wanted to purchase $400, he or she would need to pay 972 marks (1.97 × 400 = 788).

Notice that the exchange rates are given for two days. Because exchange rates are flexible, the value of currencies may rise and fall daily. For example, on Tuesday the British pound was worth $1.4375, but by Wednesday its value had risen to $1.4390. If the value of the pound rises in terms of dollars, then the value of the dollar in terms of pounds must fall. One dollar was worth .6957 British pounds on Tuesday, but only .6949 pounds on Wednesday. Although this change in the value of money may seem small, it can be an important factor in international business deals involving large sums of money.

Practicing Your Skills

Use the exchange rates shown on the table for Wednesday to answer the following questions.

1. The bicycle you wish to import costs 18,985 Japanese yen. How many American dollars will buy the yen you need?
2. You buy a pair of shoes in Italy for 34,200 lire. How much have you spent in United States dollars?
3. If you were vacationing in France and wished to exchange a $50 traveler's check, how many francs would you receive?
4. How many cruzados would it cost a Brazilian to buy a U.S.-made car worth $7,600?

Foreign Exchange Rates for a Recent Year

	Dollar Value Per Unit of Foreign Currency		Units of Currency Per Dollar	
	Wed.	Tues.	Wed.	Tues.
Australia (Dollar)	.6364	.6364	1.5713	1.5713
Brazil (Cruzado)	.0726	.0726	13.77	13.77
Britain (Pound)	1.4390	1.4375	.6949	.6957
Canada (Dollar)	.7196	.7202	1.3896	1.3885
Egypt (Pound)	.7353	.7353	1.3600	1.3600
France (Franc)	.1547	.1547	6.4645	6.4660
Greece (Drachma)	.0075	.0075	133.00	133.30
Hong Kong (Dollar)	.1284	.1282	7.7900	7.7980
India (Rupee)	.0781	.0783	12.800	12.7700
Israel (Shekel)	.6783	.6777	1.4743	1.4755
Italy (Lira)	.000732	.000732	1366.50	1366.00
Japan (Yen)	.006489	.006501	154.10	153.82
Mexico (Peso)	.001271	.001267	787.00	789.00
Norway (Krone)	.1377	.1378	7.2630	7.2570
Saudi Arabia (Riyal)	.2670	.2667	3.7450	3.7498
Spain (Peseta)	.007639	.007637	130.60	130.95
West Germany (Mark)	.5067	.5066	1.9735	1.9740

Figure 20-2: UNITED STATES BALANCE OF TRADE, 1966-1986

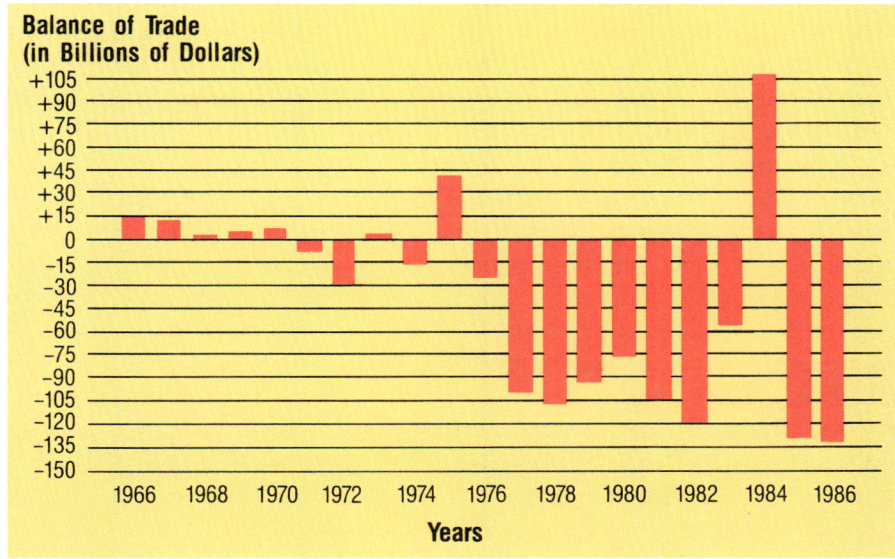

According to this graph, the United States has had trade deficits in all but three years since 1971. Based on Figure 20-1, how might the type of goods the United States imports and exports account for these deficits?

REVIEWING ECONOMIC PRINCIPLES

1. Write a sentence defining each of the following economic terms: **a.** foreign exchange markets, **b.** devaluation, **c.** depreciation, **d.** balance of trade.
2. **a.** How is the value of currency determined under the fixed rate of exchange system? **b.** Why did most countries abandon the fixed rate of exchange system in the 1970s?
3. **a.** How is the value of currency determined under a flexible rate of exchange system? **b.** Using an example, explain in a paragraph how the flexible rate of exchange works.
4. **Critical Thinking: Analyzing Concepts.** If the value of the dollar falls in relation to other countries, what would you expect to happen to American exports?

3 | RESTRICTIONS ON WORLD TRADE

Ask yourself as you read:
- What are the most common barriers that nations set to limit trade?
- What are some of the well-known tariffs that the United States has levied during its history?

The difficulties caused by different currencies are only one problem of world trade. Naturally occurring barriers involve the differences in languages and cultures between various trading partners. Some restrictions, however, are set up on purpose to discourage or limit trade. Three major barriers to world trade are: 1. tariffs, 2. quotas, and 3. embargoes.

The most commonly used barrier to free trade is the **tariff,** a tax on imports. A **revenue tariff** is one used primarily to raise income without restricting imports. Although tariffs today account for less than 2 percent of the federal government's income, they were the major source of federal funding until the early 1900s.

A **protective tariff** is one designed to raise the cost of imported goods and thereby protect domestic producers. As you learned from the law of demand, the quantity demanded of an item falls as the price rises. Higher prices for foreign goods because of tariffs mean that Americans will buy more domestic goods and fewer goods from abroad. As Figure 20-3 shows, tariff rates have been as high as 62 percent of the value of the imported goods. Tariffs are much lower today but are still used to protect such industries as textiles from foreign competition.

An alternative method for restricting imports is the quota system. An **import quota** is a restriction on the value of or the number of units of a particular good that can be brought into the country. The United States has placed quotas on imports of sugar, shoes, shirts, and cloth.

An **embargo** is a complete restriction on the import or export of a particular good. Often embargoes are enacted for political reasons. For example, in 1980 President Jimmy Carter ordered a halt of all grain sales to the Soviet Union. This was in response to Soviet intervention in Afghanistan. President Ronald Reagan lifted the grain embargo in 1981. However, he placed new restrictions on the sale to the Soviets of certain high-technology equipment such as computers. The United States has

The controversy over tariff rates has played a major role in United States history. For example, the Tariff of Abominations caused some Southerners to call for secession 40 years before the Civil War.

Figure 20-3: TARIFF RATES IN THE UNITED STATES, 1820-1986

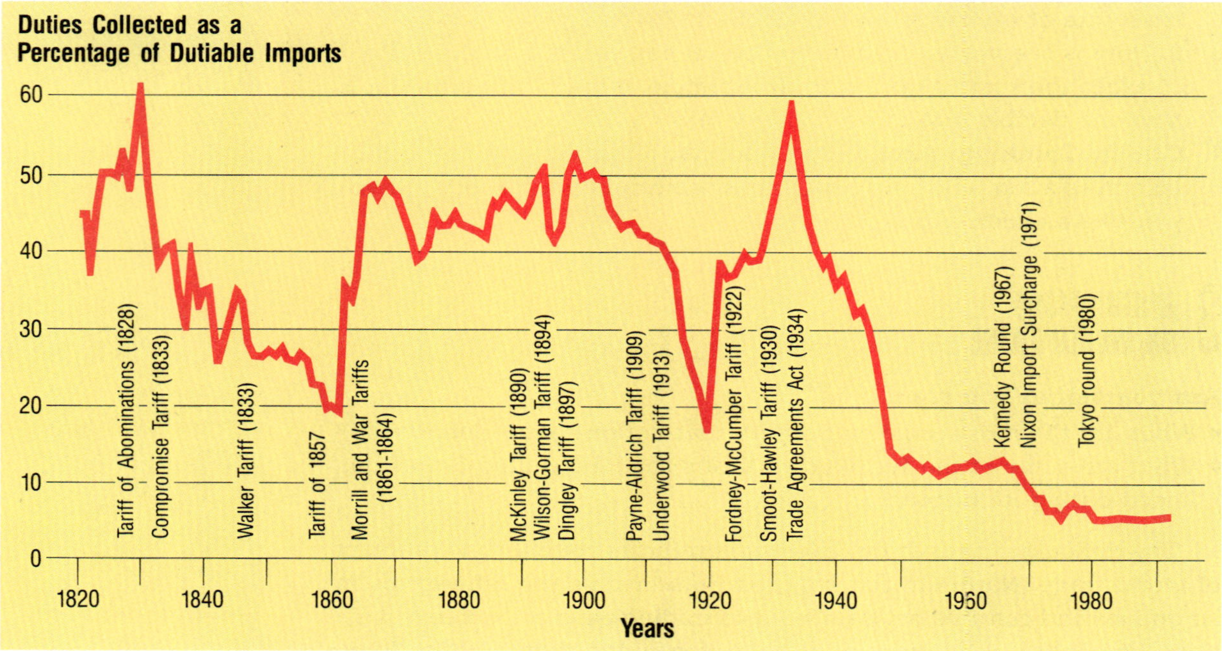

Duties Collected as a Percentage of Dutiable Imports

Labels: Tariff of Abominations (1828), Compromise Tariff (1833), Walker Tariff (1833), Tariff of 1857, Morrill and War Tariffs (1861-1864), McKinley Tariff (1890), Wilson-Gorman Tariff (1894), Dingley Tariff (1897), Payne-Aldrich Tariff (1909), Underwood Tariff (1913), Fordney-McCumber Tariff (1922), Smoot-Hawley Tariff (1930), Trade Agreements Act (1934), Kennedy Round (1967), Nixon Import Surcharge (1971), Tokyo round (1980)

Years

Source: *Statistical Abstract of the U.S., Historical Statistics of the U.S.,* Bureau of the Census

also ordered embargoes on goods from certain countries. In 1986, Congress passed a limited embargo on trade with South Africa.

REVIEWING ECONOMIC PRINCIPLES

1. What is a tariff?
2. What two natural barriers occur between international trading partners?
3. What are the reasons for enacting each of the following: **a.** revenue tariff? **b.** protective tariff? **c.** import quota? **d.** embargo?
4. According to Figure 20-3, **a.** what was the highest tariff enacted? **b.** what was the second highest tariff? **c.** For each, on what percentage of the dutiable imports were the duties collected?
5. **Critical Thinking: Inferring the Main Idea.** From 1860 to about 1915 the United States was developing into a major industrial nation. Why do you think tariffs were high during that time?

4 | ARGUMENTS AGAINST AND FOR FREE TRADE

Ask yourself as you read:
- Why are protectionists against free trade?
- What are the major international trade agreements of the 1900s?

Since World War II, the trend has been toward relaxing barriers to world trade. The pros and cons of trade restrictions are still often the subject of intense public debate. Arguments against free trade usually come under the headings of: 1. job security, 2. protection of infant industries, and 3. a strong national defense.

Under job security, **protectionists**—opponents of relaxing trade restrictions—argue that many domestic workers will be unemployed if foreign competitors are allowed to sell goods at lower prices than American firms. In the 1980s this happened in the steel industry in the United States. Competition from German and Japanese steel producers caused large layoffs at domestic steel mills.

A second argument claims that tariffs and quotas are needed as temporary protection for infant industries. These are industries that are new and developing. Protectionists believe that a young industry such as video cameras can eventually become efficient enough to compete in the world market only if foreign competition is restricted for a time.

Finally, many opponents of free trade believe that certain industries such as petroleum must be protected in the interests of national defense. They fear that the United States might be deprived of, or kept from having, critical goods in wartime if these industries were weakened because of foreign competition.

deprive (di-PRYV): to keep from having

Arguments for free trade usually involve the benefits of world specialization and the damage trade restrictions may cause a nation's export industries. Advocates of free trade claim protection from foreign competition removes incentives to improve technology and production methods. This only raises prices for everyone and unfairly protects inefficient producers. With free trade, each nation would be encouraged to specialize in those areas in which it is most efficient. Under this system, total world output would be higher than if each nation continued producing many goods, regardless of whether it did so efficiently.

Free trade advocates also note that any attempt to restrict imports into the United States necessarily hurts export industries. The fewer goods the United States imports, the less American money there is available outside the country to purchase United States exports. Also, import restrictions encourage other nations to impose similar trade barriers. When other nations impose similar trade barriers against the United States, American exporting industries lose jobs.

INTERNATIONAL TRADE AGREEMENTS

As far back as the late 1920s, international attempts have been made to reduce tariffs. In 1934, Congress passed the Reciprocal Trade Agreements Act. This law gave the President the authority to form bilateral, or two-party, agreements to reduce tariffs with other nations.

If the world's trading partners follow the trend begun after World War II, trade restrictions will continue to relax. After World War II, the world's numerous bilateral trade agreements were brought together in the General Agreement on Tariffs and Trade (GATT). The agreement was signed by 23 nations in 1947. Today member nations number more than 80. Under GATT, countries meet periodically to negotiate tariff reductions that are mutually advantageous to all members. For example, the agreements reached at the Tokyo Round, or meeting, in 1980 aimed to reduce the average level of tariffs by 30 percent during the 1980s. In the late 1980s, the Uruguay Round of tariff reductions started.

In addition to GATT, several regions in the world have their own tariff agreements. The largest is the European Economic Community (EEC), often called the European Common Market. It has eliminated almost all trade restrictions on the movement of goods between its 10 member countries. Similar agreements operate in the Central American Common Market and the West-African Economic Community.

REVIEWING ECONOMIC PRINCIPLES

1. List three arguments against and two arguments for free trade.
2. With which point of view do you generally agree? You may hold some other view. Explain your reasons in a paragraph.
3. When are opponents of free trade most likely to be listened to by their governments?
4. **Critical Thinking: Inferring the Main Idea.** Based on what you have read, what is the goal behind reducing tariffs in world trade? You will have to infer the answer.

SUMMARY OF
IMPORTANT PRINCIPLES

1
- Nations benefit from world trade because each nation differs in the type and amount of the factors of production it has available for use.
- Absolute advantage is the ability of a country, using the same amount of resources as another country, to produce more of a particular good than the other country.
- As long as a country has a comparative advantage in at least one product, it will be advantageous for that country to specialize in the production of that good. The country can then trade with other countries to obtain other goods it needs.

2
- With a fixed rate of exchange, national governments set the value of their currencies in relation to a single standard. With a flexible rate of exchange, the forces of supply and demand for goods set the prices of currencies. As a result, a currency's price may change up or down a little each day.
- Understanding how foreign currency is exchanged is important in a world of increasing international trade and travel.

3
- Four legal restrictions on world trade are: revenue tariffs, protective tariffs, import quotas, and embargoes.

4
- Arguments against free trade come under the headings of job security, protection of infant industries, and a strong national defense. Arguments for free trade involve the benefits of world specialization and the damage trade restrictions cause to a nation's export industries.
- If the world's trading partners follow the trend begun after World War II, trade restrictions will continue to relax. However, during times of economic downturn, critics of free trade will continue to press for protectionism.
- Since the late 1920s, there have been many international attempts to reduce tariffs. In 1934, the Reciprocal Trade Agreements Act gave the President the authority to enter into bilateral trade agreements. Twenty-three nations signed the General Agreement on Tariffs and Trade (GATT) in 1947. Since then, the number of members has increased to 80. One of the goals of GATT is to reduce tariffs. In 1980, GATT members agreed at the Tokyo Round to reduce the average level of tariffs by 30 percent during the 1980s.
- Several world regions have their own tariff agreements. The most important of these are the European Economic Community (EEC), often called the Common Market, the Central African Common Market, and the West-African Economic Community. These trade communities have eliminated almost all trade restrictions on the movement of goods among its members.

Putting Economics to Work

SUPPLY AND DEMAND: IMPORTING GOODS

Anne Dericho and a friend have been running a clothes boutique in their home town of San Jose, California, for a number of years. The shop is popular as a place to find inexpensive, out-of-the-ordinary clothes. Every summer, Anne goes to France, where she orders well-made, stylish dresses from a small dressmaking shop on the outskirts of Paris. Even with shipping costs and import duties, the dresses can be priced reasonably. As a result, Ann and her partner are able to sell almost all of the dresses they import and make a reasonable profit.

This year there is a problem. Ann had placed her dress order six months ago, when United States $1.00 could purchase 10 French francs. She had ordered 100 dresses at about 400 francs each. At the exchange rate of $1.00 for 10 francs, the price per dress came to $40.00. Shipping costs and duties added another $10.00, making Ann's cost about $50.00 a dress. Ann has always marked the dresses up 100 percent for a sale price of $100.00. This may sound like a lot of money, but the boutique's well-to-do clients have considered the price worth it for dresses that are chic, stylish, and well-made.

Ann's problem has arisen because the value of the dollar has fallen in value against the French franc since she placed her order. Now she can only get 5 French francs for $1.00. The dresses still cost about 400 francs a dress, but the cost in dollars has risen from $40.00 to $80.00. Ann will have to raise her prices accordingly, and she is not sure that her clients will buy at such high prices. Therefore, Ann and her friend are hesitating about having the order filled. They are also considering cancelling for now.

1. If the French franc falls to half its value in dollars, will the price that Anne has to pay for the dresses rise or fall? Why?
2. What do you think will happen to the importation of French dresses into the United States if the value of the dollar continues to fall against the French franc? Why?

CHANGES IN COMPARATIVE ADVANTAGE

Skill: Contrasting Information

 With the opening of the 20th century, the United States' comparative advantage changed from the production of certain goods to the production of different ones. Economist F. W. Taussig discusses this change in the following reading.

What, now, are the causes of industrial effectiveness and comparative advantage? To put the question in other words, what are the industries in which a comparative advantage is likely to appear? And, more particularly, in which directions is the labor of the people of the United States likely to be applied with special effectiveness?

The more common answer has been, in agriculture. A new country, with abundance of fertile land, finds its labor most effective in the extractive industries. Hence the United States long were steady exporters of wheat, meat products, cotton. Wheat is specially adapted to extensive culture, and is easily transportable; it is the commodity for which nature gives to a new country in the temperate zone a clear comparative advantage. The international trade of the United States was long determined chiefly by the country's special advantages for the production of wheat and similar agricultural staples.

It should be noted, however, that not only the natural resources told, but the manner in which they were used. From the first, inventiveness and ingenuity were shown. The United States early became the great country of agricultural machinery. . . .

That the situation began to change with the opening of the twentieth century does not need to be explained at length. The period of limitless free land was then passed, and with it the possibility of increasing agricultural production under the specially advantageous conditions of new countries. For one great agricultural article—cotton—the comparative advantage of the country indeed maintained itself, and its exports continued to play a great part in international trade. The exports of other agricultural products—wheat, corn, barley, meat products—have by no

means ceased, nor will they cease for some time. But they tend to decline. . . . Other articles grow in importance, such as copper, petroleum, iron and steel products, various manufactures. For some of these—copper, for example—the richness of our natural resources is doubtless of controlling importance. But the manner in which those natural resources are turned to account is in all cases important; and in many cases the comparative advantage of which the exports are proof rests not on the favor of nature at all, but solely on the better application of labor under conditions inherently no more promising than those of other countries.

1. How does Taussig explain the United States' comparative advantage over other countries with similar natural resources?
2. Contrast the areas in which you feel the United States enjoys a comparative advantage today with those of the 1950s described in the article.

Frank William Taussig, "The Principle of Comparative Advantage." *Selected Readings in Modern Economics.* Ed. by Asher Isaacs, C. W. McKee, and R. E. Slesinger. New York: Dryden Press, 1952.

THE TILTING BALANCE OF TRADE

Skill: Making Predictions

 One trend in the United States economy of the 1980s has been high trade deficits. Alfred E. Eckes, commissioner of the International Trade Commission, discusses this negative balance of trade and other changes in American world trade.

When I joined the International Trade Commission, which as you know is an independent agency charged with administering our import remedy laws, our trade deficit was $31 billion. That was 1981. In 1984, using the same statistical measure, the deficit was $111 billion. . . .

This year [1985] the trade deficit could be even larger, perhaps up 15 to 20 percent.

Deficits of this magnitude are unprecedented in world economic history. . . .

To appreciate fully the underlying trends, one must look at changing product patterns of trade.

Readings in Economics

Until several years ago the United States exported manufactured goods and imported raw materials and petroleum. Indeed, from the 1890s to 1971, the U.S. experienced a string of trade surpluses, brought about by exports of manufactured and capital goods. Our competitive edge in new products stirred concerns in Western Europe that they could not compete. In 1901, for example, a British writer complained that U.S. industry controlled every new industry created in the last 15 years. He wrote: "What are the chief new features in London life? They are, I take it, the telephone, a portable camera, the phonograph, the electric street car, the automobile, the typewriter, passenger lifts [elevators] in houses, and the multiplication of machine tools. In every one of these, save the petroleum automobile, the American maker is supreme; in several he is the monopolist." . . .

If an American writer were to make a similar survey in 1985, he would certainly note the supremacy of Japan in cameras, automobiles, typewriters, machine tools, telephones and other similar items on that list. I suspect it will not take 85 years for new Japans—Korea, Taiwan, China and Brazil among others—to replace Japan as the dominant low-cost supplier of standard and quality consumer items. In fact, it is already happening. . . .

In 1971, the longtime trade surplus disappeared, and a new pattern began to emerge—one in which the U.S. exports raw materials and imports manufactured products.

This gas station in Japan sells American gasoline, one of the few products Japan imports from the United States.

To an historian like myself, there is something ironic about this pattern. We export raw materials and agricultural products and import value-added products. Ironically, this is the same pattern of trade the U.S. had in the 18th century when we rebelled against the mercantilist systems of Europe.

1. If the same writer were writing this article today, what developments might he note in foreign nations' control of new industries?
2. What predictions can you make about the trade deficit of the United States in the world market?

Alfred E. Eckes, "International Trade in Turbulent Times." From a speech delivered in April 1985, Chicago. *Vital Speeches of the Day,* Vol. LI, No. 19, July 15, 1985.

RESTRICTING TRADE TO PROTECT DOMESTIC INDUSTRIES

Skill: Evaluating Information

Trade restrictions can protect manufacturers from competing with foreign firms. Adam Smith describes how such restrictions in England protected several British industries during the 18th century.

By restraining, either by high duties, or by absolute prohibitions, the importation of such goods from foreign countries as can be produced at home, the monopoly of the home market is more or less secured to the domestic industry employed in producing them. Thus the prohibition of importing either live cattle or salt provisions from foreign countries secures to the graziers [cattle grazers] of Great Britain the monopoly of the home market for butcher's meat. The high duties upon the importation of corn, which in times of moderate plenty amount to a prohibition, give a like advantage to the growers of that commodity. The prohibition of the importation of foreign woolens is equally favorable to the woolen manufacturers. The silk manufacture, though altogether employed upon foreign materials, has lately obtained the same advantage. The linen manufacture has not yet obtained it, but is making great strides towards it. Many other sorts of manufacturers have, in the same manner, obtained in Great Britain, either altogether or very nearly, a monopoly against their countrymen. The variety of goods of which the importation into Great Britain is prohibited, either absolutely or under certain circumstances, greatly exceeds what can easily be suspected by those who are not well acquainted with the laws of the customs.

That this monopoly of the home market frequently gives great encouragement to that particular species of industry which enjoys it, and frequently turns towards that employment a greater share of both the labor and stock of the society than would otherwise have gone to it, cannot be doubted. But whether it tends either to increase the general industry of the society, or to give it the most advantageous direction, is not, perhaps, altogether so evident.

1. What effect does the erection of trade barriers have on domestic producers? How might this affect the consumer?
2. What are some advantages and disadvantages of protectionism?

Adam Smith, *The Wealth of Nations*. Reprinted in *Readings in Introductory Economics*. John R. McKean and Ronald A. Wykstra. New York: Harper and Row, 1971.

FREE TRADE IS FAIR TRADE

*Skill: Identifying the Main Idea
and Supporting Details*

The Reagan administration has had a history of supporting free trade practices. In this speech by President Reagan, delivered in September 1985, the President explains why the United States supports free trade.

I'm pleased that the United States has played the critical role of insuring and promoting an open trading system since World War II, and I know that, if we ever faltered in the defense and promotion of the worldwide free trading system, that system will collapse, to the detriment of all.

But our role does not absolve [free] our trading partners from their major responsibility to support us in seeking more open, a more open trading system. No nation, even one as large and powerful as the United States can, by itself, insure a free trading system. All that we and others have done to provide for the free flow of goods and services and capital is based on cooperation. And our trading partners must join us in working to improve the system of trade that has contributed so much to economic growth and the security of our allies and of ourselves.

And may I say right here to the leaders of industry that my admiration for business in the United States is stronger than ever.

You know, sometimes in Washington there are some who seem to forget what the economy is all about. They give me reports saying that the economy does this and the economy will do that. They never talk about business. And somewhere along the way these folks in Washington have forgotten that the economy is business. Business creates new products and new services. Business creates jobs. Business creates prosperity for our communities and our nation as a whole. And business is the people that make it work. From the C.E.O. [chief executive officer] to the workers in the factories.

I know, too, that American business has never been afraid to compete. I know that, when a trading system follows the rules of free trade, when there is equal opportunity to compete, American business is as innovative, efficient, and competitive as any in the world. I also know that the American worker is as good and productive as any in the world.

And that's why, to make the international trading system work, all must abide by the rules. All must work to guarantee open markets. Above all else, free trade is, by definition, fair trade.

1. President Reagan states that for the international trading system to work, "all must abide by the rules." What are the rules to which he refers?
2. How does President Reagan equate the economy and business?

Ronald Reagan, "U.S. Trade Policy." From a speech delivered September 23, 1985, Washington, D.C. *Vital Speeches of the Day*, Vol. LII, No. 1., October 15, 1985.

20 | CHAPTER REVIEW

PRACTICING YOUR COMMUNICATION SKILLS: NEGOTIATION

International trade agreements, labor contracts, the federal budget—all are reached through negotiation. Negotiation is the settlement of a disagreement through discussion and compromise. A mediator is often chosen to help the parties settle their differences. The mediator has several responsibilities:

• to review each side's demands to make sure they are reasonable;
• to encourage the exchange of ideas and creative thinking;
• to suggest a compromise that is fair; there should be a balance between what each side gives up and what it gets in return;
• to remain impartial and open minded throughout the negotiations.

Activity: Choose an economic issue from the news and conduct mock negotiations. The class should be divided into two sides, with one student or a team of students appointed as mediator. Each side should select members to represent it at the negotiations. These representatives will present their demands and the reasons they feel they should be met. The representatives are responsible for reporting back to their groups. Each side will then vote on the compromises suggested by their representatives and the mediator.

VOCABULARY REVIEW

For each of the following definitions, write the letter of the term that correctly defines it.

a. absolute advantage
b. devaluation
c. depreciation
d. embargo
e. protectionist
f. balance of trade
g. comparative advantage

1. lowering of a currency's value in relation to other currencies _____
2. complete restriction on the import or export of a particular good _____
3. difference between the value of a nation's exports and its imports _____
4. ability of a nation to produce a product at a lower opportunity cost _____
5. drop of the price of a currency in response to supply and demand _____
6. ability of a country to use the same amount of resources as another to produce a product at less cost _____
7. one who opposes the relaxation of trade restrictions _____

PRACTICING YOUR ECONOMIC SKILLS

1. **Drawing a Bar Graph.** Use the following statistics to make a bar graph labeled "Exports from Selected Countries in a Recent Year." The statistics are: United States, $229; West Germany, $176; Japan, $152; Great Britain, $115; France, $101; USSR, $76. Dollar amounts are in billions.
2. **Calculating Percentages.** The total value of world exports for a year was $1,960 billion. What percentage of world exports did the following nations account for? **a.** France? **b.** West Germany? **c.** Japan? **d.** all six nations combined?
3. **Determining Price Advantages.** The table below contains information for three different products. For each product, you are given the price of a foreign product, the tariff on that product, and the price of a similar product produced in the United States. Decide whether the importation of each item would

	Price of Foreign Product	Tariff	Price of United States Product
Steel	$200	15%	$220
Wheat	60	10%	63
Shoes	35	10%	42

benefit American consumers.

4. **Drawing Production Possibility Graphs.**

a. Draw two graphs that show the production possibilities for the United States and West Germany of steel and wheat. On both graphs, show steel on the vertical axis and wheat on the horizontal axis. The plotting information is:

United States		West Germany	
Steel	Wheat	Steel	Wheat
400	0	300	0
300	100	200	100
200	200	100	200
100	300	0	300
0	400		

b. According to the graph of the United States, what would be the opportunity cost of 100 tons of wheat? 200 tons of steel?

c. For West Germany, what is the opportunity cost of 200 tons of steel? 100 tons of wheat?

d. Based on the graphs you have drawn, would trade for steel and wheat be advantageous between the United States and West Germany? Explain.

DISCUSSING ECONOMIC QUESTIONS

1. The Constitution forbids states the power to levy import duties. What problems do you think might arise if states were allowed to tax imports from other states and from foreign countries?

2. Based on what you have read in this chapter, what disadvantages in world trade might there be for a country whose currency has been devalued or has depreciated? Why?

3. Some economists believe that the high tariffs of the 1920s made the worldwide depression of the 1930s worse. Do you think tariffs might have contributed to the depression? Why? How? Consider the effect high tariffs have on the efficiency of world production.

4. What economic groups in a nation benefit most immediately from restrictions on international trade?

APPLYING CRITICAL THINKING SKILLS

1. **Summarizing Arguments.** Obtain a copy of Alexander Hamilton's *Report on Manufacturing* and summarize his argument for a protectionist tariff policy.

2. **Writing a Research Report.** For much of the history of the United States, tariffs have been a central issue in national politics. Choose one of the tariffs listed on Figure 20–3, and write a research report of four pages describing the tariff, its supporters and opponents, their arguments, and the outcome of the tariff.

3. **Gathering Information.** Clip articles from the newspaper for a week that involve world trade issues. The articles can be about the exchange rate, the United States trade deficit, or about specific markets or trade goods. Take notes to use as the basis of a class discussion.

READINGS

Institute for Contemporary Studies. *Tariffs, Quotas, and Trade: The Politics of Protectionism.* San Francisco: Institute for Contemporary Studies, 1979.

Johnson, E. B., Jr. "Foreign Policy Export Controls," *Department of State Bulletin,* June 1982, pp. 55–57.

Peterson, P. G. "Curing the American Export Malady." *Business Week,* 16 August 1982, p. 105.

Richardson, J. David. *Understanding International Economics: Theory and Practice.* Boston: Little, Brown, 1980.

Swartz, Thomas R., and Bonello, Frank J. *Taking Sides: Clashing Views on Controversial Economic Issues.* Guilford, Conn.: Dushkin, 1984.

CHAPTER 21

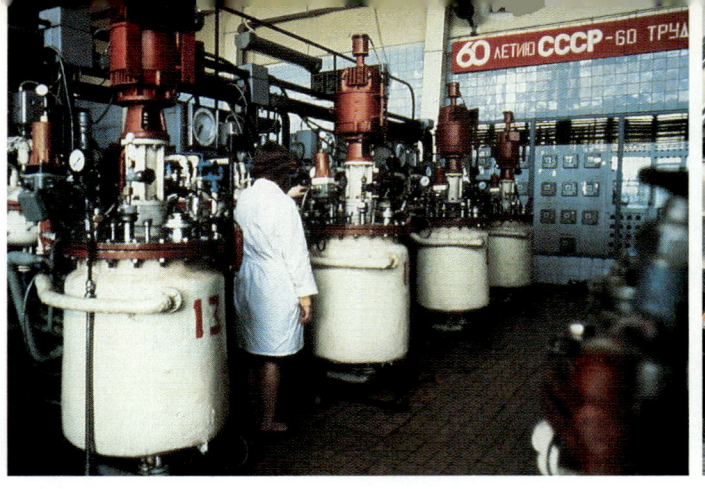

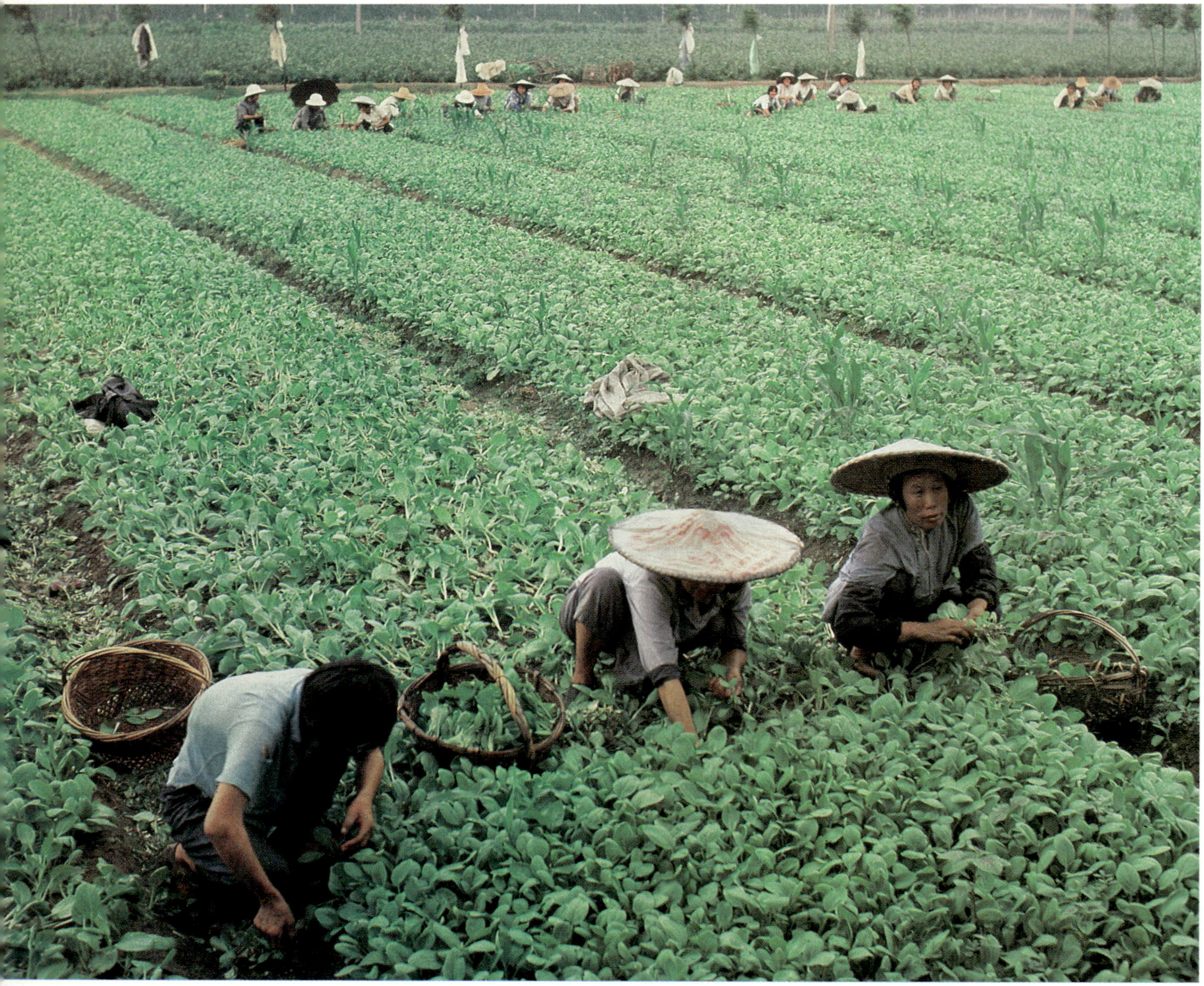

Authoritarian socialism in China and the Soviet Union, democratic socialism in Great Britain and some other European nations are among the alternatives to the market, or free enterprise, economic system in the United States.

COMPARING ECONOMIC SYSTEMS

Up until now you have been learning about the American economy. But as you read in Chapter 2, every economic system answers the four basic economic questions differently. This chapter will introduce you to the major alternatives to the market, or capitalist, economy. You will read about the beginnings of socialism and the two major types of socialism in the world today: democratic socialism and authoritarian socialism. The chapter gives examples of both economic systems in different parts of the world. Learning Economic Skills describes various ways of comparing the economies of different nations.

CHAPTER OBJECTIVES After you study the sections of this chapter, you will be able to:

1 • contrast socialism and capitalism.

2 • state Karl Marx's theory of socialism.

3 • describe how the practice of socialism has changed in the Soviet Union since Lenin.

4 • identify the changes that have occurred in other authoritarian socialist countries.

 ★ identify the problems involved in the use of statistics to compare national economies.

5 • explain why the degree of democratic socialism evident in Great Britain depends on the party in power.

 • compare and contrast authoritarian socialism and democratic socialism.

6 • summarize socialism in the Third World.

ECONOMICS VOCABULARY

socialism
proletariat
democratic socialism
authoritarian socialism
communism
privatization
Third World

Each time you buy a new sweater, change jobs, or invest in a savings bond, you are helping to determine the direction of the nation's economy. Although there is some government intervention in the American economy, it is largely the give-and-take of the marketplace that answers the four basic economic questions you read about in Chapter 2. However, as you also learned in Chapter 2, not all economies operate in this way. In command economies, the four basic questions are answered not by the market but by government.

1 | COMPARING SOCIALISM AND CAPITALISM

Ask yourself as you read:

- Why is centralized control of the decision-making process important to socialists?
- Which kind of economies have little centralized control of the decision-making process?

One way of comparing the various economic systems that exist is to look at how centralized their decision-making processes are. In Figure 21-1, the far right of the continuum represents pure capitalism. All factors of production are privately owned and controlled. All economic decisions are made by individuals reacting to the demands of the market. The government is restricted in its role in the marketplace.

To the far left is pure **socialism.** Socialism is a system in which the government owns the basic factors of production and controls how they are used. The major economic decisions about production, distribution, use of resources, and so on, within such basic industries as railroads and banking are made by government planners. They are not made by the interaction of individuals in the marketplace. For socialists, the goal of this centralized control is a more equal distribution of income among people.

In the real world, as you read in Chapter 2, neither pure capitalism nor pure socialism exists. All economies are a mix of these extremes and

continuum (kuhn-TIN-yoo-uhm): range of values; a scale

Read the paragraphs on Sweden and Tanzania in Section 5. Where would you place each on this continuum?

Figure 21-1: DEGREE OF CENTRALIZATION OF DECISION MAKING IN SELECTED NATIONS

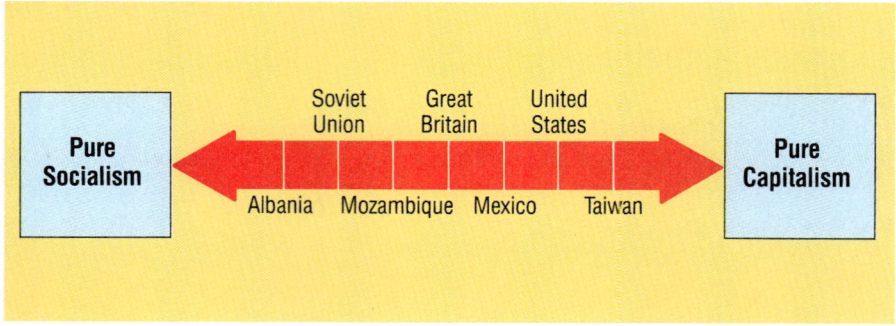

fit somewhere in between. For example, of the nations listed on the continuum, Albania has the greatest amount of government control of the economy. Taiwan, on the other hand, has the least.

As you read in Chapter 2, the United States is much nearer the pure capitalist end of the continuum. There is nonetheless some government direction of the economy. For example, government is active in planning and regulating the growth of such industries as nuclear power. As you will read later in this chapter, the Soviet Union likewise has some characteristics of capitalism. However, the Soviet Union is for the most part a socialist state. Moreover, the Soviet Union practices a particular kind of socialism.

THE BENEFITS OF CAPITALISM

Many economists like to compare the advantages and disadvantages of capitalism and socialism. Often such comparisons are based on individual values. Those who place a high value on personal freedom, initiative, and individuality prefer capitalism. Such critics point out that socialism brings with it immense government intervention in all parts of the economy and, by necessity, in people's personal lives. By definition, a socialist system is one in which government controls numerous production and pricing decisions throughout the nation.

The supporters of capitalism point out that capitalism allows for more efficiency in the marketplace and for greater rates of economic growth. Moreover, there is considerable evidence that unregulated economic systems—those that are closer to pure capitalism—have higher rates of economic growth.

Of course, capitalism as it exists in the world has some problems. Critics point out that income is unequally distributed throughout the economy. They also say that although capitalist nations have enough public goods such as highways, they do not have enough schools and museums for the general public. Such critics clearly value the political goals of socialism. They overlook the fact that regardless of their shortcomings, capitalist countries are economically healthier. Comparison of economic statistics—such as GNP, food consumption, and ownership of goods such as automobiles, for example—tells us that capitalist nations have higher living standards, more economic freedom, and higher rates of growth. In addition, a look at emigration figures and patterns tells us that more people move from socialist nations to live in capitalist nations than the reverse.

REVIEWING ECONOMIC PRINCIPLES

1. What is socialism?
2. State two ways in which capitalism differs from socialism.
3. **Critical Thinking: Making Distinctions. a.** List two countries that according to the continuum have very mixed economies.
   b. What does having a mixed economy mean?

2 | THE BEGINNINGS OF SOCIALISM

Ask yourself as you read:
- Who was Karl Marx?
- What is the dictatorship of the proletariat?

Many men and women in the 19th century labored long hours at low wages and in poor working conditions. How did Marx's theories try to explain this?

Socialism as a modern economic system grew out of protests against the problems caused by the industrial revolution of the 1800s. The rapid growth of factories gave rise to a growing class of unskilled workers, poverty, harsh working conditions, and child labor. Although there were various theories of socialism in the 19th century, Karl Marx, a German philosopher, developed socialism as it is known today.

Marx viewed history as a continuous struggle between various groups, or classes, in society. He saw this struggle in his own day as going on between capitalists—owners of the land, machines, and factories—and the **proletariat** (proh-luh-TER-ee-uht), or workers. Marx believed capitalists exploited the proletariat, or used them unfairly. According to Marx, the value of goods depends only on how much labor is used in producing them. When capitalists sold a good and kept the profit, they were taking money that rightly belonged to workers.

Despite capitalism's dominance in the 19th century, Marx believed it was doomed to fail. He thought that the business cycle would eventually tear it apart. According to Marx, capitalist economies would experience an ever-worsening series of recessions and depressions. These cycles would be most harmful to workers. At the same time, industrial power would become concentrated in the hands of a few capitalists. Eventually, the gap between the capitalist rich and the working poor would become so great that the workers would unite and overthrow capitalism.

After they had overthrown capitalism, workers would establish a new socialist system under the dictatorship of the proletariat. That is, the workers through the state would own and control the means of production. This socialist world would give way in time to an even more ideal system in which government would no longer be necessary. Workers would contribute to society to their full abilities and take in return only what they needed. Clearly, Marx did not very accurately predict what would happen in capitalist nations.

SOCIALISM SINCE MARX

In the 20th century, socialism has split into two major groups: democratic socialism and authoritarian socialism. **Democratic socialism** is a type of socialist system that works within the constitutional framework of a nation to elect socialists to office. In democratic socialist nations, government usually controls only some areas of the economy.

Authoritarian socialism, on the other hand, follows the lead of Marx. Its followers support revolution as the means to overthrow capitalism and bring about socialist goals. In authoritarian socialist nations, the entire economy is controlled by a central government. **Communism,** the term Marx applied to his ideal society, has come to mean any authoritarian socialist system.

REVIEWING ECONOMIC PRINCIPLES

1. Define the following socialist terms: **a.** proletariat, **b.** democratic socialism, **c.** authoritarian socialism, **d.** communism.
2. What was Marx's view of history?
3. Why did Marx believe that capitalism was doomed to fail?
4. Describe the two stages that Marx believed would occur after capitalism failed.
5. **Critical Thinking: Making Distinctions.** What is the difference between democratic socialism and authoritarian socialism?

3 | COMMUNISM AND THE SOVIET ECONOMIC SYSTEM

Ask yourself as you read:
- What did Lenin believe would happen in the final stage of capitalism?
- What caused the Russian Revolution?

The Union of Soviet Socialist Republics (USSR) is today the world's most powerful authoritarian socialist nation. The Soviet system has come about through revolution and gradual changes supposedly made to follow Marx's theory of socialism.

THE EARLY SOVIET ECONOMY

The most influential follower of Marx was Lenin (LEN-uhn), a Russian leader in the early 1900s. Lenin's own contribution to economic theory was based on an analysis of imperialism. Imperialism is the attempt by capitalist nations to extend their rule or authority over other nations and colonies. Lenin believed that imperialism was the final stage of capitalism. In this stage, capitalist economies would increasingly become concentrated among fewer monopolies. Capitalist nations would also have to establish more colonies to ensure supplies of raw materials and markets for finished goods. As a result, nations would have to compete for markets. Eventually, they would go to war to protect their interests. Lenin saw this struggle for economic dominance as speeding up the end of capitalism.

World War I appeared to prove Lenin's theory. It also gave Lenin and his radical followers, the Bolsheviks (BOHL-shuh-viks), their opportunity. Discontent with the rule of the czars, Russia's traditional leaders, had been growing for years, even among the wealthy. The loss of life and the shortages of food and shelter caused by the war finally led to a revolution. In early 1917, the czar was overthrown and a republic estab-

republic: nation ruled by elected representatives

527

lished. The new government, however, was short-lived. The Bolsheviks seized control in October 1917.

The Communists, as they were now called, moved quickly to put their socialist ideas into practice. The new government took control of all agriculture and the little industry there was in Russia. Farmers were forced to turn over much of what they produced for redistribution to other workers. However, the new system soon broke down. A civil war that lasted from 1918 to 1920 between the Communists and those trying to overthrow them forced Lenin to modify some Marxist theories. In 1921 he announced his New Economic Policy (NEP). It returned some decision making to managers of state-run industries. Many small businesses were returned to private ownership. Farmers could keep more of what they produced and sell it directly to customers.

modify (MAHD-luh-fy): to change partially

After Lenin died in 1924, Joseph Stalin came to power. Under him the government took over almost the complete ownership of property and control of the economy. In 1928 Stalin introduced the first of many Five-Year Plans. This first plan outlined the goals of the Soviet economy and set the pattern for its future. Rapid growth in the production of producer goods was to be stressed at the expense of consumer goods. Small privately owned farms were to be combined into large privately owned government-run collectives.

collective (kuh-LEK-tiv): farm operated by a group of workers

THE SOVIET ECONOMY TODAY

The theories of Marx, Lenin, and Stalin are still the basis of the Soviet economy. However, some changes have been introduced based on the capitalist ideas of competition and freedom of choice. Table 21-1 summarizes the major characteristics of the Soviet economic system.

During the 1950s and early 1960s, central government planners decided everything from job assignments to product design for the tens of thousands of farms and factories in the USSR. Planners would, for example, assign a quota to a factory to produce so many tractor tires or pairs of shoes. Plant managers and workers had no say in what or how much they were to produce. Nor did they receive any bonus for improving quality or bettering their quota, or goal. As a result, factories often met their quotas by making products of poor quality or in only a few sizes.

Centralized control of the economy also made it difficult for planners to decide which products should be produced and in what quantities. A mistake by a central planner in estimating quantity demanded could result in a surplus of a good in one town and a shortage of the same item in another. A truck factory might be idled for days waiting for parts because the production quota at the parts factory was too low.

Starting in the late 1960s, the government began decentralizing some economic planning. Plant managers were given more responsibility for such decisions as workers' wages and ways to increase efficiency. Instead of simply producing to meet quotas, plant managers and workers began paying attention to the type and quality of products being produced. Incentives in the form of bonuses and vacation trips

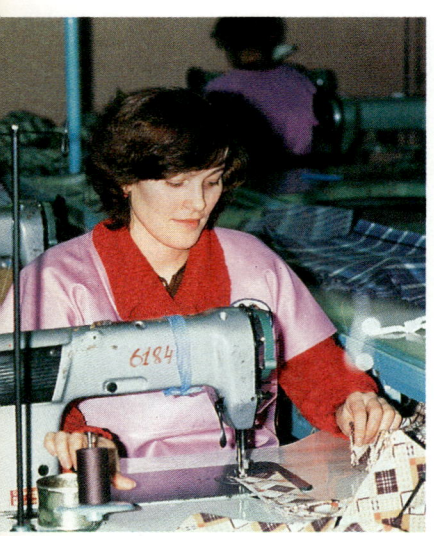

This Soviet worker is producing clothing in a state-owned factory. How does government planning affect workers in the Soviet Union today?

Table 21-1: MAJOR CHARACTERISTICS OF THE SOVIET ECONOMY

Characteristic	Description
Ownership of the factors of production	The central government owns the major factors of production. These include producer goods, such as factories, as well as natural resources, such as farmland. The government also owns the nation's transportation and communication systems, most wholesale and retail stores, and much of the housing.
Central planning	Government planners set economic policy. Decisions made by planners include allocation of resources, type and amount of production, methods of distribution, and prices charged for goods. Central planners in Moscow set long-term national production goals in the form of five-year plans. Regional and local planning councils set specific yearly quotas for each factory and farm.
Social programs	Government provides numerous social programs for all citizens, including public housing, free education, and free health care. Despite such welfare programs, living standards remain below those of many capitalist nations.
Taxes	A major source of revenue is the turnover tax—a sales tax paid on a good each time it changes hands as it moves through the production process. By varying the tax rate, the government can increase or decrease demand for certain goods. Profits of state-run enterprises are also taxed as is personal income above a certain level. The rate is higher on income earned through self-employment.
Personal economic freedom	By controlling most economic decisions, the government limits individuals' freedom to choose their economic activities. Students, for example, at an early age are placed in educational programs that will prepare them for only certain careers such as a profession or factory work. Soviet citizens cannot set up their own factories because the state controls all such enterprises. Also, workers must ask permission to take a job in another region or industry.

were increased. They were also tied directly to how "profitably" a factory was operating.

The Soviet Union also placed a new emphasis on producing consumer goods. For many years, the nation struggled to supply basic needs and build industry. As a result, the quantity demanded for consumer goods was far greater than the quantity supplied. Products, such as televisions and automobiles, were difficult to find, expensive, and often of poor quality and design. Recent Five-Year Plans have called for major increases in the resources allocated to producing consumer goods. Government planners have also begun to use market surveys— though on a small scale—to learn what consumers want.

allocate (AL-uh-kayt): to set aside for a specific purpose

Theory of Class Struggle: Karl Marx (1818–1883)

Karl Marx, in the pamphlet known as the *Communist Manifesto*, coauthored with Friedrich Engels (1848), called on the workers of the world to unite in revolt against the capitalist ruling class. According to the *Communist Manifesto*, all history was a history of class struggles. Throughout history the rulers, who were the owners of property, whether land or factories, had exploited workers. Marx believed that conflict between these two classes would continue until the capitalist system was destroyed. His ideal was a Communist society in which all people would be equal.

Marx was born in what is today West Germany and was educated at universities in Bonn and Berlin. At the age of 23 he received a doctorate in philosophy. While studying for his degree, he was deeply influenced by the ideas of philosopher George Hegel. Marx was especially interested in Hegel's view that history changes constantly. It was on this principle that Marx based his theory of historical materialism. According to this theory, the condition of the economy affects the course of people's ideas.

Between 1841 and 1848, Marx lived in Paris and Brussels. During this period, he founded and wrote for several radical journals. He returned to Germany during the revolution of 1848. When the revolution failed, he and his family fled to London where he lived for most of the rest of his life.

Without financial help from Engels and others and occasional newspaper work, Marx and his family would have starved. Marx spent his days in the library of the British Museum gathering information for his great work, *Das Kapital* (Capital). It was published in three volumes, the first in 1867. The second and third were edited by Engels and published after Marx's death.

In *Das Kapital* Marx described his theory of surplus value. To him the only true value of a good was the amount of labor used to produce it. Suppose a pair of shoes required two hours of work to make, and the worker was paid $10 per hour. If the capitalist employer sold the shoes for $40, there was $20 of surplus value. The employer kept the surplus value, which, Marx believed, rightfully belonged to the worker. He ignored the risks the capitalist was taking as well as the capitalist's job in managing the business.

Marx was not a very good predictor of the future in capitalist economies. Workers have enjoyed ever higher standards of living because capitalists have been willing to take risks and invest in new machines and new products. Marx ignored the importance of incentives. If capitalists are not rewarded by profits, or surplus value, why should they take risks? Marx misunderstood the profit motive as a way to allocate resources.

1. Describe Marx's theory of the class struggle. Has it proved correct or incorrect in capitalist economies? Why or why not?
2. What is Marx's theory of surplus value? What economic factors does it ignore?

These changes have apparently increased output, improved living conditions, and reduced poverty. Nevertheless, despite its large population and vast resources, the Soviet Union still has a standard of living below that of the large capitalist nations. Coordinating the millions of decisions of central planners remains an often impossible task. But perhaps most importantly, Soviet citizens do not enjoy the range of economic choices that are available in a capitalist economy.

REVIEWING ECONOMIC PRINCIPLES

1. Why did Lenin believe capitalism would fail?
2. **a.** How did Lenin and the Communists put their socialist ideas into practice? **b.** How did they modify some of them?
3. What economic pattern did Stalin's Five-Year Plans set?
4. What two economic problems still exist in the Soviet Union?
5. **Critical Thinking: Summarizing Main Ideas.** Summarize the activities of central planners in the Soviet economy in the 1950s and 1960s, mentioning the way the economy has been modified since. Then make a prediction about future trends.

4 | OTHER FORMS OF AUTHORITARIAN SOCIALISM

Ask yourself as you read:
- What is COMECON?
- What communist countries have introduced some capitalism into their economies?

The Soviet Union is only one of a number of nations with what economists call an authoritarian socialist, or communist, economy. Most of these nations have close economic and political ties with either the USSR or the People's Republic of China.

NATIONS UNDER SOVIET INFLUENCE

The Council for Mutual Economic Assistance (COMECON), founded in 1949, is a common market of nations aligned with the USSR. Its members are Bulgaria, Czechoslovakia, East Germany, Hungary, Poland, Romania, and the USSR, plus the non-European nations of Cuba, Mongolia, and Vietnam.

Originally most COMECON nations patterned their economies on that of the USSR. Over time, however, many have adapted capitalist ideas to their needs. Hungary in 1968, for example, put into effect the New Economic Method (NEM). It reduced central planning and introduced the profit motive into state-run industries. NEM allowed private farm plots and more consumer production. Trade with capitalist nations was encouraged. The standard of living improved.

aligned (uh-LYND): holding similar political ideas

It is often difficult to compare the success of different economies. The economy that serves the needs of one nation might not satisfy another. However, economists often do compare economic systems to see the relative success of various economic policies.

SOURCES AND TYPES OF STATISTICS

International statistics are available from a variety of sources. The United Nations collects data from many countries and publishes them in its *Statistical Yearbook.* Such United States agencies as the Bureau of the Census and the Central Intelligence Agency also provide information on other nations.

A convenient way to find statistics from these sources is to look in the international section of the *Statistical Abstract* or in such nongovernment publications as *The World Almanac and Book of Facts.* Topics covered by these statistics include population, health, education, industry, agriculture, communications, finance, and so on.

In using such sources it is important to remember that international statistics are often not as accurate as those for only one nation. Statistics for such topics as gross national product may be calculated in different ways by different nations. For example, figures on imports, may vary depending on whether shipping and insurance costs are added to the price of the products. Usually tables will have footnotes explaining differences.

SOME PROBLEMS WITH COMPARING STATISTICS

The table on p. 533 lists statistics for the United States, the Soviet Union, and Japan. The data allow you to compare different facts about these economies. However, to interpret these statistics accurately involves more than just reading them.

For example, many economists use per capita, or per person, GNP as a rough measure of a nation's economic health. Based on this statistic, you might conclude that everyone living in the United States has a higher standard of living than anyone in the Soviet Union or Japan. However, actual income per person can vary greatly within a nation.

One error to avoid is using raw statistics that are not corrected for population or other important factors. For example, the table shows that the USSR uses more crude petroleum than the United States. However, it also has a larger population. Taking this difference into account shows that the United States actually uses more petroleum per capita than the USSR.

Often two or more statistics must be considered together to give a true picture of an economy. Japan's population, for example, is about half that of the United States or the USSR. Someone with little knowledge of geography might conclude that Japan is less crowded than the two more populated nations. In fact, Japan is less than 4 percent of the size of the Soviet Union. As a result, its population per square mile is over 200 times that of the USSR.

In other cases, statistics do not tell the full story. Notice that the USSR has about seven times the number of hospital beds and about half the persons per physician as the United States. This would seem to indicate the Soviets have a better health care system. However, these raw statistics say nothing about the level of training, the availability of medicine, the amount of modern equipment in hospitals, and so on. Despite the many doctors and hospitals in the USSR, the infant mortality rate and the death rate are higher than in the United States, and life expectancy is shorter.

Practicing Your Skills

1. Which nations in the table have a negative balance of trade?
2. a. Based on the figures on steel production and consumption, which nation or nations must import much of their steel? b. Which nation is able to export the most steel?
3. What can you infer about how Japan meets most of its needs for oil and coal?

Comparative Statistics in a Recent Year for the United States, the Soviet Union, and Japan

	U.S.	USSR	Japan
General Statistics			
Population (thousands)	238,631	277,507	120,731
Area (square miles)	3,615,102	8,649,489	143,750
Population per square mile	66	32	840
Gross national product (billions of dollars)	$4,110	$1,843	$1,138
Per capita GNP (1977 dollars)	$14,000	$6,490	$9,149
Civilian labor force (millions)	120	115.2	58.5
Industry and Trade			
Imports (billions of dollars)	$325.7	$40.8	$136.1
Exports (billions of dollars)	$100.0	$45.2	$100.0
Persons working in manufacturing (millions)	19.6	30.6	11.2
Energy use (millions of metric tons of coal equivalent)	2,174.8	1,611.5	403.0
Energy used per capita (kilograms of coal equivalent)	9,304	5,900	5,397
Electric energy production (billions of kilowatt-hours)	2,368	1,408	612
Crude steel production (millions of metric tons)	76.8	152.5	97.2
Steel use (millions of metric tons)	403	145.6	500
Coal production (millions of metric tons)	660	486.8	17.6
Crude petroleum production (millions of metric tons)	427.5	616.3	0.5
Crude oil reserves (millions of barrels)	26,500	67,000	55
Food and Agriculture			
Wheat production (thousands of metric tons)	66,010	82,000	747
Rice production (thousands of metric tons)	4,523	2,500	12,958
Meat production (thousands of metric tons)	17,605	13,085	1,908
Fish catch (thousands of metric tons)	3,102	9,352	10,733
Consumer Products			
Televison sets per 1,000 persons	790	308	556
Radio per 1,000 persons	2,048	514	713
Telephones per 1,000 persons	770	98	520
Passenger cars in use (millions)	164	19	43
Health			
Life expentancy at birth (years)	75	70	76
Births during 1 year per 1,000 persons	16.2	18.1	13.7
Infant mortality rate (infants deaths per 1,000 live births)	11	31	8.9
Deaths during 1 year per 1,000 persons	8.9	10.5	6.2
Annual growth rate of population (percent)	1.0	0.8	0.5
Hospital beds per 1,000 persons	3,324	23,100	1,402
Persons per physician	549	267	735

Source: *Statistical Abstract of the U.S.*, Bureau of the Census

martial (MAHR-shuhl) **law:** rule by the military

commune (KAHM-yoon): farm operated by a group of workers

Other experiments have not been so successful. In 1980, widespread strikes forced the Polish government to allow Solidarity and other trade unions to function free from government control. Solidarity originally was a union of shipyard workers in Gdansk, but later it expanded to include workers from all over Poland. This brief experiment with sharing power came to an end in 1981. The government imposed martial law and disbanded the unions. Since then, the Polish economy has suffered from frequent shortages of food and other important products.

THE PEOPLE'S REPUBLIC OF CHINA

The People's Republic of China, the world's most populous nation, is also a major communist economy. Since the Communists took control in 1949, China has undergone a series of economic upheavals. Under its first five-year plan, land was taken from wealthy landowners and organized into communes. In 1958 a new plan, the Great Leap Forward, attempted to expand the nation's industry rapidly. The leaders soon realized that the nation lacked both the capital and skilled labor for immediate industrialization. A policy stressing agricultural development was then tried. The Cultural Revolution of the 1960s, a time of political confusion and violence, further disrupted the economy.

During the 1980s the Chinese government relaxed some of its control over the economy. It has, for example, allowed some capitalism and personal economic choice. In fact, China today, while still an authoritarian Communist government, permits a small but increasing number of privately run businesses to exist. Also, some workers are paid according to the quality of their output, and a few have been allowed to choose their own jobs. In the past, every job was assigned by the government. Other signs of capitalist influence are the opening of stock markets in Beijing and Shenyang. The collective farm, or commune, is still the basic economic unit of the nation, however.

During the 1950s, China was the nation most committed to Marx's call for worldwide socialist revolution. In the early 1960s, China broke off diplomatic relations with the USSR because it felt the Soviet Union was no longer dedicated to overthrowing capitalism. Since then, however, China has changed its radical viewpoint somewhat. It has established trade and cultural relations with many non-communist nations. It has also signed trade and other agreements with Western nations.

Like the Soviet Union, China also has close ties with a number of Communist nations. These include Albania and North Korea.

Farming in the People's Republic of China is done on large state-owned communes. Why is much of this farm work still done by hand labor?

REVIEWING ECONOMIC PRINCIPLES

1. 1.Why did the People's Republic of China abandon its program of rapid industrialization?
2. **Critical Thinking: Making a Judgment.** Write a paragraph explaining why you think Hungary modified its policies.

Table 21-2: MAJOR CHARACTERISTICS OF DEMOCRATIC SOCIALISM

Characteristic	Description
Ownership of the factors of production	The government owns some of the major factors of production. Often these are only major industries, such as oil, steel, railroads, and banking. When the government nationalizes an industry, it usually pays the owner market value. If a nonsocialist government is elected, it may sell some nationalized industries back to the private sector.
Central planning	The government engages in some planning and control of the economy. Control may affect employment and wages, prices, production levels, interest rates, and so on. Government may also plan national goals in such areas as economic growth and industrial development.
Social programs	Citizens often receive such benefits as free education and health care. Child care, disability payments, and unemployment and retirement benefits are other programs often heavily funded by government.
Taxes	A progressive income tax is often used to pay for government services. Tax rates can run as high as 80% on personal income.
Personal economic freedom	Individuals have considerably more economic freedom than under authoritarian socialism. Many production and distribution decisions are based on free market choices made by consumers. However, businesses are usually subject to more government control than those in capitalist economies. Individuals may not start businesses in industries owned by the government.

5 | DEMOCRATIC SOCIALISM

Ask yourself as you read:

- What kind of economic policies does Great Britain now follow?
- Why is Sweden sometimes called a welfare state?

Democratic socialism is the other major economic system that has grown out of Marx's theories. Table 21-2 describes some of the major characteristics of democratic-socialist nations.

SOCIALISM IN GREAT BRITAIN

Although Great Britain is considered one of the world's major capitalist nations, it has a number of socialist features. Actually, according to the theories of Marx and Lenin, Britain is more of a welfare state than a socialist economy. Legislation in the early years of the 20th century set up such social programs as pensions, health insurance, and unemployment compensation. However, it was not until the Labour Party came to power in 1945 that broad socialist policies were passed. The Labour government expanded the nation's social security system and established a free national health service. It also nationalized, or took control of, the Bank of England and such industries as steel, coal and gas, trucking, and the railroads and airlines.

In the last few decades, the degree of socialism in Great Britain has varied, depending on the political party in office. When Conservatives have been in power, the government has reduced controls on business and left much of the private sector to succeed or fail on its own. Labour Party governments also began to assist the private sector. For example, after the Conservatives came to power in the 1950s, the steel industry was resold to the private sector. A new Labour government renationalized it in 1964. In 1979, the Conservative government of Prime Minister Margaret Thatcher was elected on the promise of reducing socialist programs and encouraging private enterprise. Once in office, it reduced taxes, decreased regulation of business, and cut government spending.

Another important part of Prime Minister Thatcher's reforms has been **privatization,** a program to return many of the government-owned and -operated companies to private ownership. This increased privatization in Britain has had a great effect on other nations, encouraging many to sell their government-owned enterprises and to reduce government involvement in their economies.

SOCIALISM IN OTHER EUROPEAN NATIONS

Socialism has also been an important influence in a number of other countries in Europe. For example, France, like Great Britain, nationalized many industries following World War II. In West Germany, the Social Democrats were an important political party throughout the postwar years and gained control of the national government in 1969. In Scandanavia—Denmark, Sweden, and Norway—democratic socialism has resulted in a relatively high standard of living. Rather than nationalize industry, the socialists have concentrated on building extensive social welfare systems. For example, since the Social Democratic party came to power in 1932, Sweden has been made over into what is often called a welfare state. In addition to the programs listed in Table 21-2, there are guaranteed vacations for all workers and direct payments to families to help support each child under 16.

These various experiments with mixing capitalism and socialism have met with varying degrees of success. During the 1970s and 1980s, as inflation and unemployment increased, a number of nations joined Great Britain in questioning their commitment to socialism. In Sweden, citizens were becoming increasingly dissatisfied with the high taxes needed to pay for the nation's social programs. As a result, the socialists were voted out of office in 1986 after 44 years in power. The Social Democrats in West Germany also lost power in 1982 as the result of a worsening economy. On the other hand, a number of nations attempted to establish a new economic mix that is nearer the socialist end of the continuum. In the early 1980s, France, Spain, and Greece elected socialist governments for the first time in many years. In the late 1980s this trend toward socialism seemed to be weakening. In France, for example, the voters turned out its socialist government within a few years. The government now in power is working to revitalize the economy.

REVIEWING ECONOMIC PRINCIPLES

1. Why has Great Britain experienced shifts in its economic policies, depending on the political party in power?
2. **Critical Thinking: Making Comparisons.** Choose one of the topics from Table 21-2 and compare it with the same topic in Table 21-1. Prepare your comparison in the form of a paragraph.

6 | SOCIALISM IN THE THIRD WORLD

Ask yourself as you read:
- What are some Third World nations?
- Which Latin American nation has a Communist government?

Socialism has also played an important role in the nations of the **Third World.** These are developing nations that, in principle, are not aligned with the major Communist or capitalist nations. The focus of this influence has been on redistributing wealth from rich to poor.

LATIN AMERICA

For much of the 20th century, Central and South America have seen struggles between small groups of powerful landowners and those trying to redistribute their wealth. The first nation to translate this struggle into socialist programs was Mexico. In the decades following the Revolution of 1910, the government carried out a program of land reform. It redistributed land from the rich to the poor. During the 1930s, the government also organized state-run collective farms, supported the development of labor unions, and nationalized the oil industry.

Since the 1950s, a number of Latin American nations have enacted land reform and the nationalization of industry. For example, in the 1960s and 1970s Bolivia, Peru, and Venezuela took over industries that had been owned by businesses in the United States and Europe. Often, however, rapid changes have resulted in a violent backlash or reaction. For example, the government of Guatemala was overthrown in 1954 with American support after its elected leaders began taking over land owned by the United Fruit Company. In 1973 the elected government of Chile was also overthrown after enacting socialist programs.

backlash: reaction

Cuba is the only Latin American nation with an open and publicly declared Communist government. Since 1959, under the leadership of Fidel Castro, the Communists have nationalized all industry and organized most farmland into state-run cooperatives. Cuba's centralized economy is patterned after that of the USSR, with whom it has close military and political ties and from which it receives economic aid.

In recent years, a number of groups impatient for reform have turned to violence. For example, Marxist rebels backed by Cuba and the Soviet Union overthrew a dictatorship in Nicaragua in 1979. Although Nicaragua's leaders have followed Cuba in establishing many socialist programs, they have allowed some features of a market economy to exist. The Sandinista government of Nicaragua nevertheless remained unpopular with some groups. The continuing unrest has caused economic problems in Nicaragua. Other Latin American nations that have been fighting armed rebels who want to establish socialist governments include El Salvador, Guatemala, and Colombia.

AFRICA

In some parts of Africa, socialism has resulted in a blend of old and new ideas. Land, for example, in many areas has traditionally been considered common property. Cooperation among members of a community and close family and tribal relationships have also long been important. As new governments were established following the end of colonial rule, some leaders found that socialist ideas could be easily adapted to long-held African values.

In Tanzania, for example, the nation's first president, Julius K. Nyerere (ny-uh-REHR-ee), introduced a form of socialism called *ujamaa* (oo-jah-MAH). In Swahili, the term means a family feeling for each other. Nyerere, who described himself as a non-Marxist, carried out this program through establishing communal farms and villages. His government also nationalized major businesses such as banks, import and export firms, and food-processing plants. Most retail trade, transportation, and small industry have been left in private hands. Unfortunately, there has been little economic growth. Nyerere resigned in 1985.

Other African nations where varying degrees of socialism have been enacted peacefully include Ghana, Guinea, and Senegal. In recent years, however, socialists forces who believed in armed rebellion have come to power in a number of African nations. These include Angola, Ethiopia, the Congo, Mozambique, and Zimbabwe. In many cases, rebel groups in these nations have gained power with military help from the USSR, Cuba, or China.

Education is a high priority in most developing African nations. Can you explain why?

REVIEWING ECONOMIC PRINCIPLES

1. What is the Third World?
2. What has been the focus of political struggles in Central and South America for much of the 20th century?
3. **Critical Thinking: Making Inferences.** Why do you think some African leaders might believe socialist ideas would work in their countries?

SUMMARY OF
IMPORTANT PRINCIPLES

1
- Socialism is a system in which the government controls the major factors of production. In capitalism, economic decisions are made by individuals without government intervention.

2
- Marx viewed history as a long struggle between various groups, or classes, in society. In his own day he saw this struggle as between capitalists and workers. Eventually the gap between rich and poor would become so great that the workers would unite and overthrow capitalism. A new socialist system would be established under the dictatorship of the proletariat. Eventually this would give way to a society in which government would no longer be necessary.

3
- Lenin and the new Communist government in the USSR took complete control of all agriculture and what industry there was. The new system soon broke down, and Lenin had to reestablish some private ownership of business and return some degree of self-regulation to the managers of state-run industries. Under Stalin, rapid growth in the production of producer goods was stressed at the expense of consumer goods. The government also began to combine small privately-owned plots of land into large government-run collective farms.
- General statistics for the world are often not as accurate as those for one nation. To give a true picture, often two or more statistics must be considered.
- During the 1950s and early 1960s, central government planners made almost all decisions for the tens of thousands of government-run factories and farms in the USSR. Starting in the late 1960s, the government began decentralizing some economic planning. Emphasis shifted from simply meeting quotas to looking at the type and quality of products being produced. There was also a new emphasis on producing consumer goods.

4
- The degree of socialism in Great Britain varies depending on the political party in office. When Conservatives have been in power, the government has reduced controls on business and left much of the private sector to succeed or fail on its own. Labour Party governments have been more willing to assist the private sector and to expand social programs.

5
- Under authoritarian socialism, the government owns the major factors of production, sets economic policy through central planners, provides extensive social programs, levies taxes to control demand, and limits individuals' freedom to choose economic activities. Under democratic socialism, the government owns some of the major factors of production, engages in some planning and control of the economy, heavily funds some social programs, levies high taxes, and has little to say about individuals' freedom of economic choice.

6
- In the Third World, socialists have attempted to redistribute the wealth from the rich to the poor.

Putting Economics to Work

SUPPLY AND DEMAND: THE BLACK MARKET

David Mott is traveling in the Soviet Union with his senior class. On his first day in Moscow, a young man stops David and offers to buy a pair of American jeans for 60 rubles, or about $85. David is surprised anyone would pay so much for jeans that cost only $20 when new. Nevertheless, he turns down the offer. Over the next few days, another person asks to buy his watch. Someone else wants to swap two Soviet Army belt buckles for David's new running shoes. Although the trades sound tempting, David turns them all down.

The first chance David has to talk to a Soviet student, he asks about black market trading. The student explains that many consumer items such as cameras and sunglasses cannot be found in the state-run stores. Instead, Soviets must buy these items where they can, often from tourists. The student tells David that buying and selling outside the official economy is a widespread practice that Soviets call living *na levo,* or "on the left." Record albums, cosmetics, jewelry, and chewing gum are all available in this private market. Services are also traded. For example, a carpenter might repair a cabinet in return for first choice of some black-market theater tickets. Even information is an important commodity "on the left." A person who knows that a particular shop is about to receive a shipment of items that are in short supply may tip off others in exchange for money or a favor.

David is amazed at the extent of such private buying and selling. He now realizes that private enterprise can exist even within a command economy.

1. Why would a pair of jeans be worth so much in the USSR?
2. In the official Soviet economy, prices are set by government planners. How do you think prices are set in the black market?

THE GROWTH OF WORLD CAPITALISM
Skill: Contrasting Information

 **Nations do not always stay at the same point in the continuum between pure socialism and pure capitalism. In the 1980s, many nations shifted more toward capitalism.**

From the time of the ancient Greeks, philosophers, politicians and just plain folk have debated the best form of society and the proper role of the state in the lives of its people. For more than a century, advocates of collective ownership and strong government control of the economy have marched under the banner of socialism. Those who champion private property, individual initiative and the pursuit of profit are in the capitalist camp.

A decade ago, socialism seemed to be on the ascendency, despite some severe cracks in its façade. In Bombay and Bangkok, in Lima and Lusaka, governments were nationalizing industries and imposing ever growing and restrictive regulations on private companies. The rising tide of socialism threatened to become a tidal wave. Among superpowers, the Communist Soviet Union appeared to be gaining in international prestige and influence, while the capitalist U.S. seemed to be declining. Racked by oil crises, recession and an inflationary fever that soared to double digits, the free-enterprise system faced a doubtful, some said downright perilous, future.

All that has dramatically changed in the 1980s, as capitalism has become the spirit of the age. More and more countries are turning to free enterprise as the last, best hope for faster economic and social development. Fetters are being taken off industry. Entrepreneurship, the business of starting up companies, is in vogue. "If capitalism means allowing markets to work, then we are seeing some dramatic examples around the world," says David Henderson, chief economist for the Organization for Economic Cooperation and Development. . . .

No matter whether leaders call it private enterprise or free enterprise or privatization, the policy they are advocating today is basically capitalism.

The most fundamental distinction between socialism and capitalism is that capitalism looks to the individual to be the main actor in economic life, while socialism looks to the state to play that role. Today more and more countries are looking to the individual, while fewer and fewer think that the state can provide all the answers to economic problems. . . .

The reason that private enterprise is on the rise is clear. While capitalist nations, including the U.S. and the emerging countries of Asia, have been highly successful at creating wealth, socialism has largely proved an economic drag. Says Peter Berger, a sociologist at Boston University: "Socialist societies have been dramatically outperformed by any number of successful capitalist countries, especially in Asia."

1. Contrast the differences between socialism and capitalism, including the role of the individual in each system.
2. Why, according to this article, have many nations gained a new interest in capitalism and free enterprise?

John Greenwals, David Aikman, Christopher Redman, and Frederick Ungeheuer, "A New Age of Capitalism." *Time*, July 28, 1986. pp. 28–39.

"NOTHING TO LOSE BUT THEIR CHAINS"
Skill: Summarizing Information

 **Karl Marx, along with his friend Friedrich Engels, wrote *The Communist Manifesto*, published in 1848. In this excerpt from it, Marx explains some of the basic ideas of communism and appeals for support to the world's working class.**

A specter is haunting Europe—the specter of communism. All the powers of old Europe have entered into a holy alliance to exorcise [drive out the evil spirit of] this specter. . . .

The modern bourgeois [capitalist] society that has sprouted from the ruins of feudal society, has not done away with class antagonisms. It has but established new classes, new conditions of oppression, new forms of struggle in place of the old ones.

Readings in Economics

Our epoch, the epoch of the bourgeoisie [capitalist middle class], possesses, however, this distinctive feature: It has simplified the class antagonisms. Society as a whole is more and more splitting up into two great hostile camps, into two great classes directly facing each other—bourgeoisie and proletariat. . . .

The immediate aim of the Communists is the same as that of all the other proletarian parties: Formation of the proletariat into a class, overthrow of the bourgeois supremacy, conquest of political power by the proletariat. . . .

The distinguishing feature of communism is not the abolition of property generally, but the abolition of bourgeois property. . . .

In this sense, the theory of the Communists may be summed in the single sentence: Abolition of private property. . . .

Communists everywhere support every revolutionary movement against the existing social and political order of things.

In all these movements they bring to the front, as the leading question in each case, the property question, no matter what its degree of development at the time.

Finally, they labor everywhere for the union and agreement of the democratic parties of all countries.

The Communists disdain to conceal their views and aims. They openly declare that their ends can be attained only by the forcible overthrow of all existing social conditions. Let the ruling classes tremble at a Communist revolution. The proletarians have nothing to lose but their chains. They have a world to win.

Workingmen of all countries, unite!

1. Summarize Marx's theory of communism.
2. Explain what Marx means by "The proletarians have nothing to lose but their chains."

Karl Marx and Friedrich Engels, *The Communist Manifesto*. Northbrook, Illinois: AHM Publishing, 1955.

The writings of Marx and Engels helped inspire the Russian Revolution. Here Communist forces storm the Winter Palace at Petrograd (now Leningrad) in November 1917.

LENIN'S LETTER TO AMERICAN WORKERS

Skill: Distinguishing Fact and Opinion

 **Vladimir Lenin saw the end of capitalism approaching. In this letter addressed to the workers of America, written in 1918 during the civil war in Russia, he predicts the violent overthrow of the bourgeoisie, or capitalist middle class.**

Comrades! A Russian Bolshevik who took part in the 1905 revolution, and who lived in your country for many years afterwards, has offered to convey my letter to you. I have accepted his proposal all the more gladly because just at the present time the American revolutionary workers have to play an exceptionally important role as uncompromising enemies of American imperialism—the freshest, strongest and latest in joining in the worldwide slaughter of nations for the division of capitalist profits. . . .

The international imperialist bourgeoisie have slaughtered ten million men and maimed twenty million in "their war" [World War I], the war to decide whether the British or the German vultures are to rule the world.

If *our* war, the war of the oppressed and exploited against the oppressors and the exploiters, results in half a million or a million casualties in all countries, the bourgeoisie will say that the former casualties are justified, while the latter are criminal.

The proletariat will have something entirely different to say.

Now, amidst the horrors of the imperialist war, the proletariat is receiving a most vivid and striking illustration of the great truth taught by all revolutions and bequeathed to the workers by their best teachers, the founders of modern socialism. This truth is that no revolution can be successful unless *the resistance of the exploiters is crushed.* When we, the workers and toiling peasants, captured state power, it became our duty to crush the resistance of the exploiters. We are proud we have been doing this. We regret we are not doing it with sufficient firmness and determination.

We know that fierce resistance to the socialist revolution on the part of the bourgeoisie is inevitable in all countries, and that this resistance will *grow* with the growth of this revolution. The proletariat will crush this resistance; during the struggle against the resisting bourgeoisie it will finally mature for victory and for power. . . .

Slowly but surely the workers are adopting communist, Bolshevik tactics and are marching towards the proletarian revolution, which alone is capable of saving dying culture and dying mankind.

In short, we are invincible, because the world proletarian revolution is invincible.

N. Lenin

August 20, 1918

1. What does Lenin state the proletariat must do in order to continue their revolution?
2. Why do you think the world proletarian revolution has not occurred?

Vladimir Il'ich Lenin, *On the United States of America.* Compiled by C. Leiteizen. Moscow: Progress Publishers, 1967. pp. 332, 341, 342, 346.

THE CHINESE MOVE TO THE MARKET SYSTEM

Skill: Predicting Outcomes

 **The Chinese under leader Deng Xiaoping have transformed many aspects of their economy from centrally planned socialism to a free-enterprise market system. This article describes some reasons behind this move and some results of it.**

It is as if the world's largest convoy of lorries [trucks] were suddenly told to turn on a dime. True, the drivers of China's industrial juggernaut had been duly warned, and road signs had been repainted in recent months. But the turnabout was formally ordered only on October 20th, when the central committee issued its 16,000-word "decision." The centrally planned economy of Marx, Stalin and Mao is to be stopped in its . . . tracks and put on the market road; the traffic, if good intentions hold, will now be regulated by profits and prices rather than by bureaucrats in Peking.

No other communist country has ever tried to roll back a misguided revolution so far or so fast. The Russians are still vainly tinkering with their

Readings in Economics

hopelessly overcentralized farms and factories. The Hungarians have pioneered a route to "market socialism." . . . Indeed, the only precedent for China's change of isms is its own recent return to peasant capitalism on the farms. . . .

Over the past five years the Chinese have all but dissolved their collective agriculture and restored both decision-making and profit-making to the peasant family. The result, helped along by good weather, has been the best harvests ever, in yield per acre and per head, plus a (claimed) increase of more than 50% in real farm income. With simple faith. Mr. Deng Xiaoping and his colleagues are now setting out to apply to industry the lessons of what they did with agriculture.

Simple, however, is what an industrial reformation cannot be. In the words of October 20th, it needs "reform of every aspect of the entire economic structure." It means changing not only management methods but the managers themselves. . . . It means altering the way factories use their raw materials and sell their finished goods, the way they measure success—by profitability rather than by volume of output. . . .

Even the radical Mr. Deng insists that the commanding heights of the economy—energy and oil products, steel, newsprint, even cigarettes in a chain-smoking country—must remain under state control. But the number of products subject to compulsory planning and pricing is to be halved. The newly liberated half is to be controlled instead by economic levers such as prices, taxes and interest rates. The object of the reform is to motivate factories to produce what consumers

want to buy instead of the shoddy unsalable goods that have been piling up in Chinese warehouses.

1. What was the result when the Chinese virtually dissolved their collective agriculture system and restored control by peasant families?
2. If China is able to successfully apply some free enterprise to business and industry, what can you predict about the kind of economic system that will evolve?

"The Retreat from Marx." *The Economist*, October 27, 1984. pp. 17, 18.

WHAT HAPPENED TO SOCIALISM IN THE 20TH CENTURY?

Skill: Identifying Cause and Effect

In many cases, socialism has not replaced capitalism but has found its place within capitalist systems. Psychologist and author Erich Fromm sympathetically discusses the fate of socialism in this article written in 1958.

Socialism in the 19th century, in the Marxian and in its many other forms, wanted to create the material basis for a dignified human existence for everybody. It wanted work to direct capital, rather than capital to direct work. For socialism, work and capital were not just two economic categories, but rather they represented two principles: capital, the principle of amassed things, of *having;* and work, that of life and of man's powers, of *being* and becoming. Socialists found that in capitalism things direct life; that *having* is superior to *being;* that the past directs the present—and they wanted to reverse this relation. The aim of socialism was man's emancipation, his restoration to the unalienated, uncrippled individual who enters into a new, rich, spontaneous relationship with his fellow man and with nature. . . .

Socialism hoped for the eventual abolition of the state, so that only things, and not people, would be administered. It aimed at a classless society in which freedom and initiative would be restored to the individual. Socialism, in the 19th

Communist China now permits a limited amount of private enterprise, as in this fabric shop.

Industry is growing in Communist Yugoslavia. This worker is employed in a plant that produces medical products.

century, and until the beginning of the First World War, was the most significant humanistic and spiritual movement in Europe and America.

What happened to socialism?

It succumbed to the spirit of capitalism which it had wanted to replace. Instead of understanding it as a movement for the liberation of man, many of its adherents and its enemies alike understood it as being exclusively a movement for the *economic* improvement of the working class. The humanistic aims of socialism were forgotten, or only paid lip service to, while, as in capitalism, all the emphasis was laid on the aims of economic gain. Just as the ideals of democracy lost their spiritual roots, the idea of socialism lost its deepest root—the prophetic-messianic faith in peace, justice and the brotherhood of man.

Thus socialism became the vehicle for the workers to attain their place *within* the capitalistic structure rather than transcending it; instead of changing capitalism, socialism was absorbed by its spirit. The failure of the socialist movement became complete when in 1914 its leaders renounced international solidarity and chose the economic and military interests of their respective countries as against the ideas of internationalism and peace which had been their program.

1. What ideals of socialism does Fromm believe made it appealing?
2. How can you explain the failure of socialism in the 20th century?

Erich Fromm, *Let Man Prevail: A Socialist Manifesto and Program.* New York: The Call Association, 1960. pp. 15–17.

THIRD WORLD SOCIALISTS NEED FOREIGN CAPITAL
Skill: Drawing Conclusions

Socialism in developing nations faces the unusual question of how to promote economic development. Sociologist Barry Munslow describes how certain African socialist nations use capitalist means to develop their economies.

Looking first at Angola, we find that patterns of foreign trade three years after the revolution [in 1976] remained virtually the same as before, with 64 percent of exports going to the United States and 19 percent to Western Europe. Angola's economy and balance of payments are heavily dependent on oil revenues, and this means a reliance on Western technology for its production. Hence the process of breaking away from the world capitalist market has hardly yet begun. Indeed in July 1979 a "Law on Foreign Investment" set out . . . attractive terms for foreign capital. . . . In Mozambique, also, a clear call has been made for foreign capital. . . . Encouraging Western investment has been deemed essential, given the major development projects being proposed and the relative inflexibility and long planning cycles, as well as the limited resources, of the socialist countries. A further factor is the seeming unwillingness of the Soviet Union itself to invest sufficiently in Mozambique. Only the German Democratic Republic, Bulgaria, and Rumania have thus far made any sizable investments. This may be in part the result of an ideological dispute, with the Mozambicans rejecting the Soviet theory of the noncapitalist road of development in favor of their own theory of underdeveloped socialist states. . . .

1. How can Third World countries benefit from foreign capital?
2. How might the United States benefit by granting economic aid as part of its foreign policy toward Third World socialist nations?

Barry Munslow, "Is Socialism Possible on the Periphery?" *Monthly Review*, Vol. 35, No. 1, May 1983.

PRACTICING YOUR COMMUNICATION SKILLS: OPINION POLLING

In Chapter 12 you read about the use of samples and opinion polling in market surveys. Opinion polls are also used to analyze the public's attitudes toward government policies. The most important factors in taking a public opinion poll are choosing the right sample and asking the right questions. A poorly selected sample or poorly written question will introduce bias into your results. In taking an opinion poll, follow these tips:

- Narrow the issue you wish to analyze before you begin to write your questions.
- Design your questionnaire. A good questionnaire is a short one that can be answered quickly. A "closed" question, one that can be answered with a *yes* or *no*, is the best.
- Choose a sample that is a cross section of the population you wish to interview. Factors to consider in choosing your sample are race, sex, education, occupation, income, and location.
- Once you have taken your opinion poll, analyze your results. Compute the percentage of the sample that responded with the same opinion to each question. If you have chosen your sample carefully, you can assume that the percentages will apply within a few points to the larger population.
- Interpret the results in a written summary.

Activity: Choose an economic issue from the news such as the local budget or foreign aid to a particular country. Working in small groups, set up and conduct an opinion poll in your school.

VOCABULARY REVIEW

For each of the following definitions, write the letter of the term that correctly defines it.

a. socialism
b. proletariat
c. communism
d. Third World
e. democratic socialism

1. economic system in which the entire economy is controlled by a central government _____

2. system that works within the constitutional framework of a nation to elect socialists to office. The government controls only some areas of the economy. _____

3. workers _____

4. developing nations that are nonaligned _____

5. country in which the government owns the basic factors of production _____

PRACTICING YOUR ECONOMIC SKILLS

1. **Analyzing Data.** Colombia has a GNP of $39.6 billion and a population of 29.3 million. Venezuela's GNP is $69.7 billion, and its population, 17.3 million. **a.** Which nation has the higher per capita GNP? **b.** Do all people in this nation have a higher standard of living than those in the other nation? Explain.

2. Venezuela's GNP is more than twice that of Colombia. **a.** How much larger is its per capita GNP? **b.** What do you think accounts for this difference?

3. Although Venezuela and Colombia border each other and are about the same size, their GNPs differ greatly. What are some possible factors that could explain this?

4. The descriptions given below apply to one or more of the three types of socialism listed here. For each description, write the letter or letters of the type of socialism that best identify it.

   C. communism   T. Third World socialism
   S. socialism

   a. type of socialism that came to power mainly in highly industrial nations.
   b. socialist nations that made substantial

gains in industry but have continued to suffer continuing problems in agriculture.

c. nations whose economic progress have been hampered by high population growth rates.

d. governments established in these nations have generally been authoritarian one-party regimes.

e. nations whose socialist leaders have done much to improve health care and to increase educational opportunities.

DISCUSSING ECONOMIC QUESTIONS

1. Why do you think Soviet planners would emphasize the production of producer goods over consumer goods? For a nation that has to industrialize rapidly, does this seem a sensible course of action? How do you think consumers would react over time?

2. What advantages do you think socialists see in nationalizing major industries? Of what disadvantages can you think?

3. Today, not only socialist governments redistribute wealth to help the needy. Discuss some of the ways that capitalist nations try to redistribute income. Is redistribution of income among the important goals of the United States? Why? Could the same goals be reached without the government redistributing income?

4. Why do you think that providing worker motivation and supplying adequate numbers, kinds, and quality of consumer goods are problems for Communist central planners? What do you think these planners should do to solve their problems? Can these problems be solved without changing the structure of government in Communist nations?

APPLYING CRITICAL THINKING SKILLS

1. **Researching a Topic and Preparing a Table.** Research the following characteristics for capitalism, democratic socialism, and author-itarian socialism: degree of government ownership of the factors of production, degree of central planning, amount of social programs, taxes. Make a table using the types of economic systems as headings across the top and the characteristics down the side. Fill in the table using these rankings: high, moderate, low. List one example in each category for each system.

2. **Applying Information.** Do activity number 1 and add a fourth column called "Examples." List a country as an example for each economic system on the table.

3. **Writing a Research Report.** Select a nation with the type(s) of economic and political structures discussed in the chapter. Find out about the economic and social conditions of that nation by collecting facts on housing, food production, transportation, medical care, and the role of the government. The most reliable sources are the *Statistical Abstract of the United States*, United Nations reports, and government statistical bulletins, all of which can be found in the library. Use the information you gather to write a research report.

READINGS

Cave, Martin; McAuley, Alastair; and Thorton, Judith, eds. *New Trends in Soviet Economics.* New York: M.E. Sharpe, 1982.

Childs, Marquis, W. *Sweden: The Middle Way on Trial.* New Haven, Conn.: Yale University Press, 1984.

"China Walks the Edge of the Capitalist Road." *Business Week,* 18 October 1982, pp. 80–86.

Lekachman, Robert, and Van Loon, Borin. *Capitalism for Beginners.* New York: Pantheon, 1981.

Volgyes, Ivan. "Hungary: Socialism with a Nervous Tic." *Current History,* November 1982, pp. 362–65.

"Why Workers Won't Work in the Soviet Union." *Forbes,* 6 December 1982, pp. 138–48.

CHAPTER 22

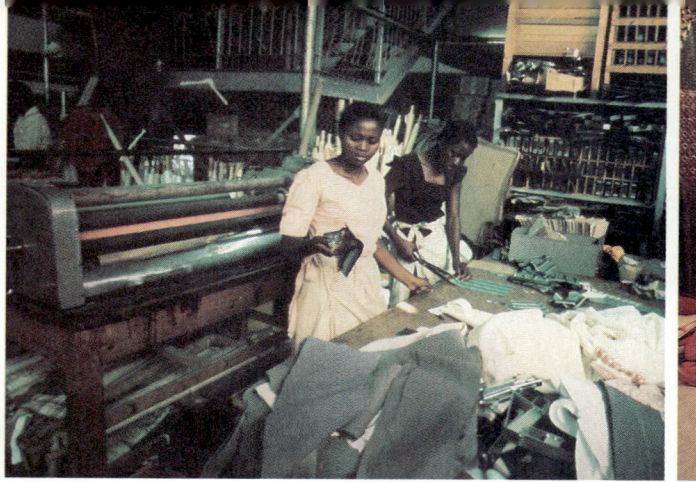

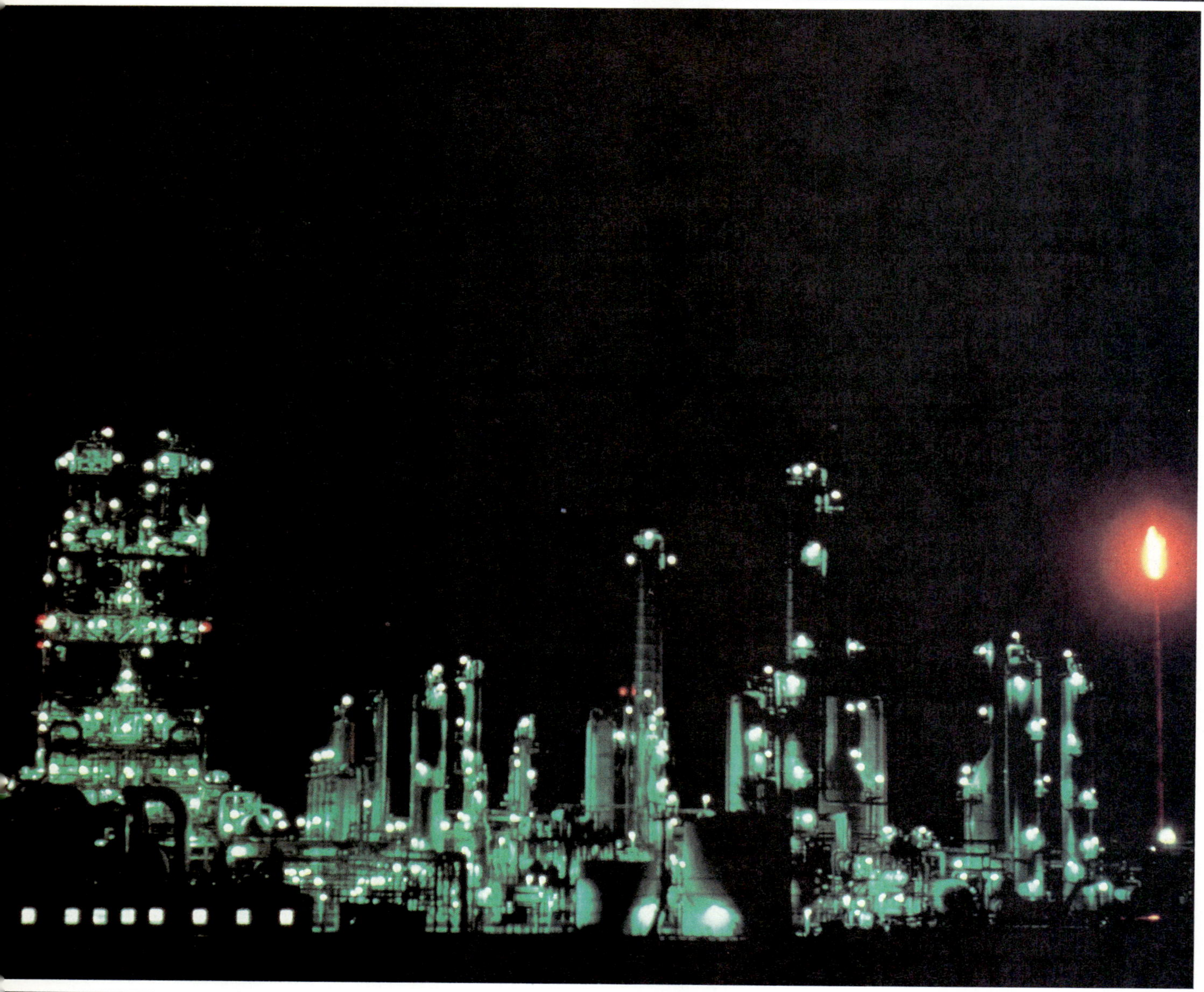

Many nations of the world, especially in Asia, Africa, and Latin America, have the labor force and natural resources needed to develop industrialized economics. These developing nations have received money capital and foreign aid from both capitalist and Communist nations.

ECONOMIC GROWTH IN DEVELOPING NATIONS

The problems Americans face are those associated with being relatively rich—urban crowding and pollution. Developing nations, however, struggle with life-threatening problems such as widespread poverty and hunger. In many cases, developing nations must deal with keeping their people alive. This chapter describes the criteria used to define a nation as *developing*. It then explains the choices these nations have available for financing their economic development. You will read about the obstacles these nations face and their need for balanced growth. The possible future for developing nations is also explored. Learning Economic Skills describes the use of statistics to interpret trends.

CHAPTER OBJECTIVES After you study the sections of this chapter, you will be able to:

1 • list five characteristics most developing nations share.

2 • explain three ways for financing economic development in developing nations.

3 • contrast the two major forms of foreign aid.
  • state four reasons for giving foreign aid.
  ★ list the problems to avoid in using statistics to recognize and interpret trends.

4 • list four obstacles to growth in developing nations.
  • explain what is meant by the term *Malthusian trap*.

5 • explain why rapid industrialization may not be the answer for all developing nations.
  • describe the possible future for developing nations.

ECONOMICS VOCABULARY

developed nation
developing nation
subsistence agriculture
foreign aid
economic assistance
multinational
technical assistance
military assistance
trend

The workers are constructing a government building in the African nation of Mali. Why do you think this developing nation is using its resources for this purpose?

subsistence (suhb-SIS-tuhns): having just enough to eat for survival

Many Americans may not realize it, but even the poorest families in the United States usually have an income far above the average income in most of the rest of the world. In fact, more than one-half of the world's population lives at or close to subsistence, that is, having just enough to eat for survival.

Out of the 168 nations in the world, only about 30 are considered **developed nations.** This group is composed of the United States, Canada, most European countries, plus Japan, Australia, New Zealand, and the Soviet Union. These nations share a relatively comfortable way of life and an economy based more on industry than agriculture. They contain about 25 percent of the world's population but account for almost 80 percent of world GNP.

The remaining three-quarters of the world's population live in **developing nations.** These are nations with less industrial development and a relatively low standard of living. Within this general definition, however, there are many differences in nations. Mexico, for example, is usually considered a developing nation. Forty percent of its work force is employed in agriculture, compared with less than 3 percent in the United States. What industry it does have is concentrated around a few major cities. The average income per person is only one-fifth that of the United States. On the other hand, Mexico is much more developed and prosperous than almost all other developing nations. In Chad, for example, 90 percent of the work force is involved in farming. Average income is only about $\frac{1}{120}$th that of the United States.

rural (RUR-uhl): in the country; away from the city

Besides differences in standard of living among developing nations, there are often great differences within a nation. For example, about 10 percent of India's population lives and works in modern cities much like those in developed nations. In rural India, however, the majority of the population never has enough to eat. The average family lives three to a room, often in mud houses. Only a fraction of these homes have running water and electricity. In this chapter, you will learn more about these nations and the difficulties they face in achieving economic development.

1 | CHARACTERISTICS OF DEVELOPING NATIONS

Ask yourself as you read:

• What are some of the characteristics of developing nations?
• How do developing nations differ from developed nations?

Despite differences, most developing nations share a number of characteristics. These include: 1. low per capita GNP, 2. an agricultural economy, 3. poor health conditions, 4. a low literacy rate, and 5. rapid population growth.

LOW PER CAPITA GNP

As you learned in Chapter 21, economists often use per capita GNP as a rough measure of a nation's prosperity. The United States and the other developed nations have per capita GNPs ranging from around $7,000 to $17,000 a year. Per capita GNP for developing nations are generally below $2,000 a year. Per capita GNP for the poorest nations—Bangladesh, Chad, and Bhutan (boo-TAHN), for example—falls even below that. Bangladesh has a per capita GNP of about $150, compared with $16,000 for the United States. Developing nations may have many natural and human resources. However, they may lack the equipment, financing, and knowledge necessary to put these resources to use. In such cases the value of their output will remain low in relation to population. They will have fewer goods and services for citizens to consume than will developed nations.

AN AGRICULTURAL ECONOMY

One reason that per capita GNP for developing nations is low is that most of their economic activity is centered on agriculture. Often families farm small plots of land with the same methods that have been used for centuries. They may have no knowledge of or access to fertilizers, modern farming methods and equipment, new types of seed or animals, and so on. Or if they have the knowledge, the technology may not exist for their particular farming needs. As a result, much of the population exists through **subsistence agriculture.** Each family grows just enough to take care of its own needs. This means no crops are available for export or to feed an industrial work force.

POOR HEALTH CONDITIONS

Poor health conditions are also common in many developing nations. A shortage of food and a lack of variety in diet cause malnutrition, or illness due to lack of food, and even starvation. Developing nations may also suffer from a shortage of modern doctors and hospitals. The few doctors available may have trouble reaching people in isolated areas and may lack medicines and equipment. The result is often a high infant mortality rate and a low life expectancy among adults. Infant mortality is measured by the number of infant deaths per 1,000 live births.

malnutrition (mal-noo-TRISH-uhn): illness due to lack of food

Table 22-1: ECONOMIC AND SOCIAL STATISTICS FOR SELECTED NATIONS IN A RECENT YEAR

	Per Capita GNP (in dollars)	Life Expectancy (in years)	Infant Mortality (per 1,000 live births)	Birth Rate (per 1,000 population)	Literacy Rate (percentage)
Afghanistan	280	35-39	217-235	50-53	11.3
Bangladesh	148	46	153	43-47	41.4
Canada	11,741	73	12	15	99.5
China (People's Republic)	441	68	NA	19-25	70.0
Colombia	1,423	59	77	28	86.3
Egypt	711	54	92	41-42	54.3
Ethiopia	161	36-44	155-200	42-52	4.8
France	10,082	73	10	14	99.5
West Germany	11,441	72	14	10	99.5
Ghana	2,382	49	115	43-47	44.8
India	261	47	125	33-35	40.3
Indonesia	583	46	114	34-35	66.9
Iran	2,641	58	112	42-44	46.6
Mexico	2,082	60	70	30-33	83.9
Netherlands	9,963	75	9	13	99.5
Nigeria	846	41	178	47-51	29.9
Sri Lanka	364	64	38	28-29	81.0
Switzerland	16,007	74	10	12	99.5
U.S.S.R.	4,882	70	31	18-20	99.5
United States	13,891	73	12	16	99.5
Zaïre	224	37-40	165-177	43-46	57.9

NA—not available

Sources: *Statistical Abstract of the U.S.;* International Demographic Data Center; Bureau of the Census

LOW LITERACY RATE

literacy (LIT-uhr-eh-see): ability to read and write

A fourth characteristic of developing nations is a low adult literacy rate—the percentage of people who are able to read and write. The citizens of many developing nations cannot read and write because their governments do not have the resources to build and maintain schools. Even where public education is offered, many children must miss school to help their families with farming. The lack of a large pool of educated workers makes it difficult to train the population for the technical and engineering jobs necessary for industrial development.

RAPID POPULATION GROWTH

A fifth characteristic—rapid population growth—is often the source of many other problems in developing nations, such as lack of food and housing. In general, developing nations have significantly higher rates of population growth than developed nations. For example, the population in the United States grows at less than 1 percent a year. The growth rate in many developing nations in Africa and Latin America is three and sometimes four times this rate. This means a nation such as Ghana, with a growth rate of 3.2 percent, will double its population in 22 years.

Table 22-1 lists statistics for these characteristics for a number of nations. As you can see, the differences between developing and developed nations are often large. For example, Americans have a life expectancy that is almost twice that of Ethiopians. In Afghanistan, the infant mortality rate is almost 18 times higher than in the United States.

REVIEWING ECONOMIC PRINCIPLES

1. Write a sentence defining each of these terms: **a.** developed nation, **b.** developing nation, **c.** subsistence agriculture.
2. Explain how each of the following would contribute to a nation's being classified as developing: **a.** low per capita GNP, **b.** an agricultural economy, **c.** poor health conditions, **d.** a low literacy rate, **e.** rapid population growth.
3. **Critical Thinking: Inferring Cause and Effect.** Choose one characteristic above. In a paragraph, explain how it contributes to keeping a nation in the category of a developing nation. You will have to infer this cause-effect relationship.

2 | THE PROCESS OF ECONOMIC DEVELOPMENT

Ask yourself as you read:
- How is economic development usually financed?
- What are some of the problems with foreign investment?

Most nations pass through three stages of economic development. The first is the agricultural stage, when most of the population has jobs in farming. The second is the manufacturing stage, when much of the population has jobs in industry. In the third stage, there is a shift of workers into the service sector—sales, food service, repair work, and so on. In its economic development, the United States has followed these stages. It began as an agricultural nation in the late 18th century and passed into an industrial economy in the late 19th century. The mid-20th century has seen the rapid growth of the service sector.

Most developing nations are still in the agricultural stage. Many have a large labor force and the natural resources necessary for an industrial economy. However, they generally lack the money, capital, and trained personnel to put these resources to work. A basic problem for many developing nations, then, is how to finance the equipment and training necessary to improve their standard of living.

personnel (per-suh-NEL): persons employed

553

FINANCING ECONOMIC DEVELOPMENT

One source of money capital is domestic savings. Many people believe that people in developing nations cannot save because they are barely subsisting. In fact, even very poor people do save something for their future. However, it may not be in a form that is useful for capital investment. For example, in a traditional economy, saving may involve storing grain that can later be traded for other goods. While this is saving, it does not provide a pool of money from which businesses can borrow for investment. Although they have some money available from domestic savings, many developing nations must look to outside sources for investment capital.

The two major outside sources are investment by foreign businesses and foreign aid from developed nations. Developing nations often have attractions for investors, such as low wage rates, few regulations on business, and abundant raw materials. Investment may include a corporation's setting up branch offices, fully owned companies, or buying into companies in developing nations.

In the decade from 1975 to 1985, American corporate investment in developing nations almost tripled, growing from $29.8 billion to $84.6 billion. Multinationals such as Exxon operates two-thirds of its gas stations outside the United States, including many in such developing nations as Guatemala and Thailand. A **multinational** is a company that does business in more than one nation. Exxon's investments also include oil wells in Indonesia, coal mines in Brazil, a copper smelter in Chile, and refineries in Jamaica, El Salvador, Argentina, Malaysia, and Kenya. General Motors manufactures diesel engines in Colombia, buses in Taiwan, and trucks in Kenya. Retailers such as Sears and F.W. Woolworth, banks such as Citicorp, and consumer-products firms such as Proctor & Gamble and Coca Cola also have major business interests in developing nations.

PROBLEMS WITH FOREIGN INVESTMENT

Foreign investments do present problems, though. From the investor's viewpoint, the political instability of many developing nations discourages significant investment. Investors know that they could lose their investment if a nation's current government is overthrown and the new leaders nationalize parts of the economy.

resent (ri-ZENT): feel injured or angry about

Problems exist from the developing nation's viewpoint as well. In nations with heavy foreign investment, citizens often resent the economic control these foreign companies have over their resources. For example, the Gulf and Western Corporation has been accused of operating a "state within a state" in the Dominican Republic. During the late 1970s, Gulf and Western owned 264,000 acres (105,600 hectares), or 8 percent of the nation's arable land. It produced one-third of the nation's sugar and had investments in livestock, tobacco, and fruit and vegetable production. The company owned resort hotels, shipping facilities, part of the nation's railway system, and more than 80 other businesses.

Local and international groups accused the corporation of, among other things, contributing to a food shortage. Supposedly Gulf and Western did this by converting farmland from growing food for local consumption to the more profitable production of sugar cane. In its defense, Gulf and Western maintained that its investments had improved the nation's standard of living. It did, however, increase fruit and vegetable production and sell some land to its employees.

Foreign aid is a second type of financing available to nations. It has played an increasingly important role in economic development.

REVIEWING ECONOMIC PRINCIPLES

1. What is a multinational?
2. What are the three stages of economic development for nations?
3. Why must most developing nations look to outside sources for investment capital?
4. List three reasons why developing nations might be attractive to foreign investors?
5. **a.** State one problem foreign investors may face. **b.** State one problem a developing nation may have with foreign investors.
6. **Critical Thinking: Identifying the Main Idea.** Besides domestic savings and foreign investment, what is a third major source of investment capital for developing nations?

3 | ASSISTANCE FROM OTHER NATIONS

Ask yourself as you read:
- What are some of the reasons for giving foreign aid?
- What are the major types of foreign aid?

Foreign aid is the money, goods, and services given by governments and private organizations to help other nations and their citizens. There are several kinds of foreign aid. **Economic assistance** consists of loans and outright grants of money or equipment to other nations to

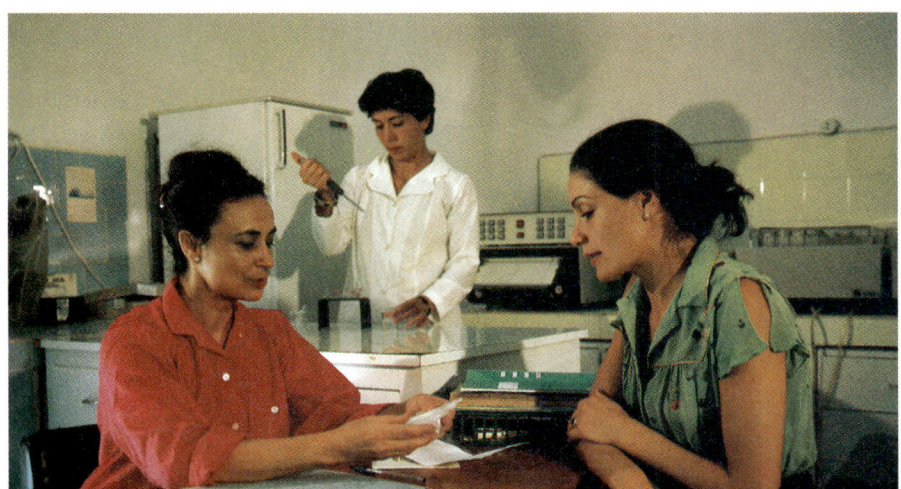

Developing nations use economic assistance to help their people as well as industrialize their economies. What benefits are these Tunisian women receiving at this health clinic built with foreign aid funds?

add to their capital resources. One use of such aid is to help build the transportation and communication systems necessary for economic development. Roads, bridges, and airports, for example, must be built to link isolated regions to the overall economy. A second use for economic assistance is to purchase the basic producer goods needed to develop both agriculture and manufacturing. These include machinery such as tractors, irrigation pumps, canning machines, and so on, that will increase a nation's productivity.

The second major form of foreign aid is **technical assistance.** Nations often provide professionals such as engineers, teachers, technicians, and so on, to teach their skills to individuals in developing nations. Such training is designed to strengthen a nation's human resources in the same way economic assistance increases a nation's capital resources.

technician (tek-NISH-uhn): expert on technical or industrial matters

When either economic or technical assistance is given to a nation's armed forces, it is called **military assistance.** For example, a country may lend a developing nation the money to purchase airplanes or tanks. Or it might make a gift of such goods. Nations such as the United States and the USSR also provide military advisers to train soldiers.

Emergency shipments of food, clothing, and medical supplies to victims of drought, earthquakes, floods, and so on, are also considered foreign aid. Governments, many private organizations, and several agencies of the United Nations provide such assistance. This type of foreign aid, however, is not directed toward economic development.

drought (DROWT): lack of rain

WHO SUPPLIES FOREIGN AID?

Many of the developed nations of the world, both capitalist and communist, offer some type of foreign aid to developing nations. The nation giving the largest amount of foreign aid is the United States. In 1986, it paid out more than $9 billion in government-sponsored foreign aid, excluding military assistance, to developing countries.

Although the dollar amount of American foreign aid has been increasing in recent years, the amount of aid after correcting for inflation has actually fallen. Expressed in constant dollars—dollars adjusted for inflation—the United States gives only about one-quarter of what it gave in the years immediately following World War II. At that time, the United States devoted most of its foreign assistance to rebuilding Europe's war-torn economy through the Marshall Plan.

In the 1950s, after European nations had regained much of their economic strength, the United States shifted the focus of its foreign-aid program to developing nations. Today most American foreign aid is sent to developing nations in the Middle East and Southeast Asia. Nations in Africa receive about 11 percent, in Latin America, 7 percent, and in East Asia and the Pacific, 5 percent.

Many of the other major capitalist nations also have foreign-aid programs. France and Great Britain, for example, have concentrated most of their aid programs on their former colonies in Africa and Asia. Japan

The United States gives more foreign aid than any other nation to developing countries. What are some reasons these ships are supplying American aid to the Asian nation of Thailand?

and West Germany both began giving aid to developing nations after their economies had recovered from World War II. Although no country gives as much foreign aid as the United States, several nations do devote a greater percentage of their GNP to foreign aid. Norway's foreign aid, for example, is about 0.8 percent of that nation's GNP. By comparison, foreign aid given by the United States is about 0.2 percent of its GNP.

Communist nations, particularly the Soviet Union and the People's Republic of China, also have foreign-aid programs. For example, the USSR provides assistance, usually in the form of low-interest loans, to developing Communist nations such as Cuba, Vietnam, and Mongolia. The USSR also offers aid to non-Communist nations in which it is trying to establish political or military influence. The Aswan Dam in Egypt and Pakistan's first iron smelter were both built with Soviet assistance. China has also sent foreign aid to non-Communist developing nations. In Africa, for example, it built and largely financed a railroad linking Zambia with a port city in Tanzania.

Some nations channel their foreign aid through a number of United Nations agencies, including the International Bank for Reconstruction and Development—usually called the World Bank. The World Bank was set up in 1945 to make loans to developing nations at low-interest rates. Two affiliates of the bank are the International Development Association (IDA) and the International Finance Corporation (IFC). The IDA lends money to nations that are the least able to obtain financing from other sources. The IFC encourages private investment in developing

Learning Economic Skills

READING A TREND

One of the most important skills required of people in business and government is recognizing and interpreting trends. A **trend** is the general movement of change over a period of time. Trends may be related to many areas of a nation's economy—GNP, consumer spending, foreign trade, demand for a product, and so on. For example, one trend in recent years has been an increase in the value of American exports. Another has been a decrease in the birth rate of developed nations. Both trends show a statistical movement in a particular direction over a number of years.

Businesspeople and government officials must often make decisions about the future based on their readings of trends. A manufacturer, for example, might decide to increase production of spare tractor parts if the trend in recent years has been toward increased exports of tractors.

As with most statistics, trends are easier to recognize if presented in graph form. There are, however, a number of factors you must consider in correctly evaluating trends.

LOOKING AT THE BIG PICTURE

When seeking a trend, it is important to have data for a long enough period of time to establish a general pattern. Otherwise, what you thought was a trend may only be a small or temporary change.

Look at the graph showing imports of industrial-grade diamonds into the United States. For the years 1970 to 1984, the general trend was toward rising levels of imports. However, if you were to draw a graph for only the years 1980 to 1983, it would indicate a downward trend. In fact, this period represents only a temporary exception to an upward trend. Concentrating on only a few years can give a false picture of the overall direction of change.

The amount of time for which you should collect data varies with different types of statistics. For rapidly changing statistics, such as stock prices, important trends can be established in only a few weeks or months. For a statistic that changes very

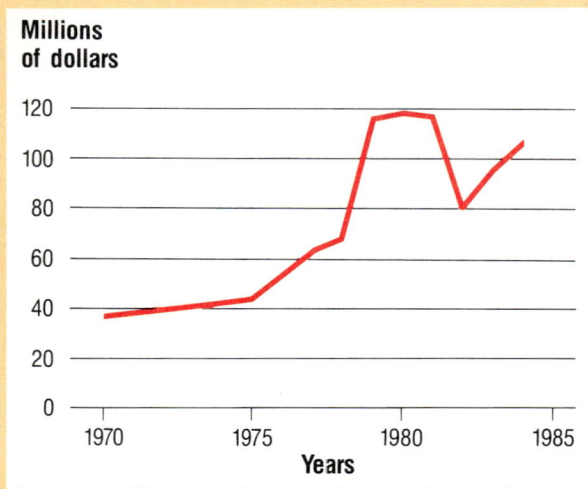

United States Imports of Industrial-Grade Diamonds, 1970-1984

slowly, such as life expectancy, 30 or 40 years may be needed to establish a trend.

How the information is to be used also helps determine the proper time period. Suppose a shop owner needs to order a shipment of Korean tape recorders within a month. In deciding whether to order now or wait a few weeks, he or she probably needs to examine the trend in exchange rates for only the past month or so. On the other hand, a decision may involve a long-term commitment such as building an automobile plant. In this case, those making the decision would examine long-term trends in car sales, wages, financing costs, and so on.

OTHER PROBLEMS TO AVOID

Two other factors you must take into account in recognizing trends are the effects of inflation and changes in population. As you learned in Chapter 14, steadily climbing GNP does not necessarily mean a nation's economy is growing. You must examine real GNP—GNP corrected for inflation—to determine the growth trend.

Likewise, the trend for most goods is to increase in price over time. However, by correcting for inflation, you can determine the more significant trend of which goods increased or decreased their price in comparison with other goods. Televisions, for example, cost more today than 20 years ago, but are nevertheless relatively less expensive.

Changes in population distort trends in much the same way as inflation. For example, from 1975 to 1983, the GNP of the Malagasy Republic increased from $1.8 billion to $2.9 billion—an increase of 62 percent. During the same time, the nation's population increased from 7.6 million to 9.6 million. As a result, per capita GNP, after correcting for inflation, decreased from $314 to $278. What at first seems a trend toward prosperity is actually a trend toward increased poverty.

Successfully recognizing and interpreting trends is really a matter of using wisely the various skills involving statistics and graphs that you have learned in this textbook. Each time you have examined and understood one of the graphs in this book dealing with a period of years, you have been reading a trend.

Practicing Your Skills

Use the two graphs on United States foreign aid to answer the following questions.

1. Based on the graph showing aid in current dollars, **a.** what has been the overall trend since 1946? **b.** what was the trend between 1956 and 1966? **c.** what was the trend between 1976 and 1986? **d.** in which ten-year period did aid increase the most over the previous period?

2. Based on the graph showing spending corrected for inflation, **a.** what has been the overall trend since 1946? **b.** in what ten-year period did spending reach the highest levels in the years after 1955?

3. Based on the two graphs, **a.** in which year was aid in current dollars the highest? **b.** in which year was aid in constant dollars the highest?

U.S. Foreign Economic Aid in Constant Dollars*, 1946-1986

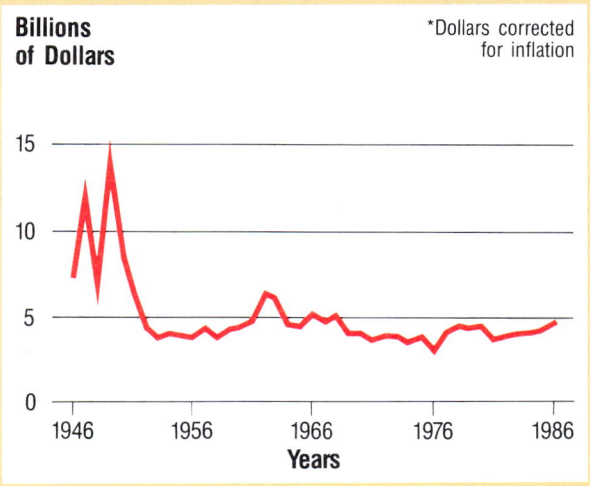

U.S. Foreign Economic Aid in Current Dollars, 1946-1986

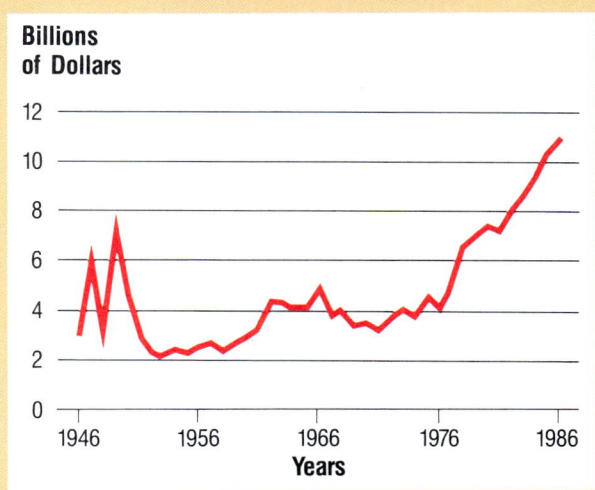

nations. In the 1980s foreign aid agencies grew increasingly alarmed as many developing nations found themselves unable to repay their foreign debts. The World Bank, for example, had to reschedule payments for several nations. The growing foreign debt has been the focus of several international meetings.

REASONS FOR GIVING FOREIGN AID

Humanitarianism is the basis of much foreign aid. The relief of human suffering is a major goal in particular of many private aid organizations. Many rich nations, including the United States, have also decided that they have a responsibility to help end world hunger and disease.

There are at least three other reasons for providing support for government-sponsored foreign aid. The first involves economics. It is usually in the best interests of developed nations to encourage international trade. American foreign aid, for example, often widens the markets for American exports and provides new opportunities for private investment. This is in part because nations are often required to spend American foreign aid on American goods and services.

Politics is also a reason for giving foreign aid. Since the 1950s, an important objective of American foreign aid and that of other major capitalist nations has been to prevent Communists from coming to power. Foreign aid has been given to make developing nations more prosperous and stable and thereby reduce the appeal of Communist arguments. The United States has also used foreign aid to build political friends that will support it in such international bodies as the United Nations.

A fourth reason for giving foreign aid is to help protect a nation's own security. Economic aid is often, in effect, a down payment on a military alliance with a developing nation. Through such alliances, or partnerships with other nations, the United States has gained overseas military bases and observation posts that it can use to gather information about the Soviet Union and other nations. However, this type of plan can backfire if a friendly government loses power. In such a situation, the military equipment given that nation would fall into the hands of the new government, one that may be hostile to the United States.

humanitarianism (hyoo-man-uh-TER-ee-uh-niz-uhm): principles or practices helpful to humanity

alliance (uh-LY-uhns): partnership between nations

REVIEWING ECONOMIC PRINCIPLES

1. What is the difference between economic assistance and technical assistance in foreign aid?
2. What are two ways in which economic assistance is used?
3. Why is some economic or technical assistance also called military assistance?
4. **Critical Thinking: Analyzing Information.** Explain why each of the following is a reason for giving foreign aid: **a.** humanitarianism. **b.** economics, **c.** politics, **d.** a nation's own security.

4 | OBSTACLES TO GROWTH IN DEVELOPING NATIONS

Ask yourself as you read:

• What are the main obstacles to economic growth in developing nations?

• Why did Indonesia fail to experience rapid economic growth?

The successful rebuilding of the European economy following World War II convinced many economists that injections, or additions, of capital into a nation could achieve rapid economic growth. As a result of this belief, billions of dollars flowed into developing nations during the 1950s and 1960s. However, aid to many of these nations failed to produce the same growth as in Europe and Japan. A number of economists, therefore, began rethinking the role of foreign aid in economic development.

Critics of foreign aid pointed out that Europe's rapid recovery following the war was a special case. In 1945, Europe already had skilled labor forces, advanced organizations such as corporations and trade groups, and experienced government bureaucracies, or offices and agencies. It lacked only the money to rebuild the physical machinery of what had been well-functioning economies. Once that money was supplied, growth was rapid. Critics today are using much the same arguments for the rapid economic growth of South Korea, Taiwan, and Hong Kong.

bureaucracy (byoo-RAHK-ruh-see): structure of agencies and officials

Many developing nations, however, face a number of obstacles to growth that are not immediately solved by injections of capital. The attitudes or beliefs of individuals, for example, are important factors in determining a nation's economy. Yet they are usually slow to change. In many developing nations, people live and work much as their ancestors

Some developing nations like South Korea have made rapid gains in industrializing their economies. Here, in this modern Korean plant, automated, computer-controlled processes are used to produce steel, from ore to finished rolled steel.

did hundreds of years before. Innovation of any sort is often viewed with suspicion. Farmers, for example, may be reluctant to accept a new way of plowing, even though it means better soil conservation and a larger harvest.

Continued rapid population growth is a second major obstacle to economic development. A high population growth rate may reduce the rate of growth of a nation's standard of living. Even if a nation's economy is growing, per capita GNP will decrease if its population is growing at a faster rate.

Sometimes nations have been held back from more rapid development through the misuse of natural or human resources. Aid may have been spent on superhighways or military equipment when it would have been better used for agricultural development. In other cases, governments have trained young people in political science and foreign diplomacy when the nation really needs more engineers and technicians. In some nations, those in power have used foreign aid to increase their own wealth rather than raise the standard of living of all the people.

Trade restrictions on imports are a fourth obstacle to growth. To develop domestic industries, many developing nations have used import restrictions such as quotas and tariffs. The result has been to prevent the purchase of cheaper foreign substitutes for what are often inefficiently produced domestic goods.

CASE STUDY: INDONESIA

When Indonesia won independence from the Netherlands in 1949, it seemed well equipped for economic growth. With a population of about 76 million, it was the world's sixth most populous nation. It was rich in minerals such as nickel, tin, bauxite, and copper, and had vast oil reserves as well as valuable farmland and rain forests. Over the next 15 years, President Achmed Sukarno (soo-KAHR-noh) obtained foreign aid totaling over $2 billion from both capitalist and communist nations. Yet at the end of this time, Indonesia's economy was a disaster.

The reasons behind this failure reveal some of the problems of trying to bring rapid growth to developing nations. One problem involved attitudes. Indonesians lacked a sense of national identity. Indonesia had been formed from several former Dutch colonies, and its people were divided by nationality, religion, and politics. These differences sometimes resulted in violent clashes. However, the major blame for economic failure can be placed on Sukarno's economic policies.

At first Sukarno was skillful in obtaining foreign aid even from rivals such as the United States and the USSR. His increasingly harsh attacks on capitalism, however, resulted in a cutoff of American foreign aid in the mid-1960s. The foreign aid that did come into the country was often wasted on projects such as sports stadiums and department stores stocked with imported goods for the rich. Nothing was done to develop Indonesia's mineral resources. The transportation system of roads and

The Malthusian Trap: Thomas Malthus (1766–1834)

In 1798, a little-known English minister named Thomas Malthus published *An Essay on the Principle of Population, As It Affects the Future Improvement of Society.* The essay summarizes Malthus' observations made while traveling in other countries. His conclusion was that "population, when unchecked, goes on doubling every 24 years, or increases in the geometric ratio." Food production, on the other hand, only increases at an arithmetic (ar-ith-MET-ik) ratio. According to Malthus, the birth rate would have to be reduced where population growth was greater than economic growth. Otherwise, eventually there would not be enough food.

The graph below illustrates Malthus' view, known as the Malthusian (mal-THOO-zhuhn) trap. The red line represents a population rising at a geometric rate. Note that it starts slowly and gradually grows steeper. The other line represents food production. As you can see, it rises in a straight line.

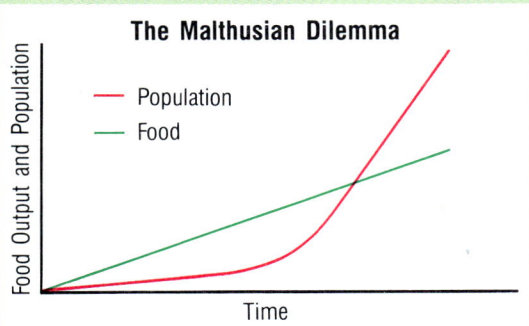

The Malthusian Dilemma

— Population
— Food

Food Output and Population

Time

In 1803 Malthus published a second edition of his essay on population. Although he modified his arguments, he still claimed that population tended to outrun the food supply. He claimed that humanity was doomed to poverty unless the rate of population growth was slowed by positive checks and/or preventive checks. Preventive checks decrease the birth rate, and positive checks increase the death rate. He listed as preventive checks such things as late marriage or no marriage at all and moral restraint. However, Malthus put much more faith in such positive checks as wars, disease, and famine.

It is not surprising that Malthus' theory was criticized severely. However, there is some truth to Malthus' theory. It accurately reflects the history of population growth and food production before the industrial revolution. Perhaps it even applies to some nations today.

The industrial revolution had a major effect on Malthus' thinking. That time in England was difficult for workers. Machines were replacing craftworkers, many of whom could not immediately find other jobs. Some people believed that England had become overpopulated.

In this century some nations have suffered and continue to suffer from overpopulation and food shortages. Nevertheless, the Malthusian theory is inaccurate for industrialized nations such as the United States. First, Malthus assumed a fixed, or unchanging, level of technology. However, improved farming technology and practices have greatly increased the supply of food. Second, the population of industrialized areas has not grown at the rate predicted by Malthus, even though people live longer. A characteristic of many industrialized nations is the leveling-off of their population growth rates. But, as the world grows "smaller," problems that affect developing nations also affect industrialized nations.

1. Describe Malthus' theory of population growth and the food supply.
2. Evaluate the validity of Malthus' ideas in today's world.

Indonesia's oil production shown in this oil refinery in Sumatra spurred that nation's economic growth. What effect did the world oil glut of the 1980s have on this developing nation?

rail lines that had been built by the Dutch was allowed to fall apart. Over a period in which the nation's population increased by one-third, rice and rubber production fell. Sukarno nationalized many businesses, which discouraged foreign investors. Heavy regulation of business, a huge government bureaucracy, and widespread corruption also contributed to the burden on the economy. Inflation was out of control. The nation's price index rose from 100 in 1953 to 3,000 only 10 years later. The government's policy of simply printing more money to pay its bills created much of the problem. By the mid-1960s, the national debt was $2.5 billion.

Indonesia's economy began to improve in the late 1960s after General Suharto (soo-HAHR-toh) replaced Sukarno. Suharto restored confidence in the government by tightening the control of money, reducing corruption, doing away with some of the vast bureaucracy, and making alliances with some Western nations. Suharto encouraged foreign aid and investment and concentrated this new capital on improving agricultural output. This increased food production allowed Indonesia to spend less money on importing food and more on buying the producer goods needed to develop industry.

By the end of the 1970s, Indonesia was one of the fastest growing economies among developing nations. This was in part due to growth in industry. Mostly, however, it was the result of increases in food output and oil production. Unfortunately, Indonesia, like many developing nations recently, has found that reliance on a few products can be dangerous. In the early 1980s, the world "oil glut" and falling prices for farm products cut deeply into the nation's trade income. Despite Indonesia's promising growth, this change, along with its rapidly growing population, make the future uncertain.

Indonesia's value as a case study lies in the variety of lessons it teaches about foreign aid. On the one hand, it illustrates that simply pouring money into a developing nation will not guarantee economic growth. On the other hand, Indonesia also shows that growth can occur if government restrictions on economic activity are reduced. Foreign aid must be used wisely in combination with domestic savings, foreign investment, and government policies that ensure economic stability. Finally, the case study points out that growth of a developing nation's economy may prove temporary if it depends on only one or two products. Changes in world market conditions have a major impact on nations with such narrowly based economies. Developed nations with broad, diverse, or varied economies are not as affected by ups and downs in the prices of specific goods.

diverse (duh-VERS): varied, made of different things

REVIEWING ECONOMIC PRINCIPLES

1. How do each of the following keep developing nations from economic growth: **a.** people's attitudes? **b.** rapid population growth? **c.** misuse of natural or human resources? **d.** trade restrictions on imports?
2. **Critical Thinking: Applying Information.** Reread the case study about Indonesia. Choose one example from it to illustrate each of the four obstacles to economic development.

5 | INDUSTRIALIZATION AND THE FUTURE

Ask yourself as you read:
- Why might it be wasteful for a developing nation to shift from agriculture to industry?
- How can developing nations cooperate to solve their economic problems?

The high standard of living of many developed nations is most often a result of their high level of industrialization. As you read earlier in this chapter, industrialization is the second stage of economic development. As a result, many developing nations have tried to improve their standard of living by shifting their resources away from agriculture to industry. Attempts at rapid industrialization, however, can prove a wasteful use of scarce resources.

For example, some developing nations have invested in steel factories and automobile plants. However, these nations do not necessarily have a comparative advantage in producing steel or automobiles. As a result, the people in these nations are worse off. Citizens receive less economic value from their resources than they would otherwise. In India, for instance, steel mills produce steel at two to three times what the resource would cost if it were imported.

Rapid economic change can also be harmful if a nation's population does not have time to adapt to new patterns of living and working. Suppose much of a nation is converted from subsistence farming to growing one crop for export. This may displace large numbers of people who are no longer needed for farming. Unable to find work in the countryside, many will migrate to the already overcrowded cities.

These traditional and modern scenes exist side by side in Bombay, India. Why is the rapid influx of displaced farmers into overcrowded cities a problem faced in many developing nations?

appropriate (uh-PROH-pree-it): proper, suitable

Another aspect of industrialization and balanced growth is the use of technology that is appropriate, or suitable, to a culture. For example, suppose most of the population in a developing nation still farms with wooden plows drawn by teams of oxen. The nation will not necessarily get the greatest benefit from buying large, sophisticated tractors. Many farmers may be unable to use such modern equipment. In addition, along with the tractors come the problems of supplying fuel, spare parts, maintenance, and so on. It may instead be better for the nation to first replace the plows currently in use with ones made of steel. Because plows are much cheaper than tractors, more of them can be bought. As a result, the benefits of modernization can be distributed more widely. This approach also allows the nation to take better advantage of its existing resources—a large population, small plots of land, and animals to pull plows.

Many economists believe industrialization is generally more beneficial if it comes about naturally. Time allows nations to adapt successfully to one stage of development before moving on to the next. Gradually, the developing nation increases its income and savings and its number of skilled and educated workers. Economic conditions reach the point where businesspeople freely decide to build factories instead of increasing farm output. This is exactly what has happened in many nations in Southeast Asia. While remaining largely agricultural, such places as Malaysia and Taiwan have developed booming industrial sectors.

THE FUTURE OF DEVELOPING NATIONS

Because of the media, information about the living standards of developed countries is known even in the remotest villages of developing nations today. These individuals know that people in other parts of the world have more food, better health conditions, better housing, and a more equal distribution of wealth.

One effect of this increased flow of information has been to convince developing nations of the benefits of working together. These nations have come to realize that compared to large developed nations such as the United States and the USSR, each developing nation has little influence over world trade. Together, however, the developing nations can and do have power in the international economic community. Paraguay and Brazil, for example, are together building the world's largest hydroelectric dam, without the use of foreign aid. Regional cooperation is apparent in areas such as the Middle East. There, Kuwait and Saudi Arabia are trying to turn the Sudan desert into the "breadbasket" of the Arab world. On an international level, the United Nations provides a forum for discussion of problems among the developing nations.

A second trend in recent years has been toward more cooperation between developed and developing nations. In 1981, the leaders of 14 developing nations and 8 developed nations, including the United States, met in Cancún, Mexico, to discuss the economic problems faced by poor nations. A major purpose of the meeting was to establish global negotiations aimed at a more equal distribution of the world's wealth and resources.

Some suggestions to achieve this goal included low tariffs for developing nations, an "income tax" on developed nations to pay for international assistance programs, and the use of profits from sea-floor mining to finance development in poor nations. As President Julius Nyerere of Tanzania told delegates, "The Third World is not asking for charity but making a proposal for dealing with a world problem. We are asking for a chance to earn our own living in a just international system."

At a meeting of the International Monetary Fund in South Korea in 1985, a plan was presented to solve some of the debt problems of developing nations. The fund would make more money available for those who were having difficulty securing loans. However, these nations would be expected to establish stable economic policies that would promote growth.

REVIEWING ECONOMIC PRINCIPLES

1. List three reasons why rapid industrialization may not be the answer for all developing nations.
2. Why do many economists believe that time is an important factor in how beneficial industrialization will be to a developing nation?
3. **Critical Thinking: Making Generalizations.** Why have some developing nations begun to work together to improve their economies?

SUMMARY OF
IMPORTANT PRINCIPLES

1
- Most developing countries share a number of characteristics: low per capita GNP, an agricultural economy, poor health conditions, a low literacy rate, and rapid population growth.

2
- The economic development of a nation may be financed through some combination of domestic savings, foreign investment, and foreign aid.

3
- Economic assistance consists of loans and outright grants of money or equipment to other nations to add to their capital resources. Technical assistance is given in the form of professionals teaching their skills to individuals in developing nations. Economic or technical assistance given to develop a nation's armed forces is called military assistance.
- There are four major reasons for giving foreign aid: the desire to relieve human suffering (humanitarianism); economic self-interest of developed nations (economics); the desire to keep communists from coming to power and to build political friends (politics); protection of a nation's own security through establishing military alliances with developing nations (security).
- When reading statistics for a trend, it is important to have data for a long enough period of time to establish a general pattern and to consider the possible effects of inflation and population changes on that data.

4
- Obstacles to growth in developing nations include: people's attitudes, continued rapid population growth, misuse of natural or human resources, trade restrictions on imports.
- According to Thomas Malthus, population increases in a geometric ratio while food production increases in an arithmetic ratio. If the population rate is not reduced drastically in places where population growth is greater than economic growth, there would not be enough food to feed the population.

5
- Rapid industrialization may not be the answer for developing nations that do not have a comparative advantage in producing some good which they decide to grow or manufacture. A nation must also be careful to choose technology that is appropriate to its culture. Rapid economic change can also be harmful if a nation's population does not have time to adapt to new patterns of living and working. Many modern economists believe that industrialization is generally more beneficial if it comes about in a nation in its own time and in the way that is best suited to the particular problems or conditions that exist in the nation.
- In recent years, developing nations have begun to work together to use their combined power in the world economic community. There has also been cooperation between developed and developing nations in trying to make life better in the nonindustrial world.

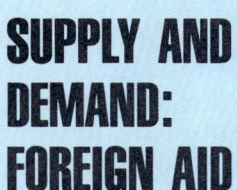

Putting Economics to Work

SUPPLY AND DEMAND: FOREIGN AID

Carl Lindbloom works on the farm after school. He often discusses U.S. programs to help developing nations with his parents. Carl's parents favor increased foreign aid. In theory, Carl agrees. However, he thinks some foreign aid should be reduced. He explains what he has read recently about the after effects of the Food for Peace program, which gives surplus farm commodities to foreign nations.

Carl points out that by giving surplus food products to another nation, the United States is disrupting the system of supply and demand in that nation. Supply and demand are supposed to signal individual farmers that increased production of food will be profitable in the future. As Carl puts it, "Take the example of wheat. If there is a reduction in the supply of wheat in any one year, for whatever reason, its price will rise. As the price rises, the profit from raising wheat also rises. This provides an incentive for those already in the farm sector to use more resources to provide more wheat for the future. It can also work as an incentive for more people to farm wheat. The result is an increase in production."

When the United States ships food to a foreign nation, the price of food there does not rise as sharply as it would without such aid. Fewer individuals will raise food because the reward is smaller.

Carl's parents are unconvinced. They admit that profit incentive is needed over the long run to develop fully a nation's agricultural potential. They point out, however, that food shipments are often made in response to emergencies such as drought or flooding. "We have to help prevent starvation."

1. Would you agree with Carl? Why or why not?
2. What effect do you think government buying of farm commodities for foreign aid have on the price of those goods in the United States?

Readings in Economics

PROFILE OF THE DEVELOPING WORLD
Skill: Making Inferences

 Economist Barbara Ward has written many books about developing nations. In this reading she describes some of their characteristics.

When we speak of developing countries, the phrase has nothing to do with levels of culture or history or contribution to mankind's heritage of civilization. The phrase in the main means simply that a society has not yet crossed the threshold to the modern, high-technology society with all the advantages and evils this passage entails. The category includes countries of immensely old and sophisticated civilizations, such as India or China—which, between them, make up a third of the human race—long-established literate and urban-oriented societies in Latin America and some of the most ancient and continuous of all the world's political units—Egypt—for instance, or Iran.

A fairly arbitrary estimate is often made which fixes at an annual income of $500 a head, the level at which a country begins to emerge fully from the pretechnological condition. But 80 per cent of the nations at and below that level have annual per capita incomes of less than $250. This figure gives a better guide to the bleak realities of personal poverty for citizens and . . . [scarce] resources for governments in developing lands. Investment to provide for the . . . increases in productivity needed for development is a third lower than in high-income countries with incomes above $1000 a year. A third of this investment is not covered by local savings and must be secured abroad. Tax revenues, another critical source of funds for investment, welfare, and amenities, are only just over half the level in developed lands.

All this is a statistical abstract of extreme shortages of resources, either private or public, for consumption and for investment. The profile gives us other evidence of pressure. For instance, nearly 60 per cent of the population is still working in agriculture, where productivity has been, until very recently, almost universally low. (The figure for the most highly developed nations—

This dam on the Volta River in the African nation of Ghana was built to fill the country's urgent need for electric power.

above $2000 per capita—is only 8 per cent of the work force.) Nearly 70 per cent of exports are still primary products, which tend . . . to fluctuate most widely and weaken most easily. Yet imports of goods and services, mainly the expensive machines and skills needed to increase productivity, are not much lower than those of the developed nations already at the $1000-a-year level.

1. Give examples of developing countries that are not yet considered modern, high-technology societies but have ancient cultures and traditions.
2. What are the characteristics of a developing nation?

Barbara Ward and Rene Dubos, *Only One Earth*. New York: W. W. Norton & Co., 1972. pp. 146, 147.

THE MECHANIZATION OF LABOR
Skill: Organizing Information

 Because of the increased wealth and higher standard of living made possible by industrialization, its negative side is sometimes ignored. In this excerpt historian Mary Beth Norton describes industrialization's effect on workers.

By 1880, when almost 5 million Americans worked in manufacturing, construction, and transportation, the status of labor had shifted dramatically from what it had been a generation earlier, when there were only 1.5 million workers in these industries. Most workers could no longer accurately be termed producers—as craftsmen and farmers had traditionally considered themselves. The enlarged working class now consisted mainly of employees—people who worked only when someone else hired them, not when or how they pleased. Whereas producers were paid by consumers according to the quality of what they produced, employees were paid wages based on time spent on the job.

As mass production subdivided manufacturing into minute tasks, workers spent their time repeating one specialized operation. . . .

No longer was it up to the worker to decide when to begin and end the work day, when to rest, and what tools and techniques to use. Especially as assembly-line production spread, employees lost their sense of independence. As a Massachusetts factory worker complained in 1879, "During working hours the men are not allowed to speak to each other, though working close together, on pain of instant discharge [loss of their jobs]. Men are hired to watch and patrol the shop."

And workers were now surrounded by others who, like themselves, worked at the same rate for the same pay, regardless of the quality of their work.

The men and women affected by these changes did not accept them passively. Workers reacted to industrialization by struggling to retain their independence and self-respect in the face of employers' ever-increasing power. . . . Artisans such as cigar makers, glass workers, and coopers . . . fought to preserve the pace and quality of their efforts and held on to such customs as appointing a fellow worker to read aloud while they worked. . . .

Employers in turn took steps to establish standards that they thought would enhance efficiency and productivity. In order to make workers docile (like machines), they supported temperance and moral reform societies, dedicated to combating supposed drinking and debauchery on and off the job. . . . And they [employers] lowered wages, forcing people to work harder and longer just to maintain the same income.

1. Describe the shift in workers' occupations as a result of industrialization.
2. What effect did industrialization have on workers?

Norton, Mary Beth, et al., *A People and a Nation: A History of the United States*, Vol. II. Boston: Houghton Mifflin, 1986. pp. 494–495.

WHAT IS NEEDED FOR SUCCESSFUL FOREIGN AID?

Skill: Understanding Cause and Effect

Foreign assistance by developed nations to developing countries, no matter how well-intended, may not always succeed in helping those countries. In this reading, Jack Sheperd, a specialist on United States foreign policy, discusses the failures of foreign-assistance programs in some African nations.

On one key issue . . . donors and Africans do agree: the aid provided during the past two decades has helped little, and the existing aid programs need reappraisal [rethinking]. Before the colonial period, African agriculture was geared to self-sufficiency in food production. Most societies fed themselves, although famines were not unheard of. . . .

During almost a century of colonial rule, African agriculture was transformed. Colonial governments favored large-scale plantation operations that produced cash crops for the benefit of the colonial power. Independent African farmers got pushed onto marginal land or, more often, into soil-poor native reserves; some had to work on the large cash-crop farms or in the town. Still, many African nations were self-sufficient with respect to food, or were even exporting food, in the early 1960s.

With independence, however, African governments promoted industrialization at the expense

Readings in Economics

of food production, while continuing the colonial pattern of producing cash crops to earn foreign exchange. Food imports increased in the two decades after most of Africa became independent, and as world prices for cash crops fell and populations grew rapidly and debts rose, many new African governments found themselves struggling to feed their people.

During the 1970s African governments inaugurated a range of projects aimed at increasing domestic-food production. The ones most widely favored—funded by the United States Agency for International Development (USAID), the World Bank, and other international agencies—were large, mechanized and highly capitalized. Moreover, investment in food production often favored crops consumed by people in the cities: wheat, rice, and sugar.

A vast portion of the aid went to what some donors now admit were "easy options"—projects that drew on donor expertise and promised a rapid rate of return. Some of the schemes involved tractors, chemical fertilizers, irrigation and large-scale state farms. Money also went into highly visible projects such as highways, hospitals in urban areas, and convention halls. But deep plowing and the use of chemical fertilizers did not increase yields, and perhaps even threatened an African farming system that had evolved over centuries. The Green Revolution, so successful in parts of Asia, did not transplant well to Africa, with its fragile soils, variable climates, and need for irrigation. Irrigation projects tended to produce a great deal of food but at a cost of $20,000 a hectare, and sometimes they drew off farm labor better used elsewhere, or spread schistosomiasis and other waterborne diseases.

1. Explain why foreign assistance to developing countries in Africa has not always had a beneficial effect on the countries receiving aid.
2. Suggest what countries offering assistance to a developing country might do to insure that their aid is useful and beneficial to the developing country.

Jack Shepherd, "When Foreign Aid Fails." *The Atlantic Monthly*, April 1985, pp. 41—46.

THE FORCE OF TRADITION

Skill: Identifying the Main Idea and Supporting Details

SECTION 4

Traditional social and political institutions often act to hinder genuine economic modernization and growth in developing countries. The author of the following reading discusses this problem in the context of Latin America.

Change always occurs. Change has taken place in Latin America. Latin America in the 1980s differs markedly from Latin America in the 1880s. Perhaps most noticeable among the changes is the presence of a significant middle class exercising a dominant role in the social, economic, and political life of each nation. Many of the most vigorous political parties spring from that class. Leaders from that class direct the potent force of nationalism, encourage industrialization and progress, and contribute to the vitality of the cities. Urban unionized laborers constitute a relatively new and important group as well. Some of them enjoy a reasonable wage and impressive social benefits. On occasion they have exerted political influence. Transportation and communication networks now cover large parts of most of the nations, giving them a greater cohesion than ever before. Increasingly Latin Americans use their own natural resources to promote national growth. . . .

To balance this assessment of change we must return to a familiar theme: despite pockets of change, a veneer of progress, and apparent modernity, much of Latin America retains the flavor of the distant past. In short, the change and modernization that have occurred in the last century have had little positive effect, particularly on the quality of life of the majority.

A major reason for this constancy is that one characteristic still dominates—and enervates—Latin America: the economies grow but do not develop. The most dynamic part of each economy remains linked to exports. The economic policies and performance strengthen institutions nurturing dependency. It is those institutional structures, minimally altered by time, that create the ever-present enigma [complicated problem] of widespread poverty amid potential wealth. . . .

Well-defined institutions from the past, enshrined [held sacred] by the elites and middle classes and which rely on the strength of the military, still prevail. . . . The Latin American experience indicates that change will require strong, determined, and well-led government to break with the past and pursue an innovative course.

1. Why do the economies of Latin American nations "grow but do not develop"?
2. Which groups in Latin American societies have prevented far-reaching changes from taking place? Why?

E. Bradford Burns, *Latin America: A Concise Interpretative History*, 4/e, © 1986, pp. 348, 349–350. Reprinted by permission of Prentice-Hall, Inc., Englewood Cliffs, NJ.

THE SOCIAL CRISIS OF RAPID INDUSTRIALIZATION

Skill: Justifying an Opinion

 **Rapid industrialization in developing nations can bring problems, including extreme inequality in income distribution and the breakdown of traditional societies. Richard J. Barnet describes these problems and the dangers they pose to other nations as well.**

There is a curious irony in what is happening in the developing countries, which was perhaps summed up best by the offhand remark of the former president of Brazil: "Brazil is doing well but the people are not." The growth rate of developing countries as a whole now exceeds that of industrial countries. . . . The prevailing development model has had perverse effects on income distribution everywhere. Some countries such as Taiwan and South Korea have for peculiar historical reasons had some success with land reform, and . . . "extremely employment-intensive growth," with the result that income distribution is somewhat better than in most other nonsocialist Third World countries. Yet even in these dubious showcases of "growth and equity" the share of the lowest 40 percent has declined and . . . is likely to decline even more sharply. Elsewhere, the export platforms with the most impressive growth—Brazil, Mexico, Iran—have exhibited highly inequitable income distribution, as the richest 5 percent cream off the dividends of development.

The argument is frequently made that the widening gap between rich and poor in such countries ought not to be a matter of great concern, because in absolute terms the poor are doing better. But it is not so clear. The situation varies greatly. Some extremely poor people huddled in urban slums would not trade places with their rural parents, but some clearly would. They are eating fewer calories and fewer proteins. Where people have exchanged a life of ordered drudgery amid familiar surroundings and community support for the uncertain existence of a city street hawker, beggar, or maid, it is not obvious that they are better off or happier, though twice as much money may jangle in their pockets as their grandparents ever saw. In a traditional society where nothing changes, most people accept their place with a certain grace. That the landlord should live in luxury and the tenant farmer in a hovel was as natural as the sunrise. But when the principle of mobility is introduced into a society and envy is stimulated to induce people to work harder and to consume more, the pain of deprivation becomes more intense and gaps begin to matter. In an industrializing world in which the principal activity is getting and spending, more and more people are becoming irrelevant to the productive process, either as producers or consumers. Almost a billion people cannot find enough work at wages adequate to provide food for their families. Every sign suggests that the number will increase dramatically. It is the monumental social problem of the planet, the cause of mass starvation, repression, and crime, petty and cosmic.

1. It is said that "ignorance is bliss." Apply this popular saying to the author's suggestion that mobility makes social inequality more painful.
2. What are the main social problems faced by developing nations?

Richard J. Barnet, *The Lean Years: Politics in the Age of Scarcity*. New York: Simon and Schuster, 1980. pp. 265, 266.

22 | CHAPTER REVIEW

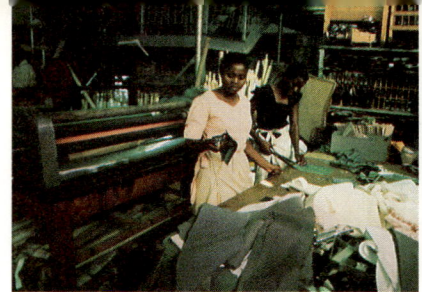

PRACTICING YOUR COMMUNICATION SKILLS: INTERVIEWING

An Interview is a valuable source of primary information. It is an interesting way to gather information for reports or class projects. You should keep in mind, though that an interview is not always factually accurate. It usually reflects a person's memories of events, opinions, and biases. To conduct an interview, follow these tips:

- Prepare the topic for the interview carefully to make sure you really need an interview.
- Decide who would be the best people to interview to gain the information you want.
- Make an appointment ahead of time to interview your subject at his or her convenience. Ask permission at this time to use a tape or video-tape recorder if you wish to record the interview.
- Before arriving at the interview, make a list of specific questions to ask.
- When you arrive, explain the purpose of the interview clearly.
- Take brief notes. It usually is not necessary to record what is said word for word.
- Do not press the person to answer questions that make him or her uncomfortable.
- Be a good listener and a careful observer. Listen to what the person says and observe how he or she expresses opinions. Do not make the interview too long.
- When you have finished, thank the person for giving you the time and information for the interview.

Activity: Choose a topic from the news and arrange an interview about it. If you choose a local issue, such as the school budget, you might interview a member of the school board. If you choose a national issue, such as foreign aid, set up an interview with a friend or relative who has served abroad in the armed forces or traveled or worked abroad.

VOCABULARY REVIEW

Write the letter of the definition in Column B that correctly defines each term in Column A.

Column A	Column B
1. military assistance	a. economic or technical assistance given to a nation's military forces
2. foreign aid	b. raising sufficient food for one's own or one's family's needs
3. subsistence agriculture	c. places with insufficient industrial development
4. developing nations	d. money, goods, and services given by one nation to another nation
5. technical assistance	e. aid in the form of professional expertise from engineers, doctors, teachers, and other specialists

PRACTICING YOUR ECONOMIC SKILLS

1. **Drawing a Line Graph. a.** Use the following statistics to make a line graph showing the value of United States investment in Brazil from 1970 to 1984: $1,526 in 1970; $4,576 in 1975; $7,704 in 1980; $8,997 in 1982; $9,026 in 1983; and $9,551 in 1984. Dollar amounts are in millions.
   b. What is the trend indicated by the graph that you have drawn?
   c. What is the percentage change in investment from 1970 to 1984?
2. **Drawing Bar Graphs.** Choose 12 nations in Table 22-1, and use the statistics to create a bar graph comparing their literacy rates. Draw a second bar graph comparing their GNP's.

DISCUSSING ECONOMIC QUESTIONS

1. Countries with relatively high standards of living are more industrialized than countries with low standards of living. Based on what you have read in this chapter, do you think developing nations should attempt to industrialize rapidly? Why or why not?
2. Many private companies have investments in developing nations. Why do you think companies invest overseas? What factors do you think companies take into consideration when they choose to invest in other nations?
3. Some developing nations believe that the development of a steel industry is important to its development into an industrialized nation. Discuss whether this is or is not a sound belief. What do nations need to become highly developed?
4. Why does the fact that a poor nation is largely dependent on agriculture often stand in the way of rapid economic growth?
5. Nations, like individuals, are influenced by rising expectations. People in almost all parts of the world today are aware of such goods as automobiles, televisions, radios, and canned goods. Imagine that you were the economic planner of a developing nation that has only a little industry. What would you do to get people to save and not buy the above goods right away? What parts of the economy would you develop first? Where would you go to obtain aid?

APPLYING CRITICAL THINKING SKILLS

1. Research a brief report on one of the following: the Marshall Plan, the International Monetary Fund's role in economic development, the Alliance for Progress.
2. Choose a developing nation with a large base of natural resources such as Brazil or Saudi Arabia and research its economic de-

velopment. Explain why development has been slow.
3. Use the "Comparative International Statistics" section of the most recent *Statistical Abstract of the U.S.* to make a table comparing five developed nations and five developing nations. For each nation, give five economic or social statistics other than the ones listed in the table on p. 552. Write a paragraph summarizing what your table shows about these nations.
4. **Making Decisions.** Suppose that you are the leader of a developing nation. Detail the economic conditions that exist in the nation. Then draw up a step-by-step plan for bringing about the economic growth of the nation.
5. **Writing a Research Report.** Choose a developing nation that has received considerable foreign aid and investment to help it develop. Research how that aid has been used and then write a report summarizing the advantages and disadvantages of foreign aid and private investment in the nation.

READINGS

Brown, Lester R. "Global Food Prospects: Setting the Record Straight." *Challenge*, November/December 1982, pp. 48–52.

"Economic Interests Which Exploit Colonial Territories Condemned." *UN Monthly Chronicle*, February 1982, pp. 41–42.

Frank, Andre G. *Crisis in the Third World*. New York: Holmes & Meier, 1981.

Higgins, Benjamin, and Higgins, Jean D. *Economic Development of a Small Planet*. New York: Norton, 1979.

Polunin, Nicholas, ed. *Growth Without Eco-disasters?* New York: Wiley, 1980.

Stockwell, Edward G., and Laidlow, Karin. *Third World Development*. Chicago: Nelson-Hall, 1981.

Ward, Barbara. *The Home of Man*. New York: Norton, 1976.

ISSUE 6

WHAT SHOULD THE UNITED STATES DO ABOUT ITS FOREIGN TRADE PROBLEMS?

After you study this Issue, you will understand arguments for and against restrictions on international trade and why they have been in the national spotlight.

balance of trade   import quotas
trade deficit   protectionism

A steady flow of foreign products into the United States has made the nation into an international marketplace. Walk into an electronics store and you will see videocassette recorders and other items with brand names such as Panasonic, Mitsubishi, Sharp, and Quasar. All of those mark products made by Japanese or Korean companies. Imports fill the shelves and bins and counters of other stores, too. Shirts from China. Bicycles, toys, clothes, and hardware from Taiwan. Shoes from Spain and Italy. Wines from France, Italy, and Germany. Carpets from India and the nations of the Middle East. Tomatoes from Mexico or the Netherlands. That is only a partial list and does not include the countless imported cars, trucks, and motorcycles seen everywhere. As one writer put it, even the steel beams used to build the store you shop in may have come from South Korea.

There is no doubt that this glittering array of products is a boon to American consumers, giving them a wide choice of quality and prices. There is, however, another side to the story and to many Americans, it is a worrisome one.

A MATTER OF BALANCE

If you study Figure 20-2, you will see what the flood of imports has done to the American bal-ance of trade—the difference between the value of a nation's exports and its imports. For most years since 1971, the United States has had a trade deficit—a greater amount of money paid out for imported goods than is earned from goods America exports—and the deficit just seems to keep growing. Some experts fear that America's deficit may reach $200 billion before 1990.

Why is a trade deficit worrisome? Because it affects the nation in a bread-and-butter way. Just one example: When Americans buy more imported clothing made in other countries than American-made clothing, American clothing makers have to close their factories and offices and lay off workers. Laid-off workers lose their spending power and that affects other businesses. The government loses tax money and also pays out more money in unemployment benefits. It should also be noted that when people in other nations buy goods produced in nations other than the United States, American companies are hurt. Why? Because exports drop and more jobs are lost. Some experts say that more than three million U.S. jobs were lost since 1971 after the deficit developed.

WHAT SHOULD BE DONE—IF ANYTHING?

Should something be done to help American business compete more effectively in the domestic and world marketplace? Answers to this question have been argued—sometimes heatedly—all across the nation and in the halls of Congress, in the offices of labor leaders and business executives, and on street corners by laid-off workers.

On one side are those who see a need for some form of protectionism—government restrictions

How the United States deals with its foreign trade problems is an important issue, as this Congressional hearing indicates.

on foreign trade in order to protect Americans from loss of business and jobs. The main protectionist measures are high tariffs, or taxes on imports, and import quotas, or limits on the value or number of products brought in from other countries. Under the Constitution, only Congress can pass such legislation and in the 1980s many attempts have been made to enact such laws.

Many Americans, including top federal government leaders and economists, are strongly opposed to protectionism, arguing that it is not a solution and has no place in world economy.

Here are major arguments on both sides:

THE PROTECTIONIST SIDE

American people believe in fair competition and even welcome it, but international competition today is definitely unfair. How can American clothing companies compete, for example, with clothing items made in countries such as China where workers are paid less than 20 cents an hour? Consumers naturally buy these cheaper goods—and put our own companies out of business. This is not fair competition. Placing tariffs on these cheap foreign goods would even out the prices and give American products a chance.

Foreign competition is also unfair because other nations do not abide by treaties in which they agree to limit amounts of goods they send to the United States. As a result, the American market is flooded with imports and the only way to give American companies equal advantage is to pass import quota laws. These laws would not keep all foreign goods out of the country. They would only limit the amount that could come to it. That way, American companies could be sure of having a share of the market. Other countries do this; why shouldn't we? Japan cut down on leather imports to help its own leather industry. It is time to take similar action in Congress!

THE FREE TRADE SIDE

Protectionist measures are not a solution to the trade deficit problem. To begin with, when one nation puts up trade barriers, other nations tend to do the same. Import restrictions therefore make export industries suffer, so nothing is gained. In addition, it should be remembered that many nations America trades with are developing nations. Free trade can help them grow into strong, independent nations whose people will not need to depend on foreign aid for support.

Moreover, the biggest loser under protectionism is the American consumer, whose spending power helps Americans in the import industry. Spending also stimulates companies to try new ways.

In the end, if certain American products cannot compete in the international markets, then American business and industry can turn to other products and new technology. Many companies are doing just that—taking part in the market system.

Discussing Economic Questions

1. What is a trade deficit—and why is it a matter of concern?
2. If you were a member of Congress, would you vote for any type of protectionist measures? If so, what type? If not, why not?
3. Do you think the reason given for free trade with developing nations is acceptable? Explain your answer.

ECONOMICS VOCABULARY/GLOSSARY

PRONUNCIATION GUIDE

/a/	/th/, /th/	go, home	EYE-land, EYE-ris TYM
/ah/	/u/	oil, boy	hwair, hwim
/ai/	/uh/	hoot, group, new	TIP, FIT
/aw/		for, imports	
/ay/		cow, round	
/ch/	/yoo/	ship, nation	
/e/	/zh/	think, three, that	JET, JEM
/ee/	mat, tap	could, wood	KAYP, KIT, SKOOL
/er/	father, star, pot	sofa, level, pencil,	FIKS
/eye/, /y/	pair, rare	lesson, sun	GOH, HOHM
/hw/	all, raw	future, fuse	OIL, BOI
/i/, /ih/ if in syllable	late, pace	measure, vision	HOOT, GROOP, NOO
by itself	chin, nature		FOR, IM-ports
/j/	pet, red	MAT, TAP	KOW, ROWND
/k/	deed, we	FAHTH-er, STAHR, PAHT	SHIP, NAY-shuhn
/ks/	bird, herd	PAIR, RAIR	THINK, THREE, THAT
/oh/	island, iris, time	AWL, RAW	CUD, WUD
/oi/	where, whim	LAYT, PAYS	SOH-fuh, LEV-uhl,
/oo/	tip, fit	CHIN, NAY-cher	PEN-suhl,
/or/	jet, gem	PET, RED	LES-uhn, SUHN
/ow/	cape, kit, school	DEED, WEE	FYOO-cher, FYOOZ
/sh/	fix	BERD, HERD	MEZH-uhr, VIZH-uhn

Pronounce consonants as you usually do when you meet them in such words as: bet, do, fat, go, have, jet, lid, mom, no, pat, run, set, tot, vim, way, yell, zoo. Stressed syllables are written in capital letters.

ability-to-pay principle: system of taxation in which those with higher incomes pay more in taxes than those with lower incomes (p. 437).

absolute advantage: ability of one country, using the same amount of resources as another country, to produce a particular product at less cost than the other country (p. 505).

accounts receivable: money owed to a business by its customers (p. 276).

agency shop: company in which employees are not required to join the union, but must pay union dues (p. 325).

aggregate (AG-ruh-git) **demand:** total demand for goods and services from all sectors of the economy—consumer, government, business, and foreign (p. 456).

agribusiness: a large corporation engaged in farming operations (p. 482).

annual percentage rate: cost of credit expressed as a yearly percentage (p. 86).

annual report: report from a corporation's management to its stockholders summarizing facts about the company's receipts, costs, and profits (p. 246).

antitrust legislation: laws to prevent new monopolies from forming and to break up those that already exist (p. 254).

arbitration (ahr-buh-TRAY-shuhn): part of negotiation process in which union and management submit the issues they cannot agree on to a third party for a final decision. Both sides agree in advance to accept the arbitrator's decision (p. 330).

articles of incorporation: document establishing a corporation: includes basic information about the corporation, the board of directors, and the stock being issued (p. 224).

assembly line: production system in which the good to be produced moves on a conveyor belt past workers who perform individual tasks in assembling it (p. 286).

asset: item of value, such as housing, car, jewelry, and so on (p. 180).

authoritarian socialism: system that supports revolution as the means to overthrow capitalism and bring about socialist goals. In such a system, the entire economy is controlled by a central government; also called communism (p. 526).

automation: use of machines supervised by people to replace human labor (p. 286).

bait and switch: deceptive advertising practice in which a store attracts customers with an ad offering a product at a low price, and then tries to sell a similar product but at a higher price (p. 61).

balance of trade: difference between the value of a nation's exports and its imports (p. 509).

bankruptcy: inability to pay debts based on the income that is received (p. 180).

bar graph: graph that compares differences between items at one point in time; can also show the change in amounts of items at different times (p. 10).

barriers to entry: obstacles to competition that prevent others from entering a market (p. 245).

barter: exchange of goods and services for other goods and services (p. 376).

base year: year used as a point of comparison for other years in a series of statistics (p. 355).

benefits received principle: system of taxation in which those who use a particular government service support it with taxes in proportion to the benefit they receive (p. 435).

blank endorsement: signature on the back of a check that allows whoever has the check to deposit or cash it (p. 388).

blue-collar worker: a person employed in crafts, manufacturing, or nonfarm labor (p. 318).

bond: certificate issued by a corporation or government in exchange for borrowed money; a bond promises to pay a stated rate of interest over a stated period of time, and to repay the full amount at the end of that time (p. 161).

boom: portion of the business cycle in which economic activity is at its highest point (p. 358).

boycott: activity in which unions urge the public not to purchase the goods or services produced by a company (p. 330).

brand name: word, picture, or logo on a product that helps customers tell it from similar products of competitors (p. 62).

budget: plan for spending and saving income (p. 88).

business cycle: periodic ups and downs in the nation's economic activity (p. 357).

capital: all property—machines, buildings, tools, and money—used to produce other goods and services (p. 6).

capital gain: increase in value of a stock or bond from the time it was bought to the time it was sold (p. 165).

capital loss: decrease in the value of a stock or bond from the time it was bought to the time it was sold (p. 166).

capitalism: system in which individuals own the factors of production and have the right to use those resources in any way they choose within the limits of the law; also called market system, free enterprise system (p. 32).

certificate of deposit: document stating amount of money deposited, the period of deposit, and interest rate. Earns more than a savings account, but a penalty is charged if money is withdrawn early (p. 158).

channels of distribution: routes by which goods are moved from producers to buyers (p. 307).

charge account: agreement that allows a customer to buy goods or services from a particular company and pay for them later (p. 84). *See also* regular charge account, revolving charge account, installment charge account.

check clearing: method by which a check that has been deposited in one depository institution is transferred to the depository institution on which it was written (p. 408).

checking account: money deposited in a bank that a person can withdraw at any time by writing a check (p. 384).

circular flow of income: flow of income from businesses to consumers in the form of wages, rent, interest, and profits, and from consumers to business in the form of payments for goods and services (p. 456).

civilian labor force: total number of people 16 years of age or older who are either employed or actively seeking work (p. 318).

closed shop: company in which only union workers may be hired; now outlawed (p. 325).

closing costs: fees charged by a lender for various costs involved with completing the sale of housing; may include fees for legal costs, taxes, and so on (p. 131).

coincident (koh-IN-suh-duhnt) **indicator:** statistic that changes at about the same time as changes in overall business activity (p. 364).

collateral (kuh-LAT-uhr-uhl): something of value that a borrower uses as a promise to repay a loan (p. 94).

collective bargaining: process by which unions and employers negotitate the conditions of employment (p. 328).

command economic system: system in which the government controls the factors of production and makes all decisions about their use (p. 29).

commercial bank: bank that offers a wide range of banking services; main functions are to accept deposits, lend money, transfer funds (p. 82).

commodity (kuh-MAHD-uh-tee) **money:** money that has a value as a commodity or a good aside from its value as money (p. 378).

common stock: share in a company that entitles the owner to a certain portion of the company's profits and to a vote in certain concerns, such as electing a board of directors (p. 160).

communism: system that supports revolution as the means to overthrow capitalism and bring about socialist goals. In such a system, the entire economy is controlled by a central government; also called authoritarian socialism (p. 527).

comparative advantage: ability of a country to produce a product at a lower opportunity cost than another country (p. 506).

comparison shopping: getting information about the types and prices of products from various stores or companies (p. 62).

competition: rivalry among producers or sellers of similar goods to win more business by offering the lowest prices or better quality (p. 35).

competitive advertising: advertising that attempts to persuade consumers that the product advertised is different from and superior to any other (p. 61).

compound interest: interest figured not only on the original funds deposited, but also on the interest those funds have earned (p. 162).

condominium (kahn-duh-MIN-ee-uhm): a single unit that is in an apartment building or in a series of townhouses and that is owned separately; common areas such as hallways, lobbies, recreational facilities, and the land on which the building is built are owned in common (p. 127).

conglomerate: large corporation made up of smaller corporations dealing in unrelated activites (p. 255).

consumer: any person or group that buys or uses goods or services to satisfy personal needs and wants (p. 56).

consumer durable: manufactured item that a person will use for a long period of time (p. 78).

consumer finance company: company that makes loans directly to individuals at high rates of interest (p. 83).

consumer goods: goods produced for individuals and sold directly to the public to be used as they are (p. 282).

consumer price index (CPI): measure of the change in price over a period of time of a specific group of goods and services used by the average household (p. 354).

consumerism: movement to educate consumers about the purchases they make and to demand better and safer products from manufacturers (p. 64).

contraction: portion of the business cycle in which economic activity is slowing down (p. 358). Also called a trough.

convenience store: store open from 16 to 24 hours a day and carrying a limited selection of goods (p. 109).

cooperative (co-op): business owned and operated by its members; cooperatives may buy and sell goods, manufacture and market products, offer services, or supply housing to members only (p. 128).

corporate charter: license to operate granted to a corporation by the state in which it is established (p. 225).

corporation: organization owned by many people but treated by the law as though it were a person; it can own property, pay taxes, make contracts, sue and be sued, and so on (p. 160).

cosigner: person who signs a loan contract along with the borrower and promises to repay the loan if the borrower does not (p. 94).

cost-of-living adjustment (COLA): part of a union contract or other arrangement that provides for an additional increase in wages each year if the general level of prices in the economy rises beyond a certain amount (p. 329).

cost-push inflation: rise in prices that results from the wage demands of labor unions and the excessive profit motive of large corporations (p. 455).

craft union: union made up of skilled workers in a specific trade or industry (p. 324).

credit: receiving of money either directly or indirectly to buy goods and services in the present with the promise to pay for them in the future (p. 78).

credit bureau: private business that investigates a person's income, current debts, character, and past history of borrowing and repaying debts to determine the risk involved in lending money to that person (p. 91).

credit card: credit device that allows a person to make purchases without paying cash (p. 84).

credit check: investigation of a person's income, current debts, character, and past history of borrowing and repaying debts (p. 91).

credit limit: maximum amount of goods or services a person or business can buy on the promise to pay in the future (p. 84).

credit union: depository institution owned and operated by its members to provide savings accounts and low-interest loans to its members only (p. 83).

death benefits: amount the insurance company pays if the insured dies while the insurance policy is in effect (p. 140).

debt financing: raising money for a business through borrowing (p. 277). *See also* short-term financing, intermediate-term financing, long-term financing.

decreasing term insurance: plan that reduces over a period of years the death benefits a company will pay (p. 140).

deductible: portion of the cost that a person must pay before the insurance company pays anything; stated on the insurance policy (p. 139).

deficit financing: spending by government that exceeds the money it takes in through taxes (p. 440).

demand: willingness and ability of a person to buy an item (p. 186).

demand curve: graph showing the amount of a product that will be bought at different prices; a visual representation of a demand schedule (p. 188).

demand deposit: money deposited in a bank that can be withdrawn at any time (p. 384).

demand-pull inflation: rise in prices that results when total demand on the part of businesses and consumers increases faster than total supply (p. 454).

demand schedule: table showing the amount of a product that will be bought at different prices (p. 188).

democratic socialism: system that works within the constitutional framework of a nation to elect socialists to office. In such a system, government controls only some areas of the economy (p. 526).

depreciate: to decline in value over time; takes place as an item wears out or becomes outdated (p. 129).

depression: major slowdown of economic activity during which millions are out of work, many businesses fail, and the economy operates at far below capacity (p. 358).

deregulation: gradual reduction in government control over business activity (p. 358).

devaluation: lowering of a currency's value in relation to other currencies by government order (p. 508).

developed nation: nation with relatively high standard of living and an economy based more on industry than on agriculture (p. 550).

developing nation: nation with little industrial development and a low standard of living (p. 550).

discount rate: interest rate the Federal Reserve charges on loans to banks (p. 441).

discretionary (dis-KRESH-uh-nairee) **income:** money income a person has left to spend on extras after basic needs have been taken care of (p. 57).

disposable income (DI): income people have left to spend or to save after all taxes have been paid (p. 57). *See also* disposable personal income.

disposable personal income (DI): income people have left to spend or to save after all taxes have been paid (p. 353). *See also* disposable income.

dividend: money return a stockholder receives on the money he or she invested in a company by buying stock (p. 161).

division of labor: breaking down of a job into small tasks. Each task may be performed by a different worker (p. 286).

double coincidence of wants: situation resulting when two individuals each want exactly what the other person has, allowing a direct exchange of goods or services (p. 376).

economic assistance: loans and outright grants of money or equipment to other nations to add to their capital resources (p. 555).

economic efficiency: the wise use of resources so that people will be better off in an economic sense (p. 39).

economic growth: expansion of the economy to produce more goods, jobs, and wealth (p. 39).

economic indicator: statistic that measures specific aspects of the economy, such as stock prices or the dollar amount of loans to be repaid (p. 364).

economic model: simplified representation of the real world; deals with the way people react to changes in the economy (p. 13).

economic system: way in which a nation uses its resources to satisfy its people's needs and wants (p. 26).

economics: study of how individuals and nations make choices about ways to use their scarce resources to fill their needs and wants (p. 4).

economies of scale: production activity in which large companies take advantage of mass production techniques that result in lower production costs (p. 268).

economy: all the activity in a nation that together affects the production, distribution, and use of goods and services (p. 13).

elastic demand: situation in which the rise or fall in the price of a product greatly affects the amount of that product people are willing to buy (p. 190).

electronic funds transfer (EFT): system of putting onto computers the various banking functions that in the past had to be handled on paper (p. 387).

embargo: complete restriction on the import or export of a particular good (p. 512).

endorse: to sign the back of a check so that it can be cleared for payment (p. 388).

entrepreneurship (ahn-truh-pruh-NER-ship)**:** ability to combine land, labor, and capital to form a new business; also the willingness to take the risks involved in forming and managing a business (p. 6).

equilibrium price: price for a product at which the amount producers are willing to supply is equal to the amount people are willing to buy. On a graph, the equilibrium price is located where the supply and demand curves meet (p. 201).

equity (EK-wuh-tee)**:** amount of money invested in property minus debts such as mortgage owed on it (p. 128).

equity financing: raising money for a company by selling stock in the company (p. 277).

excise (EK-syz) **tax:** tax on the manufacture, sale, or use within the country of specific products, such as liquor, gasoline, and automobiles (p. 143).

expansion: portion of the business cycle in which economic acitvity is increasing; also called recovery (p. 358).

export: good sold to another country (p. 504).

factors of production: resources used to produce goods and services; land, labor, and capital; some economists today include entrepreneurship and technology (p. 6).

fiat (FEE-aht) **money:** money that has value because a government fiat, or order, has established it as acceptable for payment of debts (p. 379).

finance: activity concerned with the sources and uses of money in business (p. 275).

finance charge: cost of credit expressed in dollars and cents (p. 86).

finance company: company that takes over contracts for installment debts from stores and adds a fee for collecting the debt; also makes loans directly to consumers (p. 83).

financial planning: predicting revenues and costs of a business and comparing estimated profit with the cost of investment (p. 278).

fiscal policy: federal government's set of policies concerning taxation and spending (p. 432).

fixed expense: payment that must be made; may occur only irregularly (p. 88).

fixed rate of exchange: system in which a government sets the value of its currency in relation to the currencies of other nations (p. 508).

flexible expense: payment that varies greatly from month to month (p. 89).

flexible rate of exchange: system in which the forces of supply and demand are allowed to set the price of various currencies (p. 509).

foreign aid: money, goods, and services given by governments and private organizations to help other nations (p. 555).

foreign exchange market: market that deals in buying and selling foreign currency (p. 508).

fractional reserve banking: system in which only a fraction of the deposits in a bank is kept on hand, or in reserve; the remainder is available to be lent to borrowers or otherwise invested (p. 403).

franchise: contract in which one business sells to another the right to use its name and sell its products (p. 231).

free enterprise system: system in which individuals own the factors of production and decide the answers to the basic economic questions for themselves through the interaction of individuals looking out for their own best interests; also called market economic system, capitalism (p. 34).

full employment: condition the economy is said to be in when the unemployment rate is not more than 6 percent (p. 452).

full warranty: promise by a supplier to provide for the repair or replacement of faulty merchandise within a reasonable period of time (p. 113).

generalization (jen-uhr-uh-luh-ZAY-shuhn)**:** statement that pulls together common ideas among facts and is true in most cases (p. 17).

generic (juh-NER-ik) **brand:** general name for a product rather than a specific name given by a manufacturer (p. 110).

geographic monopoly: market situation occurring when an individual seller has control over a market because of the seller's location (p. 248).

goods and services: end result of combining factors of production. Goods are the things people buy; services are the activities done for others for a fee. *Goods* is sometimes used to mean both goods and services (p. 6).

government monopoly: activity exclusive to government; market situation created by the government and protected by legal barriers to entry (p. 248).

grade: level of quality for food products (p. 114).

gross national product (GNP): total dollar value of all final goods and services produced by a nation during a given period (p. 350).

guarantee: manufacturer's promise that the product is what it is represented to be or the manufacturer will replace it (p. 113).

heavy industry: steel, coal, and other industries that manufacture goods to make other goods (p. 478).

homeowners'policy: insurance that protects a dwelling and its owners against a wide range of dangers (p. 139).

hypothesis (hy-PAHTH-uh-sis) educated guess, or prediction, that is used as the starting point for investigation (p. 17).

imperfect competition: market situation in which anyone or a group buys or sells a product in large enough amounts to affect price; includes pure monopoly, oligopoly, monopolistic competition (p. 244).

implicit GNP price deflator: price index used to remove the effects of inflation from the value of gross national product (p. 355).

implied warranty: promise that the product must do what it claims to do or the manufacturer must replace or repair it (p. 113).

import: good bought from another country for domestic use (p. 504).

import quota: restriction on the value of or on the number of units of a particular good that can be brought into a country (p. 512).

income redistribution: activity in which the government, through taxation, takes money from some people and gives it to others (p. 430).

Individual Retirement Account (IRA): private retirement plan that allows a person to save up to $2,000 of his or her earnings per year, or $2,250 for a couple with only one person working outside the home; interest on an IRA is not taxed until it is withdrawn (p. 170).

industrial union: union made up of all workers in an industry, regardless of job or skill level (p. 324).

inelastic demand: sitatuion in which the rise or fall in the price of a product does not greatly affect the amount of that product that people are willing to buy (p. 190).

inflation: prolonged increase in the general price level of goods and services (p. 354).

informative advertising: advertising that gives information about a product (p. 61).

injunction: court order preventing some activity (p. 332).

installment charge account: agreement that allows the purchase of such major items as stereos and televisions to be paid for through equal payments, or installments, over a period of time (p. 85).

installment debt: repayment of a debt divided into equal amounts, or installments, over a period of time (p. 78).

insurance: coverage by contract that spreads the losses of a few over a large group, thus protecting an individual from risk (p. 138).

interest: amount a borrower must pay for the use of someone else's money. Payment a creditor receives when lending money (pp. 78, 156).

interlocking directorate: situation occurring when the members of the boards of directors of competing corporations are the same (p. 254).

intermediate-term financing: borrowing by a business for one to ten years (p. 277).

inventory: supply of whatever items are used in a business, such as raw materials or goods for sale (p. 214).

Keogh Plan: retirement plan that allows a self-employed person to save a maximum of 15 percent of his or her income up to $30,000 a year; taxes are paid when money is withdrawn after retirement (p. 169).

labor: work performed by people (p. 6).

labor union: association of workers organized to improve wages and working conditions for its members (p. 324).

lagging indicator: statistic whose change lags behind changes in overall business activity (p. 364).

land: in economic terms, natural resources, not just surface land; all things found in nature, on or in the water and the earth. Among the most important in economic terms are land itself and mineral deposits (p. 5).

law of demand: economic rule stating that as the price of a good or service falls, a larger quantity will be bought; as the price of a good service rises, a smaller quantity will be bought (p. 186).

law of diminishing marginal utility: economic rule stating that the additional satisfaction a person gets from consuming one more unit of a product will lessen with each additional unit he or she consumes (p. 187).

law of diminishing returns: economic rule stating that, after some point, adding units of a factor of production—such as labor—to fixed factors of production—such as equipment—increases total output for a time. However, at a certain point, the extra output per each additional unit will begin to decrease (p. 274).

law of supply: economic rule stating that at higher prices a larger quantity of a product will generally be supplied than at lower prices (p. 195).

leading indicator: statistic that points to what will happen in the economy (p. 364).

lease: long-term agreement describing the terms under which property is being rented (p. 128).

legal tender: money that must by law be accepted for payment of public and private debts (p. 379).

liability insurance: insurance that pays for bodily injury and property damage (p. 138).

limited warranty: promise that provides for replacement of faulty merchandise if the consumer notifies the manufacturer within a specific period of time (p. 113).

line graph: graph showing the change in the same item over a period of time (p. 11).

line of credit: maximum amount of money that a company can borrow from a bank without having to re-apply for a loan (p. 276).

lockout: situation occurring when a company closes its doors and prevents striking workers from returning until they agree to the company's contract offer (p. 330).

long-term financing: raising money for a business to finance debts of more than ten years (p. 277).

loose money policy: policy designed to stimulate the economy by making credit inexpensive and abundant (p. 402).

M1: narrowest and simplest definition of the money supply; equals paper money and coins in circulation plus deposits in checking and checking-type accounts (p. 385).

M2: broad definition of the money supply; includes M1—currency in circulation and checking-type accounts—plus savings accounts, money market accounts, time deposits, and money market funds (p. 385).

management: job of organizing and coordinating the factors of production for maximum efficiency (p. 274).

market: freely chosen activity between buyers and sellers of goods and services (p. 29).

market economic system: system in which individuals own the factors of production and decide for themselves the answers to the basic economic questions through the interaction of individuals looking out for their own best interests; also called capitalism, free enterprise system (p. 29).

market research: job of gathering, recording, and analyzing information about the types of goods and services that people want (p. 299).

market share: percentage of total sales in a market accounted for by a single company (p. 278).

marketing: all the activities needed to move goods and services from the producer to the consumer; includes market research, advertising and promotion, distribution (p. 298).

maturity: period of time for which a certificate of deposit or bond will pay a stated rate of interest (p. 158).

mean: average of a series of items found by adding the items and then dividing by the number of items in the series (p. 37).

mechanization: combination of the labor of people and machines. Originally, machines were combined with unskilled labor to replace skilled workers (p. 286).

median (MEE-dee-uhn): midpoint in any series of numbers arranged in order. With an even number of numbers, the median is the mean of the two middle numbers (p. 37).

mediation (mee-dee-AY-shun): stage when a neutral person steps into union and management negotiations to try to get both sides to reach an agreement (p. 329).

Medicaid: state-run programs that provide free health care for people with low incomes (p. 430).

medium of exchange: use of money in exchange for goods and services (p. 376).

merger: combination occurring when one corporation buys more than half of the stock in another (p. 255). *See also* horizontal merger, vertical merger, conglomerate merger.

military assistance: economic or technical assistance given to a nation's armed forces (p. 556).

minimum wage law: law setting the lowest legal hourly wage rate that may be paid to certain types of workers (p. 321).

mixed economy: system which contains characteristics of a command economy and a pure market economy; mix varies so that any economic system leans more toward one pure type than another (p. 30).

monetarism (MAHN-uh-ter-iz-uhm) theory that deals with the relation between the amount of money placed in circulation by the Federal Reserve and the level of activity in the economy (p. 460).

monetary policy: policy that involves changing the rate of the supply of money to affect the amount of credit and, therefore, business activity in the economy (p. 402).

monetary standard: manner in which a nation assigns value to its money (p. 380).

money: anything customarily used as a medium of exchange, a unit of accounting, and a store of value (p. 376).

money market accounts: bank accounts that pay a variable amount of interest, require a minimum balance, and usually allow withdrawals at any time (p. 158).

money market fund: mutual fund that allows an individual to write checks against his or her investments (p. 167).

monopolistic competition: market situation in which there are numerous sellers, each with some control over price (p. 252).

mortgage: long-term debt owed on real property such as houses, buildings, and land; and installment debt (p. 79).

multinational: company that does business in more than one nation (p. 554).

mutual fund: investment company that pools money of many individuals to buy stocks or bonds or other investments (p. 166).

national debt: total amount of debt outstanding for the federal government (p. 441).

national income (NI): total income earned by everyone in the economy (p. 353).

national income accounting: measuring the overall economy's income and output and the interaction of its major parts—consumer, business, and government (p. 349).

natural monopoly: market situation resulting when one company drives its competitors out of business by producing goods at the lowest cost; usually found in industries that require large amounts of money to get started and where efficiency in operation is best done by one company rather than several (p. 248).

near monies: assets, such as savings accounts, that can be turned into money relatively easily and without the risk of loss of value (p. 384).

net national product (NNP): value of a nation's total output minus value lost through the wear and tear on machines and equipment (p. 352).

net weight: actual weight of food or other product without weight of the packaging (p. 112).

no-fault insurance: type of coverage stating that in the case of an accident, each driver's insurance company pays for damages and medical bills for that driver without trying to determine who was at fault (p. 139).

nonprofit corporation: organization incorporated by a state, with most of the characteristics of a corporation except that it does not pay taxes, issue stock, or operate with the idea of making a profit (p. 231).

NOW account (Negotiable Order of Withdrawal): bank account that combines checking and saving (p. 157).

oligopoly (ahl-uh-GAHP-uh-lee): industry dominated by a few suppliers that exercise some control over price (p. 250).

open-market operations: purchase and sale of United States securities by the Federal Reserve to affect the money supply (p. 412).

opportunity cost: next best alternative that had to be given up for the alternative chosen (p. 8).

organized labor: workers who are organized into labor unions (p. 479).

overdraft checking: checking-account that allows a customer to borrow money by writing checks for more money than is in his or her account (p. 387).

over-the-counter market: purchase and sale of stocks and bonds of smaller, lesser-known companies taking place outside of the organized stock exchanges (p. 165).

partnership: business that two or more individuals own and operate for their own profit (p. 220).

passbook savings account: account for which a depositor receives a booklet in which deposits, withdrawals and interest are recorded (p. 157).

patent: the right granted to an inventor for the exclusive manufacture and sale of an invention for a specified number of years (p. 248).

peak: portion of the business cycle in which economic activity is at its highest point; also called a boom (p. 358).

penetration pricing: selling a new product at a low price to attract customers away from an established product (p. 303).

percent: parts per hundred (p. 36).

perfect competition: market situation in which there are numerous buyers and sellers, and thus no one buyer or seller has control over price (p. 242).

personal income (PI): total income received by individuals before personal taxes are paid (p. 353).

picketing: activity in which striking workers walk up and down in front of a workplace carrying signs that state their disagreement with the company (p. 330).

pie graph: circle-shaped graph that shows percentages. Each section of the pie represents a percentage of the total (p. 11).

preferred stock: type of stock that guarantees the holder a certain amount of interest but does not carry with it voting rights in the company's affairs. If the company fails, preferred stockholders are paid before holders of common stock (p. 160).

premiums: fees paid for insurance (p. 138).

price elasticity of demand: situation in which demand varies according to changes in price (p. 190).

price leadership: practice of setting prices close to those charged by other companies selling similar products; found especially in industries controlled by a few large companies (p. 303).

prime rate: interest rate banks charge on loans to their best business customers (p. 411).

principal: amount of money borrowed in a loan (p. 78).

private property: goods owned by individuals or groups rather than by government (p. 35).

privatization: a program to return government-owned-and-operated companies to private ownership (p. 536).

producer goods: goods produced for business to use in making other goods (p. 282).

producer price index (PPI): measure of the change in price over time of a specific group of goods used by businesses (p. 355).

product differentiation: manufacturers' use of differences in quality and in minor features to try to differentiate between similar products (p. 251).

production: process of changing resources into goods (p. 282).

production possibilities: all the combinations of goods and services that can be produced from a fixed amount of resources during a given period of time (p. 8).

productivity: ability to produce greater quantities of goods and services in better and faster ways (p. 6).

professional: person who has a college degree and usually additional education or training (p. 319).

profit: amount of money left after all the costs of production, distribution, and taxes have been paid (p. 35).

profit incentive: desire to make money that motivates people to produce, buy, and sell goods and services that other people want (p. 35).

progressive tax: tax that takes a larger percentage of higher incomes than of lower incomes (p. 437).

proletariat (proh-luh-TER-ee-uht): term used by Karl Marx to mean the workers (p. 126).

promissory (PRAHM-uh-sor-ee) **note:** written agreement to repay a loan at a specified time with a specified rate of interest (p. 276).

promotion: use of advertising and other methods to inform customers about a new or improved product or service and to persuade them to purchase it (p. 306).

proportional tax: tax that takes the same percentage of all incomes (p. 437).

protectionist: opponent of relaxing trade restrictions (p. 513).

protective tariff: tax designed to raise the cost of imported goods and thereby to protect domestic producers (p. 512).

public assistance programs: programs that make payments to people based on need (p. 430).

public goods: goods or services supplied to everyone by the government; can be used by many individuals at the same time without reducing the benefit each person receives (p. 430).

pure monopoly: market situation in which a single seller controls the supply of a product, and thus has control over price (p. 244). *See also* geographic monopoly, government monopoly, natural monopoly, technological monopoly.

real estate taxes: taxes paid on land and buildings (p. 129).

real GNP: gross national produce corrected for inflation (p. 355).

real income: amount of goods or services a person can actually buy with his or her income (p. 189).

recession: portion of the business cycle in which a nation's output does not grow for at least six months (p. 358).

recovery: portion of the business cycle in which economic activity is increasing; also called expansion (p. 358).

registration fee: a fee paid to a state for the right to use a car (p. 142).

regressive tax: tax that takes a larger percentage of lower incomes than of higher incomes (p. 437).

regular charge account: agreement that allows a customer to buy goods or services from a particular store and to pay for them later; 30-day charge. Interest is charged on that part of the account not paid within a certain period of time (p. 84).

representative money: money not valuable in itself for nonmoney uses, but can be exchanged for some valuable item (p. 378).

reserve requirement: regulation requiring banks to keep a certain percentage of their deposits as cash or as deposits with their district Federal Reserve Bank (p. 403).

resource: anything people can use to make or obtain what they need or want (p. 4).

restrictive endorsement: signature on the back of a check that allows it to be deposited only into a specific account (p. 389).

retailer: business that sells goods directly to the public (p. 309).

revenue: money taken in by business or government (p. 224).

revenue tariff: tax on imports used primarily to raise income without restricting imports (p. 512).

revolving charge account: agreement that allows a customer to buy goods and services from a particular store and to pay for them later. Purchases may be paid off gradually, but interest is charged on the unpaid amount (p. 85).

right-to-work law: state law forbidding contracts that require employees to join a union or pay union dues (p. 325).

robotics: the sophisticated computer-controlled machinery that forms part or all of an assembly line (p. 479).

satellites: structures that orbit the earth to relay signals to and from earth stations (p. 485).

saving: nonuse of income for a period of time so that it can be used later (p. 156).

savings and loan association (S & L): depository institution that, like a commercial bank, accepts deposits and lends money to borrowers. Until recently S & Ls could make loans only for home buying or improvement; now they offer many of the same services, including checking-type accounts, as commercial banks (p. 82).

savings bank: depository institution that accepts deposits and lends money (p. 82).

savings bond: bond sold by the U.S. Treasury for less than its stated value, but when redeemed is worth purchase price plus interest (p. 164).

scarcity: condition in which people do not have enough income or resources to satisfy their every desire (p. 4).

secured loan: loan that is backed up by collateral (p. 94).

security deposit: money a tenant must pay to a landlord in advance but that is returned after the tenant has left; landlord may keep a portion to cover the cost of repairing the damages or lost rent if the tenant moves before the lease is up (p. 128).

semiskilled worker: worker who has limited training in job-related skills; can perform specific, routine tasks, often using modern technology (p. 319).

service economy: an economy in which most people are employed in the service sector (p. 478).

service sector: the sector of the economy that employs most of the United States labor force. It excludes mainly manufacturing and agriculture (p. 478).

service worker: person who provides services directly to individuals (p. 319).

shortage: situation resulting when there is a larger quantity demanded than supplied (p. 198).

short-term financing: borrowing by a business for a period of time less than a year (p. 277).

simple interest: interest figured only on the original amount deposited (p. 162).

skilled worker: person who has a trade or craft (p. 319).

smokestack industries: industries that manufacture heavy goods such as steel or automobiles (p. 478).

social cost: total cost that society must pay for any economic activity (p. 51).

social insurance programs: programs that are designed to provide insurance against the problems of old age, illness, and unemployment (p. 430).

socialism: system in which government owns the basic factors of production and controls how they are used (p. 524).

Social Security: a federal program that provides monthly payments to millions of people who are retired or unable to work (p. 430).

sole proprietorship: business owned by one person (p. 217).

special endorsement: signature on the back of a check that transfers it to another person (p. 389).

specialization (spesh-uhl-uh-ZAY-shuhn): process of a nation producing and exporting limited number of goods for which it is particularly suited (p. 505).

stabilization (stay-buh-luh-ZAY-shuhn) **policy:** attempt by the federal government to make the future more predictable for planning, saving, and investing; includes monetary policy and fiscal policy (p. 452).

stagflation: combination of inflation and low economic activity (p. 455).

standard: basis of comparison for determining quality or value of an item (p. 114).

standard of living: material well-being of an individual, group, or nation measured by the average value of goods and services used during a given period of time (p. 40).

statement savings account: bank account similar to passbook savings account except that, instead of a passbook, a monthly statement shows all transactions (p. 157).

statistics: data presented in numerical form (p. 10).

stock: share of ownership in the company that issued the stock; entitles owner to a certain part of company profits and sometimes to a vote in certain matters, such as electing a board of directors (p. 160).

stockholder: person who owns stock in a company and thus holds a claim against a certain part of its profits (p. 161).

store of value: use of money to store purchasing power for later use (p. 377).

straight life insurance: insurance that combines insurance coverage with a savings plan; also called whole life insurance or ordinary life insurance (p. 140).

strike: deliberate work stoppage by workers to force an employer to give in to their demands (p. 330).

subsistence agriculture: raising of just enough food by a family to take care of its own needs (p. 551).

supply curve: graph showing the amount of a product producers are willing to supply at different prices; visual representation of a supply schedule (p. 196).

supply schedule: table showing the amount of a product suppliers are willing to supply at various prices (p. 196).

supply-side economics: theory that emphasizes increasing the economy's ability to produce (p. 466).

surplus: situation resulting when there is a greater quantity supplied than demanded (p. 198).

tariff: tax on imports (p. 512).

tax-exempt bond: bond sold by local or state government; interest paid on the bond is not taxed (p. 164).

technical assistance: aid, in the form of professionals such as engineers, teachers, technicians, and so on, supplied by nations to teach skills to individuals in other nations (p. 556).

technological monopoly: market situation resulting when a seller develops a product or production process for which it obtains a patent; company holds exclusive rights to the new invention for a specified number of years (p. 248).

technological unemployment: unemployment resulting from the increased use of labor-saving machines (p. 342).

technology: today, use of science to develop new products and new methods for producing and distributing goods and services (p. 6).

term life insurance: insurance that provides protection during a certain period of time (p. 140).

test marketing: offering a product for sale in a small area for a limited period of time to see how well it sells before offering it nationally (p. 300).

Third World: developing nations that are not aligned with the major communist or capitalist nations (p. 537).

tight money policy: policy designed to slow the economy by making credit expensive and in short supply (p. 402).

time deposits: savings plans that require a saver to leave his or her money in it for a certain period of time (p. 158).

trade credit: credit extended by a seller to a business buying goods; allows a buyer to take possession of goods immediately and pay for them at some future date (p. 276).

trade-off: exchanging of one thing for the use of another (p. 7).

traditional economic system: system in which economic decisions are based on customs, beliefs, and ways of doing things that have been handed down from generation to generation (p. 28).

transfer payment: financial assistance by state or federal government that is not in exchange for any current productive activity by an individual; includes welfare payments, unemployment compensation, and so on (p. 353).

Treasury bill: certificate issued by the U.S. Treasury in exchange for borrowed money in minimum amounts of $10,165 and maturing during a period ranging from 3 months to one year (p. 165).

Treasury bond: certificate issued by the U.S. Treasury in exchange for borrowed money in minimum amounts of $1,000 or $5,000 and maturing in two to ten or more years (p. 165).

Treasury note: certificate issued by the U.S. Treasury in exchange for borrowed money with minimum amounts of $1,000 or $5,000 and maturing in two to ten years (p. 165).

trend: general movement of change over a period of time (p. 558).

trough (TRAWF): portion of the business cycle in which economic activity is at its lowest point (p. 358).

unemployment rate: percentage of the officially measured civilian labor force without jobs but actively looking for work (p. 452).

union shop: company in which a new employee must join the union after a certain period of time, usually three months (p. 325).

unit of accounting: use of money as a yardstick for comparing the values of goods and services in relation to one another (p. 376).

unit price: price of a product in terms of a common unit of measure. To find the unit price, divide the cost by the net weight (p. 112).

unlimited liability: legal responsibility for all debts and damages that occur when doing business; applies to sole proprietorships and partnerships (p. 218).

unsecured loan: loan not guaranteed by anything other than a promise to repay it (p. 94).

unskilled worker: worker who has no special training or education (p. 319).

usury (YOO-zhuhr-ee) **law:** law restricting the amount of interest that can be charged for credit (p. 95).

utility (yoo-TIL-uh-tee): power that a good or service has to satisfy a want (p. 187).

values: beliefs or characteristics that a person or group considers important (p. 16).

vertical merger: the merger of a business that buys from or sells to another business with that business (p. 255).

videodiscs: small disks for storing visual and printed data (p. 485).

voluntary exchange: activity practiced when a buyer and a seller exercise their economic freedoms by working out on their own the terms of an exchange (p. 186).

warehouse food store: food store that carries a limited number of brands and items, and stresses quantity purchases at lower prices (p. 109).

warranty: promise made by a manufacturer or seller to repair or replace a product at no cost to the consumer if it is found to be faulty within a certain period of time (p. 59).

welfare: public-assistance programs that include aid to families with dependent children, food stamps, and cash benefits to poor, aged, blind, or disabled people (p. 430).

white-collar worker: person employed in an office, sales, or as a professional (p. 318).

wholesaler: business that purchases large quantities of goods from producers for resale to other businesses (p. 308).

workers' compensation: state-run programs to extend payments for medical care to workers injured on the job (p. 430).

discretionary income, 57
disposable income, 57
disposable personal income (DI), 353
distribution channels, 307-9
distribution of goods and services, 27-28
dividends, 161
division of labor, 33, 286
double coincidence of wants, 376
Dow Jones Industrial Average (DJIA), 228

economic assistance, 555-56
economic development, 507, 553-55
economic efficiency, 39
economic growth, 39; environmental concerns versus, 50-52
economic indicators, 363-65
economic models, 13-14, 16
economics: Keynesian (See Keynesian theory); monetarist, 460-63; reasons for studying, 4; Smith as founder of modern, 33; supply-side, 466-67; values and, 16-17. See also economists
economic stability, 432, 452. See also stabilization policies
economic statistics. See statistics
economic systems, 25-31; American (See American economy); definition of, 26; market (capitalist), 29-32; mixed, 30-31; questions that must be answered by, 26-28; traditional, 28-29; types of, 28-31. See also capitalism; command economic system; communism; free enterprise system; socialism
economists: Heilbroner's views on, 15; schools of economic thought, 16; topics studied by, 13. See also economics
economy, definition of, 13
education, higher, 481
efficiency, economic, 39
elastic demand, 190, 193
electronic funds transfer (EFT), 387, 391
Electronic Funds Transfer Act, 391
embargos, 512-13

endorsing checks, 388-89
energy guides, 114
Engels, Friedrich, 530
entrepreneurship, as resource, 6
environmental concerns, economic growth versus, 50-52
Environmental Protection Agency (EPA), 257
Equal Credit Opportunity Act (1974), 96
equity, goal of, 39
equity financing, 277
estate tax, 436
European Economic Community (EEC; European Common Market), 514
eviction, 137
exchange rates: balance of trade and, 509; exchanging foreign currency and, 510; fixed, 508; flexible, 509
excise taxes, 143, 436, 440
expansion, 358
expenses, 215; flexible, 89
exports, 504; net, 351. See also trade

factors of production, 6, 27
Fair Credit Billing Act (1974), 97
Fair Credit Reporting Act (1970), 96
Fair Debt Collection Practices Act (1977), 97
farming. See agriculture
farm workers, 318
Federal Advisory Council (FAC), 407
federal agencies: consumers and, 67. See also regulatory agencies, federal
Federal Communications Commission (FCC), 257, 258
Federal Deposit Insurance Corporation (FDIC), 159, 381
federal government: American economy and, 32, 34, 35; banking and, 380-81; borrowing by, 440-41; budget of, 433-35; business cycles and, 362; changing role in recent years, 487, 489-91; competition encouraged by, 254-55, 257-58; Federal Reserve as fiscal agent of, 408; money and, 380-81; monopolies owned by, 248; national debt and, 498-500;

stabilization policies of (See stabilization policies). See also government; and specific topics
Federal Housing Administration (FHA) mortgages, 132
Federal Insurance Contributions Act (FICA), 436
Federal Mediation and Conciliation Service (FMCS), 331
Federal Open Market Committee (FOMC), 407, 412, 414
Federal Reserve Bank of New York, 414
Federal Reserve notes, 381, 383-84
Federal Reserve System (the Fed), 380-81, 402; Board of Governors of, 405, 407, 415; discount rate of, 411-12; functions of, 408-10; member banks of, 405-409; monetarism and, 460-63; monetary policy of, 402-3, 410-12, 414-15; open-market operations of, 412; organization of, 405, 407, 409; reserve requirements and, 403, 410-11; truth-in-lending legislation and, 409-10
Federal Savings and Loan Insurance Corporation (FSLIC), 159
Federal Trade Commission (FTC), 66, 257, 258
Federal Trade Commission Act, 255
fiat money, 379-81
finance charges: computing, 87, 90-91; definition of, 86
finance companies, loans from, 83
financial managers, 278
financial markets. See bond markets; stock markets
financial pages of the newspaper, reading, 226-28
financial planning, 278-79
financing, 275-81; choosing the right, 280-81; corporations, 225; deficit, 440-41; of economic development, 553-54; equity, 277; intermediate-term, 277, 280; long-term, 277, 280; partnerships, 221; short-term, 276, 277, 280; sole proprietorships, 219; world trade, 508-9

First Bank of the United States, 380
fiscal policy, 432; inflation and, 459-60; monetarist view of, 462; unemployment and, 458-59
fiscal year, 433
fixed rate of exchange, 508
flexible expenses, 89
flexible rate mortgage, 132
flexible rate of exchange, 509
float, 391
food: brand-name, 110; convenience, 110-11; labels on, 112; shopping for, 108-11; standards and grades of, 114
Food and Drug Administration (FDA), 67, 257
food stores, 109
food supply, Malthusian theory and, 563
Ford Motor Company, 286
foreign aid, 555-59
foreign currencies: exchanging, 510. See also exchange rates
foreign exchange markets, 508
foreign investment, 554-55
fractional reserve banking, 403
franchises, 231
freedom: of choice, 34-35; democratic socialism and, 535; of enterprise, 34; free enterprise system and, 41; as goal of market economy, 40, 41; in Soviet Union, 529
free enterprise system, 34; benefits of, 41; big business and, 268-70; critics of, 41; supply and demand in, 201-2. See also capitalism; market economic system
free trade, 33, 577; arguments for and against, 513-14
frictional unemployment, 453
Friedman, Milton, 460-62
Friedman, Rose, 461
fringe benefits, as union contract issue, 329
Frostbelt region, 482-83
full employment, 452
full warranty, 113

Galbraith, John Kenneth, 431
GATT (General Agreement on Tariffs and Trade), 514
General Motors (GM), 63
generic brands, 110
geographic monopolies, 248
gift tax, 436
Glass-Steagall Banking Act, 381

leading indicators, 364, 365

leakages, circular flow of income and, 456, 457

leases: 128-29 , 134, 136, 137

leasing, 277

lemon laws, 63

Lenin, 527

liabilities, in balance sheet, 246-47

liability: of corporations, 224; of partnerships, 221; of sole proprietorships, 218

library research, 464-65

life insurance, 140, 170

line graphs, 11

line of credit, 276

loans: from commercial banks, 82; from consumer finance companies, 83; cosigner of, 94; from credit unions, 83; from finance companies, 83; installment, 78-79; intermediate-term, 277; mortgage, 79; overdraft checking as, 387; from savings and loan associations, 82; from savings banks, 82-83; secured, 94, 276; sources of, 81-83; unsecured, 276. *See also* borrowing; credit; financing

local governments, tax-exempt bonds, 164

local unions, 325

location of a business, 282

lockout, 331

long-term financing, 277, 280

loose money policy, 402

mail-order retailers, 309

mail survey, 304-5

maintenance of automobiles, 142-43

Malthus, Thomas, 563

management: contract negotiations between labor and, 329, 331; of corporations, 224; definition of, 274; duties and responsibilities of, 274; of partnerships, 221; of sole proprietorships, 218

market economic system, 29-32; aims or goals of, 39-41. *See also* American economy; capitalism; free enterprise system

marketing, 298-300

marketing strategy (or plan), 302-3, 306-7

market research, 299-300, 304-5

Marx, Karl, 526, 530

mean, 37

mechanization, 286 , 479

median, 37

mediation, 329

Medicaid, 430

mercantilism, 33, 159

mergers, 255, 490-91

Mexico, 537

microchips, 485

Midwest Stock Exchange, 165

Mill, John Stuart, 301

minimum wage law, 321

mixed economic system, 30-31

mobile homes, 129

models, economic, 13-14; purpose of, 14, 16

monetarism, 460-63

monetary policy, 402-3; difficulties of, 414-15; tools of, 410-12

monetary standard, 380

money: commodity, 378; definition of, 376; fiat, 379-81; functions of, 376-77; history of American, 379-81, 383; as medium of exchange, 376; near, 384-85; paper, 408; representative, 378; as store of value, 377; types and characteristics of, 377-79; types of, 383-85; as unit of accounting, 376-77. *See also* currency; money supply

money market accounts, 158

money market fund, 167

money orders, 387

money supply, 385; difficulties of controlling, 414-15; expansion of, 403-5; monetarist theory and, 460-63; monetary policy and, 402-3; tools for regulating, 410-12

monopolies: antitrust legislation and, 254; geographic, 248; government, 248; importance of, 249; natural, 248; pure, 244-45, 248-49; technological, 248

monopolistic competition, 252-54; Robinson's views on, 256

mortgages, 79, 130-33; sources of, 132; types of, 132-33

municipal bonds, 441

mutual funds, 166-67, 172; reading quotations, 227

Nader, Ralph, 63

National Association of Securities Dealers Automated Quotation (NASDAQ) Index, 228, 229

National Association of Securities Dealers Automated Quotation (NASDAQ) National Market, 165

National Bank acts, 380

national banks, 409

National Credit Union Share Insurance Fund, 159

national debt, 440-41, 498-500

National Highway Traffic Safety Administration, 67

national income (NI), 353

national income accounting, 349-50

nationalization, Galbraith's call for, 431

National Labor Relations Act (Wagner Act), 327

natural monopolies, 248

near monies, 384-85

needs, 5

negotiations, labor-management, 329, 331

neighborhood businesses, 253

net exports, 351

net national product (NNP), 352-53

New Economic Method (NEM), 530

New Economic Policy (NEP), 528

New York Stock Exchange (NYSE), 165, 226

Nike company, 193

Nixon, Richard, 487

no-fault insurance, 139

nonprofit corporations, 231

Norris-LaGuardia Act, 327

NOW accounts, 157-59, 386

Nuclear Regulatory Commission (NRC), 257

Nyerere, Julius K., 538, 567

Occupational Safety and Health Administration (OSHA), 257, 258

Office of Consumer Affairs, U.S., 67

Office of Management and Budget (OMB), 433-34

older people, jobs related to the needs of, 322

oligopoly, 250-51; monopolistic competition compared to, 252-53

open-market operations, 412

opportunity costs, 7-8

Organization of Petroleum Exporting Countries (OPEC), 249, 362

organized labor. *See* labor unions

overdraft checking, 387

over-the-counter market, 165, 226

Owen, Robert, 15

ownership: of factors of production, democratic socialism and, 535; of factors of production, in Soviet Union, 529; of housing, 128, 129

paper money, 408

partnerships, 220-21

passbook savings account, 157

past due balance method, 90, 165

peak, 358

penetration pricing, 303

pension plans, 169-70

percentages, 36

perfect competition, 242-44

personal income (PI), 353

personal interviews, 305

personal satisfaction: corporations and, 225; partnerships and, 221; sole proprietorships and, 219

picketing, 331

pie graphs, 11

planning: financial, 278-79; production process and, 282, 284; in Soviet Union, 31. *See also* central planning

point-of-sale terminals, 391

points, 131

pollution, 432

population growth: in developing nations, 552-53; Malthus' theory of, 563

population shifts, regional, 482-83

Postal Service, U.S., 66, 248, 249

post-industrial economy, 478-83

preferences, demand and, 192

preferred stocks, 160, 225, 229

premiums, insurance, 138

previous balance method, 90

price elasticity of demand, 190-91

price leadership, 303

prices: consumers' responses to changes in, 13-14; forces underlying supply and demand and, 202;

ACKNOWLEDGMENTS

Cover art: © Alvis Upitis/THE IMAGE BANK

PHOTO CREDITS

ART RESOURCE: Giraudon, 44
Arthur Beck, 487
Courtesy, Benetton
THE BETTMANN ARCHIVE, 526
BLACK STAR: © Jim Balog, 2B, 373R; © Lawrence Barnes, 271TL; © Bart Bartholomew, 317R; © Dennis Brack, 401R, 420; © Andrew Holbrooke, 549L; © Lynn Johnson, 64, 516, 531TR; © Shelley Katz, 216; © Herman Kokojan, 25L, 353, 450TL; © Bob Krist, 82, 169; © Larry Mayer, 343BL; © Eiji Miyazawa, 168; © Carl Mydans, 522B; © Naoki Okamoto, 154B; © Jim Pickerell, 377, 437; © Andrew Sacks, 347L, 484; © Ron Sanford, 343TL; © Piergiorgio Sclarandis, 548B; © James Sugar, 424T; © Tom Tracy, 5, 193, 258, 355; © Peter Turnley, 24T, 528; © Fred Ward, 181BL, 181R, 480, 561; © Nick Wheeler, 253; © Arnold Zahn, 272B
CAMERAMANN INTERNATIONAL, LTD., 1BL, 144, 171, 231, 240T, 346T, 501BR, 501TR, 503TR, 544
CLICK, CHICAGO, © Billy E. Barnes, 397, © Carol Lee, 444, © Jim Pickerell, 292
BRUCE COLEMAN, © S.L. Craig, 205
COMSTOCK, 19
CULVER PICTURES, 33; 281; 324; 379; 530
DOT, © Joseph Lawton, 184T
EKM NEPENTHE, © Bob Eckert, 95
FOLIO, INC., © Linda Bartlett, 345BL, 502B; © Cynthia Foster, 550; © Fred Kligman, 425R; © Greg Pease, 271TR; © Eric Pogenpohl, 538; Richard J. Quataert, 523L
Courtesy GENERAL MOTORS, 63
THE IMAGE BANK, © Murray Alcosser, 161, 401L; © Arthur d'Arazien, 249; © Walter Bibikow, 273L; © Don Carroll, 245, 502T; © Kay Chernush, 478; © Steve Dunwell, 183BL; © Nicholas Foster, 240B; © Brett Froomer, 441; © Gary Gladstone, 183BR; © Geoffrey Gove, 345BR; © Michael Melford, 297L; © Peter Miller, 53BR; © William Rivelli, 21; © Al Satterwhite, 400B; Harald Sund, 184B; © Tom Tracy, 296B; © Alvis Upitis, 154B
THE IMAGE WORKS, Topham, 301, 359, 563
© Jane Latta, 49
© Ken Lax, 69, 85, 111, 120, 134, 189, 192, 197, 220, 311, 429/3
© Jason Lauré, 548T
LGI, © Steve Rapport, 331
© Lawrence Migdale, 3R; 284; 317T; 451TL; 476T
MONKMEYER PRESS SERVICE, © Paul Conklin, 337, 395; © Mimi Forsyth, 147; © Audrey Gottlieb, 393; © Michal Heron, 260; © Hugh Rogers, 445
THE NEW YORK TIMES, © Arthur Grace, 257; © Marilyn K. Yee, 15
ODYSSEY PRODUCTIONS, © Robert Frerck, 60; 71; 569
PHOTO RESEARCHERS, INC. © Bill Bachman, 207; © Wilhelm Braga, 545; © Van Bucher, 339; © Junebug Clark, 471; © James Foote, 518; © Farrell Grehan,

332; © F.B. Grunzweig, 265; © Richard Hutchings, 269 (inset); © Pamela Johnson, 542; © Don Kryminec, 287
THE PICTURE CUBE, © Andrew Brilliant, 99, 174; © John Goell, 233; © Phaneuf Gurdziel, 343 (inset R); © Ellis Herwig, 241L; © Lynn McLaren, 155L; © Dave Schaefer, 345TR; © L. Stimmel, 534; © Susan Van Etten, 241R
PICTURE GROUP, © Shephard Sherbell, 450BL
RAINBOW, © Hank Morgan, 271 BL; © Dan McCoy, 53TL, 93; NASA from Rainbow, 4, 345TL
SOUTHERN STOCK PHOTOS, © Gerald Fritz, 185L
STOCK, BOSTON, © J. Berndt, 239; © Eric Carle, 508; © Donald Dietz, 215, 303; © Owen Franken, 43; 271BR, 523R; © Bill Gallery, 3L; 349, 503T; © Ellis Herwig, 147, 283; © John Lei, 469; © Mike Mazzaschi, 213R; © Richard Pasley, 289, 477R; © Stacy Pick, ITR, 222
STOCKFILE, © R. Burgess, 577; © Bob Jones, Jr. 181TL; © L.S.P. 181BL; © Baron Wolman, 150
Suzann, Szasz, 213L
TAURUS PHOTOS, © Glyn Cloyd, 335; © Tim McCabe, 149; © Claire Taplin, 555
THE STOCK MARKET, © Paul Barton, 24B; © Renate V. Forster/Bilderberg, 522T; © Charles Gupton, 443; © Craig Hammell, 297R; © Ted Horowitz, 346B; © William Johnson, 212T; © Barbara Kirk, 130; © Gabe Palmer, 275, 454; © L. Stimmel, 540; © Charles West, 564
UPI/BETTMANN NEWSPHOTOS, 117; 413; 431; 461; 507
WHEELER PICTURES, © John Dominis, 299; © John Elk III, 25R; © Michael Melford, 429; © Peter Menzel, 269L, 566; © Steve Smith, 282; © Gordon Traub, 451TR
WEST STOCK, © Philip Arndal, 1TL; © Rick Bueltner, 181 (inset R), 400T; © David Falconer, 347R; © Walter Hodges, 367; © Steve Meltzer, 403; © Kim Steele, 296T; © Doug Wilson, 557
WOODFIN CAMP & ASSOCIATES, © Jim Anderson, 185R; © Craig Aurness, 1BR; © M. & E. Bernheim, 501BL; © John Blaustein, 155R; © Jacques Chenet, 183TL, 204; © Dick Durrance, 135, 243, 272T; © José Fernandez, 141; © Robert Frerck, 183TR: © George Hall, 53BL, 424B, 476B; © Michal Heron, 116, 181TL, 217; © Thomas Hopker, 501TL; © John Marmaras, 2T, 477L; © Stephanie Maze, 376; © Wally McNamee, 7; © Kim Newton, 382; © Chuck O'Rear, 316T; © Alon Reininger, 549R; © Martin Rogers, 330; © Sepp Seitz, 316B; © Lester Sloan, 425L; © Charles Thatcher, 212B

ILLUSTRATIONS

Jack Tom, 17, 58, 59, 61, 66, 67, 80, 90, 96, 97, 109, 118, 128, 131, 132, 133, 136, 142, 145, 159, 160, 164, 218, 219, 221, 224, 225, 251, 255, 256
Paul Vaccarello, 276, 277, 326, 327, 329, 365, 378, 380, 381, 386, 387, 404, 408, 436, 453, 529, 535, 552

Charts and Graphs
Eliot Bergman Inc., 9, 127, 157, 166, 191, 194, 199, 202, 306, 357, 358, 360, 361, 385, 407, 426, 427, 459, 483, 512
Hayes Cohen, 56, 79, 115, 223, 229, 308, 319, 350, 351, 405, 410, 415, 432, 434, 505, 511
Rusty Zabransky, 10, 11, 12, 188, 194, 196